Leveraging AI for Future-Ready Writing Education

Ali Sorayyaei Azar
https://orcid.org/0000-0003-3539-8250
University of Malaya, Malaysia

Rahul Kumar Ghosh
https://orcid.org/0000-0002-1814-2133
Brainware University, India

Eriona Çela
https://orcid.org/0000-0003-2710-5489
University of New York Tirana, Albania

Dorjana Flett (Klosi)
University of "Ismail Qemali" Vlora, Albania

IGI Global
Scientific Publishing
Publishing Tomorrow's Research Today

Vice President of Editorial	Melissa Wagner
Director of Acquisitions	Mikaela Felty
Director of Book Development	Jocelynn Hessler
Production Manager	Mike Brehm
Cover Design	Jose Rosado

Published in the United States of America by
IGI Global Scientific Publishing
701 East Chocolate Avenue
Hershey, PA, 17033, USA
Tel: 717-533-8845 | Fax: 717-533-7115
Website: https://www.igi-global.com E-mail: cust@igi-global.com

Library of Congress Cataloging-in-Publication Data

LCCN: 2025034470 (CIP Data Pending)
ISBN13: 9798337356013
Isbn13Softcover: 9798337356020
EISBN13: 9798337356037
British Cataloguing in Publication Data
A Cataloguing in Publication record for this book is available from the British Library.

Table of Contents

Detailed Table of Contents

tools such as interactive writing platforms, AI grammar checkers, and peer review applications enhance both the writing process and student motivation. .The findings suggest that while AI can enhance the learning process, it should support not to replace the human connection between teacher and student. Ultimately, this paper argues for a balanced, intentional use of pedagogy and AI to build future-ready writers who are not only technically sound but also imaginative, adaptable, and empowered to communicate in a rapidly evolving world.

The introduction of Artificial Intelligence (AI) into schools has introduced a lot of change, especially regarding the teaching of writing. This chapter investigates the diverse contribution of AI as it improves the writing pedagogy by providing practical writing tools, including Grammarly, ProWritingAid, Turnitin, and GPT-3. It offers guides to the educators and students about the common use of AI beyond accuracy with grammar to formative feedback, generation of ideas, revision tactics, and support in multilingual. Based on the modern research patterns, the discussion highlights the ways in which AI contributes to learner autonomy, inclusive practices, and the ability to overcome linguistic barriers. It also provides tools on how to develop a teaching profession, implement policies, and sustainably introduce of AI into institutional practices befitting the vision of Education 5.0. The chapter is an effective guide to teachers, policymakers, educational technology developers, and educational institutions in a way that is ethical, inclusive, and technologically up-to-date.

This chapter investigates the potential of artificial intelligence to revolutionize the provision of feedback on academic writing within the higher education sector,

the study examines the pedagogical, cognitive, and ethical implications of using AI in multilingual higher education. Participants largely viewed AI as a useful tool for improving linguistic accuracy, productivity, and writing confidence. They used AI throughout the writing process, particularly for grammar correction, paraphrasing, and enhancing coherence. However, participants also expressed concerns about diminished critical thinking, overreliance on AI, and the erosion of authorial voice. These concerns were further compounded by the absence of institutional guidelines to support ethical decision-making. The study emphasizes the need for AI literacy and ethical frameworks, advocating for pedagogical approaches that balance technological support with critical thinking and academic autonomy.

Chapter 9
Empowering EFL Writers Through AI: A Pedagogical Framework for AI-Enhanced Writing Instruction 191
Vivit Rosmayanti, Universitas Negeri Makassar, Indonesia

This chapter provides a practical framework for integrating artificial intelligence (AI) into English as a Foreign Language (EFL) writing classes. It encourages the use of AI tools like Grammarly, ProWritingAid, Turnitin, Quillbot, and GPT-driven assistants to provide immediate feedback and scaffolded support, helping learners develop fluency. The chapter also highlights the importance of addressing ethical concerns such as plagiarism, data privacy, and the potential diminishing of human creativity. It calls for professional development initiatives and a policy agenda to ensure fair access and equitable educational opportunities.

Chapter 10
Technology Assisted Through Virtual Robot Tutor (VTR) in Writing English Short Stories: From Tools to Innovative Pedagogy 213
Muthmainnah Muthmainnah, Universitas Al Asyariah Mandar, Indonesia
Luis Cardoso, Polytechnic Institute of Portalegre, Portugal
M. Nagalakshmi, Vels Institute of Science, Technology, and Advanced Studies, India
Eka Apriani, Institut Agama Islam Negeri (IAIN), Curup, Indonesia
Ahmad Al Yakin, Universitas Al Asyariah Mandar, Indonesia
Ali Sorayyaei Azar, Universiti Malaya, Kuala Lumpur, Malaysia
Ahmed J. Obaid, University of Kufa, Iraq

Students in English as a Foreign Language (EFL) classes have reported more individualised and innovative learning experiences with the integration of AI in hybrid classes. However, teaching narrative writing is one area where artificial intelligence is currently underutilised in Indonesia. Most existing technology-assisted approaches focus on grammar checking and output templates. Based on the findings

Scholar not only help in making research more efficient but also pose ethical issues regarding data privacy and trust in AI-based academic practices.

This chapter aims to provide readers a insight on the growing usage of artificial intelligence in academic writing. The goal of this chapter is to take a close look at the part that Artificial Intelligence plays in Education 5.0, focusing on both its pros and cons. It talks about how AI technology is getting better, how it can be used in schools, and the change towards personalisation and adaptive learning. It also talks about the ethical issues that come up when using AI in schools.A qualitative analysis of available literature is used in the study. To do this, they need to look at case studies, business reports, and real-world evidence about how AI technologies are used and how they affect education. The study looks at many uses of AI, such as using AI algorithms to choose educational material, machine learning to grade students, and natural language processing to help people learn languages. The results show that AI makes learning a lot better by allowing personalised and adaptable learning, making students more interested, and giving them feedback that is specific to them.

Artificial intelligence has revolutionized academic and research fields. Writing and editing in the creative, professional, and academic spheres are now being transformed by the application of Artificial Intelligence (AI) tools. Some AI tools like Natural Language Processing (NLP) and Large Language Models (LLMs) such as GPT, are providing content generation, summarization, and paraphrasing with high fluency and coherence. This chapter provides in-depth information about the NLP and LLMs. This chapter examines the role and applications of various available AI tools in drafting, paraphrasing and summarizing technical content with appropriate examples. This chapter also discusses various AI tools for editing which ensure domain-specific terminology, accuracy, style consistency, adherence

content creation. The shift in focus is from detection and punishment to ethics and pedagogy, guided by the notion of enabling students to use AI ethically. Case studies from Southeast Asia reveal how institutions are responding to AI concerns with inclusive pedagogies, disclosure-based policies, and frameworks for transparency and accountability. This paper argues that academic integrity accounts for the needs of diverse learners to support equitable access to institutional learning opportunities and resources. Institutions need to make the necessary changes to continuously adapt to the rapid development of AI technologies. By reimagining academic integrity, higher education can uphold its responsibilities in an AI-driven future.

The advent of sophisticated Artificial Intelligence (AI) tools has dramatically reshaped the landscape of writing, moving beyond simple content generation to offer unprecedented opportunities for pedagogical innovation. This chapter argues for a paradigm shift in writing education, advocating for the strategic integration of AI not merely as a tool for producing text, but as a catalyst for developing higher-order cognitive skills. While AI excels at automating rudimentary writing tasks, its true educational value lies in its capacity to stimulate critical thinking, enhance problem-solving abilities, and cultivate advanced analytical skills in students. We explore methodologies for designing writing assignments that leverage AI to facilitate complex decision-making, evaluate information critically, identify biases, and construct persuasive arguments grounded in evidence. Furthermore, the chapter discusses how AI can be utilized to simulate real-world scenarios, encouraging students to analyze intricate problems and formulate creative, AI-supported solutions.

it, feature extraction, as well as constructing complex deep learning systems. This study collects data based on the studies conducted in recent times and presents how automated systems are becoming more competent than the systems used before. In addition to this, it solves some grave problems that affect the interdisciplinary work, such as the imbalanced data, how the models operate, the computational requirements, ethical issues, and the challenges faced in applying the technologies in offices. The chapter also identifies the possibilities of future studies that emphasize the importance of powerful, equitable, and beneficial diagnostic technologies.

Foreword

The rapid advancement of artificial intelligence over the past decade has fundamentally altered the technological, educational, and scholarly landscape. Once confined to narrow applications, AI systems now demonstrate advanced capabilities in natural language processing, pattern recognition, adaptive learning, and generative text production. These developments have accelerated the adoption of AI across higher education, research, and professional writing environments. Universities, publishers, and research institutions increasingly rely on AI-driven tools to support writing instruction, feedback, assessment, literature review, and citation management. As a result, writing is no longer shaped solely by human cognition and pedagogy, but by complex human–machine interactions that demand new theoretical, ethical, and institutional responses.

Alongside this rapid technological progress, questions of readiness and capacity have emerged as central concerns. While AI tools are widely accessible, levels of digital literacy, pedagogical preparedness, and policy alignment vary significantly across institutions and regions. Educators are often required to integrate AI into writing instruction without sufficient guidance, training, or shared standards. At the same time, students are navigating AI-supported writing practices in environments where expectations regarding authorship, originality, and acceptable use remain unclear. These conditions underscore the need for rigorous scholarship that examines not only what AI can do, but how it should be integrated responsibly, transparently, and pedagogically into writing education and research practices.

The growing normalization of AI-assisted writing has also prompted renewed attention to foundational issues in education, including critical thinking, learner autonomy, creativity, and academic integrity. As generative systems become increasingly fluent and responsive, the distinction between support and substitution becomes more difficult to define. This has significant implications for assessment, feedback, and the development of disciplinary writing competence. Addressing these challenges requires frameworks that situate AI within established theories of learning, writing development, and sociocultural practice, while also accounting for the ethical and governance dimensions of emerging technologies.

It is within this broader context of technological acceleration, institutional adaptation, and pedagogical reconsideration that this edited volume makes a substantive contribution. The book brings together a diverse body of scholarship that examines artificial intelligence and writing from pedagogical, empirical, theoretical, ethical, and policy-oriented perspectives. Rather than approaching AI as a singular or uniform phenomenon, the chapters explore a wide range of tools, applications, and educational settings, reflecting the complexity and diversity of contemporary writing practices.

The chapters assembled in this book collectively address the pedagogical, technological, ethical, and institutional dimensions of AI-supported writing. They explore how intelligent systems are being integrated into writing instruction, feedback practices, assessment, multilingual and EFL/ESL contexts, research writing, and reference management. Importantly, the volume does not treat AI as a monolithic solution; rather, it presents nuanced analyses of specific tools, models, and frameworks that are currently shaping writing practices across educational levels and disciplinary contexts. By doing so, the book provides readers with a detailed understanding of how AI technologies operate, how they are applied in real instructional and research settings, and how their use can be aligned with established theories of learning and writing development.

A distinguishing feature of this volume is its sustained attention to ethical considerations and academic integrity. As AI tools increasingly participate in text generation, revision, and evaluation, fundamental questions arise concerning authorship, originality, accountability, data privacy, and the cultivation of critical thinking. The contributions in this book engage directly with these concerns, offering conceptual models, empirical evidence, and policy-oriented discussions that emphasize responsible use rather than uncritical adoption or outright rejection. This balanced approach supports institutions and educators seeking to move toward coherent, transparent, and pedagogically grounded strategies for AI integration.

The volume also foregrounds issues of equity, inclusion, and access in AI-enhanced writing education. Several chapters examine multilingual and multicultural learning environments, diverse learner needs, and resource-constrained contexts, demonstrating how AI can support personalization, feedback, and learner autonomy when implemented thoughtfully. At the same time, structural challenges such as uneven access, limited institutional readiness, and gaps in faculty development are critically examined. These discussions position the book as both a scholarly reference and a practical guide for curriculum designers, teacher educators, academic leaders, and policymakers.

Taken as a whole, this book offers a comprehensive and citable contribution to the literature on artificial intelligence in writing education and academic research. It systematically maps current developments, critically evaluates their implications, and identifies future directions for research and practice. As writing continues to evolve in response to intelligent technologies, this volume provides a timely and authoritative foundation for understanding how AI can be integrated in ways that are pedagogically sound, ethically responsible, and institutionally sustainable.

Hamed Taherdoost
University Canada West, Canada

Foreword

The rapid advancement of artificial intelligence (AI) has profoundly influenced nearly every domain of contemporary life, and education is no exception. Among the many areas experiencing transformation, writing education occupies a particularly complex and consequential position. Writing is not merely a technical skill but a cognitive, social, and ethical practice that shapes how knowledge is constructed, communicated, and evaluated. In this context, the thoughtful integration of AI into writing education presents both unprecedented opportunities and significant challenges.

Leveraging AI for Future-Ready Writing Education arrives at a critical moment in global educational discourse. As generative AI tools, automated feedback systems, intelligent tutoring platforms, and AI-assisted research technologies become increasingly embedded in academic and professional writing practices, educators and institutions are compelled to reconsider long-standing assumptions about authorship, originality, assessment, and academic integrity. This volume responds to these concerns with clarity, depth, and scholarly rigor.

What distinguishes this book is its balanced and human-centered approach. Rather than presenting AI as a replacement for teachers or writers, the contributors consistently position AI as a pedagogical partner—one that can support personalization, enhance feedback, foster multilingual development, and strengthen research practices when guided by sound pedagogy and ethical governance. The chapters collectively demonstrate that future-ready writing education must move beyond simplistic narratives of technological efficiency to address creativity, critical thinking, learner autonomy, and social responsibility.

The strength of this edited volume lies in its interdisciplinary and international scope. Drawing on perspectives from writing studies, applied linguistics, educational technology, ethics, policy, and cognitive science, the contributors offer theoretical frameworks, empirical investigations, systematic reviews, and practical models applicable across diverse educational contexts. Topics such as AI-supported feedback, EFL/ESL writing development, academic integrity in AI-rich environments, research writing and citation management, and emerging interdisciplinary applications are addressed with depth and coherence.

Equally noteworthy is the book's engagement with broader educational paradigms such as Education 5.0, which emphasize human-centered innovation, inclusivity, and ethical responsibility. By situating AI-enhanced writing instruction within these global frameworks, the volume provides readers with guidance that is not only timely but also sustainable and forward-looking.

This book will be of significant value to educators, researchers, curriculum designers, policymakers, and graduate students who seek to understand how AI can be responsibly integrated into writing education. It offers both conceptual clarity and practical insight, making it a meaningful contribution to ongoing debates about the future of teaching, learning, and academic communication in an AI-mediated world.

In an era where the boundaries between human authorship and machine assistance are increasingly blurred, *Leveraging AI for Future-Ready Writing Education* provides a much-needed scholarly compass. It encourages readers to engage critically with AI technologies while reaffirming the centrality of human judgment, ethical reflection, and purposeful communication. As such, this volume stands as an important and timely contribution to the evolving field of writing education.

Hind Hammouch
Sidi Mohamed Ben Abdellah University (USMBA), Fez, Morocco

Preface

OVERVIEW

Artificial Intelligence (AI) has transformed the use of education and how we write. It has had a real influence on writing pedagogy, theory, and practice in environments where writing was learned, taught, and examined as the traditional emphasis on issues of linguistic accuracy and rhetorical conventions has given its place to digital literacy, ethics, critical thinking, and the partnership between humans and AI. Combinations of AI-assisted writing helpers, computerized feedback systems, intelligent tutoring systems, and research aid tools have altered instructional expectations and student achievements.

The book *Leveraging AI for Future-Ready Writing Education* studies the changing position of AI in writing teaching and academic communication. It unites conceptual analyses, empirical investigations, pedagogical frameworks, and institutional perspectives to showcase the ways in which AI can facilitate writing skills while still supporting academic integrity, and creativity, and giving learners more control over their learning process.

GLOBAL CONTEXT

The worldwide educational institutions are at the same time experiencing and managing a rapid technological change globally that is caused by the new generative AI, machine learning, and data-driven educational technology advancements. These new changes have led to a rethinking of the traditional concepts of authorship, originality, assessment, and ethical responsibility in writing education. In the meantime, the global trend towards Education 5.0 is stressing human-centered, inclusive, and ethically supported innovation.

This book is situated in this worldwide transition and it tackles the pedagogical, technological, ethical, and policy-related aspects of AI integration in writing education. It is also a response to the increasing demand for research-informed advice on the responsible use case of AI that would get learners ready for the coming communication needs in different areas such as academic, professional, and societal ones.

TARGET AUDIENCE

This volume was created for a wide range of professionals in the field of education, including teachers, researchers, curriculum makers, and those who design educational materials, technology experts, policymakers, and post-graduate students who are involved in writing, literacy, language, and technology teaching. Besides, it can be still an important source of information for those who are looking for AI writing education approaches that are based on evidence, ethics, and pedagogy in different educational settings.

SIGNIFICANCE OF CONTRIBUTIONS

The various chapters included in this book work together to create an in-depth study of the part played by AI in writing education. Starting from basic viewpoints, the study is moved through applied practices, ethical issues and even interdisciplinary extensions.

Chapter 1: Artificial Intelligence and Academic-Based Writing Pedagogy - This chapter sets a basic viewpoint on the merging of artificial intelligence in teaching writing. It looks at personalized feedback, collaborative learning environments, and ethical considerations, thus offering a conceptual framework that helps comprehensively understand AI's contribution to writing instruction and at the same time keeping the academic responsibility high.

Chapter 2: Ink, Algorithms, and Imagination – The New Writing Trinity - The present chapter explores the ever-changing interrelationship of human creativity with AI-assisted writing. It reasserts the need to conserve human agency and interpretive skills in the context of AI-supported writing practices by underlining imagination, critical thinking, and emotional intelligence.

Chapter 3: AI and the Future of Writing Pedagogy: Pedagogical Innovation, Ethical Practice, and Institutional Readiness - The present chapter discusses the domains of pedagogy, ethics, and institutional preparedness from different angles. It is important as it provides the ways of responsible AI adoption through the use of curriculum design, faculty development, and policy frameworks.

Chapter 4: Impact of Using Effective Tools of Pedagogy and AI for Future-Ready Writing Education - The teaching and learning process in the use of AI tools combined with good teaching methods is the theme of this chapter. It insists on the necessity of the blending of teaching styles that measure up to the engagement of the learner yet do not reduce the teacher's importance at all.

Chapter 5: The Future of Writing Instruction: Opportunities and Challenges of Artificial Intelligence - A thorough examination of AI-supported writing aids and teaching methods is presented in this chapter. The significance of the chapter is in recognizing the chances and limitations together with the direction of responsible and moral use.

Chapter 6: Feedback That Feels Human: Reimagining Academic Writing Support Through Ethical AI - This chapter highlights the major role that ethical, human-centered feedback plays in AI-assisted writing scenarios. It presents models that maintain the deepness of the relationship but at the same time take advantage of the technological efficiency.

Chapter 7: Comparing Teacher and ChatGPT Feedback in EFL/ESL Writing: A Systematic Review - Through a systematic review of AI-generated and teacher feedback, this chapter provides empirical evidence. The evidence is very much needed in EFL/ESL writing contexts to support the making of pedagogical decisions based on research.

Chapter 8: Balancing Support and Autonomy in ELT Master Students' Use of AI for Academic Writing - The focus of this chapter is to analyze the views of postgraduate students regarding AI usage and to point out the necessity of a proper mix between technological aid, academic freedom and critical thinking.

Chapter 9: Empowering EFL Writers Through AI: A Pedagogical Framework for AI-Enhanced Writing Instruction - The chapter gives a rigorous pedagogical framework for AI integration in EFL writing teaching. Its relevance is in providing practical help and at the same time confronting ethical and equity issues.

Chapter 10: Technology Assisted through Virtual Robot Tutor (VTR) in Writing English Short Story - This chapter showcases novel AI applications in the teaching of narrative writing. It is a momentous step for the use of AI to go beyond mere correction and enter the territory of creativity and storytelling.

Chapter 11: Algorithmic Mentors and Multilingual Writing Development - This chapter lays out a theoretical framework that sees AI as an "algorithmic mentor." It is a major step towards the support of an equitable, multilingual, and process-centered writing pedagogy.

Chapter 12: Artificial Intelligence in Research Writing and Reference Management - This chapter explores the ways through which artificial intelligence can enhance the efficiency of research writing and the precision of citation. It is, therefore, a major factor in the recognition of the ethical and practical aspects in academic communication.

Chapter 13: Education 5.0 and AI for Academic Research and Citation Management - This chapter positions AI in the context of Education 5.0, which underlines personalization and adaptable learning as the key aspects. It helps to synchronize the research writing practices with the future educational models.

Chapter 14: AI Tools for Writing and Editing in Academia and Research - The use of AI for writing and editing support, as well as other similar applications, is thoroughly discussed in this chapter. It also covers the technical capabilities and limitations accordingly, thus being helpful in understanding them.

Chapter 15: Mapping the Evolution of Online Feedback Tools in Writing Education - This chapter provides a bibliometric analysis of online feedback tools, aiming to identify research trends, gaps, and directions for future work.

Chapter 16: Redefining Academic Integrity in the Age of AI - The significance of this chapter lies in the academic integrity frameworks re-examined in AI-rich environments by shifting the view from punitive models to ethical pedagogy and transparency.

Chapter 17: Beyond Content Creation: Emphasizing Critical Thinking and Problem-Solving with Artificial Intelligence - The chapter elaborates on AI's capability of supporting higher cognitive skills. It is centered on extracting and revisiting that machine intelligence is not questionably shifting from the status quo.

Chapter 18: Empowering Fine Arts Education with ICT to Train Primary Education Major Undergraduates - This chapter demonstrates interdisciplinary applications of AI and ICT in artistic education. They are significant as showcases of innovative pedagogical models other than language teachings.

Chapter 19: Empirical Approaches to Personality Prediction via Automated Handwriting Analysis - This chapter discusses AI-driven handwriting analysis and personality prediction, and it is important because it shows the budding interdisciplinary research connecting writing, cognition, and machine learning.

IMPACT

By offering a balanced and human-centered perspective on AI integration in writing education, *Leveraging AI for Future-Ready Writing Education* contributes to its field. The volume positions AI more as a helping hand to educators or writers, rather than a replacement, in a way that would assist in improving the pedagogy, support the development of learners, and enhance the ethical aspects of academic practices.

This book equips educators and institutions with modern tools to handle the difficult maze of AI adoption, as well as forcing them to determine from the conflicting situations the sort of changes that should be integrated on the ground. It goes further in fostering a collegial understanding of writing in conditions'; in other words: a teaching philosophy and pedagogy of AI-infused learning, and caters to the subject by enhancing practice for purpose-responsible, forewarned and futuristic learning atmospheres.

CONCLUSION

The educational practices in which we all are involved is being morphed every single day regard to artificial intelligence plying, and among them, the area of writing education suddenly finds itself positioned at a crossroad between the technological novelty and human thought. This erudite volume addresses our present juncture and offers a well-rounded scrutiny of how AI may be incorporated into writing instruction programs that best enhance the very learning of writing by bearing in mind ethical, pedagogical, and institutional.

Combining various schools of thought, empirical research, didactic models, and international case studies, the volume shifts the scholarly conversation about AI writing education. It provides educators, researchers, and institutions with help for making informed decisions in adopting AI technology within educational practices, thus foregrounding responsible use and critical engagement with learners. Finally, it builds a path towards future-ready writers who are not only already competent in everything technical or digital but who have a reflective and ethical disposition to be engaged in meaningful communication in an increasingly AI-enhanced world.

Ali Sorayyaei Azar
University of Malaya, Malaysia

Rahul Kumar Ghosh
Brainware University, India

Eriona Çela
University of New York Tirana, Albania

Dorjana Flett (Klosi)
University of "Ismail Qemali" Vlora, Albania

Acknowledgment

We would like to express our sincere gratitude to all contributing authors of the book *Leveraging AI for Future-Ready Writing Education*. We are grateful to all peer-reviewers for their invaluable insights and constructive feedback, which significantly enhanced the quality of this publication.

We wish to acknowledge our families and colleagues for their unwavering encouragement and understanding until the finalization of the book. Their support has been a cornerstone of our scholarly pursuits.

This publication is dedicated to advancing the integration of artificial intelligence in writing education, hoping that it will inspire continued innovation and scholarly discourse in this field.

Ali Sorayyaei Azar

Rahul Kumar Ghosh

Eriona Çela

Dorjana Flett (Klosi)

Chapter 1
Artificial Intelligence and Academic-Based Writing Pedagogy

Michael Oyedele Oyenuga
https://orcid.org/0000-0001-9921-5711
Woxsen University, India

ABSTRACT

The integration of artificial intelligence (AI) in writing instruction has emerged as a potent force for transforming educational practices and enhancing student outcomes. This chapter explores the applications of AI-based tools in writing pedagogy, including personalised recommendations, automated feedback, and collaborative learning environments. AI not only empowers learners by providing tailored assistance and real-time corrections but also fosters a culture of engagement and accountability in the writing process. However, the utilisation of AI in education raises significant ethical concerns, such as data privacy, academic integrity, and the risk of diminished critical thinking skills. Addressing these challenges is crucial for maximising the benefits of AI innovations in writing instruction. By examining current practices, potential barriers, and the implications of AI in writing education, this chapter aims to provide a comprehensive understanding of how these technologies can shape the future of academic writing and encourage sustainable pedagogical practices.

1. INTRODUCTION

The incorporation of artificial intelligence (AI) into the teaching of writing is no longer a speculative trend but an expanding movement. Meanwhile, AI Writing tools have been adopted in various forms by more than 60% of the world's higher education institutions as per a UNESCO report released in 2024, with Asia and North America leading in global adoption rates. This rise is symptomatic of a larger trend towards digital literacies and personalised learning settings everywhere, and particularly in post-COVID-19 educational systems (UNESCO, 2024b).

The rapid advancement of AI has had an enormous impact on educational methodologies, especially regarding the teaching of writing. Such AI-driven applications and tools are trans-

DOI: 10.4018/979-8-3373-5601-3.ch001

forming the way students approach writing, opening new possibilities for skills development and productivity (Oyenuga et al., 2024). But the embedding of AI within writing pedagogy also creates a range of risks that we need to approach reflectively, so that it does not get abused or create new problems.

Writing aids using AI, such as ChatGPT, Grammarly, or chatbot-based, generative and proofreading tools, have shown the potential to give real-time feedback or content generation support (Anh & Dieu, 2025; Ulum et al., 2024; Asad et al., 2024). Such technologies can help reduce teachers' routine instructional load and allow them to focus on higher-order thinking and critical writing skills development (Parviz, 2025; Soelistiyowati et al., 2024).

Yet despite these potential advantages, concerns remain about the impact of AI on originality, academic integrity and critical thinking. The fact that AI writing tools can produce text with ease calls into mind authenticity and the validity of student work (PAN, 2024; Ramadhan et al., 2024; Aljuaid, 2024; Murugason, 2025). Educators need to walk a line, making sure that AI supplements rather than supply those fundamental pieces of good writing instruction. In addition, ethical and social issues should be at the forefront of AI-facilitated writing instruction. Privacy, fairness and access issues should be considered to avoid the perpetuation of current educational disparities (Ербулатова et al, 2025; Apriani et al., 2024).

Real-world examples of AI bias and privacy risks further complicate adoption. For instance, grammar tools like Grammarly have been shown to penalise non-standard dialects, reinforcing linguistic hierarchies. Similarly, plagiarism detection systems such as Turnitin have flagged original work due to algorithmic misinterpretation, raising concerns about fairness and authorship attribution. These cases underscore the need for transparent governance frameworks and culturally responsive AI design.

Considering the rising influence of AI in writing instruction, collaboration between faculty, administrators and researchers is critical. This chapter examines current trends in, resistance to, and transformative possibilities for AI in writing pedagogy based on evidence-informed perspectives as well as suggestions that have positive consequences for ethical action. This chapter offers a unique contribution by synthesising cognitive and constructivist theories with AI-enhanced writing pedagogy, grounded in global case studies and low-resource contexts. It proposes a balanced, ethical, and inclusive framework for integrating AI in writing instruction, particularly relevant for emerging educational systems.

2. CONCEPTUAL UNDERSTANDING

a. AI-Based Writing Tools

The use of artificial intelligence in education, and more specifically, in writing instruction, offers considerable promise for supporting students' learning and engagement. AI-enabled writing tools, such as chatbots, automated writing assistants and grammar checkers (Fig. 1), can offer real-time feedback; help enforce correct spelling and punctuation usage as well as support academic writing idea generation, thus speeding up the work for students in different educational environments (Kong et al., 2024; Minh, 2024). Such technologies provide a tailored supportive learning environment, which meets individual student style and demands with the ability to work at the students' pace and provide personalised guidance. The pedagogical principles serving as foundations for AI tools include self-regulated learning, which encourages learners to take control of their writing without experiencing unwarranted levels of anxiety, but feel more confident (Kong et al., 2024).

Relatedly, with the advent of generative AI tools such as ChatGPT, it becomes innovative to use language instruction in ways that allow students to interact with text dynamically (Eynon & Young, 2020; Apata & Oyenuga, 2025). By means of cooperative writing and feedback chances, teachers might engender a more communicative and supportive teaching environment (Aljuaid, 2024). Nevertheless, these are also creating potential threats to academic loyalty and integrity in using AI for generating the contents since many students may misuse the technology, thus leading to issues like posing unauthenticity and originality problems (PAN, 2024; Al-Raimi et al., 2024). Understanding such challenges can help educators on the gains of using AI for writing improvement against academic integrity issues (Tian et al., 2024).

Considering these developments, it is therefore important to take a reflective and informed position towards AI writing tools in education. AI literacy must be promoted to enable educators and students alike to comprehend the impacts of AI technologies, to strike a balance between technological scaffolding and critical thinking (Abbott & Abbott, 2024). Accordingly, the collaboration in AI use can help the different educational players (stakeholders/teachers, students/administrators) to optimise their cooperation during preparing for and managing the benefits of AI-based writing instruction alongside its challenges and ethical concerns (Apata & Oyenuga, 2025).

Successful AI incorporation in writing pedagogy requires further research, training, and curricular recalibration to capitalise upon the continued evolution of such tools and increase students' writing abilities in an increasingly digital educational terrain.

AI-enhanced writing pedagogy thrives at the intersection of theory, technology, and ethics. This framework illustrates how pedagogical inputs, grounded in cognitive and constructivist models, interact with mediators like perceived value and trust, while being shaped by moderators such as ethics, infrastructure, and teacher readiness. The result is a learner-centred ecosystem that promotes satisfaction, critical thinking, and equity. For start-ups and institutions alike, this model offers a roadmap for integrating AI responsibly and reflectively into writing instruction.

To unify the chapter's pedagogical and technological dimensions, Figure 1 presents a conceptual framework that integrates cognitive and constructivist theories with AI-enhanced writing tools. This model illustrates how institutional context, ethical governance, and learner agency shape writing outcomes in digital education.

Figure 1. Conceptual Model

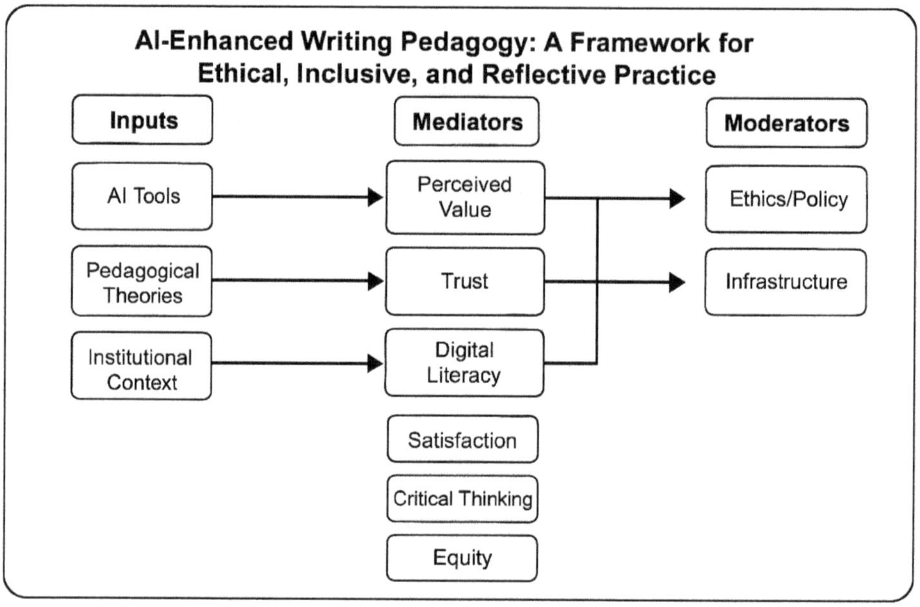

Traditional vs. AI-Augmented Writing Instruction

The landscape of writing instruction is changing in groundbreaking ways, and technology, specifically artificial intelligence (AI), is driving much of this transformation. Writing instruction has generally been dominated by top-down teacher-assisted feedback, contrived lessons and imposed testing. Although it gets the job done and does effectively pass on basic writing skills, these methods can feel impersonal and faceless to today's modern-technology super-literate children. AI-enabled writing instruction, however, is a game-changer by delivering solutions that make the learning experience better with instant and personalised feedback and guidance.

AI-supported writing tools like Grammarly have generally generated better student writing results than traditional instruction alone (Prasetya & Raharjo, 2023). Real-time corrections and recommendations; Students can learn and apply instant grammar as well as structural changes whenever they wish to do so, hence a likelihood for more thorough learning of writing conventions. Moreover, AI applications can be tailored to the writing styles and needs of negotiation that proffer a more personalised learning experience, whereas traditional approaches may fail to achieve this (Aljuaid, 2024).

Even with benefits from AI-augmented systems, there are some obstacles. There is a general worry that students are depending too much on technology for fast fixes, such as quick corrections, resulting in them not knowing the basics of language and writing, and what counts are often error-strewn papers (Aljuaid, 2024). Furthermore, though AI aids can facilitate the writing procedure greatly, they have the potential to add to problems related to originality and academic integrity (Saran, 2024). While educators must walk a tightrope of infusing AI tools in their classrooms, they need to make sure kids are still engaging deeply with the writing process, encouraging higher-order thinking and creativity alongside technical skill.

Therefore, as educational environments change, crossovers between traditional and AI-supported teaching of writing could add substantially to the learning process. Intelligent use of AI tools in curricula brings with it the opportunity for educators to provide students a resource that supports their development as writers and creators, retaining the pedagogical principles upon which effective teaching is predicated. This twofold commitment will be critical as the educational landscape evolves to accommodate technological innovations and the requirements of the 21st-century learner.

b. Cognitive and Constructivist Approaches to Writing Pedagogy

The integration of cognitive and constructivist approaches in writing pedagogy has been a subject of extensive research and debate within the field of education. These two theoretical frameworks offer distinct perspectives on how students learn and develop their writing skills, each with its own set of implications for instructional practices. These theoretical foundations directly inform the pedagogical use of AI tools. Cognitive approaches align with AI's capacity for strategy-based feedback and revision scaffolding, while constructivist principles are reflected in collaborative writing platforms and peer-supported AI environments. Together, they provide a dual lens for understanding how AI can support both skill acquisition and meaning-making in writing.

i. Cognitive Approaches to Writing Instruction

Cognitive writing instruction originated with researchers such as Linda Flower and John Hayes, who formulated the widely known Cognitive Process Theory of Writing. This theory focuses on the cognitive processes required for writing, such as planning, translating and reviewing. Cognitive-informed instruction of writing frequently involves a focus on teaching particular strategies to support students' awareness and management of these cognitive processes (Leggette et al., 2015; Zumbrunn & Krause, 2012).

One important emphasis in cognitive approaches is on direct instruction and demonstration. Teachers implementing this type of approach may give direct instruction on writing skills (e.g., grammar, organisation, and generating ideas), but then provide students with strategies for applying these skills while writing. The ideal is that learners will develop their own repertoire of strategies to deal with writing problems (Bremholm et al., 2022; Cumming, 1989).

ii. Constructivist Approaches to Writing Instruction

Constructivist theoretical perspectives on writing pedagogy, however, regard learning as an active process of meaning-making in which students construct their own understandings about writing through participation in social activity and interaction with the task of writing. The perspective highlights the value of learning from peers engaged in discussing and reviewing compositions (Zamel, 1983; Schuster, 2019).

In this case, constructivist writing instruction includes providing students with opportunities for peer feedback, group discussion, and self-reflection (Jiang & Kalyuga, 2022). The teacher's task changes from being an instructor to a mentor, helping students learn and scaffolding them as necessary (VanDerHeide, 2017; Pitenoee et al., 2017).

iii. Cognitive vs. Constructivist Writing Instruction

Table 1. Difference between Cognitive vs. Constructivist Writing Instruction

Aspect	Cognitive Approach	Constructivist Approach
Theoretical Foundation	Based on Cognitive Process Theory (Flower & Hayes), it focuses on mental processes like planning and revising.	Rooted in constructivist learning theory, it emphasises active meaning-making through social engagement.
Instructional Focus	Explicit instruction in writing strategies (e.g., grammar, organisation, idea generation).	Collaborative learning through peer feedback, group discussion, and self-reflection.
Role of the Teacher	Direct instructor and modeller of writing processes.	Facilitator who scaffolds learning and guides exploration.
Student Engagement	Individual problem-solving and strategy development.	Social interaction and co-construction of knowledge.
Learning Outcome	Development of transferable cognitive strategies for writing challenges.	Deep understanding of writing as a contextual and communicative act.
Key References	Leggette et al. (2015); Zumbrunn & Krause (2012); Bremholm et al. (2022); Cumming (1989)	Zamel (1983); Schuster (2019); Jiang & Kalyuga (2022); VanDerHeide (2017); Pitenoee et al. (2017)

Table 1 represents both cognitive and constructivist approaches offer valuable pathways to writing mastery. While cognitive instruction equips students with strategic tools for navigating the writing process, constructivist pedagogy fosters a deeper, socially grounded understanding of writing as a form of expression and dialogue. Blending these approaches can create a dynamic, inclusive, and skill-rich writing environment.

iv. Integrating Cognitive and Constructivist Approaches

Although cognitive and constructivist perspectives on writing instruction may seem contradictory, several educators see potential benefit in coordinating elements of both models. This combined approach values explicit teaching of the craft of writing but also underscores the social nature and sense-making of writing as well (Wolbers et al., 2021; Behizadeh, 2014).

Through the combination of cognitive and constructivist approaches, teachers can develop an equitable writing curriculum that meets the range of students' writing needs. Teachers, for instance, may first explicitly teach a particular technique in writing and students then practice using it through peer or self-feedback (Ng & Cheung, 2018; Rahimi & Noroozisiam, 2013).

In addition, the infusion of technological tools, such as digital writing platforms and communicative devices, can maximise the alignment between cognitive and constructivist approaches, allowing students to participate in writing as a social undertaking, drawing from corrective feedback (definition) while benefiting from responsive assistance (Slavkov 2015; Jingxin & Razali, 2020; Oyenuga & Iember 2021).

3. KEY APPLICATIONS OF AI IN WRITING PEDAGOGY

Artificial intelligence (AI) has revolutionised the field of writing instruction, providing a range of applications that enhance teaching and student writing. An illustrative example is automated feedback and grammar correction systems, such as those powered by AI (e.g., Grammarly), which provide real-time corrections to grammar, punctuation, and style; thus, students can improve their writing while also receiving immediate responses about their language use. In a randomised controlled trial involving 1,200 undergraduate students across three universities, Nazari et al. (2021) found that students using AI-powered writing assistants improved their writing scores by 18% on average, compared to those receiving traditional instructor feedback. The study likewise reported a 25% reduction in writing anxiety, suggesting that AI tools can enhance both performance and emotional engagement.

Another important use case is brainstorming and idea generation. Artificial intelligence tools may be able to help students formulate thoughts by offering a prompt or suggesting similar topics and prompts for sparking creativity. Using natural language processing, the tools can assist students in overcoming writer's block and broadening their mental models as they brainstorm papers or creative writing.

Furthermore, plagiarism control and authorship attribution have become an integrated part of writing learning. AI tools like Turnitin make it easy for educators to check originality and provide feedback on students' practice of academic honesty. Such tools are not only useful in discovering potential cases of academic dishonesty, but they also provide educational opportunities for students to learn the significance of citing sources and the ethics behind writing. If appropriately handled by these technologies, dealing with plagiarism promotes a classroom culture of honesty and accountability.

Also, AI-driven adaptive learning paths provide a personalised experience. Computers can track an individual's performance, customise assignments to needs and suggest tailored advice about how each person may improve. Such a level of personalisation gives the students responsibility for their development and leads to more effective learning outcomes. AI-based writing tutors and chatbots allow students to have personal assistance at any point in their writing process. These tools can help students at all levels of writing (from planning to revising) to identify and clarify their ideas, access support resources, and receive feedback in real time. The availability of such AI tools can increase the accessibility of writing help, especially for students who may not have ready access to in-person or traditional tutoring and writing centres.

Additionally, the use of AI in writing pedagogy has the potential to be transformative both for educators and students. By offering immediate feedback and facilitating the development of ideas, as well as maintaining academic honesty and allowing for personalised learning pathways, AI tools can enhance writing experiences while promoting critical writing growth. Nevertheless, the lecturers must strike a balance in using these gadgets and not lose sight of independent critical thought and creativity in writing practice.

Table 2. Key Applications of AI in Writing Pedagogy

Application	Function	Pedagogical Impact
Automated Feedback & Grammar Correction	Real-time feedback on grammar, punctuation, and style using tools like Grammarly.	Enhances language accuracy, fosters self-correction, and supports continuous writing improvement.
Brainstorming & Idea Development	AI-generated prompts and topic suggestions using natural language processing.	Stimulates creativity, breaks writer's block, and deepens conceptual engagement in early writing stages.
Plagiarism Detection & Authorship Analysis	Tools like Turnitin assess originality and citation practices.	Promotes academic integrity, educates on ethical writing, and reduces plagiarism risks.
Personalised Writing Support & Adaptive Learning	AI systems tailor assignments and feedback based on individual performance.	Empowers student agency, supports differentiated instruction, and improves learning outcomes.
AI-Powered Writing Tutors & Chatbots	On-demand guidance through all writing stages, offering clarification and resources.	Increases accessibility to support, enhances revision quality, and complements traditional tutoring.

Table 2 shows that AI is reshaping writing pedagogy from correction to creation. By offering real-time feedback, idea generation, plagiarism detection, and adaptive learning, these tools empower students to write with confidence, clarity, and integrity. Yet, the true power lies in how educators integrate AI, not as a replacement for critical thinking, but as a catalyst for deeper engagement, creativity, and personalised growth. The future of writing is not just digital, it's dynamic, ethical, and learner-centred.

Table 3. Empirical Studies on AI-Enhanced Writing Outcome

Study	Sample Size	Intervention	Results
Nazari et al. (2021)	1,200 students	AI writing assistant (Grammarly) in undergraduate courses	18% improvement in writing scores; 25% reduction in writing anxiety
Alharbi (2023) – Univ. of Michigan	300 students	Grammarly pilot for grammar/style feedback	Increased grammar accuracy and student confidence in revision
Tokuda et al. (2020) – Univ. of Illinois	150 students	ChatGPT chatbot for brainstorming and outlining	Enhanced idea generation and peer collaboration; improved engagement
Rao & Rao (2007) – UCLA	80 students	AI support for multilingual and neurodivergent writers	Improved vocabulary use and reduced cognitive load in writing tasks
Visbal-Cadavid et al. (2017) – Cambridge	100 students	AI plagiarism detection and authorship analysis	Strengthened academic integrity; increased awareness of citation practices

Table 3 shows the empirical studies across diverse institutions confirm that AI-enhanced writing tools can improve grammar accuracy, reduce writing anxiety, and foster deeper engagement—especially when integrated with thoughtful pedagogy. These outcomes underscore the importance of moving beyond theoretical claims to data-driven insights that shape responsible, inclusive, and effective writing instruction.

These empirical findings suggest that AI tools are most effective when embedded within pedagogically intentional frameworks. Rather than viewing AI as a standalone solution, educators must interpret these outcomes through the lens of learner autonomy, institutional readiness, and ethical scaffolding. Having explored the functional applications of AI in writing instruction, the next section turns to the pedagogical opportunities these tools create, particularly in fostering autonomy, inclusivity, and critical engagement.

4. PEDAGOGICAL OPPORTUNITIES

Building on findings from Nazari et al. (2021), this chapter argues that AI's pedagogical value lies not in automation, but in its capacity to scaffold deeper engagement. The application of artificial intelligence (AI) to writing instruction offers many pedagogical possibilities that may increase students' capacity for autonomous confidence about their own writing. Among the most prominent benefits that could result from the use of AI-assisted writing tools is their potential to offer personalised feedback based on learners' unique writing profiles and needs. This immediate response that is adapted to the individual learning helps students understand where they went wrong and gives them confidence in their right answers, as they know immediately if an answer is correct or not (Wang, 2024). Furthermore, when students receive valuable responses to their writing, they are more likely to engage in meaningful revisions and offer thoughtful and complex texts.

Artificial intelligence also makes it possible for differentiated instruction since it adapts to students' different levels of proficiency and learning preferences. Personalised learning Journey AI technologies can architect bespoke educational experiences so students can move at the pace that is just right for them and access content that relates to their own individual struggles and successes. This method creates an inclusive learning environment where every student can learn best according to their own potential (Muslimin et al., 2024). AI-assisted writing tools offer personalised feedback and adaptive learning paths, helping students refine grammar and structure. However, meta-analyses reveal that AI tools like Grammarly and ChatGPT are most effective in improving syntax and cohesion, but less effective in fostering argumentation and originality (Aljuaid, 2024; Wang, 2024). This duality underscores the need for balanced integration where AI supports technical refinement but does not replace critical thinking or creativity.

With AI, instructors also get real-time feedback to help with iterative learning. When used as a writing aide, therefore, AI tools encourage students to see how their work develops rather than understanding the process of writing development as linear. This promotes a growth mindset, which fosters students' ability to see writing as a skill that is learned and refined through continual practice (Nazari et al., 2021). While AI tools offer unprecedented support in writing instruction, their integration must be guided by pedagogic intent rather than scientific novelty. In my own teaching context, I have observed that students often rely on AI-generated suggestions without fully engaging with the reasoning behind them. This raises pivotal questions: Are we cultivating writers who think critically, or users who only correct passively? The goal of AI-enhanced pedagogy should not be to outsource cognition, but to scaffold it, empowering learners to interrogate, revise, and reflect. As educators, we must ensure that AI tools serve as catalysts for deeper engagement, not shortcuts that dilute the rigour of theoretical writing.

In addition, AI can help multilingual and neurodiverse writers by providing personalised support for their individual needs. AI tools could also offer vocabulary suggestions that raise the level of a word for those deemed requiring more challenge, possibly while gauging student proficiency in different language uses and learning styles typical to neurodivergent students. AI supports an equitable learning environment by supporting different language backgrounds and cognitive profiles of learners (Crossley et al., 2016).

The integration of AI into writing pedagogy also calls for general reform at the curriculum and policy levels. Institutions must move beyond ad hoc adoption and develop frameworks that embed AI literacy, moral use, and serious engagement into writing instruction. This includes revising assessment rubrics to account for AI-assisted outputs, training faculty to guide responsible tool use, and ensuring that policies reflect both technological innovation and academic integrity. In contexts where instructive equity is a priority, AI must be positioned not as a shortcut, but as a scaffold supporting different learners while preserving the rigour and creativity that writing education demands.

Moreover, the development of AI-powered tools makes high-quality writing assistance accessible to all. Thanks to the emergence of scalable aids for writing and sources, students at all levels can now share in the same support that has long existed only within schools or minds. This transition could level the playing field in terms of opportunities to improve writing and general academic success (Rashtchi, 2019).

The pedagogical promise of AI in teaching writing is vast and radical. Through the promotion of student autonomy and confidence, enabling differentiated instruction, offering real-time feedback, providing support to diverse writers, and democratising writing resources, AI has the potential to transform how writing is taught and learned. However, educational organisations need to be willing adopters of these innovations and do so ethically and responsibly, which allows school students a critical engagement with the opportunity for creativity.

From an institutional perspective, AI integration also affects teacher workload and instructional management. While AI tools can reduce grading time and support differentiated instruction, they also require faculty training, policy alignment, and ongoing oversight to ensure responsible use. Without adequate support, educators may experience increased cognitive and emotional labour in managing AI-enhanced classrooms. Curriculum redesign must reflect the evolving role of AI in writing instruction. This includes embedding AI literacy into learning outcomes, training faculty to guide responsible tool use, and revising assessment rubrics to account for AI-assisted outputs. Multimodal writing integrating text, visuals, and interactive media also requires pedagogical recalibration. Governance frameworks should ensure ethical use, data privacy, and equitable access, especially in low-resource contexts.

5. GLOBAL PERSPECTIVES AND CASE STUDIES

a. AI-Based Writing Pedagogy in Low-Resource Contexts

The incorporation of AI into writing pedagogy offers promising prospects for improving educational results in low-resource contexts, where access to quality instruction and learning resources is scarce(Oyenuga & Omale, 2024). But for achieving something usable in such an environment, it comes to AI writing tools, you should address some of the specific challenges and considerations.

Actual and capability offerings in low-resource settings are represented by technological infrastructure, including a reliable internet connection and possession of a digital device. Without such a prerequisite, the adoption of AI-based writing tools can be difficult (Rahayu et al., 2024). Targeted investments and community-led efforts to close these infrastructure gaps are essential to guaranteeing equitable access to AI-enhanced writing instruction.

Further, linguistic and cultural heterogeneity in many low-resource areas may complicate the successful deployment of AI-driven writing aids. These tools are usually developed using language models that have been trained on data from majority languages and cultures, and tend to neglect the nuances of local dialects and writing variations (ROA & Halim, 2024). The needs of diverse learners are at the forefront, and appropriate adaptations and localisations of AI technologies to better serve those needs are paramount in promoting inclusive and effective writing pedagogy.

In low-resource educational environments, the promise of AI in writing instruction is both inspiring and fraught. Having worked with students in settings where digital access is inconsistent and pedagogic support is stretched, I've seen firsthand how AI tools can democratize feedback and scaffold learning but only when thoughtfully deployed. For instance, in classrooms with small bandwidth or shared devices, even basic grammar checking tools can foster confidence and autonomy. Yet without culturally susceptible design and localised training, these comparable tools risk reinforcing lingual hierarchies and excluding non-dominant writing styles. The challenge is not just technological, it's pedagogic, ethical, and infrastructural.

In low-resource settings, the inclusion of AI in writing teaching must not only factor in the varied digital literacy and competence among (allow) lecturer(s) but also students. Deep training and support are essential to enable all users to effectively and make critical interpretations of AI writing tools (Moussa & Belhiah, 2024). This power-educating stance can help teachers learn how to thoughtfully incorporate AI, and be a means for students to become critical users of these technologies (Jafar et al, 2025).

Nevertheless, the possible advantages to be gained from AI-based writing pedagogy can be profound in low-resource environments. AI-generated tools can be used for personalised feedback, collaborative learning and access to a range of writing resources that might not otherwise exist (Tr n, 2024; Neshaei et al., 2025). Using these apps, teachers can meet the unique needs of their students while promoting key writing skills.

In addition, innovative technology in writing and reading instruction involving AI can have wider societal implications for developing countries. AI tools, by democratising access to quality writing support and improving academic achievement, could promote social mobility, economic growth and lift underserved communities (Le et al., 2025).

However, the use of AI is responsible and ethically vital in these applications. Questions regarding data privacy concerns, the potential for algorithmic bias and the risk of technology-based inequality demand careful consideration as trajectories are mapped that would ensure ways to benefit from AI in writing pedagogy (Xi 2024; Ekizoğlu & Demir 2025).

Simply put, AI and writing pedagogy for low-resourced contexts can be both on the obstructing side of creativity but also foster it. If infrastructure challenges, linguistic diversity, digital literacy shortages and ethical issues are confronted by educators and policy makers, the transformational powers of these technologies for writing and education may be further leveraged to promote equitable, access-based educational futures.

b. Higher Education Pilots Using AI for Writing Instruction

The use of artificial intelligence (AI) systems in writing instruction has had significant implications for colleges and universities as they consider the possible advantages and difficulties afforded by these technologies. At several universities, there have been pilot projects and initiatives to explore how AI-informed tools affect student writing outcomes and the wider writing pedagogy itself.

A good example of this is the University of Michigan, where they have implemented a pilot project utilising the Grammarly, AI-equipped writing assistant system across its undergraduate courses (Alharbi 2023). The university's objective is to explore how Grammarly's instant feedback and recommendations can improve students' grammar, style, and writing more generally. It is by offering personalised assistance throughout the act of writing process, then, that students may find themselves developing a greater degree of self-awareness as writers.

Likewise, the University of Illinois Urbana-Champaign has used AI chatbots like ChatGPT in select first-year writing courses (Tokuda et al., 2010). These chatbots are meant to keep students engaged in interactive conversations, providing advice for brainstorming and outlining and revising written work. The pilot program at the university is to learn how AI-based writing help fits into traditional instructor feedback and enhances a more productive, group-oriented learning atmosphere.

At the University of California, Los Angeles (UCLA), researchers have investigated how researchers and scholarship might advance with the inclusion of AI-driven technologies for multilingual and neurodivergent writers (Rao & Rao, 2007). The university's efforts centre on the use of AI to support students with different language abilities and learning needs, to help ensure that all have equitable access to high-quality writing instruction.

In the UK, an experimental program has been introduced by the University of Cambridge which is experimenting with various models of adopting AI in the name of detecting plagiarism and authorship analysis (Visbal-Cadavid et al., 2017) Through AI tools, the university seeks to improve academic integrity and ethical writing habits among its students by engaging students with educational resources to understand proper use of these technologies.

These pilots of higher education writing instruction are instances of profound curiosity and play with AI-enabled writing instruction in different institutional settings. Though various methods and aims may be different among the projects, they all share the overarching objective of finding ways to exploit AI techniques for transforming learning in developing writing skills, supporting personalised instruction, and addressing the differences of various types of learners as those become evident in today's learning context.

As these pilot projects develop, universities will learn much about the practical uses of AI for teaching writing as well as the pedagogical and ethical implications of incorporating A11 technology into writing instruction. The insights gained through these efforts will be used to develop larger-scale strategies and policies that can be applied to effectively and responsibly harness AI in writing pedagogy at the higher education level.

c. Student Perceptions of AI Tools in Academic Writing

Interest in the use of artificial intelligence (AI) for academic writing instruction has increased among teachers and researchers, not least in how students perceive and experience this development. The way in which students perceive these technologies is an important factor to consider for the optimal integration into curricula and for guarantees that their use will become supportive of, and not detrimental to, learning. A variety of studies have investigated different aspects of student perceptions towards AI tools in terms of effectiveness and use, as well as their effects on writing outcomes.

For example, Mahmud (2023) underscores students' favourable experiences with AI writing tools, including Wordtune. For some EFL learners, the students mentioned that their writing has become more cohesive and sophisticated over time as they used the tool, which IDC capitalised on to improve their overall writing abilities. Repeated exposure to AI through draft and feedback stages gave participants a sense of confidence, which then pushed them towards experimenting with writing in alternative ways.

In a similar vein, Wang (2024) investigated students' generative AI-assisted writing processes and found that many students enjoy receiving instant feedback from AI programs, which helps them identify errors in the writing process and adjust their writing strategies. The fact that AI tools were perceived as diminishing students' writing anxiety may imply that such tools can reduce some of the stress inherent in academic writing.

But not all of them are flattering. For some students, there is expressed concern about reliance as AI guides may serve to impede critical thinking and the ability to write proficiently (Lee, 2024). Plagiarism and originality are identified among the most important issues associated with literary quality, which causes people to cast doubt on AI-generated content (Li et al., 2024).

Additionally, the environment in which tools are applied can shape a student's perspective. For instance, in low-resource settings, the absence of access to needed technology might increase inequality of learning opportunities, which may result in scepticism around AI tools' efficacy for improving writing skills (Yan et al., 2023).

Therefore, resources indicate a strong comprehension of the consequences of AI in writing pedagogy, thereby detailing the necessity for sound AI training and ethical guidelines to facilitate student use and properly utilize AI. The critical comprehension of student views on AI writing support may help to inform better instructional practices and to address the psycho-emotional, cognitive and pragmatic dimensions of learning when dealing with AI in academic writing.

d. Teacher-Led Innovation in AI-Enhanced Writing Classrooms

The increasing incorporation of artificial intelligence (AI) into writing instruction has created openings and challenges for educators to reimagine how we can effectively deploy such technology in teaching. Teacher-led innovation is essential to the process of making sense of writing classrooms augmented with AI and to realising the value that these tools offer while keeping true to effective principles of writing pedagogy.

One component of teacher-initiated technology integration is designing customised pedagogical strategies that seamlessly integrate AI-driven writing tools. Teachers also need to think about how these two technologies could support traditional writing instruction and help students learn while still thinking critically and building autonomous writing skills (Wang, 2024; Korth et al., 2016). This may include developing limited lesson plans that walk students through using AI tools for certain tasks, like brainstorming or drafting and revision strategies, while keeping the emphasis on the writing process and creation of fundamental competencies (in writing).

In addition, teachers will be critical enablers, shaping AI literacy among students who will need to have the ability to critically interpret and assess texts produced by writing tools based on AI (Eynon & Young, 2020). Much could be gained from teaching AI literacy, explaining its capabilities and limitations to help students build a nuanced view of when and how AI use can be responsible (and when it is not), preventing over-reliance and upholding academic integrity (Kim & Kim, 2022).

Also effective in AI-augmented writing classrooms have been collaborative approaches, instances where teachers and students jointly explore AI integration. Through facilitating peer feedback, self-reflection and collaborative problem-solving, teachers can help students to develop metacognitive processes and a wider understanding of the writing process (Yan, 2023; Asad et al., 2024). This kind of interaction can also guide ongoing improvement in teaching practices, allowing teachers to understand their students' experiences and change how they teach in the light of this understanding.

Teacher-driven initiatives not only spur classroom-level innovations but can also shape institutional policies and recommendations with respect to the use of AI for writing instruction. Through professional development, sharing of best practices, and advocacy for principled approaches, teachers can help advance holistic institutional efforts to address issues surrounding data privacy and algorithmic bias or academic honesty (Osawa, 2023).

In addition, Teachers' innovation in AI-augmented writing classrooms may have broader consequences on the field of education. Through the documentation of their experiences, exploration of new pedagogical models and the communication of their findings, teachers can contribute to feeding a developing dialogue on the appropriate use of AI technologies in education (Javahery, 2025). Teacher-driven innovation is critical for managing such challenges and leveraging the affordances of AI-enhanced writing instruction. Through designing and implementing customised instructional interventions, promoting AI literacy, facilitating learning collaboration, and advocating institutional policies, educators are well-positioned to lead the way for future writing pedagogy in the digital era (Zhang & Wu, 2024).

6. CHALLENGES AND CONCERNS

While academic integrity and overreliance on AI tools are critical concerns, they are best understood as part of a broader ethical and pedagogical landscape. This section synthesizes these issues to avoid fragmentation and reinforce their interdependence.

a. Overreliance on AI and Erosion of Critical Thinking

This issue has been intensified by the evolution of artificial Intelligence (AI) in education and learning/writing pedagogy. While the AI applications have the potential to increase writing productivity, quality of written products, and personalised feedback, they might also lead to overdependence on these digital tools, which is counterproductive for fostering critical thinking and independence in students.

A challenge for AI-based writing tools in the composition classroom is that they might cause cognitive offloading as students engage too much with AI-driven suggestions and corrections. This dependence can hinder the writing process, allowing for critical thinking to improve several key cognitive tasks such as bypassing those roles in information parsing, argumentation structuration and reviewing processes. Lamimi et al (2025) emphasised that students may become passive users of AI support systems for undermining precisely the construction of thinker right that they would postulate in their academic environment.

In addition, the use of AI and writing education can result in a void between the learning process and idea expression. Once familiarised with content and solutions generated by AI, students may lack depth of understanding and inadvertently become less creative in their composing (Gonsalves, 2024). AI tools are seductive, but once they start to dominate a student's thinking process, there is a danger of creating students who can no longer think or think critically in an academic setting (Adams & Alzaabi, 2025).

Furthermore, there remain ethical questions surrounding the use of AI in writing instruction, including those of possible plagiarism and authorship. Students may face difficulty discriminating their own work and the one produced or suggested by AI, causing a tug of war in terms of moral issues pertaining to their writing (Hasan et al., 2025; Kouam, 2024).

Also, in resource-poor settings, the availability of AI tools can further increase educational disparities. Students who are ill-prepared to adequately employ these technologies may be placed at a disadvantage, thereby exacerbating disparities in writing skills and critical thinking (Hou et al., 2025). As a result, educators need to think about how to deploy AI technology fairly and in a way that guarantees all students receive support and training.

Although AI-enabled technologies have great prospects for improving writing instruction, policymakers and educators need to consider challenges such as over-reliance on technology, erosion of critical thinking skills, and ethical concerns. In response to these challenges, it is important that we advocate for ways in which the use of AI can be leveraged to its best potential within learning settings and that technological tools help enhance rather than obfuscate student engagement, creativity and critical thinking throughout the writing process.

b. Academic Integrity and Originality

The application of artificial intelligence (AI) text generation tools to academic writing has generated several concerns about academic integrity and the accentuation of original voice. As these technologies continue to develop and reach into the classroom, there is an increasing danger that students may misuse such tools to create content that is inauthentic and that threatens the integrity of academic writing.

One of the biggest worries is that AI-authored text might be used for plagiarism. The ability of the likes of ChatGPT to generate plausible-looking original text is threatening academic integrity (Buragohain & Chaudhary, 2025; Siluvai et al., 2025). Students potentially misuse these tools to avoid the writing steps and present AI-generated material as their own (Siluvai et al., 2025; Zhu, 2024), which could result in the disruption of the development of critical thinking skill sets and writing ability.

Furthermore, authorship and intellectual property are also raised issues when it comes to AI helping in academic writing. The automated production of work can also erode the distinction between human-produced and AI-originated content, making it difficult to discern what has truly been created by a person (Abbott & Abbott, 2024; Ulum, 2024). This is a big problem in publishing and in academic writing, where the integrity of the dance between wordsmithing and credit for ideas is paramount.

These are issues that need to be addressed by institutions and academics in terms of clearly laying out standards and policies on the use of AI tools in education (Lee et al, 2025). Academic integrity policies with a clear focus on AI, together with academic programs that teach students to think critically about such technologies, can reduce the risk of plagiarism and promote student insight into the ethical aspects of these technologies (Tuppal et al., 2025; Sallam, 2023).

Moreover, the introduction of AI to academic writing must be sloganized, not by downgrading the importance of critical thinking and independent writing. Over-dependence on AI-generated content may reduce students' capacity to critically analyse, articulate coherent arguments and communicate unique thoughts (Soelistiyowati et al., 2024; Wirzal et al., 2024). It is the duty of educators to find the equilibrium between grasping the advantages of AI while nurturing one's necessary cognitive skills for learning achievement (Wirzal et al., 2024; Zhu, 2024).

The implications of AI-generated academic writing demand a holistic approach that speaks to the issues concerning originality, propriety and critical analytical skill formation. In other words, through the set of clear instructions, strong emphasis on ethical application of AI, and insistence on the extreme value of independent writing, educators and institutions can navigate this changing field to ensure that integrating AI supports rather than detracts from academic writing (Parviz, 2025; Ibrahim et al., 2024).

c. Biases in AI Tools and Linguistic Homogenization, Faculty Resistance, and Data Privacy

The widespread implementation of artificial intelligence (AI) tools in education has raised several challenges and considerations to be considered to make the most of these technologies while preserving academic integrity and equity. The most fundamental problem is the bias of AI tools, homogenising language and cancelling out diverse language features students may have. Saleem et al. (2025) point to strong cultural and linguistic biases in AI writing assistance applications, including region-specific lexico-syntactic features that are erroneously categorised as mistakes. Such discrepancies may perpetuate stereotypes and sustain current inequalities if they serve only dominant varieties against marginalised languages. This raises a crucial issue: what can educators do to ensure that AI tools help amplify, rather than stifle, the linguistic diversity of their students?

Also, the resistance of faculty to AI-based tools remains a prominent issue for incorporating these technologies in writing pedagogy. A critical issue is the lack of technology being used in predictive analytics and AI-enabled applications due to unfamiliarity with these technologies among those using them (Pan, 2024), as well as unwillingness towards effectiveness, substitution quality of traditional pedagogical methods. Resistance to integrating AI tools into the teaching of writing may also be increased by insufficient training in digital pedagogy, with instructors not knowing how to use such devices in their own teaching. These fears can be reduced, and a more favourable view of incorporating AI in the classroom can be developed through an educational system that gives educators extensive training and support.

Data privacy and surveillance in learning spaces are another significant issue. AI technology sits on vast data for developing an AI product, which has brought ethical concerns such as how one should store, use or share that data (Liu & Wang, 2024). It's partly the responsibility of educators and institutions to traverse these privacy issues responsibly by following data protection laws on securing student information.

In addition, the fact that AI could inadvertently "enslave" students is a further difficulty. An over-reliance on AI-generated content might stunt the growth of critical thinking and writing skills by students for whom automated answers become their default option rather than seriously engaging with a write-up (Durak, 2025). Teachers must navigate the application of AI tools and critical thought to promote independent idea generation and creativity, so that students remain at the centre of their learning process.

Thus, though AI tools hold great promise in strengthening writing instruction, educators must be mindful of several challenges and considerations. Dealing with AI bias, faculty pushback, student privacy concerns and being able to develop writing skills independently are steps that will be necessary to facilitate the integration of AI in education. Through confronting these challenges head-on, educators can harness the potential of AI technology for writing instruction to offer students more equitable, inclusive and impactful writing pedagogy that readies them for a digital future.

7. INSTITUTIONAL AND CLASSROOM-LEVEL IMPLICATIONS

The use of artificial intelligence (AI) tools in the higher education context, especially in writing instruction, drives both institutional and classroom changes. As the use of these technologies widens, school and university administrators need to address the challenges and opportunities they bring for teaching and learning by promoting academic integrity with a new test design strategy.

a. Institutional Implications

Institutionally, AI tools create a need to develop policies and guidelines for their use. Institutions should consider how students may use AI to produce unoriginal content that undermines academic integrity (Hua, 2023). Institutions can help reduce the risk by promoting a culture of responsible use of AI. This would include creating comprehensive programs of both training for faculty and students focused on the ethical considerations in AI, the value of original work in academic writing, and the dangers posed by cheating (Khalil & Er, 2023).

Additionally, schools must establish a supportive system that guarantees AI writing tools are available to all students in an equitable manner. This may involve the provision of technology for populations who are low-income or are otherwise underserved and who do not have access (Klarin et al., 2024). Prioritising inclusivity is key to ensuring that AI tools add value to the learning experience of all students and that we can help advance diversity and equity in academic writing skills.

b. Classroom-Level Implications

At the classroom level, teachers are instrumental in how AI tools are implemented in teaching writing. Educators need to find a middle ground between utilising AI's assistance and promoting critical thinking and self-writing among students. Although AI writing tools (AWTs) can offer valuable feedback and help students develop as writers, there may be a danger of learners developing an "overreliance" on this technology and thereby losing the potential benefits that working with it offers in terms of their cognitive development (Eldakar et al., 2025; Sullivan et al., 2023). Thus, teachers need to treat AI tools as supports, guiding explicit instruction in their use so that students retain control over their writing and are situated in deeper learning environments.

Furthermore, it is crucial to promote digital literacy for students to make sense of the ethical issues of using AI tools. Teachers can promote discussion of the benefits and drawbacks of AI in writing instruction by encouraging learners to critically evaluate output generated by AI, thinking about what it means for their learning (Pan, 2024). By including education about the ethical use of AI, teachers can encourage students' consideration of academic integrity and ethical technology use.

Additionally, peer engagement and feedback can be improved by joint learning environments integrating AI tools. When faculty use AI for activities in the classroom, such as brainstorming or editing, this can create a community around students and promote more elaborate processing of the writing (Matthews & Volpe, 2023). This collaborative strategy is in accordance with constructivist pedagogies that stress the interactive and social nature of learning.

In short, AI tools in writing instruction have vast implications for the organisation and in individual classrooms. Through clear policy, ethical AI use, encouragement of digital literacy and focus on individualised instruction in educational institutions, educators can create a culture where the most powerful aspects of AI are realised whilst learners' academic integrity is nurtured and their writing skills developed. As these tools develop, consistent discussion and cooperation between educators, administrators and policymakers will be crucial to harnessing the power of AI in higher education.

8. PROSPECTS AND INNOVATIONS IN AI-BASED WRITING PEDAGOGY

The integration of artificial intelligence (AI) in writing instruction holds immense potential for transformative innovations that can enhance student learning outcomes and reshape the future of writing pedagogy. As the field continues to evolve, several key areas of prospects and innovations emerge.

a. Adaptive and Personalised Writing Assistance

One of the most anticipated innovations is the AI-based writing assistants, which can offer myriad individualised and adaptive help to students. Leveraging Machine Learning and natural language processing, the tools analyse individual writing styles, point out weak spots in their work, and provide real-time personalised feedback and advice. This degree of personalisation can help students take charge of their writing development and become more engaged with the process of writing.

b. Multimodal and Multimedia Writing Experiences

The future trajectory toward AI-driven writing instruction may also include multimodal media and multimedia integration. AI can support the natural integration of visual, audio and interactive elements in creating writing, as students experiment with different ways to express themselves and learning opportunities. This can encourage creativity, improve learning outcomes and help to better equip students for the multimodal world of online writing and communication.

c. Collaborative and Social Writing Environments

AI-powered products can also reconfigure the social life of writing instruction, creating opportunities for more collaborative and interactive kinds of learning. AI-enabled platforms could also allow students to engage in peer-to-peer feedback, conduct group brainstorming or shared revisions, and develop a sense of community and collective learning. With the help of AI in collaborative writing areas, instructors could develop fundamental competencies like critical thinking, problem solving and communication skills.

d. Automated Feedback and Assessment

AI could also transform the way feedback and assessment are given to students in writing pedagogy. AI-powered writing tools can assess student writing as it is written, providing instantaneous feedback on grammar, style, structure and substance. This can allow teachers to then focus on higher-order thinking and provide more insightful qualitative feedback to students, along with the benefits for students of using iterative drafts and self-assessment.

e Ethical and Responsible Integration

Now that AI writing tools are getting more attention, addressing the ethical and responsible use of these technologies is increasingly critical. The authors in this study suggest that the development of set guidelines and policies to regulate the ethical use of AI to foster Internet (digital) literacy and critical thinking is an important step to realising any potential benefits from AI use in writing instruction, without resulting compromise on academic integrity or insufficient learning.

f. Bridging Gaps and Promoting Equity

AI tools in writing could fill gaps related to access to high-quality instruction in writing, especially for underserved or under-resourced communities. AI has the potential to democratise access to good-quality writing assistance and can help underprivileged students improve their writing skills by delivering an affordable, scalable means of support. But of course, it's also very important to think about fairness and bias in AI and so on.

They are the corners of potential and change as AI-based writing pedagogy continues to grow, grapple with growing pains, and challenge traditional perspectives on how writing can be learned and taught. By capitalising on these advances without losing sight of sound pedagogical principles and training in key writing features, teachers can use AI's enhanced capabilities to deliver more interactive, individualised and impactful writing instruction for the 21st-century writer.

Figure 2. Prospects and Innovations in AI-Based Writing Pedagogy

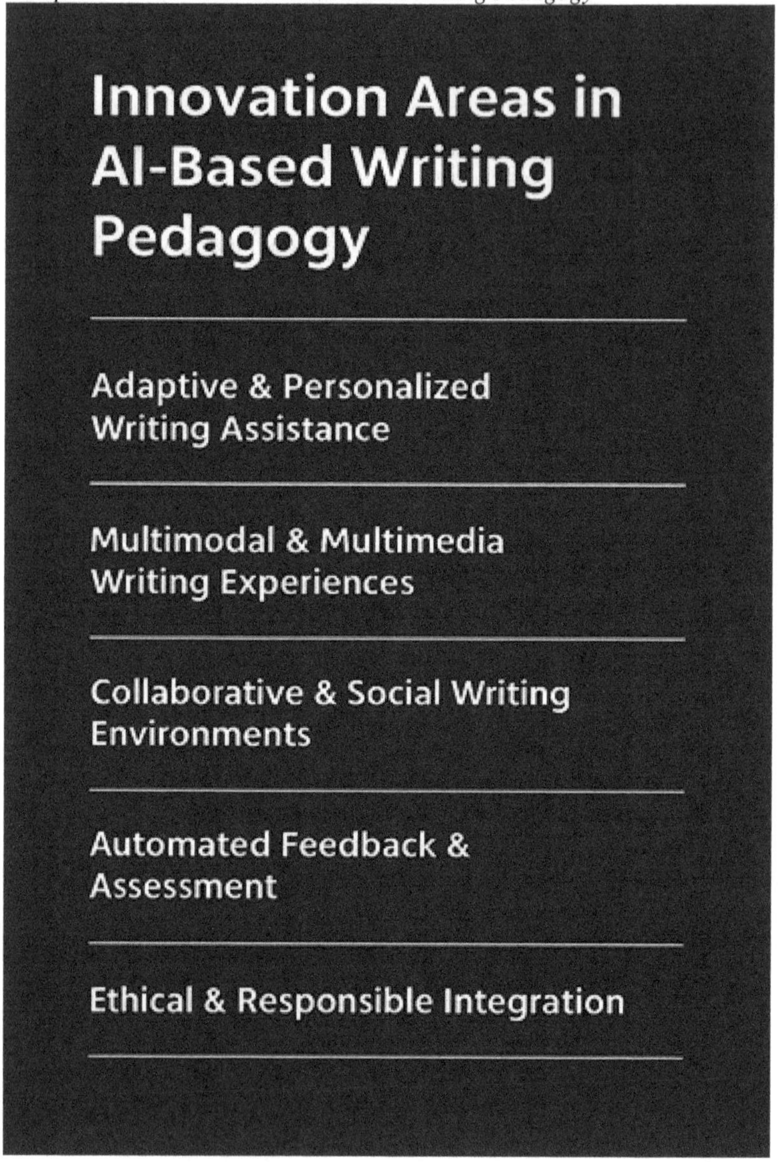

From Figure 2 the adaptive feedback to equity-driven access, these innovation areas represent the frontier of AI-enhanced writing pedagogy. Each domain invites educators to rethink how writing is taught, supported, and assessed, ensuring that technology amplifies human creativity, collaboration, and critical thinking.

8. CONCLUSION

The integration of artificial intelligence into writing pedagogy marks an important shift in how educators approach instruction, feedback, and learner engagement. Far from being a simple scientific upgrade, AI tools, when thoughtfully deployed, can scaffold critical thinking, personalise learning pathways, and democratize access to high-quality writing support. Yet, this promise is not without complexity. As this chapter has argued, the pedagogic value of AI lies not in automation alone, but in its capacity to foster deeper reflection, creativity, and moral awareness. In low-resource contexts, AI can serve as a bridge to opportunity but only if infrastructural, linguistic, and ethnic barriers are addressed through inclusive design and policy reform. Likewise, in higher education, pilot programs must evolve into evidence-based frameworks that embed AI literacy and integrity into curriculum design. Ultimately, the future of writing instruction is not about choosing between tradition and technology; it is about integrating both to cultivate writers who are not only competent but critically conscious. Educators, administrators, and policymakers must collaborate to ensure that AI-enhanced pedagogy remains learner-centred, ethically grounded, and contextually responsive. Only then can we realise the full potential of AI as a transformative force in theoretical writing education.

REFERENCES

Abbott, M., & Abbott, W. (2024). Artificial intelligence or nursing student? revisiting clues in the connectives. *Nurse Educator, 49*(6), 306–309. DOI: 10.1097/NNE.0000000000001696 PMID: 38968438

Adams, L. & Alzaabi, I. (2025). Chatgpt., 157-188. DOI: 10.4018/979-8-3373-0771-8.ch007

Al-Raimi, M., Mudhsh, B., Al-Yafaei, Y., & Al-Maashani, S. (2024). Utilizing artificial intelligence tools for improving writing skills: Exploring omani efl learners' perspectives. *Forum for Linguistic Studies, 6*(2). Advance online publication. DOI: 10.59400/fls.v6i2.1177

Alharbi, W. (2023). Ai in the foreign language classroom: A pedagogical overview of automated writing assistance tools. *Education Research International, 2023*, 1–15. DOI: 10.1155/2023/4253331

Aljuaid, H. (2024). The impact of artificial intelligence tools on academic writing instruction in higher education: A systematic review. *Arab World English Journal, 1*(1), 26–55. DOI: 10.24093/awej/ChatGPT.2

Anh, N. & Dieu, P. (2025). Teaching ai to high school students for enhancing argumentative essay writing skills., 325-348. https://doi.org/DOI: 10.4018/979-8-3693-7260-9.ch015

Apata, A. O., & Oyenuga, M. O. (2025). Undergraduates' Application of ChatGPT in Academic Writing: Perceptions, Problems and Prospects. *International Journal of Social Sciences and Management Review, 8*(3), 201–218. DOI: 10.37602/IJSSMR.2025.8312

Apata, S. B., & Oyenuga, M. O. (2025). Revolutionizing Employability: The Intersection of Digital Literacy, Inclusive Education, and Gen Z's Skill Set in the 21st Century. In Ajani, O. (Ed.), *Empowering Pre-Service Teachers to Enhance Inclusive Education Through Technology* (pp. 155–182). IGI Global Scientific Publishing., DOI: 10.4018/979-8-3693-8759-7.ch006

Apriani, E., Cardoso, L., Obaid, A., Muthmainnah, M., Wijayanti, E., Esmianti, F., & Supardan, D. (2024). Impact of ai-powered chatbots on efl students' writing skills, self-efficacy, and self-regulation: A mixed-methods study. *GERR, 1*(2), 57–72. DOI: 10.71380/GERR-08-2024-8

Asad, M., Shahzad, S., Shah, S., Sherwani, F., & Almusharraf, N. (2024). Chatgpt as artificial intelligence-based generative multimedia for english writing pedagogy: Challenges and opportunities from an educator's perspective. *International Journal of Information and Learning Technology, 41*(5), 490–506. DOI: 10.1108/IJILT-02-2024-0021

Behizadeh, N. (2014). Mitigating the dangers of a single story. *Educational Researcher, 43*(3), 125–136. DOI: 10.3102/0013189X14529604

Bremholm, J., Kabel, K., Liberg, C., & Skar, G. (2022). A review of scandinavian writing research between 2010 and 2020. *Writing & Pedagogy, 13*(1-3), 7–49. DOI: 10.1558/wap.21637

Buragohain, D., & Chaudhary, S. (2025). Navigating chatgpt in asean higher education: Ethical and pedagogical perspectives. *Computer Applications in Engineering Education, 33*(4), e70062. Advance online publication. DOI: 10.1002/cae.70062

Crossley, S., Müldner, K., & McNamara, D. (2016). Idea generation in student writing. *Written Communication*, *33*(3), 328–354. DOI: 10.1177/0741088316650178

Cumming, A. (1989). Writing expertise and second-language proficiency*. *Language Learning*, *39*(1), 81–135. DOI: 10.1111/j.1467-1770.1989.tb00592.x

Durak, H. (2025). A comparison of human-written versus AI-generated text in discussions at educational settings: Investigating features for ChatGPT, Gemini and Bingai. *European Journal of Education*, *60*(1), e70014. Advance online publication. DOI: 10.1111/ejed.70014

Ekizoğlu, M., & Demir, A. (2025). Ai-assisted writing feedback for enhancing secondary students' writing skills: an experimental study. https://doi.org/DOI: 10.21203/rs.3.rs-6430737/v1

Eldakar, M., Shehata, A., & Ammar, A. (2025). What motivates academics in Egypt toward generative ai tools? an integrated model of TAM, SCT, UTAUT2, perceived ethics, and academic integrity. *Information Development*, *41*(3), 747–765. DOI: 10.1177/02666669251314859

Ербулатова, И., Бердибаева, Д., & Ербулатов, К. (2025). Лингвистические аспекты применения ии в анализе и интерпретации текста. *Б ИТУ Хабаршысы*, *35*(3), 143–152. DOI: 10.62724/202530203

Eynon, R., & Young, E. (2020). Methodology, legend, and rhetoric: The constructions of ai by academia, industry, and policy groups for lifelong learning. *Science, Technology & Human Values*, *46*(1), 166–191. DOI: 10.1177/0162243920906475

Gonsalves, C. (2024). Generative ai's impact on critical thinking: Revisiting bloom's taxonomy. *Journal of Marketing Education*, 02734753241305980. Advance online publication. DOI: 10.1177/02734753241305980

Hasan, S., Nasreen, S., & Rasul, S. (2025). Leveraging artificial intelligence (ai) in higher education: Fostering soft skills communication, collaboration, creativity and critical thinking among university students. *IJLSS*, *3*(2), 1–7. DOI: 10.71000/c42srm97

Hou, C., Zhu, G., & Sudarshan, V. (2025). The role of critical thinking on undergraduates' reliance behaviours on generative ai in problem-solving. *British Journal of Educational Technology*, *56*(5), 1919–1941. DOI: 10.1111/bjet.13613

Hua, J. (2023). Beyond exams: Investigating ai tool impact on student attitudes, ethical awareness, and academic dishonesty in online college assessments. *International Journal of Educational Management and Development Studies*, *4*(4), 160–185. DOI: 10.53378/353030

Ibrahim, A., Taura, A., Iliyasu, A., Shogbesan, Y., & Lukman, S. (2024). Artificial intelligence (ai): Perception and utilization of ai technologies in educational assessment in nigerian universities. *Edukasiana Jurnal Inovasi Pendidikan*, *3*(3), 367–380. DOI: 10.56916/ejip.v3i3.763

Jafar, S. H., Oyedele, O. M., Nawaah, D., & Bolanle, A. S. (2025). Exploring Leadership Challenges for Adoption of Digital Innovation and Sustainability. Singh, R., Corvello, V., Coniglio, I.M. and Khan, S. (Ed.) *Innovation Ecosystems and Sustainable Technologies (Emerald Studies in Sustainable Innovation Management)*, Emerald Publishing Limited, Leeds, pp. 253-269. DOI: 10.1108/978-1-83662-368-720251012

Jai Lamimi, I., El Jemli, S., & Zeryouh, I.LAMIMI. (2025). Enhancing critical thinking: Exploring human-ai synergy in student cognitive development. *Arab World English Journal*, (1), 251–269. DOI: 10.24093/awej/AI.14

Javahery, P. (2025). Analyzing discourse patterns in chatgpt-generated ielts writing task 2 essays: a discourse analysis approach. https://doi.org/DOI: 10.21203/rs.3.rs-5608928/v1

Jiang, D., & Kalyuga, S. (2022). Learning english as a foreign language writing skills in collaborative settings: A cognitive load perspective. *Frontiers in Psychology*, *13*, 932291. Advance online publication. DOI: 10.3389/fpsyg.2022.932291 PMID: 35846619

Jingxin, G., & Razali, A. (2020). Tapping the potential of pigai automated writing evaluation (awe) program to give feedback on efl writing. *Universal Journal of Educational Research*, *8*(12B), 8334–8343. DOI: 10.13189/ujer.2020.082638

Khalil, M., & Er, E. (2023). Will chatgpt get you caught? rethinking of plagiarism detection. https://doi.org/DOI: 10.1007/978-3-031-34411-4_32

Kim, N., & Kim, M. (2022). Teacher's perceptions of using an artificial intelligence-based educational tool for scientific writing. *Frontiers in Education*, *7*, 755914. Advance online publication. DOI: 10.3389/feduc.2022.755914

Klarin, J., Hoff, E., Larsson, A., & Daukantaitė, D. (2024). Adolescents' use and perceived usefulness of generative ai for schoolwork: Exploring their relationships with executive functioning and academic achievement. *Frontiers in Artificial Intelligence*, *7*, 1415782. Advance online publication. DOI: 10.3389/frai.2024.1415782 PMID: 39263526

Kong, S., Lee, J., & Tsang, O. (2024). A pedagogical design for self-regulated learning in academic writing using text-based generative artificial intelligence tools: 6-p pedagogy of plan, prompt, preview, produce, peer-review, portfolio-tracking. Research and Practice in Technology Enhanced Learning, 19, 030. https://doi.org/DOI: 10.58459/rptel.2024.19030

Korth, B., Wimmer, J., Wilcox, B., Morrison, T., Harward, S., Peterson, N., Simmerman, S., & Pierce, L. (2016). Practices and challenges of writing instruction in k-2 classrooms: A case study of five primary grade teachers. *Early Childhood Education Journal*, *45*(2), 237–249. DOI: 10.1007/s10643-016-0774-1

Kouam, A. (2024). Ai in academic writing: Ally or foe? *International Journal of Research Publications*, *148*(1). Advance online publication. DOI: 10.47119/IJRP1001481520246427

Le, H., Shen, Y., Li, Z., Xia, M., Tang, L., Li, X., Jia, J., Wang, Q., Gašević, D., & Fan, Y. (2025). Breaking human dominance: Investigating learners' preferences for learning feedback from generative ai and human tutors. *British Journal of Educational Technology*, *56*(5), 1758–1783. DOI: 10.1111/bjet.13614

Lee, B., Ku, S., & Ko, K. (2025). ai robots promote south korean preschoolers' ai literacy and computational thinking. *Family Relations*, *74*(3), 1354–1375. DOI: 10.1111/fare.13189

Lee, S. (2024). Analyzing the use of ai writing assistants in generating texts with standard American English conventions: A case study of chatgpt and bard. *The CATESOL Journal*, *35*(1). Advance online publication. DOI: 10.5070/B5.25364

Leggette, H., Rutherford, T., Dunsford, D., & Costello, L. (2015). A review and evaluation of prominent theories of writing. *Journal of Applied Communications*, *99*(3). Advance online publication. DOI: 10.4148/1051-0834.1056

Li, J., Zong, H., Wu, E., Wu, R., Peng, Z., Zhao, J., Yang, L., Xie, H., & Shen, B. (2024). Exploring the potential of artificial intelligence to enhance the writing of English academic papers by non-native english-speaking medical students - the educational application of ChatGPT. *BMC Medical Education*, *24*(1), 736. Advance online publication. DOI: 10.1186/s12909-024-05738-y PMID: 38982429

Liu, W., & Wang, Y. (2024). The effects of using ai tools on critical thinking in english literature classes among efl learners: An intervention study. *European Journal of Education*, *59*(4), e12804. Advance online publication. DOI: 10.1111/ejed.12804

Mahmud, F. (2023). Investigating efl students' writing skills through artificial intelligence: Wordtune application as a tool. *Journal of Language Teaching and Research*, *14*(5), 1395–1404. DOI: 10.17507/jltr.1405.28

Matthews, J., & Volpe, C. (2023). Academics' perceptions of chatgpt-generated written outputs: A practical application of turing's imitation game. *Australasian Journal of Educational Technology*, *39*(5), 82–100. DOI: 10.14742/ajet.8896

Minh, A. (2024). Leveraging ChatGPT for enhancing English writing skills and critical thinking in university freshmen. Journal of Knowledge Learning and Science Technology Issn 2959-6386 (Online), 3(2), 51-62. https://doi.org/DOI: 10.60087/jklst.vol3.n2.p62

Moussa, A., & Belhiah, H. (2024). Beyond syntax: exploring moroccan undergraduate efl learners' engagement with ai-assisted writing. https://doi.org/DOI: 10.31235/osf.io/3fr45

Murugason, L. (2025). Evaluating chatgpt's influence on esl educators' teaching and motivation.. https://doi.org/DOI: 10.71284/asc.2025132

Muslimin, A., Mukminatien, N., & Maria, I. (2024). Evaluating cami ai across smar stages: Students' achievement and perceptions in efl writing instruction. *Online Learning : the Official Journal of the Online Learning Consortium*, *28*(2). Advance online publication. DOI: 10.24059/olj.v28i2.4246

Nazari, N., Shabbir, M., & Setiawan, R. (2021). Application of artificial intelligence powered digital writing assistant in higher education: Randomized controlled trial. *Heliyon*, *7*(5), e07014. DOI: 10.1016/j.heliyon.2021.e07014 PMID: 34027198

Neshaei, S., Mejia-Domenzain, P., Davis, R., & Käser, T. (2025). Metacognition meets ai: Empowering reflective writing with large language models. *British Journal of Educational Technology*, *56*(5), 1864–1896. DOI: 10.1111/bjet.13601

Ng, C., & Cheung, Y. (2018). Mediation in a socio-cognitive approach to writing for elementary students: Instructional scaffolding. *Education Sciences*, *8*(3), 92. DOI: 10.3390/educsci8030092

Osawa, K. (2023). Integrating automated written corrective feedback into e-portfolios for second language writing: Notion and notion ai. *RELC Journal*, *55*(3), 881–887. DOI: 10.1177/00336882231198913

Oyenuga, M. O., Apata, S. B., & Sulaiman, M. M. (2024). Pre-Service Teachers' Perceptions and Utilisation of Chatgpt in Higher Institutions using UTAUT Theory: Evidence from an Emerging Economy. *British Journal of Contemporary Education*, *4*(2), 28–42. DOI: 10.52589/BJCE-DBIT7S4T

Oyenuga, M. O., & Omale, S. A. (2024). Is Africa Jinxed? Exploring the Challenges of Technology Access and Adoption in Africa. *African Journal of Economic and Sustainable Development*, *7*(4), 142–161. DOI: 10.52589/AJESD-ULN1LRNF

Pan, J. (2024). Ai-driven english language learning program and academic writing integrity in the era of intelligent interface. *English Language Teaching and Linguistics Studies*, *6*(4), 120. DOI: 10.22158/eltls.v6n4p120

Parviz, M. (2025). Generative ai in the english composition classroom practical and adaptable strategies. *International Journal of Computer-Assisted Language Learning and Teaching*, *15*(1), 1–5. DOI: 10.4018/IJCALLT.386135

Pitenoee, M., Modaberi, A., & Ardestani, E. (2017). The effect of cognitive and metacognitive writing strategies on content of the iranian intermediate efl learners' writing. *Journal of Language Teaching and Research*, *8*(3), 594. DOI: 10.17507/jltr.0803.19

Prasetya, R., & Raharjo, D. (2023). Enhancing english language writing skills: An evaluation of the efficacy of grammarly application. *Journal of English Language & Studies*, *8*(2), 320. DOI: 10.30870/jels.v8i2.19294

Rahayu, R., Weda, S., Muliati, , & De Vega, N. (2024). Artificial intelligence in writing instruction: A self-determination theory perspective. *Xlinguae*, *17*(1), 234–244. DOI: 10.18355/XL.2024.17.01.16

Rahimi, M., & Noroozisiam, E. (2013). The effect of strategies-based instruction on the improvement of EFL learners' writing quality. *SAGE Open*, *3*(2), 2158244013494222. Advance online publication. DOI: 10.1177/2158244013494222

Ramadhan, R., Rahim, A., & Paris, A. (2024). Enhancing academic writing through digital tools: A systematic review. *Journal of Language and Literature Studies*, *4*(4), 707–770. DOI: 10.36312/jolls.v4i4.2342

Rao, K., & Rao, R. (2007). Perspectives in medical education 5. implementing a more integrated, interactive and interesting curriculum to improve Japanese medical education. *The Keio Journal of Medicine*, *56*(3), 75–84. DOI: 10.2302/kjm.56.75 PMID: 17906418

Rashtchi, M. (2019). Scaffolding argumentative essay writing via reader-response approach: A case study. *Asian-Pacific Journal of Second and Foreign Language Education*, *4*(1), 12. Advance online publication. DOI: 10.1186/s40862-019-0078-2

Roa, A., & Halim, S. (2024). The impact of ai-powered software on second language (l2) writing: A systematic literature review. *Research and Innovation in Applied Linguistics-Electronic Journal*, *2*(2), 138. DOI: 10.31963/rial.v2i2.4801

Saleem, T., Saleem, A., & Aslam, D. (2025). Integrating AI in Pakistani ESL classrooms: Teachers' practices, perspectives, and impact on student performance. *PLoS One*, *20*(9), e0333352. DOI: 10.1371/journal.pone.0333352 PMID: 41026767

Sallam, M. (2023). The utility of ChatGPT as an example of large language models in healthcare education, research and practice: systematic review on the future perspectives and potential limitations. https://doi.org/DOI: 10.1101/2023.02.19.23286155

Saran, A. (2024). Effect of teaching strategies on students' German writing skills at saudi international schools. *Saudi Journal of Language Studies*, *4*(1), 47–68. DOI: 10.1108/SJLS-10-2023-0049

Schuster, J. (2019). Writing instruction and assessment for struggling learners.. https://doi.org/DOI: 10.3102/1443450

Siluvai, S., Narayanan, V., Ramachandran, V., & Lazar, V. (2025). Generative pre-trained transformer: trends, applications, strengths and challenges in dentistry: a systematic review. *Healthcare Informatics Research*, *31*(2), 189–199. DOI: 10.4258/hir.2025.31.2.189 PMID: 40384070

Slavkov, N. (2015). Sociocultural theory, the l2 writing process, and google drive: Strange bedfellows? *TESL Canada Journal*, *32*(2), 80. DOI: 10.18806/tesl.v32i2.1209

Soelistiyowati, E., Permatasari, A., Nugroho, V., & Kusmulyadi, A. (2024). Enhancing college learners' writing skills through the integration of ChatGPT: Strategies, benefits, and concerns. *Eralingua Jurnal Pendidikan Bahasa Asing Dan Sastra*, *8*(1), 1. DOI: 10.26858/eralingua.v8i1.53461

Sullivan, M., Kelly, A., & McLaughlan, P. (2023). ChatGPT in higher education: Considerations for academic integrity and student learning. *Journal of Applied Learning & Teaching*, *6*(1). Advance online publication. DOI: 10.37074/jalt.2023.6.1.17

Tian, W., Ge, J., Zhao, Y., & Zheng, X. (2024). Ai chatbots in Chinese higher education: Adoption, perception, and influence among graduate students—an integrated analysis utilizing utaut and ecm models. *Frontiers in Psychology*, *15*, 1268549. Advance online publication. DOI: 10.3389/fpsyg.2024.1268549 PMID: 38384353

Tokuda, Y., Gotō, E., Otaki, J., Jacobs, J., Omata, F., Shapiro, M., Soejima, K., Ishida, Y., Ohde, S., Takahashi, O., & Fukui, T. (2010). Educational environment of university and non-university hospitals in Japan. *International Journal of Medical Education*, *1*, 10–14. DOI: 10.5116/ijme.4ba1.4034

Tr n, T. (2024). Ai tools in teaching and learning english academic writing skills. *Proceedings of the Asiacall International Conference*, 4, 170-187. https://doi.org/DOI: 10.54855/paic.23413

Tuppal, C., Atendido, M., Atendido, A., Ninobla, M., Fadlilah, S., & Roa, M. (2025). Introducing chatgpt in undergraduate research among nursing students: a quasi- experimental study. https://doi.org/DOI: 10.21203/rs.3.rs-5915492/v1

Ulum, Ö. (2024). Unveiling the layers: Analyzing chatgpt implementations in turkish state universities. *BEDU*, *5*(1), 114–134. DOI: 10.29329/bedu.2024.651.7

UNESCO. (2024). *AI in education: Global adoption trends and policy implications.* United Nations Educational, Scientific and Cultural Organization. https://unesdoc.unesco.org/

VanDerHeide, J. (2017). Classroom talk as writing instruction for learning to make writing moves in literary arguments. *Reading Research Quarterly*, *53*(3), 323–344. DOI: 10.1002/rrq.196

Visbal-Cadavid, D., Martínez-Gómez, M., & Guijarro, F. (2017). Assessing the efficiency of public universities through dea. a case study. *Sustainability (Basel)*, *9*(8), 1416. DOI: 10.3390/su9081416

Wang, C. (2024). Exploring students' generative AI-assisted writing processes: Perceptions and experiences from native and nonnative English speakers. *Technology Knowledge and Learning*, *30*(3), 1825–1846. DOI: 10.1007/s10758-024-09744-3

Wirzal, M., Nordin, N., Halim, N., & Bustam, M. (2024). Generative ai in science education: A learning revolution or a threat to academic integrity? a bibliometric analysis. *Jurnal Penelitian Dan Pengkajian Ilmu Pendidikan E-Saintika*, *8*(3), 319–351. DOI: 10.36312/e-saintika.v8i3.2127

Wolbers, K., Dostal, H., Graham, S., Branum-Martin, L., & Holcomb, L. (2021). Specialized writing instruction for deaf students: A randomized controlled trial. *Exceptional Children*, *88*(2), 185–204. DOI: 10.1177/00144029211050849

Xi, L. (2024). Research on the english writing teaching model in the ai era. *MMSE*, *6*(3), 111. DOI: 10.22158/mmse.v6n3p111

Yan, D. (2023). How ChatGPT's automatic text generation impact on learners in a l2 writing practicum: an exploratory investigation. https://doi.org/DOI: 10.35542/osf.io/s4nfz

Yan, L., Sha, L., Zhao, L., Li, Y., Martínez-Maldonado, R., Chen, G., Li, X., Jin, Y., & Gašević, D. (2023). Practical and ethical challenges of large language models in education: A systematic scoping review. *British Journal of Educational Technology*, *55*(1), 90–112. DOI: 10.1111/bjet.13370

Zamel, V. (1983). The composing processes of advanced esl students: Six case studies. *TESOL Quarterly*, *17*(2), 165. DOI: 10.2307/3586647

Zhang, L. & Wu, Z. (2024). Enhancing postgraduate academic writing skills through course reform: an action research study. Social Education Research, 217-233. https://doi.org/DOI: 10.37256/ser.5220244202

Zhu, Y. (2024). Construction of evaluation framework for classroom teaching reform of students empowered by digitalization. *Pacific International Journal*, *7*(1), 174–178. DOI: 10.55014/pij.v7i1.531

Zumbrunn, S., & Krause, K. (2012). Conversations with leaders: Principles of effective writing instruction. *The Reading Teacher*, *65*(5), 346–353. DOI: 10.1002/TRTR.01053

Chapter 2
Ink, Algorithms, and Imagination: The New Writing Trinity

Ankita Pathak
https://orcid.org/0000-0002-8068-8874
GLA University, Institute of Business Management, India

Majdi Anwar Quttainah
https://orcid.org/0000-0002-6280-1060
Kuwait University, Kuwait

ABSTRACT

Artificial intelligence is revolutionizing the writing. AI is changing every domain from journalism to scholarly publishing, AI-based tools are helping in generating abstracts, articles, and editing language with accuracy and speed.The chapter starts with explaining how large language models produce human-like text. The section includes AI's role in providing formative feedback in education, and enable the learners to refine arguments and grammar while developing confidence in writing. Practical application of AI is demonstrated through recent research. The issues of misinformation, plagiarism, and the decrease in critical thinking are also presented, with the emphasis being made on the fact that the use of automated processes might be problematic. . In the section on future trends, the viewpoint has demonstrated the significance of human skills in group writing, critical thinking, and emotional intelligence as AI continues to expand its computing capabilities.

1. INTRODUCTION

Artificial intelligence is changing the game and becoming more than just a specialised computing tool. It is also having an impact on how we produce, share, and use knowledge. While it is true that AI has the potential to impact almost every facet of education, writing is also significantly altered. Human-like text can now be produced by chatbots like ChatGPT, BERT, and LLaMA (Alipour et al., 2024). These models, having been trained on massive data sets, and able to generate coherent text, compelling arguments, and even original writing (Ilieva

DOI: 10.4018/979-8-3373-5601-3.ch002

et al., 2023). The generated content is creating difficulty in distinguishing human writing and machine-generated writing.

Writing was traditionally seen as a cognitive practice that require reflection, critical thinking, and cultural memory. With generative AI, the practice of writing is reinvented. Algorithmic systems are now contributing to various area likes scholarly essays, news reports, policy briefs, literary fiction, and educational content (Bearman et al., 2023). It produce the outputs with remarkable fluency. AI has a capacity to analyze vast quantities of information within seconds and create in adaptable language has made AI as a collaborator in human communication (Jarrahi et al., 2023).

AI has the ability to produce content that can be compared to that of a human being has also brought up the issue of authenticity, originality and the lack of the individuality of human writing i.e., emotional undertones and interpretive richness (Begum, 2025). The concept of writing has been transformed into two realities using AI. On the one hand, AI is more productive when it comes to making a draught, perfecting grammar, and simplifying the information that is challenging to comprehend. They motivate bilingual authors that assist students to develop arguments and offer timely feedback. On the other hand, the use of AI is transforming professional work process in journalism (It creates a report on financial markets and natural disasters), in academia (Jha & Singh, 2025) (it assists in synthesising the literature and writing pre-abstract) and becomes the cause of dependence on artificial structure, plagiarism, the problem of privacy of data, and the impossibility to teach students critical thinking and creativity. Such interplay between the rights of people and the development of technology might be traced in the manner in which the data is governed through the laws as the General Data Protection Regulation (GDPR). There are situations when proctoring or surveillance software is used and these raise the question of consent, equity, and transparency and underline the threat of collecting too much information. Although the generative AI is a strong, yet not flawless companion, it cannot be viewed as a disruptive threat or a revolutionary enabler. No intentionality, no consciousness or actual experience, yet, it can increase the human abilities, computational reasoning. Human creativity, criticality and moral consciousness are viewed to be inevitable, yet, not avoidable. This combination of AI and the human self would establish a certain equilibrium by preserving the diversity of the human manifestation and applying computing capacity to stimulate creativity and intellectual work (Youvan, 2024).This chapter will explain how generative AI technologies are transforming writing, learning, and content creation. Further, it will present a detailed factual review of the capabilities of generative AI, its limitations, and its influence on writers' practices in classrooms, universities, businesses, and the arts. The chapter-end questions will revolve around the themes of accountability for AI-assisted writing, safeguarding of originality, and the influence of machine-generated texts on the development of critical thinking skills, which have become significantly more prominent over time.

The chapter's emphasis will be on deepening the understanding of the impact of AI on writing and on offering a practical, realistic model for human-AI collaboration. This chapter is meant to support the readers in the correct, considerate use of AI tools rather than their imitative .

2. AI IN WRITING – CAPABILITIES AND TECHNOLOGIES

2.1 Evolution of Computational Writing Systems

Gradually but progressively the artificial intelligence in writing has evolved with the scope of stiff systems to versatile generative designs (Peckham et al., 2025). In the ancient times the writing tools were founded on the rule based systems which laid strict provisions of vocabulary, grammar, and syntax. These were mainly grammar checkers that had a small range of functionality. They were not flexible and not able to capture the natural language. The second step in development was the statistical knowledge that emerged in the 20th century. Non-probability-based algorithms started to find relationships in words and phrases by analyzing large amounts of text. This improved flexibility in using translation tools. Proper AI-generated writing relies on deep learning and transformer structures. These developments have made it easier to understand the context of longer texts (Campino, 2025).

2.2 The Architecture of Large Language Models

AI writing needs transformer architecture. This neural network structure helps connect words over long distances. Unlike other recurrent neural networks that access information one by one, transformers use self-attention (Nieminen, 2023). This method helps them understand the meaning of a word within a sentence. Parallel language processing, efficiency, and scale have led to the development of large language models (LLM) trained on billions of parameters (Naveed et al., 2025). These parameters serve as adjustable weights, supported by a vast number of terabytes of text. The models we use today have hundreds of billions of parameters, while older models only had millions. This shift has improved the coherence, variety, and context of the outputs. Large language models create responses that mimic human fluency by estimating word combinations, but they do not truly understand the text (Cai et al., 2023).

2.3 Generative Capacities and Adaptive Performance

AI writing tools can do much more than just correct grammar or predict noise (Zhang et al., 2024). With few-shot and zero-shot learning methods (Roe et al., 2023), AI models can do things with very little or even no training data. The model with same input, little prompt can write a scientific abstract, compose a poem, produce computer code, and write a news article all from the same input prompt (Gero, 2023). This adaptability shows the potential use of generative AI in multi-domain. AI is adaptive as model can change tone, structure, according to user input. These models can generate the output text for academic, professional, journalistic, and creative purposes (Beckett & Yaseen, 2023). Their ability to customize their output for the audience makes them invaluable in the education as there is a need for clarity and precision.

2.4 Multilingual and Inclusive Writing Support

AI is indifferent due to its multilingual ability. Since AI can produce content in multiple languages, it welcomes non-native speakers and provides equal access to professional and academic discourse (Santorelli & Catullo, 2023). Participation in global knowledge exchange is made easier by the inclusiveness. Since researchers have limited language skills, AI serves as a mediator, ensuring that style and coherence meet international standards. It has broadened the accessibility and promotes equity by expression of voices from various cultural backgrounds in international dialogue (Sharma et al., 2025).

2.5 Constraints and Ethical Concerns

The AI writing system has improved the process but is limited by its inherent constraints. The output relies on training data (Khalifa & Albadawy, 2024). When the data is biased, it reflects bias in gender, culture, or ideology. The text generated by LLMs is syntactically correct but it lacks intentional nor conscious (Wu et al., 2025). The output is based on probability distributions rather than actual knowledge. One negative aspect of LLMs is the lack of transparency. Users often cannot understand the reasoning behind a specific answer. It is simply impossible to follow how AI reaches its conclusions (Barman et al., 2024). Holding someone accountable for their actions and knowing what is happening are crucial in research and education (Wilf et al., 2024). This opens the door to misusing LLMs in various ways, such as creating offensive and false materials and allowing students to cheat with plagiarized papers (Scott et al., 2024). To support their arguments, writers might rely on a few phrases or even entire sentences generated by LLMs. This practice lowers the quality of writing since the paper will contain the usual repetitive phrases found in AI-generated texts. Additionally, authors may overuse AI to generate ideas or copy large sections, only making superficial edits. This can lead to academic dishonesty and plagiarism. Researchers and students may struggle to find many positive aspects of LLMs and choose to pursue other options.

2.6 Balancing Innovation with Responsibility

The technology is characterized in a scholarly article as both a burden and a support. It is capable of augmenting human inventiveness and connectivity as well as providing ease, effectiveness, and openness (Haber et al., 2025). But this improvement also poses issues of ethics, individuality, and authenticity. With such an outlook, AI would be likened to a collaborator instead of a competitor if the two are similarly appreciated. The establishment of this combination should be open, conscientious, and consistent with human command (Taneja et al., 2025). This guarantees that the creative and artistic value of writing is not lessened by the technological advance.

3. APPLICATIONS ACROSS DOMAINS

3.1 Transforming Journalism and Media Practices

In contrast, AI now creates lengthy, data-heavy articles, reversing the trend in journalism. Computer algorithms are one of the most important components of newsrooms since they give them real-time information on sports, market trends, and weather and disaster news. Media professionals can upload fact-based content in a matter of minutes because of the speed and accuracy of these algorithms.

3.2 Advancing Academic Research and Scholarship

AI tools are used in research settings to improve research processes. Artificial intelligence (AI) systems can generate literature reviews, identify knowledge gaps, and map out thematic trends (Bolanos et al., 2024). Large databases can be scanned quickly by it. AI's capabilities not only speed up the planning stages of research but also make interdisciplinary inquiry easier. It also demonstrates the unexpected connections across different fields. AI is also capable of creating preliminary manuscripts and abstracts (Tomczyk et al., 2024). It provides researchers with a practical way to get past the block and arrange their arguments more logically. It served as a scaffolding tool for doctoral students and early-career academics, helping them to refine their academic style and organise their thoughts (Molopa, 2024). The researcher can free up mental energy for critical analysis and conceptual innovation.

3.3 Enhancing Educational Practices

The application of AI in learning and writing has entirely changed the manner in which students learn and practise writing (Tajik, 2025). The AI-based platforms are used to give customised feedback on the syntax, grammar, argumentation, and structure (Adrian, 2025). The instant feedback allows students to prepare their drafts by incorporating the real feedback. The AI serves as the language learner's linguistic companion by offering vocabulary recommendations and context-based corrections. In addition to correction, it provides tailored feedback. Additionally, AI helps with curriculum development by recognising difficult subjects and offering solutions so that students can revise them. AI promotes inclusivity, particularly for students who need additional assistance. It also helps students from a variety of linguistic backgrounds. Even though the AI system boosts productivity, it must be handled carefully so that students can develop their critical and autonomous thinking skills. They shouldn't become overly accustomed to machine suggestions.

3.4 Reconfiguring Creative Industries

AI is making a significant impact on the restructuring of creative industries. Generative computers are writing stories, commercial content and even co-writing full-length novels or movies. AI's ability to create artistic work gives creative professionals the opportunity to try out different storylines, explore ideas, and accelerate the brainstorming process. Advertisers use AI to create compelling content for targeted audiences, thus creating customised work. The combination of human authors and AI-generated content in publishing and entertainment creates hybrids that challenge traditional concepts of originality. Despite the ability to generate ideas, AI lacks the emotional authenticity and experience base for human creativity. Therefore, working as a collaborator looks promising, offering linguistic opportunities and sparks of new ideas. While AI generates ideas, it ultimately remains the human writers' responsibility to make creative decisions.

4. PEDAGOGICAL IMPLICATIONS

4.1 Reimagining the Teaching–Learning Paradigm

In addition to providing technical support, AI writing questions the conventional wisdom of education (Hammer, 2024). Teachers were centralised in this traditional teaching approach, and knowledge was imparted in a step-by-step fashion (Shah, 2023). The AI, which focusses on the students, has changed this model. Students engage with computer systems in such a novel process. Students can learn at their own speed, style, and level of sophistication thanks to AI. Students can work on multiple drafts, test different argument compositions, and receive immediate feedback without having to wait for an official evaluation by using AI-based writing tools (Yigci et al., 2025). This promotes a culture of exploration and strengthens self-regulation skills, both of which are essential to the lifetime learning process (Ghomrani, 2024). Teachers have to change their roles how they facilitate intellectual interaction. Human interaction should never be replaced by technology.

4.2 Personalized Learning and the Expansion of Adaptive Feedback

The capacity of AI to produce adaptive feedback at scale can be its most transformative effect. AI offers real-time feedback on language, coherence, and logical structure, as opposed to episodic and delayed traditional grading (Yesilyurt, 2023). Feedback can motivate students to continue editing their work, much like the professional writing process of draughting and revising (Geetha, 2025). The most recent drafts are the result of revisions brought about by repeated thought. Most significantly, evaluative feedback is contextual, taking into account both the stylistic and structural issues at the surface level as well as the surface-level errors and problems. For instance, an advanced learner might be given feedback on conciseness or academically suitable tone, whereas a struggling undergraduate might be given advice on more successful transitions or evidence incorporation (Roveta et al., 2025). Such flexibility minimizes disengagement and dissatisfaction through the provision of feedback, which is tailored to the needs of students with varying levels of skills.

4.3 Second-Language Learning and Cross-Cultural Empowerment

Language learners can benefit from AI. Idioms, grammar, and cultural quirks are common problems for second language authors. AI-powered language tools provide improved vocabulary, tone modifications, and culturally appropriate phrasing (AlAfnan, 2025). This is especially helpful in academic settings when speaking correctly is just as crucial as adhering to the rules (Jesudas, 2025). Artificial intelligence (AI) systems remove discomfort and allow students to practice without feeling self-conscious by mimicking real-world conversation scenarios and providing instant feedback (Mandour, 2025). By providing language assistance at any time and from any location, these resources help reduce the need for conventional classroom training. They are helpful tools that accelerate learning and foster international academic and professional exchanges, but they cannot fully replace the depth of human education.

4.4 Transforming Assessment Practices

One area where AI integration will have a significant impact in the near future is grading (Vetrivel et al., 2025). Lexical complexity, grammar, and coherence are already being assessed by computer grading programs more quickly than by human graders (Kooli & Yusuf, 2025). However, this presents a paradox. Since they are not subject to automated grading, teachers can devote more time to mentorship and advanced skills. Conversely, it raises concerns regarding the system's legitimacy and equity. Is it possible for a machine to truly understand creativity, originality, or the ability to argue? Furthermore, the authorship issue becomes more complicated due to the widespread use of generators by students. If a student uses AI to write important parts of an essay, how much of the essay is actually theirs? These push schools to reconsider how they assess students and to put more emphasis on the process than the final product. Portfolio testing, numerous drafts, oral defenses, and reflective comments are some strategies that can be used in addition to standard exams to guarantee that critical thinking and independence are essential components of academic assessment (Samanta & Banerjee, 2025).

4.5 Developing Digital and Critical Literacy

The growing use of AI in writing highlights the importance of digital and critical literacy as core learning goals (Saddhono et al., 2024). Digital literacy is more than just being tech-savvy; it includes understanding how to use AI tools to create content, being aware of their limitations, and using their outputs responsibly. On the other hand, (Arseven & Bal, 2025) critical literacy deals with the ability to question machine-written texts by examining their accuracy, bias, and omissions. Students who lack these abilities risk losing their ability to think for themselves and becoming passive recipients of algorithmic recommendations. By integrating critical digital literacy into the curriculum, educators can guarantee that students succeed in professional environments where human judgement is needed to supplement machine insights (Costa & Joaquim, 2025). Students will be able to use AI responsibly as a result.

4.6 Evolving Role of Educators in the AI Landscape

Despite AI's widespread use, teachers continue to play a crucial role in various contexts (Salma & Ahmed, 2024). Teachers will serve as arbiters of learning. Teachers will provide a setting where technology is used responsibly and sensibly. In addition to presenting information, they must instill values like creativity, responsibility, and responsible technology use. AI will be a useful helper, and teachers can serve as their mentors (Yu, 2024). It could harm their development as a person. Teachers will have to stay up to date with the newest technological developments as a result of this evolving role. They also need to understand how their teaching will be impacted by these developments (Kallunki et al., 2024). In the rapidly evolving digital learning environment, teachers' roles as moral mentors, role models, and necessary responders are demonstrated through AI.

4.7 Challenges of Equity, Over-Reliance, and Ethical Integration

In addition, there are structural issues that have emerged from the use of AI in education. For example, students may fall behind due to the use of inadequate resources (Raza et al., 2025). There may also emerge educational inequality given the unequal access to digital infrastructure which creates further learning inequalities. Furthermore, AI, when relied on too heavily, may erode the student's ability to think critically and solve problems. There may also be a risk of addiction when students become overly attached to AI for assistance (Zhai, Wibowo, & Li, 2024). In addition to this, the unpredictable nature of algorithmic systems raises questions about equity and transparency in educational decisions (Shtayyat et al., 2025). Researchers should also be mindful of ethical issues such as AI inducing plagiarism imminently and bias that may inhibit cultural diversity in proofreading. In some cases threats may create opportunities. If AI is used with ethical intent, it has the potential to enhance educational equity and student-centeredness by providing access to resources and supporting greater inclusiveness (Ucheagwu-Okoye, 2025).

5 ETHICAL AND REGULATORY CONCERNS

5.1 Authorship and Intellectual Ownership

One of the most challenging and complex ethical issues surrounding AI and writing is authorship (Carobene et al., 2024). When a text is created with notable input from an AI system, complicated questions arise about who should be credited. Should the human user take sole credit as an author, or, in part, should the system also receive credit as a co-author? (Samuelsson, 2023). The basic assumption behind conventional definitions of intellectual property is that innovation comes from some individual human labor. The fact that AI can generate information that resembles a person's information without conscious or intentional labor complicates this premise (Mazzi, 2024). Consequently, in addition to issues of creativity related to originality, these issues evoke ethical and legal obligations, such as ownership, accountability, and copyright. The use of AI in education has harmed the reputation of academic literature in addition to all but eradicating the line of originality (Bozkurt, 2024). Therefore, publishers and academic institutions need to be more transparent about their processes in order to regain the trust of the audience.

5.2 Plagiarism and Academic Integrity

The issue that is most closely related to authorship is plagiarism. The goal of traditional plagiarism detection algorithms was to find items that were paraphrased or copied from pre-existing sources (Mulenga & Shilongo, 2024). On the other hand, even in cases when AI-generated content substantially utilizes its training data, the answer is typically novel, making traditional methods less effective in recognizing AI work (Raitskaya & Tikhonova, 2023). The integrity of education appears to be seriously threatened by such “invisible” copying. AI-generated essays that appear authentic and even feel real may be turned in by students, but they would lack creative thought (Pellerin & Ogandaga, 2024). Teachers must therefore redesign their grading schemes to prioritize thinking, process, and oral defense presentations over merely product ratings of finished work.

5.3 Bias and Fairness in AI Outputs

Large-scale textual and other digital data sets are used to train generative AI models. Thus, these datasets invariably contain cultural, gendered, and ideological presumptions that are mirrored in the AI-generated material as well (Choudhry et al., 2024). These biases may neglect underrepresented perspectives, favor dominant narratives, or subtly reinforce preconceived views. By influencing how students view language, identity, and knowledge, this could maintain current educational inequities (Kumari, 2025). In addition, the perception of machine output being objective makes biased content ever more nefarious due to the possible perception of AI-generated language being objective. Fairness therefore must require technical solutions and social intervention.

5.4 Misinformation and the Risk of Manipulation

The ethical issue arises from the ability of AI systems to generate false information. The language models generate written, well-formed, but incorrect messages based on probabilistic predictions rather than fact (Sophia, 2025). This would risk disseminating untruths and questionable citations in scholarly writing follows. Furthermore, in journalism and public discourse, this has the potential to promote disinformation campaigns and manipulate opinions (Ienca, 2023). In addition, scalable text generation increases the plausibility of misuse of AI systems to produce legislative false information, propaganda, or malicious narratives. Therefore, verification frameworks should be developed to ensure that users are exercising critical judgement rather than taking AI-generated text at face value.

5.5 Data Privacy and Surveillance Concerns

Application of AI for writing and learning involves the processing and handling of large volumes of personal data (Ergashev, 2023). Writing platforms provide the ability to process language patterns, save user entries, and track a user's progress over time. Concerns around privacy and consent remain in spite of this information being used to create more personalisation (Khan, 2024). Laws like the European Union's General Data Protection Regulation (GDPR) emphasize the importance of protecting users' rights, ensuring transparency, and reducing exploitative data practices. Debates concerning equity, dignity, and surveillance in educational settings are already being sparked by tools like computerised proctoring (Villegas-Ch & García-Ortiz, 2023). These illustrations highlight how urgently effective governance frameworks that can protect student data and promote innovation are needed.

5.6 Transparency and the Black-Box Problem

AI systems are sometimes referred to as "black boxes, "as they are hard to comprehend and don't provide explicit justifications for how their outcomes came to be (Schnitzer & Tiruwuha, 2024). Accountability is also unclear due to a lack of knowledge about how the systems operate. For example, who is at fault when an AI-generated text is biased, deceptive, or plagiarized ;the machine, the user, or the developer? This transparency issue is concerning in the academic and professional realm, where the system's entire credibility rests on trace and justification (Myers & Chater, 2024). Explainable AI is in high demand right now; thus decision-making procedures must be open and transparent. Understanding when and how to use machine aid is also very important, in addition to the fact that transparent design is one of those elements that inspires confidence (Chinnaraju, 2025).

5.7 Regulatory Frameworks and Global Governance

The difficulties that AI presents for writing cannot be attributed to a single user or institution; rather, their nature and level of difficulty call for a common regulatory framework on both a national and international scale (Park, 2023). Even though local laws (like the GDPR) provide a basis for privacy and data protection, there isn't yet a comprehensive framework that covers the ethical use of AI for communication, education, research, and other related practices. When it comes to regulation, governance falls behind policy decisions, and the lightning-fast advancement of technology leads to governance flaws (Parycek et al., 2024). If AI is to become a tool for human creativity without compromising human creativity, autonomy, fairness, or trust, good governance must find a balance between promoting innovation and upholding accountability. Besides authorship and privacy, next-generation regulatory systems must deal with more broad questions of accountability, equity, and cultural sensitivity.

5.8 Striking a Balance Between Innovation and Ethics

Ultimately, the ethical and legal concerns surrounding AI in literature present a delicate balance between creativity and responsibility. Even though the technology holds great potential for increasing diversity, creativity, and productivity, if it is implemented carelessly, it could undermine the core values of justice, honesty, and integrity. Rather than opposing AI, the challenge lies in incorporating it with ethical consciousness, responsibility, and transparency. AI can be integrated as a partner that supports human expression rather than stifles it if human judgement remains at the core of its use.

6. PERCEPTIONS AND ADOPTION

6.1 Student Perspectives and Learning Experiences

Perhaps the most frequent users of AI writing software are students, who utilize it for anything from composing essays to checking for grammar (Johnston et al., 2024). Students see these technologies as helpful coworkers who boost self-esteem by providing direction when human feedback is insufficient or delayed (Kim et al., 2025). Undergraduate students, especially those who have trouble with academic writing traditions, frequently express gratitude to AI for its capacity to improve organization, reduce complex jargon, and bolster arguments. Foreign students and second-language learners view these tools as linguistic equalizers that allow them to participate in scholarly debates that might otherwise be limited by language obstacles. Nonetheless, perspectives on the issue are not always optimistic. Because AI can inhibit the development of one's own critical thinking skills and creativity, many students remain hesitant and doubtful of using it in substantial amounts. Additionally, some students raise a number of ethical concerns around the growing use of AI within the academic sphere and assert that it is cheating, for example, when a student's work is not cited. Therefore, students tendency to fluctuate between excitement and the concern about how authentic their work is.

6.2 Educators' Attitudes and Concerns

Teachers are interested in AI writing tools, but they are also cautious and nervous (Zimotti et al., 2024). On the plus side, many people think AI is a useful teaching tool because it can give immediate feedback, differentiate instruction, and lessen the workload associated with writing assignments. These advantages allow educators to concentrate more on helping children improve their critical and creative thinking abilities (Falebita, 2025). On the other hand, in academic circles, accusations about plagiarism, intellectual laziness, and diminished originality are more common. Some educators are concerned that by using robots to accomplish their job, students may avoid the mental labor required for research and debate (Lin & Chen, 2024). Others highlight the unequal distribution of digital infrastructure, pointing out that disparities in access are creating new disparities between pupils who have access to sophisticated AI tools and those who do not. Teachers often stress how important it is for institutional policies to be transparent. Both teachers and students are left to fend for themselves in the absence of clear criteria governing permissible use of AI, which leads to inconsistent practice and misunderstanding. Thus, educators' attitudes regarding AI reflect both the technology's potential as a teaching tool and its ability to challenge established standards of academic honesty.

6.3 Researchers and Academic Professionals

In academic research, artificial intelligence is increasingly seen as a useful tool for enhancing efficiency (Qaffas, 2024). Researchers use it to condense large amounts of material, construct preliminary abstracts, and organize data-driven discoveries. By lowering the mental effort needed for repetitive tasks, AI frees up more energy for conceptual innovation and analytical investigation (Oyelude, 2024). The capacity to investigate multidisciplinary linkages will also resonate with researchers who have to traverse enormous and dispersed masses of knowledge. However, scepticism tempers adoption (Han et al., 2025). Some scholars are concerned that a heavy reliance on literature mapping or summaries produced by AI could result in superficial engagements with scholarship, undermining the depth of analysis that characterises rigorous academic work. Others draw attention to the dangers of distorted data or hallucinated citations, which can undermine confidence in academic publishing. Thus, researchers' perceptions show a cautious awareness of AI's epistemic limitations mixed with a pragmatic embrace of its efficiency.

6.4Global Perspectives on Adoption

Geographical and cultural settings also affect how AI adoption is viewed. AI easily fits into academic and professional settings by professionals and students, who usually embrace newer technologies first (Ma et al., 2024). In contrast, issues around access at times can interfere with perceptions in places with poor digital infrastructure, which may lead to problems of digital inequality. Cultural assumptions also affect adoption. Collectivist societies might see technology as a communal resource that democratizes access, while more individualist cultures might see AI as a matter of individual productivity and competitiveness (Martínek, 2024). This global diversity underscores the necessity for culturally sensitive approaches to incorporating AI into the workplace and classroom.

6.5 Balancing Enthusiasm with Ethical Awareness

There are levels of optimism and pessimism regarding AI writing tools among professionals, academics, educators, and learners (Mujtaba, 2024). Optimistic ones point to effectiveness, diversity, and empowerment, while critical ones warn against dependency, unethical ambiguity, and unequal availability. The greatest lesson from these voices is the need to strike a balance between the potential of AI and its challenges (Chubb et al., 2024). It is possible to build effective policies, which enhance digital literacy, and raise awareness of ethical use.

7. BALANCING HUMAN AND MACHINE CREATIVITY

7.1 Reconceptualizing Creativity in the Digital Age

It has long been believed that creativity is a uniquely human trait that is based on imagination, intuition, and the ability to combine seemingly unrelated concepts to create new forms (Garcia, 2024). It stems from emotional depth, cultural heritage, and lived experience that are inaccessible to machines. However, the boundaries of creativity are being renegotiated more and more as generative artificial intelligence gains traction. Poetry, prose, news articles, and even scholarly texts that appear to be authentic human work can now be produced by technologies that have been trained on massive corpora. However, probabilistic modelling rather than deliberative thought produces this type of output. It is important to recognize that AI does not "create" in the same sense as humans; it recombines patterns from historical data to produce outputs that appear to be original. Human creativity is meaning-driven, whereas machine generation is pattern-driven.

7.2 AI as an Expansive Tool for Human Imagination

AI has great potential to work as a powerful tool for enhancing human creativity, even if AI has its downsides (Ali Elfa & Dawood, 2023). Thinkers and writers often suffer from narrow viewpoints or creative blocks. Complicated wordings, AI-generated prompts, and competing plotlines can take thinkers out of the familiar, opening new avenues for exploration. Rather than thinking of AI as a competitor, it could prove beneficial to think of AI as a creative conversation partner that provides a surprising variability of language or concepts (Koivisto & Grassini, 2023). All this variability could inspire human innovators to clarify, test, or extend their own ideas. AI acts less as a source of creativity, and more as a provocation to imagination, thus providing the cognitive space in which human writers are operating.

7.3 Preserving Human Agency and Interpretive Authority

The human will should always be kept paramount when employing AI in creative pursuits (Amankwah-Amoah et al., 2024). The creative might not always be about inventing a new shape; it can also involve incorporating intentionality, interpretation, and ethics into form. It should be noted that although machine creation may have evolved stylistically, it is incapable of reflection, empathy, or cultural sensitivity. Too much reliance on algorithmic findings runs the risk of reducing writing to a technical activity that is disconnected from context or meaning. Human judgment serves as the primary criterion for evaluating worth and authenticity throughout the creative endeavor as prioritizing human interpretation promotes that AI is augmenting human intuition rather than replacing it (Saini et al., 2025).

7.4 Collaborative Models of Human–Machine Creativity

There are many areas already pointing towards the phenomenon of collaborative creativity, such as journalism, where human journalists can concentrate on serious investigative reporting with the aid of AI-generated drafts of real-time news and education where students work with comments from AI and educators assist them towards criticality and creativity (Gaur et al., 2025). In literature, writers are trying out hybrid genres and incorporating AI composed passages in their own narrative work to write multi-layered stories(Srivastava et al., 2024). These all demonstrate a division of creative labor; AI can surpass humans in terms of speed, linguistic finesse, and scope of data; while humans can surpass AI in terms of originality, depth, and cultural sensitivity. The best returns in creativity develop not out of competition but cooperation, where both partners can feed off the strengths of the other.

7.5 Cultural and Ethical Dimensions of Creativity

The Balance human and machine driven innovation can only be achieved keeping the cultural and ethical concerns away. Machine learning environments programmed with language and concepts we currently possess will generate outcomes that are homogenized that minimize non-conformist voices (Mannuru et al., 2025). Cultural means of expression and creativity will lose all definition for diversity, all for dependency upon these systems. The marketing AI-created contents as completely human-authored raises ethical and authenticity issues regarding transparency (Torrance & Tomlinson, 2025). Ongoing recognition of the AI presence matters to recognize in order to maintain integrity in educational and professional environments. Ethical work through co-creation also highlights awareness of which voices were represented and whose voices were silenced to enable AI-based content. Human creativity ought to remain vigilant to ensure that algorithms continue to encourage diversity rather than suppress it (Nowotny, 2021).

8. FUTURE DIRECTIONS

8.1 Advancing Adaptive Feedback Systems

In the future, AI writing tools will advance beyond basic corrections to become technologically intelligent teaching partners. Current systems can improve any document's grammar, spelling, and vocabulary, but future systems will employ cognitive modelling to analyse how arguments, evidence, and thought processes develop individually. Instead of merely correcting errors, the system will recognise learning patterns in the student's cognitive processes and provide recommendations for skill development and steady improvement through intentional development. For example, if a student struggles to apply evidence or counterarguments in general, the system may simply encourage introspective practice or offer models of dialectical reasoning. . AI may become a reliable collaborator for fruitful intellectual development if it shifts from providing corrective criticism to offering constructive advice. These cutting-edge technologies might even incorporate affective computing, in which an AI can identify when a pupil is disinterested or frustrated and provide creative inspiration. AI can therefore reinterpret writing assistance as a process that enhances a learner's proficiency and self-assurance.

8.2 Integration into Collaborative Writing Platforms

The writing process is increasingly a group effort, whether for academic collaboration, policy writing, or organizational projects. Digital collaboration spaces with AI tools will soon become common. These tools will serve as facilitators, editors, and mediators. They can reveal overlaps, resolve differences between disciplines, and blend contributors' different styles into a single document. These tools will speed up collaboration by giving equal importance to the views of less powerful individuals and will also make the process fairer. Additionally, AI could serve as an always available archive, tracking changes and recognizing contributions across various versions, which is important for fairness in joint projects. The emergence of AI will transform the writing process into a collaborative effort where machines will direct the organization and combination of work done by humans, rather than hiding it.

8.3 Culturally Sensitive and Inclusive AI Models

The development of contextually aware and culturally inclusive AIs may emerge as one of the most pressing areas of development. Most readings employ a worldview and reasoning strategies that value Western idioms, rhetorical strategies, and perspectives, and this is an indication of the biases of the model's authors and the training corpus. These models may be advocating for a consistent, overwritten global discourse at the expense of marginalized ways of thinking. A future AI or writing system must use multimodal, multilingual, and multicultural corpora to respect different communities' ways of expressing themselves—especially those that lean on either an Asian rhetorical network, an African oral tradition, or Indigenous storytelling. What this will entail, however, is not simply a celebration of language, but a recognition of sociopolitical contexts where bad representations that reproduce stereotypes and/or theorizing the "other" can take place. Cultural plurality will make it possible for AI to be a modality that elevates diversity rather than limits it in generating new ways to share information.

8.4 Evolving Ethical and Governance Frameworks

There will be an exponential rise in the need for strict laws as AI begins to handle more writing and communication tasks. Regulations need to address everything from ownership and data privacy to the issue of authorship itself, which includes defining the extent to which AI is accountable for the content it produces and allocating responsibility in the event of an error or misrepresentation. When an author writes or composes a piece, they may be required to include an AI or tech usage statement, whether in the academic, professional publishing, or any other expert fields. In addition, if a human and a machine collaborate on a piece of work, the question of authorship should be resolved in order to address the issue of intellectual property.Rules should also state that users get access to some form of algorithmic information. This information would help them understand how the AI-generated writing suggestions were created. Without clear and specific disclosures, it will be hard to hold companies responsible for AI-written content. They will struggle to account for tech-related issues like writing errors, bias, plagiarism, misinformation, and hate speech. The challenge will be to create governance frameworks. These frameworks should allow all stakeholders to benefit from ethical thinking while also promoting progress and preventing irresponsible use or ethical violations.

8.5 Strengthening Digital and Critical Literacy

It is just a fact that changing technology is not enough to deliver real change. Future will also need human skills development to effectively collaborate with AI. Digital literacy will evolve from the current limited definition that conforms to set procedures to one that is capable to question, evaluate, and understand AI-generated content. The primary goal of critical literacy will be to instill doubt towards machine-generated texts. It means giving users the skills to verify, find the bias, and not to over-rely on technology. These skills will be very important for educators in their teaching. It makes teachers the active thinkers and participants in the process of interaction with AI, instead of the passive users. In the workplace, critical literacy will allow the company to avoid the danger of a complete trusting in the results of machines. This will be a way to improve the communication and decision-making process. Most importantly, by fostering these skills, it is ensured that AI is a tool of empowerment, rather than one of reliance.

8.6 Synergistic Co-Creation Between Humans and Machines

The most positive scenario for the future is the emergence of a working relationship between humans and machines that will jointly create knowledge, stories, and cultural products. Recently introduced practices actually demonstrate that the biggest accomplishments may be a result of the combination of human creativity and algorithmic production, rather than the apprehension that led to the conception of this new idea. AI can be a great help to researchers to find the relationships that are not apparent in their study. Once researchers find these patterns, they can interpret them. In art fields, AI can offer a plot twist or various styles. In the end, though, writers are able to decide what connections, themes, and meanings are important to them and their readers. In school, students can use AI to create drafts, and teachers might then utilize those drafts for a continuous conversation, with the hope of guiding students toward more significant and enriched critical thinking. Such a co-creation will revolutionize creative activity, from an isolated black-box endeavor, to a cooperative way of being. The machine can create possibilities; the human can imbue those possibilities with meaning, ethics, and lived experience.

9. CONCLUSION

It is conceivable that artificial intelligence is the most significant force altering how we communicate and write today. The ability of machines to access whatever language they desire and produce sensible, appropriately responsive text is game-changing. This also raises issues and complicates our assumptions about authorship, scholarship and creativity. For the purposes of this essay, I will examine how AI does not only have the potential to act as a helpful technology in journalism, academia and teaching, but potentially, AI could be the main input into the entire process of creating and sharing knowledge. What we are witnessing is not just a story of unbridled optimism about technology or a complete retreat, but rather a careful negotiation between human input and machine output. The quickness of writing with AI brings many advantages. It can save time, make learning more accessible, allow for personalization, and create new ways to collaborate. These points are only a few of the factors we need to consider moving forward, alongside the ethical and practical risks, such as plagiarism, data and privacy concerns, algorithmic bias, and misinformation. Using technology comes with responsibility and accountability. We will need to think about what we might do with AI in our writing processes in the future.

Even though AI systems can be extremely complex, they are still primarily used as simulation tools rather than as sources of meaning. By recombining patterns in preexisting data, AI simulates meaning. It acts in this way without purpose, moral consciousness, or cultural knowledge. Human emotion, nuanced interpretation, and the capacity to portray lived experiences are the fundamental components of writing. This emphasis on human participation in the interpretation, contextualisation, and assessment of AI content emphasises how machines can support and speed up production. However, writing can only be genuinely grounded in meaning, purpose, and ethical responsibility by living people.It is possible to reframe the debate over whether AI fosters or inhibits creativity by acknowledging co-creation. AI is a partner, not an adversary, that helps us transcend our cognitive boundaries, fosters shared authorship in creative endeavours, and opens up new possibilities by providing alternative ideas. However, when creativity is moulded by human judgement and cultural insight, it achieves its full potential. A future where technology can enhance writing while the writing itself stays authentic is presented by the fusion of human creativity and computer proficiency.

In the future, the speed AI will take in the field of writing is not only to consider greater technical advancements but also to evaluate decisions made by teachers, researchers, regulatory bodies, and creators. Constructing culturally sensitive systems, governance with reliability, and extensive digital literacy will play a leading role in making sure that AI becomes a supporter of inclusiveness rather than a perpetrator of the same. The mission is to make AI part of the educational and professional environments in such ways that it would be a point of human expression and still have all the ethical rules in place. Instead of viewing AI as an enemy, societies can perceive it as a well-controlled friend and thus make use of the advantages of AI, while at the same time maintaining the richness and diversity of human communication.

The fact that AI is now so advanced that it can give up human traits like knowledge, creativity, and communication is a sign that it is taking over the writing space. AI is now asking us these questions: What does it mean to make something? How do we keep things original in the algorithm-scaled domain? How can we protect human dignity and cultural diversity as technology progresses? The answer is not to turn down AI's help, but to accept it with a critical eye. The future of writing may lie in the fusion of human imagination and AI stimulation, fostering frankness, commonality, and creativity without compromising originality, responsibility, and ethical standards.

REFERENCES

Adrian, C. T. K. (2025). Artificial Intelligence and Writing Skills.

AlAfnan, M. A. (2025). Artificial Intelligence and language: Bridging Arabic and English with technology. *Journal of Ecohumanism*, *4*(1), 240–256.

Ali Elfa, M. A., & Dawood, M. E. T. (2023). Using artificial intelligence for enhancing human creativity. *Journal of Art. Design and Music*, *2*(2), 3.

Alipour, H., Pendar, N., & Roy, K. (2024). Chatgpt alternative solutions: Large language models survey. *arXiv preprint arXiv:2403.14469*. DOI: 10.5121/csit.2024.1405114

Amankwah-Amoah, J., Abdalla, S., Mogaji, E., Elbanna, A., & Dwivedi, Y. K. (2024). The impending disruption of creative industries by generative AI: Opportunities, challenges, and research agenda. *International Journal of Information Management*, *79*, 102759. DOI: 10.1016/j.ijinfomgt.2024.102759

Arseven, T., & Bal, M. (2025). Critical literacy in artificial intelligence assisted writing instruction: A systematic review. *Thinking Skills and Creativity*, *57*, 101850. DOI: 10.1016/j.tsc.2025.101850

Audy Martínek, S. (2024). Can Individualism Survive in the Age of Artificial Intelligence? Available at *SSRN* 5149811. DOI: 10.2139/ssrn.5149811

Barman, K. G., Wood, N., & Pawlowski, P. (2024). Beyond transparency and explainability: On the need for adequate and contextualized user guidelines for LLM use. *Ethics and Information Technology*, *26*(3), 47. DOI: 10.1007/s10676-024-09778-2

Bearman, M., Ryan, J., & Ajjawi, R. (2023). Discourses of artificial intelligence in higher education: A critical literature review. *Higher Education*, *86*(2), 369–385. DOI: 10.1007/s10734-022-00937-2

Beckett, C., & Yaseen, M. (2023). Generating change: A global survey of what news organisations are doing with AI.

Begum, S. (2025). AI and Literature: The Impact of Artificial Intelligence on Creative Writing and Narrative Forms. *Journal of Social Signs Review*, *3*(06), 180–199.

Bolanos, F., Salatino, A., Osborne, F., & Motta, E. (2024). Artificial intelligence for literature reviews: Opportunities and challenges. *Artificial Intelligence Review*, *57*(10), 259. DOI: 10.1007/s10462-024-10902-3

Bozkurt, A. (2024). GenAI et al.: Cocreation, Authorship, Ownership, Academic Ethics and Integrity in a Time of Generative AI. *Open Praxis*, *16*(1), 1–10. DOI: 10.55982/openpraxis.16.1.654

Cai, Z. G., Duan, X., Haslett, D. A., Wang, S., & Pickering, M. J. (2023). Do large language models resemble humans in language use? *arXiv preprint arXiv:2303.08014*. DOI: 10.31234/osf.io/s49qv

Campino, J. (2025). Unleashing the transformers: NLP models detect AI writing in education. *Journal of Computers in Education*, *12*(2), 645–673. DOI: 10.1007/s40692-024-00325-y

Carobene, A., Padoan, A., Cabitza, F., Banfi, G., & Plebani, M. (2024). Rising adoption of artificial intelligence in scientific publishing: Evaluating the role, risks, and ethical implications in paper drafting and review process. [CCLM]. *Clinical Chemistry and Laboratory Medicine*, *62*(5), 835–843. DOI: 10.1515/cclm-2023-1136 PMID: 38019961

Chinnaraju, A. (2025). Explainable AI (XAI) for trustworthy and transparent decision-making: A theoretical framework for AI interpretability. *World Journal of Advanced Engineering Technology and Sciences*, *14*(3), 170–207. DOI: 10.30574/wjaets.2025.14.3.0106

Choudhry, M. D., Sundarrajan, M., & Sundaram, K. (2024). Bias and Fairness in Generative AI. *Generative AI and LLMs: Natural Language Processing and Generative Adversarial Networks*, 177.

Chubb, J., Reed, D., & Cowling, P. (2024). Expert views about missing AI narratives: Is there an AI story crisis? *AI & Society*, *39*(3), 1107–1126. DOI: 10.1007/s00146-022-01548-2 PMID: 36039046

Costa, P., & Joaquim, A. F. (2025). AI and Digital Literacy: Preparing Learners for a Technologically Advanced Sustainable Future. In *Rethinking Literacy in the Era of Sustainability and Artificial Intelligence* (pp. 73-98). IGI Global Scientific Publishing.

Ergashev, A. (2023). Privacy concerns and data protection in an era of ai surveillance technologies. *International Journal of Law and Criminology*, *3*(08), 71–76.

Falebita, O. (2025). Evaluating artificial intelligence anxiety among pre-service teachers in university teacher education programs. *Journal of Mathematics Instruction. Social Research and Opinion*, *4*(1), 1–16.

Garcia, M. B. (2024). The paradox of artificial creativity: Challenges and opportunities of generative AI artistry. *Creativity Research Journal*, •••, 1–14.

Gaur, S., Sharma, M., & Sharma, U. (2025). Machine Learning: A Revolution of News Writing and Digital Era. Journal of Electrical Systems, 21.

Geetha, V. (2025). AI-Driven Assessment and Feedback Systems: Transforming Education Through Intelligent Automation. *Multidisciplinary Research in Arts, Science & Commerce (Volume-23)*, 9.

Gero, K. I. (2023). *AI and the Writer: How Language Models Support Creative Writers*. Columbia University.

Haber, E., Jemielniak, D., Kurasiński, A., & Przegalińska, A. (2025). *Using AI in Academic Writing and Research: A Complete Guide to Effective and Ethical Academic AI*. Springer Nature. DOI: 10.1007/978-3-031-91705-9

Hammer, E. (2024). ChatGPT in the Classroom: The Teacher's Challenges and Opportunities in an AI Revolution.

Han, X., Xiao, S., Sheng, J., & Zhang, G. (2025). Enhancing efficiency and decision-making in higher education through intelligent commercial integration: Leveraging artificial intelligence. *Journal of the Knowledge Economy*, *16*(1), 1546–1582. DOI: 10.1007/s13132-024-01868-2

Ienca, M. (2023). On artificial intelligence and manipulation. *Topoi, 42*(3), 833–842. DOI: 10.1007/s11245-023-09940-3

Ilieva, G., Yankova, T., Klisarova-Belcheva, S., Dimitrov, A., Bratkov, M., & Angelov, D. (2023). Effects of generative chatbots in higher education. *Information (Basel), 14*(9), 492. DOI: 10.3390/info14090492

Jarrahi, M. H., Askay, D., Eshraghi, A., & Smith, P. (2023). Artificial intelligence and knowledge management: A partnership between human and AI. *Business Horizons, 66*(1), 87–99. DOI: 10.1016/j.bushor.2022.03.002

Jesudas, R. (2025, June). Empowering language learning: The role of AI in enhancing language skills. In. AIP Conference Proceedings: Vol. 3306. *No. 1* (p. 050023). AIP Publishing LLC. DOI: 10.1063/5.0278362

Jha, A., & Singh, S. R. (2025). Integrating Artificial Intelligence in Media Education: Revolutionizing Learning, Creativity, and Critical Thinking. In *Teachers' Roles and Perspectives on AI Integration in Schools* (pp. 297-328). IGI Global Scientific Publishing.

Johnston, H., Wells, R. F., Shanks, E. M., Boey, T., & Parsons, B. N. (2024). Student perspectives on the use of generative artificial intelligence technologies in higher education. *International Journal for Educational Integrity, 20*(1), 2. DOI: 10.1007/s40979-024-00149-4

Kallunki, V., Kinnunen, P., Pyörälä, E., Haarala-Muhonen, A., Katajavuori, N., & Myyry, L. (2024). Navigating the evolving landscape of teaching and learning: University faculty and staff perceptions of the artificial intelligence-altered terrain. *Education Sciences, 14*(7), 727. DOI: 10.3390/educsci14070727

Khalifa, M., & Albadawy, M. (2024). Using artificial intelligence in academic writing and research: An essential productivity tool. *Computer Methods and Programs in Biomedicine Update, 5*, 100145. DOI: 10.1016/j.cmpbup.2024.100145

Khan, W. N. (2024). Ethical challenges of AI in education: Balancing innovation with data privacy. *AI EDIFY Journal, 1*(1), 1–13.

Kim, J., Yu, S., Detrick, R., & Li, N. (2025). Exploring students' perspectives on Generative AI-assisted academic writing. *Education and Information Technologies, 30*(1), 1265–1300. DOI: 10.1007/s10639-024-12878-7

Koivisto, M., & Grassini, S. (2023). Best humans still outperform artificial intelligence in a creative divergent thinking task. *Scientific Reports, 13*(1), 13601. DOI: 10.1038/s41598-023-40858-3 PMID: 37709769

Kooli, C., & Yusuf, N. (2025). Transforming educational assessment: Insights into the use of ChatGPT and large language models in grading. *International Journal of Human-Computer Interaction, 41*(5), 3388–3399.

Kumari, N. (2025). Scalability of Generative AI Models: Challenges and Opportunities in Large-Scale Data Generation and Training. *Journal ID, 9471*(3), 1297. DOI: 10.63530/IJCSI-TR_2025_06_03_002

Lin, H., & Chen, Q. (2024). Artificial intelligence (AI)-integrated educational applications and college students' creativity and academic emotions: Students and teachers' perceptions and attitudes. *BMC Psychology*, *12*(1), 487. DOI: 10.1186/s40359-024-01979-0 PMID: 39285268

Ma, D., Akram, H., & Chen, I. H. (2024). Artificial intelligence in higher education: A cross-cultural examination of students' behavioral intentions and attitudes. *International Review of Research in Open and Distance Learning*, *25*(3), 134–157. DOI: 10.19173/irrodl.v25i3.7703

Mandour, W. S. (2025). AI-Powered Tools for Linguistic and Sentiment Analysis in Language Learning: Applications Using Google Sheets and Large Language Models. In *Using AI Tools in Text Analysis, Simplification, Classification, and Synthesis* (pp. 67-112). IGI Global Scientific Publishing.

Mannuru, N. R., Shahriar, S., Teel, Z. A., Wang, T., Lund, B. D., Tijani, S., & Vaidya, P. (2025). Artificial intelligence in developing countries: The impact of generative artificial intelligence (AI) technologies for development. *Information Development*, *41*(3), 1036–1054. DOI: 10.1177/02666669231200628

Mazzi, F. (2024). Authorship in artificial intelligence-generated works: Exploring originality in text prompts and artificial intelligence outputs through philosophical foundations of copyright and collage protection. *The Journal of World Intellectual Property*, *27*(3), 410–427. DOI: 10.1111/jwip.12310

Molopa, S. T. (2024). Artificial intelligence-based literature review adaptation. *South African Journal of Library and Information Science*, *90*(2), 1–18.

Mujtaba, B. (2024). Clarifying ethical dilemmas in sharpening students' artificial intelligence proficiency: Dispelling myths about using AI tools in higher education. *Business Ethics and Leadership*, *8*(2), 107–127. DOI: 10.61093/bel.8(2).107-127.2024

Mulenga, R., & Shilongo, H. (2024). Academic integrity in higher education: Understanding and addressing plagiarism. *Acta Pedagogia Asiana*, *3*(1), 30–43. DOI: 10.53623/apga.v3i1.337

Myers, S., & Chater, N. (2024). Interactive explainability: Black boxes, mutual understanding and what it would really mean for AI systems to be as explainable as people. *Preprint at* PsyArXiv . *io/ha37x*.DOI: 10.31234/osf.io/ha37x

Naveed, H., Khan, A. U., Qiu, S., Saqib, M., Anwar, S., Usman, M., Akhtar, N., Barnes, N., & Mian, A. (2025). A comprehensive overview of large language models. *ACM Transactions on Intelligent Systems and Technology*, *16*(5), 1–72. DOI: 10.1145/3744746

Nieminen, M. (2023). The Transformer Model and Its Impact on the Field of Natural Language Processing.

Nowotny, H. (2021). *AI we trust: Power, illusion and control of predictive algorithms*. John Wiley & Sons.

Oyelude, A. A. (2024). Artificial intelligence (AI) tools for academic research. *Library Hi Tech News*, *41*(8), 18–20. DOI: 10.1108/LHTN-08-2024-0131

Park, S. (2023). Bridging the global divide in AI regulation: A proposal for a contextual, coherent, and commensurable framework. *Wash. Int'l LJ, 33*, 216.

Parycek, P., Schmid, V., & Novak, A. S. (2024). Artificial Intelligence (AI) and automation in administrative procedures: Potentials, limitations, and framework conditions. *Journal of the Knowledge Economy, 15*(2), 8390–8415. DOI: 10.1007/s13132-023-01433-3

Peckham, O., Raines, J., Bulsink, E., Goudswaard, M., Gopsill, J., Barton, D., Nassehi, A., & Hicks, B. (2025). Artificial Intelligence in Generative Design: A Structured Review of Trends and Opportunities in Techniques and Applications. *Designs, 9*(4), 79. DOI: 10.3390/designs9040079

Qaffas, A. A. (2024). Harnessing Artificial Intelligence for Enhanced Efficiency in Academic Writing and Research. *Fusion: Practice & Applications, 16*(2).

Raitskaya, L., & Tikhonova, E. (2023). Academic integrity: Author-related and journal-related issues. *Journal of Language and Education, 9*(4 (36)), 5–10.

Raza, Z., Tahir, Z., Qamar, S., & Manan, A. (2025). The Role of AI in the Education Sector: Focusing on AI's Adaptation, Drawbacks, Implications, Trust, and Ethical Considerations. *Journal of Political Stability Archive, 3*(2), 145–165. DOI: 10.63468/jpsa.3.2.08

Roe, J., Renandya, W. A., & Jacobs, G. M. (2023). A review of AI-powered writing tools and their implications for academic integrity in the language classroom. *Journal of English and Applied Linguistics, 2*(1), 3. DOI: 10.59588/2961-3094.1035

Roveta, A., Castello, L. M., Massarino, C., Francese, A., Ugo, F., & Maconi, A. (2025). Artificial Intelligence in Medical Education: A Narrative Review on Implementation, Evaluation, and Methodological Challenges. *AI, 6*(9), 227. DOI: 10.3390/ai6090227

Saddhono, K., Suhita, R., Rakhmawati, A., Rohmadi, M., & Sukmono, I. K. (2024, November). AI and Literacy: Developing Critical Thinking and Analytical Skills in the Digital Era. In *2024 International Conference on IoT, Communication and Automation Technology (ICICAT)* (pp. 360-365). IEEE. DOI: 10.1109/ICICAT62666.2024.10922871

Saini, J., Choudhary, S., & Walia, K. (2025). The Future of AI in Decision-Making: Replacing or Assisting Humans? *International Journal of Sciences and Innovation Engineering, 2*(5), 751–778.

Salma, S. S., & Ahmed, S. M. B. (2024). Artificial Intelligence and the Evolution of Educator Roles in the Digital Technology Era. *Pakistan JL Analysis & Wisdom, 3*, 231.

Samanta, S., & Banerjee, S. (2025). *Portfolio-Based Assessment: A Holistic Method For Evaluating Higher Education Students* (No. 2025-52-02).

Samuelsson, C. S. (2023). Generative AI as a co-creator in the conception of images.

Santorelli, M., & Catullo, D. (2023). Human mobility and language: towards new multilingual approaches with ai. In *Creşterea economică în condiţiile globalizării* (pp. 151-161). DOI: 10.36004/nier.cdr.V.2023.17.16

Schnitzer, S., & Tiruwuha, M. H. (2024). Transparency in the Black Box.

Scott, B. L., Muñoz, S. M., & Scott, S. B. (2024). How whiteness operates at a hispanic serving institution: A qualitative case study of faculty, staff, and administrators. *Journal of Diversity in Higher Education, 17*(4), 563–574. DOI: 10.1037/dhe0000438

Shah, P. (2023). *AI and the Future of Education: Teaching in the Age of Artificial Intelligence.* John Wiley & Sons.

Sharma, N. (2025, June). Role of Artificial Intelligence in Intercultural Dialogue and Language: Ethical Frame works for Sustainability and Equity. In *Innovative Multidisciplinary Approaches to Global Challenges: Sustainability, Equity, and Ethics in an Interconnected World (IMASEE 2025)* (pp. 215-223). Atlantis Press.

Shtayyat, A., Gawanmeh, A., & Mashaleh, A. (2025). Risk Analysis of AI Integration in Educational Systems: Toward Ethical and Equitable Innovation. In *Examining Cybersecurity Risks Produced by Generative AI* (pp. 401-428). IGI Global Scientific Publishing.

Sophia, L. I. (2025). The Social Harms of AI-Generated Fake News: Addressing Deepfake and AI Political Manipulation. *Digital Society & Virtual Governance, 1*(1), 72–88. DOI: 10.6914/dsvg.010105

Srivastava, P., Mamodiya, U., Dutta, P. K., & Paliktzoglou, V. (2024, December). Advanced AI-Driven Thematic and Narrative Analysis: Exploring Deep Learning in Literature. In International Conference on Arts, Humanities, and Interdisciplinary Sciences (pp. 179-194). Cham: Springer Nature Switzerland.

Tajik, A. (2025). Exploring the role of AI-driven dynamic writing platforms in improving EFL learners' writing skills and fostering their motivation.

Taneja, D., Prabagaren, H., & Thomas, M. R. (2025). Al in Academia: Balancing Integrity, Ethics, and. *Pitfalls of AI Integration in Education: Skill Obsolescence, Misuse, and Bias: Skill Obsolescence, Misuse, and Bias*, 319.

Tomczyk, P., Brüggemann, P., & Vrontis, D. (2024). AI meets academia: Transforming systematic literature reviews. *EuroMed Journal of Business.* Advance online publication. DOI: 10.1108/EMJB-03-2024-0055

Torrance, A. W., & Tomlinson, B. (2025). Organic Websites: Certification of AI-Generated or Human-Written Content on the Internet. Chi.-. *Kent J. Intell. Prop., 24*, 72.

Ucheagwu-Okoye, O. M. (2025). The Role of Artificial Intelligence (AI) in Student Assessment and Evaluation in Educational Leadership in Tertiary Institutions in Anambra State. Unizik Journal of Educational Laws and Leadership Studies, 1(1).

Vetrivel, S. C., Vidhyapriya, P., & Arun, V. P. (2025). The role of AI in transforming assessment practices in education. In *AI Applications and Strategies in Teacher Education* (pp. 43–70). IGI Global.

Villegas-Ch, W., & García-Ortiz, J. (2023). Toward a comprehensive framework for ensuring security and privacy in artificial intelligence. *Electronics (Basel), 12*(18), 3786. DOI: 10.3390/electronics12183786

Wilf, S., & Wray-Lake, L. (2024). "That's how revolutions happen": Psychopolitical resistance in youth's online civic engagement. *Journal of Adolescent Research, 39*(4), 827–860. DOI: 10.1177/07435584211062121 PMID: 40969284

Wu, J., Yang, S., Zhan, R., Yuan, Y., Chao, L. S., & Wong, D. F. (2025). A survey on llm-generated text detection: Necessity, methods, and future directions. *Computational Linguistics, 51*(1), 275–338. DOI: 10.1162/coli_a_00549

Yesilyurt, Y. E. (2023). AI-enabled assessment and feedback mechanisms for language learning: Transforming pedagogy and learner experience. In *Transforming the language teaching experience in the age of AI* (pp. 25–43). IGI Global. DOI: 10.4018/978-1-6684-9893-4.ch002

Yigci, D., Eryilmaz, M., Yetisen, A. K., Tasoglu, S., & Ozcan, A. (2025). Large language model-based chatbots in higher education. *Advanced Intelligent Systems, 7*(3), 2400429. DOI: 10.1002/aisy.202400429

Youvan, D. C. (2024). Towards a Cognitive Equilibrium: The Symbiosis of Human Complexity and Artificial Intelligence.

Yu, H. (2024). The application and challenges of ChatGPT in educational transformation: New demands for teachers' roles. *Heliyon, 10*(2), e24289. DOI: 10.1016/j.heliyon.2024.e24289 PMID: 38298626

Zhai, C., Wibowo, S., & Li, L. D. (2024). The effects of over-reliance on AI dialogue systems on students' cognitive abilities: A systematic review. *Smart Learning Environments, 11*(1), 28. DOI: 10.1186/s40561-024-00316-7

Zhang, J., Zhu, C., & Zhang, Z. (2024). AI-powered language learning: The role of NLP in grammar, spelling, and pronunciation feedback. *Applied and Computational Engineering, 102*(1), 18–23. DOI: 10.54254/2755-2721/102/20240962

Zimotti, G., Frances, C., & Whitaker, L. (2024). The future of language education: Teachers' perceptions about the surge of AI writing tools. *Technology in Language Teaching & Learning, 6*(2), 1136–1136. DOI: 10.29140/tltl.v6n1.1136

Chapter 3
AI and the Future of Writing Pedagogy:
Pedagogical Innovation, Ethical Practice, and Institutional Readiness in the Age of Intelligent Tools

Manoj Govindaraj
https://orcid.org/0000-0003-2830-7875
VelTech Rangarajan Dr. Sagunthala R&D Institute of Science and Technology, India

M. S. R. Mariyappan
https://orcid.org/0000-0003-0008-9351
SRM Trichy Arts and Science College, Trichy, India

N. Mari Anand
https://orcid.org/0000-0002-6443-249X
University of Technology and Applied Sciences, Salalah, Oman

Jayendira P. Sankar
https://orcid.org/0000-0001-8435-2123
University of Technology Bahrain, Salmabad, Bahrain

Suma Godwin
Loyola College, Chennai, India

ABSTRACT

The rise of artificial intelligence (AI) is reshaping the landscape of writing pedagogy, presenting both transformative opportunities and profound challenges. This paper explores the evolving role of AI-powered tools in writing instruction, focusing on how they can support pedagogical innovation, enhance student engagement, and foster personalized learning. At the same time, it critically examines ethical concerns, including issues of academic integrity, authorship, data privacy, and algorithmic bias. The discussion extends to institutional readiness, analyzing the preparedness of educational systems to integrate AI responsibly through curriculum design, faculty development, and policy frameworks. By synthesizing emerging research, classroom

DOI: 10.4018/979-8-3373-5601-3.ch003

practices, and institutional case studies, the paper provides actionable insights into designing writing pedagogies that are ethically grounded, technologically informed, and responsive to the changing demands of the digital age.

INTRODUCTION

The emergence of artificial intelligence (AI) has created a new period of technological revolution in all industries, and education is not an exception. In this dynamic environment, the writing pedagogy, as an element of higher education literacy, critical thinking, and communication, is experiencing several opportunities and challenges. The development of AI-based applications like automated grammar checkers, predictive text developers, and large language models has already started altering the way students approach writing exercises, and teachers teach. These technologies not only suggest efficiency and customization, but also make teachers and colleges reconsider the basic pedagogical processes, ethics and institutional policies in the environment of intelligent tools.

Traditionally, writing was taught as a skill and process: as a way to express knowledge, to critically analyze, and be creative. The entry of AI makes one question ways in which these pedagogical objectives should be obtained in the context where a machine now will be able to produce consistent, argumentative, and textually diverse texts in bulk. On the one hand, AI has a prospect of democratizing the access to the writing support, allowing students with various linguistic, cognitive, and cultural backgrounds to be provided with personalized support. Individualized guidance (e.g., automated feedback systems) can be used to provide learners with real-time feedback to help them improve their writing in a manner not limited by classroom time or the availability of instructors. On the same note, AI can support differentiated learning, which means that educators can develop adaptive tasks based on different needs of students. AI, in this regard, can be viewed as a catalyst to pedagogical creativity, which encourages more interaction and reaching further limits of conventional literacy training.

Simultaneously, AI-based writing pedagogy simultaneously brings up a series of ethical dilemmas that their introduction cannot pass unnoticed. Academic integrity and authorship issues are top of the list, as a student can find the urge to utilize AI systems not as a means of learning but as a replacement to their intellectual activity. The questions of originality, plagiarism and even the definition of authorship gain a new urgency in this scenario. Furthermore, AI technologies are not neutral, as datasets and algorithms that produce them can reproduce and reinforce the current social, cultural, and linguistic biases. These biases have the danger of supporting inequities in education favoring some discourses over others. The problem of data privacy and surveillance also arises as the writing of students can be gathered, analyzed, and stored by commercial AI providers, which raises the question of the rights and control of intellectual and personal data.

Out of the classroom, the aspect of institutional preparedness is a key factor of the discourse. To make AI implementation responsible and beneficial, universities and schools need to restructure the design of the curriculum, assessment systems, and faculty education programs. Teachers need new literacies to be able to critically use AI tools and identify when and how they need to be integrated into writing instruction. The institutional policies have to change so that the application of AI in education does not contradict the values of equity, accountability, and transparency. Notably, the discussion goes beyond technical implementation to the issues of culture and trust: how institutions train students to operate in the AI in a responsible manner as a part of their educational and career lives. The present paper is located at the crossroads of pedagogical innovation, ethical practice, and institutional preparedness when it comes to defining what lies ahead of the writing pedagogy in the era of intelligent tools. It seeks to shine light on avenues of applying AI in ways that are both transformational and ethical by synthesizing existing literature, practical examples, and policy debate. This is not to put AI in a panacea or a threat, but to express a measured view on the possibilities and threats of AI and give educators, researchers and policymakers' critical information on designing writing pedagogies that are technologically aware, ethically sound and attentive to the needs of the digital era.

BACKGROUND OF THE STUDY

The growing role of artificial intelligence in education is indicative of a wider trend of creating, mediating and assessing knowledge in the digital age. Traditionally, writing pedagogy as a focus on cultivating critical thinking, imagination and communication is now converging with intelligent technologies, which are able to analyze, create and edit text with incredible quickness. An increasing number of AI-assisted devices, including grammar checkers, text generators, and adaptive writing systems, are ceasing to be the extras; they are becoming part and parcel of academic activity on both sides of the academic divide. Although these tools have the potential to offer the prospects of individual learning, accessibility, and pedagogical change, they also pose issues related to academic honesty, authorship, data control, and algorithm bias. The issue of educational institutions is thus not just to utilize the pedagogical power of AI but also to put in place mechanisms that guarantee the ethical, equitable, and responsible use of AI. It is against this changing backdrop that the study of the implications of AI in writing pedagogy, institutional preparedness and educational policy must be considered.

REVIEW OF LITERATURE

It is a multi-level meta-analysis, which concludes that automated writing evaluation (AWE) feedback improves student writing with a moderate positive effect (g 0.55 approx.), but results depend on context widely. Some of the critical moderators are the level of the learner, the type of feedback and the integration of instruction. The paper promotes considering AWE to be a versatile pedagogical technique and not a one-size-fits-all solution, and encourages mixed teacher-AWE solutions and increased concern with the tool validity in policy and curriculum development (Fleckenstein et al., 2023). They explore the concept of algorithmic bias in educational AI by tracing the origins of it through the machine learning pipeline and reporting how it affects people of color disproportionately. Their proposal is to transform the unknown bias to known bias by measurement, participatory design and policy interventions. Their taxonomy links technical decisions to social harms, and provides educators with practical strategies to ethically use AI-based tools, like AWE, in writing instruction, e.g. by using heterogeneous datasets, equity measures, and stakeholder engagement (Baker & Hawn, 2022). In order to anchor this analysis, the chapter is informed by Technological Pedagogical Content Knowledge (TPACK), which assumes that a balance of content, pedagogy, and technology knowledge is necessary to bring the integration of technology. Moreover, we also use the concepts of Social Constructivism to understand how knowledge can be constructed in collaborative and iterative ways in AI-mediated writing situations to go beyond a technical evaluation.

They synthesize the global policies of AI-in-education, and suggest the main ethical principles of such policies- transparency, accountability, privacy, equity, and learner autonomy. Through thematic analysis, they are able to present areas of agreement and areas of disagreement, and provide recommendations that are stakeholder friendly in terms of privacy impact assessment, documentation of models, oversight, and teacher training. The paper focuses on practice, both in curricular and vendor integration and institutional governance, and offers an ethical framework to implement responsible and values-based AIED practices (Nguyen et al., 2023). They discuss the way in which LLMs such as ChatGPT can support, but not substitute teaching, and propose four supportive functions, such as content provider, interlocutor, scaffolding agent, and assessor. They provide qualitative evidence and identify opportunities and risks of pedagogy like overreliance, hallucination, and equity. By focusing on teacher agency, the research proposes teacher-mediated integration, co-design of the curricula, and professional development. It puts the LLMs as a collaborator in the classroom, value proposing both applications and critical warnings of writing pedagogy (Jeon & Lee, 2023).

They present an extensive position paper on generative LLMs in education, which includes a list of opportunities, including scalable tutoring, multilingual support, and inclusive access, and risks, including hallucinations, misuse, and inequities. They suggest transparency, experimentation and collaboration across disciplines synthesizing the viewpoints of the technicians, the pedagogus and the governance. The paper focuses on weighing the benefits against the risks and warning that taking shortcuts resulting in weakening learning is dangerous. Policy implications--pilot testing, faculty training and co-constructed guidelines--provide pragmatic guidance to institutional policy, notably writing programs and assessment reform (Kasneci et al., 2023).

Reviewing the empirical research on Automated Writing Evaluation (AWE) until 2020, they found that the efficacy of using it relies on such conditions as repetition and integrated use in pedagogy. Although the results are inconsistent between settings, the review has identified gaps in research on the long-term effects, teacher mediation and qualitative interpretations of student engagement. The paper emphasizes the fact that AWE is most effective as a supplement to teacher feedback, and that automated comments should be interpreted by a human. Such recommendations are scaffolding AWE-use, monitoring progress, and linking feedback to revision-targeted instruction (Ghosh, Chakraborty, et al., 2025). They analyze the adoption of AWE systems among college students and determine that the systems are positively accepted in cases where feedback is explicit, practical, and rubric-related. Trust, nonetheless, is based on perceived correctness and teacher approval and variations are associated with confidence and proficiency. The paper emphasizes that technical quality is not enough and that successful implementation should be accompanied by faculty framing, clear direction and incorporation into pedagogy. In the teaching of writing, the results highlight the importance of modeling the use of AWE, matching feedback to assessment standards, and creating credibility in the students to be further engaged (Zhai & Ma, 2021).

They examines the consistency of large language models in the holistic scoring of essays in response to prompts and grade level and report overall consistency with human scoring, but systematic deviation, such as compressing ranges of score and subgroup differences. They advise against blind application but note that rubric calibration, fairness supervision, and hybrid human-

AI processes should be applied in high-stakes situations. The research highlights the issues of equity and validity and suggests pilot testing, post-hoc bias, adjudication, and transparency. In case of writing assessment policy, the results indicate a cautious use of AI scoring and close supervision by humans (Tate et al., 2024). It reviews design, purposes, pedagogical uses of Automated Writing Evaluation (AWE) and new feedback systems, and validity frameworks, typologies of feedback and representative tools. The chapter lays stress on evidence-based adoption which calls on educators to assess alignment with learning goals, empirical support and specificity of feedback. Effective implications would be piloting tools with set criteria of success and integrating reflective exercises to encourage students to use feedback in a metacognitive manner. As a transitional linking of technical innovation and classroom practice, the chapter offers practical advice in the choice of AWE and its integration in a responsible manner (Cotos, 2023).

They explore bias in AI-based student progress monitoring, demonstrating that predictive features are less accurate at predicting the results of groups characterized by age, disability status, and gender. Their results point to the risks of inequity with regard to formative assessment tools and note the necessity of clear documentation and remedial strategies. The authors suggest fairness audits, disaggregated reporting, and participatory evaluation involving students that are impacted. With respect to writing pedagogy, the research paper notes that analytics dashboards and predictive feedback should incorporate constraints that prevent the use of biased labels to restrict student opportunities and unfairly influence teacher expectations (Idowu et al., 2024). They perform a systematic scoping review of ChatGPT and other chatbots in higher education and find the positive effects of such tools, including research support, formative feedback, and administrative efficiency, as well as negative ones, including academic misconduct, misinformation, and privacy issues. The integration of interdisciplinary literature raises the themes of pedagogical promise, evaluation weaknesses, the digital literacy requirements, and governance issues. The paper is in favor of teacher-mediated integration, AI literacy in curriculum, and reconsidering the design of assessment. In the case of writing pedagogy, it highlights not only the opportunity in ideation and drafting assistance, but also the need to secure measures to ensure the integrity of academia and the preparedness of the institution (Dempere et al., 2023).

It is a scoping review that summarizes the literature on higher and adult learning AI literacy and classifies the curricular objectives, pedagogical practices, and evaluation methods. In 30 articles, it becomes apparent that the main topics are conceptual knowledge of AI, critical thinking regarding the role of AI in society, knowledge of how to use the tools, and ethics. The authors emphasize the elements of definitional laxity and result-oriented curricula, facilitating learning with the help of a scaffold, and assessing the results with the aid of validity tests. In the case of writing pedagogy, the review offers an approach to teaching AI as a tool, object of critique, or both with an explicit focus on outcomes, structured activities and alignment of reporting in order to promote ethically informed, critically literate writers (Laupichler et al., 2022). They provide a systematic literature review on Automated Writing Evaluation (AWE) systems, including development, empirical results and validity concerns. They complain about heterogeneity in contexts, mixed effectiveness, gaps that include longitudinal effects and differences in disciplines. The review indicates the significance of pedagogical integration, system reporting and validity based on intended use. To faculty and institutions, it provides selection criteria (alignment of rubrics, pedagogical effects), and points to research gaps, including long-term outcomes and cross-linguistic validity that are needed to make informed and large-scale use in writing pedagogy (Shi & Aryadoust, 2022).

In this research, the authors discuss the effects of AI writing aid (e.g., QuillBot, Wordtune, ChatGPT) on student writing through the analysis of qualitative interviews with EFL teachers. Educators report on improvements in coherence, structure and draft productivity, while they express their concern with the overreliance and lack of critical composition competence. The research proposes teacher scaffolding and explicit instruction on the use of the tools and integration strategies that focus on revision and metacognition. Results are used to design curricular interventions, which combine AI-generated drafts with reflective revision, example critical evaluation of recommendations, and maintain formative teacher feedback in order to facilitate substantive writing skills (Marzuki et al., 2023). They survey undergraduate and postgraduate students about their use of generative-AI in writing essays, discovering that many are familiar with it and have generally positive attitudes towards AI as an essay drafting and editing tool, which makes them more confident and more efficient. Issues of academic honesty and critical thinking are an issue. The authors suggest the instructional policies that focus on the ethical use, AI literacy, and the process-based assessment. Focusing on the student opinion, the research recommends the combination of reflective assignments and AI-literacy courses as a way of promoting responsible and scaffolded writing habits and addressing the lack of misuse (Malik et al., 2023).

The qualitative research examines the experience of lecturers and students on the application of generative AI in an Academic Writing module. The participants report that they have improved in generating, organizing, and editing their ideas, and lecturers express worries regarding dependency and lack of creativity. The paper highlights the need to focus on contextual enablers such as faculty training and a redesign of assessment and encourages low-risk pilot applications relying on reflective activities. To plan a curriculum, it offers a viable example: workshops, pilot cohorts, and deliberate reflection that will help to incorporate AI in a responsible way without causing harm to learning objectives and pedagogical values (Ghosh, Gupta, et al., 2025).

They synthetically examines the efficacy of Automated Writing Evaluation (AWE) in schools, discovering slight improvements in the quality of writing with the implementation of AWE in an iterative manner with teacher scaffolding. Standalone AWE has weak effects upon higher-order writing skills. The review recommends stricter trials and studies over time. It points out that AWE facilitates mechanical and organizational enhancements but should not substitute teacher-based instruction in rhetorical skills, programmatic designs should be made with AWE supplementing formative cycles, peer review, and grammar support and a teacher should coach substantive composition (Nunes et al., 2022).

They discuss on how students in various institutions view the use of generative-AI, which has both positive effects (brainstorming, editing, and translation) and negative effects (originality, fairness, and faculty detection). The paper suggests that to align the behavior of students and institutional integrity, the study proposes co-constructed use policies, curricular AI literacy, and clear expectations. It encourages participatory policy-making by putting students at the heart of policy-making. In the case of writing programs, practical suggestions are co-created AI-use charters and tool disclosure rubrics, which encourage responsive and reflective use of the tools and minimize insidious usage (Okonkwo & Ade-Ibijola, 2023). They investigates equity in the education algorithms, which connects technical concepts of prejudice to education results. He provides bias sources like data limitations and label biases, bias reduction techniques like data augmentation, fairness-conscious learning, and intersectional evaluation. The chapter highlights the importance of context-sensitive metrics of fairness, the concept of participatory design, and the concept of institutional monitoring, which offers practical advice to those stakeholders who adopt AI-based writing systems. Proceeds to recommend audits, stakeholder participation and disclosure to inform procurement and supervising Ferramentos of AWE and LLM tools to provide fair results to broad learner groups (Kizilcec, 2022).

It provides the survey and qualitative data about the stakeholders in the Hong Kong higher education to suggest an AI Ecological Education Policy Framework that includes pedagogical, governance, and operational aspects. This paper acknowledges ten priorities that involve training, assessment redesign and data privacy and recommends participatory policy processes involving students, faculty and administrators. The framework gives an action plan of institutional AI preparedness, infrastructure, vendor screening, faculty preparation, and assessment redesign. The way it focuses on stakeholder involvement provides effective advice on the fair and ethical use of AI in writing programs (Chan, 2023). The argument is placed in the context of well-known composition research, when writing is not just a product but rather a complex process of invention, drafting and revising, which now overlaps fundamentally with AI. The use of AI applications, including Automated Writing Evaluation (AWE) and large language models (LLMs), is an additional value to instructors since students can receive immediate feedback on style and mechanics, allowing instructors to concentrate on higher order writing and rhetorical skills.

RESEARCH QUESTIONS

1. What are the ways to use AI-driven applications to engage with writing teaching in a pedagogically innovative way and increase student interest in the process?
2. What do ethical issues such as academic integrity, authorship, and privacy, and algorithmic bias entail in implementing AI in the pedagogy of writing?
3. How ready are schools to sensibly embrace AI in writing education by developing the faculty, setting up the policies, and physical facilities?
4. What is needed is a pedagogy of writing that would strike a balance between the opportunities of technology and ethical protection in the era of intelligent tools?

OBJECTIVES

In order to examine how AI technologies can be used to facilitate innovation, personalization, and engagement in writing pedagogy.

To analyse critically such ethical issues as academic dishonesty, authorship issues, privacy concerns, writing bias based on AI-assisted writing.

In order to assess the institutional preparedness to use AI in writing instruction, it is necessary to pay attention to the curriculum design, faculty preparedness, and governance policies.

To suggest a structure in the creation of writing pedagogies that are ethically based, technologically informed, and institutionally sustainable.

METHODOLOGY

This research will take a qualitative research design based on secondary data analysis. Articles, policy reports, institutional reports, and case studies on AI in writing pedagogy are reviewed systematically, to determine patterns, themes and gaps. Primary sources can be found in peer-reviewed journals and databases, such as Scopus, Web of Science, and Google Scholar. Thematic coding and synthesis of data is conducted to analyse pedagogical innovation, ethical concern, and institutional preparedness to obtain a comprehensive and evidence-based insight into the research problem.

The Artificial Intelligence AI-Based Application that can be used to improve the Pedagogy of Writing and Student Engagement

The introduction of AI-based applications to writing pedagogy has been predominantly identified as a way to promote pedagogical change and improve student interaction. A body of research shows that AI applications like Automated Writing Evaluation (AWE) systems, large language models (LLMs), and adaptive feedback systems can serve to change writing teaching into more interactive, student-based teaching patterns. Fleckenstein et al. (2023) show AWE to affect student writing moderately positively, particularly in combination with teaching and mediation by the teacher. This demonstrates that AI is able to offer real-time and formative feedback which contributes to the repetitive quality of writing and the continued motivation of students through visible progress.

Generative AI applications, like ChatGPT, are becoming perceived as productive partners of the classroom. According to Jeon and Lee (2023), LLMs can serve as scaffolding agents, content providers, and interlocutors, thus stimulating the mechanism of language experimentation in the students in terms of their structure, argumentation, and structure. This role facilitates innovation in pedagogy since AI is placed as an assistant and not a replacement of learning. On the one hand, students receive a more advanced level of abilities in the drafting process; on the other hand, the students get a chance to evaluate AI products with a critical approach, and its evaluation skills will be improved. Marzuki et al. (2023) affirm this point of view by demonstrating that AI writing aids can enhance both the coherence and the productivity of writing, but that it should be accompanied by teacher scaffolding, which ensures against excessive reliance.

Moreover, AI-based applications can be used to support differentiated learning, providing individualized attention to students with language or cognitive needs. As Hardaker and Glenn (2025) emphasize, personalization with the help of AI can help create inclusivity and engagement, particularly in the case of multilingual or remedial learning. The customization of AI tools guarantees that students are provided with the level of assistance that corresponds to their level of competence and this leads to increased confidence and motivation. Zhai and Ma (2021) further present the argument that students tend to believe and comply with AI feedback more often when it is explicit, teacher-based, and valid. It is also possible to note that pedagogical innovation can be observed in changing the curriculum design and assessment with the assistance of AI. As Cotos (2023) states, reflective exercises can include AWE and feedback systems in them, which prompts students to not only revise their drafts, but also to think critically about the writing process. On the same note, Kasneci et al. (2023) suggest that responsive use of AI can be facilitated by faculty-based experimentation and pilot testing, so that the innovation process can be aligned with the learning needs of an institution.

But innovation has to be tempered. According to Dempere et al. (2023) and Maphoto (2024), mindless dependence on AI is likely to reduce creativity and originality. As such, AI-based writing pedagogy entails rigorously designed tasks, including reflective tasks, AI-literacy courses, and teacher mediation. These strategies will make sure that the students are proactive learners and the students enjoy interactive and adaptive features of AI. Finally, AI-based apps have the potential to revolutionize the writing pedagogy process by turning it more interactive, personal and interesting. AI empowers the writing experience, as it provides instant feedback, scaffolds the creative processes, and allows adaptive learning. However, the effective use of tools is not innovation and thus the real innovation is the use of tools by teachers; how they combine automation with human instruction, contemplation and moral action to make the use of the tools meaningful to students.

Ethical Implication of Academic Integrity, Authorship, Privacy and Algorithmic Bias in AI-Assisted Writing

Ethical aspects of artificial intelligence adoption into writing pedagogy have been the most topical issue in the educational research. The risks of AI and AI-driven improvements in efficiency and individualization are associated with the threats of academic dishonesty, authorship, data security, and algorithm bias. Such concerns are core, rather than tangential to the discussion of the responsible adoption of AI within institutions of higher learning, as they influence both the learning performance of students and institutional credibility.

Academic integrity is one of the most important ethical issues. As Jeon and Lee (2023) explain, large language models (LLMs) like ChatGPT can produce fluent and convincing texts that can be presented by the students as their own work and they will not have to study the subject anymore. This creates issues of originality and plagiarism in a way that the conventional plagiarism-detecting systems might not detect. Survey confirmed by Malik et al. (2023) that students tend to perceive generative AI as a valid tool used in drafting but confess that they do not know how to reconcile efficiency with honesty. Therefore, the policies of academic integrity should change to differentiate between the supportive and the direct replacement of student effort.

It is closely related to the issue of authorship. The process of creating the text by means of AI leaves boundaries of human and machine input unclear. According to Baker and Hawn (2022), algorithms are not neutral co-authors since they recreate bias in training data. Teachers, thus, have the dilemma of deciding authorship and credit when writing is scaffolded using the help of AI tools by students. Gustilo (2024) recommends that the institutions develop policies, which promote transparency, including disclosure rubrics: the students must specify how much AI was used to write their drafts. This maintains accountability as well as fosters digital literacy as it promotes critical thinking about the process of writing. Another important ethical issue is data privacy. A lot of AI writing programs are created by business developers who gather and archive user-created data. Nguyen et al. (2023) point out that student writing can be harvested as a source of training data, which can be a problem with intellectual property and ownership of educational information. In the absence of tough privacy controls, students will lose access to their personal and academic data. Chan (2023) also endorses institutional AI policy to encompass screening of vendors and participatory governance as a way of ensuring privacy, equity and transparency in the use of data.

These ethical dilemmas are added to by algorithmic bias that reinforces inequities in writing pedagogy. Idowu et al. (2024) demonstrate that AI-powered progress monitoring systems may be less accurate to make predictions concerning marginalized groups (by age, gender, or disability), which only strengthens the existing inequalities. Equally, Tate et al. (2024) show that automated essay scoring narrows down the range of scores and creates differences between subgroups, thus the fairness of AI-assessed education is questionable. Kizilcec (2022) suggests the following measures that should be used to reduce such risks: fairness-conscious learning, participatory design, and auditing.

Altogether, the problem of AI in writing pedagogy raises ethical concerns that imply the conflict between innovation and responsibility. Excessive use of generative tools is a threat to academic integrity, and the authorship of hybrid human-machine writing is unclear. Privacy issues reinforce the significance of institutional control and accountability of the vendors and algorithmic bias requires systemic surveillance to avoid the re-creation of educational inequalities. To adopt AI ethically, as Nguyen et al. (2023) affirm, technical protection is necessary, as well as cultural changes in teaching practice, where transparency, responsibility, and equity are deeply incorporated into the process of program content and instructions in writing. Therefore, it turns out that the concerns of such ethics is not simply the regulation of technology, but the reconsideration of the values that the digital age of writing pedagogy is built upon. The institutions should create the environment in which AI facilitates the learning process and does not threaten academic honesty, equity, and trust.

Institutional Readiness to Integrate AI: Development of Faculty, Policy Frameworks and Infrastructure

The institutional preparedness is an international issue that requires aggressive stance on policy based on international endeavours. The major organizations such as UNESCO and OECD have already issued guidelines on the importance of AI literacy training, ethical standards, and equity in order to be responsible and integrate globally. The willingness of teaching institutions to adopt writing pedagogy based on artificial intelligence (AI) is an interdisciplinary problem that includes curriculum development, faculty readiness, policy guidelines, and infrastructure. It has always been the case in literature that even though institutions understand the potential of AI in improving pedagogy, the level of readiness to embrace the potential differs significantly across settings. Institutional preparedness is therefore a technological as well as a cultural issue, and needs systemic planning, stakeholder involvement and capacity preparation. Pedagogy should no longer focus on policing AI use but on actively incorporating it into their teaching methods with new assignment design, including scaffolding assignments with AI brainstorming a low stakes outline followed by a high stakes draft. It should be taught to the students on how to critically review AI-generated work and remix it by adding their own intellectual input that their final work is an expression of human-AI synthesis.

The readiness of faculty is usually mentioned as the most significant factor in the successful implementation of AI. According to Jeon and Lee (2023), AI needs to be used as a classroom partner, not as a replacement of teaching, and this necessitates educators to acquire new mediation literacies of AI usage. In the absence of proper training, teachers can either overuse AI or use it in a manner that is detrimental to the pedagogical intent. This fear is reflected by Maphoto (2024), who says that lecturers feel that using generative AI is a good idea to ideate and write, but they also note that they worry about being dependent and less creative. Training of the faculty, reflective workshops and pilot projects are, therefore, needed to develop confidence and pedagogical control. Another important aspect of preparedness is the structure of institutional policy. Nguyen et al. (2023) review the policies of AI-in-education at the global level, stating the principles of transparency, accountability, privacy, and equity as the key ones in responsible adoption. But they too observe discrepancies within the institutions, particularly in the practice of these principles. Chan (2023) offers an AI Ecological Education Policy Framework that includes the focus on participatory governance, redesign of the assessment, and screening of vendors to protect privacy and make sure that they complement the institutional values. Okonkwo and Ade-Ibijola (2023) further state that AI-use charters created by students can be used to build trust and reduce abuse and that preparedness is a not only an administrative but also a cultural issue.

Institutional readiness also is determined by infrastructure and technical resources. In order to successfully implement AI tools in writing pedagogy, schools would need to offer access to stable digital systems, secure data management tools, and proper IT support. Kasneci et al. (2023) emphasize that pilot testing and co-constructed guidelines would avoid the situation of hasty implementation that may threaten to weaken learning outcomes. Equally, Shi and Aryadoust (2022) advise institutions to consider AI tools according to their capacity to support pedagogical aims, their validity and empirical research before adopting them at large scale. This suggests that infrastructure preparedness needs to be accompanied by stringent assessment and evidence based decision making. Another connection between institutional readiness and AI literacy development among students is present. Laupichler et al. (2022) discover that AI literacy is not appropriately taught in the majority of curriculums, and students are not equipped with the critical thinking skills to be responsible when analyzing the outputs of AI. A curriculum with AI literacy not only helps to promote responsible use of AI tools, but also equips students with the knowledge to interact with AI technologies in a wider societal context. Dempere et al. (2023) also state that AI literacy should be introduced into the design of assessments and that students should be assessed both in the writing area and in terms of their critical use of AI assistance.

Although there is increased consciousness, the literature has serious challenges. According to Idowu et al. (2024) and Tate et al. (2024), without fairness audits and oversight, unmonitored AI systems can exacerbate inequities, so fairness audits and supervision must be essential. Institutional preparedness, however, cannot be confined to making AI tools available; it should embrace a paradigm of constant monitoring, ethical supervision and consistency with equity objectives. To sum up, institutional preparedness towards AI in writing pedagogy depends on three dimensions that are interrelated: preparing faculty with AI literacies and training, creating strong and participatory policy to support writing, and providing supporting infrastructure. Most schools are trying pilot projects and ethical policies, but the only way to be really ready is through long-term investment, participatory governance, and a clear desire to make the technology implementation relevant to educational values of equity, responsibility and openness. But the very technologies that enable pedagogical innovation also present severe threats that cannot be solved only on the basis of classroom design. Thus, the efficient application of AI tools cannot be achieved without adequate, well-structured, and transparent ethical practice standards.

Striking a Balance between Technological Opportunities and the Ethical Protection in Writing Pedagogy

The main challenge of reimagining writing as a digital age is to balance the opportunities of AI that change the way writing is conducted with ethical protections. The literature identifies several key aspects previous to the application of AI tools, namely, that they need to be integrated into the pedagogical frameworks to ensure the focus on academic integrity, equity, and agency of students. This is not to rebuff or blindly accept AI, but to ensure that hybrid forms of pedagogy are formed, which combine technological possibilities and ethical safeguards. The ability of AI to deliver individualized feedback in real time to facilitate iterative writing is one of the opportunities. Fleckenstein et al. (2023) and Fan and Ma (2022) prove that Automated Writing Evaluation (AWE) can help to improve student outcomes significantly under the condition of teacher mediation. Nevertheless, the same studies emphasize that AI feedback is not able to render human insight, at least when it comes to building higher-order skills, like critical thinking, creativity, rhetorical awareness, etc. To preserve the efficiency and intellectual rigor a balanced pedagogy would thus have to use AI to obtain mechanical and organizational feedback and leave interpretive and evaluative tasks to the instructors.

Academic integrity and authorship have to be also covered by ethical protection. Jeon and Lee (2023) are cautious of overtrusting the so-called large language models (LLMs), as the author believes that this may lead to a decrease in student originality. Similar results are mentioned by Malik et al. (2023), where students express their enthusiasm about AI in drafting, yet the problems of honesty are not addressed. To achieve a middle ground, Okonkwo & Ade-Ibijola (2023) propose co-created policies of AI-use, which would stimulate the disclosure of AI help in tasks. This openness will turn AI into an openly visible, responsible learning tool, and contribute to the maintenance of authorship and integrity.

The other critical element of balance is solving the issue of algorithmic bias and equity. Baker and Hawn (2022) and Idowu et al. (2024) demonstrate that datasets and predictive models are biased, and such biases traditionally work against the disadvantaged populations, which is a matter of equity. Kizilcec (2022) suggests the use of fairness audits, participatory design and institutional monitoring as protective measures to prevent the fact that AI strengthens educational inequalities. It is by embedding these practices into writing pedagogy that AI tools can be used to make learning conditions inclusive but not exclusionary. Ethical framework also constitutes data privacy and governance. Nguyen et al. (2023) and Chan (2023) emphasize that the transparent vendor contracts and privacy evaluations should be implemented in the institutions to avoid the exploitative use of student writing information. With a combination of well-defined governance frameworks, it is possible to ensure that intellectual property is safeguarded, whilst still using AI to drive pedagogical innovation in schools.

Lastly, it is important to develop faculty and become AI-literate. Laupichler et al. (2022) believe that AI literacy should be taught as a part of the curriculum students should be taught to use AI tools not just effectively but also to be able to critique their constraints. Equally, Kasneci et al. (2023) emphasize training of the faculty and co-constructed guidelines as effective preventive measures, which are used in practice. This biliteracy, both on the side of teachers and students, is such that writing pedagogy is neither technologically deterministic nor a critical informed understanding. Finally, to find a compromise, it is necessary to develop a hybrid pedagogy that is based on three pillars: taking advantage of AI to offer personalized and adaptive learning experiences, implementing ethical safeguards including integrity policies, fairness audits, and privacy safeguards, and building digital and AI literacies in the faculty and students. In a sensible way, writing pedagogy in the AI age could embrace the opportunities of the technologies without undermining the ethical values that are at the heart of the education system.

DISCUSSIONS

The results of the literature review indicate that the combination of AI and writing pedagogy is a promising, yet challenging topic, which needs to be handled carefully. On the one hand, AI-based solutions like Automated Writing Evaluation systems, large language models, and interactive feedback mechanisms open up possibilities of pedagogical innovation by offering real-time and individualized feedback in a form of interactive feedback and increasing student engagement. These technologies make writing support more democratic, scaffold learning in diverse student groups, and promote individualized instruction that is no longer limited by the time imposed in a classroom. Nevertheless, it is evident in the literature that the effectiveness of AI in writing pedagogy depends, in any case, on its responsible implementation in which human professors play the key role as the mediators of meaning, creativity, and critical thinking. The ethical problems become one significant dimension. The problems of academic integrity, authorship, algorithmic bias, and the concept of privacy highlight the dangers of blindly following. Promoting plagiarism or causing anonymization of authorship, generative AI can also support prejudices in judgment and accessibility, and the biases inherent in datasets can strengthen disparities. Simultaneously, it is common that commercial AI devices jeopardize the student data security and require institutional control and regulation.

Such ethical issues demand collaborative policies, disclosure models, and equity audits, which safeguard students without undermining the pedagogical worth of AI. Another determinant that is final is institutional preparedness. AI integration needs faculty development, infrastructure investment, and participatory governance structures to ensure its integration is in alignment with academic principles of equity, transparency, and accountability. Lack of proper preparation means that institutions are likely to adopt AI in a manner that compromises the goals of learning or increases inequalities. The balance is then to create hybrid pedagogies to combine the opportunities presented by technology and ethical protection that encourages innovation and responsibility. Taken together, the literature demonstrates that AI in the writing pedagogy cannot be considered as a substitute to human guidance but instead, it can be used as a means to expand the scope of writing education and make it more effective.

MAIN FINDINGS

The literature review and discussion of the research questions indicate that there are a number of significant findings regarding the overlap between AI and writing pedagogy. To begin with, AI-based tools like Automated Writing Evaluation systems and large language models have a great potential to revolutionize the teaching of writing by providing real-time, personalized and adaptive feedback. This ability builds participation, democratization of the capacity to acquire writing assistance as well as inclusivity among learners with different language and cognitive groups. AI devices can become brainstorming partners, scaffolders and revisioners, thus promoting new teaching and learning methods. Meanwhile, these possibilities are also accompanied by difficult ethical issues. One of the threats to academic integrity is the urge to overuse generative AI and reduce originality and creativity. The authors question is washed out because contributions that are made by AI cannot be easily differentiated and those made by students. The commercialization of student writing data contributes to the increased issues of data privacy and security, whereas the use of algorithms poses a threat of reinforcing assessment and access inequities. These issues must be tackled by being transparent, conducting fairness audits, privacy protection, and disclosure and responsible use policies.

The results also highlight the fact that institutional preparation is not even and that most schools do not have trained faculty or supportive infrastructure and an extensive policy. To implement AI meaningfully, the institutions are needed to focus on developing faculty, AI literacy courses, and the participatory policy frameworks that will incorporate students as the stakeholders. The best possible course of action lies in hybrid models, which are human-informed with AI support to make sure that the technology serves as an addition to critical areas of writing pedagogy and not a substitution. General observations show that AI in writing pedagogy provides significant potentials of innovation and interaction but needs to be informed by ethical precautions and institutional readiness. Success is not the technology but the way it is implemented by educators and institutions into the pedagogical, cultural and ethical framework.

SUGGESTIONS

- Facilitate faculty training programs to incorporate AI literacy, so that the faculty can critically embrace and mediate AI use in writing classrooms instead of leaving students to use the tools without any supervision.
- Encourage hybrid pedagogical approaches in which AI is used to deliver mechanical and organizational feedback, whereas teachers' pay attention to higher-order capabilities, including creativity, critical thinking, and rhetorical awareness.
- Assess reflective exercises, where students report on their use of AI tools and critically reflect on them, promoting transparency, accountability and critical reflection.
- Establish institutional guidelines that create a distinction between AI as a supportive aid and AI as a replacement to student effort and keep the academic integrity intact.
- Put in place systems of participatory governance through which students, faculty, and administrators are co-creators of AI-use policy, which will foster trust and curb abuse.
- Bring AI literacy into the curriculum where students learn how to be efficient with tools and how to question their shortcomings, biases, and morals.
- Provide fairness audits and bias measures on AI application to reduce inequities in feedback, evaluation and access of various learner groups.
- Pilot design and gradual implementation plans prior to mass application to enable the institutions to check effectiveness and reasonably change policies.
- Protect privacy of data by having transparent contracts with vendors, secure infrastructure and ownership policies over writing generated by students.

- Promote an individualized learning model: AI can be applied to support the needs of multilingual, remedial, or differently abnormal students in the form of personalized scaffolding.
- Make AI-based feedback consistent with the curricular learning objectives so that technology informs, but not determines, the pedagogical practices.
- Encourage educators, technologists, and policymakers to collaborate interdisciplinary in order to make AI in writing pedagogy innovative and ethical.
- By focusing on the work that cannot be done automatically, is innovative and involves critical thought, the creativity will not be eroded by generative tools.
- Put in place surveillance measures of continual review of the effects of AI on pedagogy so that it is consistent with institutional values of equity, transparency, and accountability.
- Promote a cultural change in organisations whereby AI is not considered a substitute of human teaching but a co-worker which can add value to the learning experience.

FUTURE IMPLICATIONS OF THE STUDY

The implication of this work in the future is that AI will have a transformative and cautious application within the writing pedagogy. As smart devices become more advanced, their ability to provide personalized real-time feedback will keep further increasing the opportunities to engage with students, become more inclusive and differentiate learning. This implies that in the future people will not have to be restricted by the time available in the classroom to teach writing but can be enhanced by adaptive digital partners. The process of switching to AI in learning is irreversible, and it requires a definite, coordinated effort on the pedagogical, ethical, and institutional levels. In this paper, three recommendations have been provided towards the stakeholders: First, pedagogy should address the issues of teaching students how to work with AI in a responsible way. Second, organizations should document policies on how the use of AI, authorship, and privacy of data should be done. Lastly, the implementation of systemic professional development should be done to make sure that every faculty member is equipped with the needed AI literacy to make students follow the right direction. Simultaneously, the paper highlights the fact that an unregulated use of AI poses a threat to originality, creativity, and the authenticity of student authorship, and the role of educators is critical in mediating the use of technology. The institutions will be required to focus on teaching AI literacy to their faculty as well as students and the development of critical awareness of biases, ethical concerns, and constraints of these systems. The policy frameworks will need to change to protect academic integrity and preserve data privacy and participate governance will be needed to maintain fairness and trust, and equity audit will be required. Finally, the future of writing education will depend on hybrid models, i.e., the efficiency of AI with the invaluable human advice. In such a way, the institutions can use innovation in a responsible manner and equip the learners with the skills to survive in an age of digital technology which requires them to be not only techno-savvy but also ethical.

CONCLUSION

The paper also finds that artificial intelligence has a huge potential in changing the writing pedagogy, however, the effect that it has on the education practice is largely reliant on the way it is incorporated into the educational process. AI-based tools, like Automated Writing Evaluation systems and large language models, present more opportunities than ever before to provide personalized feedback, student activity, and inclusiveness. As scaffolding agents, content providers, and interactive partners, they can democratize the access to writing support, and they can develop new, more innovative pedagogy. Nevertheless, these benefits are closely interconnected with ethical issues in terms of academic integrity, authorship, privacy of data, and bias of algorithms. Unless closely mediated, AI will threaten the creativity, equity, and trust in the education process. The institutional preparedness is found to be a determining variable which includes faculty training, curriculum redesign, governance policies and infrastructural support. It seems that the most balanced way to go is hybrid solutions, in which AI is used to complement, rather than to replace human teaching. The adoption needs to be successful, audits on fairness, participatory policymaking, as well as developing AI literacy in students and educators. In the end, AI cannot be considered as a panacea or menace, it is a partner that in the case of responsibility will enrich the writing pedagogy. The human check and ethical protection can be embedded in the institutions to promote AI to improve the essence of education instead of degrading it.

REFERENCES

Baker, R. S., & Hawn, A. (2022). Algorithmic bias in education. *International Journal of Artificial Intelligence in Education, 32*(4), 1052–1092. DOI: 10.1007/s40593-021-00285-9

Chan, C. K. Y. (2023). A comprehensive AI policy education framework for university teaching and learning. *International Journal of Educational Technology in Higher Education, 20*(1), 38. Advance online publication. DOI: 10.1186/s41239-023-00408-3

Cotos, E. (2023). *Automated Feedback on Writing.* In *Advances in Writing Technology* (pp. ...). Springer. DOI: 10.1007/978-3-031-36033-6_22

Dempere, J., Modugu, K., Allam, H., & Ramasamy, L. K. (2023). The impact of ChatGPT on higher education. *Frontiers in Education, 8*, 1206936. DOI: 10.3389/feduc.2023.1206936

Fleckenstein, J., Zacher, J., & Schilling, S. (2023). Automated feedback and writing: A multi-level meta-analysis of effects on students' performance. *Frontiers in Artificial Intelligence, 6*, 1162454. Advance online publication. DOI: 10.3389/frai.2023.1162454 PMID: 37465061

Ghosh, R. K., Chakraborty, S., & Dutta, G. (2025). AI in Enhancing Bilingual Proficiency. In Advances in computational intelligence and robotics book series (pp. 141–176). DOI: 10.4018/979-8-3373-0275-1.ch005

Ghosh, R. K., Gupta, B., Dutta, G., & Chakraborty, S. (2025). Measuring Success: Evaluating the Impact of Reskilling and Upskilling. In Reskilling and Upskilling in the Age of AI (1st ed., pp. 200–217). DOI: 10.1201/9781003611677-11

Idowu, J. A., Koshiyama, A. S., & Treleaven, P. (2024). Investigating algorithmic bias in student progress monitoring. *Computers and Education: Artificial Intelligence, 7*, 100267. DOI: 10.1016/j.caeai.2024.100267

Jeon, J., & Lee, S. (2023). Large language models in education: A focus on the complementary relationship between human teachers and ChatGPT. *Education and Information Technologies, 28*(12), 15873–15892. Advance online publication. DOI: 10.1007/s10639-023-11834-1

Kasneci, E., Seßler, K., Küchemann, S., Bannert, M., Dementieva, D., Fischer, F., Gasser, U., Groh, G., Günnemann, S., Hüllermeier, E., Krusche, S., Kutyniok, G., Michaeli, T., Nerdel, C., Pfeffer, J., Poquet, O., Sailer, M., Schmidt, A., Seidel, T., & Kasneci, G. (2023). ChatGPT for Good? On opportunities and challenges of large language models for education. *Learning and Individual Differences, 103*, 102274. Advance online publication. DOI: 10.1016/j.lindif.2023.102274

Kizilcec, R. F. (2022). Algorithmic fairness in education. In Elliott, C. (Ed.), *The Oxford Handbook of Education and AI* (pp. 178–200). Routledge., DOI: 10.4324/9780429329067-10

Laupichler, M. C., Aster, A., Schirch, J., & Raupach, T. (2022). Artificial intelligence literacy in higher and adult education: A scoping literature review. *Computers & Education: Artificial Intelligence, 3*, 100101. DOI: 10.1016/j.caeai.2022.100101

Malik, A. R., Pratiwi, Y., Andajani, K., Numertayasa, I. W., Suharti, S., Darwis, A., & Marzuki, . (2023). Exploring artificial intelligence in academic essay: Higher education students' perspective. *International Journal of Educational Research Open, 5*, 100296. DOI: 10.1016/j.ijedro.2023.100296

Marzuki, M., Widiati, U., Rusdin, D., Darwin, , & Indrawati, I. (2023). The impact of AI writing tools on the content and organization of students' writing: EFL teachers' perspective. *Cogent Education, 10*(1), 2236469. DOI: 10.1080/2331186X.2023.2236469

Nguyen, A., Ngo, H. N., Hong, Y., Dang, B., & Nguyen, B.-P. T. (2023). Ethical principles for artificial intelligence in education. *Education and Information Technologies, 28*(4), 4221–4241. Advance online publication. DOI: 10.1007/s10639-022-11316-w PMID: 36254344

Nunes, A., Cordeiro, C., Limpo, T., & Castro, S. L. (2022). Effectiveness of automated writing evaluation systems in school settings: A systematic review. *Journal of Computer Assisted Learning, 38*(6), 1260–1277. DOI: 10.1111/jcal.12635

Okonkwo, C. M., & Ade-Ibijola, A. (2023). Students' voices on generative AI: Perceptions, benefits, and challenges in higher education. *International Journal of Educational Technology in Higher Education, 20*(1), 41. Advance online publication. DOI: 10.1186/s41239-023-00411-8

Shi, H., & Aryadoust, V. (2022). A systematic review of automated writing evaluation systems. *Education and Information Technologies, 28*(1), 771–795. DOI: 10.1007/s10639-022-11200-7

Tate, T. P., Steiss, J., Bailey, D. H., Graham, S., Moon, Y., Ritchie, D., Tseng, W., & Warschauer, M. (2024). *Can AI provide useful holistic essay scoring?* Computers & Education. *Artificial Intelligence, 7*, 100255. DOI: 10.1016/j.caeai.2024.100255

Zhai, N., & Ma, X. (2021). Automated writing evaluation (AWE) feedback: A systematic investigation of college students' acceptance. *Computer Assisted Language Learning*. Advance online publication. DOI: 10.1080/09588221.2021.1897019

Chapter 4
Impact of Using Effective Tools of Pedagogy and AI for Future-Ready Writing Education

Sanjeev Kumar
https://orcid.org/0000-0002-7375-7341
Lovely Professional University, India

ABSTRACT

As classrooms continue to evolve, educators turning to a powerful combination of modern teaching methods and artificial intelligence (AI) to make writing education more engaging, personalized, personalized writing experiences and relevant for the future. This paper explores how blending effective pedagogical tools with AI technologies reshape writing education to prepare learners for the future can help students become confident and future-ready writers. The research highlights how tools such as interactive writing platforms, AI grammar checkers, and peer review applications enhance both the writing process and student motivation. .The findings suggest that while AI can enhance the learning process, it should support not to replace the human connection between teacher and student. Ultimately, this paper argues for a balanced, intentional use of pedagogy and AI to build future-ready writers who are not only technically sound but also imaginative, adaptable, and empowered to communicate in a rapidly evolving world.

BACKGROUND OF THE STUDY

In the modern world where everything constantly changes, we learn and teach is changing very quickly, in particular in the manner in which we make students ready to write well. The business of writing is not only about grammar, structure or cursive penmanship. It is about sending intelligible thoughts, developing meaningful content and having interactions with a wider audience who is most of the time international. With the world getting computerized and interconnected, the future ready writing education is more imperative than ever(Goh et al., 2025). Two strong winds are at the center of this evolution namely modern pedagogy and arti-

DOI: 10.4018/979-8-3373-5601-3.ch004

ficial intelligence (AI). Although the two have existed in one form or the other over the years, their synergy in modern classrooms is changing our world in ways we never thought possible. This study examines the same question through the prism of effective educational resources and AI, which can be integrated to develop the set of writing abilities that are not only exemplary, but also profoundly human and futuristic(Kurban & Şahin, 2024).Contemporary learning has already moved beyond lecture based teaching to a more learner oriented paradigm of learning. The role of teachers can no longer be restricted to provision of knowledge; they are currently viewed as facilitators, mentors and guides. Such tools as project-based learning, peer feedback, storytelling, and reflective journaling all hold a lot of promise to foster a deeper level of writing skills(Baranidharan et al., 2025). These strategies not only assist students in the development of their writing mechanics, but also encourage them to think critically, have an understanding of empathizing with various voices and developing unique voice. Not only does writing then involve more than doing as an assignment, but the students also write something that they want to say(Kumar et al., 2024).

Artificial intelligence-driven technology such as grammar checkers, writing prompts, plagiarism, and even, content generators are becoming the norm. These applications are capable of providing immediate feedback, custom learning, and less pressure on instructors. They enable students to write better and in real time, experiment with different writing styles and even learn faster by making mistakes. But the true power is not only the usage of AI, but the usage of it. AI can be combined with creativity and help students when applied rationally. It is able to supplement a decent pedagogy by providing personalized recommendations as well as giving room to human discretion. A properly developed AI can highlight which sentences may be better written, but only a human being, a teacher or a student, can define whether the sentence has the purpose of the writer. And that is when humanization is important(Movahed et al., 2025).It is not surprising that AI is feared as something that will render writing lifeless. It will become of emotional expression, of expression of culture, of narration when the machine has become part of the process.However, the attitude towards AI instead of viewing it as some kind of substitute, we might implement more humanity into writing study. Educators will be able to pay more attention to mentoring, guiding and fostering creativity whereas AI will be able to complete mundane tasks or simple corrections(Kumar, 2024). In their turn, students will be able to be self-confident, discover new concepts, and be in control. The study will discuss the potential of integrating powerful pedagogical tools and AI technologies to develop the well-proportioned, humanized system of teaching writing. It emphasizes the need of empathy, morals, and critical thinking when implementing AI. It also includes consideration of issues like over- dependence on AI, ethics, and insistence on sincerity of writing by the students. But what is more important it gives examples, insights, and strategies on how to build classrooms, where technology supports the human, rather than substitutes him. Hearts and machinery will play a role in a writing classroom which is prepared to meet the future(Dhiraj & Kumar, 2023). It is high time we looked beyond pedagogy and embraced the potential that can be harnessed via AI by focusing on harnessing the best pedagogy and combining it with the power of AI not to make students better writers, but better informed, more ethical and empowered communicators.

OBJECTIVES OF THE STUDY

I. To Explore How Modern Pedagogical Approaches Support Human-Centered Writing Skills
II. To Examine the Role of AI Tools in Enhancing (Not Replacing) the Writing Process
III. To Understand the Balance between Technology and Human Connection in the Classroom
IV. To Identify Best Practices for Integrating Pedagogy and AI in Writing Education

UNDERSTANDING THE MODERN PEDAGOGICAL TOOLS

Educations have taken quite a journey together leaving chalkboards and hard lectures behind. The current state of the classrooms is more interactive, heterogeneous, and digitally connected. As this change has occurred the means by which we teach, particularly areas such as writing have changed as well. The core of this shift is contemporary educational technologies that turn students, student voices, and student learning paths to the center of education. The contemporary pedagogy is not only technology-based, but it is the way to learn(Queiroz-Neto et al., 2015). It is aimed at increasing the level of personalization, engagement, inclusiveness and meaning of education. One of the aspects of, notorious, Traditional teaching was rooted in rote learning and universal teaching. Modern pedagogy has come to realize that each student has his or her way of learning(Kirovograd Institute for Human Development & Chernenko, 2020). Not all students learn in the same manner, some prefer to visualize learning others absorb more when it comes to a discussion and most learn best when they can practice the learning in real life situations. Therefore, tools that are efficient nowadays are constructed in a manner that is flexible to respond to the differences. A project-based learning (PBL) is one of such powerful methods. It is different based on the fact that students are not writing essays or reports just to gain grades; they are solving real problems, usually with the help of teams. To give an example, they could write project proposals to community development, climate change blogs, or letters to the local leaders(Karakalpak State University, Uzbekistan & Jarilkapovich, 2025). These assignments not only require the learning of the mechanics of writing but assist the students to identify the need and effect of what they write. It makes writing live--makes it topical and actual.

A second modern device is peer collaboration and feedback. Students used to write mainly to teachers. Writing is now more shared, reviewed and perfected with the help of communication with classmates. Apps such as Google-docs, padlet or even classroom circles where students are able to view the work of one another and provide useful feedback. This process does not simply enhance writing in terms of grammar or spelling but it educates a person on the themes of empathy, critical thinking and consideration (Nancy et al., 2020). Journaling and reflections have also become a necessity. With the busy lifestyle, students rarely have some time to think. The reflective writing enables them to reflect on what they are learning, what they feel and how they grow. It can be used as digital diary or blogging, or even voice-to-text journals, either way; it is an amazing tool that helps develop not only writing skill, but also emotional intelligence. Another contemporary method with the increasing popularity is gamification(Lisova, 2024). It has such elements as challenges, points, and levels to make learning more engaging. Writing applications and sites frequently have points or rewards in case you finish a task, learn new words or correct the work(Kumar, 2023). Gamification creates the sense of playful learning by feeling without making learning less useful. Multimodal Writing Projects Multimodal writing projects are possible on digital platforms, such as Canva, Flipgrid, and Storybird. This broadens the interpretation of writing other than to the conventional paragraph and essay writing. In the world of PDP, a skill to write to various media is a significant strength to have; the skills allow students in all styles of study to be able to challenge their creativity(Department of Curriculum and Instruction, Kulliyyah of Education, International Islamic University Malaysia, Malaysia et al., 2025). But still, at the heart of contemporary pedagogy is a human relationship. It does not matter how sophisticated the tools can be, the interaction between the teacher and the student is the key to the process of learning. Capitalism has already been subjected to a long history of criticism and is still continuing to be scolded, especially in the field of pedagogy(Gorbatkova et al., 2021).

Notably, such tools can be used to create a more inclusive and equitable classroom as well. Modern tools also provide new possibilities that enable students with learning differences (or other challenges) to get involved with the work, and the same can be said about those who have language barriers or register anxiety. The aspects of modern pedagogical tools are not to substitute a teacher- they empower the teachers and students. They assist education to shift not only out of passive ways of learning, but into an environment where the students are the active creators, thinkers and communicators(Conole et al., 2004). These technologies represent a world in which people not only communicate via various mediums and through various cultures but at the speed of lightning, thus, it is even more natural that the ways of teaching writing must change, as well. Learning and accepting these tools is one of the steps in the direction of evolving writing classrooms that are not only future-ready but also profoundly human, where a student can find his or her voice in writing and courage to use(Kholoshyn et al., 2019).

ROLE OF ARTIFICIAL INTELLIGENCE IN WRITING EDUCATION

Education is not the same world as it used to be an Artificial Intelligence (AI) is one of the most significant movers in the education world. To someone, the thought of AI in learning might be a frightening concept, i.e., something stiff, mechanical, or overly technical. However, in truth, the Artificial Intelligence already actively functioning in the classrooms, particularly the way students learn to write(Marghany, 2023). A well-considered application of AI can turn into the assistant in the writing process that does not only fix the mistakes, but also makes students more confident, creative, and independent writers. First of all, we can consider what corresponding AI in writing education may entail(Dhiraj et al., 2023a). It is not about study taught by robots or essay composed by a computer at the command of students. Rather, it is about employing clever tools that have the ability to assist with the writing procedures. It is likely that you have already encountered some of them: such grammar checkers as Grammarly, writing services like ChatGPT, or word suggestions in Google Docs or Microsoft Word(Pratama & Hastuti, 2024). These are not tools to replace the writing, but these are the ones that will help you perfect the writing process. An example can be taking grammar and spelling correction. Previously, students perhaps submitted a draft, and delayed days before receiving comments after which they would make corrections. Now, it is possible to get immediate recommendations through AI that is instrumental in making students rectify mistakes (Fauziah & Minarti, 2023). It is this immediate feedback that increases learning since students do not simply correct mistakes but learn the reason behind those mistakes. This creates a more mediated knowledge of grammar, punctuation and sentence structure as time proceeds(Dhiraj et al., 2023b).

However, AI can correct mistakes in more than appearance. There are a lot of tools that provide style tips including clarity, conciseness or engagement. They are able to assist students to reuse embarrassing sentences, change or adopt tones according to audiences and develop arguments clearly. This form of guidance can give a real boost to the confidence of struggling students who may have language issues(Wahyuningsih, 2024). It is equivalent of having your own writing coach- anywhere, at anytime. Another concept is that AI may make a good concept-creator. Writer block is true even among the finest students. Motivation can be the most difficult thing sometimes, it is just the matter of starting, and then we just keep going. AI writing tools will be able to propose the outlines, supply them with topic suggestions or give those writing prompts to spark off their thinking(Al-Sofi, 2024). This does not imply that the students are cheating when they are making use of AI; it implies they are just utilizing technology to help initiate creativity amongst themselves. The voice, the story, the opinion, are all still of the student. Personalization is another significant role of AI(Abdul Rahman et al., 2022). In a traditional classroom one teacher cannot provide detailed, personal feedback to all students at all times. That gap can be filled with the help of AI. Intelligent platforms will be able to monitor the progress of students, establish the general pattern of mistakes and provide personalized recommendations according to the writing style of every student and the level they are at in the writing process. Such a specific type of assistance enables students to develop as they can, instead of getting raced or left behind. Nevertheless, despite this plethora of advantages, it is best to remember that there is a limit to AI, and it needs to be used both ethically and in a responsible way as shown in the table 01 (Kacena et al., 2024).

Table 1. Role of Artificial Intelligence in Writing

Role/Function	Description	Benefits for Students	Benefits for Teachers	Examples of AI Tools/ Applications
Automated Feedback & Assessment	AI evaluates grammar, coherence, structure, and clarity.	Immediate feedback, improved self-editing, faster learning.	Saves grading time, ensures consistency in assessment.	Grammarly, Criterion, Grammarly Classroom, Hemingway Editor
Personalized Writing Support	Tailors recommendations to individual writing strengths/ weaknesses.	Customized learning path, targeted skill improvement.	Helps differentiate instruction for diverse learners.	AI writing tutors, adaptive writing platforms
Idea Generation & Brainstorming	Generates topic ideas, outlines, and prompts.	Overcomes writer's block, enhances creativity.	Helps students start writing more easily.	ChatGPT, Ideaflow, Notion AI
Language Development & ESL Support	Supports vocabulary building, syntax, and language correctness.	Improved language proficiency, easier learning for ESL students.	Provides additional scaffolding for non-native speakers.	Duolingo Writing Tools, Grammarly ESL features
Writing Revision & Editing Guidance	Suggests revisions for clarity, tone, and structure.	Builds editing skills and improves writing quality.	Helps track student progress and common errors.	ProWritingAid, Google Docs AI suggestions
Plagiarism Detection & Academic Integrity	Detects copied content and improper citations.	Encourages original writing and ethical practices.	Prevents academic dishonesty, simplifies verification.	Turnitin, Copyleaks

continued on following page

Table 1. Continued

Role/Function	Description	Benefits for Students	Benefits for Teachers	Examples of AI Tools/ Applications
Writing Analytics & Progress Tracking	Analyzes writing trends over time.	Helps students see improvement areas.	Data-driven insights into class performance.	Learning analytics dashboards
Interactive Writing Instruction	AI acts as a tutor to explain rules, concepts, and techniques.	Reinforces classroom teaching, improves engagement.	Frees up time for deeper instruction and 1-on-1 assistance.	AI-powered writing tutors
Accessibility Support	Provides voice-to-text, text-to-speech, and adaptive interfaces.	Helps students with disabilities fully engage in writing.	Supports inclusive teaching practices.	Speech recognition tools, screen readers

A machine may advise that a sentence be altered which to the pupil means something personal or has poetry in it. It is due to this fact that it is crucial that the teaching process is not left without a teacher, who can tell the students when to listen to AI and when to listen to their instinct. The problem of authenticity is also present(Rosdiana et al., 2024). Students might be tempted to completely neglect their own train of thought in favor of AI when equipped with tools capable of producing word to word sentence structures, as well as entire paragraphs and essays. Human direction is important at that point. Students should be made to realize that as much as AI can assist them on the path towards achieving successful finishing, they will have to be the ones to provide the finishing line which is clear, honest, and original writing(Weidmann, 2024). The AI must be regarded as an accessory and not as an alternative. The most effective classrooms are the classrooms in which technology does not substitute human contact, it rather augments it. This is one case where everybody wins when students employ AI to feel more confident about what they write and teachers do the same to find more time to mentor individual students(Holmes, 2020). It is no longer about correcting mistakes but about storytelling, trying ideas, and developing real-life communication ability(Dewangan et al., 2024).Ultimately, writing is, and always will be, very human. The words can be structured and refined by AI use, but only the author can introduce meaning, purpose and emotion into the text. With thoughtful use of AI, we will be able to do more than make writing education more efficient, but more still accessible, personalized, and empowering to all learners.

INTEGRATING AI WITH PEDAGOGY

Artificial intelligence (AI) and pedagogy have ceased to be an alternative in modern education today and have started colliding, which brings new and thrilling opportunities towards altering our approaches to teaching and learning. However, this merging does not merely involve introduction of intelligent equipment to a classroom. It is the opposite of a dystopian one-dimensional model of learning based on full-scale digitalization, where technology helps, but not in the place of the teacher and the voice of students(Alqahtani & Wafula, 2025). The concept of balance is at the center of this incorporation. Educators add sentiment, impression, creativity and attachment to the classroom. AI incorporates time-saving, data feedback, and individual evaluation. Prudently combined, these strengths will be able to sustain a writing classroom which is more flexible to the needs of every single student, more communicative in its presentation, and more effective in its skills development. Consider as an option, the daily writing process. A first draft is written by a student and is submitted(Kakhkharova & Tuychieva, 2024). In conventional environment, it may take them some days before getting feedback. When using AI tools, learners can immediately receive recommendations on style, syntax, voice, and readability at the moment when they care most about what they are doing(Dr. A.Shaji George, 2023). This is where AI strengths lie in that it decreases the waiting time and gives students an opportunity to get to know how to improve during the course.The role of a teacher is also indispensible when it comes to assisting the students with the comprehension of the context, meaning, and audience. A student may be told that a sentence is awkward by an AI yet a teacher or friend can help the student introspect whether he is actually intended (Kaiser & Kaiser, 2024). This is the reason integration is important where AI covers routine part, and teachers concentrate on the higher order thinking demonstrating mentoring and encouraging creativity. An effective tool of integration is blended learning environment. The students are being involved in both methods of teaching (teacher led and AI-driven platforms) in such classrooms. Although a teacher currently conducts the talks and determines learning objectives, the AI tools allow monitoring the results, proposing specific tasks, or providing writing topics depending on the interests of the individual students(Fernández-Sánchez et al., 2025). Such hybrid model guarantees students both academic and emotional support, as well as acquisition of digital fluency that they will require in the years to come.

In addition, AI has the opportunity of assisting in differentiated instruction particularly in heterogeneous classrooms where students come at varying speeds. A student with trouble with sentence structure may be assigned additional practice in grammar, whereas a more developed child is made to be challenged by challenging rhetorical techniques or figure of speech. This type of customer reference is something which could not be done on a big degree in the past- however, AI makes that more accessible(Plate et al., 2024). Naturally, the introduction of AI into pedagogy implies the consideration of concerns. The high use of AI may transform students into over-reliant learners. To prevent it, educators must create meaningful learning experiences in which students learn how and when they should apply AI and should view it as a crutch(College of Computer Studies, University of Antique, Sibalom, Antique, Philippines et al., 2024). The curriculum should also include the idea of discussing ethics, authorship, and originality so students could become not only more efficient writers but critical digital citizens. The teachers (rather than students) should also be supported in a holistic approach. Regular training, both theoretical and teaching with AI tools, and team planning will make educators feel competent and self-sufficient. Technology should be able to support teachers and not stress them after all. Ultimately, the issue of incorporating AI into pedagogy is not the question of human or machine(Talukder et al., 2024). It is about a combination of the most useful, efficiency of technology, with the soul of human instruction. Such a combination can open strong learning experiences, in which the students write not only faster or better but also more intellectually, positively, and honestly(T P, 2024).

BLENDED LEARNING ENVIRONMENTS

The use of blended learning is much more than a fashionable buzz in contemporary education; it is a meaningful combination of classroom teaching, computer-based instructional instruments, and flexible, fun, and lasting learning. With the world having students who are already accustomed to technology being in their hands, blended learning forms a middle ground between the personal connection with the teacher and the potential of digital materials as well as development of writing skills. Consider a situation when a teacher begins a lesson by asking the students to have a brief discussion concerning persuasive writing(Jonassen et al., 2008). Then, students will sign in to an online service which provides them with writing prompts related to reading-level and interests. Students can work at their paces, some joining small groups, others meeting the teacher separately to get an additional assistance. Subsequently, they could get instant feedback in collaboration with an AI writing assistant that will allow them to identify grammar mistakes or reorganize any imperfect sentences(Gedik et al., 2013). This is what blended learning environment is all about. The advantage of blended learning is that it pays respect to the individuality of the students. Not all the students have the same pace of incoming information; some students perform well when left alone. It is that flexibility that blended learning provides. It also enables learners to work more slowly or quickly between assignments, and previous lessons whenever they require and with assistance in the form of videos, interactive activities with the instructor. However, do not get delusions that the teacher is substituted by the technology(Van Laer & Elen, 2017). Actually, it increases the role of teacher. Teachers are in a position to improve their comprehension on the improvement of each student with the help of AI tools, and learning analytics. They can do other things instead of correcting all of the grammar or format them up all the time; they can direct the students to find their voice, tone, structure and creativity of writing(Tayebinik & Puteh, 2013).

Table 2. Blended Learning Environments

Component	Description	Benefits for Students	Benefits for Teachers	Examples / Applications
Face-to-Face Instruction	Traditional in-person classroom teaching integrated with digital components.	Direct interaction, immediate feedback, social learning.	Better classroom control, opportunities for hands-on guidance.	Lectures, group discussions, lab activities.
Online Learning Modules	Students learn asynchronously through multimedia content.	Self-paced learning, flexible access to resources.	Supports differentiated and personalized instruction.	LMS modules, recorded lessons, digital readings.
Flipped Classroom	Students learn content online before class; classroom time used for active learning.	Increases engagement, improves understanding through practice.	Frees time for interactive activities and tutoring.	Pre-recorded lectures, quizzes before class.
Hybrid Courses	A scheduled mix of online and in-person sessions.	Flexible attendance, strong balance of autonomy and support.	Reduces classroom load while maintaining student interaction.	Courses with weekly online and in-person rotations.
Synchronous Online Sessions	Real-time virtual teaching via video conferencing.	Immediate clarification, real-time collaboration.	Enables remote teaching and live monitoring.	Zoom/Teams classes, virtual discussions.
Asynchronous Online Activities	Tasks completed independently at students' own pace.	Encourages independent learning and deeper exploration.	Allows flexible assignment distribution and feedback timing.	Discussion forums, online assessments, recorded demonstrations.
Digital Collaboration Tools	Platforms enabling group projects and peer interaction online.	Builds teamwork skills, increases engagement.	Simplifies monitoring group work and contributions.	Google Workspace, Microsoft 365, Padlet.

continued on following page

Table 2. Continued

Component	Description	Benefits for Students	Benefits for Teachers	Examples / Applications
Learning Management Systems (LMS)	Centralized platforms for organizing, delivering, and tracking learning.	Easy access to resources, improved organization.	Streamlines grading, communication, and analytics.	Moodle, Canvas, Blackboard.
Assessment & Analytics Tools	Online tools for formative and summative assessment with learning analytics.	Immediate results, adaptive feedback.	Data-driven insights for instructional planning.	Kahoot!, Quizizz, LMS analytics dashboards.
Technology-Enhanced Classroom Tools	Tools that blend digital media with in-class learning.	Higher engagement and interactivity.	Enhances instructional versatility.	Smartboards, AR/VR tools, digital simulations.

The other advantage of blended learning is that it helps all those in schools to get ready to face reality where one does not just write using pen and paper. The most common emails, blogs, social media posts, reports, and presentations are written today by writers of all kinds, operating on multiple platforms(Kabir et al., 2024). Being educated in a blended learning environment, students receive some experience of the digital environments, acquire skills of writing to a variety of audiences, and become capable of changing their ways of communication. Naturally, to make blended properly working, students should be informed how to use technology in a wise manner(Aspden & Helm, 2004). The digital responsibility, ethics, and balance should be included in the classroom dialogue. In that way, it is not only that students will become better writers but that they will become thoughtful and respectful digital citizens. In summary, the blended learning setting combines the benefits of the two worlds: the face-to-face experience of hot standard teaching and unique provision of the technology. When they are thought out, they will make classrooms in which every student has a chance to develop, write, and do well, in his or her own time and in his/her own words(Ellis et al., 2016).

IMPACT ON LEARNERS AND EDUCATORS

Writing pedagogy using the combination of modern pedagogy/artificial intelligence (AI) is changing in interesting and potentially unanticipated directions how classrooms work right now. This shift is not only the one concerning new tools it is also the one concerned by the individuals who would occupy them. The consequence on both learners and educators extends much beyond convenience or effectiveness. It enters into the realm of our thought, relationship, development, and pedagogy in a world, which is undergoing a high rate of change(Sakr & Abdullah, 2024). To start with, there are the learners, the engage part of any classroom. To a large number of students, writing may be a scary stuff. Either because of lack of grammar, lack of structure or even lack of the motivation to want to present a given idea, writing becomes a chore and not the development of a useful tool. However, when these two arenas successfully combine powerful pedagogical practices and versatile and helpful AI assistive technology, then something changes(Waters et al., 2018). Students learn to think of writing as an activity and not a single act. There is the feeling that they are not judged(Leandro et al., 2024).

An example of such tools is AI-powered feedback tools that help students correct their mistakes and get suggestions in real-time, when they actually require them. They have no need to wait days to have their errors in the form of red marks on a paper to make revisions therefore they get to learn in the process and correct them instantly. Such an instantaneous guidance raises the spirits and promotes a development mindset. It informs the students, Mistakes are acceptable. It is all about learning and trying again. In parallel, innovative teaching approaches that include collaborative writing, reflective journaling, project-based learning, etc. allow the students to engage emotionally with the process of writing(Dunn et al., 2009). These will include exploring their lives, communities, dreams- these will all come across as personal, meaningful and self-empowering through writing. Once pupils are listened to and taken seriously, they write because they want to be heard across the globe. The integration of AI and pedagogy also creates the picture of increased inclusion. The traditional settings may be difficult to students who have learning differences, those with language barrier or those that are anxious.However, when provided with speech-to-text, visual organizers, and other personal writing prompts, they receive the assistance they require to be engaged at full-participation levels(Harlin et al., 2009). All people are offered an opportunity to succeed, not only those who supposed to have a certain type. Writing teaching has conventionally been emotionally demanding and time consuming. Instructors used to waste their time marking up papers, correcting grammar mistakes and writing feedback, not even being always sure that the students read the feedback. The AI alters that. It will be able to fulfill menial duties such as spelling and structure checking and let the teachers concentrate on what is most useful, the facilitation of the creativity, engagement of confidence, and deep thought. The teachers no longer have to feel overpowered by the grading but become coaches and mentors. They will get more time to hold a conference with the students, talk about concepts, and support them in finding true voices(Zhong et al., 2024). AI tools provide teachers with a way to access trends of development. Teachers get quick overview of which students are struggling and require more attention, which concepts have to be repeated and where their lessons are producing the best results with data dashboard and learning analytics. Nevertheless, change does not only occur without difficulties. Other teachers are afraid that they will get replaced by robots, or fear that children will be too keen on the work and content generated by the AI. Such fears are real(Susilo et al., 2023).

However, the inclusion of teachers in the design and use of these tools makes them active contributors to the learning process, but not like in the case of passive consumers of technology. The major criteria to make the teacher feel confident and in control is professional growth and constant support to aid. Above all, the combination of AI and pedagogy introduces a possibility of better relationships. Automation of basic tasks allows students and teachers to discuss, share information and connect more. That is where the real learning takes place, in the software as well as in the trust, care and curiosity on which great education is designed. Finally, it is immensely human in the influence of this mixed approach. Students will be more interested, more self-assured and more empowered to write with meaning. Teachers are reinvigorated with energy of teaching, its purpose, and more joy. Allied, they build the classrooms, in which technology assists and people dominate, with heart and with voice, with vision(Loke et al., 2017).

CHALLENGES AND ETHICAL IMPLICATIONS FOR FUTURE-READY WRITING EDUCATION

On the one hand, these instruments are limitlessly usable: individualized studies, instant feedback, and student engagement. However, on the one hand, they also introduce a certain set of real-life challenges and moral issues which we cannot just pass over. To start with, there is the problem of excessive dependence on technology that most teachers and learners are already experiencing. It is not hard to see the reason why this occurs(Thanaraj & Gledhill, 2022). As soon as AI programs could do some grammar adjustments, offer to use different words, or even come up with whole paragraphs, certain students might start relying on the machine to think. This negates the whole point of education, which is to emerge with an ability to think, write, and express oneself using one own style. They become accustomed to clicking on accept suggestion without thinking instead of being taught on how to write better. Educators are urged to make room on discussing how AI should be applied when it comes to writing. Learners need to be taught more than how to use such devices, but when, and why, without lying or cheating in mind(Tan, 2024).

Data privacy, student safety is another issue. A majority of the AI-driven platforms gather data- writing examples, usage patterns, feedback mechanism, and use them to enhance their services. Schools and educators should be cautious in the era where a student can actually share his or her personal information and even exploit it. Selecting ethical tools, reading the privacy policy and engaging parents into the discussion should be essential steps. Students have the right to learn that their writings, as well as their digital words are safeguarded. Even though machines look neutral, they are trained on human-produced material and that material is full of stereotypes, errors, or even cultural blindness(Khine, 2024). When AI does that out of error, it is worse than beneficial. Instructors will remain custodians of sensitivity and inclusion, ensuring that technology should be used to enhance diversity and not purport to inhibit it. Another burning issue is equality. Access to advanced AI tools or the internet is not an equal task in all schools. In more affluent, technologically-endowed lessons, learners can use the latest writing technology, whereas others will work on archaic systems- nothing, in fact. This increased digital divide may expand learning disparities of students of varying backgrounds. Writing education that is ready to survive in the future must not only be innovative but also come to the collaboration to bring it to all learners, wherever they may live or earn(Cahyadi et al., 2025).Professional self and goal is one of the significant ethical implications to educators. Some teachers might fear being or becoming less valuable in their work with AI partially automating some of their duties. The truth is however the reverse. Teachers are needed as much as ever before in the technology-filled world. They would be changed to transform their role as providers of information to coaches, mentors, and moral leaders. The trick is on how to reimaging that role with confidence and clarity, to understand that not even a robot could equal the warmth of encouragement and a mentor and joy of interacting with a human being in learning(Chi et al., 2024). Last but not least we should speak about emotional and mental health. Writing does not only require skill, it is a very intimate task. Students write down their ideas, fears, dreams and narrations. Once there is AI existing in that space some may feel as they are not connected with their own voice. Different people will compare their work (which they perceive as their own) with the proposals provided by AI, and they will be discouraged. The teacher will need to pay attention to such emotional clues and remind students that vulnerability is stronger than perfection. AI has the ability to make writing shine, but it cannot become a suitable replacement of the spirit in writing. The use of AI and modern pedagogy has the potential to open incredible doors to the field of writing, but they need to be applied with caution, conscious and dialog. We should not only help students to write better but to think, to act morally, and retain an anchor in their humanity even in a high-tech world. But the aim of education is not only to educate good writers- but to educate good thinkers, good, strong people with the sense of being capable of using their voice, with responsibility and without fear(Schönwetter et al., 2020).

BEST PRACTICES AND RECOMMENDATIONS

With the digitalization of classrooms and other transformations in the world that are becoming increasingly complex, the combination of artificial intelligence (AI) and pedagogy has a potent potential to become more sensible, individualized, and future-proof in writing education. To actually achieve this shift ethically, effectively, and humanely we require more than tools. What we require is a values-based and reflective intervention. These are some of the major best practices and recommendations that can help educators, schools and institutions in this journey.

I. Purpose First, NotTechnology: It is a good idea to start with purpose before using any AI or some digital tool and ask: What learning experience do we want to create? The purpose of the tool should be clear pedagogically, be it to support grammar teaching, be encouraging creativity, or be scaffolding independent writing. You should not bring in AI just because now it is interesting; it should contribute to meaningful learning!

II. Combine the Combined forces of Machine and Man: B: AI tools are first-rate in bringing a mechanical repetition such as checking grammar, giving feedback, or proposing revisions. But they cannot fire the human parts of teaching: facilitating thinking, developing voice and fostering empathy. It should be alright to leave the bulk of the work about him to AI and what matters is taught to teachers about the depth and soul of writing. This establishes a better and humbled partnership between man and machine.

III. Learn about Digital and Ethical Literacy: Students should learn more than writing mechanics, and how to appropriately use technology. Show them how AI tools are used, teach them to analyze feedback, and save their own voice in an environment where AI becomes an assistant. Talk about subjects such as plagiarism, data privacy and responsible authorship, so the students would become a conscientious digital citizen.

IV. Make Room to Reflect and Connect with People: The best technology in the world somehow still fails to give students the time to reflect, share, and connect. Add such activities as journaling, peer and group reviews, and writing projects, one-on-one conference with a teacher. The practices maintain learning personal and relational. They help the students to remember that writing is not about being correct but rather about expression, identity and connection.

V. Promote Equity of Access and Design: Not every student has equal access to an AI tool or high-speed internet. Schools and policymakers should ensure that they reduce the digital divide by creating equal resources, training, and assistance. Additionally, AI tools should be also inclusive: culturally sensitive, available to a variety of learners, and it should not be biased. All students should be able to find the recognition of their voice and background in the tools they utilize.

VI. Train and give teachers time to support: Teachers are the movers of change but they cannot do it all alone. Present professional development in the area of technology and pedagogy. Allow some time to experiment, to collaborate, and to reflect on the part of educators. Allow them to exchange what is going on well, what it is not, and the response of students. The basis of future-ready classroom begins with an equipped and confident teacher.

VII. Create a Culture of Constant Improvement: Technology will continuously advance and our practices in teaching should be advanced as well. Promote the growth mindset among learners, as well as teachers. Stay curious. Think before testing new tools. Obtain feedbacks among students. Adjust to what is effective--not only in terms of academic achievement, but also participation, well being, and innovation. Just as writing itself never quite reaches completion, so writing education is constant and never-ending. Pedagogy and AI in an integrated environment should not be concerning the replacement of classroom experience but on the enhancements of the classroom experience. By behaving wisely ethically and humanely when using the tools, we will help students with more than producing better writing skills. We empower them to talk, think and share their stories with confidence. Not only is that future ready education, it is also human ready education.

CONCLUSION

Education is changing and so is writing instruction. Writing instruction no longer turns into dusty grammar drills or formulaic essays. Having meticulously combined the effective pedagogical instruments and artificial intelligence (AI), we are stepping into a new era, which would be more personalized, inclusive, creative, and future-ready. However, when we look at the heart of this transformation, we need to keep in mind the following fact: education is yet a deeply human experience. Contemporary pedagogy can also make us reconceptualize the major idea of classroom as a place of discovery, that of teamwork, and that of creative expression. It will enable the students to grow in their own voice, contemplate on their thoughts and to write with expressive purpose. Meanwhile, AI can contribute with a great amount of support with immediate feedback, tailored directions in learning, and access to the tools that can make students obtain more information and study on their own. As a whole, used in combination with care, pedagogy, and AI can be mutually complementary, learning to be more responsive and writing to become more interesting. This integration is an opportunity to learners. It decreases the fear of failure, offers live help and access to real-time assistance as well as creativity with the use of various writing formats, and makes education more accessible to the students with various needs. To teachers, it provides new possibilities to serve students- less time on the surface making corrections, and more time mentoring, directing, and encouraging. It is not about getting rid of teachers, it is about letting them do their jobs of connecting, guiding and cheering.

Nonetheless, although these changes are very exciting, they are not without complications. The topics of AI excessiveness, the realness of students, computer equity, and the moral duty need to be brought up openly and sensitively. Technical skills are not enough, students need to learn how valuable their ideas can be, how they should behave as digital authors, and how important it is to think critically with all the automated suggestions they are getting around the world. That is why writing education in the future should be purposeful. Technology and tools are intended to achieve higher purpose: to teach students not only to be better writers, but to be thoughtful communicator, compassionate thinker, and active member of the digital professional world. It is not a matter of making students write like machines; it is about making students write like human beings, with passion, with objectives and with clarity. When pedagogy and AI come together through writing education, it is the future of unimaginable value to the human race, as long as we can remain grounded in humanity. It is not merely to modernize how we teach writing, but humanize the future of learning. By making empathy, ethics, and student voice our point of focus, we develop writing classrooms in which every student can succeed, at not only the present time, but in the world to come as well.

REFERENCES

Abdul Rahman, N. A., Zulkornain, L. H., & Hamzah, N. H. (2022). Exploring Artificial Intelligence using Automated Writing Evaluation for Writing Skills. *Environment-Behaviour Proceedings Journal, 7*(SI9), 547–553. DOI: 10.21834/ebpj.v7iSI9.4304

Al-Sofi, B. B. M. A. (2024). Artificial intelligence-powered tools and academic writing: To use or not to use ChatGPT. *Saudi Journal of Language Studies, 4*(3), 145–161. DOI: 10.1108/SJLS-06-2024-0029

Alqahtani, N., & Wafula, Z. (2025). Artificial Intelligence Integration: Pedagogical Strategies and Policies at Leading Universities. *Innovative Higher Education, 50*(2), 665–684. DOI: 10.1007/s10755-024-09749-x

Aspden, L., & Helm, P. (2004). Making the Connection in a Blended Learning Environment. *Educational Media International, 41*(3), 245–252. DOI: 10.1080/09523980410001680851

Baranidharan, S., John, S. P., & Mohan, C. (2025). AI-Driven Pedagogies and Learning Environments in Modern Education: A PRISMA-Based Systematic Review. In Sarwar, U., Sanhong, T., Waheed Akhtar, M., & Aamir, M. (Eds.), (pp. 267–298). Advances in Computational Intelligence and Robotics. IGI Global., DOI: 10.4018/979-8-3373-1827-1.ch011

Cahyadi, T., Winarno, W., & Malau, A. G. (2025). Leadership and management training for future-ready engineers: Transforming maritime education. [RaDEn]. *Research and Development in Education, 5*(1), 111–120. DOI: 10.22219/raden.v5i1.39398

Chi, C., Md Yunus, M., & Rafiq, M., K. R., Hameed, H., & Ediyanto, E. (. (2024). A Systematic Review on Multidisciplinary Technological Approaches in Higher Education. *International Journal of Advanced Research in Future Ready Learning and Education, 36*(1), 1–10. DOI: 10.37934/frle.36.1.110

College of Computer Studies. University of Antique, Sibalom, Antique, Philippines, Mission, R., Fio, R. J., Philippine Merchant Marine School Inc., Las Pinas, Philippines, Mission, A. R., & Barangbang National High School, San Remigio, Antique, Philippines. (2024). AI-Powered Pedagogy: Integrating Artificial Intelligence in Information Technology Education for Future Workforce Readiness. *Journal of Innovative Technology Convergence, 6*(4), 69–86. DOI: 10.69478/JITC2024v6n4a06

Conole, G., Dyke, M., Oliver, M., & Seale, J. (2004). Mapping pedagogy and tools for effective learning design. *Computers & Education, 43*(1–2), 17–33. DOI: 10.1016/j.compedu.2003.12.018

Department of Curriculum and Instruction, Kulliyyah of Education, International Islamic University Malaysia, Malaysia, Ismail, H., Shazwan, N. I. M., & Kulliyyah of Education, International Islamic University Malaysia, Malaysia. (2025). *Contemporary Pedagogical Approach in Teaching Islamic Education: Navigating Challenges and Considerations*. 81–93. DOI: 10.32789/edcon.2024.3108

Dewangan, S., Kumar, S., & Tyagi, P. K. (2024). Transforming Hospitality and Tourism With AI and Innovative Technologies. In Talukder, M. B., Kumar, S., & Tyagi, P. K. (Eds.), *Advances in Hospitality, Tourism, and the Services Industry* (pp. 66–83). IGI Global., DOI: 10.4018/979-8-3693-6755-1.ch004

Dhiraj, A., & Kumar, P. D. S. (2023). Impact of E-learning on the Higher Education Sector during the COVID-19 pandemic through Pedagogy tools: An observational Study. *Revista de Educación y Derecho*, *27*(27). Advance online publication. DOI: 10.1344/REYD2023.27.40935

Dhiraj, A., Kumar, S., & Rani, D. (2023a). Social and Emotional Learning: Keys to the Success of E-Learning. In Sharma, P. C., Bansal, R., & Singh, R. (Eds.), (pp. 119–130). Advances in Educational Technologies and Instructional Design. IGI Global., DOI: 10.4018/978-1-6684-7639-0.ch008

Dhiraj, A., Kumar, S., & Rani, D. (2023b). Use of Social Media by SMEs in the Tourism Industry. In Qalati, S. A., Ostic, D., & Bansal, R. (Eds.), (pp. 221–233). Advances in Business Strategy and Competitive Advantage. IGI Global., DOI: 10.4018/978-1-6684-5770-2.ch014

Dunn, R., Honigsfeld, A., Doolan, L. S., Bostrom, L., Russo, K., Schiering, M. S., Suh, B., & Tenedero, H. (2009). Impact of Learning-Style Instructional Strategies on Students' Achievement and Attitudes: Perceptions of Educators in Diverse Institutions. *The Clearing House: A Journal of Educational Strategies, Issues and Ideas*, *82*(3), 135–140. DOI: 10.3200/TCHS.82.3.135-140

Ellis, R. A., Pardo, A., & Han, F. (2016). Quality in blended learning environments – Significant differences in how students approach learning collaborations. *Computers & Education*, *102*, 90–102. DOI: 10.1016/j.compedu.2016.07.006

Fauziah, Z., & Minarti, S. (2023). Artificial Intelligence-Assisted Writing Application for Improving Writing Skills of Islamic Education Students. *Jurnal Kependidikan Islam*, *13*(2), 119–123. DOI: 10.15642/jkpi.2023.13.2.119-123

Fernández-Sánchez, A., Lorenzo-Castiñeiras, J. J., & Sánchez-Bello, A. (2025). Navigating the Future of Pedagogy: The Integration of AI Tools in Developing Educational Assessment Rubrics. *European Journal of Education*, *60*(1), e12826. DOI: 10.1111/ejed.12826

Gedik, N., Kiraz, E., & Ozden, M. Y. (2013). Design of a blended learning environment: Considerations and implementation issues. *Australasian Journal of Educational Technology*, *29*(1). Advance online publication. DOI: 10.14742/ajet.6

George, A. S. (2023). Preparing students for an AI-driven world: Rethinking curriculum and pedagogy in the age of artificial intelligence. *Partners Universal Innovative Research Publication*, *1*(2), 112–136.

Goh, K. M., Mansor, M., Syariff, M., Fuad, D. R., & Juharyanto, J. (2025). Designing Future-Ready Education: Criteria for AI Learning Tool Selection and AI Learning Design. *Semarak International Journal of Innovation in Learning and Education*, *4*(1), 1–12. DOI: 10.37934/sijile.4.1.112a

Gorbatkova, O., Kochergina, O., & Kiryushina, O. (2021). Digital environment as effective pedagogical tool of socialization in the context of modern education. *E3S Web of Conferences, 273*, 12087. DOI: 10.1051/e3sconf/202127312087

Harlin, R., Sirota, E., & Bailey, L. (2009). Review of Research: The Impact of Teachers' Expectations on Diverse Learners'Academic Outcomes. *Childhood Education, 85*(4), 253–256. DOI: 10.1080/00094056.2009.10523092

Holmes, W. (2020). Artificial Intelligence in Education. In A. Tatnall (Ed.), *Encyclopedia of Education and Information Technologies* (pp. 88–103). Springer International Publishing. https:// doi.org/, A., Kumar, A., Mulat-Weldemeskel, E., Luthra, S., Garza-Reyes, J. A., & Yadav, S. (2025). Next-gen quality learning: How can AI technologies shape education 4.0 and 5.0 towards the SDGs from multiple stakeholders' perspective? *The TQM Journal.* https://doi.org/DOI: 10.1007/978-3-030-10576-1_107

Jarilkapovich, M. A.Karakalpak State University. (2025). The Role of Modern Education and The Teacher's Pedagogical Skills in The Application of Pedagogical Teaching Methods. *International Journal of Pedagogics, 5*(4), 266–268. DOI: 10.37547/ijp/Volume05Issue04-70

Jonassen, D., Spector, M. J., Driscoll, M., Merrill, M. D., Van Merrienboer, J., & Driscoll, M. P. (Eds.). (2008). *Handbook of Research on Educational Communications and Technology* (0 ed.). Routledge., DOI: 10.4324/9780203880869

Kabir, F., Talukder, M. B., & Kumar, S. (2024). Exchange of Cultures in the Field of Gastronomy Tourism: Evidence of Bangladesh. In Castanho, R. A., & Franco, M. (Eds.), *Advances in Hospitality, Tourism, and the Services Industry* (pp. 143–160). IGI Global., DOI: 10.4018/979-8-3693-3158-3.ch006

Kacena, M. A., Plotkin, L. I., & Fehrenbacher, J. C. (2024). The Use of Artificial Intelligence in Writing Scientific Review Articles. *Current Osteoporosis Reports, 22*(1), 115–121. DOI: 10.1007/s11914-023-00852-0 PMID: 38227177

Kaiser, G., & Kaiser, S. (2024). AI in Education: Reflections and Future Directions for Pedagogical and Andragogical Integration. In Wang, V. (Ed.), (pp. 241–260). Advances in Educational Technologies and Instructional Design. IGI Global., DOI: 10.4018/979-8-3693-6130-6.ch010

Kakhkharova, M., & Tuychieva, S. (2024, April). AI-enhanced pedagogy in higher education: redefining teaching-learning paradigms. In *2024 International Conference on Knowledge Engineering and Communication Systems (ICKECS)* (Vol. 1, pp. 1-6). IEEE.

Khine, M. S. (2024). Ethics, and the Future of Education in an AI-Driven World. In Khine, M. S. (Ed.), *Artificial Intelligence in Education* (pp. 629–735). Springer Nature Singapore., DOI: 10.1007/978-981-97-9350-1_6

Kholoshyn, I., Varfolomyeyeva, I., Hanchuk, O., Bondarenko, O., & Pikilnyak, A. (2019). *Pedagogical techniques of Earth remote sensing data application into modern school practice*. DOI: 10.31812/123456789/3262

Kirovograd Institute for Human Development, & Chernenko, O. (2020). MODERN PEDAGOGICAL TECHNOLOGIES IN HIGHER EDUCATION. *PEDAGOGY AND EDUCATION MANAGEMENT REVIEW, 2*, 52–59. DOI: 10.36690/2733-2039-2020-2-52

Kumar, S. (2023). Impact of Digitalization in Higher Education and Smart Learning Techniques. In Nadda, V., Tyagi, P. K., Moniz Vieira, R., & Tyagi, P. (Eds.), *Advances in Hospitality, Tourism, and the Services Industry* (pp. 198–207). IGI Global., DOI: 10.4018/979-8-3693-0650-5.ch013

Kumar, S. (2024). Impact of Assessment on Childhood Education Theories and Practice. In Badea, M., & Suditu, M. (Eds.), *Advances in Early Childhood and K-12 Education* (pp. 84–101). IGI Global., DOI: 10.4018/979-8-3693-0956-8.ch004

Kumar, S., Kumar, V., Kumari Bhatt, I., Kumar, S., & Attri, K. (2024). Digital transformation in tourism sector: Trends and future perspectives from a bibliometric-content analysis. *Journal of Hospitality and Tourism Insights, 7*(3), 1553–1576. DOI: 10.1108/JHTI-10-2022-0472

Kurban, C. F., & Şahin, M. (2024). Educational Implications. In C. F. Kurban & M. Şahin, *The Impact of ChatGPT on Higher Education* (pp. 153–179). Emerald Publishing Limited. DOI: 10.1108/978-1-83797-647-820241009

Leandro, G. D. S. M., Kumar, S., Jacinto Da Gama, M., Carvalho, H., & Leandro, E. (2024). Circular Economy Practices in the Hotel Sector in Luanda, Angola: Challenges and Future Perspectives. In P. K. Tyagi, V. Nadda, K. Kankaew, & K. Dube (Eds.), *Advances in Hospitality, Tourism, and the Services Industry* (pp. 54–66). IGI Global. DOI: 10.4018/979-8-3693-4042-4.ch004

Lisova, S. (2024). PEDAGOGICAL INNOVATIONS AS A TOOL FOR MODERNIZATION OF HIGHER EDUCATION: THEORETICAL ASPECT. *Zhytomyr Ivan Franko State University Journal. Pedagogical Sciences, 2*(117), 101–115. DOI: 10.35433/pedagogy.2(117).2024.9

Loke, Y.-H., Harahsheh, A. S., Krieger, A., & Olivieri, L. J. (2017). Usage of 3D models of tetralogy of Fallot for medical education: Impact on learning congenital heart disease. *BMC Medical Education, 17*(1), 54. DOI: 10.1186/s12909-017-0889-0 PMID: 28284205

Marghany, M. M. (2023). Using artificial intelligence-based instruction to develop EFL higher education students' essay writing skills. *CDELT Occasional Papers in the Development of English Education, 82*(1), 219–240. DOI: 10.21608/opde.2023.313623

Movahed, G. B., Rahmanian, F., Emarati, F., & Movahed, A. B. (2025). The Synergy of AI and Education: Opportunities and Challenges for the Future. *Applied Innovations in Industrial Management, 5*(3), 45–51. DOI: 10.63630/aiim.53.45

Nancy, W., Parimala, A., & Livingston, L. M. M. (2020). Advanced Teaching Pedagogy As Innovative Approach In Modern Education System. *Procedia Computer Science, 172*, 382–388. DOI: 10.1016/j.procs.2020.05.059

Plate, D., Melick, E., Hutson, J., & Edele, S. (2024). *Generative AI in the English Composition Classroom: Practical and Adaptable Strategies* (1st ed.). Routledge., DOI: 10.4324/9781003507949

Pratama, R. M. D., & Hastuti, D. P. (2024). The use of artificial intelligence to improve EFL students' writing skill. *English Learning Innovation, 5*(1), 13–25. DOI: 10.22219/englie.v5i1.30212

Queiroz-Neto, J. P., Sales, D. C., Pinheiro, H. S., & Neto, B. O. (2015). Using modern pedagogical tools to improve learning in technological contents. *2015 IEEE Frontiers in Education Conference (FIE)*, 1–8. DOI: 10.1109/FIE.2015.7344383

Rosdiana, S., Noercolies, M. A., & Fauzan, M. H. (2024). The Use of Artificial Intelligence in Teaching Writing Skills. *EDUCASIA: Jurnal Pendidikan, Pengajaran. Dan Pembelajaran*, *9*(1), 45–56. DOI: 10.21462/educasia.v9i1.251

Sakr, A., & Abdullah, T. (2024). Virtual, augmented reality and learning analytics impact on learners, and educators: A systematic review. *Education and Information Technologies*, *29*(15), 19913–19962. DOI: 10.1007/s10639-024-12602-5

Schönwetter, D. J., Ruge, G., McCormack, C., Kennelly, R., & Gareau-Wilson, N. (2020). A future-ready teaching philosophy: Opportunities to reflect, re-value and re-frame a teaching philosophy. *ETH Learning and Teaching Journal*, 437-443 Pages. DOI: 10.16906/LT-ETH.V2I2.180

Susilo, M. J., Sulisworo, D., & Beungacha, S. (2023). Technology and Its Impact on Education. *Buletin Edukasi Indonesia*, *2*(02), 47–54. DOI: 10.56741/bei.v2i02.285

T P, R. (2024). AI-Driven Pedagogy: Unveiling ChatGPT's Influence in Education. *Journal of Applied Science, Engineering, Technology and Management*, *2*(01), 09–14. DOI: 10.61779/jasetm.v2i1.2

Talukder, M. B., Khan, M. R., & Kumar, S. (2024). Socioeconomic Gaps and Foster Inclusive Growth: Sustainable Tourism Initiatives. In Hassan, V., Staszewska, A., & Bhartiya, S. (Eds.), *Advances in Hospitality, Tourism, and the Services Industry* (pp. 56–82). IGI Global., DOI: 10.4018/979-8-3693-5405-6.ch003

Tan, C. (2024). Future-readiness and its educational implications: A Daoist interpretation. *Research in Comparative and International Education*, *19*(2), 224–238. DOI: 10.1177/17454999241230238

Tayebinik, M., & Puteh, M. (2013). Blended Learning or E-learning? DOI: 10.48550/ARXIV.1306.4085

Thanaraj, A., & Gledhill, K. (2022). *Teaching Legal Education in the Digital Age: Pedagogical Practices to Digitally Empower Law Graduates* (1st ed.). Routledge., DOI: 10.4324/9780429351082

Van Laer, S., & Elen, J. (2017). In search of attributes that support self-regulation in blended learning environments. *Education and Information Technologies*, *22*(4), 1395–1454. DOI: 10.1007/s10639-016-9505-x

Wahyuningsih, S. (2024). Does Artificial Intelligence (AI) Play Roles in Enhancing Academic Writing? Unravelling Lecturers' Voices in Indonesian Higher Education. *Jurnal Pendidikan Progresif*, *14*(1), 489–503. DOI: 10.23960/jpp.v14.i1.202436

Waters, L., Lo, K., & Maloney, S. (2018). What impact do students have on clinical educators and the way they practise? *Advances in Health Sciences Education : Theory and Practice*, *23*(3), 611–631. DOI: 10.1007/s10459-017-9785-y PMID: 28698965

Weidmann, A. E. (2024). Artificial intelligence in academic writing and clinical pharmacy education: Consequences and opportunities. *International Journal of Clinical Pharmacy*, *46*(3), 751–754. DOI: 10.1007/s11096-024-01705-1 PMID: 38472596

Zhong, Z., Guo, H., & Qian, K. (2024). Deciphering the impact of machine learning on education: Insights from a bibliometric analysis using bibliometrix R-package. *Education and Information Technologies*, *29*(16), 21995–22022. DOI: 10.1007/s10639-024-12734-8

Chapter 5
The Future of Writing Instruction:
Opportunities and Challenges of Artificial Intelligence, Tools, Ethics, and Instructional Practices

P. Umamaheswari
https://orcid.org/0000-0003-2007-697X
SASTRA University, India

S. Nirmala
Kings College of Engineering, India

R. Mathi
https://orcid.org/0000-0003-1264-9790
SASTRA University, India

D. Rajalakshmi
SASTRA University, India

ABSTRACT

The introduction of Artificial Intelligence (AI) into schools has introduced a lot of change, especially regarding the teaching of writing. This chapter investigates the diverse contribution of AI as it improves the writing pedagogy by providing practical writing tools, including Grammarly, ProWritingAid, Turnitin, and GPT-3. It offers guides to the educators and students about the common use of AI beyond accuracy with grammar to formative feedback, generation of ideas, revision tactics, and support in multilingual. Based on the modern research patterns, the discussion highlights the ways in which AI contributes to learner autonomy, inclusive practices, and the ability to overcome linguistic barriers. It also provides tools on how to develop a teaching profession, implement policies, and sustainably introduce of AI into institutional practices befitting the vision of Education 5.0. The chapter is an effective guide to teachers, policymakers, educational technology developers, and educational institutions in a way that is ethical, inclusive, and technologically up-to-date.

DOI: 10.4018/979-8-3373-5601-3.ch005

1. INTRODUCTION

In the digital age, artificial intelligence (AI) is rapidly transforming every aspect of education, including how writing is taught and learned. Traditional approaches to writing instruction—reliant on static feedback and one-size-fits-all methodologies—are increasingly being supplemented or replaced by dynamic, AI-driven tools. These technologies provide real-time assistance, personalized feedback, and adaptive learning pathways, reshaping the classroom into an interactive and data-informed environment. As educators seek to prepare students for a future where digital literacy and communication are essential, understanding the role of AI in writing pedagogy becomes not just relevant, but imperative.

1.1 The Role of Writing in Modern Education

Writing is a cornerstone of modern education, fostering essential skills such as communication, critical thinking, creativity, and knowledge synthesis. It allows students to express their understanding, analyze complex ideas, and engage with diverse audiences. As the primary medium through which academic progress is measured and knowledge is constructed, writing has expanded beyond traditional essays to include multimodal, collaborative, and digital forms of expression. It serves not only academic purposes but also equips learners with lifelong skills required for the workplace and civic participation.

Writing is a critical skill in modern education, encompassing not only expression and communication but also critical thinking and argumentation. With the integration of AI tools like ChatGPT, Grammarly, and Copilot, writing practices (Abulibdeh et al., 2024) in higher education have transformed, offering both new opportunities and challenges. The advent of Industry 4.0 has ushered in a new era defined by automation, artificial intelligence (AI), the Internet of Things (IoT), smart factories, and cyber-physical systems, all of which are revolutionizing industrial and educational landscapes alike. While this technological transformation holds the promise of increased productivity, sustainability, and resilience, it also presents significant challenges—chief among them being the urgent demand for a digitally skilled workforce. Higher education institutions (HEIs) are expected to respond by updating curricula, enhancing digital infrastructure, and aligning educational outcomes with evolving industry requirements(Deberdt et al., 2025). Parallel to this shift is the global emphasis on Education for Sustainable Development (ESD), as outlined by the United Nations Sustainable Development Goals (SDGs), which calls for fostering responsibility toward environmental, economic, and social equity. In this context, AI technologies such as ChatGPT have emerged as transformative tools that can reshape teaching and learning, support personalized education, and drive pedagogical innovation. However, their adoption is accompanied by complex ethical concerns, the need for curriculum reform, and the requirement for continuous professional learning aligned with industry standards. Despite growing interest, literature remains limited on the broader implications of AI integration in relation to ESD, Bloom's Taxonomy, ethical frameworks, and academia-industry collaboration. Addressing this gap, recent studies emphasize the necessity of critically evaluating AI tools like ChatGPT in educational settings, not only for their instructional potential but also for their alignment with long-term sustainability and digital literacy goals.

A study conducted in Malaysia explored nursing students' use of AI tools (Jembu & Balang, 2025)in academic writing. It identified increased productivity, better grammar, and improved structure as benefits. However, students also expressed concerns about plagiarism and the lack of formal training on ethical use. Another study in Taiwan evaluated(Tseng, 2025) how tools like ChatGPT and Copilot improved the quality of nursing academic reports. The results showed enhanced writing performance and AI literacy when these tools were integrated into scaffolded teaching. However, the students sometimes submitted generic or impersonal content, indicating the need for careful pedagogical design. In Hong Kong, university students reported using generative AI (GenAI) for research writing, summarization, and brainstorming(Yeung et al., 2025). While most students viewed these tools positively for enhancing learning efficiency, they also expressed concern over diminishing critical thinking, loss of originality, and ethical risks like plagiarism.

A case study from Lebanon found (Dakakni, 2023) that a large percentage of second-language (L2) students admitted to using AI for assignments without disclosing it. This behavior raised serious ethical concerns. Instructors noted a willingness to undergo AI training—not to promote AI integration, but to detect its misuse by students. Instructional design plays a crucial role in guiding students to use writing tools responsibly. When AI tools are embedded in the curriculum within a structured, pedagogical framework, they can enhance student learning while maintaining academic integrity. The structured approach, grounded in scaffolded instruction, showed a significant improvement in AI literacy, writing cohesion, and academic presentation. A systematic review on AI (Boulhrir & Hamash, 2025) in elementary education revealed that most existing studies focused on mathematics and personalized learning. However, it emphasized the need to examine AI's impact on early writing development and ethical implications in younger age groups

Administrative staff in Hong Kong participated(Kong & Hu, 2025) in a professional development course aimed at enhancing conceptual understanding of AI. Although not specific to student writing, this study demonstrated that AI literacy, including understanding of content generation and communication, is critical for broader institutional functioning. Teachers play a pivotal role in facilitating student writing(Kong et al., 2024). However, multiple studies highlight that while educators acknowledge AI's potential, many are unprepared or hesitant to integrate it meaningfully into writing instruction. A study from South Africa examined in-service teachers' preparedness (Ayanwale et al., 2024)for AI integration in schools. Although most were aware of AI's importance, few had formal training. Many expressed uncertainty in using AI to support student writing due to ethical concerns and lack of resources. In the U.S., a study focused on K–12 teachers' use of generative AI revealed (Cheah et al., 2025)that while many used AI tools for lesson planning and assessment, few applied them during real-time classroom writing instruction.

Barriers included lack of policy, pedagogical concerns, and fear of reduced student-teacher interaction. Ethical use of AI in academic writing is a recurring concern in nearly all studies reviewed. While AI tools can assist in grammar, structure, and citation management, unregulated use may result in plagiarism, data hallucination, and overdependence. As discussions around integrating artificial intelligence (AI) into educational systems continue to evolve, there is a growing need to critically examine curriculum structures and pedagogical strategies, especially within developing regions. A recent study focusing on the Ethiopian secondary school context reviewed the existing Information Communication and Technology (ICT) curriculum to assess the extent of AI-related content and its educational integration. Using a qualitative methodology, the study analyzed the curriculum documents and conducted in-depth interviews with ten ICT educators. Findings revealed that the AI-related content is largely limited to basic definitions, lacking depth in conceptual and applied understanding. Through thematic analysis, the study identified several instructional challenges faced by educators, including limited familiarity with

AI principles and insufficient training. Notably, the research proposed strategic recommendations such as revising the curriculum to introduce AI concepts from earlier educational stages and offering structured professional development for teachers. Framed within the Five Big Ideas in AI, the study (Deriba & Sanusi, 2025)contributes valuable insights into the current state and future prospects of AI education in the Ethiopian context, while also acknowledging the need for further exploration and policy intervention.

1.2 The Advent of AI in Education

The integration of Artificial Intelligence (AI) in education marks a pivotal transformation in instructional practices. AI technologies are redefining how students learn, teachers instruct, and institutions manage academic tasks. From intelligent tutoring systems and adaptive learning platforms to data-driven assessment tools and language models, AI is automating routine processes, offering personalized feedback, and enhancing learner engagement. In writing instruction specifically, AI tools such as Grammarly, Turnitin, and GPT-3 are being increasingly employed to provide real-time feedback, detect plagiarism, and generate writing prompts. These innovations are creating new possibilities for student support while raising important questions around ethics, authorship, and pedagogical control.

The increasing use of AI-based tools such as Grammarly and ChatGPT in academic writing has sparked considerable interest due to their potential to support students across diverse disciplines. In the context of nursing education, a recent qualitative study explored (Jembu & Balang, 2025)

Exploring artificial intelligence how nursing students in Malaysia perceive these tools and what factors influence their adoption. Drawing on interviews with eleven students from both public and private universities, the study employed Braun and Clarke's thematic analysis to interpret the data. Four central themes emerged: students recognized the strengths of AI tools in enhancing productivity and writing quality; however, concerns were raised about data reliability and the risk of plagiarism. Adoption was also shaped by social influences, including peer and family support, while systemic barriers such as lack of formal training and financial limitations hindered broader use. The findings suggest that although AI tools offer clear academic benefits, ethical implications and infrastructural challenges must be thoughtfully addressed. The study contributes both theoretical insights for understanding AI integration in higher education and practical guidance for institutions aiming to implement supportive AI-driven educational policies.

The integration of Artificial Intelligence (AI) into second and foreign language (L2) education has attracted growing scholarly interest in recent years, particularly in its application to teaching productive skills like speaking and writing. However, the emotional experiences of teachers using AI tools (Seyri & Ghiasvand, 2025) in this context remain underexplored. Addressing this gap, a recent qualitative study investigated the emotional responses of Iranian English as a Foreign Language (EFL) teachers when employing AI technologies in L2 instruction. Through semi-structured interviews and narrative frames collected from 21 non-randomly selected participants, the study uncovered a range of AI-induced emotional responses. Positive emotions such as excitement, joy, confidence, and engagement were frequently reported, indicating a sense of motivation and enthusiasm linked to AI use. Conversely, negative feelings—including anxiety, frustration, and apprehension—were also prevalent, reflecting challenges related to technology adoption in the classroom. Additionally, the study identified various regulatory strategies, both antecedent-focused and response-focused, that teachers employed to manage these emotional responses. The findings underscore the importance of addressing teacher emotionality as a critical factor in the effective integration of AI technologies in L2 education and provide actionable insights for teacher support and policy development.

Artificial Intelligence (AI) is reshaping healthcare delivery through tools such as clinical decision support systems and predictive analytics. As the healthcare industry increasingly adopts AI technologies, understanding the attitudes and perceptions of future healthcare providers becomes essential. A recent quantitative study investigated(Hamad et al., 2025) nursing students' views on the usability of AI in clinical contexts, surveying 600 participants using standardized instruments: the General Attitudes Towards Artificial Intelligence Scale and the Technology Acceptance Model questionnaire. Findings revealed overwhelmingly positive attitudes toward AI, with students recognizing its usefulness and ease of use. Notably, factors such as gender, prior exposure to AI training, and academic standing significantly influenced these perceptions.

The results indicate a strong readiness among undergraduate nursing students to embrace AI in healthcare, reinforcing the need for targeted educational strategies that build competence and confidence in using AI tools within clinical practice. With the growing integration of artificial intelligence (AI) into healthcare systems, nursing professionals are increasingly concerned about the ethical implications, practical implementation, and overall impact on clinical practice. In response to these emerging needs, a recent study introduced the AI-ABCs framework, a structured model aimed at cultivating foundational AI literacy among nurse leaders, educators, and healthcare professionals. Developed through an extensive review of existing literature and expert input from the field of nursing informatics, the framework outlines three core components: A—AI Basics, B—Benefits and Challenges of AI, and C—Core Components and Terminologies *in AI*. This model serves as an accessible entry point for healthcare professionals to develop essential AI competencies. Furthermore, the AI-ABCs framework (Kobeissi et al., 2025)is positioned as a practical guide for informing policy development, curriculum design, and the ethical integration of AI technologies in both clinical and academic environments—aligning with the guidance of prominent professional organizations in the healthcare sector. As generative artificial intelligence (GenAI) tools become increasingly accessible, educators are beginning to explore their potential in formal learning environments.

A recent qualitative study examined both the opportunities and challenges of integrating GenAI (Jaber et al., 2024) into educational contexts, focusing on strategies that promote adoption among teachers and students. The study engaged 76 Canadian educators who participated in a professional development seminar on GenAI and shared their perspectives through surveys and reflective narratives. Overall, participants expressed a positive outlook on the educational use of GenAI, offering discipline-specific suggestions for its implementation. Thematic analysis highlighted three core areas of application: teaching and learning, assessment practices, and administrative functions. However, several barriers were identified, including institutional readiness, limited teacher competence in AI, and concerns about students' AI literacy and ethics. To address these issues, educators proposed solutions such as enhanced professional development, clearer policy guidelines, and improved access to AI tools and technical support.

The study further recommended adapting established frameworks—such as the TeachAI Global Initiative and the Socio-ecological Model—to guide institutions in becoming AI-ready. This includes supporting both teacher and student preparedness, fostering organizational learning, and promoting literacy transformation across educational systems. The evolving integration of artificial intelligence (AI) is significantly reshaping pharmacy practice, making pharmacists' readiness and acceptance of such technologies a key concern. A recent cross-sectional survey examined the knowledge, attitudes, and practices (KAP) of pharmacists regarding AI across a variety of work environments. Data gathered through structured questionnaires revealed that 44.8% of respondents held a moderate understanding of AI, and nearly half (49.1%) expressed favorable attitudes toward its use in pharmacy. However, only 57.3% demonstrated adequate implementation of AI in their current practices. A strong statistical correlation was observed between knowledge, attitudes, and actual practice ($p < 0.001$), suggesting that enhanced awareness and perception directly influence practical engagement with AI. The study highlights a need for structured educational initiatives to bridge existing knowledge gaps and foster a more positive outlook toward AI adoption. Additionally, systemic efforts must be made to integrate AI tools seamlessly into pharmacy workflows, thereby maximizing their potential to enhance decision-making and patient care.

1.3 Purpose and Scope of the Chapter

This chapter explores the transformative impact of AI on writing instruction, focusing on the pedagogical, technological, and ethical dimensions of this integration. It aims to provide educators, researchers, and policymakers with a comprehensive understanding of how AI tools can be harnessed to improve writing outcomes, enhance instructional efficiency, and support diverse learners. Specific tools such as Grammarly, ProWritingAid, Turnitin, and GPT-3 are examined for their instructional potential, while broader issues such as academic integrity, inclusivity, and institutional policy are critically analyzed. The chapter also presents real-world case studies, anticipates future trends, and offers actionable recommendations for sustainable and ethical AI adoption in educational contexts.

2. FOUNDATIONS: UNDERSTANDING AI AND WRITING INSTRUCTION

The integration of Artificial Intelligence (AI) in education, particularly in writing instruction, has revolutionized traditional pedagogical practices. Once a domain solely dependent on human feedback and manual correction, writing education has now embraced AI-driven tools to offer real-time assistance, individualized feedback, and adaptive learning experiences. These technologies are not merely supplementary; they are reshaping how writing is taught, learned, and evaluated across academic levels.

Figure 1. presents the AI-Driven Pedagogical Adaptation Cycle, a conceptual framework that outlines the key stages involved in incorporating AI into writing pedagogy. The cycle includes phases such as rethinking pedagogical approaches, understanding ethical implications, developing critical thinking skills, and evaluating information. This holistic cycle emphasizes that AI in education must be used thoughtfully, fostering not just better writing but also more reflective, ethical, and informed learners.

Figure 1. Adaptation cycle

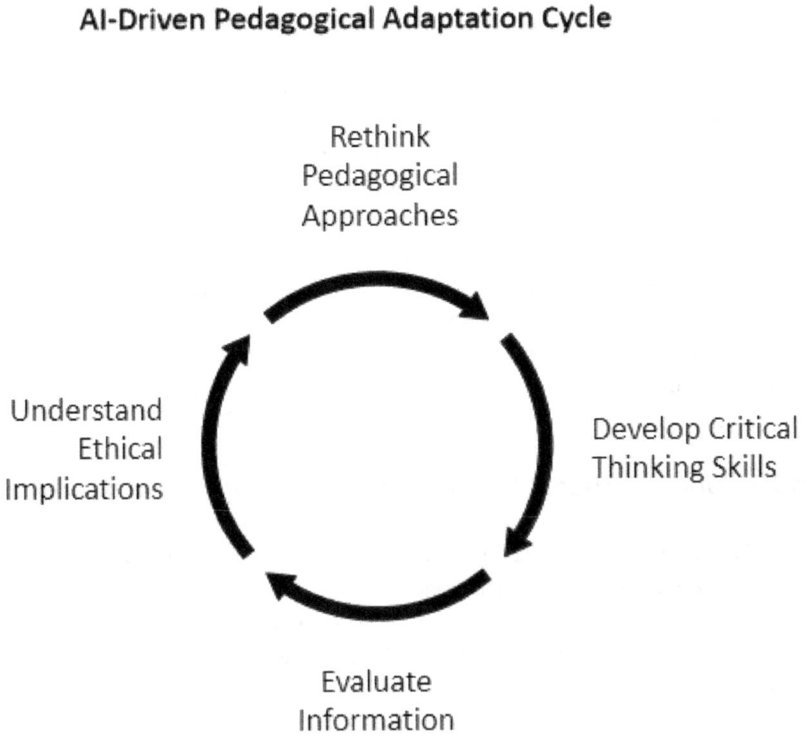

2.1 Rethinking Pedagogical Approaches with AI

The first stage of the cycle involves reimagining traditional teaching methods in light of the capabilities AI brings to the classroom. Conventional writing instruction typically follows a linear model: assign, write, review, and grade. However, AI tools disrupt this pattern by enabling continuous feedback and dynamic learning. Applications like Grammarly, QuillBot, and AI-powered writing assistants embedded in learning management systems (e.g., Turnitin Draft Coach) offer students real-time suggestions on grammar, syntax, clarity, and tone.

Educators, too, are beginning to redesign lesson plans that incorporate these tools to build writing fluency. Instead of focusing primarily on end-product assessment, instructors can now emphasize writing as a process, leveraging AI for formative feedback and encouraging iterative refinement. This shift fosters greater student engagement and accountability, allowing learners to take control of their development. Moreover, AI can support differentiated instruction. Students with different learning styles, linguistic backgrounds, or proficiency levels can benefit from tailored prompts, reading materials, and scaffolded writing activities—all powered by machine learning algorithms that track individual progress and adapt accordingly.

2.2 Developing Critical Thinking Skills

Contrary to concerns that AI might reduce students' intellectual engagement, well-designed educational AI tools can actually encourage deeper cognitive processes. For instance, tools that offer paraphrasing suggestions or summarization models do not just provide shortcuts—they can also prompt students to evaluate and reflect on alternative ways of expressing ideas.

The AI-Driven Pedagogical Adaptation Cycle acknowledges that critical thinking is central to meaningful writing instruction. AI can be used to initiate classroom discussions about *why* certain phrasing is more effective, *how* argument structure influences clarity, or *what* rhetorical strategies best suit different genres of writing. With these insights, learners are not just producing texts—they are learning to make intentional rhetorical choices, a hallmark of mature academic writing. Furthermore, AI tools often include feedback on logical consistency, plagiarism detection, and coherence analysis. This kind of input challenges students to reassess their arguments and strengthen the integrity of their work, thereby nurturing analytical reasoning and evidence-based thinking.

2.3 Understanding Ethical Implications

One of the most critical dimensions of integrating AI into writing education is fostering an awareness of its ethical use. As students gain access to increasingly sophisticated AI writing tools—including generative models like ChatGPT—they must be guided in understanding the boundaries between support and substitution. The cycle illustrated in Figure 2 emphasizes this need for ethical reflection. Students must learn about academic honesty, copyright issues, algorithmic bias, and the potential misuse of AI-generated content. Writing instructors now have a unique opportunity to incorporate digital ethics into their curriculum.

Institutions are responding to this need by updating academic integrity policies and offering AI literacy workshops. However, ethical AI use must go beyond rule-following; it should encourage students to think about the social implications of algorithmic writing and the value of authentic human expression in academic discourse.

2.4 Evaluating Information in an AI-Powered Landscape

The final stage in the cycle, *evaluating information*, speaks directly to the challenges of navigating a world saturated with automated content. AI tools can assist students in sourcing reliable information, assessing the credibility of texts, and organizing research logically. For instance, AI-powered bibliographic tools like Zotero, EndNote, and even integrated search engines in writing platforms help students streamline the research process.

But AI's role in information evaluation goes deeper. Natural Language Processing (NLP) models can summarize large bodies of text, extract key themes, and identify logical inconsistencies. Used appropriately, these features support students in becoming more discerning readers and writers.

At the same time, instructors must train students to critically evaluate AI output itself. AI is not infallible; it can generate errors, hallucinate facts, or reinforce biases. Thus, students must be taught to verify AI-generated suggestions, check sources, and understand the limitations of algorithmic assistance. In this way, AI becomes both a tool and an object of scrutiny, enriching the educational experience.

2.5 Overview of AI Technologies Relevant to Writing

Artificial Intelligence (AI) has increasingly become a transformative force in educational contexts, particularly in the domain of writing instruction. The integration of AI technologies into the writing process marks a significant shift in how educators facilitate learning and how students engage with text production. Among the array of AI applications, several core technologies stand out as particularly relevant to writing instruction: Natural Language Processing (NLP), machine learning (ML), and large language models (LLMs) such as OpenAI's GPT-3 and GPT-4. These technologies underpin many of the tools that are now being used in classrooms, writing centers, and online learning environments to support students in developing their writing skills more effectively and efficiently.

Natural Language Processing lies at the heart of AI-powered writing tools. NLP is a subfield of AI focused on the interaction between computers and human language. It enables machines to understand, interpret, generate, and respond to natural language inputs. In writing instruction, NLP powers various functions such as automated grammar correction, sentence restructuring, paraphrasing assistance, and feedback generation. Tools like Grammarly and Microsoft Editor rely heavily on NLP to detect errors in spelling, punctuation, syntax, and style, offering real-time corrections and suggestions. These features not only streamline the revision process but also provide learning opportunities for students, helping them recognize and avoid recurring mistakes.

Machine learning plays a complementary role by enabling writing tools to learn from data over time and adapt their performance accordingly. ML algorithms process vast corpora of written language and learn to identify patterns that can be used to assess writing quality, coherence, tone, and structure. Unlike rule-based systems that apply fixed grammar rules, ML-based writing assistants continuously refine their output by learning from user interactions and linguistic context. For instance, ML helps personalize writing feedback based on an individual's writing history, academic level, or subject area. This adaptability enhances the relevance and effectiveness of feedback, making AI tools more responsive to diverse learner needs.

The emergence of large language models such as GPT-3, GPT-4, and their successors represents a major advancement in AI's ability to generate and evaluate text. These models are trained on extensive datasets comprising billions of words from books, websites, and academic sources. As a result, they possess a sophisticated understanding of language use across various domains and can produce human-like text with remarkable fluency. In writing education, these models are increasingly being employed to support activities such as idea generation, essay drafting, summarization, and question answering. Students can interact with AI tools powered by LLMs to brainstorm arguments, receive model paragraphs, or clarify conceptual misunderstandings. Educators can also use these tools to demonstrate writing conventions or generate exemplars tailored to different writing genres.

Beyond assisting in the creation of text, AI technologies also facilitate assessment and feedback, both formative and summative. AI-enabled writing platforms can assess the structure, clarity, coherence, and vocabulary usage of student submissions. Some systems incorporate rubric-based scoring models to evaluate essays against preset academic standards. These automated assessments allow for timely and scalable evaluation, particularly useful in large courses or online settings. While human judgment remains essential for evaluating creativity, critical thinking, and content depth, AI tools can serve as a first layer of feedback, identifying surface-level issues and allowing educators to focus on higher-order concerns during review.

An important dimension of AI in writing instruction is its capacity for personalization. Traditional teaching methods often follow a one-size-fits-all approach, which may not meet the diverse learning needs of students. AI systems, by contrast, can adapt their support based on user data, offering tailored feedback that aligns with an individual's strengths and weaknesses. For example, an AI tool may focus more on sentence structure for one student and on coherence for another, depending on their prior submissions. This individualized support can enhance learner engagement, foster independence, and ultimately lead to improved writing outcomes.

The impact of AI technologies is also being felt in collaborative writing environments. Intelligent systems are now capable of supporting group writing tasks by managing version control, offering real-time suggestions, and tracking contributions. In addition, AI chatbots and virtual writing assistants can serve as round-the-clock tutors, answering student queries, providing tips, or guiding them through the writing process when human support is not readily available. These developments are particularly valuable in distance learning and asynchronous instructional models, where access to instructors may be limited.

Despite these advancements, it is important to approach the integration of AI in writing with a critical lens. Ethical considerations such as authorship, academic honesty, and data privacy must be addressed. The reliance on AI-generated content raises questions about student ownership and the development of authentic writing skills. Moreover, the potential for AI tools to reinforce linguistic biases present in training data must be acknowledged and mitigated through transparent design and responsible use.

2.5.1 Ethical concerns and practical strategies for responsible AI integration in education.

In order to bring together the "Theory" side of AI and the "Practice" side of AI (using AI tools) in a classroom setting, there are many ways to show teachers how to integrate AI tools in their classrooms. There are AI writing tools available such as grammar checkers such as Grammarly and/or ProWriting Aid. They help students identify grammatical errors, provide suggestions to clarify sentences and allow students to receive immediate feedback while they write. The benefits include providing students with a means to check their work, learn to edit, reflect critically and develop self-regulated learning skills; all consistent with constructivist views of student centered learning environments which value students' autonomy.

Additionally, there are several AI based platforms available such as TurnItIn which can be used to support students in developing an understanding of the importance of Academic Integrity and help them avoid plagiarism by using proper citations. Additionally, teachers can utilize these platforms to facilitate reflective classroom experiences that will allow students to review the AI generated feedback provided to them and compare it with the teacher's feedback. This allows students to evaluate the reliability and fairness of the feedback provided to them; thus connecting the theoretical discussion regarding feedback loops to hands on experience.

However, before integrating AI tools in your classroom, you must consider the ethical implications of utilizing AI tools in your teaching practices. Some of these implications include: the potential for biased algorithms to impact the student's ability to complete assignments accurately; the need to protect students' personally identifiable information when submitting assignments through online platforms; and the risk of over-reliance on automated feedback. Therefore, it is important for teachers and institutions to develop policies and procedures to provide students with transparency regarding the utilization of AI tools in the classroom and to protect students' personally identifiable information. Further, by promoting open dialogue among students, teachers and administrators regarding how AI tools make decisions can contribute to the development of digital literacy and ethical awareness among students. By merging theoretical perspectives of AI supported writing instruction with the practical strategies outlined above, educators can create an inclusive, ethically sound and pedagogically effective environment for teaching students how to write using AI.

2.6 Pedagogical Theories behind Writing Instruction

Writing instruction has long been shaped by a rich interplay of pedagogical theories that reflect evolving understandings of language, cognition, and learning. As education has moved from behaviorist models to more constructivist and sociocultural paradigms, the way writing is taught has undergone significant transformation. These theoretical underpinnings not only guide classroom practices but also inform the integration of new technologies—such as artificial intelligence—into writing instruction. A comprehensive understanding of these pedagogical foundations is essential for evaluating the effectiveness and appropriateness of AI tools in enhancing writing skills.

Early writing instruction was heavily influenced by *behaviorist theory*, which emphasized imitation, repetition, and reinforcement. In this model, writing was viewed as a set of mechanical skills—grammar, punctuation, spelling, and syntax—that students could master through drills and correction. The role of the teacher was that of a transmitter of knowledge, and assessment was focused on error detection and correction. Although now considered limited in scope, behaviorist principles laid the groundwork for structured writing curricula and continue to influence practices such as standardized testing and automated grammar correction, which align well with rule-based AI systems.

The shift towards *cognitive theories of learning*, particularly in the 1970s and 1980s, marked a major turning point in writing pedagogy. Cognitive theorists viewed writing not merely as a product but as a process involving planning, drafting, revising, and editing. Emphasis was placed on the mental strategies writers use to generate and organize ideas, manage working memory, and make decisions about language and structure. Influential models such as Flower and Hayes' cognitive process theory framed writing as a problem-solving activity, encouraging educators to teach metacognitive strategies that help students monitor and regulate their own writing processes. In today's classrooms, cognitive theories continue to support process-based writing instruction, where students are encouraged to engage in multiple drafts and receive formative feedback—practices that AI tools are increasingly equipped to support through real-time suggestions and revision prompts.

Another influential framework in writing instruction is *constructivism*, which posits that learners actively construct knowledge through experience, reflection, and interaction with their environment. Constructivist approaches to writing emphasize learner agency, contextual learning, and the role of prior knowledge. Students are seen as creators of meaning, rather than passive recipients of rules. Writing tasks are often embedded in authentic, real-world contexts that make learning meaningful and relevant. In this model, the teacher serves as a facilitator who guides students in exploring topics, organizing ideas, and expressing themselves with purpose and voice. AI-powered platforms can complement constructivist pedagogy by offering personalized feedback, scaffolding support, and opportunities for self-directed learning—provided they are used to enhance rather than replace human guidance.

Sociocultural theory, particularly Vygotsky's concept of the Zone of Proximal Development (ZPD), further deepens our understanding of writing as a socially mediated activity. According to this perspective, learning occurs through interaction with more knowledgeable others—teachers, peers, or digital tools—and is shaped by cultural and linguistic context. Writing, from a sociocultural lens, is both a cognitive and social act, deeply tied to identity, discourse communities, and language norms. Collaborative writing, peer review, and dialogue-based learning are key features of sociocultural writing instruction. With the rise of AI writing assistants, this theory highlights the importance of considering how technology mediates social interaction and supports or hinders learning within the ZPD. AI can serve as a "more knowledgeable other" when properly trained and aligned with pedagogical goals, but it can also risk isolating learners if not integrated within a collaborative framework.

Another relevant perspective is *genre theory*, which focuses on the social purposes and structural features of different types of writing. According to this approach, learning to write involves understanding the expectations and conventions of various genres—such as narratives, reports, arguments, and reflections—within specific disciplinary and cultural contexts. Genre-based pedagogy helps students identify patterns and adapt their writing for different audiences and purposes. AI tools trained on diverse textual data can offer genre-specific suggestions, modeling genre conventions and providing real-time examples. However, they must be critically evaluated to ensure they do not reinforce rigid or culturally biased representations of genre norms.

Multiliteracies theory and *critical pedagogy* offer more contemporary lenses for understanding writing instruction in the digital age. Multiliteracies emphasize the diversity of communication modes—visual, digital, textual—and the need for students to navigate multiple literacies in a globalized world. Writing is no longer limited to linear text but includes multimodal composition, web-based writing, and interaction with AI-generated content. Critical pedagogy, influenced by scholars such as Paulo Freire, challenges educators to consider issues of power, identity, and equity in writing instruction. It urges teachers to empower students through writing that engages with real-world issues and social justice. These perspectives raise important questions about the ethical use of AI in writing instruction, the ownership of AI-generated content, and the cultural biases embedded in AI training datasets.

2.7 Intersection of AI and Writing Pedagogy

The convergence of artificial intelligence (AI) and writing pedagogy represents a dynamic and evolving area within educational research and practice. As AI technologies increasingly permeate classroom settings, particularly through the integration of language-based tools such as grammar checkers, predictive text systems, and large language models, their role in shaping writing instruction becomes both more significant and more complex. This intersection invites educators, researchers, and policymakers to critically examine how AI tools align with or challenge established pedagogical theories and practices, and how they might reshape the landscape of writing instruction in the digital age.

AI's capacity to process and generate human language has made it especially relevant to writing pedagogy. Tools powered by Natural Language Processing (NLP) and machine learning can offer real-time grammar correction, style suggestions, and personalized feedback. More advanced applications, such as large language models (e.g., GPT-4), go beyond surface-level corrections to assist with content generation, paraphrasing, and even composing entire texts. While these innovations introduce powerful new affordances for learners, their integration into pedagogy must be carefully contextualized within educational objectives, ethical considerations, and student development frameworks.

At its core, writing pedagogy is concerned not only with the production of grammatically correct text, but also with critical thinking, rhetorical awareness, creativity, and voice. From this perspective, AI tools must be evaluated not just on their technical efficacy but on their pedagogical value. For instance, while AI can effectively support revision by flagging sentence-level errors or suggesting clearer phrasing, there is a risk that students may rely on it as a substitute for developing their own editing and critical reading skills. This tension underscores the need to position AI not as a replacement for instruction but as a supplementary aid that scaffolds learning when used strategically.

The intersection of AI and writing pedagogy is particularly evident in process-based and constructivist approaches to writing. Process pedagogy emphasizes recursive stages—prewriting, drafting, revising, and editing—encouraging learners to reflect on and refine their writing over time. AI tools can support this process by providing immediate, formative feedback that helps students iterate and improve their drafts. For example, an AI-powered writing assistant might help a student identify weak transitions or suggest more precise word choices during the revision stage. This aligns with the pedagogical goal of promoting metacognition and writing as an evolving, reflective process.

Similarly, constructivist and student-centered pedagogies, which emphasize active learning and individual meaning-making, find potential synergies with AI technologies that offer personalized learning experiences. Adaptive feedback systems can tailor suggestions to the learner's proficiency level, learning style, and writing history, helping students identify specific areas for growth. In collaborative writing environments, AI tools can mediate peer review by organizing comments, tracking revisions, and providing linguistic feedback that complements human input. These affordances can enhance engagement and autonomy, particularly when learners are encouraged to critically evaluate AI-generated suggestions rather than passively accepting them.

However, the intersection of AI and writing pedagogy also raises important pedagogical and ethical challenges. One major concern is the risk of homogenization in student writing. Because AI models are trained on large datasets that reflect dominant linguistic and cultural norms, the feedback and suggestions they generate may inadvertently promote standardization at the expense of individual voice, creativity, or cultural variation. From a sociocultural pedagogical perspective, this can be problematic, particularly in diverse classrooms where students bring varied linguistic identities and rhetorical traditions. Educators must therefore adopt a critical stance, guiding students to use AI tools judiciously and ensuring that writing instruction remains inclusive and culturally responsive.

Another challenge involves the authenticity and integrity of student writing. With the rise of generative AI systems capable of producing entire essays or responses to prompts, educators face new dilemmas in assessing original student work. While plagiarism detection software may evolve to detect AI-generated content, the broader pedagogical question concerns how to foster genuine authorship and ethical engagement with technology. Here, writing pedagogy must adapt to include explicit instruction on digital literacy, authorship ethics, and the responsible use of AI tools. Teaching students to reflect on when and how to use AI effectively—not simply whether to use it—can empower them to become more thoughtful and independent writers in AI-rich environments.

The pedagogical intersection with AI also extends to genre-based and multiliteracies approaches, which view writing as a contextualized and multimodal activity. AI tools can be integrated into genre instruction by offering examples of writing conventions across academic, professional, and creative contexts. They can also support multimodal composition by assisting with scriptwriting, content summarization, or caption generation for digital media. These capabilities align with the growing need to prepare students for writing in complex, media-rich environments. However, the pedagogical emphasis must remain on critical awareness—helping students understand not just how to produce different text types, but why certain conventions exist and how audience, purpose, and medium influence writing choices.

In bridging AI and writing pedagogy, educators must also consider professional development and institutional support. Teachers need training not only in how AI tools function but in how to incorporate them into pedagogical strategies that align with curricular goals. This includes understanding the limitations of AI, navigating issues of data privacy, and modeling ethical behavior in digital environments. Institutions must provide the infrastructure and policy frameworks that support the effective and responsible use of AI in writing classrooms.

The intersection of AI and writing pedagogy presents both promising opportunities and critical challenges. When thoughtfully integrated, AI technologies can enhance process-based, personalized, and collaborative approaches to writing instruction, providing timely feedback and expanding access to writing support. At the same time, educators must remain vigilant about ethical concerns, cultural inclusivity, and the preservation of core pedagogical values such as critical thinking, creativity, and authentic expression. As AI continues to evolve, its role in writing pedagogy must be shaped by a nuanced understanding of teaching and learning—one that recognizes the transformative potential of technology while reaffirming the centrality of human agency in education(Yan et al., 2025).

3. KEY AI TOOLS TRANSFORMING WRITING INSTRUCTION

Artificial intelligence tools are playing an increasingly significant role in the field of writing education. These tools assist both educators and learners by enhancing writing quality, offering real-time feedback, and supporting personalized learning. Figure.2 illustrates the various ways in which AI contributes to writing instruction, including automated grammar and style corrections, content generation, plagiarism detection, and adaptive writing suggestions. By integrating these technologies, writing education is evolving into a more efficient, engaging, and accessible process for students at all levels.

Figure 2. AI tools in Writing Education

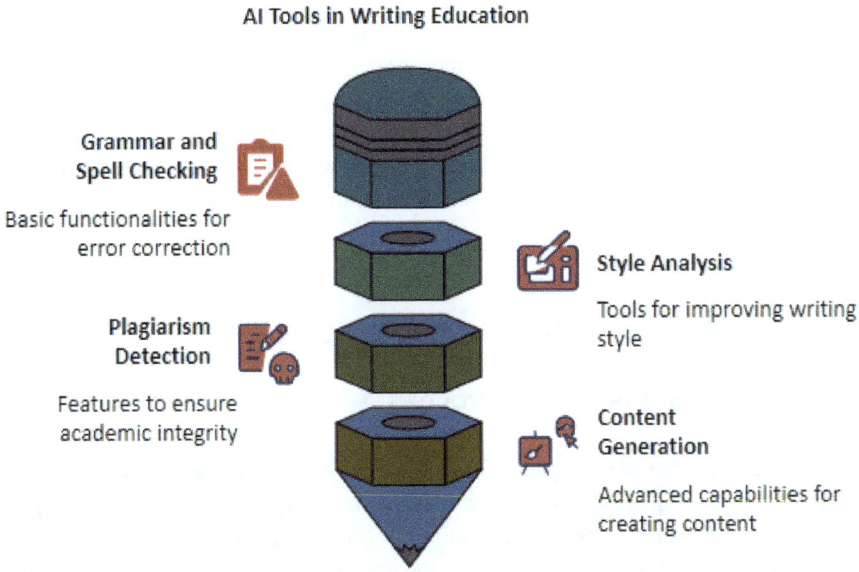

3.1 Grammarly

Grammarly is a widely used AI-driven writing assistant that helps students with grammar, spelling, punctuation, and style suggestions. It provides real-time feedback and tone analysis, which can support students in self-editing and revising their work. While helpful, reliance on Grammarly should be balanced with teacher feedback to avoid mechanical writing habits.

3.2 ProWritingAid

ProWritingAid offers similar functions to Grammarly but includes more detailed reports on readability, overused words, sentence structure, and diction. Its pedagogical strength lies in diagnostic capabilities, helping students and educators identify recurring writing issues and track improvement over time.

3.3 Turnitin

Turnitin is best known for its plagiarism detection features. However, its recent upgrades include AI-assisted feedback for grammar and argument development. Turnitin helps maintain academic integrity while offering opportunities to teach paraphrasing, citation, and responsible authorship.

3.4 GPT-3 and Other Generative Tools

Generative AI tools like GPT-3 are capable of producing coherent text in response to prompts, offering valuable support in various stages of the writing process. These tools can assist students in brainstorming ideas, generating illustrative examples, practicing peer review, and exploring diverse writing styles. While their capabilities are powerful and increasingly accessible, they also raise important ethical concerns related to authorship, originality, and academic integrity. As such, it is essential for educators to guide students in the critical and responsible use of these technologies, ensuring that AI serves as a tool for learning rather than a substitute for genuine intellectual effort.

4. TEACHING WITH AI: STRATEGIES AND SCENARIOS

4.1 Integrating AI in the Writing Process

AI tools can be seamlessly integrated into various stages of the writing process, enhancing both the efficiency and quality of student output. During the prewriting stage, tools powered by GPT-based models can support brainstorming by generating ideas, expanding on topics, or helping students formulate thesis statements. In the drafting phase, applications like Grammarly offer grammar and sentence structure suggestions, enabling writers to construct clearer, more effective prose. The revising stage benefits from platforms such as ProWritingAid or Turnitin, which provide detailed feedback on coherence, originality, and style, guiding learners toward more polished and ethically sound work. Finally, in the publishing stage, AI analytics can assist educators in assessing final drafts using institution-specific rubrics, ensuring consistency in evaluation and supporting data-informed feedback. This integration not only streamlines the writing process but also fosters greater learner autonomy and engagement.

4.2 Designing AI-Enhanced Writing Activities

AI-enhanced writing activities can be strategically designed to promote critical thinking, collaboration, and metacognitive awareness. For example, peer review workshops can be structured so that students compare their own feedback with that generated by AI tools, encouraging them to reflect on the accuracy, tone, and helpfulness of different types of feedback. Reflection journals offer another valuable approach, where students analyze and critique the feedback they receive from AI systems, fostering a deeper understanding of writing conventions and the role of automated assistance. Additionally, organizing group debates on the ethical use of AI in academic writing invites students to engage with the broader implications of emerging technologies, developing their argumentation skills while exploring real-world issues. These types of activities illustrate how AI can be integrated into writing instruction not merely as a technical aid, but as a catalyst for higher-order thinking and meaningful learning experiences.

4.3 Supporting Differentiated Instruction

AI tools offer valuable support for differentiated instruction by enabling educators to tailor writing activities to the diverse needs and skill levels of their students. For beginners, AI-powered platforms can provide real-time grammar assistance, helping them build foundational writing skills through guided correction and reinforcement. More advanced learners may engage with GPT-based tools to analyze the quality of their arguments, evaluate rhetorical effectiveness, or refine their use of academic language. For English as a Second Language (ESL) learners, AI can offer translation support, readability feedback, and vocabulary suggestions that promote language development while maintaining content comprehension. By automating aspects of feedback and support, AI allows educators to individualize instruction without significantly increasing their workload, creating a more inclusive and responsive learning environment.

4.4 Challenges in AI Integration

Despite the numerous benefits AI tools offer in writing instruction, several challenges continue to impede their effective integration into educational settings. One significant concern is the potential for over-reliance on AI, which may hinder students' development of independent writing and critical thinking skills if not used with proper guidance. Additionally, biases inherent in AI algorithms can lead to inaccurate or unfair grading and feedback, particularly for students from diverse linguistic or cultural backgrounds. Another pressing issue is that many educators feel underprepared to interpret, evaluate, or effectively integrate AI-generated outputs within their instructional practices. Addressing these challenges requires sustained professional development, equipping teachers with the knowledge and confidence to use AI tools responsibly. Furthermore, thoughtful instructional design that incorporates AI as a supportive aid—rather than a substitute for human teaching—can help ensure its ethical and pedagogically sound application in the writing classroom.

5. ETHICAL AND LEGAL CONSIDERATIONS IN AI WRITING INSTRUCTION

The integration of AI in writing instruction presents several ethical and legal challenges that educators and institutions must address. Key concerns include academic integrity, where over-reliance on AI tools may lead to issues of authorship and plagiarism. Legally, the use of AI-generated content raises questions about data privacy, intellectual property rights, and copyright infringement. To ensure responsible use, clear policies and guidelines must be established for both educators and students. Ultimately, a balanced approach that promotes transparency, accountability, and fairness is essential to uphold the integrity of educational practices in the age of AI. *Figure 3*. Ethical concerns in AI-integrated writing instruction, highlighting key areas such as data privacy, algorithmic bias, and academic integrity. The integration of AI in writing instruction presents several ethical and legal challenges that educators and institutions must address. Among the most pressing concerns are data privacy, where safeguarding student information in AI-powered platforms is crucial, and algorithmic bias, which may lead to unfair or unequal learning outcomes. Academic integrity is another key issue, as the improper use of

AI tools could compromise authorship and promote plagiarism. Legally, the use of AI-generated content raises important questions about intellectual property rights and copyright. To responsibly incorporate AI in educational settings, it is essential to develop clear policies, promote transparency, and uphold fairness—ensuring that innovation in instruction aligns with ethical standards and legal obligations.

Figure 3. Ethical concerns in AI writing

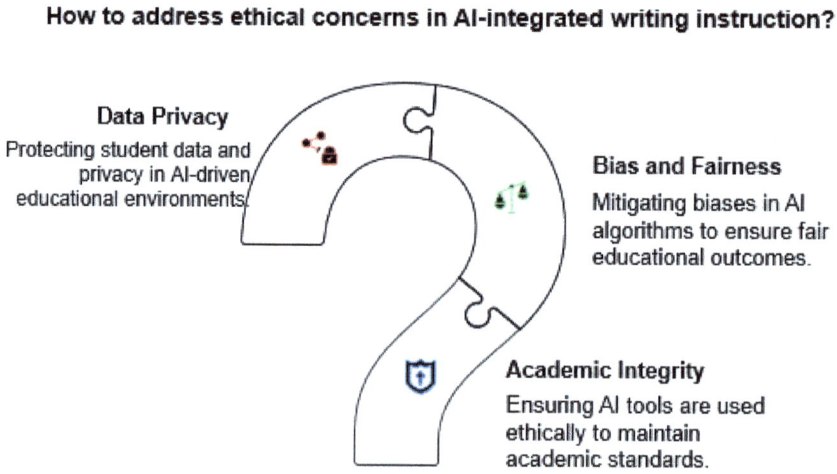

5.1 Academic Integrity and AI Usage

AI tools raise questions about the boundaries between acceptable assistance and academic dishonesty. For instance, using Grammarly for editing may be deemed acceptable, whereas relying on GPT-3 to generate entire essays could violate institutional guidelines. Educators must define and communicate clear rules regarding AI use, emphasizing transparency and attribution. Students should be encouraged to document how AI tools influenced their writing process, maintaining ownership of the intellectual work.

5.2 Authorship and Originality

As generative AI tools become more sophisticated, the concept of authorship is increasingly blurred. Who owns the text generated by GPT-3— the student, the AI, or both? Institutions and educators must guide students in understanding that while AI can assist, the core responsibility for content, structure, and critical thought must remain human. Clear policies on citation and acknowledgment of AI-generated assistance can preserve the integrity of academic work.

5.3 Bias and Fairness in AI Algorithms

AI systems are trained on vast datasets that may contain social, cultural, and linguistic biases. These biases can manifest in feedback that privileges standard language forms, overlooks multilingual expression, or reinforces stereotypes. Educators must critically evaluate the tools they adopt, advocate for transparency in algorithm design, and supplement AI feedback with culturally responsive instruction. Addressing bias also means incorporating diverse voices and writing styles into teaching models.

5.4 Data Privacy and Security

AI tools often require access to student writing and behavioral data. Institutions must ensure that the data collected is stored securely, used ethically, and governed by transparent privacy policies. Instructors should educate students about the digital footprint created through AI use and encourage informed consent. Collaboration with IT departments and legal teams is essential to vet AI vendors and comply with data protection laws such as GDPR or India's Digital Personal Data Protection Act.

5.5 Ethical Use in Assessment

Using AI tools in grading or automated assessment raises concerns about accuracy, transparency, and fairness. While AI can support formative assessment, summative grading should always involve human oversight. Educators must guard against the over-reliance on algorithmic scores, especially when evaluating creative or context-dependent writing. Establishing ethical assessment protocols that combine AI efficiency with human judgment ensures fairness and academic trust.

6. INSTITUTIONALIZING AI IN WRITING INSTRUCTION

6.1 Building a Supportive Institutional Culture

For successful integration of AI tools in writing instruction, institutions must create an environment that values innovation while upholding academic standards. This means encouraging experimentation, fostering collaboration across departments, and framing AI not as a threat but as a supplement to human creativity and pedagogical depth. Leadership must articulate a clear vision for AI adoption that aligns with institutional goals, while departments should develop local policies that reflect discipline-specific writing norms.

6.2 Professional Development and Teacher Training

Faculty training is essential for the meaningful integration of AI in writing instruction, requiring institutions to provide ongoing professional development that empowers educators with both technical proficiency and pedagogical insight. Training programs should help faculty understand the functions and limitations of AI tools, assess their alignment with instructional goals, and design writing activities that integrate AI meaningfully and ethically. Additionally, educators must be equipped to facilitate discussions on digital literacy and the ethical use of AI in academic contexts. Peer mentoring, sandbox environments, and hands-on workshops can further support instructors by offering collaborative and experiential learning opportunities, enabling them to adopt AI tools with confidence, critical awareness, and a student-centered approach.

6.3 Developing Institutional Policies and Guidelines

Institutions must develop clear and comprehensive policies to govern the use of AI in writing tasks, ensuring consistency, transparency, and academic integrity across educational settings. These policies should clearly define the distinction between AI-assisted and AI-generated content, establish guidelines outlining acceptable and prohibited uses for both students and faculty, and set standards for proper citation and disclosure when AI tools are used. Additionally, procedures must be in place for handling violations related to academic misconduct involving AI. To ensure relevance and effectiveness, such policies should be developed collaboratively, drawing on the expertise and perspectives of administrators, faculty members, students, legal advisors, and IT professionals. This inclusive approach promotes shared understanding, ethical use, and responsible integration of AI within institutional frameworks..

6.4 Infrastructure and Accessibility

Equitable access to AI tools in writing instruction demands a strong and inclusive digital infrastructure that ensures all students can benefit, regardless of their socioeconomic or physical circumstances. Institutions should provide licensed access to essential AI writing platforms and implement device loan programs or offer technical support for underserved learners who may lack personal resources. It is also vital to ensure that AI tools are compatible with assistive technologies, such as screen readers and voice recognition software, to support students with disabilities. Additionally, user interfaces must be designed to be linguistically and culturally inclusive, accommodating the diverse backgrounds of the student population. By prioritizing accessibility and inclusion, institutions can ensure that technological advancement serves as a bridge to opportunity rather than a barrier to participation.

6.5 Monitoring and Evaluation of AI Implementation

Institutional oversight is essential to ensure that the integration of AI in writing instruction remains sustainable, ethical, and aligned with educational goals. Effective evaluation frameworks should measure key indicators such as student learning outcomes, improvements in writing quality, teacher satisfaction, changes in workload, and the frequency of misuse or ethical concerns related to AI use. Additionally, institutions must assess whether AI tools are equitably accessible and effective across diverse student populations, ensuring that no group is disproportionately advantaged or marginalized. To support continuous improvement, feedback loops, annual audits, and longitudinal studies should be established, allowing institutions to monitor the impact of AI over time, address emerging challenges, and make data-informed decisions that justify ongoing investment in AI-enhanced writing programs.

7. CASE STUDIES AND REAL-WORLD APPLICATIONS

7.1 University-Level Integration: Arizona State University (ASU)

ASU incorporated Grammarly and Turnitin into its foundational writing courses through institution-wide licensing. Faculty were trained to integrate these tools meaningfully, using Grammarly for early drafts and Turnitin for final assessments. The result was improved writing quality, reduced plagiarism cases, and increased student confidence. AI tools helped instructors focus more on higher-order feedback such as argumentation and structure.

7.2 GPT-3 for Creative Writing in Finnish High Schools

A pilot project in Finland introduced GPT-3 to high school creative writing classes. Students used GPT-3 to generate story starters and explore multiple writing styles. Teachers guided them to critique AI-generated content and refine it through human revision. This not only stimulated creativity but also taught students to view AI as a collaborative partner rather than a shortcut.

7.3 Supporting Multilingual Learners in India

In rural Indian classrooms where English is taught as a second or third language, AI tools like ProWritingAid and Google Translate have been used to scaffold student writing. These tools helped learners experiment with sentence structures, vocabulary, and grammar without judgment. Teachers observed improved engagement and confidence among students who previously struggled with English composition.

7.4 Policy and Faculty Training: The UK Open University

The Open University developed a formal AI policy for all departments. It covered issues like acceptable AI usage, faculty autonomy, student consent, and data privacy. Alongside, the university implemented regular faculty workshops and AI literacy programs. This dual approach ensured that the institutional shift was not only top-down but also community-driven and pedagogically aligned.

7.5 Adult Education and AI Coaching: U.S. Community Colleges

In American community colleges serving adult learners, platforms like Ecree and WriteLab have been introduced to help learners who lack academic writing backgrounds. These tools offer instant, formative feedback on coherence, clarity, and grammar. As a result, adult learners feel more supported, and instructors can provide differentiated feedback to diverse student populations. AI serves as a bridge for learners re-entering formal education.

8. FUTURE DIRECTIONS AND SUSTAINABLE INTEGRATION

8.1 Advancing AI Capabilities for Writing Instruction

The next generation of AI tools will likely incorporate multimodal analysis, deeper semantic understanding, and personalized learner profiles. AI systems may soon be able to provide rhetorical feedback, adapt feedback to learning styles, and analyze visual content in digital writing. These advances will increase the relevance of AI in both traditional and digital composition contexts.

8.2 Redefining the Teacher's Role

As AI takes over routine evaluation tasks, teachers will evolve into mentors and facilitators. They will curate AI-enhanced writing tasks, help students interpret feedback critically, and guide them in developing writing voice and originality. This shift requires a new teacher identity grounded in coaching, digital literacy, and ethical judgment.

8.3 Scaling Access and Inclusion

Future policies must prioritize the scalability and equity of AI tools in education, ensuring that technological advancements benefit all learners rather than exacerbating existing disparities. This involves supporting open-access platforms that can be implemented in underfunded schools, making AI interfaces available in multiple languages to accommodate diverse linguistic communities, and providing targeted training for educators in low-resource settings to build capacity and confidence in using these tools. Additionally, policies must promote inclusive design practices that address the needs of learners with disabilities, ensuring compatibility with assistive technologies and universal usability. By embedding equity at the core of AI implementation, educational systems can harness AI's potential to close the digital divide and create more inclusive, accessible learning environments.

8.4 Building Collaborative Ecosystems

Sustainable integration depends on collaborations between educators, developers, policymakers, and students. Teacher input in tool design, classroom-based research, and participatory design methods can ensure AI solutions are relevant and context-sensitive. Partnerships with ed-tech companies and research institutions can foster innovation while maintaining educational integrity.

8.5 Aligning with Education 5.0 Principles

The future of writing instruction must align with the goals of Education 5.0: learner-centeredness, human-AI collaboration, sustainability, and lifelong learning. AI should be deployed not as a novelty but as a catalyst for inclusive, ethical, and forward-looking pedagogy. Educators must lead the way in shaping AI integration that reflects democratic values and human dignity.

9. CONCLUSION AND RECOMMENDATIONS

The integration of Artificial Intelligence in writing instruction represents a transformative shift in the educational landscape. From grammar correction and plagiarism detection to advanced writing analytics and idea generation, AI tools such as Grammarly, ProWritingAid, Turnitin, and GPT-3 are reshaping how writing is taught, learned, and assessed. As this chapter has demonstrated, the potential benefits of AI in writing instruction are vast—enhancing learner autonomy, providing equitable access, supporting multilingualism, and fostering critical engagement with feedback.

However, these benefits come with significant responsibilities. Ethical concerns such as academic integrity, data privacy, algorithmic bias, and over-dependence on technology must be addressed through clear policies, continuous professional development, and institutional oversight. Institutions must lead with vision—developing guidelines, offering infrastructure, and nurturing a culture that balances innovation with ethical responsibility.

Moving forward, educators should embrace their evolving roles as facilitators of AI-enhanced learning environments. Rather than fearing technological displacement, teachers can harness AI to expand their impact—guiding students to become not only better writers but also critical thinkers and responsible digital citizens.

Recommendations

1. **Policy Development:** Institutions must craft comprehensive AI usage policies, addressing academic honesty, acceptable use, and data protection.
2. **Teacher Training:** Invest in ongoing professional development to empower educators with the skills to effectively integrate and critique AI tools.
3. **Inclusive Design:** AI tools should be accessible, multilingual, and sensitive to diverse learning needs.
4. **Curriculum Integration:** Embed AI use into writing curricula through structured, scaffolded activities that promote reflection and self-regulation.
5. **Ethical Literacy:** Teach students about the ethical dimensions of using AI—ensuring responsible use and awareness of potential misuse.
6. **Evaluation and Feedback:** Continuously assess the impact of AI integration on student outcomes, teaching quality, and institutional goals.

By aligning AI implementation with pedagogical best practices, ethical frameworks, and inclusive strategies, the future of writing instruction can be one of empowerment, equity, and innovation. This chapter calls on educators, policymakers, and developers to work collaboratively to shape an AI-integrated writing pedagogy that supports both academic excellence and human dignity.

10. REFERENCES

Abulibdeh, A., Zaidan, E., & Abulibdeh, R. (2024). Navigating the confluence of artificial intelligence and education for sustainable development in the era of industry 4.0: Challenges, opportunities, and ethical dimensions. *Journal of Cleaner Production, 437*, 140527. DOI: 10.1016/j.jclepro.2023.140527

Ayanwale, M. A., Ntshangase, S. D., Adelana, O. P., Afolabi, K. W., Adam, U. A., & Olatunbosun, S. O. (2024). Navigating the future: Exploring in-service teachers' preparedness for artificial intelligence integration into South African schools. *Computers and Education: Artificial Intelligence, 7*, 100330. DOI: 10.1016/j.caeai.2024.100330

Boulhrir, T., & Hamash, M. (2025). Unpacking artificial intelligence in elementary education: A comprehensive thematic analysis systematic review. *Computers and Education: Artificial Intelligence, 9*, 100442. DOI: 10.1016/j.caeai.2025.100442

Cheah, Y. H., Lu, J., & Kim, J. (2025). Integrating generative artificial intelligence in K-12 education: Examining teachers' preparedness, practices, and barriers. *Computers and Education: Artificial Intelligence, 8*, 100363. DOI: 10.1016/j.caeai.2025.100363

Dakakni, D. (2023). Artificial intelligence in the L2 classroom: Implications and challenges on ethics and equity in higher education: A 21st century Pandora's box. *Computers & Education.*

Deberdt, R., Le Billon, P., Makinde, O., Dauvergne, P., Solwati, T., Razmi, S., Kumar, G., & Belhabib, D. (2025). Artificial intelligence and ESG in resources-intensive industries: Reviewing the use of AI in fisheries, mining, plastics, and forestry. *The Extractive Industries and Society, 23*, 101690. DOI: 10.1016/j.exis.2025.101690

Deriba, F. G., & Sanusi, I. T. (2025). Artificial intelligence in Ethiopian school curriculum: Educators' practices, challenges, and recommendations. *Computers and Education Open, 8*, 100251. DOI: 10.1016/j.caeo.2025.100251

Hamad, N. I., El-Ashry, A. M., Ibrahim, I. M., & Hassan, E. A. (2025). Embracing the future: An insight into nursing students' attitude and perception towards the usability of artificial intelligence in healthcare. *Teaching and Learning in Nursing, 20*(2), e500–e508. DOI: 10.1016/j.teln.2024.12.017

Jaber, D., Hasan, H. E., Abutaima, R., Sawan, H. M., & Al Tabbah, S. (2024). The impact of artificial intelligence on the knowledge, attitude, and practice of pharmacists across diverse settings: A cross-sectional study. *International Journal of Medical Informatics, 192*, 105656. DOI: 10.1016/j.ijmedinf.2024.105656 PMID: 39426239

Jembu, J. P., & Balang, R. V. (2025). Artificial intelligence adoption in nursing students' academic writing: A qualitative study. *Teaching and Learning in Nursing, 20*(4), e1012–e1020. Advance online publication. DOI: 10.1016/j.teln.2025.04.015

Kobeissi, M. M., Santa Maria, D. M., & Park, J. I. (2025). Artificial intelligence 101: Building literacy with the AI-ABCs framework. *Nursing Outlook, 73*(4), 102445. DOI: 10.1016/j.outlook.2025.102445 PMID: 40446514

Kong, S. C., & Hu, W. (2025). A Study of Developing Administrative Staff's Conceptual Understanding of Generative Artificial Intelligence Through Professional Development: Evaluation of a Course Using Tests, Surveys and Thematic Analysis of Reflective Writings. *Computers and Education: Artificial Intelligence*, *100444*, 100444. Advance online publication. DOI: 10.1016/j.caeai.2025.100444

Kong, S. C., Yang, Y., & Hou, C. (2024). Examining teachers' behavioural intention of using generative artificial intelligence tools for teaching and learning based on the extended technology acceptance model. *Computers and Education: Artificial Intelligence*, *7*, 100328. DOI: 10.1016/j.caeai.2024.100328

Seyri, H., & Ghiasvand, F. (2025). "Teaching is basically feeling": Unpacking EFL Teachers' perceived emotions and regulatory strategies in AI-Powered L2 speaking and writing skills instruction. *Computers and Education Open*, *8*, 100264. DOI: 10.1016/j.caeo.2025.100264

Tseng, L.-P. (2025). *Exploring artificial intelligence literacy and the use of ChatGPT and copilot in instruction on nursing academic report writing*.

Yan, J., Liu, Z., Leng, J., Zhao, J. L., Chen, C., Zhang, D., Tao, Y., Wang, Y., Liu, T., Zhang, C., Tong, Y., Mourtzis, D., & Wang, L. (2025). Human-centric artificial intelligence towards Industry 5.0: Retrospect and prospect. *Journal of Industrial Information Integration*, *47*, 100903. DOI: 10.1016/j.jii.2025.100903

Yeung, R. S. K., Tian, R., Chiu, D. K. W., & Choi, S. P.-M. (2025). University students' perceptions on how generative artificial intelligence shape learning and research practices: A case study in Hong Kong. *Journal of Academic Librarianship*, *51*(5), 103082. DOI: 10.1016/j.acalib.2025.103082

Chapter 6
Feedback That Feels Human:
Reimagining Academic Writing Support Through Ethical AI

Shikha Mann
https://orcid.org/0000-0003-0395-9164
School of Business, Indira University, Pune, India

Sakshi Mann
https://orcid.org/0009-0002-8238-5268
School of Business, Indira University, Pune, India

Tausif Mistry
https://orcid.org/0000-0003-2377-9371
School of Business, Indira University, Pune, India

Yogesh Mahajan
Symbiosis Centre for Management and Human Resource Development, India

Rita Dangre
Indira University, India

ABSTRACT

This chapter investigates the potential of artificial intelligence to revolutionize the provision of feedback on academic writing within the higher education sector, considering ethical use and collaborative participation. It also addresses the recurring difficulties associated with feedback within multilingual and multicultural classrooms, as well as reviews the empirical studies concerning AI-based writing assessment tools. Drawing from sociocultural learning theory, feedback literacy, and ethical uses of AI, the chapter proposes the Human–AI Co-Feedback Model (HACFM), which integrates the productivity of machines and the sensitivity and contextual understanding of humans. Through specific classroom and institutional examples, the model illustrates the ways AI technology could be used to improve immediacy and iteration while preserving rela-

DOI: 10.4018/979-8-3373-5601-3.ch006

tional aspects of depth, attention, inclusivity, and accountability. Policy considerations, ethical constraints, and the human side of technologically advanced feedback are the key aspects of the chapter's conclusion.

1. INTRODUCTION

Writing is both a cognitive and profoundly personal activity. It is the act of shaping thought into language, of constructing meaning in ways that embody identity and discipline. In higher education, writing functions as the primary medium of assessment and is a central site through which students develop critical thinking, disciplinary voice, and academic identity (Hyland, 2019). Yet for many learners-especially multilingual and second- or third-language writers-academic writing becomes a locus of anxiety, tension, and a sense of inadequacy. The feedback they receive, though intended to guide improvement, often compounds their struggles rather than alleviating them (Lee, 2020).

Feedback in writing education is widely recognized as essential for growth. In principle, feedback should be formative, dialogic, and oriented toward scaffolding future iterations of a text (Carless & Boud, 2018). However, in real-world university settings, feedback is frequently constrained by large class loads, limited instructor time, and institutional demands for efficiency. The result is feedback that is superficial, impersonal, or overly corrective. Many students experience such feedback not as dialogue but as evaluation-that is, as judgment devoid of growth potential (Carless & Winstone, 2020; Molloy et al., 2020).

The constraints of traditional feedback are especially felt in diverse, multilingual classrooms, where standardized norms may invisibly privilege dominant linguistic voices and disadvantage others (Lillis & Scott, 2007; Wingate & Tribble, 2012). In such contexts, students often internalize deficit views of their own language practices, while instructors-pressed for time-may default to corrective comments on grammar or style rather than engaging with students' rhetorical and ideational choices.

In recent years, artificial intelligence (AI) and automated writing evaluation (AWE) tools have been proposed as a partial remedy to the feedback bottleneck. Tools such as Grammarly, Criterion, or GPT-based writing assistants offer immediate feedback on grammar, organization, and lexical usage. Fan and Ma (2022) demonstrate through a systematic review that AWE feedback can yield positive gains in writing quality under structured pedagogical conditions. Similarly, Wei, Wang, and Dong (2023) found that structured AWE interventions led to measurable improvements in coherence, grammatical range, and lexical accuracy in a randomized controlled trial.

Despite innovations in AI, the implications of it use are still debated. Bai and Hu (2017) brought to light the feedback phenomenon of fallible AWE and how students' responses to AWE feedback varied greatly on AI generated recommendations. Some students blindly accepted and agreed with all recommendations, while others negated and countered the recommendations entirely, and a select few engaged with the AI feedback as reflection probes. This teaches that the use of feedback stems from efficacy and influence, as it can also do more harm than good, which depends on the preparatory processes of the pedagogy and the student agency put in negotiating it.

AI technology, like many others, raises certain ethical implications and concerns from a pedagogical standpoint. the concerns of unsynchrony with the cultural and stylometric forms of writing biases which biases the idiosyncrasies which AI systematically embeds are still fundamental. The application of AI within the educational sector remains unexplored in all respects of moral, ethical, and professional accountability and the allied issues of transparency and data security (Holmes et al 2022). Moreover, there exists the concern of correction dependence, Within correction dependence, writing is seen as a set of actions and a process which is required in order to achieve the end objective of satisfying and fulfilling the requirements of certain algorithms, which, in this case, downplays the entire process of writing and reduces it to just an intellectual activity.

This chapter advocates for the use of AI as a collaborator in feedback instead of a substitute for human judgment. This is framed in the context of the Human–AI Co-Feedback Model that combines the AI's efficacy with the relational, contextual, and mentorship elements of human instructors. This vision is aligned with the idea of collaborative intelligence where human creativity and machine accuracy work together to enhance learning (Sahlberg & Walker, 2021).

Such a reframing is especially crucial in today's global higher education environment, where diverse linguistic backgrounds converge. If deployed thoughtfully, AI has the potential to equalize opportunities by offering iterative scaffolding to under-resourced and multilingual students before instructor feedback. As Zou, Huang, and Xie (2023) argue, digital feedback systems can enhance writing processes, but their real value emerges when integrated into a pedagogical culture that emphasizes reflection, identity, and inclusivity.

The structure of this chapter is as follows. First, it examines the challenges of feedback in traditional writing instruction, particularly in multilingual and diverse classrooms. Second, it reviews empirical studies of AI-enabled writing feedback, outlining both benefits and limitations. Thirdly, it presents and explains a new Human–AI Co-Feedback Model as a way to combine the machine's productivity with human mentoring. Then, it presents case studies from teaching practice and the perspectives of students and instructors. The chapter then analyzes some ethical concerns as well as institutional approaches to and prospects of AI writing pedagogy.

In line with the objectives of Leveraging AI for Future-Ready Writing Education, this chapter contributes to the field by (1) Relationalizing AI feedback on writing as pedagogy, (2) a well-developed co-feedback model with solid theoretical and empirical foundations, and (3) addressing equity, voice and agency in contexts of multilingual writing.

2. PROBLEM STATEMENT AND JUSTIFICATION

Feedback is both critical and widely viewed as an unsatisfying part of the learning process filling a paradox in writing education (Carless & Boud 2018; Molloy et al, 2020). In a systems and relations context, the paradox is attributed to the charge that institutions throttle the processes of learning and improvement through feedback, often rendering interactions to be monotonous and demoralizing. Constructive feedback is challenging to provide in multilingual and heterogeneous classrooms where interaction must bridge multiple cultures and languages, and inequitable assumptions bridge the gap in feedback (Lillis & Scott 2007; Wingate & Tribble 2012).

2.1 The Feedback Dilemma

The dilemma is stark. Instructors desire to provide feedback that is formative, dialogic, and affirming, but structural constraints push them toward efficiency rather than depth. A single writing assignment in a class of 60 students, for instance, can generate hundreds of pages of student text to read and respond to. Given heavy teaching loads and administrative expectations, detailed commentary becomes nearly impossible. As Carless and Winstone (2020) emphasize, feedback is more than a technical process; it is relational, requiring trust, care, and ongoing dialogue. Yet, such relational feedback requires time-a resource in short supply in most higher education contexts.

Students, for their part, often perceive feedback as opaque or unhelpful. Studies show that they find comments cryptic, excessively focused on grammar, or inconsistent across instructors (Lee, 2020). For multilingual and first-generation learners, feedback that focuses narrowly on "errors" reinforces deficit perspectives, leading to feelings of inadequacy and reduced motivation (Hyland, 2019). What was meant to be supportive instead becomes a source of alienation. Molloy et al. (2020) argue that this is not just a matter of delivery but of literacy: both teachers and students need to develop *feedback literacy*-the capacity to understand, interpret, and use feedback productively. Without this, even the most carefully written feedback risks being misunderstood or ignored.

2.2 The Rise of AI Feedback Tools

In this context, AI-based tools have emerged as potential solutions. Automated writing evaluation (AWE) systems such as Grammarly, Criterion, and more recently, GPT-based platforms promise immediacy and scalability. They can highlight grammatical errors, suggest alternative phrasings, and provide surface-level corrections in seconds. Research indicates that such tools can indeed enhance writing performance when integrated thoughtfully. Fan and Ma (2022), in their systematic review, found that AWE feedback contributed to improvements in organization, vocabulary use, and overall text quality. Similarly, Wei, Wang, and Dong (2023) demonstrated in a randomized controlled trial that students using AWE systems outperformed control groups in coherence and lexical accuracy.

However, the benefits are not automatic. Bai and Hu (2017) documented how students responded variably to AWE feedback-some accepted all corrections uncritically, while others rejected them outright. The crucial factor was whether students were encouraged to reflect on and negotiate the feedback, rather than passively adopt it. This finding underscores that the real challenge is not the availability of AI tools but their pedagogical integration.

2.3 Risks of Algorithmic Dependence

The benefits and promise of AI produced feedback is dimmed by potential threats. An overreliance on AI feedback may lead to what Bai and Hu (2017) term "Correction Dependence," where students begin to outsource their thinking processes to the algorithm and its suggestions. Rather than using any form of active self reflection or devising their own personal strategies to revise, students have the option to click "accept" and let the tool change their writing. Although the end result may be a finished piece of writing that is grammatically and syntactically correct, the fundamental aims of writing instruction– the development of personal voice, agency, and critical literacy challenges– are suppressed.

Further, the ethical dilemmas create even more complexity. In the writing context, Holmes et al. (2022) observes that the AI instrument is seldom neutral, it incorporates biases depending on the information it is fed. It is a known fact that the AI instrument focuses on certain forms of language use and expression– in most cases, it is Anglo-American academic English and the rest of the language forms are marginalized and should be left alone. For students who emerge from certain cultural or language settings, there is a danger that they will be rendered voiceless and have to suffer from the hegemony of the monolingual ideology. The fact that in a world full of AI instruments, mechanisms and systems, a serious worry is the lack of transparency and accountability. Students are seldom told the process by which suggestions are arrived at, and worse, they have no control to determine the higher order criteria the AI tool uses to assess their work.

2.4 Why Human–AI Co-Feedback?

This chapter examines the shift toward more strategic feedback that balances the advantages and disadvantages of AI technology, thus proposing the Human-AI Co-Feedback Model. Educators across the specialty will all agree that feedback should aim at providing the best possible learning outcomes for students. This rationale is articulated through three interconnected arguments that all feedback should have.

Feedback should utilize the educational technologies that will best achieve desired learning outcomes. As Carless and Winstone (2020) indicate, meaningful engagement and listening is the heart of effective feedback. Most machines still lack the ability to completely remove the lower order thinking tasks of recitation, ma and frame, and the like. As an illustration, AI can relieve instructors of the *mechanical aspects* of providing lower-level corrective feedback, allowing them to focus on more contextually rich and developmental commentary.

In all scenarios, students should have the last say. The literature espouses the notion that students who undergo feedback from instructors as opposed to being simply passive recipients, perform much better (Carless & Boud, 2018; Lee, 2020). AI feedback, in as much as it is a type of suggestive feedback you must engage and interrogate, is not an instruction to be toed. Active learning activities where students scaffold each others' learning can teach students to not accept AI feedback uncritically.

Thirdly, the integration of AI tools needs to focus on 'ethical inclusivity'. It is imperative to implement feedback practices which recognize the cultural and linguistic identity variations in every multilingual and multicultural classroom. As Lillis and Scott (2007) and Wingate and Tribble (2012) caution, feedback that attempts to impose undue grammatical restrictions is likely to further silence already marginalized individuals. On the other hand, and used ethically, Artificial Intelligence (AI) provides tools which can facilitate multilingual learners' more confident engagement with the conventions of academic writing.

This involves open acknowledgment of the tools' shortcomings, explicit discussions of the biases of the tools, and alignment to the inclusive pedagogical objectives.

2.5 Institutional Imperatives

This chapter moves beyond practice to policy. Universities are under persistent pressure to implement AI technology driven by efficiency. The absence of ethical use frameworks reduces feedback to a mere transactional service. As Holmes et al. (2022) argue, AI in education needs to be handled with ethics regarding transparency, accountability, and learner focus. Thus, universities need to formulate policies that protect students' agency, incorporate framework literacy of AI feedback, and assess the use and effects of AI on learning.

Trust within the education system is essential, as Sahlberg and Walker (2021) argue. Trust between and among the educators, students, and the broader society is of utmost importance. Trust is easily eroded when feedback is mechanically given. The Human–AI collaboration approach augments the trust deficit: the machine offers speed and volume while the humans contribute caring, context, and warmth.

2.6 Justification for This Chapter

This chapter aims to implement the vision of Leveraging AI for Future-Ready Writing Education. The prevailing narratives of AI in writing centers on in the stale (negative) areas of detection (plagiarism) and correction (grammar) and this chapter attempts to redirect the attention of feedback as a social process. The author advocates for the use of AI in writing as feedback 'humanization' instead of 'mechanization' to encourage greater student agency.

The chapter contributes to the development of the Human–AI Co-Feedback Model. It aims to integrate the theoretical with the practical. It combines feedback literacy with academic literacies and AI ethics to propose inclusive and constructive dialogic feedback. It rests on two justifications. One is to address the persistent feedback problem in higher education. The other is to ensure that the integration of AI into writing pedagogy retains rather than diminishes the anthropogenic aspects of teaching and learning.

3. CHAPTER OBJECTIVES

The previously described arguments scrutinize the paradox within the writing pedagogy for higher education: feedback is often said to be among the most powerful influences in learner achievement, yet, for an array of systemic, interpersonal, and educational reasons, feedback almost always underdelivers.

The emergence of artificial intelligence (AI) and automated writing evaluation (AWE) systems poses new opportunities as well as new challenges. This context motivates the chapter on the basis of a number of well-defined goals that not only seek to fill existing voids but also advance the overarching goals of Leveraging AI for Future-Ready Writing Education.

3.1 To examine existing gaps in academic writing feedback

The first problem to address is obtaining detailed information about the shortcomings of feedback practices in multilingual and heterogeneous contexts. While Lee (2020) argues that feedback is vague and sometimes irrelevant, instructors have little time to attend to individualized support. These challenges become heightened in classrooms composed of students from differing linguistic and cultural backgrounds, resulting in an expectation-interpretation gap (Hyland, 2019; Lillis & Scott, 2007).

The purpose of this chapter, then, is to understand and describe how such gaps continue to exist. In doing so, it reframes the feedback the gap as an issue of feedback neglect not as teacher inaction but as feedback neglect arising from structural constraints and pedagogical mismatches.

This also reveals the feedback gaps. Feedback responses that are not well thought out have the potential to erode student confidence, while dialogic and inclusive practices can diminish agency and resilience (Molloy et al., 2020).

3.2 To discuss ways in which AI can assist formative and ethical feedback

The second objective is to critically explore how AI-enabled tools can complement, rather than replace, human feedback practices. Evidence from Fan and Ma (2022) and Wei, Wang, and Dong (2023) shows that AWE systems can improve surface-level features such as grammar and coherence, offering students real-time scaffolding that was previously unattainable at scale. However, Bai and Hu (2017) caution that students' responses to AI feedback vary considerably; without reflection and guidance, algorithmic suggestions can lead to uncritical acceptance or outright rejection.

Thus, the chapter aims to articulate *how AI can be pedagogically aligned with formative feedback practices*. Instead of viewing AI as a "fixer," it is positioned as a *thinking companion* that offers suggestions, prompts reflection, and facilitates iterative drafting. Ethical integration requires transparency, acknowledgment of tool limitations, and explicit conversations about bias, data privacy, and agency (Holmes et al., 2022). By setting this objective, the chapter underscores that AI in feedback must be adopted critically and responsibly.

3.3 To propose the Human–AI Co-Feedback Model

The purpose of this section is to describe and discuss the centrally founded concept of the Human-AI Co-Feedback Model. The model attempts to harmonize the machine's efficiency with the human's empathy and contextual judgment through the relational feedback (Carless & Winstone, 2020) and collaborative intelligence (Sahlberg & Walker, 2021) principles.

The model is composed of three primary components:

- Students' AI post-literacy enables them to appreciate both the tool's opportunities and the tool's constraints.
- Students are positioned as 'agents' who interact with suggestions made by AI and are expected to evaluate them.
- AI feedback must correspond to the course goals, assessment criteria, and instructor comments.

By creating this model, the chapter aims to offer educators a tangible set of principles for the integration of AI into feedback practices which are scalable and ethically sound.

3.4 To demonstrate real-world applications and classroom cases

A fourth objective is to show how the Human–AI Co-Feedback Model translates into practice. Literature alone is insufficient to convince skeptical educators; what matters are tangible, replicable examples of classroom use. This chapter therefore draws on case vignettes from workshops, writing labs, and reflective journals where AI tools were piloted with multilingual students.

For example, Zou, Huang, and Xie (2023) highlight the role of digital feedback systems in facilitating iterative revision cycles. Building on such evidence, the chapter will showcase how students negotiated AI feedback alongside peer and instructor responses, leading to more confident drafting. These examples aim to illustrate both successes and challenges, offering educators nuanced insights into implementation.

3.5 To explore institutional and policy implications

The fifth objective extends beyond a single classroom to focus on institutional responsibilities. While demands on universities grow to include AI technologies, usually due to some efficiency narrative, Holmes et al. (2022) insist, adopting them without an ethical framework could undermine the very idea of education. This chapter therefore aims to investigate the role of institutions in fostering AI feedback literacy through faculty development, student orientation, and a regulatory framework that balances equity and transparency.

The discussion here also positions AI feedback within the wider global framework of educational trust. Every education system, as Sahlberg and Walker (2021) put it, rests not on surveillance and control, but on trust between the various stakeholders of education - the teachers, the learners, and the institutions. If institutions aim to incorporate AI within trust-centered frameworks, they can safeguard the integrity of the educational processes and ensure that technology does not act to the detriment of educational and relational processes.

3.6 To anticipate future trends and challenges

Finally, the chapter seeks to look forward. Feedback practices are dynamic, shaped by technological advances, evolving student demographics, and global educational priorities. The objective here is to *anticipate emerging trends*-for example, adaptive AI systems capable of tailoring feedback to individual cognitive profiles, or culturally responsive feedback agents designed to support marginalized voices.

At the same time, the chapter recognizes challenges: ensuring inclusivity for neurodivergent learners, avoiding over-standardization of language norms, and addressing the potential deskilling of both students and teachers if AI takes on too dominant a role. By articulating these future challenges, the chapter positions itself not as a static account but as a forward-looking inquiry into how AI can be leveraged to co-author the future of writing pedagogy.

Summary of Objectives

In sum, the chapter has six interrelated objectives:

1. Examine existing feedback gaps in multilingual and heterogeneous classrooms.
2. Discuss pedagogically aligned uses of AI for formative, ethical feedback.
3. Propose the Human–AI Co-Feedback Model.
4. Demonstrate real-world applications and classroom case studies.
5. Explore institutional and policy implications of AI integration.

6. Anticipate future trends and challenges in AI-powered feedback.

Together, these objectives justify the chapter's contribution to both scholarship and practice. They demonstrate a commitment to not only documenting problems but also proposing actionable, ethical, and future-ready solutions for writing education.

4. CONCEPTUAL AND THEORY BASE

The challenge of integrating artificial intelligence (AI) into writing pedagogy is not only a technological issue but also a theoretical one. Without a clear conceptual foundation, AI risks being deployed in ways that reproduce inequities, mechanize learning, or diminish student agency. This chapter grounds its argument in four intersecting theoretical and conceptual frameworks: (a) sociocultural theories of learning, (b) feedback literacy and transformative feedback models, (c) ethical AI frameworks, and (d) student voice and identity in academic writing. Together, these perspectives establish a foundation for the Human–AI Co-Feedback Model proposed later in this chapter.

4.1 Sociocultural Theory of Learning

Lev Vygotsky's sociocultural theory provides a cornerstone for understanding writing as a social and dialogic process rather than a solitary act. Vygotsky (1978) argued that learning is mediated by cultural tools and social interaction, and that development occurs within the "zone of proximal development" (ZPD), where learners progress most effectively with guidance from more knowledgeable others. Writing, from this perspective, is not only a cognitive skill but also a socially situated practice shaped by dialogue, collaboration, and cultural mediation (Lantolf & Thorne, 2006).

Feedback occupies a central role in this framework. When instructors or peers provide comments, they are engaging in the scaffolding process that allows learners to extend their abilities. AI can be conceptualized as an additional mediating tool-one that, if designed ethically, can provide scaffolding in ways that expand the learner's ZPD. However, sociocultural theory also warns against viewing mediation as purely technical; the meaning of feedback emerges in the relational context between the learner, the tool, and the teacher (Donato, 2016).

In multilingual classrooms, sociocultural perspectives are particularly relevant. Writing development in a second or third language is not merely a matter of grammar acquisition but of negotiating cultural and disciplinary norms (Hyland, 2019). Feedback-whether human or AI-generated-must therefore be dialogic and culturally responsive, enabling students to engage with academic discourses without erasing their identities.

4.2 Feedback Literacy and Transformative Feedback

The second conceptual pillar is the growing body of work on feedback literacy. Carless and Boud (2018) define feedback literacy as the capacity of students to understand, interpret, and use feedback for learning. This framework shifts the focus from feedback as transmission ("teacher gives, student receives") to feedback as participation, where learners play an active role in making sense of and applying comments.

Molloy, Boud, and Henderson (2020) extend this by emphasizing the relational and affective dimensions of feedback. They argue that effective feedback practices are those that empower students, foster resilience, and support identity development, rather than those that merely highlight deficits. This resonates with the concept of *transformative feedback* (Ajjawi & Boud, 2018), where the goal is not correction but growth.

AI integration must be aligned with this literacy-oriented approach. If students are trained to see AI suggestions as authoritative corrections, they risk developing what Bai and Hu (2017) describe as "correction dependence." Conversely, if AI feedback is framed as one voice among many-alongside peer and instructor input-it can enhance feedback literacy by prompting students to reflect, evaluate, and make deliberate choices. The Human–AI Co-Feedback Model, therefore, positions AI as a facilitator of *feedback dialogue* rather than a final arbiter of correctness.

4.3 Ethical AI in Education

The third framework concerns the ethics of AI in education. Holmes et al. (2022) maintains that educational AI systems must be assessed for more than mere technical precision. Systems must also be assessed for opacity versus transparency, accountability versus evasion, and inclusion versus exclusion. They advocate for cross stakeholder approaches that AI implementations are centered on the learner, and guided ethically.

These ethical concerns are particularly salient in the writing classroom. Automated writing evaluation systems are often trained on diverse sets of texts that reinforce certain dominant usages of English. Systems are therefore at risk of perpetuating bias by reinforcing English-centric rhetorical and academic conventions, while ignoring diverse alternative conventions. Williamson and Eynon (2020) note that critical research in AI ethics has pointed to the problems of algorithmic opacity: learners and teachers are seldom provided the rationale for the feedback given to them, thus are unable to assess the feedback critically.

QUOTED By these standards, the adoption of AI feedback must concurrently be accompanied by AI literacy to both learners and teachers. AI literacy involves the critical interrogations of the limits of the systems, the biases they harbor, and the reflective practices that render algorithmic feedback transparent. In this regard, ethical AI frameworks are not adjuncts to pedagogy. They sit at the core of designing feedback systems that foster inclusion, dialogue, and empowerment.

4.4 Student Voice and Identity in Writing

The final conceptual pillar is the recognition of writing as an identity-forming process. Lillis and Scott (2007) argue that academic writing is not a neutral skill but a site of identity negotiation, where students must navigate dominant discourses while asserting their own voices. For multilingual and first-generation students, feedback can either validate or silence their identities, depending on how it is delivered (Wingate & Tribble, 2012).

Research in academic literacies has shown that deficit-oriented feedback, which emphasizes error correction without acknowledging meaning or voice, can alienate students and discourage participation (Hyland, 2019). Conversely, feedback that acknowledges students' perspectives, validates their linguistic resources, and guides them toward disciplinary participation can foster agency and confidence.

AI integration raises critical questions for this dimension of feedback. If AI systems are designed to enforce conformity to narrow linguistic norms, they risk amplifying marginalization. In a pedagogical context that emphasizes relational pedagogy, artificial intelligence can support student voice by alleviating the burden of trivial corrections, thus allowing instructors to hone in on more complex issues of argumentation, evidence, and critical engagement. As Zou, Huang, and Xie (2023) show, digital feedback systems can enable students to engage in voice and viewpoint experimentation by allowing them space for multimodal feedback at various stages of the drafting process.

4.5 Conceptual Integration: Toward the Human–AI Co-Feedback Model

Taken together, these frameworks establish the rationale for the Human–AI Co-Feedback Model.

- **From sociocultural theory**, the model inherits the emphasis on feedback as mediated, dialogic, and culturally situated.
- **From feedback literacy**, it adopts the principle of positioning students as active participants who critically engage with feedback.
- **From ethical AI frameworks**, it emphasizes transparency, inclusivity, and the importance of tool literacy.
- **From academic literacies research**, it foregrounds student voice and identity, ensuring that feedback practices nurture rather than diminish agency.

Maintaining these standpoints, the Human–AI Co-Feedback Model is designed as a pedagogical framework rather than a mere technical solution. It reconceptualizes feedback as a joint endeavor in which AI supplies immediacy and scale, while humans offer empathy, context, and validation of identity.

5. THE HUMAN–AI CO-FEEDBACK MODEL

As noted previously, the need to reconsider feedback on academic writing is even more pressing in multilingual, multicultural classrooms, where the shortcomings are more pronounced in equity, scale, and dialogic engagement.

While systems with artificial intelligence (AI) such as automated writing evaluation (AWE) systems have promise, they are inherently incapable of catering to the relational and pedagogical demands of students. This involves more than one 'hand.' Feedback models that depend solely on humans, due to time and organizational restrictions, are unable to provide the support and assistance that students expect nowadays.

The Human–AI Co-Feedback Model (HACFM) seeks to integrate the positive aspects of both human and machine feedback whilst alleviating the drawbacks of both. It proposes a feedback ecosystem where AI offers relational, contextual, and identity-affirming guidance while humans provide feedback as a scalable, instant support. Instead of viewing AI as a substitute for teachers or students, HACFM positions AI as a dialogic feedback partner to help with cycles of drafting, reflection, and revision.

5.1 Rationale for the Model

The rationale for HACFM rests on three interlinked observations:

1. **Feedback crisis in higher education**: Feedback is consistently cited as a source of student dissatisfaction, with complaints about timeliness, clarity, and usability (Lee, 2020; Molloy et al., 2020). Instructors, meanwhile, report feedback overload and struggle to maintain relational depth (Carless & Winstone, 2020).
2. **Promise and limitations of AI**: Studies have demonstrated that AWE tools can improve surface-level features of writing and enhance revision practices (Fan & Ma, 2022; Wei, Wang, & Dong, 2023). However, students vary in their responses to AI feedback, and uncritical use risks over-standardization and "correction dependence" (Bai & Hu, 2017).
3. **Theoretical imperatives**: Sociocultural theory (Vygotsky, 1978; Lantolf & Thorne, 2006), feedback literacy (Carless & Boud, 2018), and ethical AI frameworks (Holmes et al., 2022) all emphasize the need for dialogic, reflective, and inclusive practices. HACFM draws directly from these principles to ensure AI serves pedagogy rather than the reverse.

5.2 Core Pillars of HACFM

The Human–AI Co-Feedback Model is organized around *four interdependent pillars*:

Pillar 1: Immediacy and Iteration (AI-Supported)

AI tools provide students with immediate, surface-level feedback on grammar, vocabulary, coherence, and structure. By permitting instantaneous communication, Zou, Huang, and Xie (2023) observed that sustained engagement during writing is achieved through rapid iterative cycles. Still, HACFM has maintained that AI's role must be scaffolding and not authoritative.

Pillar 2: Relational Depth (Human-Supported)

The feedback given by instructors and classmates focuses on identity affirmation, feedback on the student's work, and engagement with higher-order issues like argumentation, evidence, and voice. The depth of the relationships is what Carless and Winstone (2020) call "trust-based dialogue," which surely machines cannot construct.

Pillar 3: Student Agency and Critical Engagement

Students are framed as active decision makers who assess, accept, reject, or modify AI recommendations. Reflective journals or peer discussions, for example, enable them to critically assess AI feedback. This still resonates with Carless and Boud's (2018) feedback literacy framework and ensures students cultivate judgment as opposed to fostering reliance.

Pillar 4: Ethical and Inclusive Integration

The model embeds principles of ethical AI adoption by focusing on ethical use of AI concerning transparency, accountability, and inclusivity (Holmes et al., 2022; Williamson & Eynon, 2020). It is the responsibility of teachers to explain the operational workings of AI tools, facilitate the critical examination of the output, and align the feedback practices on output so that they value rather than suppress heterogeneity, linguistic inclusion as opposed to linguistic gatekeeping (Lillis & Scott, 2007; Wingate & Tribble, 2012).

5.3 Model Diagram

Figure 1. Human–AI co-feedback model (dynamic feedback loops)

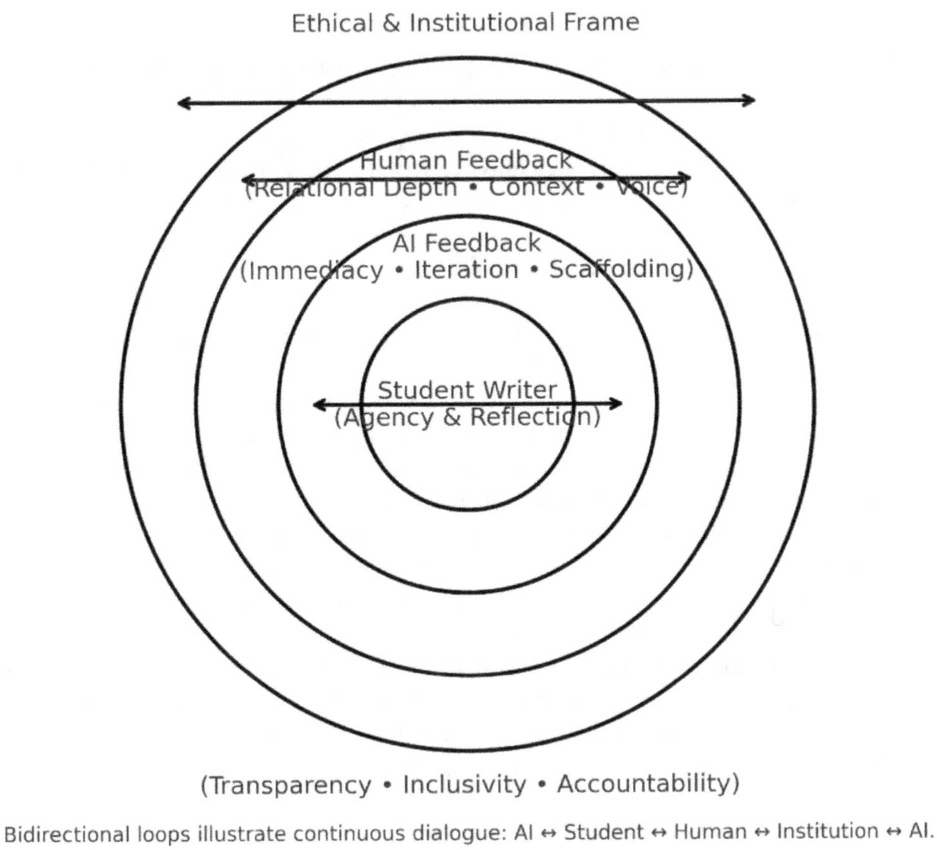

The concentric layers in Figure 1 represent the Student Writer at the core, surrounded by AI Feedback (immediacy & iteration), Human Feedback (relational depth & context), and the Ethical/

Institutional Frame (transparency & inclusivity). Bidirectional arrows illustrate the continuous dialogue among all layers.

5.4 Contrasting HACFM with Traditional Models

Tradition model have largely been:

- Instructor Centered: Feedback is provided in a unidirectional manners, mostly judgmental instead of a discourse.
- Constrained by the Clock: Evaluation comments are given several days or even weeks after the original submission which severely hampers the chances for revision or reworking.
- Negative Feedback: Feedback that focuses more on resolving the rudimentary issues instead of framing the concepts in a thoughtful or creative manner.

HACFM differs in three aspects:

1. Shared Responsibility: AI (responsiveness), the instructor (relational depth) and the learner (agency) each assume part of the responsibility of feedback.
2. Feedback as Conversation: Feedback is no longer a monologue.
3. Social Justice: AI plc(es) are thoughtfully integrated within a mosaic framework, counteracting the default position of discrimination and deficit monocultural imposition.

5.5 Practical Applications of HACFM

The implications for classroom practices and the policies for teaching suggest the following:

- In the Classroom: Students are using AI tools for text generation and in subsequent peer workshops, students draft AI commentaries for critical discussion forums. Instructors provide feedback on higher-order concerns. Students reflection logs in which they describe how they negotiate AI and human contributions.
- On the Faculty Side: Professional development workshops teach faculty strategies for reframing AI feedback as low stakes scaffolding, rather than as authoritative. Faculty learn how to integrate AI profusion with the depth of human relationships so that feedback is psychologically safe and ethically bound.
- On the Institutional Side: Developed policies and procedures delineate the ethical boundaries of AI use which protects student data and upholds accountability and transparency. Institutions provide the necessary resources such as AI literacy modules to students and faculty which empower both the learners and the instructors.

5.6 Anticipated Benefits and Challenges

Benefits:

- Timelier and more iterative feedback cycles.
- Reduced faculty burden on surface corrections.

- Increased student engagement and confidence.
- Greater inclusivity for multilingual learners.

Challenges:

- Risk of over-reliance on AI (Bai & Hu, 2017).
- Faculty resistance to AI adoption.
- Algorithmic bias reinforcing dominant norms (Holmes et al., 2022).
- Institutional gaps in policy and support.

HACFM addresses these challenges by embedding *student agency and ethical literacy* as non-negotiables.

6. CASE EXAMPLES AND CLASSROOM APPLICATIONS OF HACFM

The Human–AI Co-Feedback Model (HACFM) takes shape most clearly when seen in motion within the writing classroom. Rather than remaining a theoretical construct, it becomes a flexible practice that teachers and learners adapt to their contexts. The cases below show how HACFM's four pillars-immediacy and iteration, relational depth, student agency, and ethical inclusion-translate into action in different educational settings.

6.1 Case 1: Iterative Drafting with AI Support

At a metropolitan university, first-year undergraduates worked within a routine called *"Write Revise Reflect."* They composed short analytical essays, received automated feedback through Grammarly Premium and GPT-based suggestions, and then discussed which comments seemed helpful or misplaced. The instructor explicitly explained which aspects of feedback were rule-driven and which demanded human interpretation.

Students completed *AI Reflection Logs*, noting where they accepted, modified, or rejected feedback. This exercise strengthened what Carless and Boud (2018) describe as *student feedback literacy* and prevented the mechanical dependence warned about by Bai and Hu (2017).

During peer review sessions, attention shifted from grammar to reasoning and coherence. The combination of machine speed and human dialogue produced visible improvement. Most students said the AI helped them *notice* errors, while teacher and peer comments helped them *understand* meaning. The recursive movement-AI → Student → Human → Reflection → AI-captured HACFM's cyclical rhythm.

6.2 Case 2: Peer Collaboration through Co-Feedback Loops

In a postgraduate research-writing seminar, multilingual scholars experimented with HACFM in *Co-Feedback Triads* consisting of a Writer, an AI Reviewer, and a Human Reviewer.

1. The Writer uploaded a literature-review section to an AI assistant for structural feedback.

2. The AI Reviewer interpreted the system's suggestions aloud, linking them to disciplinary conventions.
3. The Human Reviewer offered comments on argumentation and logic.

This collaborative scaffolding reflected Vygotsky's (1978) idea of mediated learning and Donato's (2016) expansion of sociocultural support. Rather than accepting AI output passively, students negotiated its meaning, questioned inconsistencies, and refined their rhetorical voice.

By the final draft, participants displayed greater confidence in disciplinary expression and awareness of machine bias. The instructor observed more cohesive arguments and stronger authorial stance, indicating that HACFM can cultivate both competence and criticality.

6.3 Case 3: Institutional Application in Writing Centers

A Southeast Asian university writing center adopted HACFM to manage increasing demand for feedback without adding staff hours. The model paired an AI diagnostic phase with short human consultations.

Students first uploaded drafts to an automated tool for grammar and cohesion analysis. Tutors then reviewed these reports to guide focused discussions on meaning and organization. This hybrid practice resonates with Molloy, Boud, and Henderson (2020), who advocate a learning-centred approach to feedback, and aligns with Holmes et al. (2022) on ethical AI integration.

Within a semester, consultation capacity expanded by more than sixty percent. Students described AI as *quick* and tutors as *clear* and *encouraging*. Orientation sessions on data privacy and bias furthered the transparency principle highlighted by Williamson and Eynon (2020). The result was an institution that met efficiency goals without losing human connection.

6.4 Case 4: Linguistic Inclusion in Multilingual Classrooms

In a South Asian management program, HACFM supported linguistic inclusivity. Faculty introduced AI tools configured for Indian English norms so that feedback would reflect local usage rather than imported standards. Students revised drafts with the AI tool and then discussed tone and style with faculty mentors.

The immediate feedback improved fluency, while teacher conversations linked language choice to audience and intent, echoing Hyland (2019) and Lillis and Scott (2007). One learner summarized the experience: *"The AI showed me where I wrote too much; my mentor showed me why it mattered."*

Scores for clarity and confidence rose significantly, but more telling was the shift in identity. Students spoke of owning their academic voice instead of mimicking foreign models-an outcome that illustrates HACFM's agency pillar in practice.

6.5 Case 5: Faculty Development and Ethical Reflexivity

HACFM led a professional learning project called Feedback with AI at a European teacher-education institution. The workshops leveraged ethical framing from Holmes et al. (2022) and focus on Sahlberg and Walker (2021) for developing a culture of trust.

Teachers reviewed anonymized student work with AWE tools, reflected on AI's feedback philosophy, and thought about shifting their guiding feedback. Despite discontent regarding efficiency in AI vs authenticity in human feedback, discourse helped participants reshape their misconception concerning AI's capability in replacing human assistive feedback evaluation.

At semester's end, the faculty working groups designed departmental policies addressing the issues of transparency, consent to use personal data, and the ethics of data. It was an example of the ethical-institutional aspect of HACFM, and of trust and technology in an institution, both epitomizing reflective use.

6.6 Cross-Case Insights

Many critical observations hold across cases.

1. Feedback is a process hightened by AI; it is a process where human conversation adds value.
2. Reflexive activity alters feedback from a corrective process to self-governance.
3. Universal design guarantees technology augments rather than inhibits student voice.
4. Strategic scaffolding controls the governance and sustaned viability of innovation.

Together, these examples support the dialogic principles of Carless and Winstone (20020) and HACFM, as a model, continues to have a high degree ofy adaptabilty to various contexts and insitutions.

6.7 Implications for Future Practice

For HACFM to flourish, three enabling conditions are crucial.

- **AI Literacy:** Teachers and students must understand both the potential and the limits of automated systems.
- **Feedback Culture:** Open conversation and psychological safety encourage experimentation and growth.
- **Ethical Governance:** Transparent policies secure trust in digital learning environments.

When these conditions align, HACFM moves beyond method to become a mindset-one that balances speed with empathy, structure with freedom, and innovation with integrity.

7. DISCUSSION AND REFLECTION: FUTURE PATHWAYS FOR AI IN WRITING EDUCATION

The case studies within the Human–AI Co-Feedback Model (HACFM) illustrate the ways in which feedback in writing education is no longer a straight taped linear process but a complex interactive ecosystem. The model underscores that meaningful learning is not a question of automation. It is a strategic interplay between human understanding and technological functionality. This chapter is concerned with how HACFM has and will continue to guide this change and what new challenges will arise for research, policy, and pedagogy.

7.1 Reframing Feedback as an Ecosystem

Feedback has always been considered as a transfer of information from one person (the teacher) to another (the student) as a one way communicative stream. Nicol (2010) reframed it as a dialogic process of meaning-making. HACFM builds on this idea by regarding feedback as a never-ending cycle revolving around students, teachers, and intelligent systems.

This gastrodynamics of feedback concentrates on the collaboration aspect as opposed to the traditional approach of evaluation. It is also tied to Siemens' (2005) principle of connectivism, which describes learning as active engagement in dense webs of report networks. In HACFM, feedback is transported through interconnected human and digital networks which determine the amalgam of immediacy, reflection, and mutual understanding.

7.2 Balancing Efficiency and Empathy

A persistent concern in AI-based education is that automation might reduce empathy. Holmes et al. (2022) and Williamson and Eynon (2020) caution that efficiency should never overshadow humanity. HACFM proposes a pragmatic balance in which AI manages repetitive surface-level tasks and teachers focus on mentoring and conceptual depth.

Technology here is not a replacement for care but a mechanism that protects time for it. When the workload of correction decreases, teachers can attend more closely to students' intentions and struggles. Future research should examine how this balance between speed and sensitivity influences engagement and learning outcomes.

7.3 Building Feedback Literacy for the AI Age

Students benefit most when they understand both the logic and the limits of AI-generated feedback. Feedback literacy must therefore include technological discernment. Carless and Boud (2018) describe feedback literacy as awareness, engagement, and action. In the AI era, these must be accompanied by informed skepticism and reflective decision-making.

Zheng and Yu (2019) found that when learners analyze and evaluate feedback critically, they transfer learning more effectively. HACFM encourages this habit by prompting students to question automated suggestions and confirm meaning through dialogue. The result is feedback that nurtures independence instead of dependence.

7.4 Teacher Identity and Professional Renewal

The spread of AI in education is reshaping how teachers define their professional identity. For many, written feedback has long symbolized expertise. Priestley, Biesta, and Robinson (2015) describe teacher agency as the ability to act purposefully and reflectively amid change. HACFM strengthens this agency by positioning teachers as designers of feedback systems rather than passive tool users.

Lahiri and Dey (2022) argue that a pedagogy of care must evolve alongside digital transformation. Professional learning based on HACFM principles can help educators combine technical skill with ethical reflection, reinforcing both confidence and compassion.

7.5 Ethical Horizons and the Question of Trust

Ethical awareness anchors HACFM. Floridi and Cowls (2021) identify five guiding principles for responsible AI: beneficence, non-maleficence, autonomy, justice, and explicability. Policies built on these principles should aim not only for compliance but for cultures of trust.

Trust functions on three levels. Students must trust AI tools to assist without bias. Teachers must trust technology to support, not replace, their judgment. Institutions must trust educators to apply professional discretion. Sahlberg and Walker (2021) emphasize that genuine educational trust is cultivated, not imposed. HACFM embodies this ethic through transparency and shared accountability.

7.6 Inclusion and the Global Classroom

The global classroom benefits most when AI feedback systems respect diversity. Lillis and Scott (2007) remind us that equitable writing instruction recognizes multiple literacies. HACFM encourages educators to choose or design AI tools that reflect local linguistic and cultural realities.

Collaborations among teachers, technologists, and linguists can reduce bias by training algorithms on varied datasets. Such cooperation extends the reach of quality feedback to multilingual and under-resourced learners, advancing both inclusion and excellence.

7.7 Future Research and Policy Directions

Three areas deserve continued exploration.

1. **Longitudinal Research:** Examine how HACFM affects writing development, self-efficacy, and reflection across time.
2. **Cross-Cultural Comparisons:** Study how learners from different linguistic contexts perceive and use AI feedback.
3. **Policy Development:** Create institutional frameworks that balance innovation, fairness, and accountability.

Floridi and Cowls (2021) stress that ethical AI depends on coherent governance. Collaborative policymaking between educators and developers will be essential to realize that goal.

7.8 Reflection: Reclaiming the Human in the Machine Age

HACFM reminds educators that technology should serve humanity. Garrison and Vaughan (2008) observed that technology extends our reach but gains meaning only through participation. The task ahead is to use AI not as a substitute for empathy but as a catalyst for deeper human connection.

AI can identify errors; only teachers can inspire confidence and curiosity. The strength of writing education will continue to depend on how effectively humans and machines learn from each other.

8. CONCLUSION: REIMAGINING FEEDBACK FOR A HUMAN–AI FUTURE

The Human–AI Co-Feedback Model provides a framework through which feedback can remain both technologically advanced and profoundly human. Across this chapter, HACFM has shown how immediacy, empathy, agency, and ethics can work together to make writing education future-ready without losing its soul.

8.1 Revisiting the Core Idea

HACFM integrates technological precision with human understanding. AI supports the rapid revision of text, while teachers and peers ensure that reflection and emotion stay central to learning. This synthesis echoes Freire's (1970) belief that education is a dialogic act grounded in communication and empowerment.

8.2 Lessons from Practice

The classroom cases highlight three enduring lessons.

- Hybrid feedback systems expand access while preserving relational quality.
- Reflection turns correction into growth.
- Ethical transparency maintains trust among all stakeholders.

These lessons confirm that feedback is most effective when it is collaborative, reflective, and ethically anchored.

8.3 The Institutional Mandate

Institutions seeking to implement HACFM must act in three areas.

Policy: Define data protection and disclosure norms that ensure accountability.

Professional Learning: Equip educators to interpret AI feedback critically and integrate it thoughtfully.

Student Empowerment: Teach learners to use AI responsibly and to question its output.

Universities that align these three elements create feedback cultures that combine innovation with integrity.

8.4 Theoretical and Ethical Integration

The framework unites sociocultural theory, feedback literacy, and ethical AI. Vygotsky (1978) viewed learning as mediated by tools; Carless and Boud (2018) emphasized the learner's capacity to act on feedback; Floridi and Cowls (2021) and Holmes et al. (2022) outline ethical principles for responsible AI. Together, these perspectives shape feedback as a cognitive, social, and moral practice.

8.5 The Human Element

Technology cannot replace compassion or intuition. Noddings (2012) reminds educators that care is the moral foundation of teaching. Within HACFM, AI functions as a supportive tool that allows teachers to focus on dialogue, encouragement, and the subtle dimensions of growth. When applied ethically, AI makes teaching more-not less-human.

8.6 Final Reflection

The purpose of education is not to produce flawless text but to nurture thoughtful writers. HACFM demonstrates that artificial intelligence, guided by empathy and ethics, can enrich this purpose. The model envisions classrooms where technology enhances conversation, fosters reflection, and upholds dignity. The future of writing education will depend on educators who use AI not simply to correct language but to strengthen humanity within language.

REFERENCES

Ajjawi, R., & Boud, D. (2018). Examining the nature and effects of feedback dialogue. *Assessment & Evaluation in Higher Education, 43*(7), 1106–1119. DOI: 10.1080/02602938.2018.1434128

Bai, L., & Hu, G. (2017). In the face of fallible AWE feedback: How do students respond? *Educational Psychology, 37*(10), 1214–1229. DOI: 10.1080/01443410.2016.1223275

Carless, D., & Boud, D. (2018). The development of student feedback literacy: Enabling uptake of feedback. *Assessment & Evaluation in Higher Education, 43*(8), 1315–1325. DOI: 10.1080/02602938.2018.1463354

Carless, D., & Winstone, N. (2020). *Teacher feedback: A sociocultural perspective*. Routledge.

Donato, R. (2016). Sociocultural theory and the zone of proximal development. In van Deusen-Scholl, N., & Hornberger, N. (Eds.), *Encyclopedia of language and education*. Springer.

. Fan, N., & Ma, Y. (2022). The effects of automated writing evaluation (AWE) feedback on students' English writing quality: A systematic literature review. *Language Teaching Research Quarterly, 28*, 53–73. Available from ERIC (EJ1369239).

Floridi, L., & Cowls, J. (2021). A unified framework of five principles for AI in society. *Harvard Data Science Review, 3*(1). Advance online publication. DOI: 10.1162/99608f92.8cd550d1

Freire, P. (1970). Pedagogy of the oppressed. *Continuum : an Interdisciplinary Journal on Continuity of Care*.

Garrison, D. R., & Vaughan, N. D. (2008). *Blended learning in higher education: Framework, principles, and guidelines*. Jossey-Bass.

Holmes, W., Bialik, M., & Fadel, C. (2022). *Artificial intelligence in education: Promises and implications for teaching and learning* (2nd ed.). Center for Curriculum Redesign.

Hyland, K. (2019). *Second language writing*. Cambridge University Press.

Lahiri, S., & Dey, D. (2022). Pedagogy of care in digital higher education. *Educational Philosophy and Theory*. Advance online publication. DOI: 10.1080/00131857.2022.2088451

Lantolf, J. P., & Thorne, S. L. (2006). *Sociocultural theory and the genesis of second language development*. Oxford University Press.

Lee, I. (2020). *Teacher feedback in L2 writing: Issues, challenges and future directions*. Cambridge University Press., DOI: 10.1017/9781108684910

Lillis, T., & Scott, M. (2007). Defining academic literacies research: Issues of epistemology, ideology and strategy. *Journal of Applied Linguistics, 4*(1), 5–32. DOI: 10.1558/japl.v4i1.5

Molloy, E., Boud, D., & Henderson, M. (2020). Developing a learning-centred framework for feedback literacy. *Assessment & Evaluation in Higher Education, 45*(4), 527–540. DOI: 10.1080/02602938.2019.1667955

Nicol, D. (2010). From monologue to dialogue: Improving written feedback processes in mass higher education. *Assessment & Evaluation in Higher Education, 35*(5), 501–517. DOI: 10.1080/02602931003786559

Noddings, N. (2012). *The ethics of care: Personal, political, and global.* University of California Press.

Priestley, M., Biesta, G., & Robinson, S. (2015). *Teacher agency: An ecological approach.* Bloomsbury Academic. DOI: 10.4324/9781315678573-15

Sahlberg, P., & Walker, T. (2021). *In teachers we trust: The Finnish way to world-class schools.* W. W. Norton & Company.

Siemens, G. (2005). Connectivism: A learning theory for the digital age. *International Journal of Instructional Technology and Distance Learning, 2*(1), 3–10.

Vygotsky, L. S. (1978). *Mind in society: The development of higher psychological processes.* Harvard University Press.

Wei, P., Wang, X., & Dong, H. (2023). The impact of automated writing evaluation on second-language writing skills of Chinese EFL learners: A randomized controlled trial. *Frontiers in Psychology, 14*, 1249991. DOI: 10.3389/fpsyg.2023.1249991 PMID: 37842718

Williamson, B., & Eynon, R. (2020). Historical threads, missing strands, and future directions in AI in education. *Learning, Media and Technology, 45*(3), 223–235. DOI: 10.1080/17439884.2020.1798995

Wingate, U., & Tribble, C. (2012). The best of both worlds? Towards an English for Academic Purposes/Academic Literacies writing pedagogy. *Studies in Higher Education, 37*(4), 481–495. DOI: 10.1080/03075079.2010.525630

Zheng, Y., & Yu, S. (2019). What has been assessed in writing and how? Empirical evidence from *Assessing Writing* (2000–2018). *Assessing Writing, 42*, 100421. DOI: 10.1016/j.asw.2019.100421

Zou, D., Huang, Y., & Xie, H. (2023). Digital feedback systems in writing education: A meta-analysis. *Computers & Education, 197*, 104688. DOI: 10.1016/j.compedu.2023.104688

Chapter 7
Comparing Teacher and ChatGPT Feedback in EFL/ESL Writing: A Systematic Review

Maryam Hamzehloo
https://orcid.org/0000-0002-8425-802X
Tehran Payame Noor University, Iran

Ali Sorayyaei Azar
https://orcid.org/0000-0003-3539-8250
University of Malaya, Malaysia

Mahdi Hamzehloo
https://orcid.org/0000-0003-0301-5470
Mehralborz University, Iran

ABSTRACT

This systematic review investigates the use of ChatGPT-generated feedback in EFL/ESL writing. It follows the PRISMA guidelines and includes multiple databases like Scopus, Web of Science, and Google Scholar. The researchers reviewed 39 relevant studies that were published between 2022 and 2025. They addressed three main research area: first, the benefits and challenges of ChatGPT feedback in EFL/ESL writing; second, AI-generated feedback and teacher feedback are compared in terms of learners' engagement and motivation; and third, pedagogical implications and gaps in the current research are identified. Findings indicate that ChatGPT feedback enhances mechanical writing skills and promote learners' engagement. However, challenges like overreliance on AI are reported. Comparative analyses suggest that both ChatGPT and teacher feedback improve writing performance, although teacher feedback remains crucial for personalized guidance. This chapter also includes research gaps and implications for EFL/ESL pedagogy and future research directions.

DOI: 10.4018/979-8-3373-5601-3.ch007

INTRODUCTION

Over the past two decades, the landscape of feedback practices in education has been evolving rapidly with the advancement of technology. Automated feedback systems—initially based on rule-based algorithms—have gradually developed into intelligent tools powered by AI and natural language processing (NLP). These tools are increasingly integrated into educational settings to assist teachers and learners in writing assessment and feedback delivery. The growing integration of AI in education has transformed how feedback is generated, personalized, and utilized by learners.

Writing is one of the most important skills in foreign/ second language learning (EFL/ESL), and receiving feedback is an essential part of learning for students. In traditional education, teachers are the main source of providing feedback for students. Peer, teacher, and self-assessment in traditional learning have a significant role in learners' writing and speaking development (Al-Rashidi et al., 2022). Fithriani (2019) emphasized that written feedback improves L2 text quality, stimulates critical thinking, and enhances autonomy. However, these feedback practices are limited due to teachers' workload and the size of the classes. It means, an innovative alternative in writing pedagogy would be revolutionary in the field of writing language learning. With the emergence of AI, novel tools like ChatGPT deliver feedback in educational contexts.

Most recent studies highlighted the effectiveness of AI feedback tools. Wang (2024) reported that AI-generated feedback improves writing fluency and reduces learners' anxiety. Similarly, Mahapatra (2024) found that teachers have limited time in classrooms, so ChatGPT feedback can reduce their workload. He thinks AI tools can be a complementary help and improve students' academic writing. Yuan (2023) further suggested that teachers need to personalize learning, and they use chatbots in error correction. Ramezani et al. (2025) similarly concluded that AI-based corrective feedback improves grammatical and lexical resources while teacher feedback is effective in developing writing skills like organization and coherence. AI tools increase learners' motivation and self-regulation (Rahimi et al., 2025). Besides, these tools improve cognitive and behavioral skills in academic contexts (Koltovskaia et al., 2024). Moreover, Biju et al (2024) found that AI tools reduce learners' anxiety in language learning and improve their performance compared with traditional methods. Esmaeily and Mahdavi Zafarghandi (2025) suggested that AI tools improve teachers' pedagogical strategies and have a positive effect on their professional careers.

Despite the benefits that AI-generated feedback has, it has some limitations. For example, Cao and Zhong (2023) showed that while ChatGPT feedback improved the lexical resources of students, learners think teacher feedback is crucial for syntactic development. Likewise, Lee (2021) stressed that teacher feedback is necessary for students to have meaningful improvement in L2 writing.

The combination of teacher and AI feedback would be effective in ESL/EFL writing. Interestingly, AI tools' feedback cannot be replaced with teachers' feedback. Silitonga et al. (2023) argued that AI chatbots have a complementary role in providing feedback, and they cannot be a substitute for human feedback. They emphasized a balanced integration of human and AI feedback. Similarly, Fan et al. (2024) teacher feedback is vital in academic writing, and students should not replace it with other tools.

Besides writing outcomes, learners' engagement and motivation with feedback are important. Er et al. (2025) pointed out that learners think instructors' feedback is more effective in their writing performance, and it is more engaging. On the other hand, Escalante et al. (2023) observed that students prefer AI tools' feedback as it is automated and develop their writing.

Guo and Wang (2024) reported that compared to teachers, ChatGPT provided organized and content-related feedback.

AI tools also have a pedagogical role in EFL/ESL writing instruction. Li et al. (2024) noted that ChatGPT has a supplementary role in formative assessment. Ji et al (2023) argued that AI can reduce the workload of teachers and be a collaborative instructor. Polakova and Ivenz (2024) found that AI feedback improves grammatical accuracy. AI tools provide context-sensitive support and help students have a better textual organization (Yoon et al., 2023; Han et al., 2023).

Many studies showed both the benefits and limitations of AI-generated feedback in language education. While prior research found that teacher and AI feedback enhance writing skills, few studies investigated learners' engagement in EFL/ESL contexts. Moreover, integrating ChatGPT feedback with traditional feedback in a pedagogical context is not investigated. To address these gaps, this systematic review investigates three key questions.

RESEARCH QUESTIONS

1. What are the benefits and challenges of ChatGPT-generated feedback in EFL/ESL writing?
2. How does ChatGPT feedback compare to teacher feedback in terms of effectiveness, learner engagement, and acceptance?
3. What are the implications and gaps in current research on ChatGPT versus teacher feedback in EFL/ESL writing?

LITERATURE REVIEW

Effectiveness of Teacher Feedback versus ChatGPT Feedback on EFL/ESL Writing Performance

Several studies examined the perception and engagement of learners with ChatGPT feedback compared to traditional teacher feedback. Research highlights the effect of AI-based feedback on learners' motivation, confidence, and writing ability.

Many studies pointed out that AI has a positive effect on language education (Huang et al., 2023; Jin et al., 2025; Liang et al., 2023; Asadi et al., 2025; Alzubi, 2024). Several studies revealed that learners have a good perception of AI. They believe AI tools help them in their learning process (Ghimire et al., 2024; Hou et al., 2024; Mohammadi et al., 2023; Lu & Zeng, 2025). On the other hand, AI tools have some limitations in the educational context and are problematic for learners. For example, Kohenke et al. (2023) stated that teachers need to be trained before integrating AI in education. It would facilitate their job as they have a heavy workload. Besides that, students should not over-rely on AI tools if they want to improve their writing creativity (Kartal, 2023).

A number of studies revealed that ChatGPT feedback is appreciated by students. They believe it is immediate and accessible anytime and anywhere (Fakher Ajabshir, 2024; Ziaei & Tavakoli, 2025). Unlike teacher feedback, ChatGPT provides instant suggestions. It encourages students to engage more actively in writing skills (Bozorgian & Rahimi, 2025; Jafari et al., 2025; Klarin & Livaić, 2023; Zare et al., 2025). Many participants reported that interacting with ChatGPT reduced their anxiety because AI was non-judgmental and supportive (Han et al., 2023).

Some findings indicated that learners increased their motivation and engagement by using ChatGPT feedback (Ghorbandordinejad & Kenshinbay, 2024; Shahsavar et al., 2024; Zare et al., 2025). Besides, learners improve their writing skills as they receive grammar and vocabulary suggestions from ChatGPT (Alsofyan & Barzanji, 2025; Polakova & Ivenz, 2024).

Despite these positive perceptions, several studies pointed out that using AI feedback is challenging. Overreliance on AI feedback is one of the issues that has a negative effect on writing skills (Asadi et al., 2025; Bozorgian & Rahimi, 2025). Some studies reported that students need to be more critical and develop independent editing while using AI feedback (Azap, 2025; Ziaei & Tavakoli, 2025). Moreover, learners believed that teacher feedback is more effective and can develop writing organization (Mun, 2024; Zare et al., 2025; Zeevy-Solovey, 2024).

Overall, the literature revealed that learners prefer to have a blended approach and use both ChatGPT and human feedback to improve their EFL/ESL writing (Han & Li, 2024; Li, 2024; Pack & Maloney, 2023).

Learner Perceptions and Engagement with ChatGPT versus Teacher Feedback

There are a variety of studies that explore learners' perception of ChatGPT feedback compared to teacher feedback. These reports investigated learners' motivation and engagement with this kind of feedback. The results indicate both positive and negative feedback toward ChatGPT.

Many studies reported that ChatGPT feedback was fast and accessible, and useful for improving grammar and vocabulary. Students feel more independent as they can revise their work frequently. It increases learners' engagement in writing tasks as they receive instant feedback (Ghorbandordinejad & Kenshinbay, 2024; Shahsavar et al., 2024; Zare et al., 2025).

Despite many advantages that ChatGPT feedback has, it has some problems. ChatGPT feedback lacks empathy and data privacy (Fakher Ajabshir, 2024; Lee & Choi, 2024). The other issue is a technical problem that most learners face in using ChatGPT (Belda-Medina & Calvo-Ferrer, 2022). Some studies mentioned that ChatGPT feedback is not always contextually appropriate (Asadi et al., 2025; Fakher Ajabshir, 2024; Guo & Wang, 2024). Similarly, studies show that ChatGPT feedback is not accurate and reliable (Pack & Maloney, 2023; Teng, 2024; Zeevy-Solovey, 2024; Zhu et al., 2024).

On the other hand, learners generally have positive attitudes toward teacher feedback. They think it is personalized and contextualized. Teachers are a better resource for providing content organization and deeper writing issues (Azap, 2025; Shahsavar et al., 2024). Teacher feedback is more useful for learning complex issues (Aljasser, 2025; Kartal, 2023; Zare et al., 2025). Additionally, some studies emphasized that teachers' feedback motivates and engages students (Ghorbandordinejad & Kenshinbay, 2024; Zou et al., 2024).

Comparison between the two feedback types suggests that ChatGPT enhances learners' engagement. It is because of the fact that it provides immediate feedback, whereas teacher feedback motivates learners and provides deeper engagement. Some studies reported that learners need a combination of ChatGPT and teacher feedback to improve their ESL/EFL writing skills (Guo & Wang, 2024; Teng, 2024; Zeevy-Solovey, 2024; Zhu et al., 2024).

In short, learners recognized ChatGPT feedback as a supplementary tool in writing. They also believe that teachers provide motivational and context-sensitive guidance.

Pedagogical Integration of ChatGPT and AI-based Feedback in Writing Instruction

The integration of AI-based tools into EFL/ESL writing is discussed widely in recent research. AI-based tools such as ChatGPT are complementary tools in traditional education, but there are still some debates about them. Studies suggest that AI feedback is a supportive tool, but overreliance on it can have a negative effect on learners' autonomy and critical thinking.

Several studies highlighted that ChatGPT feedback should not replace teachers' feedback. While teachers should use ChatGPT for drafting and initial revisions, they should give deeper comments to students. This blended approach reduces teachers' workload and provides multiple perspectives on writing (Asadi et al., 2025; Han & Li, 2024; Shahsavar et al., 2024). Some researchers, like Ziqi et al. (2024), in their studies, pointed out that some students cannot engage with AI feedback. They stated that to address this challenge, we should consider it in our educational system.

Pedagogically, ChatGPT feedback encourages autonomous learning because students receive guidance outside of classroom hours. Some studies reported that integrating ChatGPT increases writing confidence and reduces anxiety of learners (Zare et al., 2025).

On the other hand, some studies mentioned that pedagogical integration of ChatGPT creates problems. Teachers are concerned that students are are overreliance on ChatGPT. They think that overreliance can have a negative effect on students' creativity and critical thinking (Han et al., 2023; Hossain & Al Younus, 2025). In addition, ChatGPT feedback is not completely context-sensitive and culturally appropriate (Alsofyani & Barzanji, 2025; Asadi et al., 2025; Fakher Ajabshir, 2024; Guo & Wang, 2024).

Research emphasized that effective integration requires teachers' guidance and monitoring. It means they should design the use of ChatGPT and evaluate when AI feedback is reliable. It will promote student-teacher interaction (Belda-Medina & Calvo-Ferrer, 2022).

Overall, ChatGPT should have a supplementary role in teacher feedback to enhance learners' autonomy and engagement in EFL/ESL writing rather than replacing teacher feedback. While teachers provide personalized and context-sensitive guidance, ChatGPT improves the autonomy and engagement of learners. This complementary relationship emphasized that the combination of teacher and ChatGPT feedback is more effective in writing instruction.

METHODOLOGY

This SLR analyzed studies that compare teacher and ChatGPT Feedback in the EFL/ESL writing context and focused on studies that were published between 2022 and 2025. The methodology followed the protocol of Preferred Reporting Items for Systematic Reviews and Meta-Analyses (PRISMA). It has three steps of the procedure: "identification", "screening", and "inclusion".

Data Sources and Search Strategy

To explore the current literature, the researchers had a specific searching strategy. They began with a broad scope of exploration to find relevant studies. It covered sources of teacher and ChatGPT feedback in the EFL/ESL writing context. Google Scholar was the primary search engine as it includes studies indexed in major databases such as Scopus and Web of Science.

To ensure a comprehensive search, the process moved from broad to more specific keywords. At first, initial searches with general phrases such as "feedback in EFL/ESL" had around 66,000 records. Then, studies were screened by their title, and 50,000 irrelevant studies were removed as they were not related to writing feedback. After that, the search was refined by more specific phrases such as "AI-enhanced EFL/ESL feedback," which provided approximately 3,000 results. Adding further specific keywords, "AI-enhanced EFL/ESL feedback in writing," narrowed the results to about 2,000 studies. Finally, to focus on comparing teacher and ChatGPT feedback in the EFL/ESL writing context, the keyword "comparing" was applied, resulting in a manageable set of approximately 305 studies for further screening.

The studies were context-specific, and they compared teacher and ChatGPT feedback in the EFL/ESL writing context. All of the studies were published between 2022 and 2025. In total, 39 studies were included in the review. Regarding indexing databases, 32 were indexed in Google Scholar, 19 in Scopus, and 14 in Web of Science. These numbers involve overlaps, as some studies were indexed in more than one database. It should be mentioned that 31 additional sources were cited for background information. They were not included in the total number of studies analyzed (n=39). The number of studies is shown in Figure 1.

Figure 1. Distribution of included studies by indexing database.

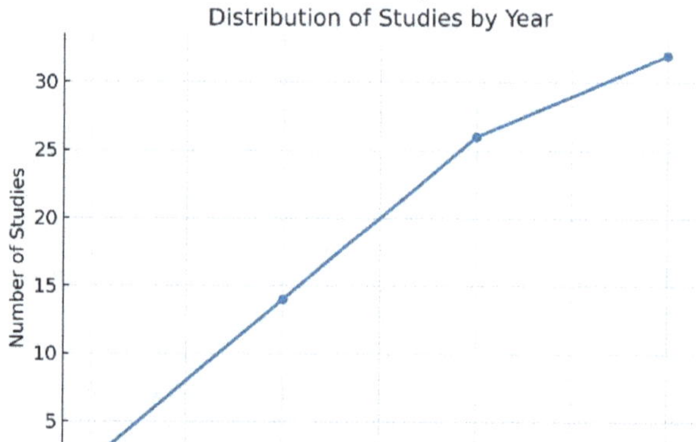

Inclusion and Exclusion Criteria

A set of inclusion and exclusion criteria was developed as researchers wanted only high-quality and relevant studies to be considered.

The following inclusion criteria were applied:

- Studies that are published between 2022 and 2025

- Studies that are in Peer-reviewed journal articles (empirical or non-empirical) and selected conference papers
- Those who are focused on teacher feedback, ChatGPT feedback, or both in EFL/ESL writing contexts
- Those that report empirical findings on writing performance, engagement, or student perceptions (for empirical studies)
- Those that are written in English

The exclusion criteria were:

- Studies that are theoretical or conceptual, and the papers that are not empirical data (except a few included for background or context)
- Studies that are outside the EFL/ESL writing context
- Studies that are not in peer-reviewed journals
- Those that are not accessible in full-text

These criteria ensured the researchers that the main resources are valid and reliable and can address the three guiding research questions.

Study Selection Process

There are four main stages to process the study selection. They are identification, screening, eligibility, and inclusion, and follow the PRISMA guidelines.

Identification: Initially, based on a broad search using keywords such as *"feedback in EFL/ESL"*, approximately 66,000 records were identified.

Screening: Around 50,000 records were removed based on their titles as they were not relevant to writing feedback. The search was then refined with more specific keywords such as *"AI-enhanced EFL/ESL feedback"* and *"AI-enhanced EFL/ESL feedback in writing"*, resulting in a manageable set of approximately 2,000 studies for further abstract screening.

Eligibility: To focus on comparing teacher and ChatGPT feedback in EFL/ESL writing, the keyword *"comparing"* was applied, narrowing the pool to about 305 studies. These were assessed for eligibility, and studies that are not related to teacher or ChatGPT feedback in EFL/ESL writing were excluded.

Inclusion: Finally, 39 studies were included in the systematic review. These studies were published between 2022 and 2025, and they were analyzed in terms of AI feedback type and thematic patterns. The full selection process is illustrated in Figure 2.

Figure 2. PRISMA flow diagram illustrating the study selection process

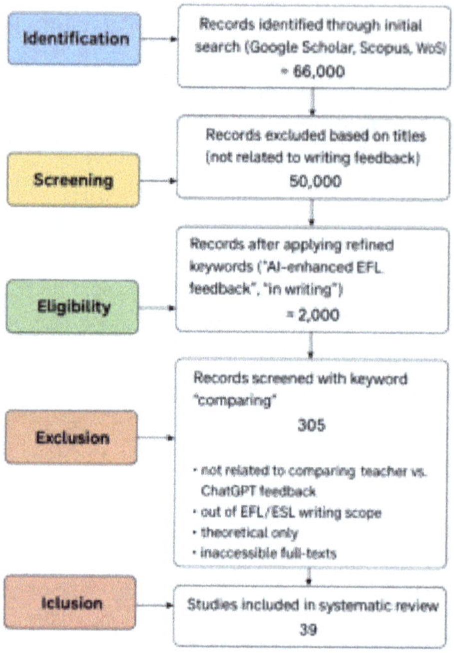

Data Extraction and Thematic Analysis

The final 39 studies were systematically analyzed in Excel form. Data extraction was performed by systematically recording relevant information for each study. By investigating characteristics such as author(s), year, country, participants, type of AI feedback, and study design, the main findings were organized into separate columns. An inductive thematic analysis was then conducted manually to identify patterns and themes emerging directly from the data. The main focus was on the benefits, challenges, and comparisons of ChatGPT feedback with human feedback. This approach enabled a comprehensive synthesis of findings across studies to address the research questions.

FINDINGS

Research question 1: What are the Benefits and Challenges of ChatGPT-generated Feedback in EFL/ESL Writing?

By reviewing these studies, some common benefits and challenges of using ChatGPT-generated feedback in EFL/ESL writing were revealed. These findings show how learners and researchers perceive educational benefits and challenges of ChatGPT- feedback tools in EFL/

ESL writing instruction. The main benefits and challenges reported in the reviewed studies are summarized in Table 1.

Benefits of ChatGPT Feedback

1. They enhance writing performance.

Many studies emphasized that one of the most important advantages of ChatGPT-generated feedback is that it can improve learners' writing performance (Asadi et al., 2025; Banihashem et al., 2024; Bozorgian & Rahimi, 2025; Elviani & Liani, 2025; Han & Li, 2024; Lu & Zeng, 2025; Polakova & Ivenz, 2024; Shahsavar et al., 2024; Teng, 2025; Zare et al., 2025; Zhu et al., 2024; Zou et al., 2024), and interestingly, it improves learners' grammar and vocabulary usage in writing (Alsofyan & Barzanji, 2025; Pariyanto & Tungka, 2025; Polakova & Ivenz, 2024). Moreover, studies indicated that ChatGPT-generated feedback improves organization of ideas (Hossain & Al Younus, 2025; Lee & Choi, 2024; Rezaei et al., 2024) and fosters metacognitive awareness and language fluency (Teng, 2025; Zare et al., 2025).

2. They are Immediacy and Accessibility.

Another notable benefits are that ChatGPT-generated feedback is immediate (Aljasser, 2025; Alsofyani & Barzanji, 2025; Fakher Ajabshir, 2024; Guo & Wang, 2024; Hossain & Al Younus, 2025; Li, 2024; Mun, 2024; Teng, 2024; Tsai et al., 2024; Zeevy-Solovey, 2024; Ziaei & Tavakoli, 2025), and accessible and user-friendly (Bozorgian & Rahimi, 2025; Jafari et al., 2025; Klarin & Livaić, 2023; Zare et al., 2025; Zeevy-Solovey, 2024). Besides, it provides personalized feedback for learners (Ghorbandordinejad & Kenshinbay, 2024; Jafari et al., 2025; Kartal, 2023; Klarin & Livaić, 2023; Zare et al., 2025), and non-judgmental (Han et al., 2023).

3. They Engage and Motivate Learners.

ChatGPT also increased learners' engagement with texts (Alsofyani & Barzanji, 2025; Ghorbandordinejad & Kenshinbay, 2024; Huang et al., 2022; Huang & Teng, 2025; Kartal, 2023; Shahsavar et al., 2024; Teng, 2024; Zare et al., 2025; Zhu et al., 2024). It also prompts learners' autonomy and motivation (Azap, 2025; Han & Li, 2024; Klarin & Livaić, 2023; Lee & Choi, 2024; Li, 2024; Lu & Zeng, 2025; Mun, 2024; Teng, 2024; Teng, 2025; Zare et al., 2025). It was also mentioned that ChatGPT feedback reduces anxiety (Zare et al., 2025) and increases learners' confidence (Lee & Choi, 2024).

4. They Give Pedagogical Support.

ChatGPT feedback can reduce teachers' workload (Guo & Wang, 2024) and increase their confidence and productivity (Ghafouri et al., 2024; Rezaei et al., 2024). It also facilitates teaching and learning processes (Jamshed et al., 2024; Pack & Maloney, 2023; Pariyanto & Tungka, 2025; Rezaei et al., 2024) and promotes student-teacher interaction (Belda-Medina & Calvo-Ferrer, 2022).

Challenges of ChatGPT-Generated Feedback

1. They Have Learner-Related Challenges.

One of the challenges that most students face is overreliance on AI feedback (Alsofyani & Barzanji, 2025; Asadi et al., 2025; Bozorgian & Rahimi, 2025; Han et al., 2023; Hossain & Al Younus, 2025; Rezaei et al., 2024; Teng, 2024; Zare et al., 2025; Ziaei & Tavakoli, 2025). Additionally, some studies mentioned that ChatGPT feedback is not personalized (Ghorbandordinejad & Kenshinbay, 2024; Han & Li, 2024).

2. They Have Quality and Accuracy Limitations.

Many studies reported that ChatGPT feedback is not always accurate and reliable (Guo & Wang, 2024; Kartal, 2023; Klarin & Livaić, 2023; Li, 2024; Pack & Maloney, 2023; Teng, 2024; Zare et al., 2025; Zeevy-Solovey, 2024; Zhu et al., 2024). Some studies mentioned that ChatGPT feedback is not contextually appropriate (Alsofyani & Barzanji, 2025; Asadi et al., 2025; Fakher Ajabshir, 2024; Guo & Wang, 2024). Besides, limited conversational depth and difficulty in handling complex writing issues are among other challenges of using ChatGPT feedback (Azap, 2025; Huang et al., 2022; Tsai et al., 2024; Ziaei & Tavakoli, 2025).

3. They Provide Pedagogical and Ethical Concerns.

Some studies illustrated that learners prefer teacher feedback (Aljasser, 2025; Mun, 2024; Zare et al., 2025; Zeevy-Solovey, 2024; Zhu et al., 2024). Some learners are concerned about ethical issues related to ChatGPT (Kartal, 2023; Li, 2024; Pack & Maloney, 2023; Rezaei et al., 2024; Shahsavar et al., 2024).

4. They Provide Technical and Emotional Limitations.

Belda-Medina & Calvo-Ferrer (2022) mentioned technical problems as a challenge in using ChatGPT for providing feedback. Some studies pointed out that lack of empathy and data privacy, and inability to process advanced tasks are among the problematic aspects of using ChatGPT feedback (Asadi et al., 2025; Fakher Ajabshir, 2024; Lee & Choi, 2024).

Table 1. Thematic Summary of Findings Addressing RQ1: Benefits and Challenges of ChatGPT Feedback

Example Studies	Description	Theme	Theme Type
Asadi et al., 2025; Banihashem et al., 2024; Bozorgian & Rahimi, 2025; Han & Li, 2024; Hossain & Al Younus, 2025; Lu & Zeng, 2025; Rezaei et al., 2024; Shahsavar et al., 2024; Zare et al., 2025; Zhu et al., 2024	ChatGPT improves learners' grammar and vocabulary. It is beneficial for organizing ideas.	Enhancement of writing performance	benefits
Aljasser, 2025; Alsofyani & Barzanji, 2025; Fakher Ajabshir, 2024; Ghorbandordinejad & Kenshinbay, 2024; Guo & Wang, 2024; Hossain & Al Younus, 2025; Jafari et al., 2025; Li, 2024; Mun, 2024; Teng, 2024; Tsai et al., 2024; Zeevy-Solovey, 2024; Ziaei & Tavakoli, 2025	ChatGPT provides immediate and accessible feedback. They are personalized and non-judgmental.	Immediacy and accessibility	benefits
Azap, 2025; Han & Li, 2024; Klarin & Livaić, 2023; Lee & Choi, 2024; Li, 2024; Lu & Zeng, 2025; Mun, 2024; Teng, 2024; Teng, 2025; Zare et al., 2025	ChatGPT increased learners' engagement and motivation. It also reduces anxiety.	Learning Engagement and Motivation	benefits
Ghafouri et al., 2024; Jamshed et al., 2024; Pack & Maloney, 2023; Pariyanto & Tungka, 2025; Rezaei et al., 2024	ChatGPT feedback can reduce teachers' workload and facilitate teaching and learning processes.	Pedagogical Support	benefits
Alsofyani & Barzanji, 2025; Ghorbandordinejad & Kenshinbay, 2024; Han & Li, 2024; Han et al., 2023; Hossain & Al Younus, 2025	Students' overreliance on AI feedback and it is not personalized.	Learner-Related Challenges	challenges
Guo & Wang, 2024; Klarin & Livaić, 2023; Li, 2024; Pack & Maloney, 2023; Teng, 2024; Zeevy-Solovey, 2024; Zhu et al., 2024	ChatGPT feedback is not always accurate and reliable, and it is not contextually appropriate.	Quality and Accuracy Limitations	challenges
Aljasser, 2025; Kartal, 2023; Li, 2024; Mun, 2024; Pack & Maloney, 2023; Rezaei et al., 2024; Shahsavar et al., 2024; Zare et al., 2025; Zeevy-Solovey, 2024; Zhu et al., 2024	Some learners prefer teacher feedback and are concerned about ethical issues related to ChatGPT.	Pedagogical and Ethical Concerns	challenges
Asadi et al., 2025; Belda-Medina & Calvo-Ferrer, 2022; Fakher Ajabshir, 2024; Lee & Choi, 2024	There is a lack of empathy and data privacy.	Technical and Emotional Limitations	challenges

Research Question 2: How Does ChatGPT Feedback Compare to Teacher Feedback in Terms of Effectiveness, Learner Engagement, and Acceptance?

By reviewing these studies, it is illustrated that EFL/ESL learners' engagement preferences in teacher and ChatGPT-generated feedback in writing tasks are different.

A Combination of Both

Several studies (Asadi et al., 2025; Guo & Wang, 2024; Han & Li, 2024; Li, 2024; Pack & Maloney, 2023; Shahsavar et al., 2024; Teng, 2024; Zeevy-Solovey, 2024; Zhu et al., 2024) indicated that learners prefer to have a combination of teacher and ChatGPT-generated feedback. These studies announced that although ChatGPT-generated feedback is beneficial, it should be combined with teachers' feedback to support learners effectively.

Both Feedback Sources Are Equally Effective

Klarin and Livaić (2023) found that there are no significant differences between teacher and ChatGPT feedback. Learners believe that both types of feedback are similarly effective in enhancing writing skills.

Teacher Preference

Several studies highlighted the advantages of teacher feedback. Some of them pointed out the personalized guidance and mentioned that teacher feedback relates to learners' needs (Belda-Medina & Calvo-Ferrer, 2022; Ghorbandordinejad & Kenshinbay, 2024; Ziaei & Tavakoli, 2025). The other advantage is content-focused support (Azap, 2025; Shahsavar et al., 2024) that makes learners choose teacher guidance. Additionally, some studies emphasized that teachers' feedback motivates and engages students (Ghorbandordinejad & Kenshinbay, 2024; Zou et al., 2024). Teacher feedback was generally perceived as more useful for learning and especially for complex issues (Aljasser, 2025; Kartal, 2023; Zare et al., 2025).

ChatGPT Preference

Conversely, some studies revealed that learners prefer ChatGPT feedback. They have different reasons for that. Some studies mentioned that it improves learners' grammar and vocabulary (Azap, 2025; Belda-Medina & Calvo-Ferrer, 2022; Ghorbandordinejad & Kenshinbay, 2024; Huang et al., 2022; Shahsavar et al., 2024). Some of them believe it increased learners' engagement, and it is immediate (Huang & Teng, 2025; Zare et al., 2025), and better text organization and cohesion the other reasons for students to prefer ChatGPT feedback (Zou et al., 2024).

Overall, both teacher and ChatGPT feedback have some advantages, and a combined approach maximizes the benefits of feedback to support EFL/ESL writing. A summary of these comparative findings is presented in Table 2.

Table 2. Summary of studies comparing ChatGPT-generated and teacher-provided feedback

Example Studies	Description	Theme	Theme Type
Azap, 2025; Belda-Medina & Calvo-Ferrer, 2022; Ghorbandordinejad & Kenshinbay, 2024; Huang & Teng, 2025; Huang et al., 2022; Shahsavar et al., 2024; Zare et al., 2025; Zou et al., 2024	ChatGPT feedback was more detailed, immediate, and useful for grammar/vocabulary than teacher feedback.	AI feedback superior	Comparison
Aljasser, 2025; Azap, 2025; Belda-Medina & Calvo-Ferrer, 2022; Ghorbandordinejad & Kenshinbay, 2024; Kartal, 2023; Shahsavar et al., 2024; Zare et al., 2025; Ziaei & Tavakoli, 2025	Teacher feedback was considered more contextual, empathetic, and reliable	Teacher feedback superior	Comparison
Asadi et al., 2025; Guo & Wang, 2024; Han & Li, 2024; Li, 2024; Pack & Maloney, 2023; Shahsavar et al., 2024; Teng, 2024; Zeevy-Solovey, 2024; Zhu et al., 2024	A combination of ChatGPT and teacher feedback produced the best results, balancing immediacy with contextual depth.	Hybrid/Complementary use	Comparison
Klarin and Livaić, 2023	No significant difference found; both ChatGPT and teacher feedback were equally effective in improving writing performance	Equal effectiveness	Comparison

Research Question 3: What are the Implications and Gaps in Current Research on ChatGPT versus Teacher Feedback in EFL/ESL Writing?

The key findings reveal that the use of ChatGPT in EFL/ESL writing has pedagogical effects. Combining ChatGPT with teacher feedback enhances writing accuracy, motivation, and engagement of learners (Klarin & Livaić, 2023; Li, 2024; Pack & Maloney, 2023; Teng, 2024). It provides immediate and accessible feedback (Bozorgian & Rahimi, 2025; Jafari et al., 2025; Klarin & Livaić, 2023; Zare et al., 2025; Zeevy-Solovey, 2024). Learners have positive experiences with ChatGPT feedback and think it increases their confidence and reduces their anxiety (Lee & Choi, 2024; Zare et al., 2025).

However, some research gaps should be considered for future study. There is not enough evidence that show long-term learning outcomes and systematic strategies for integrating ChatGPT into formal writing curricula. Future research should focus on pedagogical and ethical challenges of AI-assisted writing feedback. Moreover, studies show that students often over-reliance on AI, and they do not use it in the pre-writing stage. New studies need to investigate its AI tools on the creativity and critical thinking of students.

DISCUSSION

RQ1: Benefits and Challenges of ChatGPT Feedback

The findings of this review indicate that ChatGPT-generated feedback has many pedagogical benefits for EFL/ESL learners. Several studies pointed out that ChatGPT feedback improves grammatical, lexical, and coherence in EFL/ESL writing (Asadi et al., 2025; Bozorgian & Rahimi, 2025; Han & Li, 2024; Hossain & Al Younus, 2025; Lu & Zeng, 2025; Rezaei et al., 2024; Shahsavar et al., 2024; Zare et al., 2025; Zhu et al., 2024). Learners were also satisfied with the immediacy and accessibility of ChatGPT responses, as it enhances their autonomy and revision behavior (Aljasser, 2025; Alsofyani & Barzanji, 2025; Fakher Ajabshir, 2024; Ghorbandordinejad & Kenshinbay, 2024; Guo & Wang, 2024; Hossain & Al Younus, 2025; Jafari et al., 2025; Li, 2024; Mun, 2024; Teng, 2024; Tsai et al., 2024; Zeevy-Solovey, 2024; Ziaei & Tavakoli, 2025). This AI tool also has a motivational role and increases learners' confidence in their writing (Azap, 2025; Han & Li, 2024; Klarin & Livaić, 2023; Lee & Choi, 2024; Li, 2024; Lu & Zeng, 2025; Mun, 2024; Teng, 2024; Teng, 2025; Zare et al., 2025). Moreover, ChatGPT-generated feedback reduces teachers' workload and facilitates the teaching and learning process (Ghafouri et al., 2024; Jamshed et al., 2024; Pack & Maloney, 2023; Pariyanto & Tungka, 2025; Rezaei et al., 2024).

On the other hand, there are some challenges in using AI tools in providing feedback. Several studies mentioned that one of the disadvantages of using AI-generated tools is learners' over-reliance on these tools (Alsofyani & Barzanji, 2025; Ghorbandordinejad & Kenshinbay, 2024; Han & Li, 2024; Han et al., 2023; Hossain & Al Younus, 2025). Other studies pointed to the lack of contextual sensitivity of AI tools (Guo & Wang, 2024; Klarin & Livaić, 2023; Li, 2024; Pack & Maloney, 2023; Teng, 2024; Zeevy-Solovey, 2024; Zhu et al., 2024). Some researchers pointed to ethical and pedagogical issues that are related to AI tools (Aljasser, 2025; Kartal, 2023; Li, 2024; Mun, 2024; Pack & Maloney, 2023; Rezaei et al., 2024; Shahsavar et al., 2024; Zare et al., 2025; Zeevy-Solovey, 2024; Zhu et al., 2024). Lack of empathy and data privacy, that is technical and emotional limitation, is among the limitations of using AI-generated tools (Asadi et al., 2025; Belda-Medina & Calvo-Ferrer, 2022; Fakher Ajabshir, 2024; Lee & Choi, 2024).

These findings suggest that although ChatGPT enhances learning outcomes, it should be considered as a complementary tool rather than a replacement for human feedback.

RQ2: Comparison with Teacher Feedback

ChatGPT feedback has both advantages and limitations compared to teacher feedback. On the positive side, AI feedback is immediate and consistent, and learners can have access to it easily anytime and anywhere (Huang & Teng, 2025; Zare et al., 2025). In contrast, teacher feedback is related contextually and is personalized (Belda-Medina & Calvo-Ferrer, 2022; Ghorbandordinejad & Kenshinbay, 2024; Ziaei & Tavakoli, 2025). Some studies noted that learners appreciated ChatGPT feedback but still value motivational support and pedagogical depth of teachers' feedback (Ghorbandordinejad & Kenshinbay, 2024; Zou et al., 2024).

Importantly, some research suggested that a blended approach is appreciated, and ChatGPT and teacher feedback should be combined. For example, while AI feedback is surface-level, teachers' feedback is sensitive to cultural appropriateness (Asadi et al., 2025; Guo & Wang, 2024; Han & Li, 2024; Li, 2024; Pack & Maloney, 2023; Shahsavar et al., 2024; Teng, 2024; Zeevy-Solovey, 2024; Zhu et al., 2024). However, in some cases, learners prefer teacher feedback as they think it is more reliable and accurate compared to ChatGPT feedback (Aljasser, 2025; Kartal, 2023; Zare et al., 2025). Overall, the comparison highlights that a balanced integration of both feedback types is necessary in instructional settings.

RQ3: Pedagogical Insights and Research Gaps

The integration of ChatGPT into EFL/ESL writing provides promising opportunities. Some studies suggest that ChatGPT is an effective tool for promoting learner autonomy and reducing teachers' workload (Jamshed et al., 2024; Pariyanto & Tungka, 2025; Rezaei et al., 2024). AI-generated feedback is immediate (Bozorgian & Rahimi, 2025; Jafari et al., 2025; Klarin & Livaić, 2023; Zare et al., 2025; Zeevy-Solovey, 2024), and learners have a positive experience with it as it is not judgmental and learners can use it confidently (Lee & Choi, 2024; Zare et al., 2025).

Nevertheless, there are several research gaps. First, we need more studies on the long-term effects of ChatGPT on EFL/ESL writing development. Second, future studies should focus on the cultural and contextual diversity of EFL/ESL learners who use AI feedback. Third, more empirical work should be done on the ethical and academic integrity of ChatGPT in traditional classrooms. By addressing these gaps, we can integrate AI in language learning in a theoretical and sustainable way.

CONCLUSION

This systematic review explored the role of ChatGPT-generated feedback in EFL/ESL writing. It focused on its benefits and challenges, its comparison with teacher feedback, and pedagogical insights and research gaps in this area.

The findings revealed that ChatGPT feedback has a positive effect on writing accuracy and lexical richness. It also fosters motivation and autonomy. However, it has limitations like over-reliance and ethical concerns in AI language learning contexts.

When compared to teacher feedback, ChatGPT demonstrated advantages in speed and consistency. However, teacher feedback provided personalized and contextualized support. The two feedback types should be combined to take advantage of AI and human instructors effectively.

From a pedagogical perspective, ChatGPT enhances learner-centered writing instruction. However, there are some research gaps, particularly in terms of the long-term effects of cultural and contextual considerations.

In conclusion, ChatGPT feedback has a supportive role and not a substitutive role in EFL/ESL writing instruction. Its integration into traditional classrooms needs pedagogical design by learners and future research. We should ensure that the benefits and limitations of ChatGPT are realized in writing contexts.

IMPLICATIONS FOR PRACTICE AND POLICY

The findings suggest that ChatGPT feedback should be integrated into EFL/ESL writing as a supplementary tool. Teachers can use the advantages of ChatGPT in providing feedback to learners. As the provided feedback is immediate and extensive, teachers can devote their time to higher-order concerns. Teachers can work on the organization and rhetorical appropriateness of writing. This blended feedback model enhances students' autonomy. It also promotes their engagement and motivation in writing skills. Furthermore, teacher training programs should be provided in educational centers to help teachers integrate AI tools with their traditional methods.

In the policy level, institutions should be aware of both the potential and limitations of ChatGPT in educational contexts. Policies should make AI tools accessible for learners. In this way, students can use it easily regardless of their socioeconomic background. Additionally, institutes should improve the digital literacy of students as it develops learners' critical skills.

Finally, policymakers should support more research into the long-term impacts of AI feedback in different cultural contexts.

LIMITATIONS

This systematic literature review has some limitations that should be acknowledged. First, this review only included studies that were published between 2022 and 2025. Second, this study relied on studies that are published in English and in indexed journals. Third, the scope of the review was limited to EFL/ESL writing, and it shows that the findings cannot be generalized to other language skills or contexts where English is the first language. Fourth, most of the studies in this review reported the short-term effect of ChatGPT feedback on EFL/ESL writing. It limits the ability to conclude the long-term impact of AI tools. Finally, AI technologies are evolving rapidly, and the findings of this study may be influenced by a new version of the technology.

RECOMMENDATIONS FOR FUTURE RESEARCH

Future research should focus on the long-term effect of ChatGPT feedback on writing development. Moreover, more research is needed in diverse cultural and educational contexts because most current studies are in higher education. In addition, ethical and psychological dimensions of AI support should be investigated. Finally, different feedback models (AI-only, teacher-only, hybrid) should be compared to find the most effective integration of ChatGPT into language education. In addition, future studies could explore how AI-generated feedback can be effectively integrated into multimodal writing tasks, such as digital portfolios, visual essays, or multimedia projects, to enhance students' creativity and digital literacy skills.

Furthermore, the potential of adaptive learning systems and personalized AI tutors should be examined to understand how they can provide individualized writing support in EFL/ESL contexts. It is also important to develop teacher training protocols that enable educators to effectively mediate and evaluate AI-generated feedback in classroom settings. Finally, researchers are encouraged to adopt diverse methodological frameworks, such as mixed-methods or longitudinal designs, to provide deeper and more comprehensive insights into the long-term impact of AI-integrated feedback systems.

REFERENCES

Al-Rashidi, A. H., Asif, M., Vanani, M. G., & Aberash, A. (2022). Learner-oriented assessment (LOA) practice: The comparative study of self-assessment, peer assessment, and teacher assessment on EFL learners' writing complicity, accuracy, and fluency (CAF), speaking CAF, and attitude. *Language Testing in Asia, 12*(1), 59. DOI: 10.1186/s40468-022-00209-x

Aljasser, A. (2025). Investigating EFL students' perceptions of feedback: A comparative study of instructor and ChatGPT-generated responses in academic writing. *Education and Information Technologies, 30*(16), 1–22. DOI: 10.1007/s10639-025-13649-8

Alsofyani, A. H., & Barzanji, A. M. (2025). The effects of ChatGPT-generated feedback on Saudi EFL learners' writing skills and perception at the tertiary level: A mixed-methods study. *Journal of Educational Computing Research, 63*(2), 431–463. DOI: 10.1177/07356331241307297

Alzubi, A. A. F. (2024). Generative artificial intelligence in the EFL writing context: Students' literacy in perspective. *Qubahan Academic Journal, 4*(2), 59–69. DOI: 10.48161/qaj.v4n2a506

Asadi, M., Ebadi, S., & Mohammadi, L. (2025). The Impact of Integrating ChatGPT with Teachers' Feedback on EFL Writing Skills. *Thinking Skills and Creativity, 56*, 101766. DOI: 10.1016/j.tsc.2025.101766

Azap, S. (2025). The role of artificial intelligence in language teacher education: EFL learners' views on the concept of "ChatGPT" through metaphorical analysis. *Social Sciences & Humanities Open, 11*, 101394. DOI: 10.1016/j.ssaho.2025.101394

Banihashem, S. K., Kerman, N. T., Noroozi, O., Moon, J., & Drachsler, H. (2024). Feedback sources in essay writing: Peer-generated or AI-generated feedback? *International Journal of Educational Technology in Higher Education, 21*(1), 23. DOI: 10.1186/s41239-024-00455-4

Belda-Medina, J., & Calvo-Ferrer, J. R. (2022). Using chatbots as AI conversational partners in language learning. *Applied Sciences (Basel, Switzerland), 12*(17), 8427. DOI: 10.3390/app12178427

Biju, N., Abdelrasheed, N. S. G., Bakiyeva, K., Prasad, K. D. V., & Jember, B. (2024). Which one? AI-assisted language assessment or paper format: An exploration of the impacts on foreign language anxiety, learning attitudes, motivation, and writing performance. *Language Testing in Asia, 14*(1), 45. DOI: 10.1186/s40468-024-00322-z

Bozorgian, H., & Rahimi, H. (2025). Peer E-Feedback vs. Chatgpt-4 Generated Feedback on Academic Writing: A Case of Iranian Undergraduates.

Cao, S., & Zhong, L. (2023). Exploring the effectiveness of ChatGPT-based feedback compared with teacher feedback and self-feedback: Evidence from Chinese to English translation. *arXiv preprint arXiv:2309.01645.*

Elviani, M., & Liani, G. (2025). The Use of ChatGPT Feedback on Writing Quality: A Content Analysis of Students' Writing Assignment. *AL LUGHAWIYAAT, 6(1).*

Er, E., Akçapınar, G., Bayazıt, A., Noroozi, O., & Banihashem, S. K. (2025). Assessing student perceptions and use of instructor versus AI-generated feedback. *British Journal of Educational Technology*, *56*(3), 1074–1091. DOI: 10.1111/bjet.13558

Escalante, J., Pack, A., & Barrett, A. (2023). AI-generated feedback on writing: Insights into efficacy and ENL student preference. *International Journal of Educational Technology in Higher Education*, *20*(1), 57. DOI: 10.1186/s41239-023-00425-2

Esmaeily, J., & Mahdavi Zafarghandi, A. (2025). The Impact of AI-Driven Feedback on Iranian EFL Teachers' Reflective Practice. *Iranian Journal of English for Academic Purposes*, *14*(2), 79–94.

Fakher Ajabshir, Z. (2024). A Comparative Study of Teacher Feedback and Chatbot Feedback on Second Language Learners' Pragmalinguistic and Sociopragmatic Competences. *International Journal of Human-Computer Interaction*, •••, 1–12.

Fan, Y., Tan, S., & Lim, G. Y. W. (2024). EAP teacher feedback in the age of AI: Supporting first-year students in EFL disciplinary writing. *Australian Journal of Applied Linguistics*, *7*(3), 1943–1943. DOI: 10.29140/ajal.v7n3.1943

Fithriani, R. (2019). ZPD and the benefits of written feedback in L2 writing: Focusing on students' perceptions. *The Reading Matrix: An International Online Journal*, *19*(1), 63–73.

Ghafouri, M., Hassaskhah, J., & Mahdavi-Zafarghandi, A. (2024). From virtual assistant to writing mentor: Exploring the impact of a ChatGPT-based writing instruction protocol on EFL teachers' self-efficacy and learners' writing skill. *Language Teaching Research*, •••, 13621688241239764. DOI: 10.1177/13621688241239764

Ghimire, P. R., Neupane, B. P., & Dahal, N. (2024). Generative AI and AI tools in English language teaching and learning: An exploratory research. *English Language Teaching Perspectives*, *9*(1-2), 30–40. DOI: 10.3126/eltp.v9i1-2.68716

Ghorbandordinejad, F., & Kenshinbay, T. (2024). Exploring AI-Driven Adaptive Feedback in the Second Language Writing Skills Prompt: AI Technology in Language Teaching. *EIKI Journal of Effective Teaching Methods, 2(3).*

Guo, K., & Wang, D. (2024). To resist it or to embrace it? Examining ChatGPT's potential to support teacher feedback in EFL writing. *Education and Information Technologies*, *29*(7), 8435–8463. DOI: 10.1007/s10639-023-12146-0

Han, J., & Li, M. (2024). Exploring ChatGPT-supported teacher feedback in the EFL context. *System*, *126*, 103502. DOI: 10.1016/j.system.2024.103502

Han, J., Yoo, H., Myung, J., Kim, M., Lee, T. Y., Ahn, S. Y., . . . Answer, A. N. (2023, December). Exploring student-ChatGPT dialogue in EFL writing education. *In Thirty-seventh conference on neural information processing systems, neural information processing systems foundation.*

Han, J., Yoo, H., Myung, J., Kim, M., Lim, H., Kim, Y., . . . Oh, A. (2023). LLM-as-a-tutor in EFL Writing Education: Focusing on Evaluation of Student-LLM Interaction. *arXiv preprint arXiv:2310.05191.*

Hossain, M. K., & Al Younus, M. A. (2025). Teachers' perspectives on integrating ChatGPT into EFL writing instruction. *TESOL Communications*, *4*(1), 41–60.

Hou, X., He, S., & Cuigong, R. (2024, June). Learner Use of AI-Generated Feedback for Written Corrective Feedback in L2 Writing: Usefulness, User Proficiency and Attitude. *In Proceedings of the 2024 8th International Conference on Education and Multimedia Technology (pp.* 70-76*).* DOI: 10.1145/3678726.3678767

Huang, J., & Teng, M. F. (2025). Peer feedback and ChatGPT-generated feedback on Japanese EFL students' engagement in a foreign language writing context. *Digital Applied Linguistics*, *2*, 102469–102469. DOI: 10.29140/dal.v2.102469

Huang, W., Hew, K. F., & Fryer, L. K. (2022). Chatbots for language learning—Are they really useful? A systematic review of chatbot-supported language learning. *Journal of Computer Assisted Learning*, *38*(1), 237–257. DOI: 10.1111/jcal.12610

Huang, X., Zou, D., Cheng, G., Chen, X., & Xie, H. (2023). Trends, research issues and applications of artificial intelligence in language education. *Journal of Educational Technology & Society*, *26*(1), 112–131.

Jafari, S., Fakhraee, L., & Teimourtash, M. (2025). The Impact of Artificial Intelligence (chat GPT) on Writing Accuracy of Iranian Intermediate EFL Learners and Their Level of Motivation. *Technology Assisted Language Education*, *3*(1), 90–109.

Jamshed, M., Manjur Ahmed, A. S. M., Sarfaraj, M., & Warda, W. U. (2024). The Impact of ChatGPT on English Language Learners' Writing Skills: An Assessment of AI Feedback on Mobile. *International Journal of Interactive Mobile Technologies*, *18*(19), 18–36. DOI: 10.3991/ijim.v18i19.50361

Ji, H., Han, I., & Ko, Y. (2023). A systematic review of conversational AI in language education: Focusing on the collaboration with human teachers. *Journal of Research on Technology in Education*, *55*(1), 48–63. DOI: 10.1080/15391523.2022.2142873

Jin, F. J. Y., Maheshi, B., Lai, W., Li, Y., Gasevic, D., Chen, G., Charwat, N., Chan, P. W. K., Martinez-Maldonado, R., Gašević, D., & Tsai, Y. S. (2025). Students' Perceptions of Generative AI-Powered Learning Analytics in the Feedback Process: A Feedback Literacy Perspective. *Journal of Learning Analytics*, *12*(1), 152–168. DOI: 10.18608/jla.2025.8609

Kartal, G. (2023). Contemporary language teaching and learning with ChatGPT. *Contemporary Research in Language and Linguistics (ISSN: 2980-2253), 1(1).*

Klarin, Z., & Livaić, T. (2023). Application of artificial intelligence language model ChatGPT in higher education. *Zbornik radova Veleučilišta u Šibeniku, 17(3-4), 99-112.*

Koltovskaia, S., Rahmati, P., & Saeli, H. (2024). Graduate students' use of ChatGPT for academic text revision: Behavioral, cognitive, and affective engagement. *Journal of Second Language Writing*, *65*, 101130. DOI: 10.1016/j.jslw.2024.101130

Lee, I. (2021). The development of feedback literacy for writing teachers. *TESOL Quarterly*, *55*(3), 1048–1059. DOI: 10.1002/tesq.3012

Lee, J., & Choi, H. (2024). ChatGPT as a Tool in EFL Writing: *An Analysis of Students Usage and Perceptions. , 40(3), 3-28.*

Li, J., Huang, J., Wu, W., & Whipple, P. B. (2024). Evaluating the role of ChatGPT in enhancing EFL writing assessments in classroom settings: A preliminary investigation. *Humanities & Social Sciences Communications*, *11*(1), 1–9. DOI: 10.1057/s41599-024-03755-2

Li, M. (2024). Leveraging ChatGPT for Second Language Writing Feedback and Assessment. [IJCALLT]. *International Journal of Computer-Assisted Language Learning and Teaching*, *14*(1), 1–11. DOI: 10.4018/IJCALLT.360382

Liang, J. C., Hwang, G. J., Chen, M. R. A., & Darmawansah, D. (2023). Roles and research foci of artificial intelligence in language education: An integrated bibliographic analysis and systematic review approach. *Interactive Learning Environments*, *31*(7), 4270–4296. DOI: 10.1080/10494820.2021.1958348

Lu, D., & Zeng, Y. (2025). Exploring the use of ChatGPT-generated model texts as a feedback instrument: EFL students' text quality and perceptions. *Innovation in Language Learning and Teaching*, •••, 1–21. DOI: 10.1080/17501229.2025.2525341

Mahapatra, S. (2024). Impact of ChatGPT on ESL students' academic writing skills: A mixed methods intervention study. *Smart Learning Environments*, *11*(1), 9. DOI: 10.1186/s40561-024-00295-9

Mohammadi, R., Borna, P., & Zoghi, R. (2023). The Effect of Employing Grammarly on Iranian EFL Learners' Writing Performance. *International Journal of Research in English Education*, *8*(5), 187–197.

Mun, C. Y. (2024). EFL learners' English writing feedback and their perception of using ChatGPT. *Journal of English Teaching through Movies and Media, 25(2), 26-39.*

Pack, A., & Maloney, J. (2023). Using generative artificial intelligence for language education research: Insights from using OpenAI's ChatGPT. *TESOL Quarterly*, *57*(4), 1571–1582. DOI: 10.1002/tesq.3253

Pariyanto, P., & Tungka, N. F. (2025). ChatGPT As a Formative Feedback Tool: Improving Narrative Essay Writing Among EFL Students. *Edulitics (Education, Literature, and Linguistics). Journal*, *10*(1), 71–84.

Polakova, P., & Ivenz, P. (2024). The impact of ChatGPT feedback on the development of EFL students' writing skills. *Cogent Education*, *11*(1), 2410101. DOI: 10.1080/2331186X.2024.2410101

Rahimi, A. R., Sheyhkholeslami, M., & Pour, A. M. (2025). Uncovering personalized L2 motivation and self-regulation in ChatGPT-assisted language learning: *A hybrid PLS-SEM-ANN approach. Computers in Human Behavior Reports*, *17*, 100539. DOI: 10.1016/j.chbr.2024.100539

Ramezani, A., Bijani, H., & Oroji, M. R. (2025). Comparative Analysis of AI vs. Human Feedback Effects on IELTS Candidates' Writing Performance. *Journal of Foreign Language Teaching and Translation Studies*, *10*(1), 17–40.

Rezaei, M., Salehi, H., & Tabatabaei, O. (2024, February). Uses and misuses of ChatGPT as an AI-language model in academic writing. *In 2024 10th International Conference on Artificial Intelligence and Robotics (QICAR) (pp. 256-260). IEEE.*

Shahsavar, Z., Kafipour, R., Khojasteh, L., & Pakdel, F. (2024, December). Is artificial intelligence for everyone? Analyzing the role of ChatGPT as a writing assistant for medical students. [). Frontiers Media SA.]. *Frontiers in Education*, *9*, 1457744. DOI: 10.3389/feduc.2024.1457744

Silitonga, L. M., Hawanti, S., Aziez, F., Furqon, M., Zain, D. S. M., Anjarani, S., & Wu, T. T. (2023, August). The Impact of AI Chatbot-Based Learning on Students' Motivation in English Writing Classroom. *In International Conference on Innovative Technologies and Learning (pp. 542-549). Cham: Springer Nature Switzerland.* DOI: 10.1007/978-3-031-40113-8_53

Teng, M. F. (2024). "ChatGPT is the companion, not enemies": EFL learners' perceptions and experiences in using ChatGPT for feedback in writing. *Computers and Education: Artificial Intelligence*, *7*, 100270. DOI: 10.1016/j.caeai.2024.100270

Teng, M. F. (2025). Metacognitive awareness and EFL learners' perceptions and experiences in utilising ChatGPT for writing feedback. *European Journal of Education*, *60*(1), e12811. DOI: 10.1111/ejed.12811

Tsai, C. Y., Lin, Y. T., & Brown, I. K. (2024). Impacts of ChatGPT-assisted writing for EFL English majors: Feasibility and challenges. *Education and Information Technologies*, *29*(17), 22427–22445. DOI: 10.1007/s10639-024-12722-y

Wang, D. (2024). Teacher-versus AI-generated (Poe application) corrective feedback and language learners' writing anxiety, complexity, fluency, and accuracy. *International Review of Research in Open and Distance Learning*, *25*(3), 37–56. DOI: 10.19173/irrodl.v25i3.7646

Yoon, S. Y., Miszoglad, E., & Pierce, L. R. (2023). Evaluation of ChatGPT feedback on ELL writers' coherence and cohesion. *arXiv preprint arXiv:2310.06505.*

Yuan, Y. (2023). An empirical study of the efficacy of AI chatbots for English as a foreign language learning in primary education. *Interactive Learning Environments*, •••, 1–16.

Zare, J., Al-Issa, A., & Madiseh, F. R. (2025). Interacting with ChatGPT in essay writing: *A study of L2 learners' task motivation. ReCALL*, *37*(3), 1–18. DOI: 10.1017/S0958344025000035

Zare, J., Ranjbaran Madiseh, F., & Derakhshan, A. (2025). Generative AI and English essay writing: Exploring the role of ChatGPT in enhancing learners' task engagement. *Applied Linguistics*, •••, amaf045. DOI: 10.1093/applin/amaf045

Zeevy-Solovey, O. (2024). Comparing peer, ChatGPT, and teacher corrective feedback in EFL writing: Students' perceptions and preferences. *Technology in Language Teaching & Learning*, *6*(3), 1482–1482. DOI: 10.29140/tltl.v6n3.1482

Zhu, Y., Zhang, L., Zong, R., & Sun, H. (2024). Exploring AI-Generated Feedback on English Writing: A Case Study of ChatGPT. *US-China Foreign Language*, *22*(3), 144–153.

Ziaei, S., & Tavakoli, M. (2025). Combined Effects of Task Sequencing and Corrective Feedback on EFL Learners' Writing: A comparison between human raters and ChatGPT. *Journal of English Language Teaching and Learning*, *17*(35), 439–452.

Ziqi, C., Xinhua, Z., Qi, L., & Wei, W. (2024). L2 students' barriers in engaging with form and content-focused AI-generated feedback in revising their compositions. *Computer Assisted Language Learning*, •••, 1–21. DOI: 10.1080/09588221.2024.2422478

Zou, S., Guo, K., Wang, J., & Liu, Y. (2024). Investigating students' uptake of teacher-and ChatGPT-generated feedback in EFL writing: A comparison study. *Computer Assisted Language Learning*, •••, 1–30.

Chapter 8
Balancing Support and Autonomy in ELT Master Students' Use of AI for Academic Writing

Nakiye Üvek
Ministry of National Education, Turkey

Osman Solmaz
https://orcid.org/0000-0003-2983-1177
Dicle University, Turkey

ABSTRACT

This study examines how Master of Arts in English Language Teaching students in Türkiye perceive, justify, and incorporate artificial intelligence (AI) tools into their academic writing. Through qualitative interviews with twelve postgraduate students, the study examines the pedagogical, cognitive, and ethical implications of using AI in multilingual higher education. Participants largely viewed AI as a useful tool for improving linguistic accuracy, productivity, and writing confidence. They used AI throughout the writing process, particularly for grammar correction, paraphrasing, and enhancing coherence. However, participants also expressed concerns about diminished critical thinking, overreliance on AI, and the erosion of authorial voice. These concerns were further compounded by the absence of institutional guidelines to support ethical decision-making. The study emphasizes the need for AI literacy and ethical frameworks, advocating for pedagogical approaches that balance technological support with critical thinking and academic autonomy.

1. INTRODUCTION

Artificial Intelligence (AI) and Machine Learning (ML) are transforming higher education, opening new possibilities for language learning, writing development, and instructional design. In English as a Foreign Language (EFL) contexts, AI tools (e.g., generative text models to auto-

DOI: 10.4018/979-8-3373-5601-3.ch008

mated feedback systems) are increasingly embedded in both classroom teaching and self-directed learning (Cope et al., 2021; Huang et al., 2023). Research shows that these tools can improve grammatical accuracy, cohesion, and style while supporting idea generation, translation, and text organization (Kulaksız, 2024; Liu et al., 2023; Song & Song, 2023). For multilingual postgraduate writers, such affordances provide an additional scaffold in navigating the linguistic precision and disciplinary conventions required for advanced academic work.

However, the integration of AI into academic writing remains a pedagogical point of discussion. Scholars caution that these technologies may foster overreliance, reduce critical thinking, and homogenize writing style, while also raising concerns about academic integrity (Sabharwal et al., 2023; Zhai et al., 2024). Ethical debates focus on plagiarism, transparency, and the accuracy of AI outputs, with some studies noting that AI-generated texts often lack cultural nuance, emotional depth, and discipline-specific sophistication (Chen et al., 2022; O'Neill & Russell, 2019). In many higher education settings, the absence of clear institutional guidelines leaves students to navigate these issues independently, relying on their own judgment to balance cognitive, ethical, and technical considerations (Aljuaid, 2024). In response to these complexities, Cope et al. (2021) emphasize the importance of aligning AI integration with pedagogical values and epistemological clarity. Instead of treating AI as a neutral tool, they introduce the concept of *AI-enabled learning ecologies,* which are dynamic systems in which knowledge, assessment, and learning processes are co-constructed by humans and machines. This perspective reframes AI as not only a support mechanism, but also a participant in reshaping how writing is taught, evaluated, and ethically negotiated.

In Türkiye, AI use in EFL and English Language Teaching (ELT) programs is still emerging and uneven. Recent studies report both optimism regarding its potential to enhance engagement and writing proficiency, and caution regarding ethical risks, unequal access, and teacher preparedness (Çiftçi, 2024; Elkatmiş, 2024; Keser & Pektaş, 2024). While prior research has examined AI adoption at the undergraduate level, little is known about how postgraduate ELT students perceive and use AI in academic writing. This is a critical gap, given that postgraduate writing not only demands high-level language competence but also involves developing a scholarly identity, critical thinking skills, and professional ethics.

This study addresses that gap by examining how MA ELT students at a state university in Türkiye perceive, justify, and integrate AI tools into their academic writing. In this study, "AI tools" refers to natural language processing technologies and writing support platforms (e.g., ChatGPT, Grammarly, DeepL, and Quillbot) which were used by participants for tasks including translation, paraphrasing, grammar correction, summarization, and content refinement. The study focuses on the benefits, challenges, and ethical considerations they associate with AI use, offering insights that can inform institutional policy and pedagogical practice. It is guided by three questions: (1) How do MA ELT students perceive and justify their use of AI tools in relation to traditional academic writing practices? (2) How do they use AI tools to support their academic writing development? (3) What ethical concerns and perceived limitations do they associate with AI use in academic writing? By situating these questions within current debates on AI in language education, the study aims to contribute to the development of AI literacy training, ethical guidelines, and pedagogical strategies.

2. LITERATURE REVIEW

This literature review synthesizes emerging research on the integration of Artificial Intelligence (AI) in English as a Foreign Language (EFL) writing education, with a focus on postgraduate contexts. It is organized thematically into four strands that reflect current debates and pedagogical tensions: (1) AI in EFL writing as linguistic scaffolding, (2) AI and feedback mechanisms, (3) ethical use and academic integrity, and (4) institutional policies and governance. These strands offer a critical backdrop for understanding how prospective English language teachers navigate AI-mediated academic writing. Although studies have examined the impact of AI on linguistic development and learner motivation, few have explored how postgraduate ELT students in under-researched contexts, such as Türkiye, interpret the pedagogical, ethical, and institutional dimensions of AI. This study addresses that gap by adopting a qualitative lens and grounding its analysis in Cope et al.'s (2021) AI-enabled learning ecologies framework, which conceptualizes AI not merely as a tool, but as a co-actor in the co-construction of knowledge, authorship, and ethical practice.

2.1 AI in EFL Writing: Linguistic Support and Scaffolding

The integration of artificial intelligence (AI) into English as a foreign language (EFL) education has grown rapidly, especially in the area of academic writing instruction. AI-powered tools now provide real-time grammar corrections, vocabulary enhancements, and stylistic feedback, helping learners overcome linguistic and rhetorical obstacles in second-language writing. These capabilities are particularly important in postgraduate settings, where students must adhere to rigorous academic standards and disciplinary conventions.

A multitude of studies have underscored the linguistic scaffolding potential of these tools. For instance, Kulaksız (2024) and Zhu et al. (2024) found that generative AI tools improved grammar, cohesion, and academic tone in student writing. Sangkala and Mardonovna (2024) emphasized the efficacy of these tools for sentence-level corrections and structural refinement, while Raheem et al. (2023) underscored the importance of stylistic adjustments during the revision process. These applications extend beyond mere surface-level editing, as Mohebbi (2025) observes. AI systems adapt to learners' needs, fostering motivation and sustained engagement. In a similar vein, Solmaz (2020) demonstrated how digital annotation tools in EFL reading contexts facilitated collaborative meaning-making and fostered academic literacy through learner-driven, dialogic engagement. While not centered on AI, this work underscores the manner in which digitally mediated environments can function as a scaffold for language learning and self-regulated literacy practices. These phenomena correspond to the motivational and strategic affordances that have been observed in more recent artificial intelligence-assisted writing tools.

The writing process itself has become more iterative and exploratory with AI integration. Rad et al. (2024) and Sol and Heng (2024) describe how students utilize AI from the initial brainstorming phase to the final revisions, leveraging features such as natural language processing (NLP) and adaptive text generation. Such tools, including ChatGPT and DeepL Write, assist learners in experimenting with phrasing, coherence, and organization.

Notwithstanding these advantages, concerns regarding overreliance persist. Sabharwal et al. (2023) and Zhai et al. (2024) have expressed reservations regarding the long-term implications of AI's pervasive use, particularly with regard to the potential homogenization of writing styles and the diminution of critical thinking. Learners may unintentionally accept the outputs of algorithms without engaging with the rhetorical choices involved. In order to address this issue, O'Neill and Russell (2019) propose a blended approach, integrating AI input with human feedback. This strategy is intended to safeguard learner agency and voice in the learning process.

This study employs Cope et al.'s (2021) *AI-enabled learning ecologies*, which conceptualize AI not merely as a tool, but as an active participant in shaping how learners access, produce, and reflect on academic writing. Within these sociotechnical systems, students must continuously negotiate decisions about language, authorship, and ethical engagement, thereby highlighting the evolving nature of academic literacy in AI-rich environments.

2.2 AI and Feedback Mechanisms in Academic Writing

One of the most widely acknowledged contributions of AI tools in EFL education is their capacity to provide real-time, adaptive feedback, particularly in academic writing contexts. Tools such as Grammarly, Quillbot, and ChatGPT offer language-focused corrections on grammar, vocabulary, and sentence structure, while also assisting with coherence, cohesion, and text organization (Kulaksız, 2024; Raheem et al., 2023; Sangkala & Mardonovna, 2024). These functionalities assist EFL writers in revising and refining their texts with greater autonomy, often at a faster rate than would be possible with human feedback. In recent studies, participants identified such support as valuable for improving clarity, adherence to academic conventions, and overall writing quality (Song & Song, 2023; Zhu et al., 2024).

AI-supported feedback systems have also been found to reduce cognitive load by automating lower-order language tasks, thus freeing cognitive resources for higher-level thinking and content development (Gayed et al., 2022; Mohebbi, 2025). In the context of EFL, this scaffolding effect is particularly beneficial for learners who are confronted with the challenges of linguistic complexity and disciplinary expectations. Adaptive platforms, as discussed by Jadhav et al. (2024) and Sol and Heng (2024), adapt their feedback based on users' evolving input, thereby enabling a more iterative and personalized writing process. These tools facilitate not only surface-level accuracy but also metacognitive reflection on writing choices.

Additionally, research has identified the necessity of exercising caution with respect to over-reliance on AI feedback. Research conducted by Sabharwal et al. (2023) and Zhai et al. (2024) indicates that while AI can enhance technical accuracy, it may also result in the homogenization of writing style and the suppression of students' authorial voice. Concerns have also been raised regarding the generic nature of some AI-generated suggestions, which may lack the contextual sensitivity or critical depth provided by human instructors (Chen et al., 2022). As O'Neill and Russell (2019) contend, the most effective writing support is derived from a balance between AI-assisted feedback and human mentorship, wherein each complements the other's strengths.

A comprehensive review of the relevant literature reveals a multifaceted perspective on the efficacy of AI feedback. The literature suggests that AI feedback is efficient, accessible, and supportive, particularly for surface-level revision tasks. However, it is important to note that AI feedback cannot substitute for the pedagogical and relational dimensions of teacher feedback. These findings underscore the necessity of critical engagement with AI tools and pedagogical models that guide students in integrating automated feedback responsibly and reflectively into their academic writing processes.

2.3 Ethical Use and Academic Integrity

While AI offers linguistic and pedagogical affordances, its integration into academic writing also raises complex ethical questions concerning authorship, originality, and intellectual responsibility. As AI systems become more sophisticated, the distinction between authentic student authorship and algorithmically generated text has become increasingly challenging, thereby prompting debates concerning the acceptable scope of assistance in higher education (Aljuaid, 2024; Solmaz, 2023). In EFL contexts, where learners must navigate linguistic and cultural asymmetries, these questions are further complicated by varying levels of digital literacies and institutional guidance.

Scholars emphasize that the ethical implications of AI in writing are closely tied to issues of academic integrity, transparency, and responsible use. As Nguyen et al. (2024) emphasize, the necessity of clearly articulated policies and AI literacy programs is paramount to assist students in making informed decisions regarding the utilization of such tools. In a similar vein, Solmaz (2023) and Wang (2024) argue that the integration of AI within educational frameworks must be supported by pedagogical frameworks that encourage critical evaluation and ethical reflection. This ensures that technology enhances rather than undermines cognitive engagement and scholarly integrity. Without such scaffolding, students may risk developing dependency on AI feedback or engaging in unintentional misconduct due to unclear institutional expectations.

Concerns regarding privacy, bias, and misinformation also influence the discourse surrounding the ethical use of AI. Mohebbi (2025) offers a critical perspective on the potential limitations of generative models, highlighting their capacity to reproduce bias and factual inaccuracies inherent in their training data. This phenomenon has the potential to distort students' comprehension of disciplinary discourse. Chen et al. (2022) similarly warn that automated systems lack the sociocultural awareness necessary to represent the contextual nuances of human communication, potentially leading to homogenized and decontextualized writing. These risks underscore the necessity for human oversight and ethical safeguards to accompany technological adoption in academic settings.

At a conceptual level, Cope et al.'s (2021) notion of AI-enabled learning ecologies offers a productive lens for interpreting these ethical dynamics. Within such ecologies, students navigate learning environments co-populated by human and non-human actors, continually negotiating the boundaries of autonomy and assistance. Consequently, ethical literacy can be conceptualized as a form of ecological agency, defined as the capacity to discern when to depend on, inquire about, or resist AI contributions in the pursuit of authentic academic work. This perspective situates ethics not as a static rule set but as an ongoing process of critical judgment, shaped by institutional culture, personal values, and technological mediation.

In essence, the current body of literature emphasizes that the effective integration of ethical AI in the field of EFL academic writing necessitates more than a mere awareness of plagiarism. It demands a reflective engagement with fundamental questions of authorship, fairness, and accountability. The development of these competencies through explicit policy guidance, curricular integration, and AI literacy education remains a central challenge for institutions and educators alike.

2.4 Institutional and Contextual Perspectives: Global and Turkish Insights

Recent research across global and local contexts has revealed a complex, evolving relationship between AI tools and academic writing in EFL education. While the advantages of AI (e.g., enhanced engagement, linguistic assistance, and customized learning) are documented, scholars persist in articulating concerns regarding its ethical implementation, overreliance, and deficiencies in institutional readiness. This section reviews seminal international and Turkish studies that provide the contextual foundation for the present research.

In a variety of international contexts, the integration of AI within higher education has been met with a range of responses, including both enthusiasm and caution. For instance, Kim et al. (2020) reported that U.S. students exhibited a greater propensity to adopt AI in higher education when they held favorable perceptions of AI teaching assistants. In a similar vein, Chen et al. (2022) observed that in Taiwan, the integration of AI into instruction enhanced learners' oral fluency, vocabulary, and personalization, particularly through the use of robotics and adaptive learning systems. In Indonesia, Butarbutar (2024) observed that educators regarded AI as a beneficial support system that augmented learner efficiency and engagement. Tools such as chatbots and adaptive writing platforms were praised for their accessibility and the consistency of their feedback.

However, across these contexts, several limitations persisted. Butarbutar (2024) underscored the limitations of AI tools in acquiring sufficient contextual and cultural understanding, thereby giving rise to ethical concerns regarding privacy and overdependence. In China, An et al. (2023) documented high levels of support for AI among EFL teachers, but also found persistent apprehension surrounding data privacy, student autonomy, and the absence of clear institutional guidelines. These studies underscore a recurring theme: The efficacy of AI is contingent not solely on its technical capabilities, but also on the presence of robust governance frameworks, comprehensive teacher training programs, and a clear ethical framework guiding its utilization.

In Türkiye, emerging research similarly reflects both promise and hesitation in adopting AI for academic writing and language instruction. In the context of primary education, Aktay et al. (2023) observed that fourth-grade students regarded ChatGPT as both accurate and accessible, despite its limited integration into classroom routines. In a large-scale survey, Çayak (2024) found that higher AI literacy among teachers correlated with more favorable attitudes. However, discrepancies in access and digital readiness continued to challenge equitable integration.

A mounting body of research has emerged on the subject of postgraduate EFL students, indicating a growing interest among this demographic at the university level. Elkatmiş (2024) observed that MA students found ChatGPT to be a source of motivation and creativity. Keser and Pektaş (2024) highlighted the strengths of combining AI-generated feedback, which was valued for its immediacy and clarity, with human feedback that offered deeper contextual understanding. Kulaksız (2024) demonstrated that ChatGPT could improve grammar, vocabulary, and cohesion among high school students, although Karabulut (2024) found that similar tools had no measurable effect on writing proficiency in preparatory classes, despite positive student attitudes. From an instructional design perspective, Aslan (2025) demonstrated that AI-generated lesson plans in EFL have the potential to match the clarity and effectiveness of teacher-created materials. However, these tools continue to exhibit cultural and contextual limitations. Across these Turkish studies, researchers consistently argue for the implementation of ethical safeguards, the establishment of stronger policy frameworks, and the provision of targeted professional development to support the responsible adoption of AI in language education.

A synthesis of global and Turkish studies reveals that while AI offers significant potential to enhance writing support and student motivation, its pedagogical impact is dependent on meticulous integration, teacher mediation, and institutional alignment. The present study builds on these insights by examining how Turkish MA ELT students navigate this landscape, shedding light on their lived experiences, ethical concerns, and educational expectations in the context of emerging AI-supported writing practices.

3. METHODOLOGY

This section outlines the qualitative approach used to examine MA ELT students' perceptions, practices, and ethical considerations in using AI for academic writing, detailing the research design, participants, data collection, and thematic analysis.

3.1 Research Design and Questions

This study adopted a qualitative research design to investigate the perceptions, practices, and ethical considerations of MA English Language Teaching (ELT) students regarding the integration of artificial intelligence (AI) into academic writing. A qualitative approach was chosen for its capacity to capture the depth, nuance, and contextual complexity of participants' lived experiences, particularly within a discipline shaped by rapidly evolving digital tools.

Data were collected through semi-structured interviews, a method that balances consistency with flexibility by combining pre-determined prompts with opportunities for participants to elaborate on emerging themes. This format was especially suited to exploring how students position AI relative to traditional academic writing, how they employ it to support linguistic and cognitive development, and the ethical boundaries they perceive in its use.

The study was guided by three research questions:

1. How do MA English Language Teaching (ELT) students perceive and justify their use of AI tools in relation to traditional academic writing practices?
2. How do MA ELT students use AI tools to support their academic writing development?
3. What ethical concerns and perceived limitations do MA ELT students associate with the use of AI in academic writing?

These questions addressed both the affordances of AI—such as linguistic support, time efficiency, and engagement with digital literacies—and the challenges it presents, including risks of dependency, threats to authenticity, and implications for academic integrity. By framing AI adoption as part of a broader negotiation between efficiency, creativity, and scholarly identity, the design positioned student perspectives at the center of the analysis.

3.2. Context of the Study and Participants

This research was conducted in the English Language Teaching (ELT) master's program at a state university in Türkiye, focusing on how postgraduate students integrate AI into their academic writing. Although the university offers digital infrastructure, including campus-wide internet, smart boards, and computer labs, it lacks formal AI training and institutional policies. Consequently, AI use remains at the discretion of individual students, with tools informally adopted for tasks such as rephrasing, summarizing, and proofreading. This growing informal use reflects a broader need for flexible, personalized writing support in postgraduate study.

The present study employed purposive sampling to recruit twelve MA ELT students from a state university in Türkiye. All participants voluntarily agreed to participate following an invitation shared by the first author. While a small number of male students were enrolled in the program at the time, none of them opted to participate or had withdrawn from the course during the data collection period. Consequently, the final sample comprised exclusively female participants. This composition reflects the gender distribution of the cohort and was not a selection criterion; however, it necessarily shapes the lens through which the findings should be interpreted. All participants exhibited comparable English proficiency, demonstrated active engagement in graduate-level academic writing, and had prior experience using AI tools in educational contexts. The respondents reported utilizing AI not only in academic coursework but also in their daily communication and professional teaching activities. The purposes of these tools ranged from idea generation and argument structuring to improving linguistic accuracy, coherence, and citation practices. The participants' experience with AI tools ranged from six months to over two years, enabling a comparison of how duration influenced their engagement, purposes, and attitudes. In the absence of institutional guidelines, participants relied on personal judgment to navigate the ethical boundaries of AI use, underscoring the need for clearer policies, training, and support from universities.

The study employed purposive sampling to recruit twelve female MA ELT students, all with comparable English proficiency, active engagement in graduate-level writing, and prior experience using AI in academic contexts. Participants also reported employing AI in coursework, daily communication, and professional teaching roles. Their reasons for using AI varied—from idea generation and argument structuring to improving linguistic accuracy, coherence, and citation practices—with experience ranging from six months to over two years. This variation allowed for comparison of how usage duration shaped engagement, purposes, and attitudes. In the absence of institutional guidelines, participants relied on personal judgment to navigate ethical and appropriate use, underscoring the need for universities to establish clear policies, training, and ethical frameworks.

3.3. Data Collection

The present study adopted a qualitative research design to explore the integration of artificial intelligence (AI) into academic writing instruction among MA students in English Language Teaching (ELT). The data were collected exclusively through semi-structured individual interviews. These interviews were selected for their capacity to generate rich, detailed accounts while maintaining consistency across participants. The semi-structured format was characterized by a balanced structure and flexibility. It provided a consistent framework for all interviews, yet the open-ended nature of the format allowed participants to elaborate on their experiences and for the researcher to follow emerging lines of inquiry. The interview guide encompassed three primary domains: The participants' motivations and rationales for using AI tools, the manner in which they incorporated these tools into their academic writing processes, and their ethical reflections and concerns are the focal points of this study. This approach has proven to be particularly effective in capturing reflective accounts and exploring the ethical considerations surrounding AI use, offering nuanced insights that would have been difficult to obtain through more rigid or purely quantitative methods. The resulting data were closely aligned with the study's aims, contributing meaningfully to discussions on technology-enhanced learning in higher education.

Semi-structured interviews were conducted with 12 ELT master's students who had prior experience using AI tools in academic writing, each lasting 25–35 minutes and guided by ten core questions with additional follow-ups as needed (see Appendix A). The interviews explored views on AI-assisted versus traditional writing methods, impacts on proficiency, cognitive engagement, and critical thinking, as well as ethical concerns such as originality, plagiarism, and dependency. Participants reported benefits including improved grammar, coherence, and overall quality, alongside challenges like over-reliance, reduced originality, and weakened critical thinking. Reviewed for clarity by the thesis supervisor and refined through peer feedback, the interviews yielded rich, first-hand insights into the pedagogical and ethical implications of AI in academic writing, underscoring the need for clear institutional guidelines and offering a foundation for further research on technology's role in reshaping ELT writing instruction and student engagement.

The data collection process adhered to established ethical and academic standards to ensure the quality and credibility of the research. Ethical approval was obtained from the Ethics Committee of the university, and the study was conducted during the 2024–2025 academic year following a qualitative research design. Informed consent was secured from all participants, who were provided with a detailed explanation of the study's purpose, voluntary nature, and confidentiality measures. Consent forms were distributed electronically, and participation was confirmed prior to data collection.

Semi-structured interviews served as the sole method of data collection and were conducted online via Zoom to accommodate participants' schedules and enhance accessibility. The decision to use an online format was based on considerations of convenience, flexibility, and the ability to include participants regardless of physical location. All interviews were conducted in English, as participants were enrolled in the English Language Teaching (ELT) master's program. Each session lasted approximately 25 to 35 minutes. At the beginning of each interview, participants were reminded that the session would be audio-recorded for academic use only, and their verbal consent was obtained before recording commenced. The interviews took place over a two-month period. Each session was recorded in both audio and video format. During the interviews, the researcher also took field notes and memos to document immediate reflections, notable observations, and potential themes. Upon completion of the data collection, all recordings were transcribed verbatim to ensure accuracy and comprehensiveness in representing participants' responses. These transcripts served as the primary data source for analysis. To ensure the protection of participants' privacy, all digital recordings and transcripts were stored on a password-protected device, accessible only to the researcher. This step ensured that confidentiality and data integrity were maintained throughout the research process. In summary, the data collection procedure was carried out in a systematic, ethical, and transparent manner, contributing to the credibility, depth, and contextual richness of the study's qualitative findings.

3.4 Data Analysis

The qualitative data generated through semi-structured interviews were analyzed using thematic analysis, following the six-phase framework outlined by Braun and Clarke (2006). This approach was selected for its flexibility and rigor in identifying, analyzing, and reporting patterns within qualitative datasets, and for its capacity to accommodate both semantic (explicit) and latent (underlying) meanings in participants' accounts. It provided a structured yet adaptable process aligned with the study's aim of examining MA ELT students' perceptions, practices, and ethical considerations in using AI for academic writing.

The analysis began with the verbatim transcription of all interview recordings by the researcher, a process undertaken not only to ensure accuracy but also to develop early familiarity with the data. Direct engagement with the transcripts allowed the researcher to note emerging ideas, potential connections, and points of emphasis, thereby reducing the risk of misinterpretation. Once transcribed, the data were read and re-read in full to gain a holistic understanding before initial coding commenced. These first-cycle codes represented recurring words, concepts, and patterns directly drawn from the participants' language.

MAXQDA software was used to support the coding process and to manage the large volume of qualitative data efficiently (Kuckartz & Rädiker, 2019). The software enabled systematic organization, retrieval, and comparison of codes, and its visual tools facilitated the exploration of relationships between themes. Importantly, MAXQDA maintained a detailed audit trail of analytic decisions, enhancing transparency and reproducibility. Codes were iteratively reviewed and refined, with related codes clustered into broader thematic categories that captured both the diversity and commonality in participants' experiences.

Throughout the process, memoing was used to document analytical reflections, methodological decisions, and evolving interpretations (Saldaña, 2021). These memos helped track the development of ideas, record shifts in thematic boundaries, and address researcher reflexivity, ensuring that interpretations remained grounded in the participants' own words and contexts. Once candidate themes were identified, they were reviewed against the entire dataset to ensure internal coherence and alignment with the research questions.

Credibility was further strengthened through a member-checking process in which participants were invited to review summaries of the findings and confirm their accuracy. This step not only validated the thematic interpretations but also allowed participants to clarify or expand on their perspectives. The final analysis produced three overarching themes: (1) Perceptions and Motivations Behind AI Use, (2) AI-Supported Academic Writing Development, and (3) Risks, Drawbacks, and Ethical Tensions. Each theme encompassed subthemes including writing proficiency, critical thinking, engagement, ethical concerns, and time management. These themes, derived through a combination of iterative coding, software-assisted data management, and continuous reflexive engagement, form the analytical foundation for the findings presented in the next section.

4. FINDINGS

This section reports the results of the study, which explored how MA students in English Language Teaching (ELT) perceive, employ, and critically evaluate artificial intelligence (AI) tools in academic writing. Drawing on qualitative data from semi-structured interviews, the analysis examines students' motivations, experiences, and ethical considerations, offering insight into the ways AI is integrated into their writing processes.

4.1 Perceptions and Motivations Behind AI Use

The participants' attitudes toward AI in academic writing exhibited a range of expressions, from enthusiastic adoption to cautious skepticism. For many, AI has functioned as a beneficial assistant, enhancing efficiency, reducing stress, and sustaining engagement. One participant (S8) characterized it as *"a game changer,"* while another (S12) observed that effective use *"helps you get the most beneficial part... and reduce the risk."* Concerns regarding ethical and cognitive implications were also voiced by other parties. S5 acknowledged that while AI enhanced efficiency and grammatical accuracy, it also impeded their critical thinking process and, at times, engendered a sense of self-doubt, leading them to question their professional credibility.

It has been reported that students have utilized AI for a variety of creative and technical purposes. These purposes include brainstorming, paraphrasing, grammar correction, summarizing, translation, and feedback. It was further explained that AI can be utilized to fill the gaps that are left by traditional tools. For instance, S10 was valued for its ability to process extensive PDFs and facilitate idea generation during periods of inactivity. S2 found it to be particularly beneficial for vocabulary recall and stylistic enhancement. They argued that, given its alignment with technological progress, academia should embrace AI.

A recurring theme was the immediacy of feedback, particularly in contrast to delays in traditional writing processes. S4 described the convenience of *"just asking AI to give me feedback on certain points"* rather than waiting for teacher input, using it for summarizing, proofreading, translation, and adjusting tone. S9 likewise valued paraphrasing, translating, and synonym suggestions, but emphasized the need for critical evaluation—*"check them and choose the best one"*—modifying outputs when necessary. S3 reported using grammar checkers and language models to revise sentence structure, tone, and clarity, while tracking progress and reviewing past feedback. For them, AI was effective for automating repetitive tasks like proofreading or formatting but should enhance, not replace, traditional practices.

When comparing AI-assisted and traditional writing, participants consistently described the latter as more cognitively demanding, time-consuming, and emotionally taxing—particularly when working in a second language without immediate support. Outlining and structuring were identified as burdensome; S12 described *"creating an outline"* as *"really a burden,"* while S11 noted that *"outlining, structuring, framework... it can feel exhausting."* The slower pace of teacher feedback in traditional contexts was also discouraging. S7 explained, *"Traditional methods do this in a longer period, which sometimes feels discouraging,"* contrasting this with AI's *"instant feedback"* that made them feel they were *"learning in real time."*

AI-assisted writing was thus perceived as more manageable, efficient, and less stressful. Several students reported reduced anxiety due to real-time guidance and corrective support. S6 emphasized that AI *"helps students who are not confident with their writing... it makes them feel they can actually complete a task,"* while S12 described feeling *"more comfortable while writing with AI."* For many, AI functioned as a linguistic scaffold, enabling clearer expression and coherence when *"chains of thought [were] broken"* (S11). S7 highlighted *Grammarly*'s grammar detection as particularly useful, while others appreciated rephrasing and restructuring suggestions for enhancing tone and flow.

In summary, students regarded AI as a pragmatic and inspirational adjunct to conventional academic writing, aiding them in composing with greater clarity, expediency, and self-assurance. As S3 concluded, *"We can't avoid it. It's going to be part of academic writing from now on."* These evolving practices underscore students' construction of flexible, AI-enhanced learning ecologies (Cope et al., 2021), in which diverse tools are mobilized to bridge feedback gaps, reduce stress, and support linguistic performance.

4.2 AI-Supported Academic Writing Development

This section explores the *ways* in which *AI* tools have been utilized to support students' academic writing, with a focus on the enhancement of language accuracy, the provision of immediate feedback, and the mitigation of anxiety. Participants described AI as a linguistic and motivational scaffold that compensated for deficiencies in traditional instruction. While acknowledging its efficiency and accessibility, they underscored the necessity for balance to prevent excessive reliance and to sustain independent skill development.

4.2.1 AI as Linguistic and Motivational Scaffold

Participants described traditional academic writing as cognitively demanding, time-consuming, and often emotionally exhausting, especially when it is undertaken without timely support. Many participants noted the challenge of navigating all stages of the writing process independently, from research and outlining to drafting and revision. S8 noted that academic writing *"is more time-consuming... you have to do every bit on your own,"* while S3 cited the "*limited immediacy of feedback*" as a barrier to maintaining productivity. The pressure on teachers is further compounded by delays in receiving feedback, which can be attributed to academic workloads or institutional constraints. As S4 acknowledged, *"Immediate feedback is difficult because it's a workload for teachers and professionals,"* particularly in large cohorts. This absence of prompt assistance, coupled with the linguistic intricacy characteristic of academic materials, frequently impeded students' self-assurance and fluency.

In this context, AI tools were widely regarded as accessible, responsive scaffolds that compensated for the slow or inconsistent feedback characteristic of traditional settings. Participants highlighted the potential of AI to offer on-demand grammar correction, paraphrasing, vocabulary suggestions, and formatting assistance, thereby mitigating the apprehension associated with seeking assistance. S8 articulated that the act of soliciting feedback was somewhat distressing, whereas AI provided an environment devoid of risk, thereby facilitating experimental endeavors. For S11, this assistance encompassed more than mere technical support; it also included emotional encouragement: *"Sometimes I ask ChatGPT, 'Please give me some encouraging sentences,' like 'I can do it,' and it gives me."*

These tools were particularly valued for their role in enhancing the linguistic aspects of academic writing. As indicated by the participants' reports, gains were made in the areas of vocabulary precision, grammatical accuracy, fluency, and clarity by the non-native English speakers. S2 articulated a common challenge, stating, *"Sometimes I know what I want to say, but I do not know how to say it in the right academic way."* The integration of AI has been instrumental in addressing this disparity by proposing alternative approaches, enhancing sentence transitions, and calibrating tone for formal compositions. S12 reflected, *"Before AI, my sentences were really short and simple... but now I can write more clearly."* Furthermore, S1 noted that the implementation of AI-generated suggestions has facilitated more fluid transitions between paragraphs.

Repeated use has also been demonstrated to support linguistic awareness and longer-term development. A number of students characterized AI as a comparative model, one that facilitates learning through the use of contrast. As S9 explained, *"I compare the sentences, and I see that this translation or this paraphrase is better than my writing in these ways."* However, some participants *(e.g.,* S8*)* expressed uncertainty regarding the origin of the observed improvement, speculating whether it stemmed from AI exposure or the intensive academic reading required in their MA program.

Despite the linguistic and motivational benefits that have been demonstrated, students have expressed concerns regarding the potential for overreliance. A number of respondents reported feelings of excessive reliance on AI, particularly in domains such as paraphrasing and sentence construction. S5 acknowledged the potential consequences of excessive use, expressing concern over the possible loss of their own creativity. S2 also voiced apprehensions about a potential decline in their paraphrasing abilities. In response, participants described strategies for preserving authorship. These strategies included the utilization of artificial intelligence solely for grammar and vocabulary refinement, while maintaining full control over content generation. As S11 articulated: *"My ideas are mine, but the grammar and vocabulary, I let AI help with that part."*

In summary, participants positioned AI as both a linguistic aid and a motivational scaffold that mitigated the cognitive and emotional burden of traditional academic writing. This approach has been shown to facilitate more precise expression, reduce anxiety, and maintain engagement, particularly in the absence of immediate human feedback. However, these benefits were tempered by concerns regarding skill attrition and dependency, thereby reinforcing the necessity for judicious and deliberate utilization. These practices reflect how students selectively integrate AI into their personal learning ecologies, in response to the limitations of institutional scaffolding, by cultivating individually tailored support systems (Cope et al., 2021).

4.2.2 Cognitive and Strategic Engagement with AI

The participants articulated a nuanced comprehension of AI's cognitive and strategic function in academic writing. On the one hand, the integration of AI has been met with appreciation for its ability to alleviate the intimidation associated with academic tasks, providing scaffolding for vocabulary and structure, and facilitating a more engaging and efficient workflow. Conversely, concerns have been raised regarding its capacity to diminish independent thinking, reduce creative effort, and cultivate overreliance.

When utilized deliberately, AI was regarded as a valuable intellectual collaborator and a source of motivation. The program has been shown to assist students in overcoming writer's block, refining their arguments, and managing their workload by freeing up mental energy for more complex tasks. S10 characterized it as *"less intimidating and more dynamic,"* elaborating that while AI provided assistance, *"I still had to think critically and structure my work logically."* In a similar vein, S2 noted that AI *"powers my abilities"* during moments of creative block, offering reassurance through alternative options.

However, several participants cautioned against the potential consequences of AI assuming an excessively substantial cognitive role, namely the possibility of diminished effort and increased passivity. S7 remarked that it *"limits one's critical thinking"* and provides *"less space for further thinking on one's own,"* while S4 admitted that writing could become *"revising the work from the AI"* rather than generating original content. S5 elucidated the distinction between utilizing AI as a conversational partner and allowing it to function as a proxy thinker: *"When I come to a conclusion by myself... I don't forget it. It's mine. But when AI thinks in place of me critically... I forget it... It's not my own idea."*

The predominant emphasis across accounts was on maintaining equilibrium, a notion that emerged as a recurring theme in the participants' reflections. The efficacy of AI was most evident when it served as a complement to, rather than a substitute for, active cognitive engagement. As S11 concisely articulated, *"The key word is balance... use it as a guide, but not as an assistant."*

A range of AI tools were employed by participants across the writing process, in accordance with strategic considerations. *ChatGPT* has been adopted universally for brainstorming, feedback, and stylistic refinement. *DeepL* assisted with translation and cross-linguistic adjustment, while *Grammarly*, *Quillbot*, and *ChatPDF* supported grammar correction, paraphrasing, and content extraction, respectively. Students frequently integrated a variety of tools, adapting them to particular stages in the writing process, including outlining, proofreading, and formatting citations.

Additionally, participants emphasized the significance of prompting skills in ensuring the effective utilization of AI. S1 engaged in proactive efforts to ensure the efficacy of prompt engineering, thereby facilitating the generation of pertinent and consistent outputs: *"I'm working on how to give prompts in a strong way... I want to improve myself in giving coherent and cohesive messages to it."*

The significance of meticulously designed prompts was also emphasized by several other participants. S12 noted that the program "lacks the provision of citations or resources for those who may not be good at writing prompts," while S6 underscored the significance of effective sentence structuring and clarity. Prompting, therefore, can be regarded as both a technical and a cognitive skill, with the quality of AI-generated responses being influenced by the efficacy of the prompting process.

In response to concerns regarding overreliance, a significant number of students have devised self-regulation strategies with the objective of preserving originality, academic integrity, and critical thinking. These included staged use of artificial intelligence (e.g., utilizing AI for brainstorming but not for drafting), verifying AI output against scholarly sources, and reserving core idea development for independent work. For instance, S11 employed AI at the inception and conclusion of the writing process, yet deliberately suspended its utilization during the central drafting phases.

The table below (Table 1) synthesizes the most frequently cited strategies employed by students to balance the affordances of AI with cognitive and academic integrity.

Table 1. Strategies to Balance the Use of AI

Category of Balancing Action	Frequency
Strategic AI Integration (e.g., using AI for outlining, summarizing, or proofreading specific sections)	9
Human Skill Development (e.g., actively developing critical thinking skills, practicing writing independently)	8
Blending AI with Traditional Academic Practices (e.g., combining AI with traditional research methods, using books alongside AI)	4

continued on following page

Table 1. Continued

Category of Balancing Action	Frequency
Awareness of AI Limitations (e.g., verifying AI output, correcting AI-generated mistakes)	3
Maintaining Originality & Authorship (e.g., ensuring personal voice, limiting AI's influence during core writing phases)	2
External Support & Guidance (e.g., seeking mentorship, taking AI literacy courses)	2

Time pressure emerged as a prevalent motivator for the utilization of AI. Participants lauded the efficacy of AI in facilitating expeditious planning and revision, particularly in circumstances characterized by stringent deadlines. S5 articulated this efficiency in a straightforward manner: *"Time is the reason for me to use AI. There are no other reasons... Instead of finding some peers for review, I can just go and ask AI, make this text sound more professional and more academic."*

Overall, participants regarded AI as a malleable and progressive component of their writing process, necessitating both technical expertise and reflective judgment. The cognitive and strategic value of AI does not lie solely in the tools themselves, but rather in students' ability to utilize them with intention, discipline, and a robust sense of authorship. Such practices exemplify learners' agentive negotiation of AI within complex, evolving learning ecologies (Cope et al., 2021), where tools, skills, and values are blended to serve specific academic goals.

4.3 Risks, Drawbacks, and Ethical Tensions

This section outlines the perceived risks and ethical dilemmas students encountered when integrating AI into academic writing, highlighting a generally cautious, reflective stance toward its use.

4.3.1 Reduced Effort, Overreliance, and Skill Decline

Many participants expressed concern that the convenience of AI could lead to a reduction in personal effort and, consequently, a gradual decline in essential academic skills such as critical thinking, creativity, and independent writing. This phenomenon has been characterized as a form of *"academic laziness,"* where the expediency and accessibility of AI has led to a tendency to bypass more profound cognitive engagement. One participant (S2) acknowledged an escalating reliance on the technology, while another (S4) cautioned that excessive use can lead to inactivity.

Time pressure and heavy workloads were seen to amplify this tendency. S5 acknowledged that, in circumstances where resources such as energy and time were limited, the appeal of AI was particularly strong, characterizing it as a *"shortcut"* that was deliberately sought to be avoided. It was observed by several participants (e.g., S7, S9) that while grammar support was found to be beneficial, the utilization of AI in a non-reflexive manner has the potential to hinder *"creative thinking"* and promote passivity.

A number of respondents reflected on perceived declines in their learning and writing quality. S5 asserted that they had previously been *"a better writer before using AI,"* and S6 cautioned that excessive reliance on AI could potentially result in students' inability to articulate the origins of their own work, thereby risking *"ignorance in front of academic people."* Conversely, for others, such realizations precipitated feelings of guilt and led to self-regulation. One participant (S11) disclosed that, subsequent to utilizing AI extensively for an urgent assignment, they experienced a sense of uncertainty regarding the extent to which they had acquired new skills, expressing concern over a potential decline in *"critical thinking and creativity."*

Beyond the reduced effort, students identified a deficiency in AI's capacity to generate original or meaningful ideas. As stated by S12, *"AI does not produce original content."* Furthermore, S2 noted that it lacks depth and has the potential to influence users' writing styles subconsciously. The role of prompting skill as a pivotal variable is also noteworthy. Substandard prompts have the potential to yield outputs that are either irrelevant or misleading, thereby compromising the overall quality of the writing.

Notwithstanding these concerns, a minority expressed a more balanced perspective. S1 characterized their approach to working with AI as a form of *"collaborative expertise,* " leveraging AI as an instrument to enhance, rather than supplant, their own contributions.

In summary, participants regarded AI's efficiency as a double-edged sword, signifying that while it offers clear productivity benefits, there are risks to its sustained use, including the potential for hindering intellectual effort and skill development if it is used uncritically. These tensions further illustrate the delicate balance students must manage within their AI-mediated learning ecologies, where short-term gains can challenge longer-term goals of autonomy and deep learning (Cope et al., 2021).

4.3.2 Ethical Considerations and Academic Integrity

Participants expressed notable uncertainty regarding the formal status of AI use within their programs, which contributed to hesitation, inconsistent practices, and, in some cases, feelings of guilt. The absence of explicit institutional guidelines left students unsure whether AI-assisted work might be considered academically dishonest. One student (S11) recounted being advised by a professor to refrain from utilizing AI, suggesting that instructors might be more receptive to its limited, assistive application. However, the ambiguity surrounding this directive has led to uncertainty among students.

Concerns about plagiarism, authorship, and authenticity were central to participants' reflections. Several emphasised the need to verify and adapt AI-generated content to preserve academic integrity. S6 cautioned that AI *"could be additive, corrective, idea giver, but it cannot be your writing altogether... you have to make some decisions about what to write and what not to write."* Similarly, S8 described her strategy of *"double-check[ing] everything"* and rewriting in her own words to avoid plagiarism.

For some participants, the potential loss of individuality was equally troubling, especially if many students relied on AI for similar topics. As S5 warned, *"If we are all using AI for the same topic... it won't be unique."* Others pointed to the risk of institutional scrutiny, with S1 noting that some professors had warned students they might run assignments through plagiarism detection software specifically to identify AI-generated text.

Across accounts, participants stressed that ethical AI use requires transparency, critical engagement, and a commitment to originality. Many advocated for universities to provide explicit policies and targeted training on responsible AI integration—guidance that would help students use AI as a supportive, assistive tool while safeguarding independent thought, personal authorship, and scholarly integrity. In the absence of such guidance, students were often left to develop their own ethical boundaries within fragmented learning ecologies, navigating tensions between institutional expectations, personal values, and peer norms (Cope et al., 2021).

4.3.3 Limitations of AI Outputs: Accuracy and Emotional Depth

While participants acknowledged AI's grammatical precision and structural clarity, many noted that its outputs lacked the emotional depth and nuance characteristic of human-authored writing. One participant (S12) characterized AI responses as *"mainly shallow,"* indicating the necessity for additional effort to elicit meaningful interpretation. It has been observed by others (e.g., S1, S10) that AI frequently lacks the capacity to convey context or human perspective, resulting in writing that is perceived as distant or impersonal. For some, this phenomenon led to emotional disengagement, as evidenced by S5's reported disconnection from work that no longer aligned with their personal expression.

The importance of human mentorship was frequently emphasized, particularly for developing coherent arguments and a distinctive academic voice. As one student (S3) noted, conventional feedback provided "deeper insights into logic and argumentation" that AI could not replicate.

Concerns regarding factual accuracy were also prevalent. Participants reported that AI occasionally generated outdated or fabricated information, necessitating time-consuming verification. As indicated by the findings of several students (e.g., S6, S9), a cross-checking process of AI outputs with academic sources is recommended. In addition, the necessity of verifying even minor details, particularly in circumstances where accuracy is paramount, has been underscored by other students (S4, S8).

While the value of AI as a supportive writing aid was acknowledged, participants reached a consensus that its outputs require critical human oversight. This is necessary not only to ensure factual accuracy and contextual relevance but also to infuse the emotional resonance, disciplinary nuance, and personal authorship that AI alone cannot provide.

When considered as a sum, the participants' accounts reflect a multifaceted engagement with AI tools. This engagement highlights clear benefits for linguistic support, cognitive scaffolding, and motivation. However, it also reveals tensions around ethical use, critical thinking, and academic integrity. Taken together, these findings demonstrate how students construct and inhabit hybrid learning ecologies that blend algorithmic tools with reflective judgment, disciplinary expectations, and human mentorship (Cope et al., 2021). Table 2 provides a synopsis of the primary functions, reported benefits, and key concerns associated with each domain of AI use.

Table 2. Summary of AI Use in Academic Writing: Use Themes, Functions, Benefits, and Concerns (as reported by participants)

Use Theme	Primary Functions	Reported Benefits	Key Risks / Concerns
Linguistic Enhancement	Grammar correction, paraphrasing, vocabulary suggestions, tone adjustment, sentence restructuring	Improved clarity, fluency, cohesion, and academic tone; learning through comparison	Overreliance; diminished creativity or personal style; uncertainty over source of improvement
Cognitive Support & Idea Generation	Brainstorming, outlining, writer's block relief, idea refinement	Aids productivity, reduces overwhelm, supports complex thinking when used intentionally	Passive engagement; loss of authorship; decline in critical and independent thinking
Feedback & Motivational Scaffolding	Instant feedback, encouragement, emotional reassurance	Reduced anxiety; sustained engagement; support in absence of timely human feedback	Feedback may lack depth; emotional detachment from writing
Academic Integrity Management	Rewriting AI outputs, checking for plagiarism, maintaining originality	Preserves ethical standards; promotes critical engagement with AI content	Institutional ambiguity; fear of misconduct; sameness if used widely
Strategic & Technical Engagement	Prompt crafting, selective AI use across writing stages, citation formatting	Enables agency and intentionality; increases output relevance and precision	Poor prompting skills yield poor results; dependence on AI's structure or logic
Efficiency & Time Management	Task automation (proofreading, summarizing), workflow acceleration	Increased speed and reduced workload, especially under deadlines	Temptation to shortcut deep engagement; risk of superficial or generic writing
Verification & Accuracy Checking	Cross-checking AI outputs with scholarly sources	Ensures factual reliability; reinforces academic standards	Fabricated or outdated info; time-consuming verification; reliance on user's own diligence

5. DISCUSSION

This study investigated how Master of Arts in English Language Teaching (MA ELT) students in Türkiye perceive, justify, and integrate artificial intelligence (AI) tools into their academic writing. The study also examined the pedagogical, cognitive, and ethical implications of this integration in a multilingual postgraduate context. Through the lens of Cope et al.'s (2021) AI-enabled learning ecologies, this study explores how learners navigate dynamic sociotechnical environments where human actors (e.g., supervisors and peers) and non-human actors (e.g., ChatGPT and Grammarly) influence academic practice. By examining students' motivations, reservations, and strategies, the study illuminates how AI reshapes, rather than merely supports, the postgraduate writing process by offering scaffolds and constraints for academic development. The findings point to a complex, and at times contradictory, relationship between AI use and academic writing development. While participants consistently valued AI for its immediacy, linguistic scaffolding, and motivational support, they also voiced concerns over overreliance, diminished critical thinking, and the erosion of personal authorial voice. These tensions reflect a broader pedagogical challenge: leveraging AI's affordances without undermining the intellectual autonomy, creativity, and scholarly integrity that advanced academic writing demands. This concern aligns with Cope et al.'s (2021) call for pedagogically grounded AI use, where technology supports rather than reshapes core educational values and learning processes.

Overall, the study revealed a variety of views on the role of AI in academic writing, which were largely positive. Echoing Gayed et al. (2022), almost all participants regarded AI as a valuable resource for improving the quality of their work. In line with Sangkala and Mardonovna (2024), they frequently identified grammar correction, phrase suggestions, and structural adjustments as essential functions that enhanced clarity, coherence, and adherence to academic conventions. The results also align with Kulaksız (2024) and Zhu et al. (2024), who found that generative AI tools provide immediate feedback on grammar, vocabulary, and coherence, thus reducing cognitive load and supporting more fluent academic communication. Consistent with Song and Song's (2023) findings, participants described AI not only as a time-saving aid but also as a motivational resource, countering the demotivating aspects often associated with traditional writing tasks. This was especially evident when timely feedback from supervisors was unavailable, reinforcing Rad et al.'s (2024) conclusion that real-time support can help students internalize academic writing norms more effectively. This finding also aligned with Çayak's (2024) study, where Turkish EFL students experienced reduced writing anxiety and increased confidence when AI tools were embedded in a process-based writing approach.

Participants' motivations for AI adoption were often rooted in limitations of traditional academic writing practices, particularly time constraints and restricted access to feedback from peers or faculty. In this regard, AI functioned as a bridge between the demands of conventional postgraduate writing and the realities of an evolving higher education landscape, offering both practical support and emotional reassurance. Yet, many students stressed the importance of preserving their academic voice, which is consistent with Aljuaid's (2024) argument for maintaining a balance between technological assistance and the rigor, originality, and creativity central to traditional academic pedagogy.

At the same time, ethical and cognitive concerns significantly shaped participants' perceptions. Several people expressed concerns about plagiarism, reduced critical thinking skills, and potential dependency on AI tools. These concerns echo the ongoing scholarly debates about academic integrity in the digital age. The absence of clear institutional guidelines further complicated matters, forcing students to rely on their own judgment to determine what constitutes acceptable use. This ambiguity blurred the line between academic misconduct and responsible engagement, creating uncertainty over what level of AI assistance was permissible. While no participant reported deliberate misuse, several expressed confusion about whether using AI for sentence restructuring or paraphrasing could be seen as unethical, especially in the absence of formal guidance. This lack of clarity places undue pressure on learners to self-regulate, increasing the risk of both unintentional misuse and unnecessary anxiety. This finding aligns with the work of Nguyen et al. (2024), who emphasize the need for clearly articulated policies and AI literacy training to promote responsible engagement. Teachers' generally positive beliefs about AI are well-documented, though most advocate for AI as a complement—not a substitute—for human mentorship (Butarbutar, 2024). This balance mirrors the findings of this study, where participants emphasized both AI's utility and the irreplaceable value of human feedback. These findings also reinforce Nguyen et al.'s (2024) and Solmaz's (2023) argument that developing AI literacy is a crucial component of preparing students to use such tools critically and responsibly. Participants' calls for dedicated instruction on AI-integrated academic writing further highlight the need for formal, structured approaches that promote ethical engagement, critical evaluation, and reflective practice in technology-enhanced learning environments.

All twelve participants—despite holding varied attitudes toward AI—reported using such tools to support their academic writing development. This aligns with Mohebbi's (2025) observation that AI-driven applications enhance language learning by fostering engagement, delivering immediate feedback, and enabling personalized learning experiences. Similarly, Raheem et al. (2023) emphasize that AI writing assistants can improve texts by analyzing style and suggesting structural refinements. Participants' integration of AI across multiple stages of the writing process, from prewriting to final revision, reflects Sol and Heng's (2024) finding that AI makes writing more iterative and interactive. In line with Khalifa and Albadawy (2024), students described using AI to boost productivity through editing assistance, feedback management, and organizational support. More than half primarily engaged AI for language-focused tasks—such as grammar correction, vocabulary enhancement, and sentence restructuring—while others leveraged it for comprehension-oriented purposes, including summarizing readings and clarifying complex academic material.

AI use extended into the prewriting phase for brainstorming and outline generation, as well as the revision stage for refining clarity, coherence, and correctness. Several participants reported incidental learning through repeated exposure to AI-generated outputs, noting that rephrased sentences and model structures helped internalize syntactic accuracy and academic style. Others emphasized AI's value in simplifying dense scholarly texts, thereby improving comprehension and making advanced concepts more accessible. These findings support ElSayary's (2024) view that generative AI can enhance metacognitive awareness by prompting reflection on writing choices. They also align with Jadhav et al.'s (2024) scaffolding model, wherein technological tools adjust their support in response to the learner's evolving needs.

At the same time, the study identified several ethical concerns and limitations, with the trustworthiness of AI-generated content emerging as a prominent issue. Many participants encountered factual inaccuracies, inappropriate tone, or overly generic language, underscoring the necessity of human verification. This concern echoes Zhai et al.'s (2024) warning that AI outputs can lack originality and homogenize writing style. In line with Wang's (2024) finding that digital literacy shapes both technostress and productivity, participants reflected on the cognitive and emotional implications of AI use. While valuing its efficiency and linguistic support, several expressed concern over diminished critical engagement and a growing dependence on automated suggestions. Consistent with Nguyen et al. (2024), they warned that overreliance could compromise originality, with one student describing feeling "like a fraud" after extensive AI use. Another key theme was the absence of institutional policy on AI use, which left students uncertain about acceptable practice. Echoing Elkatmiş (2024), participants stressed that AI integration should be accompanied by ethical frameworks and training. However, in contrast to findings by Werdiningsih et al. (2024), this lack of formal guidance did not appear to foster unethical behavior, as students relied on personal values, academic integrity norms, and teacher feedback to guide responsible use.

Participants also raised equity-related concerns, noting that students who avoided AI often felt disadvantaged compared to peers whose AI-assisted work appeared more polished. While participants did not explicitly discuss the cost or versioning of AI tools, this disparity implicitly points to broader access issues. The advanced features of paid AI tools, such as enhanced feedback quality and faster response times, may contribute to uneven writing outcomes. These unspoken differences, shaped by socioeconomic background, institutional support, and digital literacy, raise questions about fairness in academic assessment and the invisibility of AI-enhanced advantages. A further limitation concerned AI's lack of emotional depth and personal voice, echoing Aslan's (2025) observation that AI-generated texts, while technically correct, can lack warmth, sophistication, and authenticity. In practice, many participants mirrored O'Neill and Russell's (2019) recommendation to blend AI with human feedback—employing AI primarily for grammar correction, sentence restructuring, and coherence enhancement—yet they cautioned that sustained overreliance could weaken critical thinking and independent writing skills. Concerns over bias and misinformation also emerged, aligning with Mohebbi's (2025) warning that AI outputs may perpetuate stereotypes or factual inaccuracies due to limitations in training data. In addition, the majority expressed apprehension about AI-induced academic laziness; while one participant viewed AI as motivating and used it to refine prompting skills, most felt its convenience reduced personal effort and deep engagement. This perspective reinforces Sabharwal et al.'s (2023) caution that overreliance can diminish motivation and long-term skill development, underscoring the need for AI literacy and ethical awareness as essential components of sustainable academic writing practices. Finally, teacher preparedness also emerged as an equity issue. While some participants had instructors who addressed AI use explicitly, others received little or no guidance, leading to inconsistent classroom norms. This unevenness mirrors broader digital divides in educator readiness and institutional policy.

These findings can be further interpreted through Cope et al.'s (2021) conception of AI-enabled learning ecologies. In these ecologies, learners negotiate knowledge and meaning within environments co-populated by human guidance and algorithmic influence. In this study, participants demonstrated ecological agency by making decisions about when and how to use AI. Sometimes they leveraged its efficiency and accuracy; at other times, they resisted it to preserve their authorial voice or uphold academic integrity. Their narratives reflect ecological literacy, where students evaluate the epistemic, ethical, and cognitive benefits of AI tools within institutional ambiguity and personal values. This underscores the importance of pedagogical models that support such decision-making, fostering critical engagement rather than dependence in evolving AI-mediated academic ecosystems.

In sum, the findings across research questions suggest a balance between AI's affordances and its potential risks in postgraduate EFL academic writing. For MA ELT students, AI tools functioned as linguistic scaffolds, productivity aids, and confidence boosters, yet they also raised concerns about overreliance, diminished originality, and ethical ambiguity in the absence of institutional guidance. These results align with global scholarship advocating for AI as a complement—not a substitute—for human mentorship and critical engagement. They also highlight the urgency of embedding AI literacy, ethical frameworks, and balanced pedagogical models into higher education to ensure that technological support strengthens rather than supplants the cognitive and creative processes central to scholarly writing.

6. CONCLUSION, LIMITATIONS, AND IMPLICATIONS

This study investigated how MA ELT students in Türkiye perceive, justify, and integrate AI into their academic writing, illuminating both its pedagogical affordances and its potential risks. Participants valued AI for its immediacy, linguistic scaffolding, and ability to reduce cognitive load, particularly in contexts where timely human feedback was unavailable. At the same time, they voiced concerns about overreliance, diminished critical thinking, and erosion of authorial voice, while the absence of institutional guidelines introduced uncertainty and ethical ambiguity. These findings reinforce the global call for balanced AI integration, where technological capabilities complement, rather than replace, human expertise. They also underscore the importance of embedding AI literacy, ethical frameworks, and pedagogical models that protect scholarly integrity while leveraging AI's ability to improve multilingual academic writing.

These findings highlight the urgent need for institutional policies and governance structures that promote the ethical and effective use of AI in higher education. Without formal guidelines, participants were unsure about what constitutes responsible engagement, so they relied on personal values or informal instructor advice. Institutions can address this gap by adopting or adapting global AI literacy frameworks, such as those proposed by European Commission and OECD (2025). These frameworks outline principles for the ethical, inclusive, and transparent use of AI in education. Universities should prioritize developing clear generative AI policies, coupled with training for students and educators, to promote responsible use, reduce technostress, and foster academic integrity. Institutional AI governance should also consider issues of equity, access, and cultural contexts to ensure that all learners benefit from AI without amplifying digital divides.

Since all of the participants were prospective English teachers, their experiences with AI tools carry important implications for teacher education. While many participants saw AI as a useful writing tool, they also expressed ambivalence about its role in learning and assessment. This dual perspective, as both learners and future instructors, suggests that beliefs formed during postgraduate study may influence future teaching practices. If teachers view AI as a shortcut or a threat, they may avoid integrating it into their pedagogy. Therefore, teacher education programs should address the technical, epistemological, ethical, and pedagogical dimensions of AI. Pre-service training should include critical reflection on the role of AI in language learning, especially its impact on voice, creativity, and learner agency. This can enable future educators to make informed, context-sensitive decisions about its classroom use.

To bridge the gap between theory and practice, the findings support several practical interventions. For example, AI-integrated writing workshops can teach students to use tools like ChatGPT and Grammarly critically, helping them understand both the tools' strengths and limitations. Scaffolded activities, such as side-by-side revision comparisons, guided feedback tasks, and critical prompting exercises, can encourage learners to reflect on AI output while maintaining control over their voice and meaning. Integrating AI literacy into writing curricula alongside instruction in citation, paraphrasing, and source evaluation can encourage ethical use and metacognitive awareness. Importantly, instructors should not frame AI as a shortcut to fluency, but rather as a partner in the writing process that must be used intentionally and reflectively within clear academic boundaries.

As with all empirical research, this study has limitations that should be considered when interpreting its findings. The qualitative design, based on semi-structured interviews, prioritized participants' subjective experiences over the technical capabilities or algorithmic performance of AI tools. The sample consisted of twelve female Master of Arts in English Language Teaching (MA ELT) students, all of whom had teaching experience or related academic backgrounds. This gender composition reflects the demographics of the program at the time of data collection, where female enrollment was predominant. As such, while the study does not aim for statistical generalizability, it offers transferable insights into how postgraduate EFL students engage with

AI tools in academic writing. Nonetheless, the education-focused profile of the participants may have influenced the nature of their reflections, and the reliance on self-reported data introduces the possibility of response bias. Moreover, as the study was conducted within a single institution in Türkiye, its findings may be shaped by local cultural and institutional norms that limit their applicability across broader higher education contexts.

Despite these constraints, the study contributes to ongoing debates on technology-enhanced learning by offering nuanced insights into how future English teachers navigate AI's benefits and risks in academic writing. The results point to several avenues for future research: expanding the participant pool to include more diverse backgrounds and disciplines; conducting cross-cultural comparisons to examine how educational norms influence AI adoption; and exploring the effects of specific tools (e.g., DeepL, Grammarly, or Turnitin) on writing quality, efficiency, and cognitive engagement. Longitudinal studies could track how attitudes, competencies, and ethical considerations evolve over time, while experimental designs might measure AI's direct impact on critical thinking, originality, and stylistic development. Given participants' recurring concerns over plagiarism and academic honesty, further work should examine how students and educators define and operationalize responsible AI use. Finally, research into pedagogical interventions, such as AI-integrated writing workshops and ethical use guidelines, could inform strategies that preserve intellectual autonomy while maximizing the educational value of AI in EFL academic writing contexts.

REFERENCES

Aljuaid, H. (2024). The impact of artificial intelligence tools on academic writing instruction in higher education: *A systematic review. Arab World English Journal (AWEJ), Special Issue on ChatGPT*, 26-55.

An, X., Chai, C. S., Li, Y., Zhou, Y., Shen, X., Zheng, C., & Chen, M. (2023). Modeling English teachers' behavioral intention to use artificial intelligence in middle schools. *Education and Information Technologies*, *28*(5), 5187–5208. DOI: 10.1007/s10639-022-11286-z

Aslan, K. (2025). *A Comparison of Lesson Plans From Artificial Intelligence and English Language Teachers* (Unpublished Master's thesis). Dicle University, Turkiye.

Braun, V., & Clarke, V. (2006). Using thematic analysis in psychology. *Qualitative Research in Psychology*, *3*(2), 77–101. DOI: 10.1191/1478088706qp063oa

Butarbutar, R. (2024). Artificial intelligence for language learning and teaching: A narrative literature study. *Englisia: Journal of Language, Education, and Humanities*, *12*(1), 147–163. DOI: 10.22373/ej.v12i1.23211

Çayak, S. (2024). Investigating the relationship between teachers' attitudes toward artificial intelligence and their artificial intelligence literacy. *Journal of Educational Technology & Online Learning*, *7*(4), 367–383. DOI: 10.31681/jetol.1490307

Chen, Y. L., Hsu, C. C., Lin, C. Y., & Hsu, H. H. (2022). Robot-Assisted Language Learning: Integrating Artificial Intelligence and Virtual Reality into English Tour Guide Practice. *Education Sciences*, *12*(7), 437. DOI: 10.3390/educsci12070437

Çiftçi, A. (2024). *AI-assisted teaching: Practices and perspectives of instructors on using AI tools in ELT* (Unpublished master's thesis). Maltepe University, Türkiye.

Cope, B., Kalantzis, M., & Searsmith, D. (2021). Artificial intelligence for education: Knowledge and its assessment in AI-enabled learning ecologies. *Educational Philosophy and Theory*, *53*(12), 1229–1245. DOI: 10.1080/00131857.2020.1728732

Elkatmiş, M. (2024). Chat GPT and creative writing: Experiences of master's students in enhancing. *International Journal of Contemporary Educational Research*, *11*(3), 321–336. DOI: 10.52380/ijcer.2024.11.3.597

ElSayary, A. (2024). Integrating Generative AI in Active Learning Environments: Enhancing Metacognition and Technological Skills. *Journal of Systemics, Cybernetics and Informatics*, *22*(3), 34–37. DOI: 10.54808/JSCI.22.03.34

Gayed, J. M., Carlon, M. K. J., Oriola, A. M., & Cross, J. S. (2022). Exploring an AI-based writing Assistant's impact on English language learners. *Computers and Education: Artificial Intelligence*, *3*, 100055. DOI: 10.1016/j.caeai.2022.100055

Huang, X., Zou, D., Cheng, G., Chen, X., & Xie, H. (2023). Trends, research issues and applications of artificial intelligence in language education. *Journal of Educational Technology & Society*, *26*(1), 112–131.

Jadhav, S., Vhatkar, S., & Aalam, Z. (2024). Bridging the gap: Exploring the revolutionary application of GenAI in language teaching and learning. *Journal of Electrical Systems, 20*(4s, 4S), 2185–2193. DOI: 10.52783/jes.2325

Karabulut, E. (2024). *Analysing the effects of AI-powered chatbots on the writing skills of English preparatory class students: An experimental study* (Unpublished Master's thesis). Ondokuz Mayıs University, Türkiye.

Keser, K., & Pektaş, R. (2024). Human vs. AI Feedback on Academic Writing: A Comparative Study in Turkish Context. In Özkan, Y. (Ed.), *English Studies: A Multifaceted Lens* (pp. 190–203). Black Swan Press.

Khalifa, M., & Albadawy, M. (2024). Using artificial intelligence in academic writing and research: An essential productivity tool. *Computer Methods and Programs in Biomedicine Update, 4*, 100145. DOI: 10.1016/j.cmpbup.2024.100145

Kim, J., Merrill, K., Xu, K., & Sellnow, D. D. (2020). My teacher is a machine: Understanding students' perceptions of AI teaching assistants in online education. *International Journal of Human-Computer Interaction, 36*(20), 1902–1911. DOI: 10.1080/10447318.2020.1801227

Kuckartz, U., & Rädiker, S. (2019). *Analyzing qualitative data with MAXQDA*. Springer International Publishing. DOI: 10.1007/978-3-030-15671-8

Kulaksız, G. C. (2024). *Artificial intelligence-based language modelling: The effect of ChatGPT application on writing skills in the context of teaching English as a foreign language* (Unpublished Master's thesis). Bursa Uludağ University, Türkiye.

Liu, C., Hou, J., Tu, Y. F., Wang, Y., & Hwang, G. J. (2023). Incorporating a reflective thinking promoting mechanism into artificial intelligence-supported English writing environments. *Interactive Learning Environments, 31*(9), 5614–5632. DOI: 10.1080/10494820.2021.2012812

Mohebbi, A. (2025). Enabling learner independence and self-regulation in language education using AI tools: A systematic review. *Cogent Education, 12*(1), 2433814. DOI: 10.1080/2331186X.2024.2433814

Nguyen, A., Hong, Y., Dang, B., & Huang, X. (2024). Human-AI collaboration patterns in AI-assisted academic writing. *Studies in Higher Education, 49*(5), 847–864. DOI: 10.1080/03075079.2024.2323593

O'Neill, R., & Russell, A. (2019). Stop! Grammar time: University students' perceptions of the automated feedback program Grammarly. *Australasian Journal of Educational Technology, 35*(1), 42–56. DOI: 10.14742/ajet.3795

OECD. (2025). Empowering learners for the age of AI: An AI literacy framework for primary and secondary education (Review draft). OECD. Paris. https://ailiteracyframework.org

Rad, H. S., Alipour, R., & Jafarpour, A. (2024). Using artificial intelligence to foster students' writing feedback literacy, engagement, and outcome: A case of Wordtune application. *Interactive Learning Environments, 32*(9), 5020–5040. DOI: 10.1080/10494820.2023.2208170

Raheem, B. R., Anjum, F., & Ghafar, Z. N. (2023). Exploring the profound impact of artificial intelligence applications (Quillbot, Grammarly and ChatGPT) on English academic writing: A Systematic Review. [IJIR]. *International Journal of Integrative Research, 1*(10), 599–622.

Sabharwal, D., Kabha, R., & Srivastava, K. (2023). Artificial intelligence (ai)-powered virtual assistants and their effect on human productivity and laziness: Study on students of delhi-ncr (india) & fujairah (uae). *Journal of Content. Community and Communication, 17*(9), 162–174. DOI: 10.31620/JCCC.06.23/12

Saldaña, J. (2021). *The coding manual for qualitative researchers* (4th ed.). SAGE.

Sangkala, I., & Mardonovna, N. S. (2024). Artificial intelligence as a personalized tutor in language learning: A systematic review. *Klasikal: Journal of Education. Language Teaching And Science, 6*(2), 565–576.

Sol, K., & Heng, K. (2024). AI-powered chatbots as personalized academic writing assistants for non-native English speakers. In Peters, M. A., & Heraud, R. (Eds.), *Encyclopedia of educational innovation* (pp. 1–5). Springer., DOI: 10.1007/978-981-13-2262-4_313-1

Solmaz, O. (2020). The Nature and Potential of Digital Collaborative Reading Practices for Developing EFL Proficiency. *IOJET: International Online Journal of Education and Teaching, 7*(4), 1283–1298.

Solmaz, O. (2023). AI Literacies in Language Education: Meeting Challenges, Embracing Transformations. In Bakla, A., & Çakır, İ. (Eds.), *ChatGPT in Foreign Language Education and Translation Studies* (pp. 167–188). Anı Publishing.

Song, C., & Song, Y. (2023). Enhancing academic writing skills and motivation: Assessing the efficacy of ChatGPT in AI-assisted language learning for EFL students. *Frontiers in Psychology, 14*, 1260843. DOI: 10.3389/fpsyg.2023.1260843 PMID: 38162975

Wang, J. (2024). The effect of Chinese EFL students' digital literacy on their Technostress and Academic Productivity. *The Asia-Pacific Education Researcher, 33*(4), 987–996. DOI: 10.1007/s40299-023-00794-2

Werdiningsih, I., Marzuki, , & Rusdin, D. (2024). Balancing AI and authenticity: EFL students' experiences with ChatGPT in academic writing. *Cogent Arts & Humanities, 11*(1), 2392388. Advance online publication. DOI: 10.1080/23311983.2024.2392388

Zhai, C., Wibowo, S., & Li, L. D. (2024). The effects of over-reliance on AI dialogue systems on students' cognitive abilities: A systematic review. *Smart Learning Environments, 11*(1), 28. DOI: 10.1186/s40561-024-00316-7

Zhu, Y., Zhang, L., Zong, R., & Sun, H. (2024). Exploring AI-generated feedback on English writing: A case study of ChatGPT. *US-China Foreign Language, 22*(3), 144–153.

Chapter 9

Empowering EFL Writers Through AI:
A Pedagogical Framework for AI-Enhanced Writing Instruction

Vivit Rosmayanti
https://orcid.org/0000-0002-3648-9878
Universitas Negeri Makassar, Indonesia

ABSTRACT

This chapter provides a practical framework for integrating artificial intelligence (AI) into English as a Foreign Language (EFL) writing classes. It encourages the use of AI tools like Grammarly, ProWritingAid, Turnitin, Quillbot, and GPT-driven assistants to provide immediate feedback and scaffolded support, helping learners develop fluency. The chapter also highlights the importance of addressing ethical concerns such as plagiarism, data privacy, and the potential diminishing of human creativity. It calls for professional development initiatives and a policy agenda to ensure fair access and equitable educational opportunities.

INTRODUCTION

The integration of artificial intelligence technologies into educational practices, particularly in writing instruction, has transformed pedagogy and student learning in unprecedented ways. For teachers of English as a Foreign Language, AI technologies have developed, and to assist these teachers, new challenges and issues have emerged. The instruction of writing has relied upon methodologies that, to a large extent, have failed to give adequate support to students grappling with the complexities of the production of a language in a foreign context. Nevertheless, the advent of AI technologies has started to revise the teaching of writing and the methodologies teachers employ.

There are persistent problems in the writing of EFL learners, such as inadequate lexical knowledge, poorly developed sentence patterns, and low self-confidence in writing. The language problems that many EFL learners face in communicative English are pivotal to the students'

DOI: 10.4018/979-8-3373-5601-3.ch009

failure and disengagement with a writing task. Recent studies have indicated that these issues are particularly salient to learners and underscore the need to address them.

Artificial intelligence has great potential to improve tailored assistance, prompt feedback, and even writing self-efficacy and self-efficacy in learners (Wale & Kassahun, 2024; Song & Song, 2023; Pratama & Sulistiyo, 2024). Furthermore, AI writing programs aid learners in word suggestions, grammar corrections, and overall writing. These features of AI writing programs facilitate the process of language acquisition (Wu, 2024; Zhao, 2022).

In this chapter, I intend to discuss some key objectives. First, I aim to outline a more empowering teaching approach and instructional design for AI tools integration in writing for EFL learners. Also, I will seek to provide a detailed understanding of the integration of various AI writing tools, including generative AI, in the teaching of English as a foreign language. The proposed framework reiterates the integration of AI tools with strategy alteration to meet the needs of EFL students to improve the experience (Xi, 2024; Pratama & Sulistiyo, 2024). This chapter adds to the discourse on the ethical implications of the use of AI in education, focusing on issues of educational integrity, the tension between scaffolding students and allowing them to freely articulate their thoughts in written form (Pan, 2024; Parviz, 2025).

Integrating AI into writing instruction has students learning competencies that extend well beyond the mechanics of writing. The technology fosters critical thinking, self-regulation, and creativity, all of which substantiate the need for students' training on the discerning use, as opposed to the passive use, of these technologies (Kong et al., 2024; Chen, 2023). The adoption of a self-regulated learning framework, in particular, is motivational as it encourages students to take responsibility for their learning, while AI technology is used to write. This assists learning in writing purportedly AI technologies (Ratih & Kastuhandani, 2024; Utami et al., 2023). This chapter will articulate the self-determination theory approach as a framework to examine how AI technology can unlock the potential of EFL writers and, in the process, make the learning experience more self-directed and intrinsic (Rahayu et al., 2024; Minh, 2024).

The rapid development of AI presents new possibilities for instruction in EFL writing. EFL students' varied and complex learning challenges warrant a shift in teaching pedagogy to embrace the potential of new technologies. This chapter aims to do two things. First, it presents a comprehensive approach to teaching writing with AI. Second, it demonstrates how teaching writing with AI can lead to enhanced student confidence, empowerment, and engagement in the process of learning a language. The impact of AI on teaching and research is profound, transforming language teaching in ways that address contemporary students' needs and challenges (Wang, 2024; Moussa & Belhiah, 2024; Pratama & Sulistiyo, 2024).

THEORETICAL FOUNDATIONS

The variety of writing teaching theories has brought noticeable changes within English Language Teaching (ELT) and it has taken people time to recognize the challenges involved in teaching students to write well. The Process Writing Approach, the Genre-Based Approach, and the Product Approach are the three main ways to write. The current discussion revolves around these three approaches. Each of these approaches offers unique insights and methods to developing the writing skills of students learning English as a foreign language (EFL).

The Process Writing Approach emphasizes the cyclic character of writing. It emphasizes the importance of planning, drafting, revising, and editing. This encourages students to recognize that writing is a non-linear process that shifts in different directions, rather than a straight line (Kadmiry, 2021; Bhowmik, 2021). Kadmiry states that this method heightens students' intrinsic motivation because it fosters ownership of the writing process and collaboration through peer feedback loops (Kadmiry, 2021). Conversely, the Product Approach is centered on the outcomes of the writing tasks, prioritizing traditional academic correctness and structure when assessing students. This approach can simplify the process of teaching; however, it sometimes lacks the necessary depth that encourages students to engage in thoughtful analysis or innovation (Bhowmik, 2021).

The Genre-Based Approach integrates the Process and Product theories and suggests that writing be a contextualized activity in specific genres, each of which has its particular guidelines and expectations (Zohbie & Bhowmik, 2024). This approach not only equips students to compose texts in a specific genre but also ensures that they appreciate the different styles that can be used in writing within different contexts (Hassan, 2020). Genre-based approaches in writing instruction are shown to be effective in developing audience awareness and employing specific rhetorical techniques, which, in turn, enhance the writing skills of EFL students (Hanušová et al., 2020).

As a consequence of the evolution of teaching strategies, the field of writing instruction has expanded the scope of educational foundations to include digital literacy as a fundamental aspect. For contemporary EFL learners, digital literacy, which encompasses the ability to utilize various digital tools and spaces effectively, is of critical importance. Recent advancements in AI have prompted the concept of 'AI literacy,' the ability to use AI applications in learning and writing responsibly. For EFL learners, AI literacy involves using AI responsibly, critically evaluating AI-generated content, and intentionally polishing their writing (Song & Song, 2023). With the growing use of AI tools such as ChatGPT in classrooms, teaching students to distinguish between quality and poor AI-enhanced writing has become a top priority.

The designed model of Education 5.0 is a visionary change concerning human-machine interfaces in collaboration. This model fosters collaborative engagements between learners and educational AIs, with each party contributing particular capabilities. Using the Education 5.0 paradigm, teachers can rethink their methods in teaching English writing by transforming the lesson from a speech to a conversation, where AI can serve as a partner in the learning process (Song & Song, 2023). The collaborative interaction of the machine and the human encourages learners to pursue the higher-order questioning of the language and the writing mechanics (Nazim & Mohammad, 2022). The AI motivates them to learn more and, in the end, integrate the more complex writing mechanics through deeper learning, and, in particular, for English as a Foreign Language learners.

Additionally, as EFL teachers use these new frameworks, they should be aware of issues that come with AI reliance. To ensure the right level of digital literacy and AI literacy, critical thinking must also be taught so students can meaningfully engage with AI outputs and maintain the authenticity and voice of their writing (Song & Song, 2023; Nazim & Mohammad, 2022). As the educational world transforms, the careful balance of these components becomes crucial.

Integration thus becomes essential in writing EFL teaching, as a result of the complicated connection between digital literacy, pedagogical theories, and the principles of Education 5.0. By enhancing the Process Writing, Genre-Based, and Product Approaches, and introducing AI tools, teachers are able to provide a balance in the EFL writing instruction framework and empower students within the shifting educational landscape.

LANDSCAPE OF AI TOOLS FOR WRITING

The rapid evolution of artificial intelligence technologies, especially in the realm of AI-assisted writing tools, has provided learners in EFL contexts with remarkable new opportunities for engaging with texts in ways that will enhance their writing proficiency. Grammarly, ProWritingAid, Quillbot, Turnitin, and ChatGPT each claim significant writing assistance, each for different reasons. Each assistant has different qualities that forbetter and for worse, impact EFL writers, helping with different aspects of writing.

Grammarly remains a reference and a standard in writing-assistant programs. As a primary function, it analyzes and corrects written texts. It identifies, corrects, and provides real-time suggestions for spelling and grammar and offers alternative, clearer ways of composing text according to the user's goals. Grammarly tends to provide EFL learners with real-time feedback that their cognition of the target language and their editing skills have improved substantially (Moybeka et al., 2023). Effectiveness, though, is certainly a function of proficiency, and some learners might become overly reliant on Grammarly, failing to develop and maintain necessary independent editing skills (Alzahrani & Alotaibi, 2024).

ProWritingAid, like Grammarly, also analyzes texts for grammar and style, but offers more in-depth advanced writing analysis tools. It includes reviews of a document's writing style, organization, and overall readability, along with suggestions for improvements. ProWritingAid assists EFL learners with developing linguistic proficiency and correct composition skills (Moussa & Belhiah, 2024). Yet, some learners might perceive the program's comprehensive feedback as overwhelming and, therefore, a disincentive for engaging in deconstructive writing (Al-Raimi et al., 2024). Quillbot provides other functionalities. Quillbot assists users in writing revisions and the production of clearer text. It is particularly valuable for EFL writers struggling with limited vocabulary, as it provides suggestions for synonyms and rephrasing, which fosters proficiency and expressiveness (Dergaa et al., 2023).

Quillbot assists users in producing varied sentence structures, but, unlike ProWritingAid, it does not provide attention to coherence and cohesion principles in writing. This lack of substantive linguistic guidance may cause errors, especially for students with limited linguistic proficiency for the target language (Mudawy, 2024).

Turnitin serves its primary role in identifying plagiarism, but also provides feedback. It encourages academic honesty along with the understanding of the importance of originality for EFL writers. Feedback guides students for improvement in the use of sources and proper citation (Nazari et al., 2021). However, focusing disproportionately on plagiarism detection without attention to the creative aspects of writing could discourage imaginative processes (Babanoğlu et al., 2025).

Recent advances, particularly in the form of ChatGPT and tools using GPT, are remarkable achievements in the area of AI. These conversational AI tools are able to generate text, respond to queries, and provide suggestions in a conversation. During the writing process, EFL students can use ChatGPT to generate ideas, organize their writing, and expand their vocabulary.

Research indicates that employing AI tools, such as ChatGPT, can alleviate students' anxiety and encourage more creativity in their writing (Song & Song, 2023). Nonetheless, certain issues may arise, including dependency on AIs for content generation, which can inhibit students' ability to find their authentic writing voice and develop critical thinking (Kostka & Toncelli, 2023; Ekizoğlu & Demir, 2025; Roy & Swargiary, 2024).

The provided advantages and disadvantages indicate that AI technologies are great teaching, writing, and composition tools and that their implementation requires precise integration into lesson plans. Presumably, the greatest concern is balance; the potential for AI's immediate feedback and content generation capabilities must be weighed against students' need to write and articulate their thoughts in higher-order, more nuanced forms. The role of EFL teachers as guides in the optimal use of these technologies is invaluable.

Training individuals to engage in critical thinking regarding received suggestions rather than accepting them at face value is essential (Baskara, 2023; Amin, 2023; Harunasari, 2023). In today's rapidly evolving context, the effective utilization of AI technologies can enhance the writing experience for EFL (English as a Foreign Language) learners, as they face challenges in establishing new communication competencies while navigating language acquisition.

PEDAGOGICAL FRAMEWORK FOR AI-ENHANCED WRITING

Stages of AI-Integrated Writing Instruction

Incorporating AI in teaching EFL writing can enhance student learning experiences. This section describes an AI teaching framework focused on writing, which includes four parts: prewriting, drafting, revising and editing, and feedback and reflections. For each component, different AI resources will be employed to assist writers in different stages. For preliminary activities, AI resources like ChatGPT can assist in brainstorming and organizing thoughts and ideas. During this stage, EFL learners can collaborate and expand on ideas. As learners engage in ChatGPT, they can devise certain writing task prompts, which will be useful.

As noted in (Salimi & Hajinia, 2024; Launonen et al., 2024), different perspectives could promote idea generation, foster creativity, and deepen comprehension of various topics. When faced with a complex task, this kind of facilitative assistance is critical; particularly for students struggling with the linguistic components of a task or those with limited English proficiency. Students grappling with the idea generation or the writing block that results from a perceived lack of words or difficulty articulating ideas will find this support particularly helpful.

The drafting process requires the writer to first develop ideas and then arrange and elaborate on them in structured paragraphs. At this stage, AI writing tools, particularly ChatGPT, can support students with the structural organization of their drafts. They are able to provide writing templates for various genres and corresponding outlining rules. This scope of support will assist EFL learners with the challenges of sentence and paragraph organization (Sarıcaoğlu, 2022). In addition, AI sentence expansion tools will assist learners with fluency and overall draft improvement (Schmidt-Fajlik, 2023). Drafting students will benefit from AI-powered suggestions that enhance their vocabulary and enrich their sentence structures and overall writing.

Clarity and precision in written work come from the revision and editing stages. For this stage, Grammarly and ProWritingAid serve crucial functions. They offer comprehensive assessments on grammar, punctuation, and style (Wahyuda & Putera, 2022). The readability analysis and contextual suggestions in these software programs aid students in fine-tuning their drafts and aligning them with the conventions of standard written English. EFL learners benefit greatly from these resources, as the prompt feedback helps them grasp the rules of language and the quality of their writing more deeply, thereby identifying and addressing their common errors (Basaula, 2024). However, these automating systems must be integrated within a broader pedagogical framework that helps students develop their own editing skills, rather than depending solely on automated systems (Malakar & Leeladharan, 2024).

Finally, ensuring students' ability to self-assess their writing and learn from it is critical. AI tools can assist students in this stage; however, the teacher's role is still highly relevant. Teachers should guide students in understanding AI feedback and outlining the self-assessment, calling on students to identify the learning and decide on the actionable next steps to take (Sarıcaoğlu, 2022). Teachers encourage students to think critically about the AI feedback, thereby developing a reflective attitude, which is essential in the writing process. This approach provides the students with an opportunity to engage collaboratively about the AI feedback and, in the process, engage in peer review. Through discussion and the reinforcement of the peer review process, students learn about the various components of the writing process. This approach highlights the collaborative aspect of writing in the EFL classroom.

The Teacher's Role as a Facilitator and Guide in the Ethical use of AI

Educators assist students in morally integrating AI-assisted technologies in their writing. This permits students to consider possible ethical implications. While educators consider the introduction of new AI technologies in their classrooms, it will be equally important to precisely identify the ethical implications students will need to unpack. This involves providing students with the requisite information and critical thinking necessary to navigate the challenging landscape of AI-assisted writing.

The introduction of AI technologies will, without a doubt, expand the opportunities for personalized learning in education and the provision of real-time customized feedback. Yet the expected benefits will come with ethical concerns that educators will need to address, including but not limited to privacy, data inequality, and biases that are deep-rooted in most AI systems (Bibi, 2024; Asrifan et al, 2026). Many students have not received formal ethical AI writing instruction, which subsequently indoctrinates and confuses students with a warped understanding of academic integrity as they attempt to misuse and unethically integrate technology into their academic work (Pan, 2024; Rosmayanti et al, 2023).

Illustrating the importance of integrity in digital writing will enable teachers to suggest guidelines for the ethical use of AI-based writing technologies in the absence of formal instructional guidelines. This includes a discussion of fundamental principles of AI ethics such as transparency, accountability, and fairness, while also stating that it is up to the user to evaluate the AI's outputs and offer critical feedback (Pan, 2024). For instance, educators can discuss how the algorithms of AI systems can reflect biases present in the training data, resulting in the generation of language that is less diverse and inclusive (Russell et al., 2022). Encouraging these conversations is important because it teaches students to understand and interrogate the rationale underlying AI recommendations and the implications of uncritical reliance on AI.

Adopting a methodical way of including ethics in the use of AI tools develops a feeling of ownership and accountability in students. Educators can stimulate students' interest in ethics through the use of 'real-world' unethical AI use case studies, students' discussions, and group work on unethical AI use situations (Choi et al., 2024). Such active involvement is crucial not only for learning the ethics of a given subject but also for developing the essential higher-order skills of critical reasoning needed for rational decision-making in the use of AI tools.

Having teachers attend professional development workshops on the ethical implications of AI in the classroom has a positive ripple effect in assisting students (Meylani, 2024). Teacher ethical AI training sets forth ongoing teacher training. By removing ethical AI training from the classroom setting, teachers can facilitate AI ethics classroom discussions. As stewards of academic ethics, teachers themselves should demonstrate ethical AI use by working through ethical issues in an openly guided manner (D'Souza et al., 2024). Establishing clear AI classroom use policies is a necessary, though insufficient, step to guide ethical AI use in the classroom.

Considering a set of guidelines regarding permitted uses of AI may be instructive for schools. Such guidelines may inform teachers and learners of the ethical boundaries within which AI instruments may be employed. These regulations should center on the principles of fairness, respect, and transparency, which will improve understanding of the ethical considerations regarding AI use (Knowles, 2021).

To summarize, the instructional facilitator role regarding responsible AI use and the associated challenges it entails is undoubtedly complex. However, teachers can prepare students for the responsible use of AI through the instruction of core ethical values, the promotion of critical inquiry, and the establishment of comprehensive policies. This approach affords students a clear understanding of the ethical implications of AI, and thus, the responsible use of technology will improve their writing while observing the school's ethical standards.

Integration Model in the ELT Lesson Plan

Incorporating AI in ELT offers transformative potential within the field. For AI to be effectively integrated within lesson planning, a comprehensive framework detailing the steps and considerations associated with the planning process is essential. This section outlines a comprehensive framework designed for ELT lesson planning that emphasizes the need for integration within structured formats, distinct activities, as well as the contribution of teachers and students, respectively.

Aligning the use of AI tools with set learning objectives is a critical consideration in the integration framework. This alignment ensures that the intended use of the tools is closely related to the learning outcomes to be achieved. Akbarani, 2024. For instance, AI is useful in vocabulary acquisition and language practice. This stipulates that lesson objective-focused tools are critical to the goal of each lesson. A lesson plan starts with an introduction phase where teachers present the topic and objectives, followed by interactive brainstorming where students use AI tools such as ChatGPT to generate ideas and topic-related vocabulary(Gyawali & Mehandroo, 2022). This phase is essential in piquing students' interest and stimulating engagement.

In the lesson design, after the introduction, the model proposes an interactive instructional component that fuses AI tools with active learning strategies. In this example, teachers are able to employ AI-based writing tools such as Grammarly or ProWritingAid to assist in the writing of students' papers at the drafting stage. Such tools provide students with instant feedback on the grammatical and stylistic components of their writing, and also demonstrate that writing is a process, as students are prompted to revise their drafts—and in some cases revise their drafts significantly—based on AI feedback (Mambu, 2022). In this sense, the drafting stage of writing achieves a balance between the use of technology and the individual author's personal expression, as it fosters autonomous learning and the ability to reason analytically.

For the integration model to be even more cohesive, lesson plans should incorporate classroom tasks involving group work structured around students' sharing their work and their AI-generated ideas with each other. Cooperative tasks are designed to foster peer feedback and dialogue, thereby enhancing the learning environment by establishing a community of practice in which the teacher and the classmates act as resources and support systems for one another (Idapalapati, 2024). In this phase, teachers have the opportunity to enhance learning by engaging in Socratic dialogue, providing needed scaffolding, and encouraging students to engage in critical discourse around each other's ideas and writing.

During the final stages of the lesson, which include revision and editing, the objective of employing AI tools ought to be the enhancement of students' work. This section entails students utilizing AI to implement modifications and receive instant feedback on those adjustments. In addition, students should engage in reflective thinking on the modification process they undertook (Fitria, 2021). The role of the teacher cannot be underestimated, as they guide the students in the process of work revision, emphasize the need for criticality concerning AI revision proposals, and ensure that students fully understand and assume the responsibility of authorship.

Assessment and reflection, as the final elements of the lesson, have to be integrated. Moreover, students ought to be allowed to consider the effectiveness of the AI tools they employed during the pre-writing stage once the lesson is completed. This should include an assessment of how AI assistance impacted their writing, as well as the value and mechanics of the language they used (Muthmainnah et al., 2022). These reflections should be teacher-guided, where the students are offered a space to discuss their AI language learning.

In closing, the AI integration model for ELT lesson planning is not more than the expected minimum that demonstrates how teachers can appropriately incorporate AI technology into their teaching. Ensuring that AI tools align with learning objectives, fostering collaborative activities, and promoting an examination of the role of technology are ways teachers assist EFL students with important connections to writing instruction. Therefore, as technologies with AI characteristics advance, there will be a need to revise and augment instructional designs to meaningfully incorporate AI so that students can learn a language effectively in today's educational context. (Gyawali & Mehandroo, 2022; Akbarani, 2024; Muthmainnah et al., 2022; Idapalapati, 2024; Fitria, 2021).

CASE EXAMPLES IN EFL CLASSROOMS

Integrating AI tools into EFL writing classrooms has fostered greater interest in writing instruction and increased student autonomy and empowerment. Here, I present brief case studies related to writing instruction in the AI era to illustrate the innovations and transformations in students' writing, the range of issues they address in their writing, and their attitudes toward AI as a writing aid in developing their writing.

Small studies on the use of AI writing tools, specifically ChatGPT and Grammarly, in the writing instruction of intermediate-level Indonesian EFL students have yielded positive results. In the initial phase of the study, students participated in a workshop that instructed them on the use of these tools for brainstorming, drafting, self-editing, and overall quality enhancement in writing. In subsequent lessons, students completed practice-based assignments that required them to write using AI tools and methods discussed in the workshop. Positive results have been attributed to the students' increased interest and motivation to write in the assigned tasks, as evidenced in the pre- and post-tests of the writing sample (Tajik, 2025).

Consider one of the students' writing samples before and after the intervention. Before the incorporation of AI tools, the student demonstrated weaknesses in constructing overly simplistic paragraphs, including excessive run-ons, poor transitions, and grammatical inaccuracies. This student subsequently revised their writing using ChatGPT and Grammarly, which improved the writing in grammar, clarity, and cohesion. The revisions to this writing sample indicate considerable improvement in the student's writing skills, which can be attributed to the AI tools available for constructing more sophisticated sentences and diverse word choices (Nazari et al., 2021).

In the advanced writing class, the instructor employed an integrated approach utilizing combined peer-review sessions with the AI tool ProWritingAid. The instructor designed the exercise to focus not only on the technical aspects of writing but also on the rhetorical aspects, such as audience awareness and argument construction. This collaborative editing approach also facilitated self-assessment, as students used AI tools to evaluate their writing before the peer feedback session (Tajik, 2025).

Interviews conducted with advanced students in the EFL program reflect a positive attitude towards the use of AI in their writing; many indicated that AI writing tools not only helped them draft their essays but also helped bolster their self-confidence. As one student wrote, "Grammarly helped me notice my recurring mistakes, and now I feel confident enough to write long essays" (Lai, 2025). Others explained that AI tools helped them think more creatively and experiment with diverse styles, perspectives, and patterns in their writing.

Still, students expressed some concerns about the disadvantages of AI. Some of my respondents mentioned that their reliance on AI tools had gotten to the point where the tools did their thinking for them. This indicates that educators need to emphasize the importance of maintaining one's unique writing style and voice and that even AI needs to be used deliberately rather than passively.

Overall, there is no denying that AI tools enhance the EFL writing classroom and offer a myriad of advantages like improving the clarity, precision, and interest level of student writing. The advancements made by students in their writing indicate the potential of AI in aiding the acquisition of new languages, particularly EFL. Moreover, the students' reflections reveal a lack of developed critical thinking skills and self-sufficiency in their writing. Therefore, teachers should strive to provide structures that encourage students to engage purposefully with AI, balancing the benefits of the technology with the authentic expression of students' voices in their writing endeavors.

CHALLENGES AND ETHICAL CONSIDERATIONS

One of the main worries about using AI tools in writing lessons is that students might copy other people's work or rely too much on them. As AI writing help gets better and better, EFL learners might unintentionally rely on these tools to make content that is very similar to what is already out there, which could lead to plagiarism. This worry is made worse by how easy it is for students to get AI-generated suggestions, which can make them do work that isn't original or creative. Also, automating writing can make the process of drafting, revising, and improving one's work less effective, which can hurt the growth of important writing skills. Teachers need to create a culture of academic honesty by teaching students about the consequences of plagiarism and pushing for a balance between using AI tools and developing their creative skills (Seo et al., 2021).

One major problem with using AI technologies in education is that not everyone has the same access to technology, especially in diverse EFL settings. Students who come from poor backgrounds or who live in remote areas may not have the tools they need to use AI tools effectively, like high-speed internet and modern devices. This digital divide can make the differences in educational outcomes even worse, which means that AI-assisted writing instruction won't help students who are already behind. To make sure that everyone has fair access to technology, policymakers and schools need to work together to solve this problem. Some examples of initiatives are giving resources to areas that don't have enough, giving training that uses devices that are easy to use, and making educational platforms that are open to all students (Subaveerapandiyan et al., 2023; Kumar & Suthar, 2024).

Also, both teachers and students need to be able to understand AI. To encourage responsible use among students, it's important to know what AI can and can't do. Teachers often find it hard to teach students how to use AI because many of them don't have the right training to use AI effectively in language instruction. Not being ready can lead to inconsistent or ineffective use of AI tools in the classroom, which can harm students' learning. So, teachers need to keep learning and getting better at using AI tools so that they can help their students learn how to use them critically (Barua et al., 2022; Sapci & Sapci, 2020).

To deal with these problems, it's important to come up with plans that raise ethical awareness and encourage the responsible use of AI. When teachers use AI in their classrooms, they can use frameworks that stress ethical issues like fairness, accountability, and openness. This entails involving students in dialogues regarding the importance of these ethical principles, steering discussions on the consequences of AI errors, and orchestrating activities that promote contemplation on their utilization of AI tools. Integrating ethical dilemmas into classroom discourse enables students to confront the moral ramifications of technology, thereby fostering critical thinking and awareness (Williams et al., 2022; Aghaziarati et al., 2023).

Also, creating a space where students can think about things can help them understand how they use AI tools. For example, giving students reflective assignments that make them think about how they used AI in a writing task and how it affected their learning can help them use these tools responsibly. Teachers can help students talk about AI's role in writing by encouraging conversations that look at both the pros and cons of relying too much on AI tools (Akgün & Greenhow, 2021).

In conclusion, AI presents promising prospects for the improvement of EFL writing instruction; however, educators must remain cognizant of the associated challenges and ethical implications inherent in its implementation. Educators can create a framework that encourages both the responsible use of AI tools and the growth of responsible future users by talking about the dangers of plagiarism and over-reliance, addressing equity issues, promoting AI literacy, and putting strategies for ethical awareness into action. In the end, teaching students to use AI in a smart and ethical way will lead to more fair and rewarding learning experiences for them.

IMPLICATION FOR TEACHER DEVELOPMENT AND POLICY

In light of the rapid pace of technological change, ELT teachers must receive professional training. As AI tools keep getting better, teachers need to know exactly how to use them to help their students learn languages and write better. Professional development programs ought to incorporate training on the functionalities of diverse AI tools, cultivating pedagogical expertise that is congruent with these innovations (Alruqi and AlHarbi, 2022). Workshops, online courses, and collaborative learning opportunities can help teachers learn about AI technology and think critically about its ethical implications (Gregersen et al., 2021). Institutions still need to provide ongoing support that focuses on both how well AI tools work and how they can be used in the classroom (Oh et al., 2021).

Schools and colleges are very important when it comes to making rules about how to use AI in language classes. They create frameworks that promote responsible technology integration while protecting academic integrity (Gregersen et al., 2021). Policies should make clear what is acceptable use of AI, with a focus on practices that encourage students to be original, creative, and think critically. Institutions can make sure that teachers and students use AI tools responsibly and don't break academic ethics by setting clear rules. Additionally, institutions ought to collaborate with educators to foster a sense of ownership and accountability in policy implementation, ensuring that these regulations align with real classroom experiences and the challenges encountered by educators (Pagallo et al., 2022).

As institutions create and enforce these rules, it is important to make long-term suggestions for how to use AI in ELT programs in a way that is sustainable. First, policies need to be constantly checked and changed as technology changes quickly. Institutions can improve their plans and make changes that need to be made by getting regular feedback from teachers and students (Pagallo et al., 2022). It is essential that educational policies remain adaptable and responsive to the changing landscape of AI applications within the classroom. Second, encouraging partnerships between schools and tech companies could lead to the creation of customized resources that help students reach their specific learning goals. This would make sure that technology is always in line with educational goals, rather than existing on its own (Carrasco et al., 2025).

Institutions should also put inclusivity and fairness first when thinking about AI in education. This entails the allocation of resources to mitigate the digital divide, guaranteeing that all students have access to essential technologies, and cultivating environments conducive to the benefits of AI interventions for all learners (Ozor et al., 2025). Also, professional development should focus on culturally responsive practices that teach teachers and students how to use technology in a way that takes into account different cultural backgrounds and learning styles (Theodorou et al., 2022).

Finally, it is important for teachers and students to be more aware of ethics in order to use technology responsibly. Schools should include ethics education in their teacher training and development programs. This should include topics like how AI affects writing, why it's important to avoid plagiarism, and how to encourage independent critical thinking (Ibrahim et al., 2023).

By incorporating ethical considerations into AI-related pedagogy, institutions can develop a generation of educators and learners equipped to navigate the complexities of AI technologies with integrity and discernment.

In conclusion, the consequences for teacher development and policy regarding the incorporation of AI in ELT are significant. It is critical that educational authorities prioritize professional development programs that provide educators with the requisite skills and knowledge to proficiently employ AI tools. At the same time, institutions must actively work to create clear rules about how AI can be used, creating a space that encourages new ideas while also encouraging moral responsibility. Long-term plans should focus on fairness, inclusion, and sustainability to make sure that AI makes education better instead of making problems worse. These efforts can help make the future of English Language Teaching more informed, open to everyone, and ethically aware of how AI technologies can change things.

CONCLUSION

AI has a lot of educational benefits when it comes to teaching EFL writing. AI technologies, including grammar and style checking tools like Grammarly and AI-assisted brainstorming tools like ChatGPT, give learners quick feedback, which helps them at many points in the writing process. Zaugg (2024) Aghaziarati et al. (2023). This feedback not only helps students improve their writing mechanics, but it also encourages them to learn on their own by letting them try out different language options, which improves their vocabulary and their ability to use the target language in a more advanced way. Additionally, employing AI tools can cultivate a more stimulating and interactive educational atmosphere that encourages students to actively engage in their writing assignments, thereby enhancing their confidence and proficiency in English (Göçen & AYDEMİR, 2020; Konyrova, 2024).

But it's important to find a balance between using technology and keeping the human touch that is so important for learning. Teachers play an important role as facilitators and mentors. They give students not only the pedagogical guidance they need but also the emotional support they need to deal with the difficulties of learning a new language. A teacher makes sure that each student gets individualized instruction, feedback on their work, and the assurance that AI tools are not a replacement for meaningful interactions between teachers and students. In this context, educators can leverage AI to enhance their teaching while preserving the fundamental human attributes of empathy, encouragement, and genuine engagement (Guo et al., 2020).

The goal for the future should be to give learners more power, not to replace traditional ways of learning with AI. This means creating a culture in schools that sees AI as a tool that can make boring tasks easier and boost creativity, rather than as a disruptive force (Aparicio-Gómez et al., 2024). As AI technologies continue to evolve, it is imperative that educators focus on equipping students with critical thinking and digital literacy skills that will enable them to engage with these tools responsibly and effectively. By encouraging the growth of analytical skills, teachers get students ready to tell the difference between AI-generated content and use these tools to express their own thoughts and ideas in writing.

In conclusion, AI offers a substantial opportunity to improve EFL writing instruction via personalized feedback and heightened learner engagement; however, it is crucial to maintain a balance between technological integration and conventional pedagogical methods. Putting more focus on teachers' roles in the learning process and creating an environment that gives students power will make sure that AI is a useful tool that adds to their educational journeys instead of taking away from the basic parts of meaningful learning. As we look to the future, it is important to push for the long-term use of AI in EFL classrooms that respects and enhances the human side of teaching. This will help students do well in a world that is becoming more digital.

REFERENCES

Aghaziarati, A., Nejatifar, S., & Abedi, A. (2023). Artificial intelligence in education: investigating teacher attitudes. aitechbesosci, 1(1), 35-42. https://doi.org/DOI: 10.61838/kman.aitech.1.1.6

Akbarani, R. (2024). Use of artificial intelligence in english language teaching. *International Journal of English Learning and Applied Linguistics (Ijelal), 4*(1), 14–23. DOI: 10.21111/ijelal.v4i1.10756

Akgün, S., & Greenhow, C. (2021). Artificial intelligence in education: Addressing ethical challenges in k-12 settings. *AI and Ethics, 2*(3), 431–440. DOI: 10.1007/s43681-021-00096-7 PMID: 34790956

Al-Raimi, M., Mudhsh, B., Al-Yafaei, Y., & Al-Maashani, S. (2024). Utilizing artificial intelligence tools for improving writing skills: Exploring omani efl learners' perspectives. *Forum for Linguistic Studies, 6*(2). Advance online publication. DOI: 10.59400/fls.v6i2.1177

Alruqi, S., & AlHarbi, M. (2022). Teachers' perceptions towards professional development training courses: Exploring the effects on teachers' performance in the saudi context. *Theory and Practice in Language Studies, 12*(9), 1723–1735. DOI: 10.17507/tpls.1209.04

Alzahrani, F., & Alotaibi, H. (2024). The impact of artificial intelligence on enhancing efl writing skills among high school students. *Journal of Educational and Human Sciences, 34*. Advance online publication. DOI: 10.33193/JEAHS.34.2024.482

Amin, M. (2023). Ai and chat gpt in language teaching: Enhancing efl classroom support and transforming assessment techniques. *International Journal of Higher Education Pedagogies, 4*(4), 1–15. DOI: 10.33422/ijhep.v4i4.554

Aparicio-Gómez, O., Aparicio-Gómez, C., & Feigenblatt, v. (2024). Tejiendo conexiones: la simbiosis transformadora entre aprendizaje e inteligencia artificial. Hachetetepé Revista Científica De Educación Y Comunicación, (28). https://doi.org/DOI: 10.25267/Hachetetepe.2024.i28.1103

Asrifan, A., Sudirman, R., Rosmayanti, V., & Sulolipu, A. A. (2026). Navigating Ethical AI: Ensuring Fairness in Educational Technologies. In *Foundations and Frameworks for AI in Education* (pp. 27-52). IGI Global Scientific Publishing.DOI: 10.4018/979-8-3373-2397-8.ch002

Babanoğlu, M., Karataş, T., & Dündar, E. (2025). Envisioning the future of ai-assisted efl teaching and learning: Conceptual representations of prospective teachers. *SAGE Open, 15*(2), 21582440251341590. Advance online publication. DOI: 10.1177/21582440251341590

Barua, P., Vicnesh, J., Gururajan, R., Oh, S., Palmer, E., Azizan, M., Kadri, N. A., & Acharya, U. (2022). Artificial intelligence enabled personalised assistive tools to enhance education of children with neurodevelopmental disorders—A review. *International Journal of Environmental Research and Public Health, 19*(3), 1192. DOI: 10.3390/ijerph19031192 PMID: 35162220

Basaula, A. (2024). Secondary level students' lived experience of being involved in academic writing in elt classroom. *Ganeshman Darpan, 9*(1), 56–65. DOI: 10.3126/gd.v9i1.68545

Baskara, F. (2023). Integrating chatgpt into efl writing instruction: Benefits and challenges. *International Journal on E-Learning*, *5*(1), 44–55. DOI: 10.31763/ijele.v5i1.858

Bhowmik, S. (2021). Writing instruction in an efl context: Learning to write or writing to learn language? *Belta Journal*, *5*(1), 30–42. DOI: 10.36832/beltaj.2021.0501.03

Bibi, A. (2024). Navigating the ethical landscape: ai integration in education. EATP, 1579-1585. https://doi.org/DOI: 10.53555/kuey.v30i6.5546

Carrasco, D., Alcántara, M., Várgas, C., Espino, B., Cabrera, C., Valdera, A., & Córdova, L. (2025). Sustainability of ai-assisted mental health intervention: A review of the literature from 2020–2025. *International Journal of Environmental Research and Public Health*, *22*(9), 1382. DOI: 10.3390/ijerph22091382 PMID: 41007526

Chen, J. (2023). Reform of english writing teaching method under the background of big data and artificial intelligence. *International Journal of e-Collaboration*, *19*(4), 1–16. DOI: 10.4018/IJeC.316828

Choi, J., Yang, E., & Goo, E. (2024). The effects of an ethics education program on artificial intelligence among middle school students: Analysis of perception and attitude changes. *Applied Sciences (Basel, Switzerland)*, *14*(4), 1588. DOI: 10.3390/app14041588

D'Souza, R., Mathew, M., Mishra, V., & Surapaneni, K. (2024). Twelve tips for addressing ethical concerns in the implementation of artificial intelligence in medical education. *Medical Education Online*, *29*(1), 2330250. Advance online publication. DOI: 10.1080/10872981.2024.2330250 PMID: 38566608

Dergaa, I., Chamari, K., Żmijewski, P., & Saad, H. (2023). From human writing to artificial intelligence generated text: Examining the prospects and potential threats of chatgpt in academic writing. *Biology of Sport*, *40*(2), 615–622. DOI: 10.5114/biolsport.2023.125623 PMID: 37077800

Ekizoğlu, M., & Demir, A. (2025). Ai-assisted writing feedback for enhancing secondary students' writing skills: an experimental study. https://doi.org/DOI: 10.21203/rs.3.rs-6430737/v1

Fitria, T. (2021). The use technology based on artificial intelligence in english teaching and learning). *Elt Echo the Journal of English Language Teaching in Foreign Language Context*, *6*(2). Advance online publication. DOI: 10.24235/eltecho.v6i2.9299

Göçen, A., & Aydemir, F. (2020). Artificial intelligence in education and schools. *Research on Education and Media*, *12*(1), 13–21. DOI: 10.2478/rem-2020-0003

Gregersen, T., Mercer, S., & MacIntyre, P. (2021). Language teacher perspectives on stress and coping. *Foreign Language Annals*, *54*(4), 1145–1163. DOI: 10.1111/flan.12544

Guo, Y., Hao, Z., Zhao, S., Gong, J., & Yang, F. (2020). Artificial intelligence in health care: Bibliometric analysis. *Journal of Medical Internet Research*, *22*(7), e18228. DOI: 10.2196/18228 PMID: 32723713

Gyawali, Y., & Mehandroo, M. (2022). Artificial intelligence in english language teaching: Navigating the future with emerging perspectives. *Journal of Language and Linguistics in Society*, (26), 21–27. DOI: 10.55529/jlls.26.21.27

Hanušová, S., Dontcheva-Navrátilová, O., Vališová, M., & Matulová, M. (2020). Process genre approach to l2 academic writing: an intervention study. Xlinguae, 30-51. https://doi.org/DOI: 10.18355/XL.2020.13.04.03

Harunasari, S. (2023). Examining the effectiveness of ai-integrated approach in efl writing: A case of chatgpt. *International Journal of Progressive Sciences and Technologies*, *39*(2), 357. DOI: 10.52155/ijpsat.v39.2.5516

Hassan, N. (2020). Using the genre-based approach for developing efl writing skills among student teachers at faculty of education students. , 31(12305), 23-47. https://doi.org/DOI: 10.21608/jfeb.2020.174655

Ibrahim, S., Aziz, A., Said, N., & Ismail, H. (2023). Malaysian english language teachers' willingness, readiness, needs and wants to develop graphic oral history elt materials. *International Journal of Learning Teaching and Educational Research*, *22*(5), 101–118. DOI: 10.26803/ijlter.22.5.5

Idapalapati, S.Srinivasa Rao Idapalapati. (2024). Ai integration in elt as a disruptive mechanism. *International Journal of Science and Research Archive*, *12*(1), 922–933. DOI: 10.30574/ijsra.2024.12.1.0941

Kadmiry, M. (2021). The comparison between the process-oriented approach and the product-oriented approach in teaching writing the case of moroccan efl students in preparatory classes for the grandes ecoles. https://doi.org/DOI: 10.31235/osf.io/4aebr

Knowles, M. (2021). Five motivating concerns for ai ethics instruction. *Proceedings of the Association for Information Science and Technology*, *58*(1), 472–476. DOI: 10.1002/pra2.481

Kong, S., Lee, J., & Tsang, O. (2024). A pedagogical design for self-regulated learning in academic writing using text-based generative artificial intelligence tools: 6-p pedagogy of plan, prompt, preview, produce, peer-review, portfolio-tracking. Research and Practice in Technology Enhanced Learning, 19, 030. https://doi.org/DOI: 10.58459/rptel.2024.19030

Konyrova, L. (2024). The evolution of language learning: Exploring ai's impact on teaching english as a second language. *Eurasian Science Review*, *2*(2), 133–138. DOI: 10.63034/esr-42

Kostka, I. and Toncelli, R. (2023). Exploring applications of chatgpt to english language teaching: opportunities, challenges, and recommendations. Teaching English as a Second or Foreign Language--Tesl-Ej, 27(3). https://doi.org/DOI: 10.55593/ej.27107int

Kumar, D., & Suthar, N. (2024). Ethical and legal challenges of ai in marketing: An exploration of solutions. *Journal of Information Communication and Ethics in Society*, *22*(1), 124–144. DOI: 10.1108/JICES-05-2023-0068

Lai, Z. (2025). The impact of ai-assisted blended learning on writing efficacy and resilience. *International Journal of Computer-Assisted Language Learning and Teaching*, *15*(1), 1–21. DOI: 10.4018/IJCALLT.377174

Launonen, P., Talalakina, E., & Dubova, G. (2024). Students' perceptions of using chatgpt for academic writing in english. *Półrocznik Językoznawczy Tertium*, *9*(1), 219–249. DOI: 10.7592/Tertium.2024.9.1.274

Malakar, P., & Leeladharan, M. (2024). Generative ai tools for collaborative content creation. *DESIDOC Journal of Library and Information Technology*, *44*(3), 151–157. DOI: 10.14429/djlit.44.3.19698

Mambu, J. (2022). Co-constructing a critical elt curriculum: A case study in an indonesian-based english language teacher education program. *TESOL Journal*, *13*(3), e667. Advance online publication. DOI: 10.1002/tesj.667

Meylani, R. (2024). Artificial intelligence in the education of teachers: A qualitative synthesis of the cutting-edge research literature. *Journal of Computer and Education Research*, *12*(24), 600–637. DOI: 10.18009/jcer.1477709

Minh, A. (2024). Leveraging chatgpt for enhancing english writing skills and critical thinking in university freshmen. Journal of Knowledge Learning and Science Technology Issn 2959-6386 (Online), 3(2), 51-62. https://doi.org/DOI: 10.60087/jklst.vol3.n2.p62

Moussa, A., & Belhiah, H. (2024). Beyond syntax: exploring moroccan undergraduate efl learners' engagement with ai-assisted writing. https://doi.org/DOI: 10.31235/osf.io/3fr45
Moussa, A., & Belhiah, H. (2024). Beyond syntax: exploring moroccan undergraduate efl learners' engagement with ai-assisted writing. https://doi.org/DOI: 10.31235/osf.io/3fr45
Moybeka, A., Syariatin, N., Tatipang, D., Mushthoza, D., Dewi, N., & Tineh, S. (2023). Artificial intelligence and english classroom: the implications of ai toward efl students' motivation. Edumaspul - Jurnal Pendidikan, 7(2), 2444-2454. https://doi.org/DOI: 10.33487/edumaspul.v7i2.6669

Mudawy, A. (2024). Investigating efl faculty members' perceptions of integrating artificial intelligence applications to improve the research writing process: a case study at majmaah university. https://doi.org/DOI: 10.31235/osf.io/k4ub8

Muthmainnah, M., Seraj, P., & Oteir, I. (2022). Playing with ai to investigate human-computer interaction technology and improving critical thinking skills to pursue 21st century age. *Education Research International*, *2022*, 1–17. DOI: 10.1155/2022/6468995

Nazari, N., Shabbir, M., & Setiawan, R. (2021). Application of artificial intelligence powered digital writing assistant in higher education: Randomized controlled trial. *Heliyon*, *7*(5), e07014. DOI: 10.1016/j.heliyon.2021.e07014 PMID: 34027198
Nazari, N., Shabbir, M., & Setiawan, R. (2021). Application of artificial intelligence powered digital writing assistant in higher education: Randomized controlled trial. *Heliyon*, *7*(5), e07014. DOI: 10.1016/j.heliyon.2021.e07014 PMID: 34027198
Nazim, M., & Mohammad, T. (2022). Implications of design thinking in an efl classroom: Writing in context. *Theory and Practice in Language Studies*, *12*(12), 2723–2730. DOI: 10.17507/tpls.1212.31

Oh, Y., Zhang, J., Fang, M., & Fukuoka, Y. (2021). A systematic review of artificial intelligence chatbots for promoting physical activity, healthy diet, and weight loss. *The International Journal of Behavioral Nutrition and Physical Activity*, *18*(1), 160. Advance online publication. DOI: 10.1186/s12966-021-01224-6 PMID: 34895247

Ozor, N., Nwakaire, J., Nyambane, A., Muhatiah, W., & Nwobodo, C. (2025). Enhancing africa's agriculture and food systems through responsible and gender inclusive ai innovation: Insights from ai4afs network. *Frontiers in Artificial Intelligence*, *7*, 1472236. Advance online publication. DOI: 10.3389/frai.2024.1472236 PMID: 39917548

Pagallo, U., Ciani, J., & Durante, M. (2022). The environmental challenges of ai in eu law: Lessons learned from the artificial intelligence act (aia) with its drawbacks. *Transforming Government*, *16*(3), 359–376. DOI: 10.1108/TG-07-2021-0121

Pan, J.PAN. (2024). Ai-driven english language learning program and academic writing integrity in the era of intelligent interface. *English Language Teaching and Linguistics Studies*, *6*(4), 120. DOI: 10.22158/eltls.v6n4p120

Parviz, M. (2025). Generative ai in the english composition classroom practical and adaptable strategies. *International Journal of Computer-Assisted Language Learning and Teaching*, *15*(1), 1–5. DOI: 10.4018/IJCALLT.386135

Pratama, A., & Sulistiyo, U. (2024). A systematic review of artificial intelligence in enhancing english foreign learners' writing skill. *PIJED*, *3*(2), 170–181. DOI: 10.59175/pijed.v3i2.299

Rahayu, R., Weda, S., Muliati, , & De Vega, N. (2024). Artificial intelligence in writing instruction: A self-determination theory perspective. *Xlinguae*, *17*(1), 234–244. DOI: 10.18355/XL.2024.17.01.16

Ratih, M., & Kastuhandani, F. (2024). Students' lived experiences in utilizing artificial intelligence for thesis writing. Nusra Jurnal Penelitian Dan Ilmu Pendidikan, 5(2), 760-769. https://doi.org/ DOI: 10.55681/nusra.v5i2.2696

Rosmayanti, V., Patak, A. A., & Noni, N. (2023). Integrating Technology into ESP Instruction: Teaching English for Pharmacy Students. *The Journal of AsiaTEFL*, *20*(2), 475–484. DOI: 10.18823/asiatefl.2023.20.2.18.475

Roy, K., & Swargiary, K. (2024). Chatgpt impact on efl indian undergraduates. https://doi.org/ DOI: 10.20944/preprints202405.0130.v2

Russell, R., Novak, L., Patel, M., Garvey, K., Craig, K., Jackson, G., & Miller, B. (2022). Competencies for the use of artificial intelligence–based tools by health care professionals. *Academic Medicine*, *98*(3), 348–356. DOI: 10.1097/ACM.0000000000004963 PMID: 36731054

Salimi, E., & Hajinia, M. (2024). Llms and academic writing in practice: exploring participants' utilization of gpt during an ai-assisted course on writing research papers. https://doi.org/DOI: 10.21203/rs.3.rs-5534554/v1

Sapci, A., & Sapci, H. (2020). Artificial intelligence education and tools for medical and health informatics students: Systematic review. *JMIR Medical Education*, *6*(1), e19285. DOI: 10.2196/19285 PMID: 32602844

Sarıcaoğlu, A. (2022). Towards teaching undergraduate-level disciplinary writing in english majors: A genre-based approach. *RumeliDe Dil ve Edebiyat Arastirmalari Dergisi*, (26), 1024–1038. DOI: 10.29000/rumelide.1074517

Schmidt-Fajlik, R. (2023). Chatgpt as a grammar checker for japanese english language learners: A comparison with grammarly and prowritingaid. *AsiaCALL Online Journal*, *14*(1), 105–119. DOI: 10.54855/acoj.231417

Seo, K., Tang, J., Roll, I., Fels, S., & Yoon, D. (2021). The impact of artificial intelligence on learner–instructor interaction in online learning. *International Journal of Educational Technology in Higher Education*, *18*(1), 54. Advance online publication. DOI: 10.1186/s41239-021-00292-9 PMID: 34778540

Song, C., & Song, Y. (2023). Enhancing academic writing skills and motivation: Assessing the efficacy of chatgpt in ai-assisted language learning for efl students. *Frontiers in Psychology*, *14*, 1260843. Advance online publication. DOI: 10.3389/fpsyg.2023.1260843 PMID: 38162975

Subaveerapandiyan, A., Paladhi, M., & Maruthaveeran, V. (2023). Evaluating ai literacy proficiency among lis researchers in asean. *Library Hi Tech News*, *41*(4), 6–8. DOI: 10.1108/LHTN-07-2023-0121

Tajik, A. (2025). Exploring the role of ai-driven dynamic writing platforms in improving efl learners' writing skills and fostering their motivation. https://doi.org/DOI: 10.21203/rs.3.rs-5788599/v1

Theodorou, A., Nieves, J., & Dignum, V. (2022). Good ai for good: how ai strategies of the nordic countries address the sustainable development goals. https://doi.org//arxiv.2210.09010DOI: 10.48550

Utami, S., Andayani, A., Winarni, R., & Sumarwati, S. (2023). Utilization of artificial intelligence technology in an academic writing class: How do indonesian students perceive? *Contemporary Educational Technology*, *15*(4), ep450. DOI: 10.30935/cedtech/13419

Wahyuda, M., & Putera, A. (2022). The effectiveness of prowritingaid toward students writing skills in senior high school. *English Edu Journal of English Teaching and Learning*, *1*(1), 26–34. DOI: 10.18860/jetl.v1i1.1624

Wale, B., & Kassahun, Y. (2024). The transformative power of ai writing technologies: Enhancing efl writing instruction through the integrative use of writerly and google docs. *Human Behavior and Emerging Technologies*, *2024*, 1–15. DOI: 10.1155/2024/9221377

Wang, C. (2024). Exploring students' generative ai-assisted writing processes: Perceptions and experiences from native and nonnative english speakers. *Technology Knowledge and Learning*, *30*(3), 1825–1846. DOI: 10.1007/s10758-024-09744-3

Williams, R., Ali, S., Devasia, N., DiPaola, D., Hong, J., Kaputsos, S., Jordan, B., & Breazeal, C. (2022). Ai + ethics curricula for middle school youth: Lessons learned from three project-based curricula. *International Journal of Artificial Intelligence in Education, 33*(2), 325–383. DOI: 10.1007/s40593-022-00298-y PMID: 35935456

Wu, L. (2024). Ai-based writing tools: Empowering students to achieve writing success. *Advances in Educational Technology and Psychology, 8*(2). Advance online publication. DOI: 10.23977/aetp.2024.080206

Xi, L. (2024). Research on the english writing teaching model in the ai era. *MMSE, 6*(3), 111. DOI: 10.22158/mmse.v6n3p111

Zaugg, T. (2024). Embracing innovation in education: investigating the use and impact of artificial intelligent assistants among preservice teachers. https://doi.org/DOI: 10.21203/rs.3.rs-5032655/v1

Zhao, X. (2022). Leveraging artificial intelligence (ai) technology for english writing: Introducing wordtune as a digital writing assistant for efl writers. *RELC Journal, 54*(3), 890–894. DOI: 10.1177/00336882221094089

Zohbie, A., & Bhowmik, S. (2024). Using a genre-based approach to teach writing to elementary esl students: A boon or a barrier? *TESOL Journal, 15*(4), e819. Advance online publication. DOI: 10.1002/tesj.819

KEY TERMS AND DEFINITIONS

Artificial Intelligence (AI): A field of computer science concerned with the development of computer systems capable of performing functions that, under normal circumstances, would require the intellectual faculties of a human being, including learning, reasoning, problem-solving, and comprehension of language.

AI Literacy: The capacity to comprehend, assess, and utilize artificial intelligence in a contextualized and responsible manner, particularly in academic settings and other forms of writing.

ChatGPT: A product of OpenAI, this is a generative AI language processing model that helps in brainstorming, drafting, editing, and generating assignments, as well as in writing tasks for learners of the English language.

Digital Literacy: The ability and the right to use digital tools and technologies for communication, learning, and the creation of content, including a consideration of ethical and critical perspectives.

EFL Writing: The process of constructing written material in English by learners who are non-native speakers of the language, typically with the aid of specific instructional methods and appropriate technologies.

Ethical AI Use: The use of AI technologies that is responsible, fair, and considerate of privacy, transparency, plagiarism avoidance, academic integrity, and ethical use in education.

Feedback Loop: The system in which learners revise their writing and receive corrections/input from AI tools, along with feedback that helps them adjust their work, improves their overall performance.

Process Writing Approach: A teaching method that emphasizes writing as a recursive process that includes planning, drafting, revising, and editing, rather than concentrating on just the finished product.

Self-Regulated Learning: A learner-centered approach in which a student sets a goal, then tracks and self-evaluates their progress, refining the strategy to achieve the targeted learning outcome, often assisted by AI.

Writing Empowerment: The strengthening of a learner's confidence, autonomy, and creativity in writing, which occurs through constructive feedback and critical engagement combined with the responsible use of AI.

Chapter 10
Technology Assisted Through Virtual Robot Tutor (VTR) in Writing English Short Stories:
From Tools to Innovative Pedagogy

Muthmainnah Muthmainnah
https://orcid.org/0000-0003-3170-2374
Universitas Al Asyariah Mandar, Indonesia

Luis Cardoso
https://orcid.org/0000-0003-3748-5593
Polytechnic Institute of Portalegre, Portugal

M. Nagalakshmi
Vels Institute of Science, Technology, and Advanced Studies, India

Eka Apriani
https://orcid.org/0000-0002-8427-2817
Institut Agama Islam Negeri (IAIN), Curup, Indonesia

Ahmad Al Yakin
https://orcid.org/0000-0003-3170-2374
Universitas Al Asyariah Mandar, Indonesia

Ali Sorayyaei Azar
https://orcid.org/0000-0003-3539-8250
Universiti Malaya, Kuala Lumpur, Malaysia

Ahmed J. Obaid
https://orcid.org/0000-0003-0376-5546
University of Kufa, Iraq

ABSTRACT

Students in English as a Foreign Language (EFL) classes have reported more individualised and innovative learning experiences with the integration of AI in hybrid classes. However, teaching narrative writing is one area where artificial intelligence is currently underutilised in Indonesia. Most existing technology-assisted approaches focus on grammar checking and output templates. Based on the findings of this study indicates that VRT is more than just a technological tool; learning VRT assists students in storyboarding, brainstorming, and self-editing through practical dialogic feedback. AI-assisted VRT can be a versatile and scalable tool for teaching writing in resource-constrained EFL environments, such as in Indonesia. This study contributes

DOI: 10.4018/979-8-3373-5601-3.ch010

to the credibility of incorporating intelligent agents into EFL classrooms as a means to foster students' autonomy, creativity, and narrative skills. This solution helps educators, legislators, and instructional designers improve student performance in writing instruction in the digital age.

INTRODUCTION

GenAI has transformed EFL training by using intelligent technology in the classroom to enhance effective language acquisition. While crucial for academic achievement and successful communication in general, teaching EFL students to write effectively remains a significant challenge, particularly for EFL students in ASEAN and Indonesia. NLP and LLM have emerged as viable options for educators seeking to enhance their students' writing skills through the integration of AI and robotics into the classroom. Therefore, writing short stories is a valuable strategy for students to practise their writing, editing, and analytical skills. Students' creative capacity, analytical thinking, grammatical proficiency, and practical competence are all enhanced through this activity (Muthmainnah et al., 2025). This study introduces a unique approach to teaching students short narrative writing skills in English, utilising a Virtual Robot Tutor (VRT). This approach integrates cutting-edge technological resources with modern teaching methods for the 21st century. Educators worldwide and in Indonesia are seriously considering incorporating robotic agents and artificial intelligence (AI) into higher education in a practical manner. This can lead to increased active student engagement, more personalised instruction, and the provision of necessary scaffolding (Aditya, D., & Otermans, 2025; Ren & Wu, 2025).

Interactive and multimodal interfaces make it simple to converse, obtain feedback, boost communication, and connect with others emotionally (Muthmainnah et al., 2024). Virtual robot tutors can be screen-based avatars or social robots. Such tools can be useful in English as a foreign language (EFL) writing since they offer immediate feedback on mistakes and assist with mental activities like editing, droughting, and concept organisation. Particularly relevant for narrative writing, where students need to strike a balance between originality, grammar correctness, and a practical grasp of story structure, are these abilities. According to Jin (2025) and Shahzad et al. (2025), students' perspectives on writing as a means of communication rather than only an evaluation tool can be shifted by the use of digital tools in language writing settings. Unfortunately, in Indonesia, students of English as a foreign language (EFL) are typically confined to using passive writing tools like grammar checkers or learning through templates because the use of AI-based technology in EFL instruction is still little understood, particularly in the context of creative writing.

In the class, using intelligent agents like VRT in writing lessons is still in its early stages, the *"Merdeka Belajar"* curriculum put out by the Indonesian Ministry of Education has helped students understand how to use technology. Research has mainly focused on various forms of online writing tools, mobile learning applications, and Learning Management Systems (LMS) (Ikhsan et al., 2025; Morady et al., 2025; Oubibi et al., 2025; Pakdel et al., 2025). Recent research including Li et al. (2025), Hsieh et al. (2025), and Derakhshan, et al. (2025); Nuemaihom et al., 2025; Li et al., 2025) suggests that students can benefit from working with virtual instructors that employ dialogic systems and natural language processing (NLP) to enhance their collaborative writing, story-building, and adaption skills. Also, unlike many Indonesian classrooms, several of this research have taken place at schools that have access to a wealth of technology and resources.

Improving the accessibility of AI-assisted writing instruction in the Indonesian EFL setting is the primary objective of this work. Literacy isn't enough for today's students. Their proficiency with technology will also help them write creatively and analytically. The rapid advancement of technology and the ever-changing ways in which individuals learn make this talent crucial.

It was already crucial to learn independently and with technology throughout the COVID-19 pandemic era. A decent, up-to-date education is quite difficult to get by, as this pandemic has also demonstrated. To bridge the gap between analogue and digital methods of teaching English as a foreign language in Indonesia, this article presents a Virtual Robot Tutor for composing short stories. The strength of this study is that it provides a creative language teaching strategy that can be applied in all types of schools. This study is important and applicable in presenting an innovation in teaching English short story writing that combines process-based methodology with AI-driven VRT. The proposed model maximizes the function of VRT to provide personalized, real-time, and multi-modal feedback, as stated by Babaoğlu et al. (2025). The proposed VRT writing learning model differs from the existing conventional methodologies, which mostly use teacher-centered training and manual feedback. Here, students have more freedom to express themselves creatively and imaginatively as a result. Furthermore, this study explores the specific difficulties faced by Indonesian EFL students, with an emphasis on their concerns regarding the consistency of their stories, their grammatical accuracy, and their confidence in expressing themselves creatively. Third, this study contributes to the literature on Human-Robot Interaction (HRI) in the classroom by examining the effects of VRT on students' emotions and learning outcomes (Muthmainnah et al., 2025). This study concludes by providing several recommendations to Indonesian educators and instructors on how to use AI-based technologies in a reasonable and appropriate manner, depending on the circumstances.

The theoretical basis for this chapter is derived from Chen's (2025) sociocognitive model of writing, which states that writing is a complex process that requires prewriting, translation, and revision. Through the integration of virtual tutoring (VRT), a distributed cognition paradigm is established in which a robot instructor helps students develop more independent and efficient cognitive patterns. By conversing with students, demonstrating activities, offering ideas, and providing feedback, a more knowledgeable other (MKO) VRT enhances learning and learning outcomes. This type of approach is beneficial in general, but especially in situations where a human teacher is unable or unwilling to provide direct feedback. An optimal strategy is to follow Vygotsky's ZPD model. The presence of a robot tutor can offer social and emotional support, which can help students feel more comfortable and confident when writing (Serholt et al., 2021). This chapter seeks to fill a substantial gap in English as a Foreign Language (EFL) teaching in Indonesia by exploring the potential of technology, specifically virtual robot tutors, to transform from a mere tool into a crucial aspect of a new paradigm in modern education. Adapting to recent technological developments, this work seeks to demonstrate, both theoretically and practically, that intelligent virtual agents can help students hone their creative writing skills in a practical, efficient, and relevant manner. This study presents a future-orientated strategy for global English language teaching that combines the advantages of AI with the goal of effective narrative writing training.

VIRTUAL ROBOT TUTOR (VTR) PRACTICES IN EFL

Integrating VRT, or virtual robot tutors, in this study aims to create an effective online learning environment where the software mimics the actions of a human teacher. An avatar or intelligent interface on a screen or device represents VRT, distinguishing it from a real humanoid robot. Research has indicated that VRT can significantly improve communication, adaptive learning, and individual engagement. Using machine learning, affective computing, speech recognition, and natural language processing (NLP), these tutors can understand students' speech and respond appropriately (Liu et al., 2025; Pham & Tran, 2025). Math, physics, and ESL classes are just a few examples of the many classes that can benefit from using VRT. Visual response tools (VRT) can help ESL students with better sentence construction, vocabulary, grammar, and story organization (Moran & Pyles, 2025).Unlike static educational platforms or digital worksheets, VRT, with its learning activities, facilitates direct discussions between educators and students. Writing assignments requiring language, creativity, and analysis work particularly well with the platform's modelling, guidance, and correction capabilities.

Anand et al. (2025) showed that students' writing motivation, ability to memorize previously taught content, enthusiasm for writing, and writing anxiety can be improved by utilising VRT as an effective virtual peer or mentor. Qin and Chuaychoowong (2025) found that students' descriptive writing skills improved when they used a robot tutor to lead structured discussions. Furthermore, Serholt et al. (2021) found that students remained engaged longer in open-ended activities like story writing due to the "human nature" of these virtual agents. Technology-assisted language learning (TALL) has revolutionized writing instruction in EFL classrooms. With the help of AI interventions, students can learn independently, receive immediate feedback, and express themselves in various ways.

Tools such as AI-based feedback systems, grammar checkers, word processors, and smartphone apps make these developments possible. For example, according to Khatoony et al. (2025), students can benefit from collaborative writing platforms like ChatGPT in many ways, including story structure, automatic error correction, word suggestions, and more. Tutorial learning systems, skill-practice platforms, and intelligent tutoring systems (ITS) are three main categories of computer-assisted language learning (CALL) systems that assist writers (Zhai, 2025). The most advanced type is ITS, which uses artificial intelligence to adapt its responses to learner speech in real time. Vehicle-to-pedestrian communication (VRT) systems integrate embodied interaction with discourse systems. Because many students struggle to generate ideas, organize them in a logical sequence, and create a smooth flow in their creative writing, their potential is crucial in this field. These advances have not eliminated the prevalence of teacher-centred approaches, textbooks, and manual feedback in many English as a Foreign Language (EFL) classroom in Indonesia (Mohsen et al., 2025).

Accuracy, rather than fluidity or originality, remains the primary goal. Furthermore, teachers lack the necessary skills in digital pedagogy and easy access to smart technology, which hinders their ability to effectively utilise VRT in the classroom. Thus, new teaching methods, particularly in creative writing, do not make extensive use of electronic resources, even when available. Furthermore, VRT complements and enhances existing technology-assisted practices in teaching English as a foreign language writing, as described in the Table 1 below.

Table 1. Connecting Virtual Robot Tutors and Technology-Assisted EFL Writing

Component	Technology-Assisted Efl Writing (Ta-Efl)	Virtual Robot Tutor (Vrt)	Pedagogical Shift
Feedback Mechanism	Automated correction (e.g., Grammarly, MS Word)	Real-time dialogic feedback and adaptive scaffolding	From static correction to dynamic dialogue
Interaction Type	One-way system (user-tool)	Two-way interactive tutoring (learner-VRT dialogue)	From passive use to active engagement
Cognitive Support	Grammar, vocabulary, and structure templates	Narrative logic building, idea generation, sequencing	From accuracy-only to holistic writing support
Emotional Engagement	Minimal (interface only)	Embodied agent offers affective feedback (e.g., encouragement, prompts)	From impersonal to relational interaction
Creative Facilitation	Templates and prompts	Story prompts, co-creation, brainstorming with VRT	From structured output to co-creative production
Learner Autonomy	Limited (tool-dependency)	High (learner-led interaction, VRT follows learner direction)	From tool dependency to self-regulated learning
Creative Facilitation	Templates and prompts	Story prompts, co-creation, brainstorming with VRT	From structured output to co-creative production
Learner Autonomy	Limited (tool-dependency)	High (learner-led interaction, VRT follows learner direction)	From tool dependency to self-regulated learning
Pedagogical Role of Technology	Supplementary tool	Co-tutor and learning partner	From support tool to pedagogical agent

Source: Adaptation from Nuemaihom et al., 2025.

Table 1 shows how virtual robot tutors transform conventional methods of using technology to aid language learning. Unlike tools like Grammarly and Google Translate, which only provide translation or correction services, the advantages of VRT platforms encourage communication between students, much like in a classroom. Cognitive tasks such as organising, brainstorming, and refining story elements are also facilitated by VRT; VRT goes beyond simply validating language.

The ability to consistently use creativity, empathy, and a variety of language skills is crucial in short story writing, necessitating this modification. This freedom to express oneself freely and engage in direct dialogic inquiry is what distinguishes short story writing from essay writing. Turvey and Pachler (2025); (Man et al., 2025) stated that static platforms are less effective in fostering higher-order thinking and creativity than dialogic and multimodal settings

WRITING IN EFL: CHALLENGES AND NEEDS

There is a common misconception in many English as a foreign language (EFL) class, particularly in Southeast Asian nations like Indonesia, that writing is a process rather than an art form, and that students should not be allowed much leeway to be creative or make changes to their work (Liu & Xiao, 2025); (Yang & Chano, 2025). According to Xiao et al. (2025),. Students can enhance their fluency, passion in writing, storytelling abilities, and self-expression via the underappreciated practice of writing short tales.

According to Geetha (2025), students should be guided through the writing cycle stages including prewriting, draughting, revising, and editing with the use of structured coaching and constructive criticism. The personal support that EFL students require to develop their writing over time is unfortunately lacking in many Indonesian classrooms due to teacher workloads, huge class sizes, and a lack of class time (Pardede, 2025). Because of this knowledge gap, writing courses should include intelligent and scalable technologies like Virtual Robot Tutors (VRTs) to help students with their writing, provide them constructive criticism, and tailor their support to their specific needs. In 2025,

In this study, "Virtual Robot Tutors" (VRTs) are digital agents like ChatGPT, Gemini, or Cici bot that mimic human instructors in conversation and interaction. These agents are typically powered by artificial intelligence (AI) and based on avatars (Muthmainnah et al., 2025). As intelligent tutors, VRTs can converse with students to keep them engaged while they write, offer real-time feedback, and walk them through the steps of the writing process. Their development incorporates elements of affective computing, machine learning, and natural language processing (NLP). "Your beginning is less interesting" is one example of how they might offer structural assistance. Do you wish to include persons or events? In line with sociocognitive theories of learning, such as the Zone of Proximal Development (ZPD) proposed by Lev Vygotsky, this type of interactive scaffolding is appropriate. Beyond what they are currently capable of, pupils in the ZPD receive assistance. Because the virtual instructor seemed so much like a real person, students were more engaged and able to regulate their own behaviour when using it (Rigopouli et al., 2025). The use of a robot tutor improved the flow and creativity of students' academic writing papers, according to Apriani et al. (2025).

According to studies conducted by Corbeil (2025), a feedback system powered by artificial intelligence helped students improve their writing. This technique provided pupils with more frequent, faster, and individually tailored feedback. I find the iterative and dialogic process of writing stories using VRT fascinating. As they write and revise, the students will gain from comments, questions, and explanations about the story's reasoning. Using VRT is getting easier for all of these things. Whether it's serving as a guide, a collaborator, or even an audience, VRT can take on many roles to enrich the creative process. Unlike the two passive grammar checkers, QuillBot and Grammarly, this one actively checks for errors. Video Review of All Lessons in EFL Writing The widespread use of artificial intelligence (AI) in the field of education has opened up new opportunities for teaching and learning English as a foreign language (EFL), particularly in the area of writing (Hubbard & Schulze, 2025). Use of learning technologies based on Virtual Robot Tutors (VRTs) is an intriguing new development. Conversational AI, natural language processing, and multimodal interfaces are the means by which these VRTs improve EFL proficiency (Nuemaihom et al., 2025). These AI-enabled agents can provide students personalized feedback while they work through difficult writing tasks like droughting, editing, and story commentary. The use of virtual reality trainers (VRTs) is on the rise as a potential new approach to teaching languages, particularly for encouraging creative writing styles like short stories, as part of the movement away from teacher-centered models and towards learner-driven, technology-mediated environments. In EFL classes, writing is seen as a crucial skill; students are required to have a firm grasp of the language's syntax and vocabulary as well as critical thinking, logical thought structure, and the ability to draw readers in with vivid imagery. Countries like Indonesia often have exam-orientated curricula, large class sizes, and insufficient individualized instruction, which means that pupils rarely have opportunities to write meaningfully (Chen et al., 2022). As a result, students' writing lacks narrative depth and expressive fluidity and is instead formulaic. We need methods of instruction that can be customized to meet the specific needs of every student while yet being broadly applicable.

Virtual robot teachers powered by artificial intelligence are perfect for fixing this. One novel technique for EFL instruction is the employment of VRTs, or virtual robot tutors, to help students learn the language. You may find a lot of VTRs or virtual teaching robots in the Google Play Store. These VTRs typically look like avatars and try to mimic human professors (Muthmainnah et al., 2025). What differentiates VRTs from static tools like grammar and spellcheckers is their ability to evaluate conversations in real time and provide feedback that is relevant to the current context. According to García et al. (2025), intelligent tutoring systems (ITS) typically use techniques such as natural language understanding (NLU), conversation management, affective computing, and learner modelling to personalize the learning process for each student. Video response tools (VRTs) are great for teaching writing because of all the helpful features they offer. They can do things like ask students guiding questions, organize tale segments, correct language faults, suggest better terminology, and keep students engaged to make classes more dynamic and exciting.

The foundation of VRT applications is a natural language processing system that listens to the student's speech, searches for grammatical patterns, and verifies that it is clear. After that, a machine learning model analyses the data by comparing it to a large language database or a writing rubric, and then it generates useful comments. For example, if a student writes, "The boy went to the market," VRT can detect where the subject-verb agreement is lacking, with a statement such as "Let's look at the verb tenses," VRT can then launch into a structured interview. Is it proper to say something "went" when it has already happened? In addition to correcting errors, this approach of teaching draws students' attention to the language and linguistics they are studying. With the ability to monitor the student's progress, VRT can tailor its support to meet their needs. Starting the next session with a mini-lesson or an example story that shows the process is a great way for VRT to help students who are struggling with the structuring of a discussion. Lio et al. (2025) and Fung et al. (2025) conducted research on the use of artificial intelligence (AI) in English as a foreign language (EFL) class.

Their findings demonstrated that students who collaborated with robot tutors to enhance their story structure, character creation, and narrative flow were able to generate better writing. Alghasab (2025) also found that an AI-based coaching system improved students' English writing by giving them immediate editing signals, which led to more creative and grammatically correct writing. As the authors put it, the computer would be able to ask, "What happens next?" Asking genuine questions like "How does the character feel?" was crucial for students' narrative development. These results show that VRT improves student motivation and learning, not human instructors. Educators in the field of English as a foreign language (EFL) believe that the use of video response technology (VRT) to create short stories in EFL is in line with the process writing model and sociocultural learning theory. Writing teaching that is process-orientated often involves repetitive procedures such as prewriting, droughting, revising, and editing (Alsharif, 2025). Virtual reality therapy (VRT) is useful at every level. Students can use VRT to find ideas or writing prompts that are related to their interests. As they write, students can use VRT to generate word ideas and structure their stories. VRT can ask, "Where does your story turn?" during the revision process. Alternatively, "How can I make the ending more unexpected?" Finally, VRT may analyse the syntax and offer alternate languages as part of the editing process. This dynamic, ever-changing interaction helps students understand their writing better in terms of style, subject matter, and structure. Brazant (2024) asserts that the instructional design of VRT has a substantial impact on Vygotsky's concept of the Zone of Proximal Development (ZPD). The prevailing view in this school of thought is that students retain more information when presented with materials that highlight the differences between their current level of competence and that which they could achieve with the use of technology tools. Virtual reality technology (VRT) acts as a "more knowledgeable other" by providing quick feedback and personalized assistance. Such an approach helps students internalize and apply writing skills to many activities. This feature is crucial in ESL classrooms since students studying the language often lack confidence and cannot afford to study with native speakers. Learning to take risks, improve language skills, and hone storytelling abilities can all be accomplished through repeated practice with a supportive VRT in low-stakes encounters.

Furthermore, the idea of who writes and who reads is consistent with VRT's dialogic nature (Wilkins et al., 2025). Writing is inherently interactive and targeted towards a hypothetical readership, according to Samala et al. (2025). This approach towards communication is reinforced by VRT since it pretends to be a reader or co-writer and asks questions to either clarify or offer suggestions for how to enhance the narrative's style or tone. It teaches kids that writing is about more than simply putting words on paper; it's a means of expression. Constructed ethically and dialogically, human-robot interactions in the classroom can empower students to take charge of their own learning and increase their level of engagement (Liang & Hwang, 2025). Although this is encouraging, video response technology is currently underutilized in English as a foreign language (EFL) writing classrooms, particularly in resource-constrained countries like Indonesia.

The CALLEdA model is applied in IT-integrated learning, focussing on how AI is utilised in the classroom through flexible and practical instruction. The goal of the VRT-based instructional design is to improve writing skills in TAM. The TAM model is modified into the open CALLEdA model, which ensures that VRT interventions in the classroom are maximised, in line with TAM (Davis 1985), which is the evolution of traditional to modern learning systems. Access to robot-based learning technology focuses on teachers' knowledge of RALL (robot-assisted language learning) interventions, utilizing AI features in EFL learning. Muthmainnah et al. (2025) stated that RALL is a practical, efficient, and effective transformation of EFL learning using a hybrid or hyflex model modality that can help students learn more personally, independently, and comfortably. RALL is a pedagogical tool that plays a crucial role in improving EFL skills, and the CALLEdA model presents concrete learning stages for implementing VRT in EFL classes as a tutoring tool for maximising learning.

Most Indonesian schools do not use AI-integrated teaching methods, and written education is still mainly focused on tests and teachers. Creative writing assignments, such as short tales, are frequently omitted in favors of more standardized essay formats, such as expository or argumentative pieces. Because of class sizes that are too big and instructors that lack proper training, English as a foreign language (EFL) students also do not receive adequate feedback on their writing, when teachers faced with such a situation, VRT provides a scalable solution that can help students receive continual tailored guidance without putting too much strain on teachers. Given the importance of incorporating visual rhetoric techniques (VRT) into the process-orientated instructional stages of EFL writing classes, this framework presents a six-step methodology utilising CALLEdA to teach EFL students writing and the art of short story writing, with VRT incorporated into each stage.

Stage 1: Generate Ideas and Develop Strategies

The brainstorming session in the VRT class includes various questions, introducing graphs or describing graphs, introducing language, and providing opportunities for students to build fictional characters or start practical stories. An example of a stimulus given is "Imagine I am a dragon who has lost its fire." The VRT can play the role of a fictional person and ask interesting questions. How could that be done? The hope is that this approach can encourage new perspectives and create the possibility of a compelling and interesting story. Research by Chang et al. (2010) shows that students can benefit from including a robot teacher in their stories, both as a main character and as a way to spark their imagination and ideas before writing.

Stage 2: Writing (Conceptualizing the Story)

At this stage, to help students write better stories, teachers provide structural templates, transition words, and opening phrases using VRT. One technique for providing students with alternatives within this method is to ask questions such as, "Would you like to add more dialogue or describe the setting?" Furthermore, this technique offers students diction choices, including more evocative synonyms and descriptors. Students are asked to interact with the VRT, providing prompts or appropriate directions to help them become more independent writers without overwhelming them. The next stage involves students working with their groupmates to refine the content, organization, and consistency. When a story is incoherent, characters are not fully developed, or important parts are missing, students can recognize that the author is using VRT. During the design and editing process, teachers may want students to suggest new storylines or provide more background on their characters' struggles and inner feelings. Solving problems and developing new strategies are key components of the revision stage. This phase can now be directly assisted by VRT. The first step is editing (including mechanics, vocabulary, and grammar).

Step 4: Layout and Editing

Currently, VRT can provide explicit feedback on errors, contextual explanations of grammatical errors, alternative word choices, and demonstrations of correct sentence structure. In addition to correcting, VRT explains, asks questions, and provides examples, all of which contribute to student learning. Students who work with a knowledgeable tutor retain more information when they discuss their mistakes rather than just hear them, according to Menshikova et al. (2025).

Step 5: Discuss and Reflect on Student Writing

Class blogs and other forms of storytelling between students are highly encouraged. To help you structure your story or generate ideas for visuals or titles, VRT is a great tool to use. Students can engage in self-reflection through VRT, asking questions such as "What did you enjoy most about your story?" which can inspire new ideas. In this phase, students apply constructivist principles by presenting their work to an audience; this helps them view writing as more than just a formal academic task.

Phase 6: Critique

Students may receive general comments or a rubric from the VRT after they complete their story. Examples of directed mini-lessons the VRT can provide students include "The student might want to practice using more descriptive verbs" and similar suggestions. Furthermore, the VRT is able to recall past events and modify its future communication style based on those memories.

Unlike static feedback systems, Yin et al. (2023) found that an AI system that provides adaptive feedback improves a person's writing ability.

This study highlights a significant knowledge gap about EFL in Indonesia. While interactive digital scaffolding can be beneficial, it is not commonly used in Indonesian EFL classrooms. Students often struggle to gather feedback on their work when they are nearing the end of the writing process. Rather than teaching students how to write, most writing classes in Indonesia emphasize the final product. There is a lack of resources (both financial and human) and education (in terms of how to use technology) for educators.

Indonesian students often lack confidence and practice in accepting constructive criticism, especially in narrative and other forms of artistic expression. The majority of students primarily use AI for grammar correction, rather than integrating it into a more comprehensive teaching strategy. Although VRT can solve logistical and pedagogical problems in the classroom, it is still not widely used in Indonesia. The use of VRT can improve students' writing abilities and demonstrate the efficacy of AI-assisted creative instruction on a larger scale, as this study uncovers a new method for teaching creative writing to students in Indonesia.

RESEARCH METHOD

This study aimed to evaluate the effectiveness of "Cici Bot", a virtual robot tutor (VRT), in assisting EFL students with the composition of short English stories using a quantitative research approach and a pre-experimental design. The primary goal was to find out if students could improve their creativity, coherence, and linguistic accuracy while writing short stories with the help of VRT as an instructional tool. How students felt about utilizing an AI-based tool to assist them in writing structured short tales was also investigated in the study.

Participants

This study involved 25 first-year students from the Department of Pancasila and Citizenship Education, Al Asyariah Mandar University, Indonesia. English II is a compulsory course for these students, and its primary objective was to improve their academic and everyday English skills. All participants scored in the mid-range on the university-administered English placement test. Furthermore, students were characterised by a lack of practice using digital writing tools, or artificial intelligence, in class. All participants provided written informed consent, and the study was approved by the relevant ethics body. Participants confirmed their participation before the study began.The acronym CALLEdA—Connect, Activate, Listen, Learn, Explore, Develop, and Assess—describes the virtual reality (VR)-assisted teaching methodology used in this study. We can use this model to map out our strategy for using Cici Bot, an AI writing tool, to write short stories. The procedure is outlined in the Table 2 below:

Table 2. CALLEdA learning flow

CALLEdA Stage	Description
Connect	Students are introduced to the topic and objectives of narrative writing.
Activate	Learners brainstorm ideas and prior knowledge through Cici Bot prompts.
Listen	Students engage with short story examples curated and read aloud by the bot.
Learn	The bot introduces elements of story writing (e.g., setting, characters, plot).
Explore	Students interact with the bot to outline their stories collaboratively.
develop	Learners write their short story drafts with real-time support from the bot.
Assess	The bot provides formative feedback, followed by teacher-led peer assessment.

Integrating AI in the classroom in a structured, student-centered manner is the goal of CALLEdA-based learning. To help students develop their narratives, this teaching style also utilises the AI-powered Cicibot for discussion.The most important methods used in this study were, first, an observation sheet and, second, a Likert-scale survey.

1. Classroom Observation Sheet

Observing the VRT-based English as a Foreign Language (EFL) learning process in the classroom, the researchers recorded writing sessions during which Cicibot was used. During the observations, we looked for indicators of student engagement and interaction with the bot based on their behaviour, cognition, and emotions. Table 3 below shows the indicators used to compile the observation sheet:

Table 3. Observation sheet of VTR in EFL class

No	Observation Indicators	Scoring Scale
1	Student initiates interaction with the VRT	1 = No, 2 = Yes
2	Student responds to feedback or questions from the bot	1 = Never to 5 = Always
3	Student revises or edits writing based on bot's suggestions	1 = Never to 5 = Always
4	Student expresses enthusiasm or motivation during interaction	1 = Low to 5 = High
5	Student completes the writing task in collaboration with bot	1 = Not Completed to 5 = Fully Completed

Observations were conducted by the lecturer, and one trained assistant collected data from the observation sheets to ensure that different people rated the same thing in the same way.

2. Questionnaire

The supplementary instrument was a questionnaire survey consisting of twenty-one statements rated using a 5-point Likert scale, with 1 indicating "strongly disagree" and 5 indicating "strongly agree". The purpose of this survey was to measure the extent to which EFL students felt comfortable integrating VRT into their work. The survey consisted of five sections: (1) Usefulness; (2) Usability; (3) Quality of Interaction; (4) Improved Writing Ability; and (5) Engagement and

Motivation. Here are some examples of items for each dimension:(1) Ideation Value: "The Cici bot helped me organise my thoughts better." Second, usability: "The bot interface is easy to use and understand." Third, engagement level: "The bot asked relevant and valuable questions about my story." Fourth, improving one's ability to put thoughts on paper: "Interacting with the bot helped me learn new words." Engagement and Motivation (5): "Using the bot made me want to write more than in a regular class." A pilot study confirmed the reliability of the questionnaire (Cronbach's Alpha = 0.84), and two experts in educational technology and teaching English as a foreign language verified its content validity.

The Procedure for Collecting Data

Over 14 weeks, data collection followed a set plan for pre-treatment, treatment, and post-treatment. The steps in the process were as follows:

1. Pre-Treatment Phase

The students had to write a short story without assistance as part of a pre-test. We used their scores as a starting point. This session also included observation notes to learn about how the children wrote initially.

2.Treatment Phase: The students learnt to use the CALLEdA approach, with Cici Bot as their main writing assistant. Each session covered one or more parts of the writing process, such as setting the scene, building characters, or organizing dialogue. Students talked to the bot in class and outside the classroom. The teacher monitored and wrote down behavioural signs on the observation sheet.

3. Post-Treatment Phase

Students worked on writing exercises for the post-test that were almost the same level of difficulty as the pre-test. They also filled out a 20-item Likert scale survey. Two different raters used criteria to view the post-test writing samples. The rubric looked at how well the ideas were organized, grammatical, creative, and coherent.

4. All data, including writing samples, observation scores, and questionnaires, were recorded in Microsoft Excel and then sent to SPSS for analysis.

Data Analysis

This study used SPSS version 26 to view the data we had collected. We used the following statistical methods:

1. To summarize students' answers on the questionnaire, we used descriptive statistics such as mean and standard deviation.
    3. We conducted Reliability Testing using Cronbach's Alpha to ensure that the questionnaire was consistent. For all inferential analyses, a significance level of $p < .05$ was used.

4. Ethical consideration

Students were selected to take part in the study. All students were informed about the purpose of the study and that they could leave at any time. The university's research ethics board gave the green light for the study, and the data was anonymized to protect privacy.

FINDINGS AND DISCUSSION

Building on previous research on the potential of AI to aid learning, this study adds to the growing body of evidence suggesting that students can benefit from AI-based writing support in developing their creative capacities and mastering advanced grammar concepts. How to maximize the effectiveness of robotic teachers in the classroom. In their view, AI evaluation relies heavily on data collected from learner perceptions and organized observations. Building on a constructivist framework, the CALLEdA teaching paradigm focuses on student engagement and self-reflection in contexts enhanced by artificial intelligence.

Table 4. Descriptive Statistics

Statements	N	Min	Max	Mean	SD
1. The Cici bot helped me organize my thoughts better.	25	4.00	5.00	4.6400	.48990
2. Using the bot made my writing tasks more effective.	25	4.00	5.00	4.6400	.48990
3. The bot provided useful suggestions that improved the content of my writing.	25	4.00	5.00	4.6400	.48990
4. the bot was a valuable tool for supporting my writing process.	25	4.00	5.00	4.4400	.50662
5. The bot interface is easy to use and understandable.	25	4.00	5.00	4.8000	.40825
6. I could quickly learn how to interact with the bot without difficulty.	25	4.00	5.00	4.7600	.43589
7. The instructions and functions of the bot were clear and straightforward.	25	4.00	5.00	4.8400	.37417
8. I did not face major technical problems when using the bot.	25	3.00	5.00	4.4000	.76376
9. The bot asked relevant and helpful questions about my story.	25	2.00	5.00	4.2400	.87939
10. The feedback I received from the bot was meaningful and easy to follow.	25	3.00	5.00	4.0800	.40000
11. Interacting with the bot felt like a supportive conversation.	25	4.00	5.00	4.6000	.50000
12. The bot's responses were appropriate for my writing needs.	25	4.00	5.00	4.5600	.50662
13. Interacting with the bot helped me learn new words.	25	3.00	5.00	4.3200	.74833
14. The bot encouraged me to write more accurately in English.	25	3.00	5.00	4.1600	.89815
15. Using the bot improved the overall structure of my writing.	25	3.00	5.00	4.1600	.89815
16. The experience with the bot helped me develop better writing strategies.	25	3.00	5.00	4.1600	.89815
17. Using the bot made me want to write more than in regular lessons.	25	3.00	5.00	4.0000	.57735
18. The bot made the writing activity more enjoyable.	25	3.00	5.00	4.1600	.68799
19. I felt more motivated to complete my writing tasks when using the bot.	25	4.00	5.00	4.4800	.50990
20. I would like to use the bot again in future writing activities.	25	4.00	5.00	4.4800	.50990
Valid N (listwise)	25				

Virtual conversational agents and artificial intelligence (AI) are increasingly being researched for their potential applications in English as a Foreign Language (EFL) classroom. This study aimed to determine how students felt about "Cicibot", a Virtual Reality Tutor (VRT) they used to help them write short stories for their English as a Foreign Language (EFL) class. Fifteen students completed a twenty-item survey assessing five aspects: perceived usefulness, ease of use, quality of interaction, motivation/engagement, and development of writing skills. Each item was rated using a five-point Likert scale, with 1 representing "strongly disagree" and 5 representing "strongly agree". Using descriptive statistics (mean, standard deviation, minimum and maximum values), we can observe the results of this study, which relate to students' opinions about the usefulness, usability, and purpose of the bot. When assessing the first indicator, "How practical is the bot's effectiveness as a writing assistant?", four factors were taken into account.

Overall, respondents felt that the Cici bot helped them organize their ideas better (M = 4.64, SD = 0.49), that the bot made better use of their writing time (M = 4.64, SD = 0.49), that their writing improved significantly (M = 4.64, SD = 0.49) due to the bot's helpful suggestions, and that respondents responded generally positively, saying the bot was an excellent writing tool (M = 4.44, SD = 0.50). Statistics for Indicator 1 can be found in Table 1. Mean scores (all greater than 4.4) indicate that students saw substantial improvements in efficiency, organization, and content quality. The data show a low standard deviation, indicating consistency among participants. The indicative statements cover two aspects related to user experience. Respondents stated that the bot interface was very user-friendly and easy to understand (M = 4.80, SD = 0.41); I had no problems interacting with the bot (M = 4.76, SD = 0.43) after some time (M = 4.84, SD = 0.37); the bot's instructions and features were easy to understand and use; and, based on my experience (M = 4.40, SD = 0.76), there were no significant technical issues. Several items in the dataset scored very high for the usability of this VTR.

The fact that the first three criteria were universally agreed upon demonstrates how intuitive the tool is. There may have been some usability issues for some users, but overall the scores were lower (4.40) and the variability was greater (SD = 0.76). Furthermore, in indicator 3, interaction quality, all four factors were used to evaluate the nature of the contact: regarding my story, the bot asked relevant and helpful questions (M = 4.24, SD = 0.88); regarding the bot's feedback, the feedback was helpful and straightforward (M = 4.08, SD = 0.40); feedback on the bot was quite encouraging (M = 4.60, SD = 0.50); and on how well the bot met my writing needs (M = 4.56, SD = 0.51). With a standard deviation of 0.88 for the first element, students' varying assessments of the depth of the bot's conversations likely reflect better overall results. Statistical data indicating characteristics related to skill development indicate that Indicator 4, which is strengthening written expression skills, received somewhat lower, though still quite satisfactory, ratings. "I can refine my writing technique with the bot" (M = 4.16, SD = 0.89).

The structure of my writing has improved" (M = 4.16, SD = 0.89), "I use more precise English as prompted by the bot" (M = 4.32, SD = 0.75), and "I can improve my vocabulary through conversations with the bot" (M = 4.32, SD = 0.75). The larger standard deviation indicates that there is considerable variation in how learners perceive their own writing development. This variation could be attributed to varying levels of initial competence or individual differences in learning methods. Question 5 asks about what inspires and engages individuals. In the final section, we examine what motivates people. Mean score result 4.16 and standard deviation of 0.69, respondents generally reported that the bot improved their writing skills. They also reported that the bot made them feel more motivated to complete their writing assignments (M = 4.48,

SD = 0.51) and were interested in using it for future writing assignments (M = 4.48, SD = 0.51). While most agreed that the bot's usability and ease of use were important, these results suggest that it is the bot's ability to increase happiness and motivation that is truly important.

Figure 1. Distribution of Average Scores

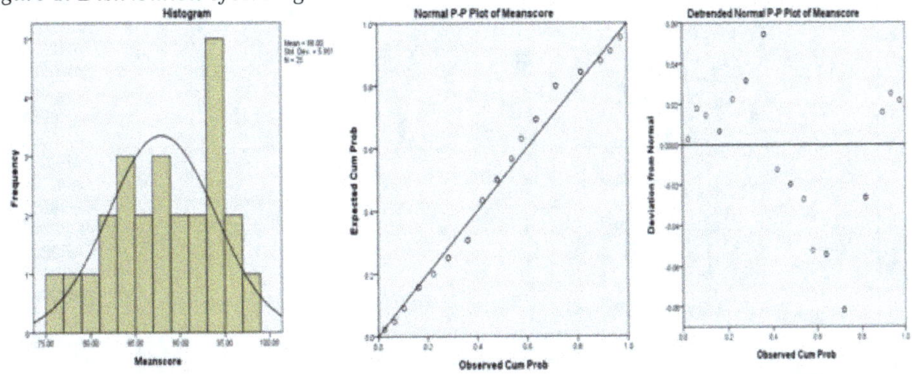

The data displayed by the histogram in Figure 1 shows the distribution of mean scores from the dataset (N = 25). The recorded scores had a width of 5.951 standard deviations, ranging from 75.00 to 100.00. The mean was 88.00. The histogram shows that scores arranged in the interval between 85 and 95 have a cluster of numbers. The fact that five individuals reached the most common score range, the 95th percentile or higher, is significant. The distribution is significantly skewed toward the positive, as there were fewer scores in the lower range (75-80) compared to the upper range (90-100).

These results indicate a low level of dispersion and a strong central tendency. The strong clustering around the higher scores indicates that participants generally had a positive view of the bot experience, which is significant from an educational research perspective. The tool's effectiveness is reliable due to the high clustering, which indicates a consistent positive response pattern. In Figure 1, we can see the mean score represented by a Normal Probability-Probability (P-P) plot.

In Figure 2, we can see how the cumulative probability of the data compares to what we would expect from a normally distributed data set. If a data point lies on the diagonal, which represents an ideal distribution, we can say that it is closer to a normal distribution. In the graph, you can see the detrended mean score data presented in a normal P-P plot. Typically, a detrended number strengthens the argument that the data set is normal.

Figure 2. Sequence chart of the questionnaire

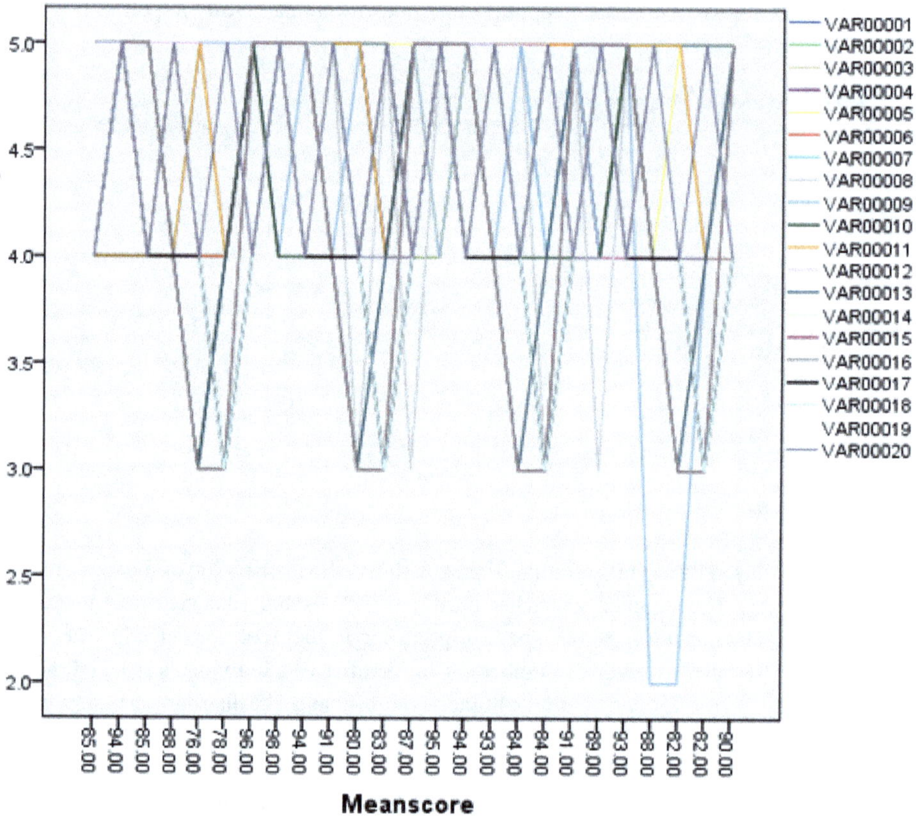

Figure 2 provides visual evidence supporting the aforementioned descriptive figures. As the histogram shows, with mean scores concentrated in the high range (above 85), the majority of students had a very favourable experience with the bot. Consistent with the descriptive statistics, most items received mean ratings of 4.16–4.84 on a 5-point scale.

A more parametric approach could be considered, given that all items align with the diagonal line, despite the small sample size (25 students). Users consistently rated the virtual reality tool (VRT) or chatbot intervention (CiciBot) favourably across multiple dimensions, including usability, ease of use, interaction quality, writing improvement, and motivation. This suggests that the tool was highly effective. The average rating data, above 4.0, indicates that students found the bot easy to use and a powerful learning tool that helped them engage more with the subject and improve their writing skills.

Table 5. Reliability Statistics

Cronbach's Alpha	N of Items
.797	20

AS Table 4, Twenty items, each with a 5-point Likert scale, make up this survey's dependability results. These elements include qualities such as perceived utility, simplicity of use, motivation/engagement, and enhanced writing abilities. The study found that the instrument's reliability was 0.797 when using Cronbach's alpha, which is greater than the requirement of 0.70 for social science research.

The measures used to gauge students' perceptions of chatbot-assisted writing had excellent internal consistency, suggesting that the notions under evaluation were consistent. The possible total score ranged from 76 to 98, with a standard deviation of 5.95 as peer Table 5. The majority of pupils seemed to enjoy using the chatbot. This consistent positive impression, characterized by a high central tendency and limited variability, supports the dependability findings.

Table 6. Descriptive Statistics

	N	Min	Max	Mean	SD
Meanscore	25	76.00	98.00	88.0000	5.95119
Valid N (listwise)	25				

All of the data, including descriptive statistics, reliability analyses, and line graphs, points to the same conclusion: students thought the chatbot was a great learning tool since it was interesting, instructive, and easy to use. Despite its excellent use and engagement, the tool had less of an impact on improving deeper writing skills, as seen by the varied item-level replies. With a Cronbach's Alpha of .797, the instrument is sufficiently reliable, and the chatbot's high mean score (M = 88.00) demonstrates its ability to improve EFL writing instruction.

Discussion

Based on the findings, the study shown students' positive reactions to the VRT chatbot in EFL writing classes. The data showed that most people were satisfied with the bot's use; average scores were higher than 4.0 in every category. Prior research has demonstrated that conversational AI can facilitate language learning through the provision of tailored feedback, alleviation of fear, and enhancement of learner agency (Wang, 2025). The study also found that the bot had great usability ratings, which means that it helped undergraduates with content production and assignment organization in a practical way. This agrees with the results of Ding and Yusof (2025), who found that students improved their writing's structure and substance with the help of an AI-based feedback system.

One of the most important factors in determining whether a tool will be used again is how valuable people think it is, as stated in the Technology Acceptance Model (TAM). This shows that students will likely use the same kinds of technology to help them improve their writing in future classes. Consistent with the high overall ratings achieved for ease of use, this study emphasises the significance of user-friendly interfaces for the uptake of technology in education. With high mean ratings (M > 4.7) across usability items, the technological design is one of the system's strengths. Nevertheless, owing to a number of technical difficulties, the system's reliability could be improved (SD = 0.76). The reason being, learning is frequently impeded by technological obstacles.

Undergraduates encounter difficulties in technical writing and ethical concerns like plagiarism when using the virtual robot-based writing process, despite the program ease of use. In addition, the favorable evaluations of interaction quality show a greater degree of diversity. The majority of students found the chatbot to be helpful, and its relevant assertions were supported by a higher standard deviation of 0.88. This exemplifies the difficulties of implementing NLP in instructional chatbots, since the system is prone to misunderstanding context, especially in the case of unsuccessful prompts. Smart questioning and responses tailored to the current circumstances can further enhance the standard of interactions. The moderate scores for writing progress show one small but important detail. Every single student felt that they made significant improvement in their language abilities after using the programmed, and they all thought it was simple and helpful. Affective supports, like motivation and organization, seem to lag behind improvements in linguistic correctness. Chatbots can boost self-assurance and fluency, but they can't fix major grammar mistakes (Javed, 2024), so it might be useful to use QuillBot or another tool for that. Different skill levels may have different effects, as there seems to be a wide variety in the outcomes. Vocabulary exercises, for instance, might help students with lower proficiency levels more than those with higher levels, whereas students with higher levels might think the comments are too broad.

An analysis of descriptive data revealed that VRT chatbot users were satisfied with their experience as EFL writers. Results showed that most people were satisfied with the bot's use; average scores were higher than 4.0 in every category. According to Boğaz (2024), earlier research has demonstrated that conversational AI can facilitate language acquisition through the provision of tailored feedback, alleviation of fear, and enhancement of learners' autonomy. The bot was found to have great usability ratings, which means it really helped undergraduates with content production and assignment organization, according to this study. Wang et al. (2021) found that students improved their writing with the use of an AI-based feedback system, and our results are in line with that. The Technology Acceptance Model (TAM) states that one of the most important factors in determining whether a tool will be used again is how useful people think it is (Al-Adwan et al., 2025). Students are likely to use these kinds of technology in future classes if they want to get better at writing, according to the research.

The high mean ratings (M > 4.7) across usability items, the technological design is one of the system's strengths. The system's dependability may be enhanced, nonetheless, because of a number of technical issues (SD = 0.76). The reason being, learning is frequently impeded by technological obstacles. While the application is user-friendly, undergraduates may encounter difficulties with technical writing and ethical concerns like plagiarism when utilizing virtual robots for writing assignments. In addition, there is a wider range of positive evaluations for interaction quality. The chatbot's informative utterances demonstrated that the majority of students found it useful (a greater standard deviation of 0.88). This shows that educational chatbots using natural language processing (NLP) have their limitations, especially when it comes to unsuccessful prompts and the system's inability to recognize context. The quality of conversations can be even better with adaptive inquiry and responses that are responsive to context.

There is a small but important aspect that the moderate writing growth scores show. Every single student felt that they made significant improvement in their language abilities after using the program, and they all thought it was simple and helpful. It would appear that improvements in emotional support, such as motivation and organization, are not keeping pace with advancements in linguistic correctness. While chatbots can boost confidence and fluency, this study's results are comparable to those of Grab (2025) in that they cannot fix severe grammatical mistakes; thus, it may be beneficial to use other program like QuillBot. Different skill levels may have different effects, as there seems to be a wide variety in the outcomes. Vocabulary drills may help students with lower competence levels more than those with higher levels, and students with higher levels may find the comments to be overly broad. The study emphasizes the importance of perceived usefulness and simplicity of use as factors that determine the adoption of educational technology, in line with the Technology Adoption Model (TAM).

This model is consistent with these findings. Students seem to have a favorable view of this bot based on the high averages of its usefulness (M = 4.64) and ease of use (M = 4.80). These impressions are constant across groups with little volatility, as evidenced by the histogram and plot, so we can have confidence in the results. High scores tend to cluster together, which could mean that the AI teaching system is successful in getting people to stick around for a while. The trend-reduced results show a little outlier, which might be attributable to individual student backgrounds or experiences. Statement 8 stated: "I didn't encounter any significant technical issues when using the bot." It is conceivable that a small subset of students encountered slight technical difficulties (M = 4.40, SD = 0.76) these findings in line with Hwang et al. (2025) found that AI can be effective in writing, and this study emphasizes that educational interventions will necessarily have some heterogeneity in this regard. With modest variability, limited skewness, and substantial clustering of high scores, the data set appears to be fairly normal according to the histogram and P-P plot. In line with the descriptive data, these outcomes support the idea that the chatbot intervention was generally well-received.

The consistent responses and high central tendency show that the bot could be beneficial and pedagogically significant in teaching English as a foreign language writing. The Cici bot is supposedly both technically possible and educationally beneficial, and its images back up this claim. These results, when combined with theories like TAM and CALL, show that instructional technology driven by AI can significantly enhance language learning results. The chatbot (Cici bot) was highly regarded by students in this study for its usefulness in teaching writing in English as a foreign language. There was substantial agreement on usability claims, such as "The instructions and functions of the bot were clear and straightforward" (M = 4.84, SD = .37), but all items got high mean scores. The findings are consistent with the Technology Acceptance Model (TAM), which posits that perceived ease of use is a key component in technology adoption. The ease and transparency of the interface have a direct impact on the level of engagement, retention, and overall satisfaction with digital learning environments experienced by learners (Syamala et al., 2025). This study regularly found that learners had a favorable experience with the chatbot, and the high results are a direct result of its usability. Students were lukewarm at best when asked whether the chatbot helped them improve their writing, despite its high grades for general assistance with organization and structure (M = 4.64).

The chatbot was only able to assist with basic language skills, as indicated by the lower means of questions like "Using the bot improved the overall structure of my writing" (M = 4.16, SD = .89) and "Interacting with the bot helped me learn new words" (M = 4.32, SD = .75).

In a similar vein, Marzuki et al. (2023) found that while AI-driven writing tools are fantastic at reducing students' fear of writing and maintaining their motivation, they fall short when it comes to fostering the higher-order cognitive processes essential to second language acquisition. Although students did well with the chatbot's organizational help and immediate feedback, it appeared to have less success scaffolding complex writing processes or increasing students' lexical knowledge; therefore, pedagogical supplementation is required. The chatbot's ability to keep learners engaged and motivated was a particularly remarkable finding. Statements like "I would like to use the bot again in future writing activities" (M = 4.48, SD = .51) and "I felt more motivated to complete my writing tasks when using the bot" (M = 4.48, SD = .51) demonstrate the bot's motivating value.

The study similar to Self-Determination Theory (SDT) (Deci & Ryan, 2000), a learner who is more engaged is one whose demands for autonomy, competence, and relatedness are met. This aligns with these findings. By giving immediate, personalized responses and doing away with the necessity for people to work alone on writing assignments, chatbots and other kinds of interactive technology promote this type of setting. Also, the study on digital learning and gamification have shown that interactive learning promotes intrinsic motivation. These results showing near-ceiling motivating ratings and line chart patterns suggest that Cici Bot may have acted as both a learning tool and an engagement motivator. With a mean score of 88.00 (SD = 5.95), it is clear that interacting with the chatbot was beneficial to the learning process. Low dispersion and a nearly normal distribution are indicators of student agreement, as are P-P plots and the histogram. According to this statistical pattern, the majority of people gave positive answers, and only a handful of outliers affected the overall result. Where detrended plots and specific measures (such as interaction quality) displayed minor changes, students' critical reflections were more complex. These patterns reveal both the tool's general success and its areas of improvement, which is really useful. A number of important conclusions can be drawn from the findings. Design implications. The chatbot failed miserably at providing deep language scaffolding, despite its effectiveness with motivation and usability. Adaptive feedback methods and contextualized vocabulary assistance could solve this problem. Research on the use of AI in the classroom has shown promising similar results by (Reddig et al., 2025) findings.

The ethics and considerations of using VRT in EFL classes stem from teachers' concerns about students' dependence on VRT and the potential for teachers to be completely replaced by it. Therefore, designing EFL learning using the CALLEdA model can help teachers and students achieve a balance and collaboration between human intelligence and artificial intelligence in a more humane and harmonious way. Furthermore, this study provides an opportunity for EFL learning evaluations to be more focused on independent practice, encouraging students to use AI wisely, as a partner and intelligent learning tool that helps students be more creative in expressing their ideas and insights.

EFL students' interest in VRT stems from their collaborative learning partner, unbounded by time and space, in a way that humans cannot. However, internet access limits VRTs and hinders their ability to understand user emotions. They sometimes fail to understand instructions if prompts are inappropriate, and they operate according to need-based prompts. Therefore, VRTs act as peer tutors and companions for students in learning EFL accurately.

One such study found that systems with natural language processing capabilities may personalize their feedback based on students' individual language competence levels. As an adjunct to more conventional forms of education, chatbots can make learning more engaging by providing students with instantaneous feedback. Critical thinking, reasoning, and developing one's style are all aspects of writing that necessitate scaffolding provided by the instructor. Overall, the findings corroborate what is already known from research on AI-assisted learning: students value these tools for what they can do right away, how interactive they are, and the motivation they provide, but their potential to improve language competence is still largely untapped. The captivating features of AI technologies in education cause them to be widely used, as pointed out by Zawacki-Richter et al. (2019); however, for these technologies to truly revolutionize education, they need to be carefully integrated into existing pedagogical frameworks. Chatbots like Cici Bot are great tools to have on hand in EFL classrooms, but they shouldn't be thought of as a substitute for human teachers.

REFERENCES

Aditya, D., & Otermans, P. C. (2025). A Review of AI-Enabled Personalised Teaching (2021–2025): Progress, Impact, and Future Directions. *Journal of the Kenya National Commission for UNESCO*.

Al-Adwan, A. S., Meet, R. K., Anand, S., Shukla, G. P., Alsharif, R., & Dabbaghia, M. (2025). Understanding continuous use intention of technology among higher education teachers in emerging economy: Evidence from integrated TAM, TPACK, and UTAUT model. *Studies in Higher Education, 50*(3), 505–524. DOI: 10.1080/03075079.2024.2343955

Alghasab, M. B. (2025). English as a foreign language (EFL) secondary school students' use of artificial intelligence (AI) tools for developing writing skills: Unveiling practices and perceptions. *Cogent Education, 12*(1), 2505304. DOI: 10.1080/2331186X.2025.2505304

Alsharif, S. A. N. (2025). *A Proposed Model of Automated, Peer, and Teacher (APT) Feedback and Its Impact on L2 Learners' Engagement and Writing Performance Changes Over Time* (Doctoral dissertation, University of Southampton).

Anand, S., Reddy, K. A., Reddy, P. A., Srinivas, C. S., & Rao, S. N. (2025, February). Vidhya: A Virtual Tutor for Enhancing English Education in Rural Areas of India. In *2025 10th International Conference on Signal Processing and Communication (ICSC)* (pp. 591-597). IEEE. DOI: 10.1109/ICSC64553.2025.10967876

Boğaz, N. (2024). *Examining the Perceptions of EFL Instructors on AI Integration in an English Preparatory School* (Master's thesis, Middle East Technical University (Turkey)).

Brazant, K. J. (2024). Disrupting the discourse: Applying critical race theory as a conceptual framework for reflecting on learning and teaching in higher education. *Equity in Education & Society*, *3*(1), 61–75.

Chen, J. (2025). *Writing and Revising in Second Language Classrooms: The Role of Self-Regulation in Cultivating Expert Writers*. Springer Nature.

Chen, Y. L., Hsu, C. C., Lin, C. Y., & Hsu, H. H. (2022). Robot-assisted language learning: Integrating artificial intelligence and virtual reality into English tour guide practice. *Education Sciences, 12*(7), 437. DOI: 10.3390/educsci12070437

Corbeil, J. R. (2025). The Future of Learning: AI-Driven Education in 2040. In *Teaching and Learning in the Age of Generative AI* (pp. 362–390). Routledge. DOI: 10.4324/9781032688602-22

Derakhshan, A., Teo, T., Saeedy Robat, E., Janebi Enayat, M., & Jahanbakhsh, A. A. (2025). Robot-assisted language learning: A meta-analysis. *Review of Educational Research, 95*(4), 747–774. DOI: 10.3102/00346543241247227

Ding, D., & Yusof, M. B. (2025). Investigating the role of AI-powered conversation bots in enhancing L2 speaking skills and reducing speaking anxiety: A mixed methods study. *Humanities & Social Sciences Communications, 12*(1), 1–16. DOI: 10.1057/s41599-025-05550-z

Fung, K. Y., Fung, K. C., Lui, T. L. R., Sin, K. F., Lee, L. H., Qu, H., & Song, S. (2025). Exploring the impact of robot interaction on learning engagement: A comparative study of two multi-modal robots. *Smart Learning Environments, 12*(1), 12. DOI: 10.1186/s40561-024-00362-1

García-Méndez, S., de Arriba-Pérez, F., & Somoza-López, M. D. C. (2025). A review on the use of large language models as virtual tutors. *Science & Education, 34*(2), 877–892. DOI: 10.1007/s11191-024-00530-2

Geetha, R. (2025). Digital Pedagogy and Cognitive Writing in English Language Classroom. In *Thinking Skills in Higher Education* (pp. 245–259). Springer. DOI: 10.1007/978-981-96-5600-4_19

Hsieh, W. M., Yeh, H. C., & Chen, N. S. (2025). Impact of a robot and tangible object (R&T) integrated learning system on elementary EFL learners' English pronunciation and willingness to communicate. *Computer Assisted Language Learning, 38*(4), 773–798. DOI: 10.1080/09588221.2023.2228357

Hubbard, P., & Schulze, M. (2025). AI and the Future of Language Teaching. *International Journal of Computer-Assisted Language Learning and Teaching, 15*(1), 1–17. DOI: 10.4018/IJCALLT.378304

Hwang, H., Chang, X., & Sun, J. (2025). Generative AI is useful for second language writing, but when, why, and for how long do learners use it? *Journal of Second Language Writing, 69*, 101230. DOI: 10.1016/j.jslw.2025.101230

Ikhsan, I., Husnaini, A. N., & Lopo, F. L. (2025). Strategies for implementing ai in LMS to improve the effectiveness and personalization of digital learning. *The Journal of Academic Science, 2*(3), 944–953. DOI: 10.59613/qp3e7d30

Javed, F. (2024). The Evolution of Artificial Intelligence in Teaching and Learning of English Language in Higher Education: Challenges, Risks, and Ethical Considerations. In *The Evolution of Artificial Intelligence in Higher Education: Challenges, Risks, and Ethical Considerations* (pp. 249-276). Emerald Publishing Limited.

Jin, S. (2025). Writing in the digital age: Understanding the relationship between social media use and college students' writing skills and anxiety. *Humanities & Social Sciences Communications, 12*(1), 1–11. DOI: 10.1057/s41599-025-05443-1

Khatoony, S., Mall-Amiri, B., & Kolahi, S. (2025). Developing a New Augmented Reality Mobile Application to Improve School-Age EFL Learners' Vocabulary Acquisition. *Technology Assisted Language Education, 3*(2), 120–143.

Li, H., Kang, M., & Liu, J. (2025). Exploring Chinese EFL Teachers' Perceptions of the Potentials and Challenges of Robot-Assisted Language Learning. *European Journal of Education, 60*(4), e70226. DOI: 10.1111/ejed.70226

Liang, J. C., & Hwang, G. J. (2025). Embodied social agency in human-robot collaboration for promoting EFL learners' persuasive communication and bodily-emotional awareness: A functional linguistics perspective. *Education and Information Technologies, 30*(17), 1–45. DOI: 10.1007/s10639-025-13747-7

Liu, V., Latif, E., & Zhai, X. (2025). Advancing education through tutoring systems: A systematic literature review. *arXiv preprint arXiv:2503.09748.*

Liu, X., & Xiao, Y. (2025). Chinese university teachers' engagement with generative AI in different stages of foreign language teaching: A qualitative enquiry through the prism of ADDIE. *Education and Information Technologies, 30*(1), 485–508. DOI: 10.1007/s10639-024-13117-9

Man, S. S., Fang, Y., Chan, A. H. S., & Han, J. (2025). VR technology acceptance for English learning amongst secondary school students: Role of classroom climate and language learning anxiety. *Education and Information Technologies, 30*(4), 4131–4155. DOI: 10.1007/s10639-024-12969-5

Marzuki, W., Widiati, U., Rusdin, D., Darwin, , & Indrawati, I. (2023). The impact of AI writing tools on the content and organization of students' writing: EFL teachers' perspective. *Cogent Education, 10*(2), 2236469. Advance online publication. DOI: 10.1080/2331186X.2023.2236469

Menshikova, M., Bonacci, I., & Scarozza, D. (2025). Rethinking Tutoring Activities in the New Normal: New Ways of Tutoring and Evolution of The Tutor's Profile. *Procedia Computer Science, 253*, 1515–1524. DOI: 10.1016/j.procs.2025.01.213

Mohsen, M. A., Mahdi, H. S., AlThebi, S. H., Alkhammash, R., & Alsharani, A. (2025). A scientometric study of computer-assisted pronunciation training in second language acquisition: Technological affordances and research trends. *Humanities & Social Sciences Communications, 12*(1), 1–11. DOI: 10.1057/s41599-025-04474-y

Morady Moghaddam, M., Esmaeilpour, F., & Ranjbaran, F. (2025). Insights into mobile assisted language learning research in Iran: A decade review (2010–2023). *Education and Information Technologies, 30*(2), 2155–2181. DOI: 10.1007/s10639-024-12879-6

Moran, C. M., & Pyles, D. G. (2025). Teachers First: Building AI Literacy to Address Mundane Tasks and Enhance Creative Applications in Secondary English Classrooms. In *Reimagining Literacy in the Age of AI* (pp. 49-72). Chapman and Hall/CRC.

Muthmainnah, M., Al Yakin, A., & Seraj, P. M. I. (2024, September). Integrating Robot-Based Resources to Foster Computational Thinking and Communication. In *Sustainable Development through Machine Learning, AI and IoT: Second International Conference, ICSD 2024, Virtual Event, April 27–28, 2024* []. Springer Nature.]. *Proceedings, 2196*, 70.

Muthmainnah, M., Cardoso, L., Marzuki, A. G., & Al Yakin, A. (2025). A new innovative metaverse ecosystem: VR-based human interaction enhances EFL learners' transferable skills. *Discover Sustainability, 6*(1), 156. DOI: 10.1007/s43621-025-00913-7

Nuemaihom, A., Al Yakin, A., Seraj, P. M. I., Asad, M. M., & Elngar, A. A. (2025). In-Depth Analysis of Artificial Intelligence Practices: Robot Tutors and Federated Learning Approach in English Education. In *Artificial Intelligence Using Federated Learning* (pp. 16-36). CRC Press.

Oubibi, M., Hryshayeva, K., & Huang, R. (2025). Enhancing postgraduate digital academic writing proficiency: The interplay of artificial intelligence tools and ChatGPT. *Interactive Learning Environments, 33*(6), 1–19. DOI: 10.1080/10494820.2025.2454445

Pakdel, F., Khojasteh, L., Kafipour, R., & Shahsavar, Z. (2025). Navigating AI writing tools in medical education: A SWOT analysis of L2 academic writing perspectives. *Language Teaching Research*, •••, 13621688251322953. DOI: 10.1177/13621688251322953

Pardede, P. (2025). Recent Research on Creative Writing Learning in Indonesian EFL Settings: A Systematic Literature Review. *Journal of English Teaching*, *11*(2), 150–167. DOI: 10.33541/jet.v11i2.6971

Pham, N. T. B., & Tran, T. M. (2025). Students' Perceptions of AI Language Models as Virtual Assistants in Learning Writing-A Case Study at a Tertiary Institution. *International Journal of TESOL & Education*, *5*(2), 87–115. DOI: 10.54855/ijte.25525

Qin, Z., & Chuaychoowong, M. (2025). Artificial Intelligence in EFL Education in China: A Systematic Review of Trends, Gaps, and Future Directions (2015-2024). *Language Teaching Research*, *49*, 59–89. DOI: 10.32038/ltrq.2025.49.04

Reddig, J. M., Arora, A., & MacLellan, C. J. (2025). Generating In-Context, Personalized Feedback for Intelligent Tutors with Large Language Models. *International Journal of Artificial Intelligence in Education*, *35*(6), 3459–3500. Advance online publication. DOI: 10.1007/s40593-025-00505-6

Ren, X., & Wu, M. L. (2025). Examining teaching competencies and challenges while integrating artificial intelligence in higher education. *TechTrends*, *69*(3), 1–20. DOI: 10.1007/s11528-025-01055-3

Rigopouli, K., Kotsifakos, D., & Psaromiligkos, Y. (2025). Vygotsky's creativity options and ideas in 21st-century technology-enhanced learning design. *Education Sciences*, *15*(2), 257. DOI: 10.3390/educsci15020257

Samala, A. D., Rawas, S., Wang, T., Reed, J. M., Kim, J., Howard, N. J., & Ertz, M. (2025). Unveiling the landscape of generative artificial intelligence in education: A comprehensive taxonomy of applications, challenges, and future prospects. *Education and Information Technologies*, *30*(3), 3239–3278. DOI: 10.1007/s10639-024-12936-0

Shahzad, S. K., Panhawar, A. H., & Ansari, S. (2025). Project-based learning and digital literacy integration: Investigating task design and student collaboration in developing academic writing and thesis skills in EFL classrooms. *Research Journal in Translation, Literature, Linguistics, and Education, 1*(3), 18-31.

Syamala, S., Shrivastava, A., & Karmakar, S. (2025). Identifying interface design factors impacting user experience in digital learning platforms-A pilot study. *Social Sciences & Humanities Open*, *11*, 101662. DOI: 10.1016/j.ssaho.2025.101662

Turvey, K., & Pachler, N. (2025). A topological exploration of convergence/divergence of human-mediated and algorithmically mediated pedagogy. *British Journal of Educational Technology*, bjet.70007. DOI: 10.1111/bjet.70007

Wang, Y. (2025). Reducing anxiety, promoting enjoyment and enhancing overall English proficiency: The impact of AI-assisted language learning in Chinese EFL contexts. *British Educational Research Journal*, berj.4187. DOI: 10.1002/berj.4187

Wilkins, K., Bennett, L., & Marshall, H. (2025). Story Thinking and the Real-world Applications of Sci-fi and Fantasy Writing.

Xiao, F., Zhu, S., & Xin, W. (2025). Exploring the landscape of generative AI (ChatGPT)-powered writing instruction in English as a foreign language education: A scoping review. *ECNU Review of Education*, 20965311241310881.

Yang, L., & Chano, J. (2025). The Impacts of Blended Learning on English Language Proficiency in Higher Education: A Systematic Literature Review. *Higher Education Studies*, *15*(2), 83–96. DOI: 10.5539/hes.v15n2p83

Zhai, Y. (2025). Computer-assisted English teaching model for improving learning performance of college students. *Journal of Computational Methods in Sciences and Engineering*, 14727978251361524.

Chapter 11
Algorithmic Mentors and Multilingual Writing Development:
An Activity Theoretic Framework for AI-Mediated Collaborative Revision

S. Henry Kishore
https://orcid.org/0000-0002-5749-8167
Sri Krishna arts and Science College, India

Jacintha Maria Florence
https://orcid.org/0009-0005-4447-7841
Nirmala College for Women, India

ABSTRACT

This chapter reinterprets generative AI within the framework of Activity Theory (AT), transitioning from an independent text creator to a designated 'algorithmic mentor' that supports diagnostic reasoning, genre-sensitive explanation, and metacognitive uptake in multilingual revision. It shares a theory-building, design-based account to update writing studies that link sociocultural writing development, peer-mediated revision, translanguaging and growing literature on feedback in AI-supported environments. It suggests design principles for eight projects to situate a five-phase "trialogue" coordinating authorial intent, peer diagnosis, and AI consultation. K -12/ university scenarios show equity-oriented orchestration, transparency protocols, and process-focused assessment approaches. Contributions involve an AT model of AI-mediated writing practice, a routine that privileges explanation over replacement, multilingual designs validating translanguaging/code meshing in writing for multilingual students, and governance principles for privacy, fairness, and integrity.

DOI: 10.4018/979-8-3373-5601-3.ch011

1. INTRODUCTION

Generative Artificial Intelligence (AI) has intensified an inherent contradiction found in writing instruction. The educational goal is not only to generate fluent, grammatical prose, but also to develop agentive writers who analyse rhetorical situations, provide rationales for revision, and adapt arguments to audiences. Today's LLMs can produce competent text with the click of a button, but the value of writing instruction is in the strategic, metacognitive, and social development of writers, or as Bereiter and Scardamalia (1987) describe it, the move from knowledge telling to knowledge transforming. This tension between "writing as product" and "writing as development" poses a dilemma for multilingual and emergent bilingual writers alike, who construct meaning alongside linguistic repertoires, cultural rhetorics, and genre expectations (García & Wei, 2014; Horner et al., 2011).

Contemporary debates around AI and instruction often exist in crude binaries: prohibited (more or less for integrity and combating cognitive offloading), or a wholesale invitation (for access to ample and quality feedback). Emerging scholarship suggests a more promising middle ground: position AI to scaffold learners—acting as a learning mediator—instead of as a text ghostwriter or overwriter (Bender et al., 2021; Kasneci et al., 2023; Cotton et al., 2024). In this position, AI extends socially distributed labour of revision, but does not replace human authorship.

We work through our position using Activity Theory (AT), a sociocultural model of learning as tool-mediated, object-oriented activity occurring in rule-governed communities and divisions of labour. Concerning writing instruction, the integration of AI is one set of activity within the writing activity system and all that comprises it, changing the object (what counts as writing), mediating artefacts (LLMs, platforms, rubrics), rules (attribution and academic integrity), communities (classrooms, disciplines), and divisions of labour (author, peer, teacher, tool), often producing contradictions in writing activity systems that require design-based resolutions. We articulate role constraints, transparency mechanisms, and equity-by-design infrastructures to engage these system elements for equitable developmental purposes. In this way, this article makes several technological contributions.

The first is to bring the landscape of AT-based theory to bear on algorithmic mentorship, in order to resolve recurrent contradictions present in AI-mediated writing activity systems. Second, we operationalize the account through research-based, principled frameworks and three-space coordination routines, which merge writer intent, learner peer diagnosis, and AI-constrained algorithms to support transitions. Finally, we suggest governance constructs and a research agenda that address privacy, fairness, equity, and long-term development. These contributions extend established cognitive and sociocultural theories of composing (Hayes, 2012; Hayes & Flower, 1980), checked against emerging evidence in peer feedback and academic integrity in the era of AI (Ghosh, Chakraborty, et al., 2025; Sperber et al., 2025; Baig et al., 2024).

2. THEORETICAL FOUNDATIONS

This section integrates the theoretical perspectives that underpin the proposal of algorithmic mentors for writing development in the chapter. It begins with a synthesis of cognitive, process, and sociocultural models of writing, drawing particularly on Activity Theory to define composing as a tool-mediated activity. It continues with a review of literature on collaborative revision and peer feedback, as well as translanguaging and multilingual writing, to highlight the dialogic and multilingual aspects of writers' meaning-making. All of this is then positioned within the context of existing debates regarding AI in writing pedagogy, including automated writing evaluation systems and language models, to justify a mentor-constrained approach to AI-mediated revision.

2.1 Writing Development as Sociocultural, Tool-Mediated Activity

Process Process models conceptualise composing as a recursive orchestration of planning, translating, and revising under the influence of metacognitive control (Hayes & Flower, 1980; Hayes, 2012). Sociocultural models broaden the process view of composing by emphasising mediation by artefacts, communities, and genres; writing development is situated, dialogic, and distributed across people and tools (Prior, 2006; Russell, 1997). Activity Theory (AT) represents an integration of these conceptual orientations by modelling how the goals, rules, roles, and outcomes of any given writing activity can be reconfigured by tools.

In this frame, LLMs are better conceptualised as tutors who support diagnostic reasoning in composing, offering explicit rationales and audience-aware decision-making—characteristics associated with expert writers—rather than as automated generators of text.

2.2 Collaborative Revision and the Epistemic Value of Dialogue

It has been robustly established that well-scaffolded peer review improves text quality and promotes writer development; the quality of dialogic negotiation—diagnosis, rationale, proposal, and uptake—predicts substantive revision (Min, 2006; Nelson & Schunn, 2009; Storch, 2013; Graham et al., 2020). Recent studies show LLMs can scaffold feedback literacy and expand student reviewers' strategy repertoire, contingent on designs that counsel against wholesale rewriting and centre explanation (Guo, 2024; Sperber et al., 2025). In this respect, algorithmic mentorship elevates feedback literacy and metacognitive uptake over product substitution.

2.3 Translanguaging and Multilingual Writing

Translanguaging reconceptualizes language difference as a resource, justifying the mobilization of entire linguistic repertoires for ideation, stance, and adaptation to audience (García & Wei, 2014). Research documents how multilingual writers value their use of code-meshing and metalinguistic reflection, so that their linguistic repertoires can result in greater accuracy and lexical sophistication, as well as increased rhetorical flexibility (Storch & Wigglesworth, 2010; Wigglesworth & Storch, 2012). More recent research in EAP writing similarly frames translanguaging as a multilingual pedagogy that disrupts monolingual ideologies. Thus, algorithmic mentors ought to support multilingual planning (Tastanbek, 2024), contrastive rhetorical analysis, and voice preservation, rather than homogenization.

2.4 AI in Writing Pedagogy: From Automated Scoring to Mentor-Constrained Mediation

The historical emphasis of automated writing evaluation (AWE) on surface features has triggered validity and equity concerns (Stevenson & Phakiti, 2019; Wilson & Czik, 2016).

Large Language Models (LLMs) indicate a developmental shift in our design space from fixed metrics of writing to dialogic mediation of revision. However, this also creates new risks and potential violations related to cognitive offloading, stylistic homogenization, and writing integrity that require intentional orchestration on the part of the instructor (Bender et al., 2021; Cotton et al., 2024; Baig et al., 2024). Activity Theory (AT) helps surface and resolve contradictions by connecting learning goals with artefacts, rules, and roles.

2.5 Contrasting Feedback Regimes: AWE, Unconstrained LLM, and Mentor-Constrained LLM

The study compares three feedback regimes, all of which are currently shaping writing instruction: automated writing evaluation (AWE) systems, unconstrained LLM rewriting, and the mentor-constrained LLM design developed in this chapter. AWE and unconstrained LLM use bring power and efficiency to the writing instruction process, but they typically value product quality over visibility into the writing process, authorial agency, and beliefs about equity. The mentor-constrained LLM design aims to keep the benefits of AI while drawing from feedback practices that are aligned with process-centred, ethically accountable pedagogy.

Table 1. Contrasting Feedback Regimes in AI-Mediated Writing

Feature	Automated Writing Evaluation (AWE)	Unconstrained LLM Rewriting	Mentor-Constrained LLM (this chapter)
Primary Goal	Surface - feature scoring	Rapid product generation	Process-centred diagnostic mentoring
Typical Artifacts	Scores, trait ratings	Overwritten drafts	Prompt logs, revision memos, tracked changes
Main Risks	Validity, surface focus	Cognitive offload, homogenized voice	Still: dependence, equity gaps if poorly implemented
Equity/Privacy	Centralised scoring systems	Data exposure to 3rd-party tools	Local, policy-aligned, transparent logs

(Source: *Author's original synthesis*)

The first two columns demonstrate how AWE systems and unconstrained LLM rewriting prioritize evaluation and productivity over learning. AWE tools tend to produce scores and trait ratings oriented toward surface correctness and fidelity to rubrics, which limits writers' attention to aspects that can be easily measured. Even though unconstrained LLM rewriting can produce well-edited text very quickly, it can erase the decision-making of the writer, obscure authorship, and may even impose a homogeneous linguistic and rhetorical voice.

The mentor-constrained LLM design in this chapter explicitly addresses these risks. This design uses families of prompts to constrain AI to clarifying issues, modelling alternative responses, simulating audience responses, and providing multilingual planning. Through the generation of process artefacts—prompt logs, tracked revisions, revision memos—the LLM design documents how writers think about feedback.

These artefacts are fed directly into the trialogue interaction routine and the process-centred assessment framework that shifts the focus toward the teacher's evaluation of diagnostic thinking, strategic uptake, and ethical attribution instead of only rewarding polished output.

2.6 Contributions of this Chapter

This This chapter describes three interrelated contributions to the AI-mediated design of writing instruction. First, it presents an Activity-Theoretic account of algorithmic mentors, which reconceptualizes large language models as role-bounded mediators of revision rather than autonomous text generators. By conceptualizing LLMs as one mediating artefact in the writing activity system in conjunction with other mediating artefacts, it identifies common contradictions around objects, rules, community, and division of labour—contradictions that authorship, equity, and assessment can produce with unmediated AI usage—and shows how authorship, equity, and assessment can instead be supported by clear, parameterized roles.

Second, it introduces a five-phase trialogic interaction routine—Intent Articulation, Peer Diagnosis, AI Consultancy, Revision, and Revision Memo—that combines participation of students, peers, and the AI around common artefacts: comments, prompt logs, tracked changes, and reflective memos.

Third, it presents a process-centred assessment and governance framework that complements the above practices and ties these practices educationally to institutional responsibilities. An analytic rubric weights revision coverage and depth, diagnostic reasoning, strategic uptake, multilingual and metalinguistic strategies, and accountable use and attribution, while a set of guidelines discusses logging, disclosure, data governance, and equity monitoring, illustrating how teachers and institutions can audit AI-mediated writing without reverting to collapsed product-only assessment. In total, these contributions tie together theory, pedagogy, assessment, and policy into a cohesive model of mentor-locked AI for writing development.

3. CONCEPTUAL FRAMEWORK: ALGORITHMIC MENTORS AS MEDIATING ARTIFACTS

3.1 Definition and Role Constraints

Algorithmic Algorithmic mentors are LLM systems explicitly designed to simulate expert revision strategies: identifying rhetorical issues, articulating genre expectations, modelling potential options with trade-offs, and simulating audience response—but not to replace authors. Two areas of constraints are primary:

(a) *Functional role-boundedness*, privileging diagnostic explanation over replacement text; and
(b) *Metacognitive transparency* through traces of process (prompt logs, response histories, and memos of authorial revision) that make decision-making visible and assessable.

The next section translates this conceptualisation into a trialogue interaction routine and a set of mentor-constrained prompt families that realise these constraints in classroom practice.

3.2 Activity-Theoretic Analysis of Contradictions

Activity-Theoretic Activity-Theoretic (AT) analysis prioritizes contradictions as mechanisms for change (Engeström, 2001). Some of the tensions related to AI-mediated writing activity systems include:

- **Subject–Object:** Students are very focused on the grade given, while the teacher is focused on students' learning.
- **Artefact–Object:** In utilizing AI text, the object is shifted from traditional development to deliverables.
- **Rules–Community:** Institutional bans of AI text versus communities of practice that normalize its use.
- **Division of Labour:** The roles of author and evaluator have become blurred.

Our design targets these contradictions by emphasizing the role of process evidence in assessment, requiring transparent indication of tool mediation, preserving the teacher's orchestration and authority, and facilitating equitable access to tools supported at the institutional level. As shown in Figure 1, the Activity-Theoretic model frames the student-author, tools, and outcomes as interdependent components mediated through rules, community, and division of labour.

The following classic Engeström triangle illustrates in Figure 1, shows how the algorithmic mentor is positioned along the Subject–Object edge as a mediating artefact that shapes—but does not replace—authorship. The system of writing activity includes the Subject (student-author) located on the lower left, Object/Outcomes at the top of the triangle, and Rules, Community, and Division of Labour indicated in the lower band. In order to emphasize the algorithmic mentor's role as a mediating artefact (LLMs, rubrics, platforms) that shapes action while maintaining authorship, the Subject–Object link (the pedagogic assignment) is made visible as Mediating Artefacts. Alt Text: "Triangle of Subject, Object/Outcomes, and lower band (Rules, Community, Division of Labour) showing Mediating Artefacts indicated along the Subject–Object edge."

Subject (student-author) Rules Community Division of Labour

Figure 1. Activity-Theoretic Model: Algorithmic Mentors as Mediating Artifacts (Source: Adapted from Engeström (2001); redrawn by the author)

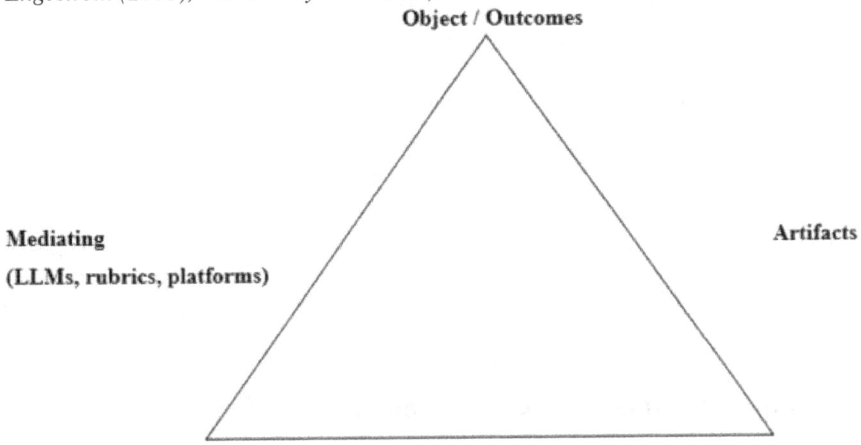

A classic Engeström triangle illustrates, the algorithmic mentor is positioned along the Subject–Object edge as a mediating artifact that shapes—but does not replace—authorship. The system of writing activity: Subject (student-author) is located on the lower left, Object/Outcomes is located at the top of the triangle, and Rules, Community, and Division of Labour are indicated in the lower band. In order to emphasize the algorithmic mentor's role as a mediating artifact (LLMs, rubrics, platforms) that shapes action while maintaining authorship, the Subject→Object link (the pedagogic assignment) is made visible as Mediating Artifacts. Alt Text: "Triangle of Subject, Object/Outcomes, and lower band (Rules, Community, Division of Labour) show Mediating Artifacts indicated along the Subject–Object edge."

4. DESIGN PRINCIPLES FOR RESPONSIBLE AI-FACILITATED COLLABORATIVE REVISION

4.1 Principle 1. Valuing process-based evidence over superficial polish.

Assessment should emphasize process-based indicators of learning rather than simply the end product. Evaluative emphasis must be placed on visible indicators of revision behaviours (tracked changes, version histories, AI prompt–response logs, reflective revision memos) to ensure grading criteria are based on observable cognitive effort and iterative learning rather than stylistic polish.

4.2 Principle 2. Make transparent attribution practices the standard.

Students must be required to document the technologies used for revisions, what the technologies were used for, how they were prompted, and the reasons for accepting, changing, or rejecting AI suggestions. This systematic transparency creates a culture of responsibility, academic integrity, and metacognition regarding the ethics and epistemology of human–AI co-learning.

4.3 Principle 3. Acknowledge the legitimacy of translanguaging and code-meshing.

Instructional design must formalize multilingual pre-writing, writing, and post-writing through rhetorical negotiation. Providing students with the opportunity to utilize multiple language repertoires, as well as to discuss cross-linguistic rhetorical analyses, supports communication with particular audiences, as well as engagement with institutional expectations and differentials.

4.4 Principle 4. Provide feedback that explains instead of or in contrast to text replacement.

AI tools need to be limited to diagnostic and intellectual purposes—to identify issues, explain what rules might be involved, suggest alternative strategies, and describe the pros and cons of various suggestions. With this system, students can build critical thinking skills about what "revision" means.

4.5 Principle 5. Keep humans performing pedagogical functions ("humans in the loop").

Instructors are needed to organize the pedagogy and will establish task order, norms, timing, and analytics. AI should be used as a supplemental scaffold so that teaching practice can remain humanistic, contextualized in the classroom, and oriented toward advocating for good ethical practices.

4.6 Principle 6. Center equity in AI-based learning design.

Equity-based implementation must include institutional responsibility for fair access to AI, which means in-class time with institutional supports. Ongoing analysis should track cyclical access, engagement, participation, or learning-outcome inequities to prevent algorithms or access to infrastructure from exacerbating inequities in access to AI.

4.7 Principle 7. Protect data privacy from low exposure and tool ethics.

To responsibly utilize AI, it is preferable to use systems that are locally hosted or supervised by institutional governance with robust data protections. A "privacy by design" ethos must be built into the provider and accompanying institutions, with data deletion, user consent, and clear descriptions of data use to ensure safeguards against surveillance, profiling, or unjustified data retention.

4.8 Principle 8. Align assessment criteria with authentic learning outcomes.

Rubrics for assessment must identify and reward predictive reasoning and ethical use of tools. The intention is that assessment promotes higher-order cognitive, linguistic, and ethical engagement beyond mechanical task completion.

4.9 Activity-Theoretic Contradictions and Algorithmic Mentorship Solutions:

The study's main theoretical takeaway is how Activity Theory (AT) can diagnose and design for the contradictions created when generative AI enters the ecology of writing instruction.

Each aspect of the activity system—object, mediating artefacts, rules, community, division of labour, and outcomes—points to a distinct form of contradiction introduced with AI, alongside a design principle of algorithmic mentorship which portrays AI as a pedagogically bounded mediator, rather than as an autonomous producer of text.

i. Object: From development to deliverables

Under AI mediation, the object of writing activity is relocated from developmental learning to polished deliverables. This change represents the traditional contradiction between "writing as process" and "writing as product" (Bereiter & Scardamalia, 1987).

Algorithmic mentorship re-establishes the object in process evidence and strategic uptake, nudging teachers to inspect the manner in which students engage with revision, not what AI can produce (Cotton et al., 2024; Guo, 2024). Revision logs, prompt traces, and reflective memos become valid evidence of learning.

ii. Mediating Artifacts: From replacement to reasoning

At the level of mediating artefacts, AI has the potential to replace human reasoning by offering ready-made resolutions on demand. Within the algorithmic-mentorship framing, LLMs are re-envisioned as role-bounded mentors who explicate alternatives and model expert diagnostic reasoning while avoiding the substitution of the authorship workload (Sperber et al., 2025). This resolution aligns with sociocultural understandings of tools functioning as metacognitive control scaffolds rather than as independent agents (Prior, 2006; Russell, 1997).

iii. Rules: Integrity and attribution norms

Institutional norms are frequently ambiguous on acceptable AI use, generating conjectures about the integrity expected collectively in contrast to what happens in practice in class (Cotton et al., 2024). By design, the resolution requires documentation and transparency about AI mediation and prompting (with rationale), as well as accounting for the work of AI. This transparency reshapes integrity from a punishment-centred framework toward metacognitive and ethical action with discernible co-regulation (Winstone & Carless, 2019).

iv. Community: Normalizing versus banning

In the practice community, tensions exist between banning AI and normalizing its uncritical use (Bender et al., 2021; Baig et al., 2024). The algorithmic-mentorship approach alleviates tensions through co-produced agreements and policies negotiated collectively, with teachers positioned as orchestrators (Dillenbourg & Jermann, 2010). The proposition foregrounds collaborative governance and co-responsibility to acknowledge equitable, ethical, and educationally oriented use of AI.

v. Division of labour: Authorship and evaluation

Integration with AI blurs the lines among author, peer, and evaluator (Guo et al., 2025). The design solution offers explicit delineation of roles to differentiate what belongs to the student-author, what is aided by AI, and what belongs to the teacher, in ways that reinforce human support and evaluative agency. Teachers hold the pedagogical centre in orchestrating what Engeström (2001) calls "humans-in-the-loop of situated activity."

vi. Outcomes: Voice and equity

The final outcome contradiction concerns the homogenized style of output and the unequal growth of learning based on differential access and capabilities that students may have (García & Wei, 2014; Tastanbek, 2024). Algorithmic mentorship includes prompts that preserve voice alongside mechanics and that monitor equity to ensure multilingual and culturally diverse voices do not become flattened (Storch & Wigglesworth, 2010). Institutional structures should provide equitable access and continuous auditing of participation and performance data (Slade & Prinsloo, 2013). As shown in Table 2, the AT elements reveal how AI-induced contradictions emerge and how algorithmic mentorship offers design resolutions.

Table 2. AT Elements, Typical Contradictions, and Design Resolutions

AT Element	Typical AI-Induced Contradiction	Design Resolution (Algorithmic Mentorship)
Object	Shift from development to polished deliverables	Assess **processes** and **strategic uptake**; weight revision evidence
Mediating Artifacts	AI replaces human reasoning	**Role-bounded AI** that explains and models alternatives
Rules	Ambiguous integrity and attribution norms	**Mandatory disclosure** of AI use with **rationale** and **logs**
Community	Normalization vs. prohibition tensions	**Co-created policies; teacher-led orchestration**
Division of Labour	Blurred authorship and evaluation	**Explicit roles** for author/peer/AI; **teacher oversight**
Outcomes	Homogenized voice; inequitable gains	**Voice-preservation prompts**; **equity monitoring** and access

(Source: *Author's compilation*)

Table 2, therefore, acts as both diagnostic schema and design blueprint for the responsible application of AI in practice. The table outlines contradictions mapped to mentor-constrained resolutions in AT—what Engeström (2001) refers to as expansive learning—turning tensions into avenues for pedagogical innovation. Algorithmic mentorship uses structures to convert disruption created by AI into organized growth and metacognitive follow-up through co-constructed integrity and equitable orchestration of writing as dialogic, tool-mediated, socially distributed growth.

5. THE TRIALOGUE INTERACTION ROUTINE: STUDENT–PEER–AI COLLABORATION

The operational core consists of a five-phase cycle that integrates authorial self-assessment with dialogic peer review and AI consultation, capped by a mentor. Each phase generates assessable artefacts that make learning observable while allowing for authorial agency through reasoned uptake decisions.

The trialogue phases of algorithmic mentorship represented in Table 3 illustrate the Trialogue Interaction Routine, which is the working hub of the algorithmic-mentorship framework suggested by the study. Based in Activity Theory (Engeström, 2001), the trialogue framework positions three interacting agents—the student-author, the peer reviewer, and the AI mentor—into a recursive cycle of writing development framed by metacognition, feedback literacy, and ethical co-learning (Guo, 2024; Sperber et al., 2025).

Each of the five phases—Intent Articulation, Peer Diagnosis, AI Consultancy, Revision, and Revision Memo—produces concrete artefacts that bring observable and assessable evidence of learning, addressing persistent concerns around observing the cognitive and collaborative processes of writing (Hayes & Flower, 1980; Winstone & Carless, 2019).

a. Intent Articulation: Grounding Metacognition and Audience Awareness

The first phase grounds the author as an intentional, reflective agent. By articulating writing goals, expected audience, and issues of concern using an intent note (in any language), the learner externalizes their metacognitive awareness. The intent articulation phase serves to establish the dialogues needed to orient peers and the AI to the writer's rhetorical situation (Bereiter & Scardamalia, 1987). In multilingual classrooms, intent articulation validates translanguaging as a cognitive resource rather than a deviation (García & Wei, 2014), allowing the writer to use their entire linguistic repertoire to ideate and to frame areas of difficulty (Tastanbek, 2024).

b. Peer Diagnosis: Advancing Feedback Literacy via Dialogic Negotiation

In the second phase, peer reviewers pinpoint two to three areas for enhancement and provide rationales that leverage text evidence. This phase realizes dialogic negotiation—diagnostic reasoning, rationale, and uptake—as indicators of insightful revision (Min, 2006; Nelson & Schunn, 2009; Storch, 2013). Annotated commentary provides learners space to develop their feedback literacy and to engage in the acknowledgement of audience positioning and evaluative reasoning in socially distributed contexts (Graham et al., 2020). Peer diagnosis fits within a sociocultural model of learning wherein learning occurs in a community of practice and shared inquiry (Prior, 2006; Russell, 1997).

c. AI Consultancy: Role-Bound Explaining and Diagnostic Modelling

In this phase of AI consultancy, we define the unique contribution of algorithmic mentorship. Here, the author and the AI collaboratively search for explanations, genre modelling, and alternative ways of writing while (importantly) not replacing the author's text. The prompt-response trace collaboratively produced is a process artefact that communicates diagnostic reasoning (Guo, 2024; Sperber et al., 2025). This design anticipates the role-bounded mediator: AI functions as a tutor of diagnostic reasoning, rather than as an agent that replaces the writer's text (Bender et al., 2021). The AI models reasoning as an expert diagnostician—explaining a rule of rhetoric, genre-related expectations, and reactions in relation to audiences—while still maintaining authorship.

d. Revision: Enacted Agency and Strategic Uptake

In the fourth phase, the author receives input from peers and AI and makes decisions about revision next steps—whether to keep, change, or remove material—while documenting their decisions through tracked versions. In this phase, the act of revision becomes a visible example of strategic uptake (Winstone & Carless, 2019)—moving from mechanical correcting and editing to an intentional restructuring of meaning. The author gains awareness of both global reorganization and local work on meaning. This shift from mechanical knowledge-telling to intentional knowledge-transforming supports writing as a different way of knowing (Bereiter & Scardamalia, 1987).

e. Revision Memo: Externalizing Metacognition and Ethical Reflection

Externalizing In the final phase, each student consolidates their learning into a revision memo. The author writes and shares a 200–300-word revision memo summarizing their colleagues' input and outlining multilingual next steps. The memo serves two purposes: it provides evidence of metacognition in the revision process and constitutes summative evidence of learning and development. Process-based data can be connected to evaluative frameworks (Faigley & Witte, 1981). The revision memo records the author's rationale for revisions and provides an ethical framing of authorship by documenting how AI contributed and how the author exercised agency in accepting, adapting, or rejecting suggestions. The memo culminates in reflection on what the author learned, what changed, and how their writing will continue to advance. It offers practical value and visibility of learning while also serving as interpretable, equitable evidence of development for the teacher (Cotton et al., 2024; Dillenbourg & Jermann, 2010).

As summarized in Table 3, the trialogue routine outlines the interactional sequence among the author, peer, and AI mentor, along with the artefacts and pedagogical functions associated with each phase.

Table 3. Trialogue Phases, Actors, Artifacts, and Functions

Phase	Primary Actor(s)	Core Activity	Artifacts/Evidence	Pedagogical Function
1. Intent Articulation	Author	State goals, audience, concerns	Intent note (any language)	Activate metacognition; orient reviewers
2. Peer Diagnosis	Peer(s)	Identify strengths; 2–3 growth areas with reasons	Annotated comments	Develop feedback literacy; audience response
3. AI Consultancy	Author + AI	Request **explanations**, options, genre modelling; **no rewrite**	Prompt/response trace	Expand repertoire; model expert diagnosis
4. Revision	Author	Accept/modify/reject; implement global + local changes	Tracked versions	Exercise agency; perform strategic revision
5. Revision Memo	Author	Explain decisions; multilingual strategies; next steps	200–300-word memo	Externalize metacognition; central assessment evidence

(Source: *Author's compilation.)*

"Instructors can use this table as a checklist when designing assignments, confirming that each phase elicits the core activity, artefacts, and pedagogical functions shown here."

Taken together, the sequence of five phases constitutes a transparent, evidence-producing cycle of learning. Each phase emphasizes a different aspect of learning, such as metacognition, feedback literacy, diagnostic reasoning, strategic uptake, and ethical reflection, while maintaining visible authorship. The organization of these phases also aligns with Dillenbourg and Jermann's (2010) discussion of pedagogical orchestration, as they relate to harmonizing human and AI engagement across the cycle.

Collectively, the phases reconfigure the writing classroom through equitable and dialogically transparent practices that clarify and document text for the purposes of increasing visibility, preserving authorial voices, and cultivating ethical collaboration with AI at all levels of writing proficiency. Linking the trialogue phases to Activity Theory highlights Engeström's (2001) notion of an expansive cycle of learning, in which contradictions among tools, rules, and roles become drivers for transforming educational practice. The study captures generative-AI mediation in collaborative writing interventions that adjust for the humanness of rhetorical and multilingual stances of authorship. As illustrated in Figure 2, the trialogue interaction routine sequences five phases of author–peer–AI collaboration supported by two distinct feedback loops that guide revision and metacognitive reflection.

Figure 2. The Trialogue Interaction Routine: Student–Peer–AI Collaboration

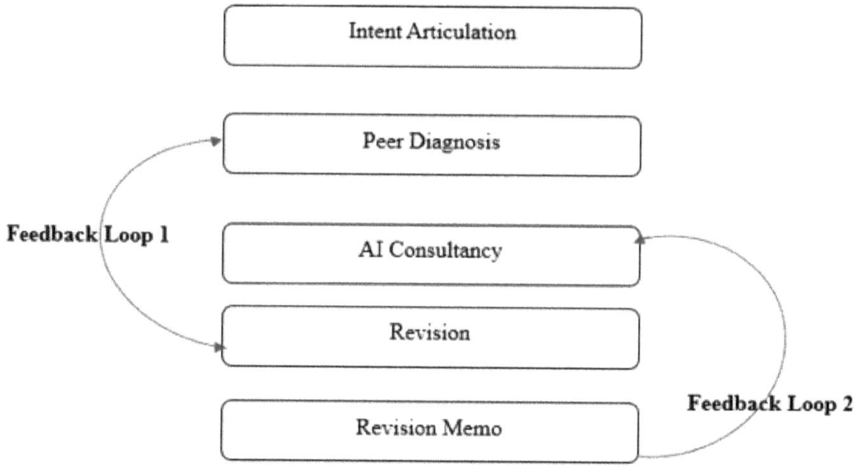

(Source: Author's original figure, drawing on Dillenbourg & Jermann (2010) and Winstone & Carless (2019))

"Teachers can use this figure to plan a sequence of weekly activities, ensuring that each phase of the trialogue corresponds to class time and produces the artefacts listed in Table 3."

As shown in Figure 2, the routine coordinates author intent, peer diagnosis, and constrained AI consultancy into a recursive cycle. Rather than presenting AI as an autonomous text generator, the model situates it within a pedagogically constrained ecology that enhances rather than replaces human agency—a principle central to the study's argument for AI-mediated, process-centric, and socially distributed writing development.

6. PROMPT FAMILIES FOR MENTOR-ROLE CONSTRAINT

Prompt families assist in operationalizing the mentor role by channelling AI toward explanation-first mediation and away from complete summarizing or rewriting. Prompts are closely tied to rhetorical challenges, require rationales tied to genre and/or audience, and instruct AI not to provide replacement text. Prompt families include diagnostic explanation, strategic alternatives with associated costs of change, genre modelling and rhetorical analysis, audience simulation, multilingual planning and contrastive rhetoric, and voice-preservation prompts. Each family is bound to a specific cognitive function and observable artefact of learning so that instructors can assess uptake without merging authorship into automated substitution. Additionally, the table illustrates the commitment to Activity Theory in practice through particular interactional moves in the trialogue routine (author–peer–AI).

i. Diagnostic Explanation

Definition. Prompts in this family ask the AI to identify a problem and defend its relevance (e.g., requiring the AI to tie a detected weakness to genre or audience expectations) instead of providing sentences to replace the identified problem.

Importance. This situates revision as a form of disciplined diagnostic reasoning, not superficial editing. Diagnostic explanation invites warrants ("why this matters here") that writers weigh against their intent and reader needs, which is an indicator of the thinking expert composers engage in.

What to look for. Outcome indicators include clear reasoning points bound to genre and audience. In practice, we see these warrants in revision memos and margin notes where the writer cites the diagnostic, shows where it applies, and highlights a response (accepted, adapted, rejected).

ii. Strategic Alternatives

Definition. Instead of providing a singular fix, the AI offers multiple, viable options while simultaneously making the trade-offs explicit (e.g., precision vs. accessibility, concision vs. nuance).

Importance. Providing a design space creates deliberative agency, slowing the process down and avoiding narrowly mimicked closing moves. In this vein, it pushes writers to select tactics that best support their rhetorical situation.

What to look for. Expected outcomes are visible in rationale-based selection and adaptive moves. These appear in version histories and revision memos where writers articulate why one option was selected over others, how they tailored AI suggestions back into their own voice, and why they rejected or deferred otherwise plausible options.

iii. Genre Modelling

Definition. Prompts require the AI to identify genre moves, naming patterns (for example, claim–warrant–evidence; synthesis-before-gap) and exemplifying them with illustrative but non-substitutive sentences.

Importance. By externalizing genre structure, we support metapragmatic awareness while enabling writers to evaluate structural architecture, rather than merely sentence-level persuasion.

What to look for. Indicators include the use of genre-aligned structures in revisions, visible in resegmented sections, reconstituted paragraphs, or added signposting of genre-aligned moves. Look in memos to ascertain the rationale for structural revision.

iv. Audience Simulation (Reader Questions)

Definition. Here the AI is tasked with perspective-taking to surface likely questions a reader would ask at specific points in the text.

Importance. Anticipating questions trains situation analysis and helps authors calibrate background information in sections that are dense with evidence or complex concepts.

What to look for. Evidence includes anticipated reader questions in AI-generated prompts and subsequent targeted additions (for example, bridging definitions or clarifying methods). Look in author memos for reader-related rationales for added material.

v. Audience Simulation (Reader Objections)

Definition. A complementary simulation, in which the AI role-plays a critical reader to surface objections (counter-evidence, rival explanations, boundary cases).

Importance. This activity builds argumentative robustness while reducing confirmation bias, as it prompts the writer to consider counter-positions before committing to revision.

What to look for. Outcomes include pre-emptive qualification and strengthened warrants, where sections are added or revised to engage counterarguments, with clear links to objections surfaced in the AI prompts and taken up by the author.

vi. Multilingual Planning

Definition. Prompts make explicit use of L1/L2 resources for ideation, clarification of concepts, and problem-solving, followed by presentation to audience in the target language.

Importance. By exploiting translanguaging as a cognitive resource, we can expand the space for invention and be more precise and deliberate in stance-taking for the intended audience.

What to look for. Indicators of this activity include visible translanguaging in intent notes, notes on prompts, and target-language presentations that show ideas first incubated in L1/L2.

vii. Voice Preservation

Definition. Prompts constrain the AI to judge clarity of thought or argumentative tension, and to comment on intonation, style, and diction while not wholesale rephrasing.

Importance. Voice is an important feature of authorship and provides resistance to homogenization; it is an essential feature of what makes us who we are as scholars. To make the best arguments requires tightening the logic of exposition while keeping the writer's voice.

What to look for. Outcomes include maintenance of stylistic features alongside improved clarity. Evidence can be seen in revision memos noting "clarity without voice loss" and in revised texts where rhythm and phrasing remain recognizably the author's, but with fewer obstacles to comprehension. As outlined in *Table 4*, the prompt families used in mentor-constrained AI consultancy each serve a distinct pedagogical purpose and produce specific, observable outcome indicators in students' revisions.

Table 4. Prompt Families and Expected Outcomes

Prompt Family	Primary Purpose	Example Outcome Indicators
Diagnostic explanation	Identify problems and **explain why** they matter	Clear rationales tied to **genre** and **audience** expectations
Strategic alternatives	Offer multiple options with **trade-offs**	Writer's **reasoned selection** and adaptation
Genre modelling	Make rhetorical **moves/patterns** visible	Use of **genre-aligned structures** in revisions
Audience simulation	Perspective-taking and situation analysis	Anticipation of **reader questions/objections**
Audience simulation	Perspective-taking and situation analysis	Anticipation of **reader questions/objections**

continued on following page

Table 4. Continued

Prompt Family	Primary Purpose	Example Outcome Indicators
Multilingual planning	Leverage L1/L2 for ideation/problem-solving	Visible **translanguaging**; audience-appropriate TL presentation
Voice preservation	Retain authorial style while tightening argument	Maintenance of **stylistic features** with improved clarity

(***Source:*** *Author's compilation.*)

"This table can guide the selection of mentor-constrained prompts when particular issues arise in a draft, such as unclear structure, weak audience awareness, or underdeveloped multilingual strategies."

Collectively, these prompt families put into practice the paper's role-bound conception of algorithmic mentorship: they call upon LLMs to facilitate consistency, explanation, options, modelling, perspective-taking, multilingual invention, and voice care—not to overwrite text. The "Example Outcome Indicators" column, importantly, anchors each family to assessable traces—prompt logs, annotated rationales, tracked revisions, and reflective memos—so that assessment can validly prioritize and weigh process evidence and strategic uptake over attractive polish.

7. MULTILINGUAL PEDAGOGIES WITH ALGORITHMIC MENTORING

Algorithmic mentoring focuses on translanguaging as a legitimate and generative resource for ideation and rhetorical problem-solving while guiding writers toward audience-responsive presentation. Pedagogical designs include multilingual intent notes, code-meshed brainstorming, error-as-inquiry routines, and contrastive rhetorical analysis. Collectively, these practices build lexically precise, rhetorically flexible, and identity-affirming voice (García & Wei, 2014; Tastanbek, 2024).

7.1 Practical Multilingual Routines

To render translanguaging principles actionable within classroom practice, the algorithmic mentoring framework is accompanied by a small number of multilingual routines that can be integrated into any major writing assignment. The first routine is an intent-note template completed by students in whatever language or languages feel most natural during the planning stage. The template prompts four short fields: Audience ("Who am I writing for?"), Main claim ("What do I most want them to understand or feel?"), What I am worried about (e.g., argument, evidence, tone, or language), and Languages I used in planning and why (e.g., brainstorming in L1, drafting in L2, switching languages for particular sources). This note accompanies the draft in the peer diagnosis, AI consulting, and revision memo, thus making multilingual reasoning visible and relevant across the trialogue.

The second routine is a contrastive rhetoric grid that students use while engaged in revision for genre and audience. On a simple three-column grid—Move in this genre, How I would say it in L1, and How I will say it in the target language—students map important rhetorical moves like making a claim, signalling stance, and integrating sources. The grid can be completed independently or with peers, and then used to generate genre-modelling or audience-simulation prompts for the algorithmic mentor, so AI support is based on students' own multilingual comparisons rather than replacing them.

The third routine is a short voice-preserving checklist that students tick through each time they use AI: Did I ask AI to comment on clarity, structure, or examples, rather than rewriting entire paragraphs? Does the final text still sound like me, with some phrasing that reflects my linguistic background? Did I restore or adapt AI-suggested wording so that it does not feel generic or unlike myself? Have I made clear any time AI had some part in the work? The intention of these templates is to help students incorporate their multilingual resources into the trialogue cycle as central to writer development, so that AI mediation supports rather than flattens students' voices.

8. ORCHESTRATING AI-MEDIATE REVISION: TEACHER ROLE AND CLASSROOM STRUCTURES

Teacher Sustained impact is derived from pedagogical orchestration rather than tool features (Dillenbourg & Jermann, 2010). Meaningful orchestration involves: co-creating use norms and attribution protocols with students; scheduling time in class to ensure access and reduce inequity; curating exemplars and counter-exemplars; formative interpretation of process analytics (for reflection, not ranking); and ongoing professional learning communities for teachers. Teacher agency is important at all times; the educator determines the tasks, timing, and feedback intended to keep learning-oriented goals and authorial agency intact, ensuring AI-mediated revision supports learning and does not replace discipline-specific judgement and student voice.

8.1 Implementation Playbook: Classroom Use of the Trialogue Routine

To To support practical adoption, the trialogue routine can be conducted as a five-week cycle coinciding with a standard writing assignment.

- **Week 1.** The teacher sets norms by establishing institutional AI policies, clarifying what attribution involves, and inviting students to think of their AI system as an "algorithmic mentor" constrained to helping rather than ghost-writing. The teacher also provides sample prompt logs and disclosure language.
- **Week 2.** Students write a first draft and attach a brief intent note in any language that names their audience, sets goals, and names concerns; the teacher models at least one strong intent note and provides feedback on a small sample of notes.
- **Week 3.** Class time is set aside for peer diagnosis; students exchange drafts and provide two to four targeted comments directly connected to dimensions of the rubric, addressing global concerns first before sentence-level edits.
- **Week 4.** Students engage in AI consultancy (in class) using only the mentor-constrained prompt families described earlier, asking their AI system for explanations, alternatives, genre models, audience simulations, multilingual planning, and voice-preserving suggestions, while saving prompt-response logs.
- **Week 5.** Students revise their drafts using tracked changes, write a 200–300-word revision memo explaining how they acted on peer and AI suggestions and which suggestions

they rejected (and why), and submit the revised draft, memo, prompt log, and tracked changes as integrated evidence of their thinking and writing for the assignment.

This five-week cycle can be compressed to fit shorter assignments or repeated for multiple tasks, while maintaining a similar routine.

8.2 Minimal Tool Checklist

The The implementation discussed above assumes only a minimal essential set of tools that should be assembled in most institutional contexts. Teachers should have a writing platform that supports accessible version history and tracked changes (e.g., a word processor or cloud document editor), a simple way of logging prompts and AI responses (e.g., a copy-and-paste template or image-upload area in an LMS), and a revision-memo template that prompts students to connect specific changes to peer and AI comments.

9. ASSESSMENT SUPPORTS THE WORK OF LEARNERS

To To counter product substitution and offloading risk, assessment needs to recognize process evidence and strategic reasoning as a substantial share of meaning. We offer an analytic rubric that assesses the following: (a) the coverage and depth of revisions; (b) diagnostic reasoning; (c) strategic uptake and agency; (d) multilingual strategy and metalinguistic awareness; and (e) ethical use and attribution (Faigley & Witte, 1981; Winstone & Carless, 2019). A short memo (200–300 words) provides core evidence for metacognition, making visible the rationales, decision points, and ethical choices underpinning the move from the initial text to the revised text. As detailed in Table 5, the analytic rubric evaluates students' process-centred writing development across five dimensions.

Table 5. Analytic Rubric (Process-Centred Assessment)

Dimension	Weight	Exemplary (4)	Proficient (3)	Developing (2)	Emerging (1)
Revision Coverage & Depth	25%	Multiple **global** revisions plus strategic local refinements; clear alignment with goals and audience	Mix of global/ local revisions with purposeful improvement	Primarily local edits with limited restructuring	Minimal change; surface correction
Diagnostic Reasoning	20%	Sophisticated diagnosis with **genre/audience** rationales. *For example, the revision memo cites specific peer and AI comments, explains why each mattered, and justifies keeping or altering ideas.*	Major issues identified with clear reasons	Vague or generic diagnoses	Minimal/absent diagnosis
Strategic Uptake & Agency	25%	Judicious accept/ modify/reject with substantive rationales; **voice preserved**	Mostly appropriate uptake; occasional uncritical acceptance / rejection	Inconsistent uptake; limited rationale	Wholesale adoption/rejection
Multilingual Strategy & Metalinguistic	15%	Productive **translanguaging**; explicit reasoning about register, stance, evidentiality	Evidence of multilingual strategy; metalinguistic reflection	Limited or implicit strategies	No visible strategy
Ethical Use & Attribution	15%	Precise, transparent documentation; **policy-aligned**; reflective commentary on mediation. *For example, the student consistently discloses AI use, distinguishes original and AI-supported wording, and reflects on the appropriateness of that support.*	Minor omissions; generally aligned	Partial/unclear attribution; policy ambiguity	Violations/misrepresentation

(Source: *Author's original rubric*)

"Teachers can use this rubric both for summative scoring and for planning feedback and workshops that target the dimensions where students most often score at Developing or Emerging levels."

9.1 Rubric Calibration and Use of Process Artifacts

9.1.a Inter-rater Calibration

In To promote trustworthy use of the analytic rubric, instructors are encouraged to develop a straightforward inter-rater calibration routine at the beginning of each term. Two teachers, or a teacher and researcher, can independently score a small set of anonymized trialogue cases (including a draft with tracked changes, an associated prompt log, and revision memo) and then compare independent judgements to determine where they scored differently across dimensions—for example, diagnostic reasoning, strategic uptake, or ethical use and attribution.

Scores can be compared and any discrepancies used to clarify the rubric notes with examples or decision rules, including potential sources of evidence to support judgements on shared cases. This brief collaborative calibration exercise can be repeated periodically and can also serve as professional development, so that scores received by students are grounded in shared interpretations rather than idiosyncratic intuitions.

9.1.b Linking Rubric to Artifacts

The rubric is designed to work directly with the artefacts created during the trialogue routine. Drafts and their tracked-change histories yield primary evidence for the Revision Coverage & Depth dimension, demonstrating how comprehensively and intentionally texts were revised. Prompt logs and AI–student exchanges provide evidence for Diagnostic Reasoning and Ethical Use & Attribution in terms of how students framed problems, assessed suggestions, and documented their interaction with AI. Revision memos, lastly, are the primary source for assessing Strategic Uptake & Agency and Multilingual Strategy & Metalinguistic Awareness because they require students to comment on which peer and AI suggestions they took up, discarded, and how they used their entire linguistic repertoire.

Evaluating these artefacts in concert helps raters attend to processes of learning, rather than only to the final product. The above data are graphically portrayed in Figure 3, which displays the dimension weights within the process-centred review rubric. The figure shows the proportionate value assigned to each analytic dimension when assessing learner performance. The rubric gives most weight to Coverage/Depth (25%) and Uptake/Agency (25%) because they are considered the most direct measures of conceptual understanding and agency. Diagnosis (20%) measures how well students can understand and critique ideas, while Multilingual Strategy (15%) and Ethical Use (15%) address aspects of inclusive and accountable communication. Collectively, these weighted dimensions represent a balanced approach to assessment design that integrates cognitive depth, diagnostic acuity, agency, linguistic plurality, and ethical awareness.

As illustrated in Figure 3, the process-centred assessment rubric assigns proportional weights to each dimension, highlighting the importance of revision coverage, diagnostic reasoning, strategic uptake, multilingual strategy, and ethical use in evaluating learner development.

Figure 3. Dimension Weights within the Process-Centred Review Rubric – Source: Author's original figure

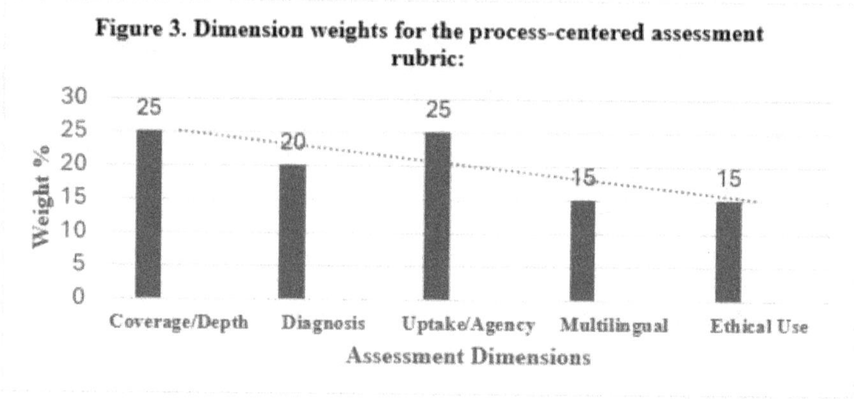

"Because Revision Coverage & Depth and Strategic Uptake are weighted highest, lesson time and sample analyses should prioritise global revision and justification of change decisions, with multilingual and ethical-use activities woven through these focal areas."

9.2 Using Visual Tools for Instructional Decisions

The figures and tables in the chapter are constructed as tools for teachers rather than decorative summaries. Figure 1 and the accompanying table map where algorithmic mentors sit within the writing activity system to direct instructor decision-making regarding which elements of practice to reconsider once AI enters the equation. Collectively, Table 3 and Figure 2 provide a planning template for lessons: each phase of the trialogue can be mapped to one or more course sessions and checked against the artefacts listed to ensure drafts, comments, prompt logs, tracked changes, and revision memos have all been generated. Table 4 becomes a prompt-selection guide for teachers and students; when they encounter a particular issue within a draft, they can choose a mentor-constrained prompt family—for example, genre-modelling prompts when structure is unclear or audience-simulation prompts when stance and register are misaligned.

Table 5 and Figure 3 both support assessment and intervention; the rubric makes visible which dimensions of process are weighted, and the weight distribution provides focus on where time and feedback should be spent in instruction if particular dimensions, like revision coverage or strategic uptake, carry the most weight. Taken together, these visuals function as concise tools for moving from theoretical commitments to concrete decisions about tasks, classroom routines, and feedback emphasis.

10. LEARNING ANALYTICS, DATA GOVERNANCE, AND PRIVACY

When oriented to be contextually useful and used formatively, student-facing analytics—such as visualizations of revision pathways, evidence of prompt-strategy trajectories, and indicators of feedback quality—can promote self-regulation. All indicators should remain auditable and traceable to evidence in drafts and system logs, and they should include prompts for structured reflection that cue students' focus on strategy and decision-making. Data-governance models should be predicated on principles of data minimization and purposeful renewal, reside in local or institution-controlled AI instances, and respect students' rights to deletion and portability, to ensure compliance with applicable regulations (Rubel & Jones, 2016; Slade & Prinsloo, 2013). Analytics, in this paradigm, should inform reflection and growth—not ranking or surveillance.

10.1 Equity and Privacy Indicators for Algorithmic Mentoring

Algorithmic mentoring implementation should include straightforward, measurable metrics to bring equity from an aspirational principle to a principle of practice. At the course level, teachers can keep track of approximate minutes or access per student to AI-enabled tools during lesson time and note if any students continue to show barriers to participation through inconsistent device, connectivity, or language access. Where peer-review records are visible to the teacher, they can note patterns of participation and distributions of feedback—for example, who comments, who receives comments, and whether drafts submitted by multilingual or minoritised students attract parity of engagement in terms of quality and level of peer feedback. Rubric-based scores associated with the artefacts of the trialogue—diagnostic comments, AI-supported revisions, and revision memos (Kapitzke & Doughty, 2023)—for different learner groups (e.g., prior proficiency band or language background) can then be compared to check whether the iteration of mentor-constrained design is closing or widening attainment gaps. This is always with the understanding that metrics are not being used to rank students, but to understand inequities structurally, provide equitable support, and shift task design, time allocation, and access arrangements.

Equity monitoring needs to be linked to specified governance and data-protection policy. Course documentation should include a statement indicating: the period of time for which prompt logs, AI responses, drafts with tracked changes, and revision memos will be kept (a potential option is for the period of the module plus the appeals period); who can see them (students and auditors); and that students can request redaction or deletion of identifiable text or information not related to their assessment, subject to institutional policy. Prompt logs and artefacts are used for learner analytics and feedback practice, and for improvement of the course being studied rather than for high-stakes ranking outside the course context.

A syllabus or assignment-sheet statement could provide students with meaningful guidance similar to:

> *"In this module, we are using prompt logs, drafts, and revision memos related to use of AI to understand how students are developing their writing strategies and to improve our teaching. These will only be reviewed by you and the teaching team, kept only for the module and routine quality-assurance processes, and will never be used to inform high-stakes ranking or punishment outside of this process. You may ask about, amend, or request deletion of identifiable remarks or information, as per institutional policy."*

In this way, governance and analytics commitments have measurable outcomes and a transparent way of being shared with students.

11. CLASSROOM SCENARIOS

i) Scenario A: Secondary (Tamil—English)

In a Grade 10 English class in Chennai, students compose opinion editorials using local or urban content. Writers create intent notes in Tamil, English, or code-meshed forms, and then provide diagnostic feedback to peers tied directly to audience needs and genre conventions. Within a scaffolded interface, authors can query the AI for evidence-generating strategies (e.g., examples tied to local legislation, civic reports, or comparisons), as the AI offers generative strategies for aiding the author rather than rewriting entire paragraphs, thereby leaving the author's capabilities intact. Writers generate localized evidence and adjust tone while maintaining voice. After revision, each author composes a reflection memo that captures key decisions, multilingual use, and rationales.

ii) Scenario B: First-Year University (Arabic—French—English)

Students develop a 2,000-word literature review in English. Peers identify student work as "list-like" summaries that miss opportunities to synthesize sources. Authors then invoke AI and ask genre-modelling prompts to help surface synthesis moves—comparison and contrast, gap identification, progression through theory. The AI illustrates these moves with non-substitutive sentences. Authors then reorder and synthesize across sources through dialogical positioning, while maintaining signature phrasing through voice-preservation prompts.

12. LIMITATIONS, RISKS, AND MANAGEMENT STRATEGIES

Primary risks include cognitive offload and dependence; stylistic homogenization; opacity and bias; privacy risk; and misaligned policy. Management strategies include mentor-role limitations; banks of voices and rubricized attention to voice; explanation-first prompts; regular monitoring for equity; privacy-first implementation with local and/or institutional control and opt-out options; and co-creation of policy with an attribution model (Bender et al., 2021; Cotton et al., 2024; Bond et al., 2024).

13. IMPLEMENTATION FRAMEWORK FOR INSTITUTIONS AND EDUCATORS

i) **Policy & Capacity.** Establish a policy for AI use and attribution that includes stakeholder input; provide secure infrastructure and device lending; and offer targeted faculty development.

ii) **Curriculum Alignment.** Redesign tasks around collaborative revision; embed the trialogue; and deploy process-oriented rubrics and exemplar methods.
iii) **Classroom Implementation.** Co-create norms for AI use; provide structured in-class time for AI-mediated activities; model prompting; and provide low-stakes rounds for formative outcomes before summative work.
iv) **Formative Iteration.** Interpret framework-linked process artefacts with students; monitor for equity; and use analytics formatively.
v) **Summative Analysis and Distribution.** Evaluate change and outcomes; document lessons learned; and use emerging knowledge about policy implications, alongside further data collection, for longitudinal analysis.

14. RECOMMENDATIONS FOR FUTURE INVESTIGATION

Using the Activity-Theoretic framework and constraints of mentor-designed AI in this research, we recommend six overlapping approaches to build an evidence base for equitable, developmentally-focused AI mediation in writing.

i. Longitudinal developmental effects of mentor-designed AI on independent revision

Future work is needed to develop empirically rigorous, longitudinal mixed-methods designs that examine how mentor-designed AI (MC-AI) influences learners' independent revision. Multi-wave data that integrates keystroke logging, process-tracing artefacts (e.g., prompt/response histories), and delayed transfer tasks could support growth-curve modelling of the depth and durability of revision. Qualitative components (stimulated recall, think-alouds, revision memos) should provide insights into shifts in metacognitive regulation and sustained depth in independent writing conducted "cold," without AI.

ii. Equity implications of language profile, SES, and previous opportunity through participatory design

Equity analysis should consider learners' language profile, socioeconomic status, and histories of opportunity by combining outcomes-equity metrics with process-equity measures (access time, uptake, participation). Participatory and co-design methodologies with marginalised learners should surface contextual constraints and community-valued outcomes. For example, constraints imposed by mentors, transparency practices, or access models may need to be shaped by those experiencing greatest disadvantage.

iii. Multilingual development via translanguaging in AI-mediated revision

Future research is needed to understand how translanguaging during AI-mediated revision develops learners' metalinguistic awareness and rhetorical flexibility. Mixed-methods, corpus-analytic, and ethnographic approaches could interrogate episodes of code-meshing, cross-linguistic problem-solving, and shifts in stance across audiences and genres. Repeated measures of metapragmatic reflection, genre-move control, and audience adaptation can reveal whether MC-AI accelerates multilingual writers' strategic repertoire while avoiding homogenisation of voice.

iv. Trajectories of teacher orchestration and professional learning communities

Ethnographic and practitioner-inquiry studies could map how teachers' appropriation and refinement of orchestration moves (norm-setting, role-splitting, prompt modelling, evidence use, etc.) develop over semesters and how, if at all, professional learning communities (PLCs) mediate that change. Potential data sources might include video-based micro-analysis of classroom interaction, orchestration teaching logs, and PLC artefacts to trace trajectories of teacher expertise in MC-AI efforts.

v. Fairness auditing of AI feedback and genre-specific biases at the classroom level

There is a need for classroom-based auditing protocols for detecting and reducing systematic differences in the quality of AI feedback across genres, linguistic varieties (i.e., dialects), and learner identities. Designs could involve counterfactual testing of prompts (e.g., swapping dialects or names), analyses of distributions of error types, and checks against expert judgements as calibration. Iterative bias-mitigation strategies (e.g., prompt constraints, genre-sensitive exemplars, human-in-the-loop overrides) will need to be assessed for their effectiveness and practicality at the point of instruction.

vi. Comparative utility and cost-utility of feedback regimes

Multi-arm comparative studies that contrast unconstrained AI, AI feedback constrained by mentorship, peer feedback only, and hybrids of mentored peer feedback and AI feedback should be used to estimate differential impact on text quality, process evidence, transfer, and equity. Cluster-randomized or stepped-wedge trials could be coupled with economic evaluations (e.g., total cost of ownership, time-on-task, incremental cost-utility) to inform sustainable decision-making at course and institutional levels. Collectively, these priority areas foreground durable development, distributive justice, and instructional practicality, moving us toward a systematic research agenda that might support responsible, classroom-ready algorithmic mentorship in multilingual writing.

14.1 Framework Derivation and Validation Plan

The design framework introduced in this chapter originates from an integrative synthesis of several prominent strands of literature, including Activity Theory, process- and sociocultural-oriented models of writing, research on collaborative peer review, translanguaging-focused studies of multilingual composing, and new work on automated writing evaluation and large language models in education. By mapping typical contradictions in AI-mediated writing activity systems—relating to goals, tools, rules, community, and division of labour—these strands were translated into design principles that connect to specific roles for algorithmic mentors, the five-phase trialogue routine, and the mentor-constrained prompt families described in this chapter. Validation of the framework will occur through classroom pilots in multilingual, writing-intensive classes where the routine is utilized as a whole. The data over the course of this research will include prompt logs from mentors, interaction traces from AI and students, drafts with tracked changes, completed prompts, revision memos and rubric scores, and teacher and student reflections on their experience.

15. CONCLUSION

Configured as algorithmic mentors in an Activity-Theoretic design, LLMs can foster dialogic, multilingual, and metacognitively rich revision. By limiting role functionality to explanation-first mediation, requiring transparent attribution, validating translanguaging, designing for equity and privacy, and re-weighting assessment towards process, we can reposition AI toward developmental objectives. The trialogue routine and framework provided here offer a principled avenue for responsible deployment, while the research agenda proposes rigorous, longitudinal, and equity-attentive evidence to support classroom-ready algorithmic mentorship in multilingual writing.

REFERENCES

Baig, M. I.. (2024). ChatGPT in higher education: A systematic literature review. *Computers in Human Behavior, 152*, 107326. DOI: 10.1016/j.chb.2024.107326

Bender, E. M., Gebru, T., McMillan-Major, A., & Shmitchell, S. (2021). On the dangers of stochastic parrots: Can language models be too big? In *Proceedings of the 2021 ACM Conference on Fairness, Accountability, and Transparency* (pp. 610–623). https://doi.org/DOI: 10.1145/3442188.3445922

Bereiter, C., & Scardamalia, M. (1987). *The psychology of written composition*. Lawrence Erlbaum Associates.

Bond, M., Khosravi, H., De Laat, M., Bergdahl, N., Negrea, V., Oxley, E., Pham, P., Chong, S. W., & Siemens, G. (2024). A meta systematic review of artificial intelligence in higher education. *International Journal of Educational Technology in Higher Education, 21*(1), 31. DOI: 10.1186/s41239-023-00436-z

Cotton, D. R. E., Cotton, P. A., & Shipway, J. R. (2024). Chatting and cheating: Ensuring academic integrity in the era of ChatGPT. *Innovations in Education and Teaching International, 61*(2), 146–155. DOI: 10.1080/14703297.2023.2190148

Dillenbourg, P., & Jermann, P. (2010). Technology for classroom orchestration. In Khine, M. S., & Saleh, I. M. (Eds.), *New science of learning* (pp. 525–552). Springer. DOI: 10.1007/978-1-4419-5716-0_26

Engeström, Y. (2001). Expansive learning at work: Toward an activity-theoretical reconceptualization. *Journal of Education and Work, 14*(1), 133–156. DOI: 10.1080/13639080020028747

Faigley, L., & Witte, S. (1981). Analyzing revision. *College Composition and Communication, 32*(4), 400–414. DOI: 10.58680/ccc198115887

García, O., & Wei, L. (2014). *Translanguaging: Language, bilingualism and education*. Palgrave Macmillan. DOI: 10.1057/9781137385765

Ghosh, R. K., Chakraborty, S., & Dutta, G. (2025). AI in Enhancing Bilingual Proficiency. In Advances in computational intelligence and robotics book series (pp. 141–176). DOI: 10.4018/979-8-3373-0275-1.ch005

Graham, S., Kiuhara, S. A., & MacKay, M. (2020). The effects of writing on learning in science, social studies, and mathematics: A meta-analysis. *Review of Educational Research, 90*(2), 179–226. DOI: 10.3102/0034654320914744

Guo, K. (2024). EvaluMate: Using AI to support students' feedback literacy in peer review. *Computers & Education, 208*, 104877. DOI: 10.1016/j.compedu.2024.104877

Guo, K., Zhang, E. D., Li, D., & Yu, S. (2025). Using AI-supported peer review to enhance feedback literacy. *British Journal of Educational Technology, 56*(2), 451–469. DOI: 10.1111/bjet.13540

Hayes, J. R. (2012). Modeling and remodeling writing. *Written Communication, 29*(3), 369–388. DOI: 10.1177/0741088312451260

Hayes, J. R., & Flower, L. S. (1980). Identifying the organization of writing processes. In Gregg, L. W., & Steinberg, E. R. (Eds.), *Cognitive processes in writing* (pp. 3–30). Lawrence Erlbaum Associates.

Horner, B., Lu, M.-Z., Royster, J. J., & Trimbur, J. (2011). Language difference in writing: Toward a translingual approach. *College English, 73*(3), 303–321. DOI: 10.58680/ce201113403

Kasneci, E., Sessler, K., Küchemann, S., Bannert, M., & Sesagiri Raamkumar, A.. (2023). ChatGPT for good? On opportunities and challenges of large language models for education. *International Journal of Artificial Intelligence in Education, 33*, 1–24.

Min, H.-T. (2006). The effects of trained peer review on EFL students' revision types and writing quality. *Journal of Second Language Writing, 15*(2), 118–141. DOI: 10.1016/j.jslw.2006.01.003

Nelson, M. M., & Schunn, C. D. (2009). The nature of feedback: How different types of peer feedback affect writing performance. *Instructional Science, 37*(4), 375–401. DOI: 10.1007/s11251-008-9053-x

Prior, P. (2006). A sociocultural theory of writing. In MacArthur, C. A., Graham, S., & Fitzgerald, J. (Eds.), *Handbook of writing research* (pp. 54–66). Guilford Press.

Rubel, A., & Jones, K. M. L. (2016). Student privacy in learning analytics: An information ethics perspective. *The Information Society, 32*(2), 143–159. DOI: 10.1080/01972243.2016.1130502

Russell, D. R. (1997). Rethinking genre in school and society: An activity theory analysis. *Written Communication, 14*(4), 504–554. DOI: 10.1177/0741088397014004004

Slade, S., & Prinsloo, P. (2013). Learning analytics: Ethical issues and dilemmas. *The American Behavioral Scientist, 57*(10), 1510–1529. DOI: 10.1177/0002764213479366

Sperber, L.. (2025). Peer and AI Review + Reflection (PAIRR): A human-centered approach to integrating AI feedback. *Computers and Composition, 76*, 102921. DOI: 10.1016/j.compcom.2025.102921

Stevenson, M., & Phakiti, A. (2019). Automated writing evaluation for EFL/ESL: A synthesis of the literature. *Language Assessment Quarterly, 16*(4–5), 389–409.

Storch, N. (2013). *Collaborative writing in L2 classrooms*. Multilingual Matters.

Storch, N., & Wigglesworth, G. (2010). Learners' processing, uptake, and retention of corrective feedback on writing. *Studies in Second Language Acquisition, 32*(2), 303–334. DOI: 10.1017/S0272263109990532

Tastanbek, S. (2024). Translanguaging pedagogy in EAP writing: A multilingual Qazaq instructor's perspective. *Journal of Second Language Writing, 63*, 101075. DOI: 10.1016/j.jslw.2023.101075

Wigglesworth, G., & Storch, N. (2012). What role for collaboration in writing and writing feedback? *Journal of Second Language Writing, 21*(4), 364–374. DOI: 10.1016/j.jslw.2012.09.005

Wilson, J., & Czik, A. (2016). Automated essay evaluation and the teaching of writing: Critical considerations. *Assessing Writing*, *29*, 90–97.

Winstone, N. E., & Carless, D. (2019). *Designing effective feedback processes in higher education: A learning-focused approach*. Routledge. DOI: 10.4324/9781351115940

Chapter 12
Artificial Intelligence in Research Writing and Reference Management

Subhadip Nandi
https://orcid.org/0009-0009-8087-3306
Brainware University, India

Indranil Sarkar
https://orcid.org/0000-0002-0472-6533
Guru Nanak Institute of Technology, India

Gourab Dutta
https://orcid.org/0000-0003-4493-6508
Brainware University, India

Sandip Chakraborty
https://orcid.org/0009-0000-1166-0846
Brainware University, India

ABSTRACT

The development of technology has been a major factor in the change and improvement of academic research, thanks to AI-powered tools that are now available for literature review, management of citations, and detection of plagiarism. Using natural language processing (NLP) and machine learning, AI systems are capable of increasing the precision of research works, automating the process of reference formatting, and keeping the integrity of citations. Research tools like Zotero, Mendeley, and Semantic Scholar not only help in making research more efficient but also pose ethical issues regarding data privacy and trust in AI-based academic practices.

1. INTRODUCTION

In today's data-driven academic environment, researchers face a deluge of scholarly information, rapidly changing citation paradigms, and increasingly stringent demands on ethical writing.

DOI: 10.4018/979-8-3373-5601-3.ch012

Thus, with the multiplication of domain-specific literature outputs, the traditional ways of literature review, referencing, and citation formatting have turned from cumbersome to erroneous, inefficient, and inefficient. This has posed a rather paramount need for the intelligent automation of scholarly tasks. AI is fast becoming one of the main game changers in the realm of academic research and citation management, especially through NLP and machine learning(Dash et al., 2019). An AI tool can be embedded at any step in the research lifecycle: locating and retrieving literature, language analysis, summarizing research findings, reference formatting, plagiarism detection, or assessing originality of writing. Citation managers, once static repositories for storing bibliographic entries, have transformed into AI-powered tools capable of recommending references to match your current work, searching for incorrectly formatted citations in real time, and even binding into word processors and academic publishing tools. This confluence of AI and academic research allows for greater productivity while maintaining accuracy, consistency, and adherence to scholarly standards. This is a huge benefit from the perspective of early career researchers and non-native English speakers who confront challenges in dealing with complex citation styles and norms of academic writing. On the ethical front, AI has a dual role: it aids accurate citation and protects against academic misconduct. Plagiarism detection systems can detect copied or poorly paraphrased content that has been stored in huge repositories. Higher-end systems can analyze whether citations are supportive, neutral, or critical, thus revealing the quality of engagement with the literature. These functions ensure academic integrity and let the authors amend and improve their manuscripts even before formal review. By analyzing context, comparing texts, and tracking the provenance of citations, AI has redefined both the conceptualization of originality and the practice of scholarly referencing simultaneously. While AI also benefits the academic environment through smoother integration into academic workflows, it is not without its share of certain issues. Important ethical questions come into play regarding issues like algorithmic bias, data privacy, intellectual property, and uncritical reliance upon automation. If these concerns are not addressed with the right intent, they can erode the very fabric of academic inquiry instead of buttressing it. Therefore, while AI has hitherto shown tremendous potential in streamlining operations and enhancing quality, it should be accompanied by sensible implementation strategies and institutional policies that promote transparency and fairness. AI was incorporated into the research domain and is indisputably diversified with a spotlight on citation management and plagiarism detection(Radu, 2019). It dives deeper into how scholarly communication is being redone with AI tools while comparing the operational features of some of the dominant citation platforms. The chapter will further apply its scrutiny in interdisciplinary settings of teaching and research, thereby providing researchers, educators, and academic establishments with an overarching understanding of how to effectively utilize AI in an ethical manner within research workflows.

2. OBJECTIVE

The central aim of this chapter is to explain how artificial intelligence (AI) is changing the way academic research is done, with a focus on the identification, management, and detection of plagiarism in the context of textual literature. By making us of AI-powered tools, the chapter should be able to show that automation and intelligent algorithms can reduce the work force greatly, increase the quality of scholarly communities, and sustain evidence-based decision-making practices all over the disciplines. Another major goal is to present the value of AI in practice through actual cases, thereby providing the proof that the integration of AI into the daily academic routines of researchers, students, and academic institutions pays off. Furthermore, there is an intention to engage in a critical analysis of the ethical, pedagogical, and methodological issues brought about by the use of AI in academic settings such as the issue of data privacy, the integrity of authorship and the presence of bias in the algorithm. Last but not least, this paper is a means of discussing the upcoming tendencies and the directions that the academic writing, publishing, and research integrity as affected by AI may be undergoing in the years to come.

3. ROLE OF AI IN ACADEMIC RESEARCH

Artificial intelligence has been tremendously reshaping the landscape of academic research by bringing intelligent solutions to age-old problems faced by scholars, academicians, and institutions. In the past, research was sometimes saddled with processes that were time-consuming and boring, such as manual literature searching, reading till midnight, building blocks of references, or organizing research data. With the advent of AI, however-currently dominated by natural language processing, deep learning, and semantics analysis-hardware configurations around ages are fast becoming automated and accelerated, freeing research workers to focus more on inquiry, critical thinking, and genuine contribution. AI, at one time, was unheard of in academia, but now is slowly becoming the knowledge discovery, curation, and dissemination backbone. Some of the more obvious impacts of AI are streamlining research processes, particularly literature discovery(Dwivedi et al., 2019). The older processes of keyword searches in academic databases have begun to give way to, or have been augmented by, semantic search engines that aim to understand what sort of activity or objective is implied by the research query. Such systems retrieve documents that may be devoid of actual keyword mention but are very much aligned with the researcher's construct by way of intent. Especially useful in interdisciplinary work are these translator-like functions that bridge terminological variations used across disciplines describing related phenomena. AI tools give an even bigger opportunity than traditionally found limited literature to conduct a thorough literature review.Processing, synthesizing, and making sense of literature data is another way AI assists researchers: such powerful tools now process through thousands of documents, extracting metadata, summarizing findings, highlighting gaps in the research, and even mapping out trends in huge corpora. For instance, Elicit and Scite.ai can interpret academic claims and compare them across sources and provide structured insights into how certain hypotheses have been tested, supported, challenged, or refuted. This analytical capability assists researchers in creating links between studies and thus in formulating more refined and better-informed research questions. In pragmatic disciplines such as healthcare, economics, or climate science, such a synthesis provided by AI would accelerate policy formulation and decision-making at the pragmatic level(Baduge et al., 2022). AI supports the personalization of the research process. Based on the user's search history, reading habits, and citation patterns, AI systems can recommend fairly research-related papers, authors, and journals. The recommendations are not sorted by popularity or citation counts but rather by relevance to the user's context, boosting the efficiency of navigating the academic landscape. Systems in citation management such as Mendeley and Zotero have begun incorporating machine learning models that recommend literature and ease the burden of managing bibliographies, thus smoothing and facilitating the research writing process. This individualized assistance is beneficial for most early-career researchers who are still relatively new in the academic landscape. Another significant function of AI lies in promoting interdisciplinary collaboration-interacting across different areas, using knowledge graphs and semantic analysis, to suggest potential novel research avenues bridging disciplinary divides. This is pivotal in solving global problems - sustainability, digital health, ethical AI - whose solutions require input from vastly different academic perspectives. AI acts as a cognitive bridge that unites different silos, building awareness for interdisciplinary synergy. AI enhances the purposes of productivity and the quality of research. The use of tools for grammar, stylistic improvements, citation formatting, and collaborative editing during manuscript preparation is already widely accepted. AI-powered applications like Grammarly, Turnitin, and ChatGPT improve clarity, cut down redundancy, and enhance logic and flow in academic writing. These provide non-native English speakers the tools to develop reputable scholarly works, evidencing inclusivity and diversity in the global academic publishing sphere. Meanwhile, AI-powered solutions ensure compliance with academic standards and formatting styles and ethical guidelines, thereby taking away what would be considered a heavy administrative burden from researchers and editors alike.

Still, as we think about these advances, it becomes necessary to highlight that with every development comes the discussion of how to keep AI research ethically sound in academic contexts. There remain all kinds of concerns with bias in data, depending too much on systems, and the algorithmic decision-making being so opaque(Bednarz&Manwaring, 2021). The researcher needs to understand the limitations of the tool and employ the tools as augments rather than substitutes for human judgment and critical thinking. Institutions ought to go forth to provide digital literacy and support the crafting of framework for the responsible use of AI in research settings.AI-powered research changes the working of academic research by promising research to be faster and efficient while also opening new avenues of discovery, collaboration, and innovation. As AI tools get more advanced and accessible, they will be instrumental in shaping the future landscape of research if embraced by the scholarly world and institutions with balanced enthusiasm, critical awareness, and moral positions.

4. OVERVIEW OF AI-BASED CITATION MANAGEMENT TOOLS

Citation management was and still is an important building block for academic research: it helped scholars to order their sources in some discipline-specific methods, a mode of defense against plagiarism, and standardization for publication. Yet, with an increase in complexity of academic writing as well as the enormous expansion of literature across disciplines, manual citation management has become an increasingly inefficient approach prone to errors. To combat the issues, Artificial Intelligence came into the picture in citation management tools of the 21st century, thus transforming the manner in which scholars collect, store, format, and work on bibliographic data. These systems do much more than provide citations alone: They offer intelligent help in library organization, offer source recommendations, fix formatting mistakes, and even spot inconsistencies in the use of a referencing style. The appearance of smart citation tools has eased the heavy cognitive and administrative workload involved in academic writing. Contemporary tools such as Mendeley, Zotero, EndNote, and RefWorks now have AI features empowering them with abilities in the automatic extraction of metadata, duplicate identification, and conversion of style (Kalisdha, 2023). If a user uploads a PDF or inputs a DOI, for example, the AI back end can immediately pull the citation details-full or partial, comprising title, author, journal name, year of publication, volume, and so forth-with almost no manual keying in. Such applications also provide smooth integration with word processors such as Microsoft Word and Google Docs, thus allowing citations to be inserted progressively and bibliographies to be updated as they get drafted and revised, ensuring that the document remains consistent in its formatting and avoids any inadvertent errors(Vergara &Karpukhin, 2022). Artificial Intelligence has added to the customer experience within citation tools by allowing intelligent organization and tailored recommendations. Thus, machine learning algorithms identify the reading habits of a user, his favorite journals, and his citation history to recommend relevant articles, propose citation clusters, and auto-tag documents for better classification. In a collaborative research setting, the tool facilitates shared libraries and synchronized annotations to jointly manage references and notes across institutional or geographic boundaries. Such group intelligence is highly favorable for interdisciplinary or large-scale projects wherein several contributors work with a wide array of sources. Every AI-powered citation tool offers a degree of specialization that caters to various types of users(Dwivedi et al., 2020). Zotero, being open-source, is highly flexible and community-driven and thus suits individual researchers and educators. Mendeley, powered by Elsevier, pairs the citation engine with academic networking features and thus makes recommendations based on aggregated reading behavior across user profiles. EndNote is the go-to option in environments where strong research is required owing to its highly customizable capabilities coupled with journal-specific formatting templates. RefWorks is often adopted at the institutional level for its cloud infrastructure and robust integration with library systems. Despite these differences, however, the same arc can be seen with the embedding of AI into the academic workflow for a smarter and quicker bibliographic management. Moreover, style conversion has been brought with precision into AI-powered tools(Raschka et al., 2020). Academic disciplines require rigorous obedience to citation styles such as APA, MLA, Chicago, IEEE, or Vancouver, and AI engines now can do the task of swiftly converting references among these styles. This comes in handy mostly when researchers are submitting documents to various journals with different demands, thus saving immense time and effort, the latter spent on conversion work. The advanced AI tools can further check the correctness of citations by cross-referencing them with databases such as CrossRef or PubMed, thereby verifying the validity and completeness of bibliographic entries. These verification capabilities also avoid the possibility of citing papers that have been withdrawn or outdated versions of documents. In recent-years, there has been an expansion in the capacity and scope of citation management software to encompass plagiarism detection systems and AI writing assistants. This unity permits the researchers to not only cite correctly but also to write more ethically and efficiently. For example, a researcher while drafting a manuscript might be getting real-time prompts about missing citations or be warned that the passage bears similarities to a previously published work. Through mechanisms like this, the scholar will be encouraged to pay heed to academic integrity and improve the overall quality of scholarly output. Now, as these tools keep moving forward, we are stepping towards a shift where they are turn into smart research assistants fostering the intent to scholarly publication. The merging of AI with citation management is hardly just a touch of another technological panacea on a long-standing problem; a far more pertinent metaphor would characterize the emergence of these tools as a confluence where bibliographic rigor, writing efficiency, and scholarly ethics meet(Staiano, 2021). However, in order for the researcher to reap the full benefits from these

AI-powered tools, they must acquire some digital literacy so that they do not mindlessly comply with the suggestions of these software programs. By embracing AI-powered citation management in an informed and thoughtful fashion, the academia can move towards higher levels of productivity, collaboration, and integrity.

5. NATURAL LANGUAGE PROCESSING FOR LITERATURE DISCOVERY

Natural Language Processing (NLP) has accepted the role of another disruptive force in the traditional working method of research in literature discovery. Traditionally, few keyword-based searches through academic databases, library catalogs, digital libraries, and other possible information sources were used by scholars in identifying any literature. Although, to some extent, these approaches could suffice; they would not entertain the whiles of rigid syntax, lack of semantic nutshell, and inability to fathom the researcher's real intent. NLP solves some of these problems and thus conversing with machines to understand, interpret, and generate human language with full awareness of context(Caldarini et al., 2022). This shifts academic search tools toward semantic understandings rather than mere keyword matching and thus leads to finer control over literature retrieval with better precision and relevance. The core of NLP utility in literature discovery is semantic search. Instead of searching for exact phrases, an NLP-powered system looks at the meaning and intent of the queries to retrieve documents exhibiting relevant conceptual relations such that terminology discrimination exists. This factor becomes more relevant in interdisciplinary fields where difference in vocabularies exists to define the same phenomena. So, for example, a researcher intent on searching "remote learning effectiveness" may be led to relevant literature that speaks of "virtual classrooms," "e-learning retention," or "digital pedagogy", even though these terms differ from those used in his/her searches(Zawacki-Richter et al., 2019). Classic tools of this kind include Semantic Scholar, Elicit, and Connected Papers, which utilize NLP-devised algorithms to cluster, link, and recommend research papers essentially based on concept similarity. Another strength of NLP research in literature discovery is the automatic summarization ability of literature research. With the exponential growth of published literature, it is becoming increasingly difficult for researchers to read every relevant paper in full. NLP technology can view the abstract, introduction, and conclusion of a paper and generate a summary that concentrates on key results, methodology, and implications. This facilitates the screening process and channels coordination toward the most promising sources. Some highly advanced platforms can even juxtapose the summaries of many papers to bring out dissenting views or shared research gaps, which engenders a more efficient framework for synthesizing knowledge from separate studies. Topic modeling is yet another NLP-based technique serving an important function in handling vast amounts of academic literature. It identifies the themes covered and provides groupings of articles by analyzing the distribution and co-occurrence of terms with respect to the documents. It is particularly useful for systematic reviews and meta-analyses, where researchers are faced with massive, often non-continuous datasets. By the application of models such as Latent Dirichlet Allocation (LDA), literature can be grouped automatically into topics like "machine learning in medicine," "neural networks for image recognition," and "ethics in AI," rather than manually tagged. In this way, it directs an organized, comprehensive view of the research landscape. Citation context analysis is another glimmer of an emerging application made possible with NLP that outstrips the counting of citation frequency. It rather analyzes the citation that takes place in either a positive or a negative manner. As an example, research could cite a source as a backstop to its own study, express a criticism of it, or simply provide background. By analyzing the surrounding text, tools such as Scite.ai assist in categorizing the nature of citations and therefore piece together how subsequent research has been steered by a particular work. LINGO is an NLP technology that recognizes different language contexts and can be used to enhance conversational quality analysis and improve pronunciations of individual words or phrases. Next comes the whole AI transformation, which promises to further revolutionize the question-answering space. Another leap-frog moment that can make NLP-based measures relevant is conversational AI interfaces. Some large language model (LLM)-powered tools allow the user to ask: "What are recent trends in AI for public health?" A curated response with paper recommendations, summaries, and follow-up question suggestions will be given. Standard databases are completely passive stores of data with little to no machine intelligence in provides a space for knowledge exploration possibilities. This dialogic interaction supports exploratory learning and aligns closely with how human researchers naturally think, ask, and evolve their inquiries. However, despite advantages, the employment of NLP techniques in academic research poses its challenges. Because of ambiguity in language, domain-specific jargon, and varied quality of source data, an NLP system can produce erroneous interpretations or give irrelevant results.Most NLP systems that exist in the current day have been trained primarily on English-language content data, which presents a language barrier for academic researchers working in other languages and possibly skewing discovery toward English-dominant publications. Yet more transparency is needed regarding how NLP algorithms decide to rank and filter results because opaque decision processes may inadvertently increase bias or limit access to a diversity of views. Far from dystopic, NLP has, for literature discovery, changed paradigms on a very far-reaching level. Therefore, when finding, assessing, and organizing scholarly information, researchers' endeavors are efficiently translated into a more comprehensive and intelligent research endeavor. There remains the glimmer of hope for democratizing knowledge discovery, helping interdisciplinary research, and supporting more inclusive and innovative scholarship as these technologies evolve and become more accessible.

6. AI IN REFERENCE FORMATTING AND PLAGIARISM DETECTION

Referencing is an intricate and demanding topic that involves academic writing. It carries with it the need for a high level of precision from the writer on whose reference is given, the correct style to be used, and absolute consistency in the whole manuscript. Traditionally, researchers would sift through style manuals to format citations manually according to the prescribed style-AOA, MLA, Chicago, IEEE, and others-or even use static citation generators. However, with the arrival of AI in the realm of reference management, the whole landscape was changed dramatically. Reference and citation management is now done via an automated and intelligent tool that, in turn, minimizes the time spent by scholars and reduces the chances for human error. These tools interpret a style guide and, in the interim, quickly incorporate any style guide changes that writers may implement during the writing process to ensure that all in-text citations and bibliography entries are correct and up to date. AI citation and bibliographic tools like Zotero, Mendeley, EndNote, and RefWorks offer much more besides mere citation insertion. They analyze a digital source, such as a PDF file, DOI, or URL, and identify key bibliographic elements: they determine the authors, the publication year, the journal title, and others; all of this information is subsequently formatted in conformity with the user's chosen citation style and inserted directly into the user's document through an integrated plugin for word processors. The AI algorithms behind these tools also help identify inconsistencies in the user's bibliographic data that could include missing fields or duplicate entries and recommend corrections for these issues(Nicholls et al., 2021). From here on, this proactive approach substantially speeds up the referencing process and ensures the confronting of many different publisher requirements from across disciplines. Most of these AI-assisted citation platforms will automatically suggest switching styles with very little action from the user. A complete manuscript in IEEE style disappears within seconds, leaving behind the new style in APA or MLA, yet keeping the structure of the document. This variation will be especially useful when multiple journals with conflicting formats are submitted to by a researcher. Such transformations give a competitive edge in a high-pressure academic environment where deadlines are tight and any slip-up in formatting leads to rejection. This AI also keeps references consistent in collaborative writing projects with multiple authors using different software or citation habits, leading to a consistent and professional output. Beyond mere formatting, the AI assists in keeping the academic integrity through advanced plagiarism detection. Plagiarism is a serious concern in scholarly communication, intent or unintended. AI detection systems such as Turnitin, iThenticate, Grammarly, and Unicheck have re-conceptualized the ability to unearth unoriginal material by pitting the submitted text against the vast databases of academic literature, websites, and previously submitted documents. While traditional plagiarism checkers limit their scope to string-matching techniques, these modern AI detectors engage in semantic analysis, machine learning, and pattern recognition to sniff out paraphrased content, improper citations, and subtle rewordings that would otherwise escape detection. These tools can recognize suspicious similarities and produce detailed similarity reports specifying which sections are problematic, which sources they are matched to, and how to calculate originality scores in percentage. This presentation of evidence gives the researchers an opportunity to correct the weak parts before turning it in. For instructors and publishing houses, the emphasis is laid on making a strong quality control machine. On the advanced scale, AI could provide authorship analysis to spot inconsistencies in writing style and tone, which could be indicative of ghostwriting or unauthorized assistance, thus supporting efforts toward transparency, authorship ethics, and originality in research. Integrating plagiarism-detection into citation management workflows has another way of gaining efficiency and reliability(Foltýnek et al., 2020). Most reference tools include or support export into integrated plagiarism services. This way researchers end up judging citations, attributions, and content originality on one platform, instead of making all these matters stay fragmented across different tools. This consolidation thus patches up some of the fragmentation in the research process and facilitates evolution towards all-in-one academic writing solutions. While the benefits of AI in citation formatting and plagiarism detection cannot be argued against, their limitations and ethical concerns come to the table as well. False positives do happen, especially with phrases in common use in academic writing or definitions that are considered standard. Likewise, excessive reliance on AI might end up in fostering merely superficial grasp of citation culture among most early career researchers. Then there is this concern of data security, for many services for plagiarism detection retain submitted papers; this itself raises questions pertaining to intellectual property rights and consent. Thus, such tools need to be considered as support systems and not substitutes for scholarly diligence or ethical responsibility. In essence, AI has, in mass, changed the way reference management and academic integrity are handled. While AI automates mostly-or entirely-all the cumbersome formatting tasks and offers highly advanced plagiarism checks, it promises a smoother, more precise, and more ethical way of writing. Joining AI technologies with research workflows means that these technologies can ease the entire activity of writing and research while producing quality output that leaves scholars free to dive into more creative and analytical aspects. As AI technologies continue to evolve, their focus in academic circles to back up accuracy, transparency, and originality will certainly increase.

7. CASE STUDIES

The impact of AI software in academic research and citation management is perhaps best illustrated through real-life case studies or practical applications. With such examples, it can be showcased how AI works to ease research workflows, as well as how it conversely improves the level, speed, and credibility of scholarly outputs in diverse academic contexts. In a situation of graduate research, for instance, a master's graduate in public health was confronted with conducting a literature review on hundreds of journal articles concerning COVID-19 vaccine effectiveness. Through the assistance of AI tools such as Elicit and Semantic Scholar, the student was able to input natural-language queries to receive a curated list of semantically relevant papers-many of them ranked based on research design strength and sample size-that summarized each paper's findings with little room for the student's intervention in screening and synthesizing. By integrating Zotero with the word processor, citations were managed during writing, allowing for a smooth switch between APA and Vancouver styles as the target journal guidelines specified(Khabib, 2022). This case presented further evidence of AI assisting in speeding up scholarly accuracy, especially with research urgent with time and strongly data-based. Another citation management problem began to present itself when an interdisciplinary team involving computer scientists and humanities scholars researched AI ethics. They ended up using Mendeley for shared library features where scholars from different disciplinary backgrounds could annotate PDFs, tag sources, and receive AI recommendations for additional articles. As the literature review developed, the AI began to detect overlaps across disciplines- for example, papers that dealt with algorithmic fairness in both technical and philosophical terms. As a consequence, cross-referencing increased significantly, and sources were included that otherwise might have been overlooked because of disciplinary silos. By acting as a unifying guide to the development of the research narrative, the AI proved to be instrumental in an integrated literature synthesis, demonstrating the benefit of intelligent citation systems for interdisciplinary projects. At the institutional level, many universities have adopted AI-driven citation and plagiarism detection software as part of their undergraduate research training. A mid-sized liberal arts college, for example, embedded Turnitin and RefWorks into its academic writing courses, where students were taught to build citation libraries, insert formatted references in essays, and employ plagiarism reports to inform their revision of drafts before the final submission. This has gone on to enhance citation-level accuracy over time and, furthermore, decreased events of student plagiarism, whether intentional or not. Visual feedback was provided by AI-generated similarity reports pinpointing problematic areas and encouraging reflective learning and deeper engagement between students and the source material. This integration speaks to how AI can contribute to forming ethical research conduct practices from the earliest phases of academic life. In systematic review and evidence-based policymaking domains, the promise shown by AI tools is likewise transformative. When carrying out a rapid systematic review on the mental health effects of lockdown during the COVID-19 pandemic, a medical research group utilized an AI-aided tool Rayyan. The software utilized machine learning algorithms to prioritize abstracts in accordance with inclusion criteria as defined by the team. It flagged duplicate entries, highlighted keyword relevance, and permitted team members to perform joint screening of research through a cloud-based environment. Traditional manual time taken for such a review was curtailed drastically, and the report found favorable acceptance for publication in a peer-reviewed journal. This presents an example of three pressing public health questions that can benefit from AI speeding up research processes without sacrificing methodological rigor. In the academic-publishing landscape, AI tools have found various uses. Latter-day submission to a high-impact journal in data science saw the use of Mendeley Cite during manuscript preparation. The AI system suggested in-text citations within the context and formatted the references according to the journal standards for submission. The editorial team of the journal used iThenticate during peer review to check for manuscript originality. The reports generated were precise and quite exhaustive, highlighting both the fine-line acceptable overlaps, such as common terminologies, and less acceptable passages that have been edited subsequently. The well-worked submission process in itself lays an illustration of how the AI solutions can give opportunities to authors and editors alike by enhancing the transparency and compliance of workflows in academic publishing, as well as affording better efficiency.There are more complicated courses of action with ethical overtones where AI forensic authorship may detect the possibility of academic misconduct. At a large research university, a doctoral thesis was flagged for rampant stylistic inconsistencies. An AI authorship analysis that evaluates sentence structure, lexical choice, and syntactic rhythm detected such disparities among chapters(Alharbi, 2023). Upon further investigation, some portions were found to have been ghostwritten. The AI tool's findings helped substantiate the Academic Integrity Policy enforcement of the institution. It shows that AI is not just for convenience and efficiency—it ensures that ethical standards are upheld within academia. The common thread through all these varying scenarios is that AI tools are no longer just technological adjuncts but rather integral partners in the research and writing process. They improve discoverability, ease the collaborative processes of writing, ensure citation validity, and safeguard integrity. As these tools become more sophisticated and accessible, the range of useful applications for them will only increase, making research more inclusive, transparent, and attuned to the ever-changing needs of scholarly communication.

Public health investigators on a project related to COVID-19 vaccine effectiveness made time-sensitive data needs in a rapid systematic review task. BY the help of Elicit and Rayyan, the incorporated AI platforms, they could go over around 1,500 abstracts in several hours instead of weeks. The AI system did the work of reporting identical publications, giving cues and distinctions, and by inclusion probability, arranging the articles. The NLP task was the priority first. Research-related items were extracted in the first place by NLP-generated summaries.Therefore, the crew handed in a one-third time high-quality evidence synthesis, pushing the health authorities towards their policy steps in a quicker manner.

A diverse group made up of computer scientists, sociologists, and philosophers, worked together in a large project concerning AI-ethics, sharing Mendeley's libraries through advanced AI algorithms. By means of artificial intelligence, they discovered that there were common areas (for instance, fairness of algorithms, and socio-technical damages) among the disciplines and that the team had missed references to different domains. The former led to the isolation of research and the latter became the fusion of technical and humanistic points of view, reflected in a coherent final literature review.

The manuscript of a data-science study put together by a research organization underwent the use of Mendeley Cite as well as automatic citation-checking tools during preparation. The AI came up with in-text citations by taking the context of the paragraph into account and rectified the mismatches automatically.

Upon the submission of the paper for peer review, the journal opted to utilize authenticate for the purpose of originality verification. The report of the AI called attention to the existence of some minor plagiarism incidents and some repetition of paraphrased content, and thus, gave authors a second chance at editing before acceptance (Kurzweil, 2025).

. This way of working, which was very effective, not only saved the journal's editorial time but also resulted in a much cleaner and particularly not infringing upon any laws submission, which proves AI to be of value to not only authors but also publishers.

At a major research university a sizable Ph. D. thesis was notable for its differences in writing diction. AI tools, designed to authenticate authorship, were applied to analyze the sentence structure, lexical diversity, and stylistic markers. The equipment found absolutely no similarity in the levels of these parameters between different chapters—some were like a robot's voice and some were like a human's voice. Later on, the human authorship could not be verified.The situation provides an example of how AI-based forensic tools, used by educational institutions for certification purposes, can bring to light plagiarism and thereby, rescue the originality of high-stake academic work.

8. PRACTICAL APPLICATIONS

The case studies taken together, show how the AI technology has become the main player in the recent academic research and also, points out the fact that it can cut the time for tasks that require human work, such as literature checking, citation formatting, and plagiarism detection, considerably (Grassini, 2023). The adoption of the machines in these tasks allows the researchers to instead get more involved with the core activities of their work such as the development of analytical tools, theories and research methods. Through this development, the scholars can still be on the rigorous side, but they will be able to work faster and produce their quality outputs all the same even faster, as far as busy fields like public health are concerned. The use of AI in scholarly writing assures the precision and consistency of the content. As the technology constantly monitors grammar, spelling, punctuation, and other writing-related issues, the resulting content will meet the high standard required of scholarly writing. AI can also be of great help in the organization of bibliographic details so that all references are in a uniform format as stipulated by various style manuals and a specific set of guidelines from a given journal or publisher. Thus, even when an author is new to a particular style guide, with AI, it is possible to have the manuscript written in the perfect format, slimming chances of rejection due to formatting discrepancies. By its complexity, AI, however, relieves the burden of a lot of work, such as that of the author juggling between different styles of citation. AI makes it easier for researchers in various fields to collaborate in research and to exchange information. This technology also brings better recommendations among all and thus, leading to more integrated and complete research. The functionality of Mendeley or Zotero aids in connecting the dots between research papers with different jargon or belonging to different disciplines and thereby encouraging the sharing of knowledge and mutual learning. An additional notable result is the reduction in the number of unethical research practices, of which AI is a major contributor. The detection of similarity of grants, author analysis, and the citation tracking, all made by AI systems, are just some of the ways that institutions can fight against academic misconduct(Cheng et al., 2021). And, this is how the community will be more aware of the negative impact that they can potentially bring about to their field, thus, AI is replacing the unethical practices with good norms, not only in a professional but to a whole new level by educating the youth and new researchers, to develop the right behavior. AI is being introduced in undergraduate writing courses which are excellent examples showing the value of the technology being utilized in the formation of the students' ethical competencies.

9. CHALLENGES AND ETHICAL CONSIDERATIONS

AI-powered tools have transformed the way academic research and citation management are conducted. They present their own set of initial challenges and ethical considerations that must be laid on the forefront. As these technologies increasingly diffuse in scholarly workflows, it is paramount to consider their implications for privacy of data, authorship, intellectual responsibility, and research integrity in addition to mere utility. One predicament that emerges with increased use of AI systems is over-reliance and neglect of human critical thought and academic rigor(Hutchinson et al., 2022). AI can efficiently suggest sources, summarize literature, and format citations-an act that lacks a replacement for the researcher's duty to judge the quality, credibility, and relevance of these sources. Automation creates convenience; however, while chiefly useful for indoctrinating literature from surface-level engagement with it, this aggravates this issue especially with younger academics who might take results given by the AI at face value. This passive way of consuming information erodes essential academic skills-i.e., critical reading, the ability to think analytically, and to lay out arguments based on sound evidence. Algorithmic bias constitutes another major concern. If AI tools are systems trained on huge datasets, skewed-incomplete, or overly affirmative of certain regions, languages, or academic disciplines-then these recommendations too borrow from their respective biases. Favoring, for instance, citations from Western journals or English language publications that, while high in impact, lack thematic diversity serves to marginalize research entities of the Global South or non-English speaking scholars. This form of bias furthers the epistemic inequalities and blocks avenues for inclusive academic discussion. Unless and until there are deliberate efforts in place for diversifying training data sets and transparent AI design processes, these tools, wittingly or unwittingly, will serve as a hindrance to the redress of systemic inequities in global scholarship(Huang et al., 2022). Privacy and data security take the center stage when AI tools process private materials-constituting unpublished manuscripts, student submissions, or sensitive research data. Most plagiarism detection services and AI-based citation managers keep a copy of user content stored somewhere within the network for purposes of refining the algorithm or for cross-checking in the future. This varies privacy concerns relating to ownership, consent, and potential misuse of such daunting content. It is incumbent on researchers that they must become aware of where and how their data is kept, and whether the data, once in storage, bears any identification or is shared; also to question whether there is suitable legal protection of their intellectual property. Institutions and software producers must create frameworks compliant with data protection laws while providing clear-cut privacy policies that constitute a guarantee for the users.Authorship integrity is also under threat in an era where text-generation tools start paraphrasing content and even lend a hand in the drafting of entire sections of academic work. On the one hand, these can be a boon for those who have English as a second language or for boosting one's productivity, but these do end up clouding the distinction between human input and machine contribution(Dwivedi et al., 2022). How much AI assistance is ethical in scholarly writing is a question yet to be answered. Journals and other academic bodies should draft clear regulations on when to disclose that AI was used in research and writing so that transparency is ensured and so responsible researchers using these tools are not unfairly discriminated against. Another problem remains concealed in the lack of clarity surrounding the inner operations of AI systems, hence called the "black box" phenomena. Most users do not know how AI algorithms arrive at particular recommendations or rankings of sources, or even at the degree of textual similarity. This lack of transparency becomes inconvenient when such outputs influence core academic decisions---like citing literature, determining how to paraphrase, or approving a manuscript in an originality check. When researchers themselves remain ignorant on the very logic or even on what might be the limitations of the tools they are using, they may indeed turn into one of the culprits propagating errors or misunderstands. There is, therefore, an increasing call for explainable AI in academic scenarios, wherein decisions ought to be subject to audit, justify-able, and uphold scholarly values. The integration of AI tools also poses a dilemma for educational uses. Meanwhile, obtaining paraphrasing engines, citation generators, and summarization tools puts forth certain dilemmas to educators who are expected to walk a tightrope between encouraging digital literacy and putting forward checks against its misuse. The problem of depending too much on AI for the execution of academic assignments can be detrimental to the students' learning of basic research and writing skills. Thus, they must embrace this pedagogy during which ethical use of AI is discussed so that students themselves will be guided as to transparency in AI use, reflection on when AI use is appropriate, and choosing the best tool for the right job. Imparting to students some measure of judgment on AI outputs and on when to embrace or shy away from automation must become an instrument in nurturing the ethical scholar of tomorrow.

10. FUTURE TRENDS AND RESEARCH DIRECTIONS

As the adoption of Artificial Intelligence in academia continues to evolve, the future of AI-driven tools for research and citation management promises drastic changes. These advances are envisioned to go beyond the mere automation to intelligent systems that complement cognitive workflows, support ethical decision-making, and personalize the academic experience. The road of this particular innovation pivots the transformation of AI from a mere facilitator to a joint collaborator in the creation of scholarly knowledge(Kraus et al., 2023). The rise in the horizon of the AI-based research assistant, equipped with reasoning and dialogical capacities, will be among some of the biggest transformational trends. While the current systems are static, next-generation AI systems will work dynamically with researchers in the interaction. These systems will leverage LLMs and domain-specific ontologies to help scholars generate hypotheses, evaluate arguments, suggest methodological approaches, and even highlight logical fallacies found in drafts of manuscripts. They will be able to work as intelligent collaborators that learn interactively and evolve with the researcher's disciplinary background and domain interests, writing style, and citation preference. If implemented well, such systems will not only speed up the research process but also advance critical thinking and academic reflection. Another important trend will be the integration of AI with real-time bibliometric and altmetric analytics. Future citation tools may continuously monitor the impact, relevance, and reception of cited works ironically through social media, through preprint servers, via open peer-review platforms, or through citation indexes. Researchers will be able to visualize the scholarly conversation in evolution around a topic and manifest changes in influence, making further data-informed decisions on literature to interact with. Such trend supports a dynamically and socially engaged citation practice done from the perspective of both academic value and social relevance-an area where the applications could be very handy in public policy, education, and health fields.Multilingual and cross-cultural AI research tools will gain traction. Today, most AI-driven platforms are biased toward English language content, excluding a significant amount of valuable research done in other languages. Future breakthroughs in machine translation, cross-lingual NLP, and culture-adaptive AI systems will narrow this divide by helping academics access, cite, and engage with literature from around the world. This will promote inclusive scholarship and bring underrepresented voices to the global academic discourse. AI tool development supporting indigenous languages and region-specific journals will go a long way toward democratizing knowledge production. Whereas the integration of AI with blockchain and decentralized identity technologies might open a whole new chapter in citation verification and intellectual property management. Researchers could timestamp every citation on an immutable ledger and track its evolution in real-time to allow works to be fully put to complement the right. Citation royalties or permissions for copyrighted works may then be issued automatically through smart contracts, thus giving the power back to the authors and thereby boosting the transparency of the citation economy. They will undoubtedly come in handy in collaborative open-access contexts where trust is dependent on the provenance of data and attribution. Ethics-aware and explainable AI systems will become a crucial part of future research environments. As AI increasingly assumes a significant role in shaping literature reviews, structuring research questions, and formatting publications, increased transparency around the workings of these systems is going to be demanded by users and institutions alike. Researchers will expect that tools offer explanations for why certain citations, content summaries, and plagiarism flags were suggested to them, not simply present the recommendations themselves. This increased transparency supports the building of trust, the enforcement of accountability practices across academia, and weighing down the risks of blindly following the respective algorithmic recommendations. From a pedagogic standpoint, embedding AI education into academic training and research methodology will certainly be a future development(Karataş&Yüce, 2024). Universities will likely develop modules teaching responsible AI use, data ethics, and human-AI collaborative research. Students and faculty alike will need to develop not just digital literacy but algorithmic literacy: the ability to perceive how AI systems impact decisions made within academic research. This set of educational strategies will extend researchers' capacities to critically engage with the study tools themselves; hence guarantee that the adequate use of technology corresponds with the ideals underpinning academic integrity and epistemic responsibility. Finally, research on the psychological and sociocultural effects of AI in academia will grow into a very fertile area of inquiry. As researchers become more and more dependent upon intelligent systems, big questions will be raised concerning the cognitive effects of automation, the evolving definition of authorship, and the metamorphosis of academic labor. Meta-research will provide a reflective perspective on the implications of integrating AI in order to guide institutional policy in favor of human agency, creativity, and fairness in academic work.To conclude, the future of

AI in research and citation management is broad, interdisciplinary, and ethically thorny. It has the potential to give new meaning to how knowledge is accessed, organized, and shared-but only if these technologies are developed and employed with critical foresight. Ongoing innovations must be complemented by inclusive design, transparent governance, and continuous dialogue between technologists and academicians. As AI ventures further into the academic terrain, the research community must therefore remain fluid yet vigilant, ensuring that these tools are in fact vehicles of thoughtful, equitable, and impactful scholarship.

11. CONCLUSION

Infusing artificial intelligence in research and citation management applications marks a serene reflection in the way knowledge is produced, curated, and disseminated in the digital era. AI tools have gone far enough to serve the scientist as intelligent partners-from literature discovery and semantic analysis to dynamic citation formatting and plagiarism detection-because these tools evolved much beyond mere automation. These changes have led to faster research, greater accuracy, and better accessibility, especially for early-career scholars, interdisciplinary research students, and nonnative speakers. On the ethical and practical front, they present dilemmas of data privacy, authorship legitimacy, algorithmic bias, and academic reliance on machine intelligence. While it is persuasive to claim that AI specimen constitutes an ultimate paradigm, their potential is jointly realized through consciousness, critical engagement, and institutional guidelines that ensure responsible usage. With the academic ecosystem evolving, AI undeniably will have to turn toward the center of attention, not to see itself claim a replacement for human insight but rather to support intellectual refinement and ensure inclusiveness and the maintenance of scholarly communication standards. It is precisely the manner in which we will embrace the scholarly future within that crossroads. While here, we have to balance innovation with ever-established values of ethical scholarship and human-centric inquiry.

REFERENCES

Alharbi, W. (2023). AI in the Foreign Language Classroom: A Pedagogical Overview of Automated Writing Assistance Tools. *Education Research International, 2023*, 1–15. DOI: 10.1155/2023/4253331

Baduge, S. K., Thilakarathna, S., Perera, J. S., Arashpour, M., Sharafi, P., Teodosio, B., Shringi, A., & Mendis, P. (2022). Artificial intelligence and smart vision for building and construction 4.0: Machine and deep learning methods and applications. *Automation in Construction, 141*, 104440. DOI: 10.1016/j.autcon.2022.104440

Bednarz, Z., & Manwaring, K. (2021). Risky Business: Legal implications of emerging technologies affecting consumers of financial services. In *Nomos VerlagsgesellschaftmbH& Co. KG eBooks* (pp. 59–74). DOI: 10.5771/9783748926979-59

Caldarini, G., Jaf, S., & McGarry, K. (2022). A literature survey of recent advances in chatbots. *Information (Basel), 13*(1), 41. DOI: 10.3390/info13010041

Cheng, L., Varshney, K. R., & Liu, H. (2021). Socially Responsible AI algorithms: Issues, purposes, and challenges. *Journal of Artificial Intelligence Research, 71*, 1137–1181. DOI: 10.1613/jair.1.12814

Dash, S., Shakyawar, S. K., Sharma, M., & Kaushik, S. (2019). Big data in healthcare: Management, analysis and future prospects. *Journal of Big Data, 6*(1), 54. Advance online publication. DOI: 10.1186/s40537-019-0217-0

Dwivedi, Y. K., Hughes, L., Baabdullah, A. M., Ribeiro-Navarrete, S., Giannakis, M., Al-Debei, M. M., Dennehy, D., Metri, B., Buhalis, D., Cheung, C. M., Conboy, K., Doyle, R., Dubey, R., Dutot, V., Felix, R., Goyal, D., Gustafsson, A., Hinsch, C., Jebabli, I., & Wamba, S. F. (2022). Metaverse beyond the hype: Multidisciplinary perspectives on emerging challenges, opportunities, and agenda for research, practice and policy. *International Journal of Information Management, 66*, 102542. DOI: 10.1016/j.ijinfomgt.2022.102542

Dwivedi, Y. K., Hughes, L., Ismagilova, E., Aarts, G., Coombs, C., Crick, T., Duan, Y., Dwivedi, R., Edwards, J., Eirug, A., Galanos, V., Ilavarasan, P. V., Janssen, M., Jones, P., Kar, A. K., Kizgin, H., Kronemann, B., Lal, B., Lucini, B., & Williams, M. D. (2019). Artificial Intelligence (AI): Multidisciplinary perspectives on emerging challenges, opportunities, and agenda for research, practice and policy. *International Journal of Information Management, 57*, 101994. DOI: 10.1016/j.ijinfomgt.2019.08.002

Dwivedi, Y. K., Ismagilova, E., Hughes, D. L., Carlson, J., Filieri, R., Jacobson, J., Jain, V., Karjaluoto, H., Kefi, H., Krishen, A. S., Kumar, V., Rahman, M. M., Raman, R., Rauschnabel, P. A., Rowley, J., Salo, J., Tran, G. A., & Wang, Y. (2020). Setting the future of digital and social media marketing research: Perspectives and research propositions. *International Journal of Information Management, 59*, 102168. DOI: 10.1016/j.ijinfomgt.2020.102168

Foltýnek, T., Dlabolová, D., Anohina-Naumeca, A., Razı, S., Kravjar, J., Kamzola, L., Guerrero-Dib, J., Çelik, Ö., & Weber-Wulff, D. (2020). Testing of support tools for plagiarism detection. *International Journal of Educational Technology in Higher Education, 17*(1), 46. Advance online publication. DOI: 10.1186/s41239-020-00192-4

Grassini, S. (2023). Shaping the Future of Education: Exploring the potential and consequences of AI and ChatGPT in educational settings. *Education Sciences, 13*(7), 692. DOI: 10.3390/educsci13070692

Huang, C., Zhang, Z., Mao, B., & Yao, X. (2022). An Overview of Artificial intelligence ethics. *IEEE Transactions on Artificial Intelligence, 4*(4), 799–819. DOI: 10.1109/TAI.2022.3194503

Hutchinson, B., Rostamzadeh, N., Greer, C., Heller, K., & Prabhakaran, V. (2022). Evaluation gaps in machine learning practice. *2022 ACM Conference on Fairness, Accountability, and Transparency*, 1859–1876. DOI: 10.1145/3531146.3533233

Kalisdha, A. (2023). The Future of Library Science Research: Tools and Databases. *International Journal for Research in Applied Science and Engineering Technology, 11*(11), 700–707. DOI: 10.22214/ijraset.2023.56602

Karataş, F., & Yüce, E. (2024). AI and the Future of Teaching: Preservice Teachers' Reflections on the Use of Artificial Intelligence in Open and Distributed Learning. *International Review of Research in Open and Distance Learning, 25*(3), 304–325. DOI: 10.19173/irrodl.v25i3.7785

Khabib, S. (2022). Introducing artificial intelligence (AI)-based digital writing assistants for teachers in writing scientific articles. *Deleted Journal, 1*(2), 114–124. DOI: 10.12928/tefl.v1i2.249

Kraus, S., Kumar, S., Lim, W. M., Kaur, J., Sharma, A., & Schiavone, F. (2023). From moon landing to metaverse: Tracing the evolution of Technological Forecasting and Social Change. *Technological Forecasting and Social Change, 189*, 122381. DOI: 10.1016/j.techfore.2023.122381

Kurzweil, R. (2025). The Singularity Is Nearer: When We Merge with AI. *Perspectives on Science and Christian Faith, 77*(1), 75–76. DOI: 10.56315/PSCF3-25Kurzweil

Nicholls, J., Kuppa, A., & Le-Khac, N. (2021). Financial Cybercrime: A comprehensive survey of deep learning approaches to tackle the evolving financial crime landscape. *IEEE Access : Practical Innovations, Open Solutions, 9*, 163965–163986. DOI: 10.1109/ACCESS.2021.3134076

Radu, R. (2019). Negotiating internet governance. In *Oxford University Press eBooks*. DOI: 10.1093/oso/9780198833079.001.0001

Raschka, S., Patterson, J., & Nolet, C. (2020). Machine learning in Python: Main developments and technology trends in data science, machine learning, and artificial intelligence. *Information (Basel), 11*(4), 193. DOI: 10.3390/info11040193

Staiano, M. F. (2021). *CRITICAL DIALOGUES Human rights, democracy and pandemic perspectives*. DOI: 10.55658/gpcds978-65-00-40218-6

Vergara, J., &Karpukhin, S. (2022). *Reimagining Nabokov*. DOI: 10.3998/mpub.12734225

Zawacki-Richter, O., Marín, V. I., Bond, M., & Gouverneur, F. (2019). Systematic review of research on artificial intelligence applications in higher education – where are the educators? *International Journal of Educational Technology in Higher Education*, *16*(1), 39. Advance online publication. DOI: 10.1186/s41239-019-0171-0

Chapter 13
Education 5.0 and AI for Academic Research and Citation Management

Jyoti Rana
https://orcid.org/0000-0001-7474-3702
Amity University, India

Rahul Gahlot
College of Engineering and Applied Science, University of Cincinnati, USA

Ruchi Jain
https://orcid.org/0000-0001-5148-7654
Amity School of Business, Amity University, India

Jonika Lamba
Independent Researcher, India

ABSTRACT

This chapter aims to provide readers a insight on the growing usage of artificial intelligence in academic writing. The goal of this chapter is to take a close look at the part that Artificial Intelligence plays in Education 5.0, focusing on both its pros and cons. It talks about how AI technology is getting better, how it can be used in schools, and the change towards personalisation and adaptive learning. It also talks about the ethical issues that come up when using AI in schools.A qualitative analysis of available literature is used in the study. To do this, they need to look at case studies, business reports, and real-world evidence about how AI technologies are used and how they affect education. The study looks at many uses of AI, such as using AI algorithms to choose educational material, machine learning to grade students, and natural language processing to help people learn languages. The results show that AI makes learning a lot better by allowing personalised and adaptable learning, making students more interested, and giving them feedback that is specific to them.

DOI: 10.4018/979-8-3373-5601-3.ch013

INTRODUCTION

Scientific writing is an important part of education because it uses a methodical way to express ideas (Benavides et al.,2020). Researchers and teachers often use it in academic writing to make arguments based on evidence and logical reasoning. It lets writers look at ideas in depth, which leads to a clear hypothesis or conclusion. Different fields uses scientific writing for different reasons. For example, scientists use it to explain their study and findings, while literary critics use it to make critiques based on evidence (Aler Tubella et al.,2024, Hu, 2025). Different writers and fields have different problems when it comes to academic writing. It is important to be able to handle a lot of material, complicated ideas, theories, and real-world data in academic writing (Anwar & Ahyarudin, 2023). This requires a insightful grasp of the topic and the ability to explain difficult ideas to the reader. Scholarly writing must follow strict rules for accuracy, proof, and logical structure. There must be trustworthy proof for each claim. Also, it can be hard to understand the formal tone and exact words used in academic writing, especially for beginners (Çela et al., 2025). To meet the changing needs of students in the 21st century, it has become necessary to use cutting-edge tools in education (Mustafa et al.,2024).

Transition on Education 4.0 to Education 5.0

Education 4.0 and Education 5.0 is at the front of this transformative journey. It promises a pedagogical revolution in which Artificial Intelligence (AI) plays a key role, bringing about personalised and flexible learning experiences (Esiyok et al.,2025). The different stages of education's history can be quickly viewed together. In the early days of education, there was a traditional "one size fits all" method that focused on memorisation and teacher-centered instruction. Multimedia and technology were brought into classes during Education 2.0, which led to more interactive and interesting learning experiences (Al-Emran er al., 2025). Education 3.0 pushed for learning that is focused on the student, shared spaces, and the use of web-based tools. It set the stage for the current era of digital education. With the arrival of Education 4.0, technologies like AI, the Internet of Things (IoT), big data analytics, and cloud computing have come together. In particular, AI is becoming a force for change in education, with the ability to make learning experiences more personalised based on each student's needs and preferences. Using AI not only makes personalised learning paths easier, but it also makes it possible for systems to change based on the learner's success, which makes the learning process more efficient and effective (Matthew et al.,2023).The change from Education 4.0 to the new Education 5.0 shows a stronger dedication to crafting personalised learning experiences for each student. Education 5.0 imagines a world where human intelligence and AI work together to improve students' cognitive abilities in a way that goes beyond the limits of traditional education (Cao et al.,2025). This stage marks the beginning of a time when AI is an important part of learning and is easily integrated into teaching methods to improve students' ability to be creative, think critically, and solve problems. AI is becoming more popular in education because it can handle huge amounts of data and come up with ideas that help create personalised learning paths (Shukla et al.,2025). AI subsets called machine learning algorithms look at how each student learns, what they like, and what they're good at. This lets teachers change the lessons and activities to fit the needs of each student. This change from a standardised to a personalised approach breaks away from the limits of traditional education and gives each student a unique educational journey (De Villiers,

2024). These systems use real-time data to change the pace, topic, and way lessons are taught based on how well the student is doing and how well they understand the material.is adaptability makes sure that students can learn at their own pace and get extra help or challenges as needed, making the learning process more effective and open to everyone.

Technological Touchpoints in Education 5.0

AI also helps people learn important skills for the 21st century by encouraging hands-on and collaborative learning. By combining virtual reality (VR) and augmented reality (AR) technologies that are driven by AI, students can play simulations that are more realistic and immersive than what they can do in a regular classroom.not only helps students understand the material better, but it also encourages imaginatioan, teamwork, and problem-solving, all of which are important for success in today's global world. Studies looked into how AI-powered teaching systems affected how well students did in school in a range of subjects.The results showed that students who worked with AI trainers did significantly better in school than students who worked with regular teachers.Individualised feedback and personalised learning paths provided by AI systems were found to be key factors in the noted rises in student success. Also, the new studies looked into how AI can help make education more fair and open to everyone.The study showed that AI-powered adaptive learning tools could help close the achievement gap between students from disadvantaged groups (Ayeni et al.,2024). This lets teachers give more individualised help to students from a wide range of backgrounds, creating a more fair learning environment. Despite the fact that AI has a lot of promise in education, it also has some problems and limits. Some new writings have made people worry about the moral effects of using AI programmes in schools (Malla et al.,2025). For example, study has shown that AI-based assessment tools might have algorithmic bias, which could make education even less fair without meaning to. Additionally, concerns about data protection and security have become important factors to think about when AI technologies are used in schools. New developments in AI research, like shared learning and differential privacy, show promise for ways to deal with privacy issues while keeping the benefits of personalised learning (Cañavate et al.,2025). Experts say that teachers can use AI to help students learn better while keeping private information safe by spreading out the training of AI models and using privacy-protecting methods.

A lot of problems need to be fixed before AI can be used responsibly and fairly in schools. These problems include ethical concerns, data privacy issues, and the fact that AI programmes might be biassed. It is very important for the success and long-term viability of AI-driven education to find a balance between new technologies and moral concerns.The goal of this study paper is to look into the complicated web of Education 4.0 and 5.0 and look at how AI could change personalised and adaptive learning environments. New directions in AI research, like shared learning and differential privacy, show promise for ways to deal with privacy issues while keeping the benefits of personalised learning. Educators can use AI to help students learn better while keeping private information safe by spreading out the training of AI models and using privacy-protecting methods (Corbin et al.,2025).Ethical concerns, worries about data privacy, and the chance of biases in AI systems are big problems that need to be fixed before AI can be used fairly and responsibly in schools. Finding a balance between new technologies and moral concerns is very important for AI-driven education to work and last (Uribe et al.,2024). This study adds to the conversation about how to best use AI to improve education by looking at the present situation, problems, and possible futures of AI integration in education.

LITERATURE REVIEW

The term "Education 4.0" refers to the use of new technologies, especially AI), in schools. It builds on the previous industrial changes in education, which were Education 1.0 (traditional classroom teaching), Education 2.0 (computers and the internet), and Education 3.0 (collaborative learning on the web)(Jaboob et al., 2025). Using AI, big data, the Internet of Things (IoT), and other cutting-edge technologies, Education 4.0 tries to create a learning setting that is both dynamic and flexible. In Education 4.0, AI has many uses and affects many parts of the educational system (Rachmad, 2019).

EDUCATION 5.0 EVOLUTION

Digital change and modernisation have made the education industry a bigger part of the world's economic growth. This transition happened because new technologies are always getting better in various areas. AI, Big Data, Robotics, Automation, and the Internet of Things (IoT) are all significant aspects of Industry 4.0. This is why Culot et al. (2020) provide us a detailed look into Industry 4.0, which helps us comprehend how intricate modern industrial technologies are(Qin and Zhang, 2025). Their results show how crucial it is for teachers to make lesson plans that are both up-to-date with technology and able to adapt to changes in the field (Andres et al., 2022). The European Commission just started Industry 5.0 to celebrate the tenth anniversary of Industry 4.0. There are currently two industrial revolutions going on at the same time, each with its own purposes in different fields (Ye et al., 2024) . This is because of the drive to Industry 5.0. Industry 5.0 is the name of this new phase. It comes before Education 5.0, which wants to transform AI-enhanced education more like the way individuals think (Kumar et al., 2024). Rahim (2021) says that the main parts of Education 5.0 include research, innovation, community service, and industrialisation. Lantada (2020) also believes to keep ethics, morals, conscience, and humanitarianism at the top of the list of things that the next generation of engineers should be able to do. However, recent research shows that the implementation of Education 5.0 has been slowed down by a lack of curriculum updates, a poor understanding of the Education 5.0 doctrine, a lack of involvement from stakeholders, a lack of academic capacity, and a short amount of time set aside for the activity (Munikwa & Mapara, 2022). Because of this, a lot of professors are hesitant to make changes to Education 5.0 at universities, which makes the transformation process much harder (Muzira & Muzira, 2020). Also, according to teachers' thoughts on adapting to Education 5.0, money for building industrial parks and innovation centres to assist AI-driven education is a key priority (Muzira & Bondai, 2020). Saihi et al.'s (2024) recent study looks at the most important elements that are driving digital transformation in maintenance. It also gives us ideas about the skills and methods we need to implement digital technologies. These results are in line with Education 5.0's goals of including digital literacy with transformation skills in schools, which will help create a workforce that can easily navigate the digital world of today's businesses. In this regard, Spencer (2023) talks on how technology changes the way people work, showing both the good and bad sides.

Learn in your own way

AI in Education 4.0 is great at making sure that each student has a great time learning.AI systems understand each student's unique learning styles, preferences, and skills by looking at a lot of data.It makes it easier to make personalised learning paths, which make sure that students get tasks and content that are right for them (Kumar, 2024). Adaptive learning platforms, which are driven by AI, change the level of difficulty and speed of lessons based on how well each student is doing, which helps them understand and remember more (Bozkurt and Gursoy, 2025).

Smart tools for tutoring

Intelligent teaching systems that are run by AI help students in real time and in a way that is unique to them.Based on how each student does, these tools give them advice, feedback, and extra help. Smart teaching systems help students learn better and more efficiently by checking their progress often and changing based on their learning styles (Stolpe and Hallström, 2024).

Putting administrative chores on computers

AI makes administrative jobs easier, which gives teachers more time to teach and mentor. AI systems can take care of boring tasks like marking, keeping track of attendance, and allocating resources automatically.not only saves time but also lowers the chance of mistakes, which lets teachers focus on more important parts of their jobs (Mrida et al.,2025).

Better growth of curriculum

AI looks at a lot of educational data to find patterns, holes, and places where lessons could be better.This method is based on data, which gives teachers the power to make more useful and effective teaching materials. Additionally, AI algorithms evaluate the effectiveness of various teaching methods and suggest changes that will improve general learning outcomes (Obenza et al., 2024).

Early intervention and statistics for learning

By looking at achievement data, AI tools can find students who are at risk of falling behind or having trouble learning (Cabrera et al.,2025). Using predictive analytics, early intervention tools find students who might have problems and give them the help they need.is proactive method stops students from having trouble in school and makes sure they get help when they need it (Hur, 2025).

Processing language to get feedback

Natural language processing (NLP) systems that are powered by AI read students' homework and give them immediate input (Lee et al., 2025).It speeds up the grading process and gives students helpful feedback on their work, which encourages them to keep getting better. Moreover, NLP can be used to create language-learning apps that offer personalised language practice and feedback(Pears and Shields, 2025).

Teaching methods have come a long way since Education 4.0. Education 5.0 builds on the ideas behind Education 4.0 and adds new methods and tools. At its core, Education 5.0 uses advanced AI tools to change the way people learn. AI is different from its predecessor in that it is now the main tool used to acquire, process, and apply information. One big difference between Education 4.0 and 5.0 is that AI apps are now more advanced and used by many people. In Education 4.0, (Soyler et al.,2025) AI mostly helped with paperwork, tests, and making personalised learning suggestions for each student based on data collected from previous records. But in Education 5.0, AI-powered technologies are used in almost every part of education (Sperling et al.,2024). These technologies change how lessons are planned, how material is delivered, how engaged students are, and how they are graded. AI algorithms change learning paths on the fly based on each student's success, preferences, and preferred ways of learning(Giannakos et al.,2024). This makes learning very personalised. AI is also used in Education 5.0 to encourage collaborative and hands-on learning settings (Temsah et al.,2025). Education 4.0 focused on passive learning, where students just took in information. Education 5.0, on the other hand, encourages interactive, hands-on learning through AI-powered virtual worlds, simulations, and immersive technologies (Perkins et al.,2024).These tools let students interact with course materials, try out difficult ideas, and work together with others in virtual classes, going beyond the limits of regular classrooms.

Education 5.0 makes AI a core part that fundamentally changes things for personalised learning and data analysis.In the same way, Indian institutions need to take a strategies to getting rid of resistance and improving the technology skills of their professors and researchers in order to implement Education 5.0.Based upon the literature review in education 5.0 Fig 1 is made below.

Figure 1. represents the major 7 aspect of education 5.0 (made by authors)

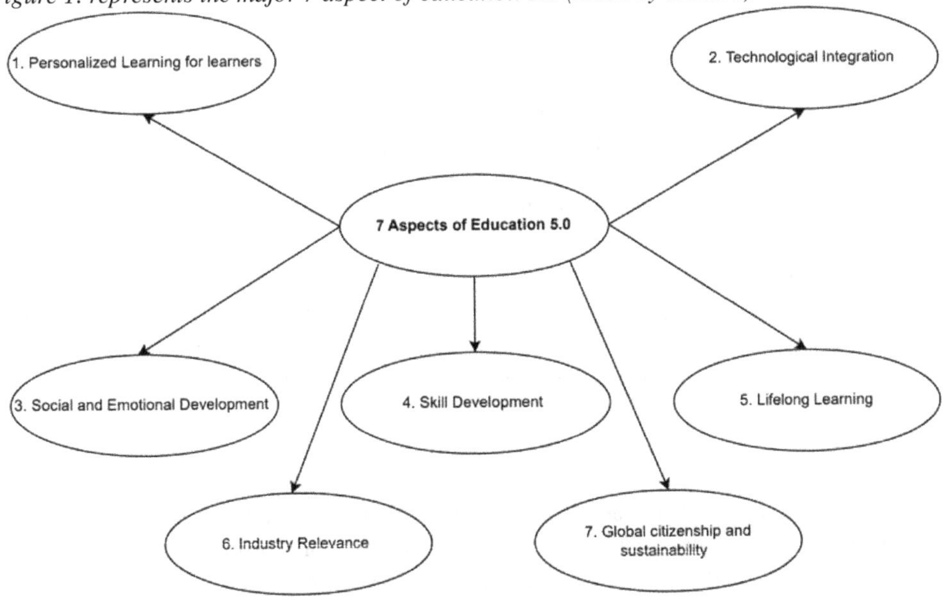

Education 5.0 is a move towards a more personalised, learner-centered approach to learning that uses digital technologies to make the experience better and meet the changing requirements of society (Ferrigno et al.,2023). It stresses leveraging technology to make the learning environment more human, with an emphasis on building social and emotional skills combined with academic knowledge (Gaur, et al.,2023). This model's goal is to give students the skills and information they need for the 21st century and beyond, encouraging them to keep studying and be active members of society(León et al., 2023).

WHY AI IS IMPORTANT IN EDUCATION 5.0

The field of AI has been constantly changing and improving in many areas, with schooling being one of the most important. Here are some important places where AI is having a big effect on the field (Harcourt et al.,2024).

Smart and personalised learning

In AI in Education 5.0, personalised and flexible learning is given a lot of attention. Advanced AI algorithms look at each person's learning styles, preferences, and performance data to make material that is uniquely tailored to them.It makes sure that every student gets a customised lesson plan that fits the way they learn and the speed at which they learn (Montuori et al.,2025).

Using predictive analytics to help with early prevention

The use of predictive analytics for early assistance is a key part of AI in Education 5.0. AI algorithms look at trends and data from the past to find possible learning gaps or problems(Al-Zahrani, 2024). Then, teachers can step in and offer extra help, making sure that students stay on track with their learning goals (Triansyah et al.,2023).

Putting together augmented reality (AR) and virtual reality (VR)

Augmented reality (AR) and virtual reality (VR) are used in AI in Education 5.0 to make learning more engaging.These technologies are more advanced than traditional ones because they let students connect with learning materials in three-dimensional spaces. This makes them more interested and helps them understand difficult topics better (Gupta, 2025).

Game play and simulations In AI in Education 5.0

simulations and game-like features are seamlessly built into the learning process. Educational platforms keep students interested and make learning fun by adding game-like features (Strielkowski et al.,2025). Simulations let you get realworld experience in a virtual setting. This is especially helpful for topics like science and engineering that need real-world applications (Corpuz et al.,2025).

Lifelong learning and getting better at things

AI in Education 5.0 creates personalised learning paths for academic success and skill development needed in the 21st-century industry (Nguyen et al.,2024). This is because it knows how important it is to keep learning and improving skills throughout life.

Ethical AI and schooling for everyone

When it comes to AI in Education 5.0, ethics and inclusion are very important. The creation and use of AI-like systems must follow rules that put fairness, transparency, and responsibility first. A lot of work goes into making sure that AIpowered learning tools meet the needs of all kinds of students and don't reinforce biases (Cukurova, 2025).

Lifelong learning and holistic growth

Education 5.0 recognises how important it is to raise well-rounded people who can adapt to a world that changes quickly. Adaptive learning models encourage lifelong learning by teaching skills like critical thinking, problem-solving, collaboration, and adaptability. This creates a mindset of always learning outside of formal school settings (Nelson, et al.,2020).

SEL stands for Social and Emotional Learning.

Education 5.0 is different from earlier ways of teaching because it puts a lot of emphasis on social and emotional learning. Adaptive learning models include parts that check on and care for students' mental health, giving them support and tools to learn important life skills like self-awareness, empathy, and resilience (Mohebbi, 2025).

AI TOOLS IN ACADEMIC WRITING

Academic writing is an important part of research that involves organising thoughts, making arguments based on evidence, and using logic. But it can be hard to deal with a lot of information and complicated thoughts (Çela et al.,2025). Integrating AI into academic writing is becoming more and more significant since it helps solve these problems. The goal of this review is to look at certain areas where AI is a big help with academic writing (Gupta et al., 2022).

Writing for school and research is an important part of both, and it involves a systematic way of getting ideas across. Researchers and educators typically use it in academic writing to back up their claims with facts and sound reasoning (Pedro et al.,2019). This type of writing helps people get a better grasp of a problem. It helps authors think about concepts in depth, which leads to a clear theory or conclusion (Babu, 2024). Academic writing is used for different things in different fields. Scientists use it to talk about their work and findings, while literary critics use it to write evaluations that are based on facts. But writing for school can be hard, and the issues are different for each writer and field. When you write for school, you have to deal with a lot of information, sophisticated ideas, theories, and real-world data in a way that is simple and easy to understand (Mobo et al., 2025). This takes not just a lot of knowledge about the topic, but also the ability to make complicated ideas easy to understand for the reader (He et al., 2021). Academic writing must be very accurate, have a lot of proof, and follow a logical pattern. There must be credible proof to back up every claim. Also, it can be hard to learn how to write in a professional way and use the right words in academic writing, especially for beginners (Emanuel, 2013). It's very important to keep academic integrity by properly acknowledging and referencing sources, but it can take a lot of time and be hard, especially for people who don't speak English as their first language (Hensley, 2011).

The "publish or perish" mentality in academia puts a lot of stress on people and might make them burn out. Writers need to find a balance between giving information and keeping the reader interested (Karataş et al., 2025). It might be hard to be innovative and creative when you have a lot of work to do in a short amount of time. Structural coherence is particularly crucial in academic writing, especially in big papers like theses and dissertations. This means that you need to make sure your concepts make sense (Malfatti, 2025). You need to find a way to combine your need for coherence with your ability to manage your time well, as academic writing often gets in the way of other things you need to complete. When you write for school, you usually have to make changes based on what your peers and advisors say. You need to be able to take criticism and use feedback well for this to work (Sungur et al.,2013). When writers perform interdisciplinary study, they have to deal with the difficulty of merging different methods, terms, and ideas from different domains, which makes their work more difficult. Because of these problems, AI (Rana et al., 2024) is now an essential tool for writing in school. Writing helpers that use AI (Rana et al.,

2023) can aid with grammar, organisation, citations, and following the rules of your field. These tools are not only useful, but they are also essential for making academic writing more efficient and high-quality. They let writers focus on the most important and new parts of their research. So, even if academic writing can be hard, AI technologies make it much easier and help you get more done faster(Ferrigno et al.,2024) . This chapter shows the most important ways that AI tools can help with academic writing. It shows how important they are for spreading knowledge, boosting productivity, and adding to academic conversation (Rana et al., 2022).

There are currently more and more AI programmes that help with academic writing and research, and each one is made to satisfy a different need. Zotero, Mendeley, and EndNote are all great tools for managing literature, organising research materials, making citations, and working with word processors. But these technologies don't help with writing or making text. Grammarly and OpenAI's ChatGPT are two highly significant tools for making writing better (Makda, 2025). They have AI-powered grammatical checks, plagiarism detection, and text generation tools that are necessary for writing clear and original academic content. But they don't have any tools for managing references or analysing data (Vartiainen et al.,2025). Turnitin and Copyscape are the best at finding plagiarism since they use large databases to check the originality of academic papers. But they can only check for plagiarism; they can't analyse text or analyse data (Zafrullah et al.,2024). Tableau makes a tremendous difference in data analysis because it turns hard-to-understand data into easy-to-understand graphs. Tableau is great at displaying data, but it can't create content with AI. Researchers can now use AI-powered tools like ArXiv and Semantic Scholar to find and summarise relevant academic publications. These tools keep them up to date on the latest advancements in their domains. NVivo, MAXQDA, Leximancer, Quirkos, ATLAS. ti, and Dedoose are some of the most popular tools for qualitative data analysis. They can automatically code, analyse sentiment, and find patterns in large amounts of text data (Pritiprada et al., 2025). Both Provalis Research and RapidMiner use AI and text analytics together to make it easier to undertake deep qualitative analysis. These technologies all have their own AI features and integrations, and the research project picks the one that best fits its demands. This shows how AI can be used in many different ways in scientific writing and research (Verma, 2018).

AI tools for managing citations

This section points out AI tools for easy citation mamagemnet like Trinka AI is a complete writing assistant that helps you find sources, organise your work correctly, and make your writing clearer overall. It has a citation generator built in (Steele, 2008).

Scholarcy is a study assistant that helps with managing citations, summarising articles, and keeping track of research progress. Sourcely shows how AI is changing the way academics handle citations in 2025 by combining automation with an easy-to-use interface. This tool is made to make correct citations in styles like APA, MLA, and Chicago (Garrett et al.,2020).One great thing about Sourcely is that it can make multiple sources at once, which is especially useful for big research projects. Its smart algorithms automatically pull and arrange source information, so you don't have to. This cuts down on mistakes made by hand and makes sure everything follows current academic standards.Sourcely integrates with well-known writing programmes so users can add references, make citations, and send bibliographies all without having to switch between programmes. Its autocite tool finds and formats citations from different types of sources, which saves you time and effort (Wang et al.,2025). Sourcely checks sources and often changes reference styles to keep up with changing standards to protect academic honesty. Its simple interface is made to work for both new and experienced researchers, striking a good mix between ease of use and usefulness.Sourcely is all about automation and integration. The next tool, AI Blaze, has tools that are designed to help people work together on research projects. AI Blaze is a useful Chrome extension that was made to make citing sources easier for students and experts in the year 2025 (Runco, 2025). It saves time and cuts down on mistakes by automating the process of making citations straight from online sources. This makes academic research more efficient.You can make notes in real time with AI Blaze in either APA or MLA styles as you browse. Since it works perfectly with Chrome, it won't get in the way of your work.AI Blaze is unique because it can make sources right away while you browse, which makes it great for quick online research. It is important to double-check the links, though, because the tool depends on the web sources it uses being correct (Vrouwenvelder, et al.,2025).That being said, AI Blaze does have some flaws. It can't handle bulk quotations or sources that aren't on the web, so it's not as good for projects that need to use a lot of different kinds of sources. On the other hand, its focused method works well for managing citations from online sources (Rizki et al.,2025).Semantic Scholar is a search engine that uses AI to index and organise scientific books. This makes it easier to find sources and keep track of citations. There is a tool called Paper Digest that can summarise and cite research papers, find related citations, and highlight important findings. This is Scite AI, a tool that helps people find the right citation style and makes sure they are correct (Yim et al.,2025). Zotero is one of the best tools for managing citations. It works with both web browsers and word processors and lets users gather sources, organise them, and reference them. Mendeley is an AI-powered reference manager and social network for researchers that makes it easier to manage citations, work together, and find relevant study Safitri and Fithriani, 2024). According to the source, this is an academic search assistant driven by AI that has features like reverse search and different pricing plans (Walters, 2025). It makes sense to have an AI-powered reference editor and academic note-taker that can do things like retrieve documents, do semantic search, and connect to Google Search. scienceOS is a free AI reference manager that sorts citations and turns literature collections into study indexes that can be shared (García-Rudolph et al.,2025).

DISCUSSION

This study reveals AI is a very useful tool for boosting productivity and has totally transformed academic writing and research in six domains. Some of these are Concept Development and Research Design, Content Development and Structuring, Review of Literature and Synthesis, Data Analysis, Editing, and Ethical Compliance. AI changes how ideas are developed and research is planned by giving useful information and improving methods. It improves the quality of material by helping with writing and analysing emotional tone. AI's capacity to handle massive data sets makes sure that literature reviews and data management are thorough and accurate. AI also makes the publishing process easier and helps researchers follow ethical guidelines while sharing their work (Howard and Tummon, 2025).

Based on these results, there are a few important suggestions that come to mind. First, to get the most out of AI tools, schools and academics need to use them more extensively in their study. This integration should not only be ubiquitous, but also deep, so that AI's ability to change things affects every part of academic activity. Second, it is very important to employ AI in a way that is fair and open. Researchers must utilise AI tools in a way that keeps their work original and high-quality and doesn't degrade academic excellence (Supa'at and Ihsan, 2023). Third, there is a real requirement for enough time to train and adapt. Researchers need these things to learn how to use AI technologies well, which will help them get the most out of their academic work. Also, it's important to find the right balance between using AI and human understanding, especially when it comes to coming up with new ideas and designing research. This balance is important to make sure that AI doesn't take away from the creativity and critical thinking that comes with being human. Finally, the field of AI in academia is continually developing, therefore research and development must go on.

Future research will focus on making AI tools better for making predictions and hypotheses, setting up ethical rules for using AI, figuring out the best ways for humans and AI to work together, finding out how AI can help with data management, analysis, editing, and communication. To solve problems, improve tools, and make sure that AI is used ethically in academia, exploration must continue.

Integration of cutting edge technologies like AI into education to make learning more personalised and flexible is what Education 4.0 and 5.0 mean. However, there are some problems with putting AI into schooling. To solve this problem, one possible solution is to create strong AI algorithms that can correctly figure out what each student needs and make learning experiences fit those needs (Hashmi & Bal, 2024).machine learning techniques are needed to look at huge amounts of data, such as student success, preferences, and learning styles, in order to make personalised learning paths. To address concerns about the collection and use of sensitive student data in AI-powered educational platforms, it is also important to set up complete data protection and security frameworks. Enforcing strict rules for data anonymization, encryption, and user consent can help protect students' privacy and make AI-driven personalised learning work better.For educators, technologists, lawmakers, and industry stakeholders to come up with and use effective AI-integrated educational solutions, they need to work together.

Working together across different fields can lead to the creation of new tools and methods for using AI to enhance teaching and learning while taking into account moral, social, and cultural issues. To make sure teachers have the skills and information they need to use AI tools effectively in the classroom, it is also important to fund teacher professional development programmes. Training programmes should focus on helping teachers understand how AI can work with traditional teaching methods and giving them the tools and support they need to use AI-powered devices in their lessons. Also, making sure that everyone has equal access to educational tools that use AI is very important for reducing differences in how well people learn.It means fixing problems with the digital gap by making sure all students have access to a stable internet connection and the right hardware. Also, making AI-powered platforms that are welcoming to everyone, taking into account things like different language backgrounds, disabilities, and financial backgrounds, can help make sure that all students can benefit from personalised learning. Finally, it is important for educational organisations to encourage a culture of experimentation and new ideas in order to make AI-integrated learning environments better all the time. Supporting and allowing teachers to try out different AI tools and teaching methods while also letting them work together and share their knowledge with others can help find the best ways to use AI for personalised and flexible learning.Education systems can get past problems and fully utilise AI for personalised and adaptable learning in the age of Education 4.0 and 5.0 by looking at it from different angles, including technological, pedagogical, ethical, and social ones.

RECOMMENDATIONS FOR FUTURE RESEARCH

Even though the possibilities of using AI in education are bright, there are still some areas that need more study and exploration. To start, ethical issues like fairness, transparency, and responsibility in AI algorithms and decision-making processes need to be thought about to make sure that AI is used responsibly in schools. Getting rid of biases in AI systems and protecting the safety of student data are very important for fostering trust and acceptance. Also, study should focus on closing the digital divide so that all students have equal access to AI-powered learning tools.it includes efforts to close the gap in technology and internet access, especially in areas that are already struggling.

To help shape the way we teach in the future, we also need to study how well AI helps people learn new things and improve their skills over time, as well as how it affects their mental and emotional health. Future study should also look into new ways to use AI in education, like quantum computing and integrating brain-computer interfaces, to make learning more personalised and help kids learn better. To fully use AI's ability to shape the future of education and prepare students for success in a world that is always changing, researchers, teachers, policymakers, and technology developers must work together.

CONCLUSION

Since Education 4.0, there have been a lot of changes in how we teach. Education 5.0 adds new tools and methods to the ideas that were in Education 4.0. At its core, Education 5.0 changes the way people learn by using cutting edge tools for AI. AI is different from its predecessor because it is now the main way that people get knowledge, process it, and use it. AI apps are now more advanced and many people use them, which is a big change between Education 4.0 and 5.0. As part of Education 4.0, AI mostly helped with paperwork, tests, and making personalised learning ideas for each student based on information gathered from past work. A lot of the things that are used in education today are driven by AI in Education 5.0. These technologies have changed how lessons are planned, how students are engaged, how they are graded, and how the subject is taught. AI programmes change students' learning paths instantly based on how well they are doing, what they like, and how they like to learn. This makes learning very specific to each person. AI is also used in Education 5.0 to inspire students to work together and learn by doing. Passive learning, in which students just took in knowledge, was a big part of Education 4.0. With Education 5.0, on the other hand, AI-powered virtual worlds, simulations, and immersive technologies make learning more participatory and hands-on.With these tools, students can connect with course materials, try out hard ideas, and work with others in virtual classes, which isn't possible in regular classrooms. AI is a big part of Education 5.0, which changes everything for personalised learning and data analysis. A lot has changed in the way we teach since Education 4.0. Ed 5.0 builds on the ideas in Ed 4.0 by adding new tools and ways of doing things. The main idea behind Education 5.0 is to use cutting edge (AI) tools to change the way people learn. AI is different from the one that came before it because it is now the major way that people learn, process, and use information. A big difference between Education 4.0 and 5.0 is that AI apps are now better and more people use them. As part of Education 4.0, AI mostly helped with paperwork, tests, and coming up with unique ways for each student to learn based on what they had already done. AI is at the heart of a lot of the things that are used in schools today (3.0). With these new tools, teachers can now plan lessons, keep students interested, grade them, and teach the subject in new ways. AI systems change the way students learn right away based on what they like, how well they are doing, and how they like to learn. This makes it possible for everyone to learn in their own way. In Education 5.0, AI is also used to get kids to work together and do things to learn. A big part of Education 4.0 was passive learning, in which students did nothing but take in information. In Education 5.0, on the other hand, virtual worlds, simulations, and immersive technologies driven by AI make learning more interactive and hands-on.You can connect to course materials, try out hard ideas, and work with other students in virtual classes with these tools, which isn't possible in real schools.AI plays a big role in Education 5.0, which changes everything about how people learn and how data is analysed. Getting better at social skills. Teachers can spend more time on their students' overall growth while AI takes care of routine jobs and creates personalised learning experiences. Data privacy, ethical concerns, and the digital gap are all very important issues that need your full attention.It is very important to make sure that AI systems are open, fair, and follow social rules. To build trust among stakeholders, it's also important to address worries about data protection and privacy.The digital gap is still a big problem, affecting underserved groups through differences in technology and internet access. The goal of Education 5.0 should be to make sure that everyone can benefit from AI in education, no matter their socioeconomic background.AI changes academic writing and research in a big way in several fields. Suggestions include using AI tools more widely in research processes, stressing ethical and open use, giving researchers enough training, and keeping a balance between AI usefulness and human intuition. To deal with new problems and moral issues that come up while using AI in academia, research and development must continue.

REFERENCES

Al-Emran, M., Al-Qaysi, N., Al-Sharafi, M. A., Khoshkam, M., Foroughi, B., & Ghobakhloo, M. (2025). Role of perceived threats and knowledge management in shaping generative AI use in education and its impact on social sustainability. *International Journal of Management Education, 23*(1), 101105. DOI: 10.1016/j.ijme.2024.101105

Al-Zahrani, A. M. (2024). Unveiling the shadows: Beyond the hype of AI in education. *Heliyon, 10*(9), e30696. DOI: 10.1016/j.heliyon.2024.e30696

Andres, B., Sempere-Ripoll, F., Esteso, A., & Alemany, M. M. E. (2022). Mapping between industry 5.0 and education 5.0. In *Edulearn22 Proceedings* (pp. 2921–2926). IATED. DOI: 10.21125/edulearn.2022.0739

Anwar, M. R., & Ahyarudin, H. A. (2023). Ai-powered arabic language education in the era of society 5.0. [ITSDI]. *IAIC Transactions on Sustainable Digital Innovation, 5*(1), 50–57. DOI: 10.34306/itsdi.v5i1.607

Ayeni, O. O., Al Hamad, N. M., Chisom, O. N., Osawaru, B., & Adewusi, O. E. (2024). AI in education: A review of personalized learning and educational technology. *GSC Advanced Research and Reviews, 18*(2), 261–271. DOI: 10.30574/gscarr.2024.18.2.0062

Babu, B. V. (2024). *Education 5.0: an overview*. Advances in Technological Innovations in Higher Education. DOI: 10.1201/9781003376699-13

Benavides, L. M. C., Johnny, A. T. A., Martín, D. A. S., John, W. B. B., & Burgos, D. (2020). Digital transformation in higher education institutions: A systematic literature review. *Sensors (Basel), 20*(11), 3291. DOI: 10.3390/s20113291

Bozkurt, V., & Gursoy, D. (2025). The artificial intelligence paradox: Opportunity or threat for humanity? *International Journal of Human-Computer Interaction, 41*(1), 174–187. DOI: 10.1080/10447318.2023.2297114

Cabrera, B. C. C., Leal, M. C., Martínez, J. A. S. A., Soto, A. L. R., Sepulveda, J., Valencia, J., Garcés-Giraldo, L. F., & Valencia-Arias, A. (2025). Artificial Intelligence (AI) and Learning Management Systems (LMS): A bibliometric analysis. *Journal of Infrastructure, Policy and Development, 9*(1), 8029. DOI: 10.24294/jipd8029

Cañavate, J., Martínez-Marroquín, E., & Colom, X. (2025). Engineering a sustainable future through the integration of generative AI in engineering education. *Sustainability (Basel), 17*(7), 3201. DOI: 10.3390/su17073201

Cao, Z., Zhang, L., Huang, Y., & Sivertsen, G. (2025). How does scientific research influence policymaking? A study of four types of citation pathways between research articles and AI policy documents. *Journal of the Association for Information Science and Technology, 76*(10), 1340–1356. DOI: 10.1002/asi.25006

Çela, E., Fonkam, M. M., Eappen, P., & Vajjhala, N. R. (2025). *Current Trends in Smart Classrooms and Sustainable Internet of Things*. Designing Sustainable Internet of Things Solutions for Smart Industries.

Çela, E., Potluri, R. M., & Vajjhala, N. R. (2025). *A Comprehensive Meta-Analysis of IoT Integration for Data-Driven Decision Making in Education*. Designing Sustainable Internet of Things Solutions for Smart Industries.

Çela, E., Vajjhala, N. R., Eappen, P., & Vedishchev, A. "Artificial Intelligence in Vocational Education and Training." In *Transforming Vocational Education and Training Using AI*, pp. 1-16. IGI Global Scientific Publishing, 2025.

Çela, E., Vedishchev, A., & Vajjhala, N. R. "Strategies for Secure Knowledge Management: An In-Depth Analysis of Educational Data Protection Trends and Themes." In *Cybersecurity in Knowledge Management*, pp. 49-64. CRC Press, 2025.

Corbin, T., Dawson, P., Nicola-Richmond, K., & Partridge, H. (2025). 'Where's the line? It's an absurd line': Towards a framework for acceptable uses of AI in assessment. *Assessment & Evaluation in Higher Education*, •••, 1–13. DOI: 10.1080/02602938.2025.2553340

Corpuz, L. O., Lardizabal, E. N., Torno, A. G., Gabayan, V. P.Jr, Pandey, P., & Bautista, R. G. (2025). Dreams and Wishes: The Dawn of AI in the Education Setting. *American Journal of Educational Research*, *13*(1), 17–22. DOI: 10.12691/education-13-1-2

Cukurova, M. (2025). The interplay of learning, analytics and artificial intelligence in education: A vision for hybrid intelligence. *British Journal of Educational Technology*, *56*(2), 469–488. DOI: 10.1111/bjet.13514

Culot, G., Nassimbeni, G., Orzes, G., & Sartor, M. (2020). Behind the definition of Industry 4.0: Analysis and open questions. *International Journal of Production Economics*, *226*, 107617. DOI: 10.1016/j.ijpe.2020.107617

De Villiers, C. (2024). The impact of society 5.0 on curriculum development in higher education. *Journal of Ethics in Higher Education*, *4*(4), 1–25. DOI: 10.26034/fr.jehe.2024.5953

Emanuel, J. (2013). Users and citation management tools: Use and support. *RSR. Reference Services Review*, *41*(4), 639–659. DOI: 10.1108/RSR-02-2013-0007

Esiyok, E., Gokcearslan, S., & Kucukergin, K. G. (2025). Acceptance of educational use of AI chatbots in the context of self-directed learning with technology and ICT self-efficacy of undergraduate students. *International Journal of Human-Computer Interaction*, *41*(1), 641–650. DOI: 10.1080/10447318.2024.2303557

Ferrigno, G., Di Paola, N., Oguntegbe, K. F., & Kraus, S. (2023). Value creation in the metaverse age: A thematic analysis of press releases. *International Journal of Entrepreneurial Behaviour & Research*, *29*(11), 337–363. DOI: 10.1108/IJEBR-01-2023-0039

Ferrigno, G., Martin, X., & Dagnino, G. B. (2024). Explaining the interplay of value creation and value appropriation in strategic alliances: A developmental perspective. *International Journal of Management Reviews*, *26*(2), 232–253. DOI: 10.1111/ijmr.12351

García-Rudolph, A., Sanchez-Pinsach, D., Opisso, E., & Soler, M. D. (2025). Exploring new educational approaches in neuropathic pain: Assessing accuracy and consistency of artificial intelligence responses from GPT-3.5 and GPT-4. *Pain Medicine*, *26*(1), 48–50. DOI: 10.1093/pm/pnae094

Garrett, N., Beard, N., & Fiesler, C. "More than" If Time Allows" the role of ethics in AI education." In *Proceedings of the AAAI/ACM Conference on AI, Ethics, and Society*, pp. 272-278. 2020. DOI: 10.1145/3375627.3375868

Gaur, L., Rana, J., & Jhanjhi, N. Z. (2023). *"Digital twin and healthcare research agenda and bibliometric analysis." Digital Twins and Healthcare: Trends*. Techniques, and Challenges.

Giannakos, M., Azevedo, R., Brusilovsky, P., Cukurova, M., Dimitriadis, Y., Hernandez-Leo, D., Järvelä, S., Mavrikis, M., & Rienties, B. (2024). The promise and challenges of generative AI in education. *Behaviour & Information Technology*, •••, 1–27.

Gupta, S., Jaiswal, A., Paramasivam, A., & Kotecha, J. "Academic writing challenges and supports: Perspectives of international doctoral students and their supervisors." In *Frontiers in Education*, vol. 7, p. 891534. Frontiers Media SA, 2022. DOI: 10.3389/feduc.2022.891534

Gupta, V. (2025). AI experimentation policy for libraries: Balancing innovation and data privacy. *Public Library Quarterly*, •••, 1–21.

Harcourt, E., Loxley, J., & Stanson, B. (2024). Automated learning of finegrained citation patterns in open source large language models.

Hashmi, N., & Bal, A. S. (2024). Generative AI in higher education and beyond. *Business Horizons*, *67*(5), 607–614. DOI: 10.1016/j.bushor.2024.05.005

He, L., Yang, N., Xu, L., Ping, F., Li, W., Sun, Q., Li, Y., Zhu, H., & Zhang, H. (2021). Synchronous distance education vs traditional education for health science students: A systematic review and meta-analysis. *Medical Education*, *55*(3), 293–308. DOI: 10.1111/medu.14364

Hensley, M. K. (2011). Citation management software: Features and futures. *Reference and User Services Quarterly*, *50*(3), 204–208. DOI: 10.5860/rusq.50n3.204

Howard, K., & Tummon, N. (2025). Understanding student citation literacy: A multi-method approach. *Public Services Quarterly*, *21*(2), 85–103. DOI: 10.1080/15228959.2025.2467715

Hu, Y. (2025). Generative AI, communication, and stereotypes: Learning critical AI literacy through experience, analysis, and reflection. *Communication Teacher*, *39*(1), 6–12. DOI: 10.1080/17404622.2024.2397065

Hur, J. W. (2025). Fostering AI literacy: Overcoming concerns and nurturing confidence among preservice teachers. *Information and Learning Science*, *126*(1/2), 56–74. DOI: 10.1108/ILS-11-2023-0170

Jaboob, M., Hazaimeh, M., & Al-Ansi, A. M. (2025). Integration of generative AI techniques and applications in student behavior and cognitive achievement in Arab higher education. *International Journal of Human-Computer Interaction*, *41*(1), 353–366. DOI: 10.1080/10447318.2023.2300016

Karataş, F., Eriçok, B., & Tanrikulu, L. (2025). Reshaping curriculum adaptation in the age of artificial intelligence: Mapping teachers' AI-driven curriculum adaptation patterns. *British Educational Research Journal*, *51*(1), 154–180. DOI: 10.1002/berj.4068

Kumar, Alok. "Management Education 5.0, the NEP and AI: The Unwired Connection." *ADHYAYAN: A JOURNAL OF MANAGEMENT SCIENCES* 14, no. 02 (2024): 16-22.

Kumar, N., Antoniraj, S., Jayanthi, S., Mirdula, S., & Saravanakumar Selvaraj, N. Rajkumar, and K. R. Senthilkumar. "Educational technology and libraries supporting online learning." In *AI-Assisted Library Reconstruction*, pp. 209-237. IGI Global, 2024.

Lantada, A. D. (2020). Engineering education 5.0: Continuously evolving engineering education. *International Journal of Engineering Education*, *36*(6), 1814–1832.

Lee, S., Law, M., & Hoffman, G. (2025). Lee, Seo-young, Matthew Law, and Guy Hoffman. "When and how to use AI in the design process? Implications for human-AI design collaboration.". *International Journal of Human-Computer Interaction*, *41*(2), 1569–1584. DOI: 10.1080/10447318.2024.2353451

León-Gómez, A., Jorge, A. M. F., & Santos-Jaén, J. M. (2023). A bibliometric analysis of sustainability education in tourism universities. *SAGE Open*, *13*(3), 21582440231193215. DOI: 10.1177/21582440231193215

Makda, F. (2025). Digital education: Mapping the landscape of virtual teaching in higher education–a bibliometric review. *Education and Information Technologies*, *30*(2), 2547–2575. DOI: 10.1007/s10639-024-12899-2

Malfatti, F. I. (2025). ChatGPT, Education, and Understanding. *Social Epistemology*, •••, 1–15.

Malla, A., Shah, J. N., Giri, B., Khadka, K., & Gurung, S. (2025). Citation and referencing in research writing publication: A guide for selecting the reference management software. *Journal of Chitwan Medical College*, *15*(2), 91–100.

Matthew, U. O., Bakare, K. M., Ebong, G. N., Ndukwu, C. C., & Nwanakwaugwu, A. C.Ugochukwu Okwudili MatthewKafayat Motomori BakareGodwin Nse EbongCharles Chukwuebuka NdukwuAndrew Chinonso Nwanakwaugwu. (2023). Generative Artificial Intelligence (AI) Educational Pedagogy Development: Conversational AI with User-Centric ChatGPT4. *Journal of Trends in Computer Science and Smart Technology*, *5*(4), 401–418. DOI: 10.36548/jtcsst.2023.4.003

Mobo, F. D., Azar, A. S., & Ana, L. R. G. "The Synergy of AI and Robotics in Modern Education." In *Innovations in Educational Robotics: Advancing AI for Sustainable Development*, pp. 69-86. IGI Global Scientific Publishing, 2025. DOI: 10.4018/979-8-3693-6165-8.ch004

Mohebbi, A. (2025). Enabling learner independence and self-regulation in language education using AI tools: A systematic review. *Cogent Education*, *12*(1), 2433814. DOI: 10.1080/2331186X.2024.2433814

Montuori, R., & Gilabert-Sansalvador, L. (2025). "EMPOWERING ARCHITECTURE STUDENTS IN CITATION MANAGEMENT." In *INTED2025 Proceedings*, pp. 3681-3686. IATED. DOI: 10.21125/inted.2025.0929

Mrida, M. S. H., Rahman, M. A., & Alam, M. S. (2025). AI-Driven Data Analytics and Automation: A Systematic Literature Review of Industry Applications. *Strategic Data Management and Innovation*, *2*(01), 21–40. DOI: 10.71292/sdmi.v2i01.9

Munikwa, S., & Mapara, J. The Case of Chinhoyi University of Technology. (2022). Grappling with education 5.0 curriculum development in Zimbabwean higher education. The case of Chinhoyi University of Technology. *Journal of African Education*, *3*(2), 181–203. DOI: 10.31920/2633-2930/2022/v3n2a7

Mustafa, M. Y., Tlili, A., Lampropoulos, G., Huang, R., Jandrić, P., Zhao, J., Salha, S., Xu, L., Panda, S., Kinshuk, , López-Pernas, S., & Saqr, M. (2024). A systematic review of literature reviews on artificial intelligence in education (AIED): A roadmap to a future research agenda. *Smart Learning Environments*, *11*(1), 59. DOI: 10.1186/s40561-024-00350-5

Muzira, D. R., & Bondai, B. M. (2020). Perception of educators towards the adoption of education 5.0: A case of a state university in Zimbabwe. East African Journal of education and social sciences, 1(2), 43-53.

Muzira, D. R., & Muzira, R. (2020). An assessment of educators' level of concern on the adoption of education 5.0: A case of one university in Zimbabwe. *Current Journal of Applied Science and Technology*, *39*(17), 22–32. DOI: 10.9734/cjast/2020/v39i1730749

Nelson, M. J., & Hoover, A. K. (2020). "Notes on using Google Colaboratory in AI education." In *Proceedings of the 2020 ACM conference on innovation and Technology in Computer Science Education*, pp. 533-534. DOI: 10.1145/3341525.3393997

Nguyen, A., Hong, Y., Dang, B., & Huang, X. (2024). Human-AI collaboration patterns in AI-assisted academic writing. *Studies in Higher Education*, *49*(5), 847–864. DOI: 10.1080/03075079.2024.2323593

Obenza, B. N., Salvahan, A., Rios, A. N., Solo, A., Alburo, R. A., & Gabila, R. J. (2024). University students' perception and use of ChatGPT: Generative artificial intelligence (AI) in higher education. *International Journal of Human-Computer Studies*, *5*(12), 5–18.

Pears, R., & Shields, G. (2025). *Cite them right: the essential referencing guide*. Bloomsbury Publishing.

Pedro, Francesc, Miguel Subosa, Axel Rivas, and Paula Valverde. "Artificial intelligence in education: Challenges and opportunities for sustainable development." (2019).

Perkins, M., Furze, L., Roe, J., & MacVaugh, J. (2024). The Artificial Intelligence Assessment Scale (AIAS): A framework for ethical integration of generative AI in educational assessment. *Journal of University Teaching & Learning Practice*, *21*(6), 49–66. DOI: 10.53761/q3azde36

Pritiprada, P., Satpathy, I., Azar, A. S., & Patnaik, B. C. M. "RoboRevolution: Transforming Education for Sustainable Futures." In *Innovations in Educational Robotics: Advancing AI for Sustainable Development*, pp. 157-172. IGI Global Scientific Publishing, 2025. DOI: 10.4018/979-8-3693-6165-8.ch008

Qin, Q., & Zhang, S. (2025). Visualizing the knowledge mapping of artificial intelligence in education: A systematic review. *Education and Information Technologies*, *30*(1), 449–483. DOI: 10.1007/s10639-024-13076-1

Rachmad, Y. E. (2019). Transforming Workforce Skills in the Era of Society 5.0: Integrating Technology and Artificial Intelligence in Competency Development.

Rahim, M. N. (2021). Post-pandemic of Covid-19 and the need for transforming education 5.0 in Afghanistan higher education. *Utamax: Journal of Ultimate Research and Trends in Education*, *3*(1), 29–39. DOI: 10.31849/utamax.v3i1.6166

Rana, J., Gaur, L., & Santosh, K. C. "Classifying customers' journey from online reviews of Amazon fresh via sentiment analysis and topic modelling." In *2022 3rd International Conference on Computation, Automation and Knowledge Management (ICCAKM)*, pp. 1-6. IEEE, 2022. DOI: 10.1109/ICCAKM54721.2022.9990124

Rana, J., Gaur, L., Singh, G., Awan, U., & Rasheed, M. I. (2022). Reinforcing customer journey through artificial intelligence: A review and research agenda. *International Journal of Emerging Markets*, *17*(7), 1738–1758. DOI: 10.1108/IJOEM-08-2021-1214

Rana, J., Jain, R., & Nehra, V. (2024). Utility and acceptability of AI-enabled Chatbots on the online customer journey. *International Journal of Computing and Digital Systems*, *15*(1), 323–335. DOI: 10.12785/ijcds/150125

Rana, J., Jain, R., & Santosh, K. C. (2023). Automation and AI-enabled customer journey: A bibliometric analysis. *Vision (Basel)*, •••, 09722629221149854. DOI: 10.1177/09722629221149854

Rizki, D. P., & Hannin, P. N. S. (2025). Mendeley-Based Training to Improve Reference Management and Citation Formatting in Sociology Students. *Room of Civil Society Development*, *4*(2), 309–319. DOI: 10.59110/rcsd.565

Runco, M. A. (2025). Updating the standard definition of creativity to account for the artificial creativity of AI. *Creativity Research Journal*, *37*(1), 1–5. DOI: 10.1080/10400419.2023.2257977

Safitri, M., & Fithriani, R. (2024). Exploring Higher Education EFL Students' Perception of AI Writing Tools in the 5.0 Era. *Cetta: Jurnal Ilmu Pendidikan*, *7*(1), 267–276. DOI: 10.37329/cetta.v7i1.3158

Saihi, Afef, Ben-Daya, Mohamed, & Hariga, Moncer, and Rami As' ad. "A Structural equation modeling analysis of generative AI chatbots adoption among students and educators in higher education." *Computers and Education: Artificial Intelligence* 7 (2024): 100274.

Shukla, P., Naik, S., Obi, I., Backus, J., Rasche, N., & Parson, P. "Rethinking Citation of AI Sources in Student-AI Collaboration within HCI Design Education." *arXiv preprint arXiv:2506.08467* (2025). DOI: 10.1145/3742901.3742909

Soyler, A., Burmaoglu, S., & Kidak, L. B. (2025). The evolutionary path of medical waste management research: Insights from co-citation and co-word analysis. *Waste Management & Research*, *43*(1), 3–15. DOI: 10.1177/0734242X241227378

Spencer, D. A. (2023). Technology and work: Past lessons and future directions. *Technology in Society*, *74*, 102294. DOI: 10.1016/j.techsoc.2023.102294

Sperling, K., Stenberg, C.-J., McGrath, C., Åkerfeldt, A., Heintz, F., & Stenliden, L. (2024). In search of artificial intelligence (AI) literacy in teacher education: A scoping review. *Computers and Education Open*, *6*, 100169. DOI: 10.1016/j.caeo.2024.100169

Steele, S. E. (2008). Bibliographic citation management software as a tool for building knowledge. *Journal of Wound, Ostomy, and Continence Nursing*, *35*(5), 463–468. DOI: 10.1097/01.WON.0000335956.45311.69

Stolpe, K., & Hallström, J. (2024). Artificial intelligence literacy for technology education. *Computers and Education Open*, *6*, 100159. DOI: 10.1016/j.caeo.2024.100159

Strielkowski, W., Grebennikova, V., Lisovskiy, A., Rakhimova, G., & Vasileva, T. (2025). AI-driven adaptive learning for sustainable educational transformation. *Sustainable Development (Bradford)*, *33*(2), 1921–1947. DOI: 10.1002/sd.3221

Sungur, M. O., & Seyhan, T. Ö. (2013). Writing references and using citation management software. *Turkish Journal of Urology*, *39*(Suppl 1), 25.

(2023). Supa'at, Supa'at, and Ihsan Ihsan. "The challenges of elementary education in society 5.0 era." [IJSL]. *International Journal of Social Learning*, *3*(3), 341–360.

Temsah, A., Alhasan, K., Altamimi, I., Jamal, A., Al-Eyadhy, A., Malki, K. H., & Temsah, M.-H. (2025). DeepSeek in healthcare: Revealing opportunities and steering challenges of a new open-source artificial intelligence frontier. *Cureus*, *17*(2). Advance online publication. DOI: 10.7759/cureus.79221

Triansyah, Fadli Agus, Ilham Muhammad, Andi Rabuandika, Kartika Dwi Pratiwi Siregar, Nurhuda Teapon, and Mohammad Syahru Assabana. "Bibliometric analysis: Artificial intelligence (AI) in high school education." *Jurnal Ilmiah Pendidikan dan Pembelajaran* 7, no. 1 (2023): 112-123.

Tubella, A., Andrea, M. M.-C., & Nieves, J. C. (2024). How to teach responsible AI in Higher Education: Challenges and opportunities. *Ethics and Information Technology*, *26*(1), 3. DOI: 10.1007/s10676-023-09733-7

Uribe, S. E., Maldupa, I., Kavadella, A., El Tantawi, M., Chaurasia, A., Fontana, M., Marino, R., Innes, N., & Schwendicke, F. (2024). Artificial intelligence chatbots and large language models in dental education: Worldwide survey of educators. *European Journal of Dental Education*, *28*(4), 865–876. DOI: 10.1111/eje.13009

Vartiainen, H., Valtonen, T., Kahila, J., & Tedre, M. (2025). ChatGPT and imaginaries of the future of education: Insights of Finnish teacher educators. *Information and Learning Science*, *126*(1/2), 75–90. DOI: 10.1108/ILS-10-2023-0146

Verma, M. (2018). Artificial intelligence and its scope in different areas with special reference to the field of education. *Online Submission*, *3*(1), 5–10.

Vrouwenvelder, K., Raia, N. H., & Thomer, A. K. (2025). Obstacles to Dataset Citation Using Bibliographic Management Software. *Data Science Journal, 24*, 24. DOI: 10.5334/dsj-2025-017

Walters, W. H. (2025). Gauging scholars' acceptance of Open Access journals by examining the relationship between perceived quality and citation impact. *Science, 9*(4), 1–18.

Wang, C., Wang, H., Li, Y., Dai, J., Gu, X., & Yu, T. (2025). Factors influencing university students' behavioral intention to use generative artificial intelligence: Integrating the theory of planned behavior and AI literacy. *International Journal of Human-Computer Interaction, 41*(11), 6649–6671. DOI: 10.1080/10447318.2024.2383033

Ye, J.-H., He, Z., Bai, B., & Wu, Y.-F. (2024). Sustainability of Technical and Vocational Education and Training (TVET) along with Vocational Psychology. *Behavioral Sciences (Basel, Switzerland), 14*(10), 859. DOI: 10.3390/bs14100859

Yim, I. H. Y., & Su, J. (2025). Artificial intelligence (AI) learning tools in K-12 education: A scoping review. *Journal of Computers in Education, 12*(1), 93–131.

Zafrullah, Z., Meisya, A., & Ayuni, R. T. (2024). Artificial intelligence as a learning media in English education: Bibliometric using biblioshiny analysis (2009-2023). *ELTR Journal, 8*(1), 71–81. DOI: 10.37147/eltr.v8i1.179

Chapter 14
AI Tools for Writing and Editing in Academia and Research

Shilpi Lavania
https://orcid.org/0000-0001-8923-1646
Institute of Engineering and Technology, Dr. Bhimrao Ambedkar University, Agra, India

A. K. Verma
Hindustan College of Science and Technology, Farah, India

Rex B. Basuel
Pangasinan State University, Philippines

ABSTRACT

Artificial intelligence has revolutionized academic and research fields. Writing and editing in the creative, professional, and academic spheres are now being transformed by the application of Artificial Intelligence (AI) tools. Some AI tools like Natural Language Processing (NLP) and Large Language Models (LLMs) such as GPT, are providing content generation, summarization, and paraphrasing with high fluency and coherence. This chapter provides in-depth information about the NLP and LLMs. This chapter examines the role and applications of various available AI tools in drafting, paraphrasing and summarizing technical content with appropriate examples. This chapter also discusses various AI tools for editing which ensure domain-specific terminology, accuracy, style consistency, adherence to documentation standards, plagiarismfree text and tools to enhance the human like writing style with tone adjustment of the document. This chapter also provides a deep understanding of the prompt engineering.

1. INTRODUCTION

The rapid evolution of Artificial Intelligence (AI) has instigated a significant transformation across several fields. Academia and research are also no exception. In recent years, the integration of AI has brought a striking paradigm shift in knowledge creation, refinement, and dispersion

DOI: 10.4018/979-8-3373-5601-3.ch014

(Clemson University, n.d.). Advanced tools have been developed that offers refine writing quality and facilitate research process. These advanced developments and integration of the technology are proven to be a great assistance to students, faculty, and researchers alike, offering tools that can enhance writing quality and streamline the research process. (Nasution et al., 2024). This technological wave promises to redefine the boundaries of scholarly productivity and innovation, presenting both unprecedented opportunities and new challenges for the global research community.

Advanced technologies like Large Language Models (LLMs) and Natural Language Processing (NLP) are at the core of this transformation. NLP provides the foundational framework that enables machines to comprehend, interpret, and manipulate human language, while LLMs, such as the well-known Generative Pre-trained Transformer (GPT) models, serve as powerful engines trained on enormous text and code datasets. Together, these technologies have enabled a new generation of tools that can generate content, summarize and paraphrase with remarkable coherence precision and fluency, fundamentally changing the landscape of academic communication. (Launonen et al., 2024).

The integration of AI into the academic workflow offers dual benefits: it increases the efficiency of the research process while simultaneously improves the quality of the written work. Grammar correction, plagiarism detection, and citation formatting that once use to be considered as laborious and time-consuming tasks are now automated by AI-driven tools. These tools facilitate the researchers to concentrate on the more intellectually demanding aspects of their work, such as conceptual development and critical analysis. (Sadang & Palompon, 2021). For example, AI can assist in the initial stages of research by helping to generating and refining search terms or by creating concept maps to visualize the complex connections between different sources, promoting a more thorough and sophisticated comprehension of the existing literature. (Clemson University, n.d.).

However, there are complications and worries associated with the increasing dependency on AI in academic writing. While these tools offer many advantages, they also raise serious concerns about academic integrity, the possibility of over-reliance, and the long-term effects on students' and researchers' development of critical thinking and writing abilities. (Lópes et al., 2024). The ethical considerations surrounding authorship, data privacy, and the originality of AI-generated content are at the center of this discussion. A balanced, knowledgeable viewpoint that appropriately uses AI's power is necessary to navigate this new terrain.

Therefore, this chapter aims to provide a comprehensive guide for academics and researchers exploring the rapidly evolving field of Artificial Intelligence (AI) in academic writing and research. It highlights the importance of Prompt Engineering in producing high-quality technical writing and gives a foundational understanding of the underlying technologies, such as Natural Language Processing (NLP) and Large Language Models (LLMs). The chapter further reviews a wide range of AI tools designed for writing, editing, paraphrasing, and image generation, supported with practical examples. Additionally, it addresses important concerns related to plagiarism detection and ethical writing practices in the era of AI. Overall, this chapter provides readers the knowledge and skills required to use AI tools effectively, responsibly, and ethically. Following are the key objectives of the chapter:

- It gives the fundamental ideas and applications of LLMs and NLP in academic and technical writing.

- It explains the fundamentals and importance of Prompt Engineering with appropriate examples.
- It identifies and evaluates important AI tools for writing, editing, paraphrasing, and image generation.
- Provides the significance of AI-based plagiarism detection systems and their importance in maintaining academic integrity.
- It discusses the essential ethical principles for responsible and effective application of AI in research and writing.

2. NATURAL LANGUAGE PROCESSING (NLP) AND ITS APPLICATIONS

Natural Language Processing (NLP) is a specialized field of artificial intelligence that provides computers the ability to comprehend, interpret, and generate meaningful and practical human language (Géron, 2017, Gaunov et al., 2024). It bridges the gap between computer comprehension and human communication; it enables machines to process speech and text like human. One of its key applications is automatic grammar and style correction, where programs like Grammarly and Language Tool examine content for tone, sentence structure, and grammatical problems to ensure high-quality writing. Additionally, researchers can use AI-based summarizing and paraphrasing tools to reduce the length of articles or rewrite challenging content without sacrificing its meaning.

Most of the AI-powered writing and editing applications rely on this fundamental technology to function. NLP enables a wide range of applications that are particularly beneficial for academic and research writing by enabling machines to process and analyze enormous volumes of text and speech data. A model of NLP system is shown in figure 1.

Figure 1. A basic NLP system Model

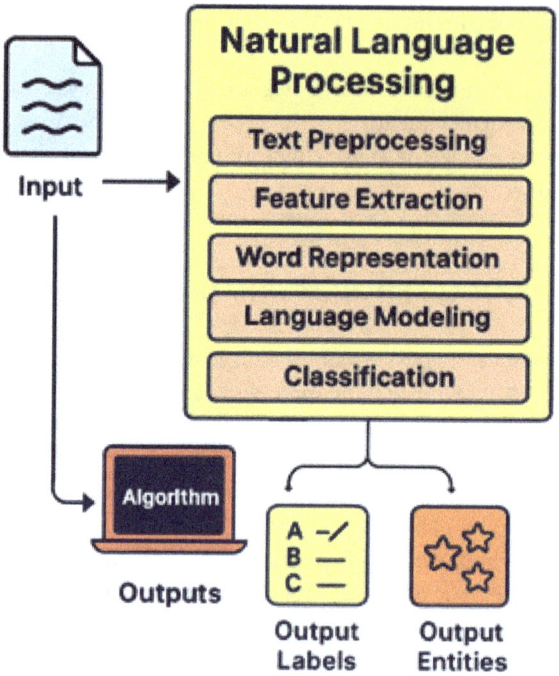

2.1 Key NLP Applications in Academic Writing and Research

NLP applications in AI tools have become integral part of writing and editing in the field of academic and research. These tools offer a variety of features from content generation to grammar checks and also improves efficiency, accuracy, and creativity in the writing process, The integration of AI in academic writing has not only streamlined the workflow but also has addressed challenges such as linguistic limitations and ethical concerns.

2.1.1 Content Generation and Enhancement

AI tools like ChatGPT and BARD are used for academic text creation, assisting idea generation, and in improving writing style. These technologies are especially helpful for writing preliminary research paper drafts because these can provide coherent and contextually relevant content. AI-driven applications also assist in content organization and structuring, ensuring logical flow and coherence in academic writing. (Khalifa & Albadawy, 2024).

2.1.2 Grammar and Style Improvement

Tools such as Grammarly utilizes NLP to provide grammar checks, style recommendations, and language improvements, which are essential for non-native English speakers and for maintaining high-quality academic writing standards (Guo & Zaini, 2024). These tools assist in enhancing the language, ensuring clarity, and improving the overall readability of academic documents. (Churi et al., 2022)). Figure 2 depicts the grammatical structure of sentences using syntactic parse trees.

Figure 2. An example of a syntactic parse tree, which models the grammatical structure of a sentence. This analysis is fundamental for grammar and style improvement tools. Adapted from "Speech and Language Processing," by D. Jurafsky and J. H. Martin, 2025, Prentice Hall.

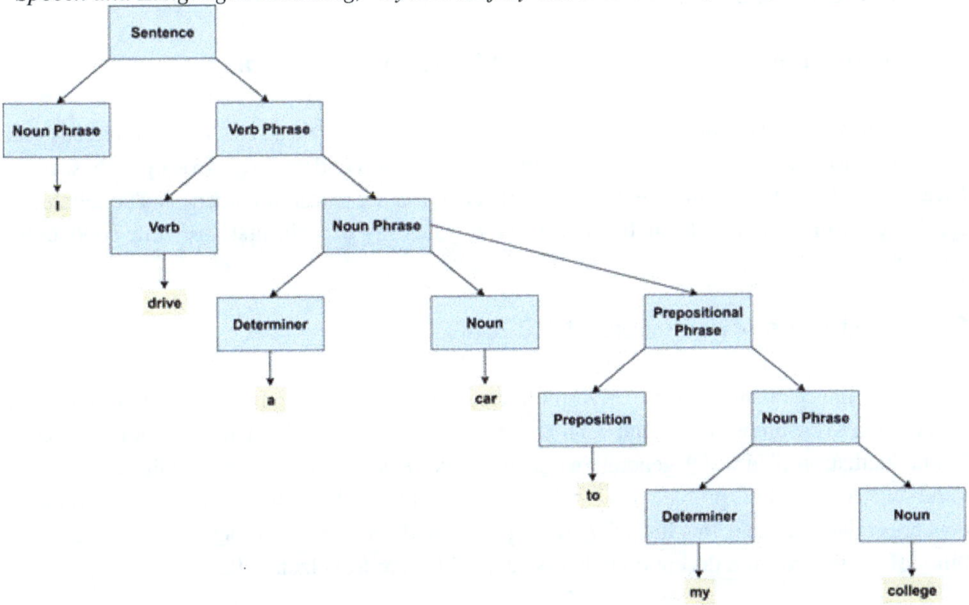

2.1.3 Literature Review and Data Analysis

Automated literature searches and data synthesis are made possible by AI technologies, which drastically reduces the time needed for these processes. This is accomplished by using advanced NLP methods that can process and analyse huge volume of text. (Effah Kwabena, 2023). Additionally, NLP tools facilitate literature synthesis and critical analysis. These tools help researchers by providing thorough insights and summaries. (Agrawal, 2024).

2.1.4 Editing and Formatting

AI tools help in document editing and formatting, ensuring that specific academic standards and guidelines are followed. This covers the generation of bibliographies and citation management(Biondi-Zoccai, 2025). By streamlining the editing process, these programs saves the time of and allow them to concentrate more on the quality of the text rather than formatting specifics (Khalifa & Albadawy, 2024).

2.1.5 Ethical Considerations and Challenges

On the one hand where AI tools offer numerous advantages, they also pose ethical challenges such as potential biases in training datasets and the risk of over dependency on AI-generated content. These issues necessitate proper guidelines to be formed and deployed for the responsible application and uses of AI. (Guo & Zaini, 2024). The excessive use of AI also raises serious concern about the loss of critical thinking skills and the ambiguity in authorship accountability (Biondi-Zoccai et al., 2025).

2.2 **Current Limitations, Biases, and Mitigation Strategies**

The substantial advantages of AI-powered NLP tools have attracted the academicians and researchers to enhance efficiency of the writing in academics and research. However, these tools have several limitations and potential biases that can impact research outcomes. The reliability and integrity of the research can be improved by addressing these limitations while conducting research.

2.2.1 Limitations of AI-Powered NLP Tools

Over-reliance on automation can result in errors because AI systems frequently need human supervision to ensure accuracy and context-appropriate operation (Memarian & Doleck, 2024). "AI hallucinations," in which generative models generate outputs that are misleading or factually unreliable, are a serious problem (Sakib, 2024). Additionally, the application of AI raises ethical concerns related to academic integrity. The AI generated content sometimes increases the possibility of plagiarized and deception (Elaiess, 2024; Meça & Shkëlzeni, 2023).

2.2.2 Potential Biases in AI-Powered NLP Tools

NLP algorithms can inherit and amplify biases from their training data, leading to skewed results that misinterpret some populations or perspectives (Flores, 2023). For instance, unfair treatment and the maintenance of stereotypes might be caused by gender bias. Repeatability and dependability of research findings may be impacted by algorithmic bias introduced during model building, particularly when the training of the model is done on limited datasets. (Samala & Rawas, 2024).

2.2.3 Strategies to Address Limitations and Biases

Combining human expertise with AI tools through effective oversight and collaboration helps to reduce errors and ensure appropriate contextual outputs (Memarian & Doleck, 2024; Rashidov & Rashidova, 2024). It's also crucial to provide reliable tools for bias detection and elimination using a variety of datasets and applying different mitigation strategies(Guo & Zaini,

2024). Establishing ethical frameworks and guidelines can help govern the use of AI, promoting transparency and accountability (Elaiess, 2024; Rashidov & Rashidova, 2024). Lastly, improving researchers' AI literacy through instruction and training can encourage more responsible and efficient use of these tools.

3. LARGE LANGUAGE MODELS (LLMs) IN TECHNICAL CONTENT CREATION

LLMs are a class of artificial intelligence models designed to understand, develop, and manipulate the human language in an exceedingly sophisticated manner. Deep learning architectures, notably the Transformer model, proposed by Vaswani in 2017(Vaswani et al., 2017), serve as the foundation for LLMs. These models are trained on huge volumes of textual data from a diverse source, including books, research papers, websites, and other written materials. The core principle behind LLMs is their ability to predict the subsequent word in a sequence, which allows them to generate coherent and contextually relevant content. Over time, these models have evolved to manage increasingly complicated linguistic tasks, such as answering queries, summarising documents, translating languages, and engaging in conversations. (Geroimenko, 2025).

The ability of Large language models to understand precise linguistic patterns, such as idiomatic expressions, syntactic structures, and semantic links between words, is one of the key innovations in their development. To achieve this understanding, the model utilizes billions or even trillions of parameters, which are numerical values that help to assess the importance of particular words and phrases according to their context. As a result, LLMs are capable of performing tasks such as inference, conclusions, and reasoning over extended passages rather than simple text generation. However, their effectiveness heavily relies on diversity of the training data. The effectiveness of these models may introduce biases if the data is inaccurate or not indicative. (Geroimenko, 2025).

Despite their significant potential, LLMs also pose unique challenges. These are probabilistic models and do not rely on actual knowledge but instead, they use patterns identified in data. This can lead to issues like generating false information, providing overconfident yet inaccurate responses, or failing to recognize their own knowledge gaps. Additionally, the substantial computing power required to train and run LLMs raises concerns regarding the models' accessibility and their potential environmental effects. However, as more research in this area is conducted, LLMs could further transform various industries, including communication, healthcare, education and entertainment, by improving human–computer interaction in unprecedented ways. (Geroimenko, 2025).

3.1 Fundamentals of LLM

The Transformer architecture, which serves as the foundation for large language models (LLMs), makes use of self-attention mechanisms to understand the relationships between words and phrases, irrespective of their distance in the text. Figure 3 illustrates the various steps involved in content generation, a flow chart of various steps involved in content generation using LLM (Brown et al., 2020; "Daniel Jurafsky and James H. Martin, 2025; Ouyang et al., 2022) and Figure 4 shows a Transformer upon which LLMs are built.

Figure 3. Steps of content generation using LLMs

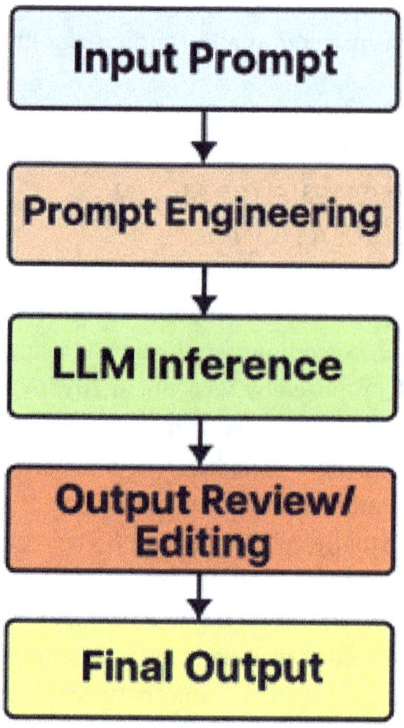

Figure 4. Conceptual workflow of a transformer used in LLMs

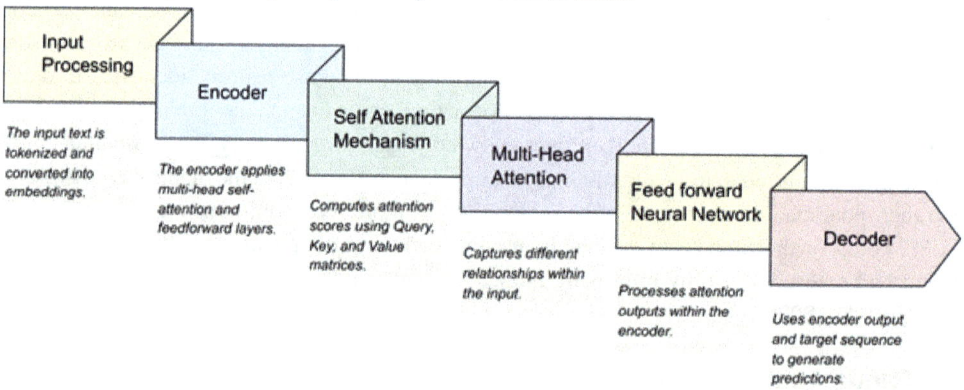

Preprocessing and Input

i. A text as a prompt that "Explain cloud computing in simple terms," is entered as input by the user.

ii. To standardize formatting, punctuation, and characters, the system performs text normalization.
iii. Text normalization ensures, the input is processed consistently before being sent to the neural network.

Tokenization

i. Byte pair encoding (BPE) or sentence piece is used to divide the text into discrete parts known as tokens.
ii. Example: "Cryogenic temperatures refer to extremely low temperatures."-> ["Cryogenic", "temperatures", "refers", "to", "extremely", "low", "temperatures", "."].
iii. Every token is associated with a distinct numeric ID that the model recognizes.

Positional and Embedding Encoding

i. Token IDs when transformed into dense numerical representations that capture meaning, are known as embedding vectors.
ii. The addition of positional encodings maintains the sequence's word order.
iii. This results in a numerical matrix that represents the meaning of words and order.

Transformer Layers

i. The embeddings are passed through multiple transformer blocks, each containing:

Multi-Head Self-Attention: Calculates how each word relates to others in the sentence.

Where, Q, K, V are query, key and value matrices respectively. is dimensionality of key vectors,
Feed-Forward Network (FFN): Adds non-linear transformations for deeper understanding.
Residual Connections & Normalization: Maintain gradient stability and coherence across layers.

ii. After several layers, the model produces a context vector representing the overall meaning of the prompt.

Context Encoding

The final representation of every token, after going through N levels, forms a context vector, that serves as a comprehensive numerical synthesis of the prompt. This vector encodes:

i. Grammar and syntax

ii. Relationships with semantics
iii. Knowledge of the world (from pretraining)
iv. Context and intent

Decoding: Token-by-Token Generation

Now, in the autoregressive generation phase, the model predicts one token at a time. For each step t:

i. Determine the probability distribution across all potential subsequent tokens:

ii. Apply the top-p, top-k, temperature, and penalties output configuration settings.
iii. Choose or sample the next token that seems most likely.
iv. To the input sequence, append that token.
v. For the following prediction, feed it back into the model.

This continues until a stop condition, a stop string, limit length, or end-of-sequence (EOS) token is satisfied.

Sampling and Output Configuration

In this stage parameters mentioned in Table 1 are tuned to guide the decoder to traverse the probability landscape:

Table 1. Backend parameters which are tuned

Parameters	Functions
Temperature	Controls randomness in sampling
Top-k / Top-p	Restricts next-token candidates
Frequency / Presence Penalties	Restricts next-token candidates
Stop Sequences	Forces output cutoff
Max Tokens	Limits length

Detokenization

In this step the model detokenizes the earlier generated token IDs and converts the numeric IDs into words that can be read by humans with the help of vocabulary map.

Output post-processing

This step performs grammar correction and formatting. This step also filters and checks for privacy, toxicity or bias detection concerns.

Reinforcement Learning from Human Feedback (RLHF)

i. Models are fine-tuned using RLHF, where human annotators rate responses.
ii. The model is then optimized (via Proximal Policy Optimization, PPO) to maximize expected human satisfaction.

3.2 Major LLMs

- **GPT4/ GPT 5 (Open AI):** GPT models are general-purpose LLMs created by OpenAI that are employed in code generation, reasoning, and content production. Trained using multimodal data (text, image, and code) and trillions of text tokens. Better contextual awareness, reasoning, and adaptive memory for challenging tasks are all introduced by GPT-5.
- **PaLM 2 (Google DeepMind):** PaLM 2 belongs to Google's large model series, which are utilized in Bard, the company's AI chatbot. It enables a wide range of applications, including knowledge- based tasks, reasoning, and translation. Versions of PaLM 2 vary in size and functionality (e.g., Gecko,Otter, Bison).
- **Gemini (Google DeepMind):** Google's next-generation big models include Gemini, which is the replacement for PaLM. Integrated into Google products like Bard and other enterprise AI solutions, it is made for increased generalization and multimodal capabilities.
- **Claude 4.5 (Anthropic):** The most recent Claude model, Claude Sonnet 4.5, was released in September 2025. It is a strong hybrid reasoning model that excels in computer usage and coding and may be used to create sophisticated AI agents. Opus 4 and Sonnet 4, the latter of which was released in May 2025, were part of the Claude 4 family, which it builds upon.
- **LLaMA (Meta):** LLaMa 4, the most recent version, was made available by Meta in April 2025. The LLaMa 4 series of models come in several sizes and is multimodal, which means it can handle both images and text. Among the variations are LLaMa 4 Maverick, which has more parameters, and LLaMa 4 Scout, which has a wide context window.
- **Grok (xAI):** Grok 4 is the latest model which was released in July 2025. The Grok 4 Fast, a more contemporary model, was released in September 2025. With its sophisticated reasoning, real-time data integration, and native tool usage, Grok 4 and Grok 4 Fast offer a substantial performance boost that enables it to solve complicated problems with ease and produce cutting-edge results on academic benchmarks.
- *Falcon 180B, including the Falcon 2 and Falcon 3 series (Technology Innovation Institute, UAE)*

Falcon 180B (2023): 3.5 trillion tokens from the Refined Web dataset were used to train the first large scale open-weight model, which had 180 billion parameters. By utilizing a decoder only Transformer with rotary position embeddings (RoPE), it achieves reasoning and multilingual performance that is on par with GPT-3.5.

Falcon 2 Series (2024): This generation, which was released in parameter variations 11B and 40B, improved speed and efficiency by introducing Mixture of Experts (MoE) and multi-query attention. Falcon 2 models are appropriate for real-time inference and applications such as code generation, RAG, and conversational AI since they support quantization.

Falcon 3 Series (2025): Falcon's capabilities will be extended to multimodal understanding (text, image, and audio) in the next version. With emphasis on factual alignment, long-context processing, and instruction tailoring, it seeks to compete with more sophisticated systems like GPT-4 and Gemini 1.5.

4 IMPORTANCE OF PROMPT ENGINEERING

The ability of users to effectively communicate with an AI model is a critical aspect of any AI-driven content-generating system. This communication gap is bridged by prompt engineering, which transforms human intent into a structured input format that machine learning algorithms, particularly large language models (LLMs), can understand accurately. Prompt engineering is the science of creating, evaluating, and refining prompts to get the most accurate, inventive, and relevant results from an AI model. It is not just about providing instructions (Geroimenko, 2025; Oppenlaender et al., 2024).

A large language model utilizes the input as a text prompt (sometimes with additional modalities like image prompts) that the model uses to predict a particular output. For writing a prompt it doesn't require anyone to be an expert in data science or machine learning. However, writing an effective prompt can be challenging sometimes. For a model, its training data, configurations, word choice, style and tone, structure, and context are all important factors that impact the efficacy of the model response to the prompt as input. Consequently, the process of quick engineering is iterative. The model's capacity to produce useful results may be hampered by inadequate prompts, which might result in unclear and wrong responses (Geroimenko, 2025; Lee & Palmer, 2025).

4.1 Prompting Techniques

Recall from the previous section which clearly states that an LLM is a prediction engine. After receiving sequential text as input, the model uses the data it was trained on to predict what the next token should be. By appending the previously predicted token to the end of the sequential text to predict the subsequent token, the LLM is operationalized to perform this action repeatedly. The link between what was in the prior tokens and what the LLM saw during training is the basis for the subsequent token prediction. The act of creating excellent prompts that direct LLMs to provide precise outputs is known as prompt engineering. This procedure entails experimenting to determine the ideal prompt, maximizing prompt length, and assessing a prompt's structure and writing style considering the assignment. LLMs are not completely accurate. They can predict the next likely text more accurately if the prompt text is clear. Additionally, certain methods that leverage on the training and operation of LLMs will assist in obtaining appropriate results from LLMs. Following are the various prompting techniques (Geroimenko, 2025; Lee Boonstra, 2024):

• General Prompting/ Zero-Shot

A special case of general prompting known as "zero-shot prompting". It is used when the model completes the task without the use of an example or specific training data. Instead, it utilizes its semantic knowledge of natural language instructions to infer how to do the task.

Prompt: Classify the sentiment of this review: "The movie was outstanding and emotional."
Output: POSITIVE
Model: GPT-5 Mini OpenAI

• One-shot and few-shot

Examples are useful when developing prompts for AI models. These examples can help the model in understanding the request. When it is required to guide the model toward a specific output structure or pattern, examples are particularly helpful.

One-shot: As the name suggests, a one-shot prompt only offers one example. The idea is that the model can best accomplish the task by imitating an example.

One-shot Prompt: Translate the following English sentence to Hindi.
Example: English: "Hello"
Hindi: "Namskar"
Now Translate this: English: "Good morning"
hindi:?
Output: " "
Model: GPT-5 Mini OpenAI

Few-shot: A few-shot technique assists the model by giving it several examples. This method demonstrates a pattern that the model must follow. Although the concept is like one-shot, the probability that the model will follow the pattern is increased when the desired pattern is reflected in the examples several times.

Few-shot Prompt: Translate the following English sentences to Hindi.

Example 1:

English: "Hello"
Hindi: "Namaskar"

Example 2:

English: "How are you?"
Hindi: " ?"

Example 3:

English: “Good morning”
Hindi “ ”
Now translate this:
English: “Good night”
Hindi:?
Output: “ ”
Model: GPT-5 Mini OpenAI

- System, Contextual and Role prompting

System Prompting: The language model's general context and goal are established via system prompting. It outlines the “big picture” of what the model must accomplish, such as categorizing reviews or translating languages.

Example:
System Prompt: You are an expert German translator. Always translate English sentences into formal German and do not include any kind of explanations. The only task is to translate English to German language.
User Prompt: It's a beautiful morning today.
Output: “Es ist heute ein schöner Morgen”.

□ Contextual Prompting

Contextual prompting offers particulars or background knowledge relevant to the task or discourse at hand. It enables the model to understand the complex nature of the question and modify the solution appropriately.

Example:

Contextual Prompt: Today the newly admitted students are coming to university to attend induction program. You are writing a welcome speech for these students. The speech must be inspiring, innovative and warm.

User Prompt: Write a short welcome note.

Output:

“Dear Students,

A very warm welcome to our university! Today marks the beginning of an exciting journey filled with learning, discovery, and growth. Embrace every opportunity, stay curious, and believe in your potential. Together, let’s create memories, explore new ideas, and shape a future full of success and inspiration.

Welcome to your new beginning!”

□ Role Prompting

The language model is given a certain identity or character to assume through role prompting. This helps the model in producing answers that align with the designated role and the knowledge and behaviour that go along with it.

Example:

Role Prompt: You are a professional career counsellor with 15 years of experience guiding college students.

User Prompt: I am a final year student of electronics & communication engineering branch. I am very confused about the job-oriented course which I should take.

Output: Since you are in Electronics & Communication Engineering (ECE), there are several job-oriented courses that can enhance your employability and align with current industry trends. Here's a short, focused version of career guidance for an ECE final-year student:

Top Job-Oriented Courses for ECE Students

- o Embedded Systems & Hardware
- o Embedded Systems Design, VLSI, FPGA Programming
- o Software & Programming
- o Python/ C++, IoT Software Development
- o Networking & Communication
- o 5G, Network Security, IoT Networking
- o Emerging Technologies
- o AI/ ML for Embedded Systems, Robotics, Cloud/ Edge Computing
- o Certifications
- o CCNA/ CCNP, ARM/Intel Embedded, AWS IoT/ Cloud

Tip: Focus on 1–2 areas of interest, do hands-on projects, and combine with certifications for better job prospects.

• Step-back prompting

Asking the AI to halt, analyse or reconsider before responding is known as step-back prompting. You can "step back" to examine reasoning, clarify assumptions, or break a problem down into smaller parts rather than leaping directly to a solution. This frequently increases accuracy, particularly for difficult or complex topics.

Step-back Prompt: Before finding the range of a projectile motion launched at 25 m/s at 45 degrees, recall the formula for projectile motion. Then compute step-by-step before giving the result.

Output:

Recall the formula (step-back): Where R is range, u is launch speed, $\theta$is launch angle, and g is gravitational acceleration. Identify values:

Round (practical): $R \approx 63.78$ m (assuming no air resistance, level ground).

- Chain of Thought (CoT) Prompting

A method for enhancing LLMs' thinking ability is Chain of Thought (CoT) prompting, which creates intermediate reasoning processes. As a result, the LLM produces more precise responses.

CoT Prompt: A is taller than B, and B is taller than C. Who is the shortest? Think step-by-step before answering.

Output:

Chain of Thought:

A > B > C (in height).
The last person in order is the shortest.
Final Answer: C.

- Tree of Thoughts (ToT) Prompting

Tree of Thoughts prompting expands on Chain of Thought (CoT) prompting. ToT allows the model to explore several potential reasoning branches, resembling a tree, rather than just following a single linear reasoning path. The model then determines which branch leads to the optimal solution. It enables the model to think more like a human brainstorming, weighing several possibilities, quickly examining each, and then selecting the most sensible or ideal course of action.

Tree of Thoughts Prompt: List two or three different strategies to reduce city pollution, analyse their pros and cons, and choose the best one.

Output:

Strategies:

Promote public transport — less traffic & emissions.
Enforce industrial emission norms — quick air quality gains.
Encourage electric vehicles — long-term clean transport.

Best:

A mix of better public transport + EV promotion gives effective and sustainable pollution reduction.

4.2 Importance of Prompt Engineering for Content Generation in Research and Education with Example

Prompt engineering has gained momentum in many fields, but its potential is arguably most revolutionary in the field of academics and research. Large Language Models (LLMs) are being used by academicians and researchers more than ever before for a variety of tasks, including creating literature reviews, coding simulations, summarizing complex scientific articles, and even creating quiz questions or grant submissions.

4.2.1 Prompt Engineering in Research

• *Transforming Research Workflows*

Prompt engineering enables researchers to extract more precise, appropriate, and insightful outputs from huge language models and other generative AI systems. Through a well-structured prompt, researchers can boost productivity and save time for critical analysis by automating repetitive operations such as translation, information extraction and for generating summaries. (Chen et al., 2025; *Prompt Engineering: Overview and Guide*, 2025).

• *Enhancing Accuracy and Reproducibility*

• Careful rapid engineering has improved the accuracy and dependability of AI-generated results. This is essential in research environments where repeatability and transparency are crucial. For example, in the field of chemistry, researchers have applied rapid engineering as discussed to prevent model "hallucinations" and enhance the reasoning capabilities of AI assistants when analyzing experimental data and synthesizing literature. (Luo et al., 2025; Shah, 2025).

• *Risks and Scientific rigor*

• The careless use of rapid engineering methods poses serious risks such as the generation of feedback loops, overfitting hypotheses, and unverifiable results. Thus, to prevent biases and ensuring reliable outcomes, rapid engineering in scientific research must adhere to strict, transparent, and recurring methods. (Shah, 2025).

Examples:

Target: Literature Review and Knowledge Discovery

Prompt: "Summarize five peer-reviewed papers published between 2022–2024 on machine learning applications in structural health monitoring, highlighting methodology and outcomes."

Target: Research Design and Hypothesis Generation

Prompt: "Suggest three research hypotheses related to renewable energy storage, based on recent advancements in lithium-ion battery technology."

Target: Data Analysis and Interpretation

Prompt: "Interpret the following regression results and explain whether the independent variables significantly affect the dependent variable at 5% significance."

4.2.2 Prompt Engineering in Education

Teaching and Curriculum Design

- Prompt engineering helps teachers in quickly creating structured lesson plans, relevant examples, and learning materials. It allows educators to align curricular objectives and student learning levels with AI-generated content. Well-organized content increases the student engagement in the classroom and saves preparation time. (Lee & Palmer, 2025; Leung, 2024).

Prompt Example: "Design a 30-minute lecture plan on P-n Junction diode for engineering first year students, including applications of the diode."

• *Supporting Personalized Learning*

AI can modify explanations according to a learner's age, background, or comprehension when prompts are effective. Depending on their needs, students receive notes, tests, or condensed explanations. This encourages self-directed learning and enhances understanding for a variety of learners (Federiakin et al., 2024).

Prompt Example: "Explain the concept of creation of depletion layer in a P-n junction diode."

• *Improving Critical Thinking and Creativity*

Encouraging students to explore, analyse, and generate ideas by using AI questions fosters creativity. Students can create essay ideas, compare different perspectives, or simulate real-world situations. This approach enhances critical thinking and innovative problem-solving skills. (Federiakin et al., 2024).

Prompt Example: "Explain how a P–N junction diode behaves under forward and reverse bias and discuss the current flow."

• *Teacher Training for AI integration in Classroom*

Prompt engineering assists teachers understand how to successfully integrate AI into their teaching. AI-generated training materials can highlight advanced classroom techniques and modern teaching practices. This technological development allows teachers to maintain their creative and technological proficiency. (Sharon Hall, n.d.).

Prompt Example: "Create a workshop plan for teachers on integrating AI tools like ChatGPT into daily teaching."

5 AI TOOLS FOR WRITING AND EDITING

Artificial intelligence (AI) systems have completely changed the way individuals write, edit, and convey ideas. The way individuals write, edit, and communicate ideas has been completely transformed by artificial intelligence (AI) systems. These tools analyze text, correct grammar, and improve clarity by utilizing machine learning and natural language processing (NLP) techniques. With minimal effort, they assist users in generating organized, logical, and professional documents. AI tools are particularly helpful in efficient drafting of theses and articles in academic and research contexts. They provide valuable suggestions for enhancing vocabulary, tone, and style. Additionally, they save time by automating tedious tasks, formatting and proofreading. As a result, writers can focus more on creativity, critical thinking, and the quality of their work. In today's digital academic environment, AI-powered writing and editing tools have become essential. This section provides information about various tools available for content creation, paraphrasing, grammar, clarity, and image generation.

5.1 AI Tools for Content Generation

Digital communication and creativity have evolved primarily due to AI technologies for content generation. From blogs, articles, and essays to advertisements and social media captions, natural language processing can produce a wide range of content with excellent fluency and context awareness. These AI-powered tools enhance output, maintain consistency, and ensure content quality, providing valuable support to researchers, writers, and marketers. AI-powered solutions also assess user intent, optimize for search engines, and modify tone or style to appeal to audiences. They enable content creators to concentrate more on strategy, creativity, and innovation by automating repetitive writing activities. Table 2 provides a list of AI tools available for generating content.

Table 2. AI tools available for generating content

Sl. No.	Tools	Specifications	Source
1	ChatGPT	Multi-style writing, brainstorming, drafting, rewriting	https://chat.openai.com/
2	Surfer AI	SEO insights, competitor analysis, collaborative editing	https://surferseo.com/
3	Jasper	voice adaption, multilingual	https://www.jasper.ai/
4	Hyperwrite	AutoWrite, TypeAhead, research assistant, personalization	https://www.hyperwriteai.com/
5	Bramework	Keyword recommendations (Semrush), outlines, WordPress	https://www.bramework.com/
6	Perplexity AI	Real-time info retrieval with source citations, summarization, conversational search; emerging creative features	https://www.perplexity.ai/
7	GitHub Copilot	AI-assisted code and technical content generation: docs, comments, code explanations, test case writing	https://github.com/features/copilot

5.2 AI Tools for Content Paraphrasing

AI tools for content paraphrasing have become essential for writers, researchers, and students seeking to rephrase text effectively while preserving its original meaning. These technologies examine phrase structures and semantics using machine learning techniques and natural language processing (NLP) to produce original, plagiarism-free content. They aid in improving readability, clarity, and audience-appropriate tone and complexity. In fields where originality and accuracy are crucial, such as academic writing, content marketing, and SEO, paraphrasing tools are quite helpful. AI-powered paraphrasers save time, preserve coherence, and guarantee that concepts are presented in original and captivating ways by automating linguistic transformation.

To accommodate various writing requirements, they also provide a variety of rewriting modes, including formal, creative, and brief. For further improvement, a lot of tools additionally offer synonym recommendations and grammar correction. They let non-native speakers communicate ideas in a natural and fluid way. Content authenticity is ensured through integration with plagiarism detectors. All things considered, AI paraphrasing tools are essential allies in the current digital writing environment. Table 3 shows various AI tools available for content paraphrasing.

Table 3. AI tools available for content paraphrasing

Sl. No.	Tools	Specifications	Website
1	QuillBot	Multiple paraphrasing modes (Standard, Fluency, Creative), synonym suggestions, fine control over rephrasing depth	https://quillbot.com
2	Paraphraser.io	Accurate paraphrasing, multilingual support, intelligent synonym replacement	https://paraphraser.io
3	SEO Tools Centre	SEO-focused paraphrasing to maintain keyword density	https://seotoolscentre.com/paraphrasing-tool
4	Wordtune	Contextual grammar, tone and style preservation, human-like paraphrasing	https://www.wordtune.com
5	WordAi	Plagiarism-free rewriting, machine learning-based content understanding	https://www.wordai.com
6	Spinbot	Automatic text rewriting, simple and free to use	https://spinbot.com
7	Grammarly	AI paraphrasing with grammar and clarity improvement	https://www.grammarly.com/grammarly-paraphrasing-tool

5.3 AI Tools for Grammer, Clarity and Style

To improve the calibre and professionalism of written communication, artificial intelligence tools for grammar, clarity, and style are essential. These programs identify grammar mistakes, punctuation problems, and difficult phrasing by utilizing deep learning algorithms, artificial intelligence, and natural language processing (NLP). They include recommendations for enhancing sentence structure, clarity, tone, and readability in addition to basic correction. Students, professionals, and content producers frequently utilize these tools to polish manuscripts and guarantee flawless writing. Numerous AI writing assistants enable users speak more effectively, confidently, and in a polished, reader-friendly way by offering real-time feedback, context-based suggestions, and tone adjustments. Table 4 provides various tools available for grammar and styling.

Table 4. AI tools available for Grammer, Clarity and Style

Sl. No.	Tools	Specifications	Website
1	Grammarly	Advanced grammar, spelling, tone detection, style improvements, plagiarism check	https://www.grammarly.com
2	LanguageTool	Multilingual grammar and style checker, AI sentence rephraser, custom style guide	https://languagetool.org
3	Wordtune	Contextual grammar and clarity improvements, tone adjustment, paraphrasing	https://www.wordtune.com
4	Antidote	Grammar and style correction, dictionaries, writing guides, bilingual English/French support	https://antidote.info
5	Hemingway Editor	Focus on readability, sentence structure, simplicity, adverbs, passive voice	https://hemingwayapp.com

continued on following page

Table 4. Continued

Sl. No.	Tools	Specifications	Website
6	Trinka	Academic and technical writing focus, advanced grammar checks, style, word count optimization	https://www.trinka.ai
7	Ahrefs Grammar Checker	Grammar, punctuation, style fixes, rewriting and expanding suggestions	https://ahrefs.com/writing-tools/grammar-checker

5.4 AI Tools for Image Generation

Artificial intelligence (AI) techniques for image generation have transformed digital design, art, and creative media by allowing machines to create high quality images from basic text prompts or ideas. These tools, which are driven by sophisticated deep learning models like diffusion models and Generative Adversarial Networks (GANs), can produce realistic images, digital paintings, 3D representations, and abstract art in a matter of seconds. Their comprehension of context, style, colour composition, and viewpoint enables users to create personalized images for research, marketing, teaching, and enjoyment. While corporations employ AI for rapid content development and design prototyping, artists use it to explore new creative directions. Additionally, these tools are user-friendly and adaptable due to their editing options, which include upscaling, style transfer, and background replacement. By blending human imagination with machine intelligence, AI image generation tools democratize creativity, reduce production costs, and redefine the boundaries of visual expression in the digital age. Table 5 provides a list of AI Tools for Image Generation.

Table 5. AI tools available for Image Generation

Sl. No.	Tools	Specifications	Website
1	DALL·E 3	Handles long, complex prompts; conversational style; photorealistic and artistic image creation	https://openai.com/dall-e-3
2	Midjourney	High-quality artistic images; Discord and web app interface; subscription-based	https://midjourney.com
3	Adobe Firefly	Integrated with Adobe Creative Cloud; stylistic customization; editing tools	https://firefly.adobe.com
4	Stable Diffusion	Open source with extensive customization; downloadable and hosted platforms	https://stability.ai
5	Leonardo AI	Web and mobile apps; creator-friendly with various stylistic options	https://leonardo.ai
6	Freepik AI Image Generator	Combines newest AI image models; subscription includes many features	https://www.freepik.com/ai-image-generator
7	Canva AI Image Generator	Easy-to-use design tool with AI image creation; free and paid plans	https://www.canva.com/ai-image-generator
8	Meta AI	Integrated within Facebook, Instagram, WhatsApp; good for casual social media image creation	https://meta.ai
9	Nano Banana (Google Gemini)	Editing-focused AI image generator with integration in Google AI ecosystem	https://pollo.ai

6 PLAGIARISM AND ETHICAL CONSIDERATIONS

Plagiarism is defined as the act of presenting someone else's thoughts, words, information, or artistic creations as one's own without providing credit. This behaviour violates the principles of integrity, equity, and decency that are essential in both academic and professional environments. In the digital era, retrieving and replicating information has become easier due to the availability of plenty of online resources and availability of AI-based content creation tools. However, this convenience also increases the risk of both accidental and intentional plagiarism, highlighting the need for greater awareness and accountability among researchers, teachers, and students. In the process of avoiding plagiarism, ethical considerations also include maintaining transparency, properly citing original authors, guaranteeing the veracity of data reporting, and refraining or falsifying information.

In 2017, Merriam-Webster Online Dictionary stated the definition of Plagiarism as "to steal and pass off (the ideas or words of another) as one's own: use (another's production) without crediting the source (Merriam-Webster, 2025). Another striking definition was given by Stanford University in 2012 as "use, without giving reasonable and appropriate credit to or acknowledging the author or source, of another person's original work, whether such work is made up of code, formulas, ideas, language, research, strategies, writing, or other form". Plagiarism typically entails deceit and theft. Meuschke & Gipp (2013), however, believe that since plagiarism is not always deliberate, it is not always theft. Inadequate citation frequently leads to plagiarism (Meuschke & Gipp, 2013).

Few basic types of Plagiarism (AIJR, 2025.) that everyone scholar must be aware of to avoid it happening and enhance the quality of work are as follows:

Intentional Plagiarism: The most unethical kind of duplication is when somebody deliberately or intentionally commit plagiarism and is also referred as direct plagiarism. When someone purposefully takes content or writing work from another author and publishes it with their name, then it is called plagiarism. A researcher or scholar must be aware that there are two primary categories of intentional plagiarism. The first one is the Complete plagiarism, where all the text is reproduced and used in the new source. On the other hand, the second kind, sometimes referred to as partial plagiarism where some content is unique and some is copied from other sources (AIJR, 2025).

Source Manipulation: It is the kind of plagiarism when someone copies content from a specific source but cites it deceptively or with secondary references, it's known as source manipulation plagiarism. This is one of the more critical types of plagiarism and is sometimes referred to as deceptive citation. Misleading citations are illegal, and it affects the authenticity of the research.

Mosaic Plagiarism: "Mosaic plagiarism" is the practice of incorporating text and phrases from other sources into one's own writing and modifying sentences without providing credit or quotation marks. This kind of plagiarism is sometimes referred to as patchwriting, and it mostly happens when researchers fail to properly paraphrase.

Self-Plegirism: Recycling or reusing one's own specific words from previously published works is known as self-plagiarism. A writer's published work is, in fact, their intellectual property. However, one should be aware that this work can only be published or reused with correct citation. Otherwise, it will only have the same consequences as outright plagiarism.

Accidental Plagiarism: Accidental plagiarism is when author uses comparable terms, word groups, and/or sentence structures without giving credit, or when they fail to cite their sources, misquote them, or inadvertently paraphrase them. The author is indeed accountable for plagiarism even if they have no malicious intent. Unintentional plagiarism is treated with the same seriousness as other forms of plagiarism and carries the similar consequences.

6.1 AI Tools to detect plagiarism

Plagiarism has evolved in the digital age, expanding beyond basic copy-paste to paraphrasing, translation, and even work produced by artificial intelligence. Artificial intelligence has transformed plagiarism detection, yet traditional technologies frequently fall short of capturing these complexities. AI finds latent connections in meaning, structure, and style in addition to exact matches by using natural language processing (NLP), semantic analysis, and machine learning (ML). AI, therefore, emerges as a strong ally for publishers, scholars, and educators in preserving academic integrity and originality. AI based tools identify text plagiarism by a systematic procedure that uses natural language processing and complex algorithms to analyse incoming text against large databases, detecting skilled paraphrasing and noticeable copying. The flow chart depicted in the Figure 5 gives a clear illustration of the processing steps used by any AI tool in detection of plagiarism and AI generated content and Table 6 provides a list of AI tools to detect plagiarism.

Figure 5. Processing steps in detection of plagiarism and AI generated content

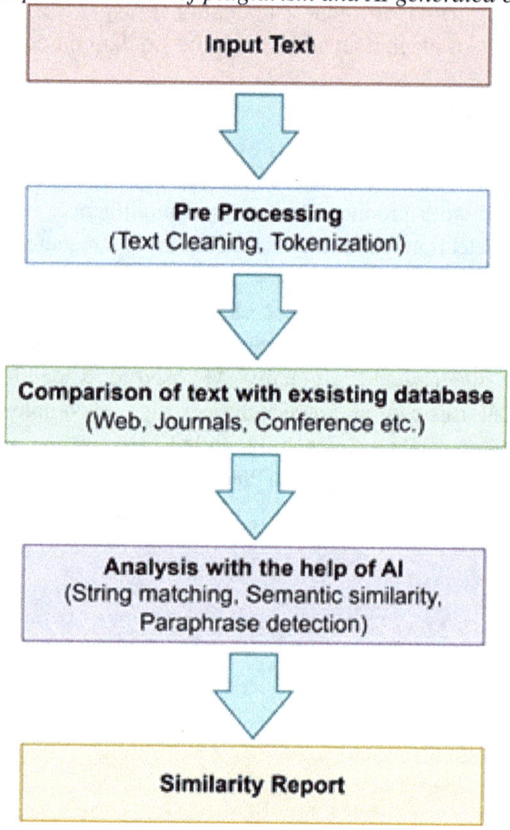

Table 6. Tools for Plagiarism detection

Sl. No.	Tools	Specifications	Reference
1	Turnitin	Plagiarism detection and AI text detection, good for academic and research.	https://www.turnitin.com/
2	Grammarly	Grammer help, AI text detection	https://www.grammarly.com/
3	Copyleaks	Plagiarism detection, AI text detection and it also supports the paraphrased content.	https://copyleaks.com/
4	Scribbr	Specially designed for academic and research for plagiarism detection as well as the AI generated content.	https://www.scribbr.com/
5	Prepostseo	Paraphrase detection, plagiarism checkers	https://www.prepostseo.com/
6	Winston AI	advanced plagiarism detection with AI-driven analysis	https://gowinston.ai/
7	GPTZero	AI Detector	https://www.zerogpt.com/

6.2 Writing Ethics in the era of AI

Writing in academics and research has completely transformed with the integration of AI In recent years. Technology adaption in Text generation, analysis, and distribution of information have introduced substantial changes in various academic and research field. The ability of AI to assist researchers in writing research papers is among its most fascinating scholarly uses. AI-powered solutions provide a wide range of capabilities, such as data analysis, literature review, drafting, and editing, which expedite the research process and increase productivity.

However, several ethical issues are raised with the increasing integration of AI into academia and research, which calls for cautious consideration (Ateriya et al., 2025; Chetwynd, 2024; Mondal & Mondal, 2023; Ong et al., 2024). Following are various cases published or reported in various newspaper or websites in academic or research writing where malicious use of AI has been found:

Case 1: Inaccurate authorship and misattributed AI-generated articles in GIJIR

According to a study, the Global International Journal of Innovative Research (GIJIR) published several AI-generated articles under the names of actual researchers who did not author them (Spinellis, 2025).

Case 2: Non-scientific illustrations

AI-generated figures that are medically futile or nonsensical imagery (such as grotesquely large rat genitals) were included in a Frontiers publication. The figures were produced via Midjourney which is a platform dedicated to image generation using prompts. In response to public criticism, it was later retracted (Elisabeth Bik, 2024).

Case 3: Regenerate Response artifacts

A Google researcher's paper on arXiv was withdrawn when people pointed out instances of plagiarism and AI-indicative sentences ("Regenerate response," etc.) that indicates the content was created by an LLM and used without the necessary disclosure.

Case 4: Neurosurgical Review 2024 / Saveetha University-retractions

Numerous commentaries, letters, and small articles were retracted because it was traced that these were being generated by large language models (LLMs) without disclosure, especially from authors affiliated with Saveetha University (Chellapandian & Jeyachandran, 2024).

These are few instances which have been listed, and these cases are increasing day by day. This shows that it is the right time to introduce some ethical measures for the use of AI in research and academic writing. The core ethical issues that AI has introduced in the academic writing and research are(OpenAI et al., 2024; UNESCO, 2021):

- AI-generated content may replicate patterns from existing data. This gives rise to plagiarism and doubts are being raised about originality of the research work.

- Responsibility for accuracy and accountability remains with the writer even if the content is AI generated.
- Mostly, the writers hiding that the AI uses and provides misleading information about the source.
- AI models are biased with the training data. It raises the concern on the correct and accurate information.
- The use of AI has in research and academic writing has initiated a debate on Intellectual Property (IP) Rights. The improper use of AI has initiated a valid question that who owns AI-generated text-the one who developed the tool, the end-user, or it belong to no one?

Thus, it can be inferred that the integration of artificial intelligence into research and academic work offers unparalleled opportunities for efficiency, innovation, and knowledge generation. The advancements in technology come with important ethical responsibilities. One major concern is plagiarism, as AI-generated content can be mistakenly or intentionally presented as original work, which threatens academic integrity and intellectual honesty. As a result, researchers and students must acknowledge the use of AI assistance, verify the accuracy of its outputs, and treat AI-generated content as a supportive tool rather than a substitute for human effort. Ethical usage also involves respecting data privacy, avoiding the introduction of biases present in AI models, and ensuring transparency regarding authorship and contributions. Institutions, educators, and policymakers play a crucial role in establishing clear guidelines that balance innovation with accountability. By following these principles, the academic community can utilize AI as a powerful instrument for learning, exploration, and discovery while upholding the values of originality, credibility, and ethical responsibility. Ultimately, responsible use of AI in academia is not just about compliance; it is a commitment to fostering integrity, trust, and sustainable advancement in knowledge creation. It is essential to ensure that technology enhances rather than undermines scholarly rigor.

7 CONCLUSION

The evolution of AI tools has significantly transformed the landscape of writing and editing in academia and research. Technologies like natural language processing (NLP), enable machines to produce, comprehend, and interpret human language accurately. LLMs, such as GPT-5, built on NLP technologies, may summarize complex research findings, generate contextually appropriate writing, and even assist with manuscript drafting. These tools are utilized across various fields, enhancing productivity, reducing manual labour, and fostering creativity in scholarly writing. The effective use of these technologies relies heavily on prompt engineering, which shapes how AI processes and interprets user inputs. AI can support a range of academic tasks—both structured and open-ended—through techniques like zero-shot, one-shot, and few-shot prompting. For example, a researcher can generate a well-crafted prompt to summarize a literature review, ensuring that the AI's output is clear and thorough while adhering to the research context.AI tools for writing and editing further support academics by suggesting improvements in grammar, clarity, and style, as well as aiding in citation management and content organization. Automated solutions can simplify drafting and revising, freeing up researchers to concentrate on creative contributions rather than tedious editing duties. Examples of such tools include Grammarly,

QuillBot, and Zotero-integrated AI assistants. By helping non-native English speakers create polished manuscripts appropriate for worldwide publication, these tools promote diversity in addition to efficiency. The integration of AI in academic writing brings remarkable efficiency and creative potential, but it also requires careful attention to plagiarism and ethical considerations. AI-generated content can inadvertently be misappropriated, making transparency, proper acknowledgment, factual verification, and data privacy essential. Researchers remain accountable for all AI-assisted work, ensuring integrity and credibility. When used responsibly with precise prompting and oversight, AI tools for writing and editing not only streamline scholarly tasks but also enhance creativity, learning, and collaboration, signalling a future where human intellect and AI work together to advance knowledge.

REFERENCES

Agrawal, V., Bhardwaj, S., Pathak, N., Dixit, J. K., Agarwal, S., & Momin, M. (2024). *Augmenting Research.* IGI Global., DOI: 10.4018/979-8-3693-1798-3.ch003

AIJR. (2025). Plagiarism, its Types, Consequences, & Prevention. AIJR Publisher. Retrieved September 30, 2025, from https://aijr.org/blog/

Ateriya, N., Sonwani, N. S., Thakur, K. S., Kumar, A., & Verma, S. K. (2025). Exploring the ethical landscape of AI in academic writing. *Egyptian Journal of Forensic Sciences, 15*(1), 36. DOI: 10.1186/s41935-025-00453-1

Bik, E. (2024, February 15). The rat with the big balls and the enormous penis – how Frontiers published a paper with botched AI-generated images. Science Integrity Digest. https://scienceintegritydigest.com/2024/02/15/the-rat-with-the-big-balls-and-enormous-penis-how-frontiers-published-a-paper-with-botched-ai-generated-images/?utm_source=chatgpt.com

Biondi-Zoccai, G.. (2025). The impact of artificial intelligence on academic writing: A guide for authors and editors. *European Journal of Clinical Investigation.*

Boonstra, L. (2025). Prompt engineering. Google, https://www. kaggle. com/whitepaper-prompt-engineering

Brown, T. B., Mann, B., Ryder, N., Subbiah, M., Kaplan, J., Dhariwal, P., Neelakantan, A., Shyam, P., Sastry, G., Askell, A., Agarwal, S., Herbert-Voss, A., Krueger, G., Henighan, T., Child, R., Ramesh, A., Ziegler, D. M., Wu, J., Winter, C., & Amodei, D. (2020). Language Models are Few-Shot Learners. https://arxiv.org/abs/2005.14165

Chellapandian, H., & Jeyachandran, S. (2024). RETRACTED ARTICLE: Comment on "Struggle with traumatic spinal cord injury: a need for improved surgical and rehabilitation services.". *Neurosurgical Review, 47*(1), 637. DOI: 10.1007/s10143-024-02861-8 PMID: 39294472

Chen, B., Zhang, Z., Langrené, N., & Zhu, S. (2025). Unleashing the potential of prompt engineering for large language models. *Patterns (New York, N.Y.), 6*(6), 101260. DOI: 10.1016/j.patter.2025.101260 PMID: 40575123

Chen, B., Zhang, Z., Langrené, N., & Zhu, S. (2025). Unleashing the potential of prompt engineering for large language models. *Patterns (New York, N.Y.), 6*(6), 101260. DOI: 10.1016/j.patter.2025.101260 PMID: 40575123

Chetwynd, E. (2024). Ethical Use of Artificial Intelligence for Scientific Writing: Current Trends. *Journal of Human Lactation, 40*(2), 211–215. DOI: 10.1177/08903344241235160 PMID: 38482810

Churi, P. P., Joshi, S., Elhoseny, M., & Omrane, A. (2022). *Artificial Intelligence in Higher Education.* CRC Press., DOI: 10.1201/9781003184157

Clemson University. (n.d.). AI in academic writing. Retrieved July 26, 2025, from https://www.clemson.edu/centers-institutes/writing/writing-resources/writing-resources/ai-in-academic-writing.html

Effah Kwabena, A., Wiafe, O.-B., Boakye-Danquah, J., Asare, B., & Frimpong, A. F. B. (2023). An automated method for developing search strategies for systematic review using Natural Language Processing (NLP). https://doi.org/https://doi.org/10.1016/j.mex.2022.101935

Elaiess, R. (2024). *Academic Integrity in the Age of Artificial Intelligence: Exploring Ethical Challenges in a Digital Era. International Journal of Academic Multidisciplinary Research.* IJAMR.

Federiakin, D., Molerov, D., Zlatkin-Troitschanskaia, O., & Maur, A. (2024). Prompt engineering as a new 21st century skill. *Frontiers in Education, 9*, 1366434. Advance online publication. DOI: 10.3389/feduc.2024.1366434

Flores, L., Kim, S., & Young, S. D. (2023). Addressing bias in artificial intelligence for public health surveillance. Journal of Medical Ethics, jme-108875. https://doi.org/DOI: 10.1136/jme-2022-108875

Gaunov, S. R., Baymuradov, U. G., & Sitnikov, S. Yu. (2024). Machine learning in python: using tensorflow and scikit-learn libraries. Èkonomika i Upravlenie: Problemy, Rešeniâ, 12/8(153), 72–81. https://doi.org/DOI: 10.36871/ek.up.p.r.2024.12.08.009

Geroimenko, V. (2025). *The Essential Guide to Prompt Engineering.* Springer Nature Switzerland., DOI: 10.1007/978-3-031-86206-9

Géron, A. (2017). Hands-On Machine Learning with Scikit-Learn and TensorFlow: Concepts, Tools, and Techniques to Build Intelligent Systems. https://www.amazon.com/Hands-Machine-Learning-Scikit-Learn-TensorFlow/dp/1491962291

Guo, H. Y., & Zaini, S. H. (2024). Artificial Intelligence in Academic Writing: A Literature Review. *Asian Pendidikan, 4*(4), 46–55. DOI: 10.53797/aspen.v4i2.6.2024

Hall, S. (n.d.). *Prompt Engineering for Teachers: Making the Most of AI, Part 1.* Thinking Teachers Teaching Thinkers. Retrieved October 10, 2025, from https://teachersfirst.com/blog/2024/07/prompt-engineering-for-teachers-making-the-most-of-ai-part-1/

Jurafsky, D., & Martin, J. H. (2025). *Speech and Language Processing: An Introduction to Natural Language Processing* (3rd ed.). Computational Linguistics, and Speech Recognition., https://web.stanford.edu/~jurafsky/slp3/

Khalifa, M., & Albadawy, M. (2024). Using artificial intelligence in academic writing and research: An essential productivity tool. *Computer Methods and Programs in Biomedicine Update, 5*, 100145. DOI: 10.1016/j.cmpbup.2024.100145

Launonen, P., Talalakina, E., & Dubova, G. (2024). Students' Perceptions of Using ChatGPT for Academic Writing in English. *Półrocznik Językoznawczy Tertium, 9*(1), 219–249. DOI: 10.7592/Tertium.2024.9.1.274

Lee, D., & Palmer, E. (2025). Prompt engineering in higher education: A systematic review to help inform curricula. *International Journal of Educational Technology in Higher Education, 22*(1), 7. DOI: 10.1186/s41239-025-00503-7

Leung, C. H. (2024). Promoting optimal learning with ChatGPT: A comprehensive exploration of prompt engineering in education. *Asian Journal of Contemporary Education*, *8*(2), 104–114. DOI: 10.55493/5052.v8i2.5101
Leung, C. H. (2024). Promoting optimal learning with ChatGPT: A comprehensive exploration of prompt engineering in education. *Asian Journal of Contemporary Education*, *8*(2), 104–114. DOI: 10.55493/5052.v8i2.5101
López, C., Comas Forgas, R., & Cerdá-Navarro, A. (2024). A PhD dissertation in education written by artificial intelligence? Revista Brasileira de Educação, 29. https://doi.org/DOI: 10.1590/s1413-24782024290066

Luo, F., Zhang, J., Wang, Q., & Yang, C. (2025). Leveraging Prompt Engineering in Large Language Models for Accelerating Chemical Research. *ACS Central Science*, *11*(4), 511–519. DOI: 10.1021/acscentsci.4c01935 PMID: 40290144
Luo, F., Zhang, J., Wang, Q., & Yang, C. (2025). Leveraging Prompt Engineering in Large Language Models for Accelerating Chemical Research. *ACS Central Science*, *11*(4), 511–519. DOI: 10.1021/acscentsci.4c01935 PMID: 40290144
Meça, A., & Shkëlzeni, V. (2023). The ethical implications of AI in higher education. *Journal of Academic Ethics*.

Memarian, B., & Doleck, T. (2024). Human-in-the-loop in artificial intelligence in education: A review and entity-relationship (ER) analysis. Computers in Human Behavior Artificial Humans. https://doi.org/DOI: 10.1016/j.chbah.2024.100053

Merriam-Webster. (2025, September 30). Plagiarize. Https://Www.Merriam-Webster.Com/Dictionary/Plagiarize

Meuschke, N., & Gipp, B. (2013). State of the Art in Detecting Academic Plagiarism. *International Journal for Educational Integrity*, *9*(1), 50–71. DOI: 10.21913/IJEI.v9i1.847

Mondal, H., & Mondal, S. (2023). ChatGPT in academic writing: Maximizing its benefits and minimizing the risks. *Indian Journal of Ophthalmology*, *71*(12), 3600–3606. DOI: 10.4103/IJO.IJO_718_23 PMID: 37991290

Nasution, K. Y., Sihite, R. A., & Hartati, R. (2024). Exploring the Role and Benefits of ChatGPT AI in Enhancing Students' Fiction Writing Literacy: Insights from Learner Experiences. *Fonologi Jurnal Ilmuan Bahasa Dan Sastra Inggris*, *2*(4), 141–153. DOI: 10.61132/fonologi.v2i4.1219

Ong, J. C. L., Chang, S. Y.-H., William, W., Butte, A. J., Shah, N. H., Chew, L. S. T., Liu, N., Doshi-Velez, F., Lu, W., Savulescu, J., & Ting, D. S. W. (2024). Ethical and regulatory challenges of large language models in medicine. *The Lancet. Digital Health*, *6*(6), e428–e432. DOI: 10.1016/S2589-7500(24)00061-X PMID: 38658283

Open, A. I., Achiam, J., Adler, S., Agarwal, S., Ahmad, L., Akkaya, I., Aleman, F. L., Almeida, D., Altenschmidt, J., Altman, S., Anadkat, S., Avila, R., Babuschkin, I., Balaji, S., Balcom, V., Baltescu, P., Bao, H., Bavarian, M., Belgum, J., & Zoph, B. (2024). *GPT-4 Technical Report*. https://arxiv.org/abs/2303.08774

Oppenlaender, J., Linder, R., & Silvennoinen, J. (2024). Prompting AI Art: An Investigation into the Creative Skill of Prompt Engineering. https://arxiv.org/abs/2303.13534

Ouyang, L., Wu, J., Jiang, X., Almeida, D., Wainwright, C. L., Mishkin, P., Zhang, C., Agarwal, S., Slama, K., Ray, A., Schulman, J., Hilton, J., Kelton, F., Miller, L., Simens, M., Askell, A., Welinder, P., Christiano, P., Leike, J., & Lowe, R. (2022). Training language models to follow instructions with human feedback. https://arxiv.org/abs/2203.02155

Rashidov, J., & Rashidova, F. (2024). The role of human oversight in AI-driven research. *AI and Ethics.*

Sadang, J. M., & Palompon, D. R. (2021). The development of Need-Threat Internal Resiliency Theory in COVID-19 crisis utilizing deductive axiomatic approach. 7(2), 72–77. https://doi.org/ DOI: 10.33546/bnj.1300

Sakib, S. M. N. (2024). *Bane and Boon of Hallucinations in the Context of Generative AI.* IGI Global., DOI: 10.4018/979-8-3693-2643-5.ch016

Samala, A. D., & Rawas, S. (2024). Bias in artificial intelligence: Smart solutions for detection, mitigation, and ethical strategies in real-world applications. *IAES International Journal of Artificial Intelligence, 14*(1), 32. DOI: 10.11591/ijai.v14.i1.pp32-43

Shah, C. (2025). From Prompt Engineering to Prompt Science with Humans in the Loop. *Communications of the ACM*, 3709599. Advance online publication. DOI: 10.1145/3709599

Spinellis, D. (2025). False authorship: An explorative case study around an AI-generated article published under my name. *Research Integrity and Peer Review, 10*(1), 8. DOI: 10.1186/s41073-025-00165-z PMID: 40420142

UNESCO. (2021). *Draft text of the recommendation on the ethics of artificial intelligence.*

Vaswani, A., Shazeer, N., Parmar, N., Uszkoreit, J., Jones, L., Gomez, A. N., & Kaiser, Ł. ukasz, & Polosukhin, I. (2017). Attention is All you Need. In I. Guyon, U. Von Luxburg, S. Bengio, H.

Chapter 15
Mapping the Evolution of Online Feedback Tools in Writing Education: A Bibliometric Analysis (2000–2024)

Hassan Abuhassna
https://orcid.org/0000-0002-5774-3652
Sunway University, Malaysia

Conie Toh
https://orcid.org/0009-0003-3287-9507
Sunway University, Malaysia

Farah Naaz Abd Yunos
Sunway University, Malaysia

Mohammad Abdul Hammed Qatawneh
https://orcid.org/0000-0001-5226-636X
University of Malaya, Malaysia

Ahmed Almabhouh
https://orcid.org/0009-0006-0765-8667
Al Aqsa University, Palestine

ABSTRACT

This study maps the evolution of online feedback tools in writing education, focusing on historical development, technological innovations, and pedagogical impacts between 2000 and 2024. A bibliometric analysis was conducted using the Scopus database, covering 241 documents from an initial 577. Guided by the PRISMA framework, data were analyzed with R Studio (Bibliometrix), VOSviewer, to produce descriptive statistics, co-authorship networks, keyword analyses, and thematic maps. Results reveal steady growth, with sharp increases in the last decade, particularly post-COVID-19. Influential sources such as Lecture Notes in Computer Science and Computers and Education dominate, while key scholars like Noroozi and Biemans drive contributions from Wageningen University. Trending topics show a shift from error correction to multimodality and

DOI: 10.4018/979-8-3373-5601-3.ch015

AI integration, while factorial analysis highlights four clusters: pedagogy, technology, higher education, and methodology. Persistent challenges include uneven engagement, cultural barriers, limited teacher readiness, and geographical imbalances.

1. INTRODUCTION

Online feedback tools have become central to writing education, reshaping how learners receive, process, and act on feedback across increasingly digital learning environments. These tools support scalable and timely formative assessment while fostering autonomy, engagement, and self-regulation in writing tasks (Tian & Zhou, 2020; Farnia et al., 2025; Nourinezhad et al., 2021). Over the last fifteen years, the landscape has shifted from basic digital platforms toward sophisticated, AI-enabled and multimodal ecosystems that interweave teacher, peer, and automated feedback—yet questions remain about balancing these approaches and optimizing them for diverse contexts (Zhang & Zhang, 2025; Osawa, 2024; Alnasser, 2022; Thi & Nikolov, 2022; Janar & Nozima, 2022; Cheng & Liu, 2022).

In writing education, "online feedback tools" refer to digital platforms and software applications that facilitate the provision, receipt, and revision of feedback on student writing in web-based or blended learning contexts. These tools may support teacher-to-student, peer-to-peer, or automated feedback interactions, and are characterised by features such as asynchronous comments, tracked revisions, integrated rubrics, and data-driven visualisations of writing progress. For instance, an online peer-review system allows learners to upload drafts, receive structured feedback from classmates and the instructor, and revise accordingly (Douglas et al., 2021). Meanwhile, automated writing evaluation (AWE) systems provide algorithmically generated feedback on writing features such as grammar, cohesion and argumentation. More broadly, online feedback tools serve as part of the feedback loop in digital writing environments, enabling continuous interaction, scaffolding and iteration beyond the physical classroom. Understanding their key components and functionality is essential before tracing their evolution and historical deployment in writing education. See figure 1 below:

Figure 1. Online feedback tools for writing education key components

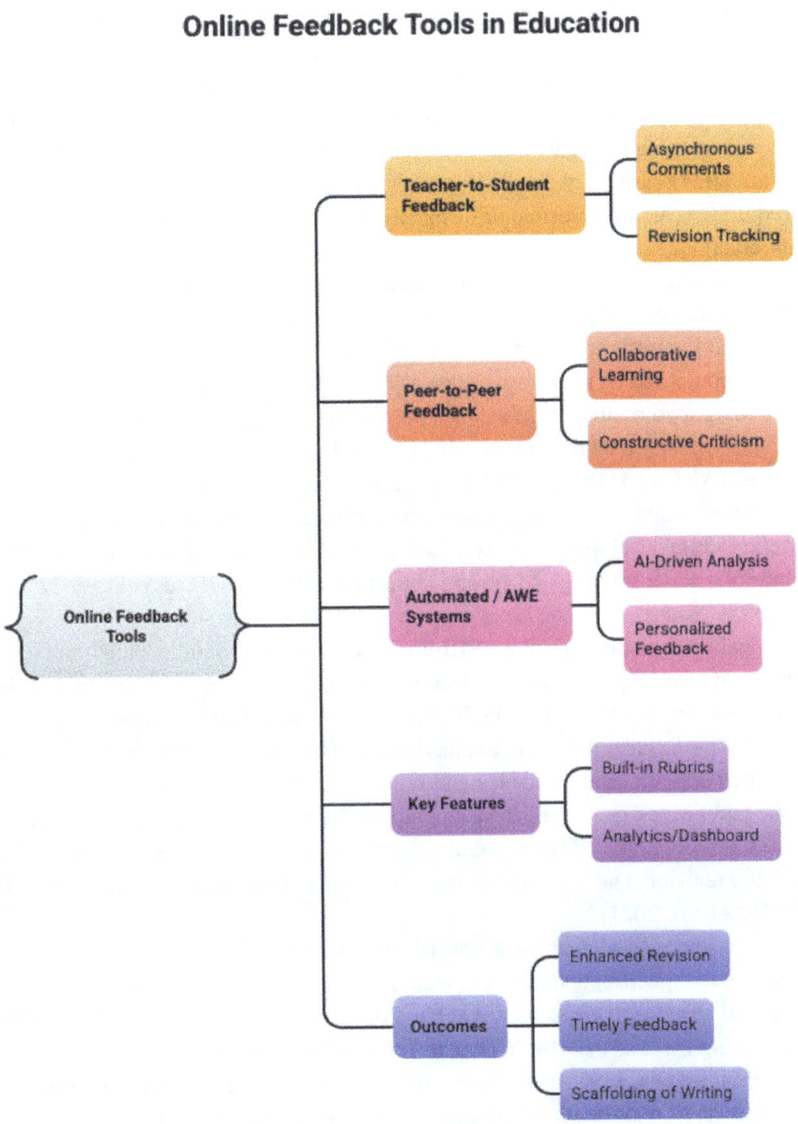

Historically, early work (2010–2015) introduced foundational online writing systems emphasizing writer–reader interaction and "feedback of feedback" (Lan et al., 2011), alongside semi-automated marking solutions for formative assessment (Burrows & Shortis, 2011) and combinations of automated written corrective feedback (AWCF) with asynchronous computer-mediated communication that improved complexity, accuracy, and motivation in writing (Tan et al.,

2023). As digital platforms proliferated, studies contrasted instructivist clarity with constructivist benefits for higher-order thinking, signaling a methodological and pedagogical diversification in online feedback research (Hopton, 2013; Strobl, 2014).

Between 2015 and 2020, expansion accelerated through learning management systems (e.g., Schoology/Edmodo) that enabled online teacher and peer feedback—though with mixed performance relative to conventional approaches (Saiful et al., 2019; Wihastyanang et al., 2020). Quality improved when learners received peer-feedback training (Do, 2024), while automated tools such as *Write & Improve* gained traction for individualized, motivating feedback at scale (Taskiran et al., 2024). Crucially, feedback modes broadened beyond text to audio, screencast, and video, requiring structured, formative designs and multiple revision cycles to realize benefits (Liang et al., 2025).

From 2020 onward, the COVID-19 pandemic acted as a digital catalyst, rapidly normalizing online feedback practices while exposing infrastructural disparities and digital-literacy gaps across regions and institutions (Mospan, 2023; Thapaliya & Hrytsuk, 2023; Sedrakyan et al., 2023). In this period, AI-driven platforms such as Notion AI and Virtual Writing Tutor (Song et al., 2023) and integrated multimodal feedback became more prevalent, supporting autonomous learning and self-regulation while underscoring the need to tailor strategies to local contexts and faculty practices (Alawad & Hamid, 2025; Singaram et al., 2024). Adoption and effectiveness varied with resources and pedagogical norms, with private institutions often reporting higher feedback quality, while developing contexts faced infrastructure-related constraints, highlighting the importance of teacher training and capacity building (Gonzalez-Torres et al., 2022; Krasniqi & Përvetica, 2024; Sousa et al., 2022).

Technologically, the field has progressed from typed comments to audio, video, and screencast modalities that can raise engagement and revision rates—though evidence about superiority over text for learning outcomes is mixed (Bakla, 2020; Cunningham, 2019; Mahoney et al., 2019; Yiğit & Seferoğlu, 2023). Automated Writing Evaluation (AWE) and AI-assisted feedback deliver fast, scalable input that supports independence and reduces teacher workload, but can be perceived as mechanistic and limited in content-focused guidance (Zein et al., 2025; Yu, 2023; Liu, 2022; Wang, 2025). Multimodal platforms and collaborative tools such as Google Docs enable genre awareness, richer revision, and socio-emotional support in hybrid or fully online courses (Ching & Simon, 2025; Akoto, 2021).

Pedagogically, there is a clear shift toward process-oriented, learner-centred approaches that value formative, specific, and dialogic feedback, with technology mediating scaffolding, collaboration, and reflection (Çiçek & Kayaoğlu, 2024; Budiman, 2025; Kulprasit, 2024; Ryan et al., 2021; Semingson et al., 2016). Yet mismatches between student preferences and teacher practices can blunt impact, reinforcing the need for alignment and training (Abdel Latif et al., 2024). Evidence shows multimodal feedback (typed, audio, video) can enhance engagement, relationships, and writing outcomes; flipped designs paired with audiovisual feedback further improve performance (Nourinezhad et al., 2021; Cunningham & Link, 2021; Saeed et al., 2024).

At the same time, sociocultural and proficiency factors shape how learners engage with teacher and automated feedback—teachers' linguistic backgrounds, translanguaging practices, and learners' feedback literacy all mediate participation and uptake (Lee, 2014; Cheng & Zhang, 2021; Li & Wang, 2024; Liu & Storch, 2023; Zhang et al., 2024). Persistent challenges revolve around the time-intensive nature of dialogic teacher feedback, workload pressures, variable student use of feedback, and methodological limitations around peer-feedback implementations

(Högemann et al., 2021; Liang et al., 2025). Interventions such as combining automated with teacher/peer feedback (Shibani, 2017), FLOOP-supported peer review (Janar & Nozima, 2022), and AI-focused professional development (Wardat & Akour, 2025; Asadi et al., 2025) can mitigate some constraints and build feedback literacy. Yet key gaps remain: the socio-emotional dimensions of feedback (Chong, 2018), multimodal feedback literacy (Jiang et al., 2024), adaptive feedback systems, and the need for longitudinal work in underrepresented regions and levels of education (Chin & Chew, 2021).

Building upon these insights and addressing the identified gaps, the present study seeks to systematically map the intellectual and thematic structure of research on online feedback tools in writing education. To guide this investigation, the following research questions are formulated:

1. How has research on online feedback tools in writing education evolved in terms of publication volume between 2000 and 2024?
2. Which journals, conference proceedings, or publishers have been the most influential sources for disseminating research on online feedback in writing education?
3. Who are the most productive and influential authors in this field, and which universities or institutions have contributed the most to advancing research on online feedback tools in writing education?
4. What are the most frequently studied or trending topics within the domain of online feedback tools in writing education, and how have these topics shifted over time?
5. What thematic clusters emerge from the co-occurrence and factorial analysis of keywords, and how do these clusters reflect the intellectual structure and research frontiers of the field?

2. LITERATURE REVIEW

The increasing integration of online feedback tools in writing education has attracted significant scholarly attention, yet many critical issues remain unresolved. While the Introduction mapped the broad evolution of online feedback tools, this section consolidates other dimensions highlighted in prior work to clarify persistent challenges and research gaps.

2.1. Student Engagement and Cultural Dimensions

A substantial challenge in online feedback lies in student engagement. While feedback is widely acknowledged as essential, many learners fail to consistently act upon the input provided (Jansen et al., 2025). This disengagement is not merely individual but also shaped by cultural and contextual dynamics. For example, Al-Ghazali (2015) demonstrated how peer feedback practices are deeply mediated by social norms in Gulf contexts, influencing both the uptake and perceived value of comments. Similarly, Thi Van Pham (2022) found that peer feedback in online learning environments faced variable effectiveness depending on cultural expectations of hierarchy and collaboration. These findings underscore that online feedback cannot be divorced from the sociocultural realities in which it operates.

2.2. Peer Feedback Opportunities and Barriers

Peer-driven platforms such as Google Docs and e-portfolios have opened new spaces for collaborative writing, yet questions of trust, quality, and emotional safety persist. Chen (2016) synthesized ESL/EFL studies and revealed that while technology-enhanced peer feedback can improve writing quality, limited training and usability issues often undermine outcomes. Le et al. (2025) emphasized anonymity as a preferred mechanism among Vietnamese EFL learners to reduce discomfort in giving honest feedback, though this creates trade-offs in accountability. Guardado and Shi (2007) earlier showed that despite the potential benefits, students often perceived online peer feedback as uneven in quality and emotionally taxing. Collectively, these studies suggest that while peer feedback tools hold promise, they require scaffolded literacy development and culturally responsive design.

2.3. Teacher Competencies and Pedagogical Constraints

Teachers' readiness and competencies are another recurrent barrier. Montiel and Gomez-Zermeño (2022) reported that even during the pandemic, many educators lacked the ICT skills necessary to leverage digital platforms effectively. Beyond technical competence, culturally-situated approaches to feedback remain underdeveloped. Ghosh, Chakraborty, et al. (2025) proposed a multi-peer, community-based framework to build culturally responsive feedback literacy, but empirical testing of such models is limited. Çiçek and Kayaoğlu (2024) highlighted how feedback type (form vs. content) impacts learner proficiency development differently, reinforcing the need for teachers to align strategies with learner levels. Together, these findings illustrate the tension between growing technological opportunities and limited teacher capacity to exploit them fully.

2.4. Research Methodology and Theoretical Gaps

Despite an expanding body of literature, methodological and theoretical shortcomings persist. Many studies remain short-term, small-scale, and cross-sectional, limiting understanding of sustained impacts (Chong, 2018). Zhang and Zou (2023) reviewed research on technology-enhanced peer feedback and found that most work failed to systematically apply robust frameworks, often overlooking activity theory or sociocultural theory to guide analysis. Similarly, Cuocci et al. (2023) replicated Chen's synthesis and reaffirmed the need for more systematic meta-analyses in feedback research. Chin and Chew (2021) profiled the research landscape and confirmed a geographical skew toward digitally advanced regions, with limited data from underrepresented contexts such as Africa, Latin America, and Southeast Asia.

2.5. Problem Statement and Research Gap

Taken together, these studies reveal several unresolved issues:

- Student engagement with feedback remains inconsistent, often undermined by cultural norms, emotional discomfort, or lack of training (Al-Ghazali, 2015; Le et al., 2025).

- Peer feedback quality varies widely, with concerns about reliability, trust, and cultural acceptance persisting across different contexts (Thi Van Pham, 2022; Guardado & Shi, 2007).
- Teacher competencies in ICT and feedback pedagogy lag behind technological innovation, creating a disconnect between tools and actual classroom practices (Gao & Chen, 2025).
- Methodological gaps remain, with limited longitudinal, large-scale, or theory-driven studies to assess the long-term and cross-cultural impact of feedback tools (Chong, 2018; Zhang & Zou, 2023).
- Geographical imbalances in research outputs persist, leaving entire educational regions underrepresented (Chin & Chew, 2021).
- Thus, while online feedback tools have expanded rapidly, the field suffers from fragmentation, uneven adoption, and insufficiently theorized evidence bases.

2.6. Positioning the Present Study

This bibliometric analysis directly addresses these gaps by systematically mapping the evolution of online feedback tools in writing education between 2000 and 2024. Unlike prior small-scale or localized studies, bibliometric mapping provides a global, data-driven synthesis that identifies publication trends, key authors, leading institutions, dominant themes, and emerging research frontiers. By doing so, it clarifies where the field has matured and where critical research opportunities remain, particularly regarding sustained engagement, culturally adaptive models, and equitable representation across global contexts.

3. METHODOLOGY

This bibliometric analysis followed the PRISMA guidelines (Preferred Reporting Items for Systematic Reviews and Meta-Analyses; Page et al., 2021) to ensure transparency and rigor throughout the identification, screening, eligibility, and inclusion stages. The Scopus database was selected due to its extensive coverage of peer-reviewed publications and robust indexing standards. To process and analyze the data, we employed a combination of R Studio (Bibliometrix package), VOSviewer, and Microsoft Excel, enabling both descriptive statistics and advanced visualizations of co-authorship, co-occurrence, and thematic evolution networks. In line with prior bibliometric research in related domains (Van et al., 2021; Abuhassna et al., 2024; Dan et al., 2026; Li et al., 2026; Pan et al., 2026), this study adopted a similar methodological rigor to enhance comparability and replicability. The study relied solely on **Scopus** to ensure data consistency, reliability, and reproducibility. Scopus was selected as it is one of the largest and most comprehensive databases, offering standardized metadata for bibliometric analysis. Integrating multiple databases (e.g., Web of Science) often introduces duplication and inconsistencies in citation formats and author records. Using a single, high-quality source aligns with established bibliometric practices (Aria & Cuccurullo, 2017; Donthu et al., 2021) and ensures methodological transparency without compromising analytical validity. The overall methodological process, structured around PRISMA stages, is illustrated in Figure 2.

Figure 2. PRISMA Framework

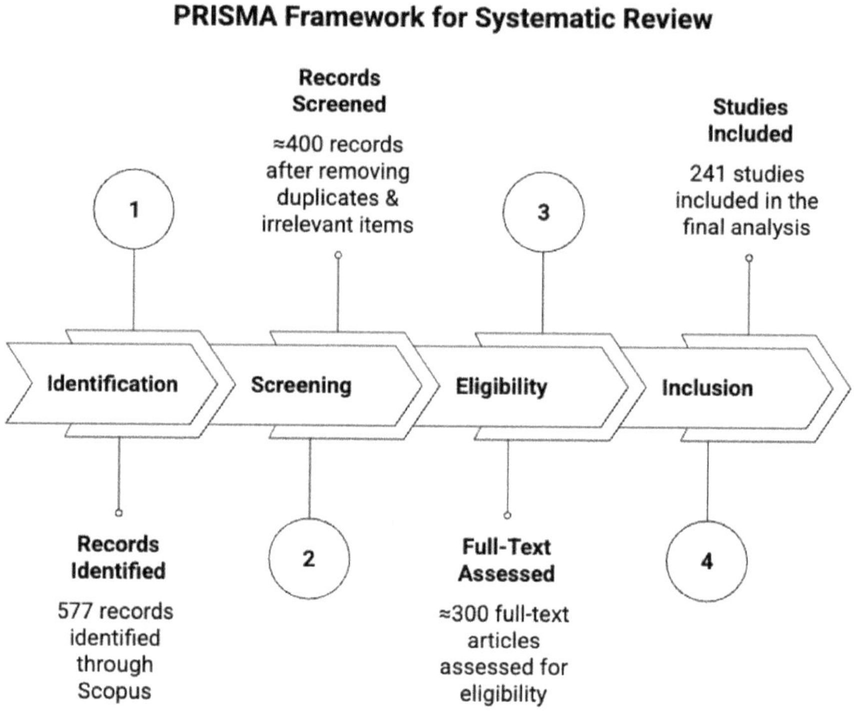

3.1. Identification Stage

At the identification stage, a comprehensive query was developed to capture publications on online feedback tools in writing education between the years 2000 and 2024. The search was conducted on 4 September 2025, and an initial 577 documents were retrieved. The query string applied in Scopus is presented in Table 1.

Table 1. Scopus Query Applied in the Study

Category	Criteria Applied	Query Evidence	Notes
Database	Scopus	—	Comprehensive and peer-reviewed coverage
Date of Search	4 September 2025	—	—
Timeframe	2000–2024	PUBYEAR > 1999 AND PUBYEAR < 2025	Ensures only publications within 2000–2024

continued on following page

Table 1. Continued

Category	Criteria Applied	Query Evidence	Notes
Keywords (Title, Abstract, Keywords)	*Online Feedback* AND *Writing Education*	TITLE-ABS-KEY (Online Feedback AND Writing Education)	Core search terms
Subject Areas	Social Sciences (SOCI), Computer Science (COMP), Arts & Humanities (ARTS)	(LIMIT-TO (SUBJAREA, "SOCI") OR LIMIT-TO (SUBJAREA, "COMP") OR LIMIT-TO (SUBJAREA, "ARTS"))	Restricted to relevant academic domains
Document Types	Articles, Conference Papers, Book Chapters, Conference Reviews	(LIMIT-TO (DOCTYPE, "ar") OR LIMIT-TO (DOCTYPE, "cp") OR LIMIT-TO (DOCTYPE, "ch") OR LIMIT-TO (DOCTYPE, "cr"))	Excluded editorials, letters, notes, etc.
Language	English only	LIMIT-TO (LANGUAGE, "English")	Ensured consistent interpretation
Initial Search Results	577 documents retrieved	—	Before applying screening/ eligibility criteria
Final Dataset	241 documents included	—	After applying inclusion and exclusion criteria

3.2. Screening and Eligibility Stage

The documents were screened for relevance based on their *titles, abstracts, and keywords.* Articles not directly related to writing education, online feedback mechanisms, or pedagogical applications were excluded. Additionally, only documents in the *English language* were retained.

3.3. Inclusion and Exclusion Criteria

To refine the dataset, a set of inclusion and exclusion criteria was applied, as detailed in *Table 2*.

Table 2. Inclusion and Exclusion Criteria

Criteria Type	Inclusion	Exclusion
Timeframe	Publications between 2000–2024	Publications before 2000 or after 2024
Document Type	Articles, conference papers, conference reviews, and book chapters	Editorials, notes, reviews, letters, theses, and non-peer-reviewed content
Language	English	Non-English documents
Subject Areas	Social Sciences, Computer Science, Arts & Humanities	Publications outside these domains
Content Relevance	Focus on online feedback tools, writing education, higher education, or pedagogy	Publications unrelated to feedback, writing, or education contexts

As shown in table 2 after applying these criteria, the dataset was refined from 577 initial records to a final 241 eligible documents for analysis

3.4. Data Analysis

The final dataset was exported from Scopus in CSV format. The data were then cleaned and standardized using Microsoft Excel to remove duplicates, correct author name variations, unify institutional affiliations, and ensure the consistency of bibliographic fields (e.g., title, source, year, DOI). For the bibliometric analysis, the Bibliometrix package (Aria & Cuccurullo, 2017) within R Studio (Version 4.3.2) was employed to conduct descriptive and performance analyses. This included the computation of publication trends, annual scientific production, most productive authors, prolific institutions, and leading sources. Subsequently, VOSviewer (v1.6.20) was utilized for network analysis and visualization. The workflow followed these main steps:

1. Data Import and Pre-Processing: The Scopus CSV file was imported into VOSviewer to extract bibliographic coupling, co-citation, and keyword-co-occurrence relationships.
2. Network Construction: Separate maps were generated for *authors*, *countries*, *sources*, and *keywords*, each filtered by a minimum occurrence threshold (≥ 5 documents per node) to ensure meaningful representation.
3. Clustering and Normalization: The association-strength normalization method was applied to cluster nodes, revealing thematic and collaborative linkages.
4. Visualization and Interpretation: The resulting networks were exported as high-resolution SVG images and interpreted alongside quantitative indicators from Bibliometrix to identify research frontiers, emerging themes, and influential contributors in the field of online feedback tools in writing education.

4. RESULTS

The results of this bibliometric analysis provide a comprehensive overview of the research landscape surrounding online feedback tools in writing education between 2000 and 2024. Guided by the research questions, the findings highlight both descriptive patterns and conceptual structures within the field. The analysis begins with an examination of annual publication trends to capture the evolution of scholarly output over time. It then identifies the most influential sources, shedding light on journals, conference proceedings, and publishers that have served as key platforms for dissemination. Attention is also given to the most productive authors and universities, thereby recognizing leading contributors and institutions in this domain. Furthermore, trending topics are analyzed to reveal the thematic directions that have shaped discourse across different periods. Finally, a factorial analysis of keyword co-occurrence provides insight into the intellectual structure of the field and emerging research frontiers.

4.1. Annual Publication Trends (RQ1)

Understanding the annual scientific production is essential for identifying the developmental trajectory of research on online feedback tools in writing education. The distribution of publications over time illustrates how scholarly interest in this domain has evolved, indicating both early explorations and more recent expansions in research activity.

Figure 3. The annual distributions of the publications in the field of Online Feedback and Writing Education

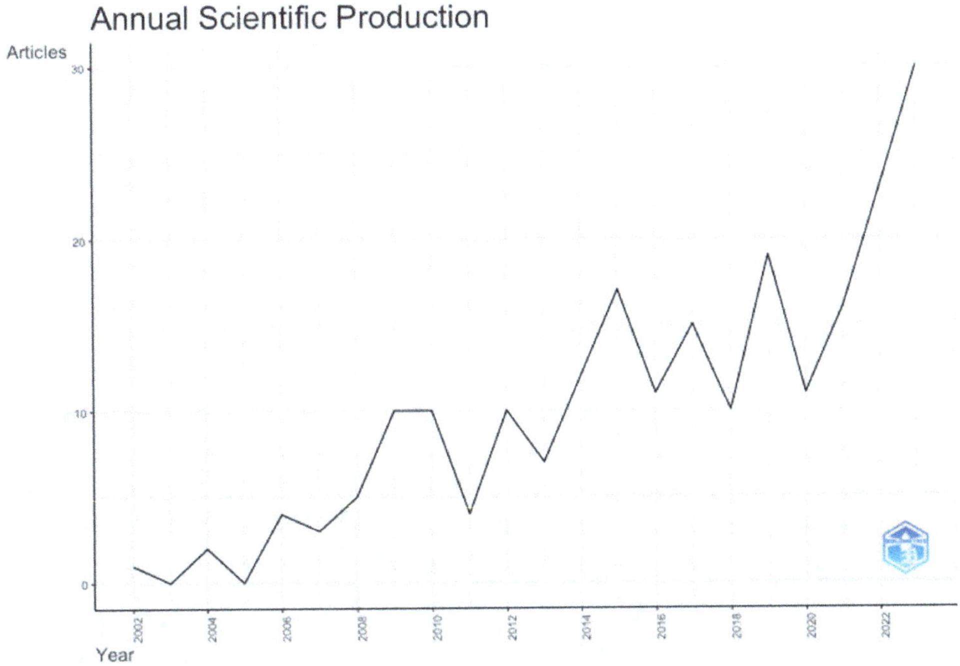

As shown in Figure 3, research in this field began modestly in the early 2000s, with only one article in 2002 and sporadic contributions until 2007. A noticeable rise occurred in 2009 and 2010, each recording 10 publications, marking the first wave of significant attention to online feedback in writing education. After a temporary decline in 2011, output stabilized between 7–12 articles annually from 2012 to 2014, before experiencing a steady upward trajectory.

The peak years of growth emerged after 2015, with notable spikes in 2015 (17 articles), 2019 (19 articles), and 2021 (16 articles). The momentum accelerated further in the last two years, with 23 publications in 2022 and a record 30 publications in 2023, the highest level across the entire study period. This pattern suggests an increasing global recognition of the role of online feedback tools in writing education, particularly in the context of digital transformation and post-pandemic educational shifts.

4.2. Most Relevant Sources (RQ2)

Identifying the most relevant sources provides insight into the primary platforms through which knowledge on online feedback tools in writing education is disseminated. Journals and conference proceedings play a vital role in shaping the research discourse, influencing citation practices, and determining the visibility of studies within the academic community.

Figure 4. The most relevant Sources in the field of Online Feedback and Writing Education

As presented in Figure 4 and Table 3, the leading outlet is Lecture Notes in Computer Science with 11 publications, reflecting the strong link between technological development and its application in education. This is followed by Computers and Education, one of the highest-impact journals in the field, contributing 7 publications and confirming its central role in advancing technology-enhanced learning research.

Conference proceedings also feature prominently, with both the ACM International Conference Proceedings Series and CEUR Workshop Proceedings contributing 6 publications each, demonstrating the significance of conferences as venues for presenting emerging research. Other specialized journals such as Internet and Higher Education and Nurse Education Today (each with 4 publications) highlight the diverse disciplinary reach of online feedback research, spanning higher education and professional training contexts.

Additionally, reputable journals such as the British Journal of Educational Technology, International Journal of Emerging Technologies in Learning, and Frontiers in Education Conference Proceedings each recorded 3 publications, further underlining the interdisciplinary nature of the field. Collectively, these findings show that the research domain is supported by a combination of high-impact journals and conference proceedings, reflecting both theoretical contributions and practice-driven insights.

4.3. Most Productive Authors (RQ3)

Examining the most productive authors provides valuable insights into the intellectual leadership and institutional hubs that have shaped the development of online feedback tools in writing education. The findings, summarized in Table 3, highlight the leading scholars, their publication volume, most cited contributions, and affiliated institutions.

Table 3. Authors production over time

	Most productive authors	TP	Most cited article	TC	Affiliation
1	Noroozi, O.	8	Relations between scripted online peer feedback processes and quality of written argumentative essay	141	Wageningen University & Research, Wageningen, Netherlands
2	Biemans, H.J.A.	4	Students' online argumentative peer feedback, essay writing, and content learning: does gender matter?	90	Wageningen University & Research, Wageningen, Netherlands
3	Ahoniemi, T.	3	ALOHA - A grading tool for semi-automatic assessment of mass programming courses	21	Tuxera, Espoo, Finland
4	Banihashem, S.K.	3	Online peer feedback patterns of success and failure in argumentative essay writing	67	Open Universiteit, Heerlen, Netherlands
5	Issa, T.	3	Promoting human-computer interaction and usability guidelines and principles through reflective journal assessment	4	Curtin University, Perth, Australia
6	Admiraal, W.	2	Streaming video to enhance students' reflection in dance education	124	Centre for the Study of Professions, Oslo, Norway
7	Anquetil, E.	2	Multi-criteria handwriting quality analysis with online fuzzy models	26	Institut de Recherche en Informatique et Systèmes Aléatoires, Rennes, France
8	Backer, P.R.	2	Efficacy of an online writing program on URM students in engineering	1	San Jose State University, San Jose, United States
9	Campbell, C.W.	2	To peer or not to peer: A controlled peer-editing intervention measuring writing self-efficacy in South Korean higher education	9	Dongguk University, Seoul, Seoul, South Korea
10	Cheng, G.	2	The impact of online automated feedback on students' reflective journal writing in an EFL course	71	The Education University of Hong Kong, Hong Kong, China

TP*= total publication in this field of study, TC*= total citation for the most cited article

As illustrated in Table 3, Noroozi, O. stands out as the most prolific researcher with 8 publications, and his most cited article, *Relations between scripted online peer feedback processes and quality of written argumentative essay*, has received 141 citations. His affiliation with Wageningen University & Research, Netherlands, positions this institution as a central hub for online feedback research. Closely linked, Biemans, H.J.A. (also from Wageningen University & Research) contributed 4 publications, with his widely cited work on gender differences in peer feedback and essay writing accumulating 90 citations.

Other key contributors include Ahoniemi, T. (Tuxera, Finland) with 3 publications, focusing on semi-automated grading tools in programming courses, and Banihashem, S.K. (Open Universiteit, Netherlands), whose research on success and failure patterns in argumentative essay writing has been cited 67 times. Similarly, Issa, T. (Curtin University, Australia) has 3 publications emphasizing human–computer interaction and reflective learning, albeit with lower citation counts.

Scholars with 2 publications each have also enriched the field significantly. Admiraal, W. (Oslo, Norway) produced impactful work on video-based reflection in dance education with 124 citations, one of the highest citation counts in the dataset. Anquetil, E. (Rennes, France) focused on handwriting quality analysis with fuzzy models (26 citations). Backer, P.R. (San Jose State University, USA) studied online writing programs for underrepresented minorities in engineering, while Campbell, C.W. (Dongguk University, South Korea) examined peer-editing interventions and writing self-efficacy. Cheng, G. (Education University of Hong Kong) contributed significantly with 71 citations for his work on automated feedback in EFL reflective journal writing. Figure 5 shows the most productive authors in the field of Online Feedback and Writing Education.

Figure 5. The most productive authors in the field of Online Feedback and Writing Education

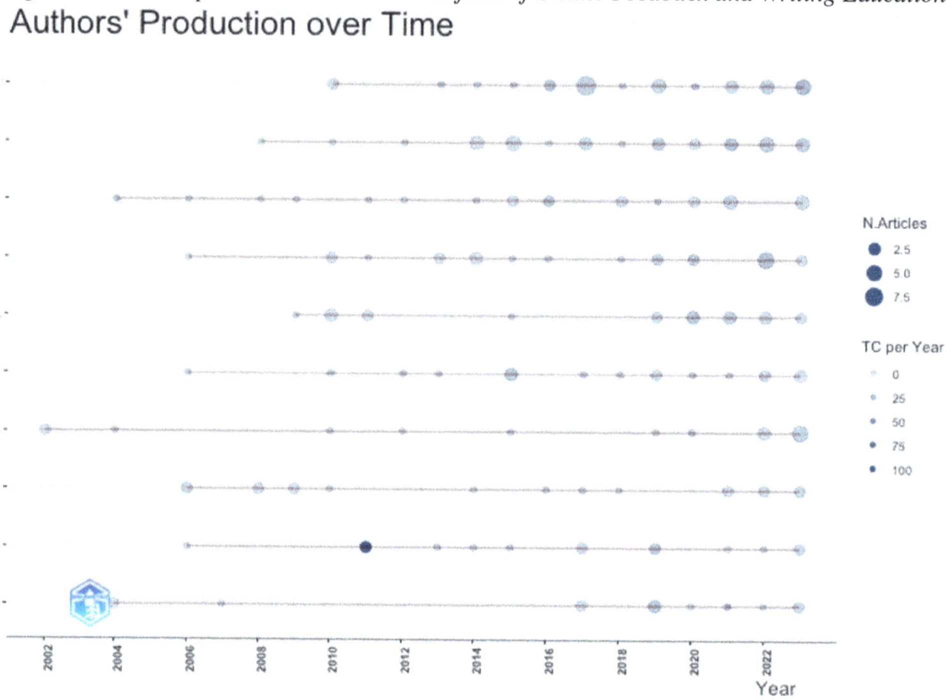

Collectively, these findings reveal a diverse network of scholars and institutions across Europe, Asia, and North America contributing to the field. The high citation impact of several works, particularly those of Noroozi, Biemans, Admiraal, and Cheng, indicates that research on online feedback tools in writing education has not only grown in volume but also achieved strong academic influence across disciplines and geographic regions.

4.4. Most Productive Universities (RQ4)

Analyzing the most productive universities provides insight into the institutional hubs driving scholarship in online feedback tools for writing education. Universities with a high output not only serve as research leaders but also foster collaborations, attract international partnerships, and influence the direction of pedagogical and technological innovations in this field.

Figure 6. The most productive Univerisites in the field of Online Feedback and Writing Education

As illustrated in Figure 6, the most productive institution is The University of Hong Kong, with 14 publications, followed closely by Wageningen University & Research, Netherlands, with 13 publications. These two institutions stand out as the primary centers of excellence, consistently producing impactful research and contributing significantly to both theoretical and applied aspects of online feedback.

Other institutions making notable contributions include the Open University (UK), University of Oulu (Finland), and Curtin University (Australia), each of which has demonstrated steady engagement with the topic through multiple outputs. Additionally, universities such as San Jose State University (USA), Dongguk University (South Korea), and the Education University of Hong Kong (China) also appear prominently, reflecting the global spread of research activity across Europe, Asia, and North America.

The data suggest that while a few institutions dominate in terms of volume, the field is broadly supported by international collaborations and cross-disciplinary initiatives, reinforcing its interdisciplinary and global nature. The prominence of Wageningen University further aligns with the strong individual contributions of scholars such as Noroozi and Biemans (see Section 4.3), emphasizing its institutional leadership.

4.5. Trending Topics (RQ5)

Analyzing trending topics provides insights into the evolving thematic priorities within the field of online feedback tools in writing education. By tracing the emergence and frequency of key terms, we can identify how scholarly attention has shifted over time and which concepts have become central to the discourse.

Figure 7. The most trending Topics in the field of Online Feedback and Writing Education

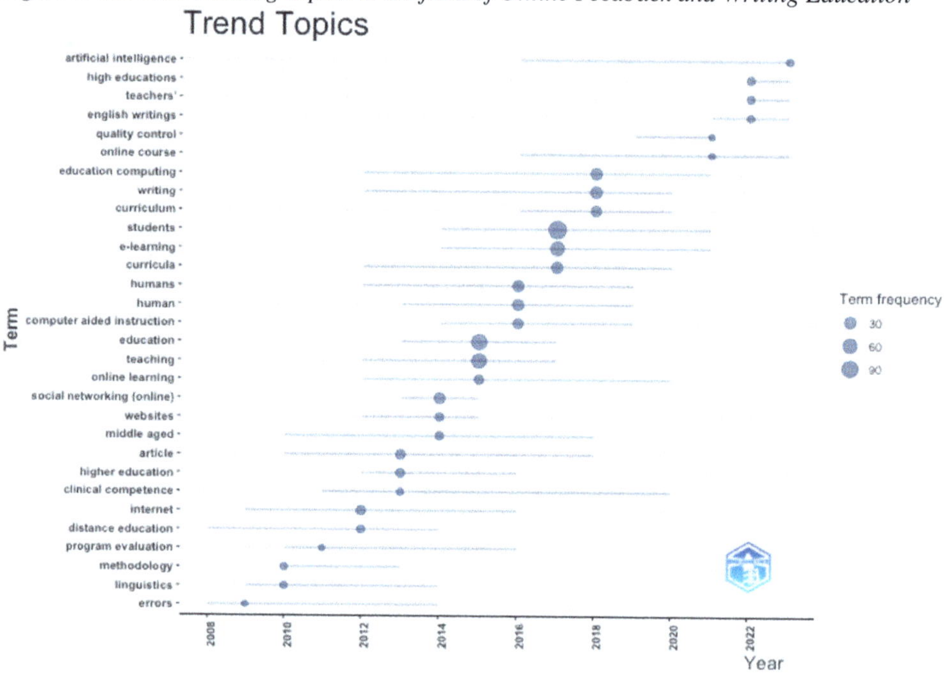

As illustrated in Figure 7, early research (2002–2010) focused on foundational themes such as distance education, errors, and methodology, reflecting initial explorations of online and computer-assisted feedback systems. Between 2011 and 2015, the field expanded toward applied themes, with frequent attention to teaching, assessment, learning environments, and social networking tools, signaling the integration of online feedback into broader e-learning contexts.

From 2016 onwards, the discourse grew more diverse and sophisticated, with emerging focus areas such as curriculum design, quality control, and clinical competence, particularly within professional and higher education settings. The period after 2020 saw a sharp rise in interest around artificial intelligence, high education contexts, and teachers' roles, aligning with global trends in digital transformation and post-pandemic adaptations in teaching and learning.

Overall, the trending topics highlight a clear trajectory: from early emphasis on basic feedback mechanisms toward technology-enhanced, data-driven, and AI-supported feedback practices, positioning online feedback tools as a critical element of modern writing education.

4.6. Factorial Analysis of Keywords (RQ6)

A factorial analysis of keywords helps uncover the intellectual structure of the field by grouping related concepts into thematic clusters. This approach highlights how different research strands interact, overlap, and evolve, offering insights into both established areas and emerging frontiers in online feedback and writing education.

Figure 8. Factorial analysis of the main keywords in the field of Online Feedback and Writing Education

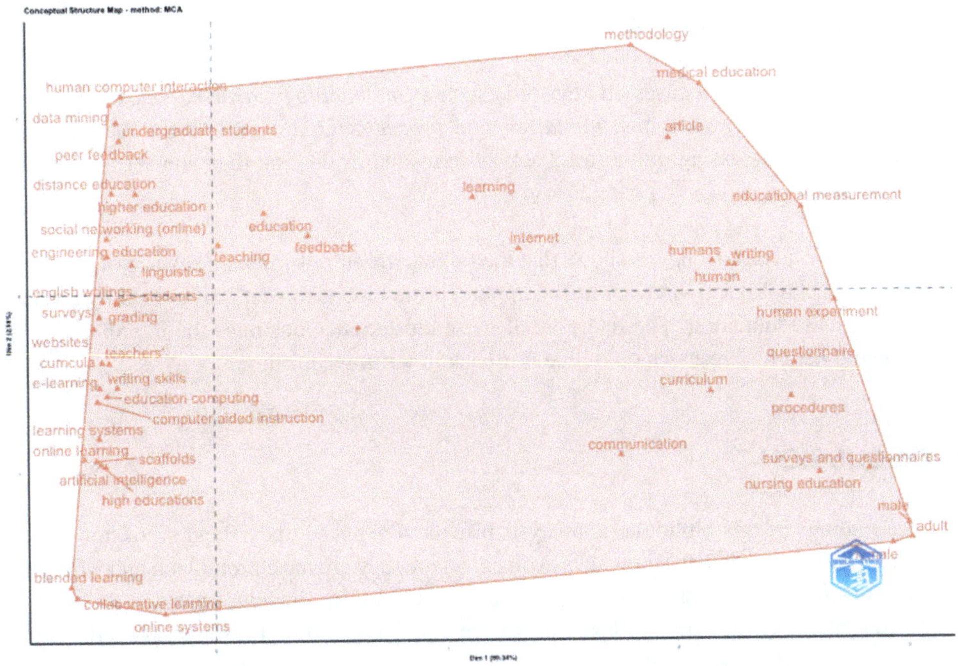

As shown in Figure 8, the factorial analysis reveals several distinct clusters of research focus:

1. Pedagogical and Feedback Practices

- This cluster includes terms such as *feedback*, *peer feedback*, *teaching*, *education*, *learning skills*, and *writing education.* It reflects the pedagogical emphasis of the field, particularly on how online feedback shapes learning processes, skill development, and instructional practices.

2. Technology-Enhanced Learning and Systems

- Keywords such as *e-learning*, *online systems*, *computer-assisted instruction*, *blended learning*, *collaborative learning*, and *artificial intelligence* indicate the central role of technology in facilitating online feedback. This cluster underscores the intersection of educational technology with feedback-driven pedagogies.

3. Higher Education and Professional Training

o Terms like *curriculum, higher education, medical education, nursing education, adult learning*, and *human-computer interaction* point to applied contexts where online feedback is being integrated. These keywords highlight the expansion of online feedback into professional fields and lifelong learning.

4. Methodology and Research Design

o A separate strand focuses on keywords such as *methodology, article, educational measurement, surveys and questionnaires*, and *procedures*. This reflects the methodological rigor in assessing online feedback systems and evaluating their impact on learning outcomes.

Overall, the factorial analysis shows that the field is structured around a balance of pedagogical inquiry, technological innovation, and applied professional contexts, supported by a strong methodological foundation. The interplay of these clusters demonstrates the interdisciplinary and evolving nature of research on online feedback in writing education.

5. DISCUSSION

The findings of this bibliometric analysis provide a nuanced understanding of how online feedback tools in writing education have evolved, where they are most prominent, and what gaps remain. By situating the results against prior studies, several key insights emerge.

Beyond numerical growth and clustering patterns, the findings reveal a progressive pedagogical shift in writing education from instructor-centric feedback toward collaborative, technology-mediated, and AI-supported ecosystems. The dominance of clusters related to automated feedback, peer collaboration, and multimodal feedback literacy highlights how digital platforms are reshaping both teaching roles and learner agency. This transition reflects a move toward dialogic and data-informed pedagogy, where feedback operates as a continuous learning loop rather than a one-time evaluation. Furthermore, emerging AI-driven tools signal new research directions focused on feedback personalization, ethical use of automation, and professional development for educators, ensuring that technology enhances, rather than replaces, the human dimension of academic writing.

5.1. Growth of Research and Shifts in Focus

The steady increase in publications, particularly after 2015 and with sharp peaks in 2019, 2022, and 2023, confirms that online feedback has become an established field of inquiry. This growth reflects both global digitalization and the impact of the COVID-19 pandemic in accelerating reliance on digital platforms (Mospan, 2023; Thapaliya & Hrytsuk, 2023; Sedrakyan et al., 2023). Earlier concerns about reliability and trust in peer feedback (Guardado & Shi, 2007; Al-Ghazali, 2015) have gradually shifted toward exploring multimodal, AI-supported, and large-scale approaches (Osawa, 2024; Zein et al., 2025). The timeline demonstrates that online feedback has moved from *experimental classroom tools* to becoming an integral element of mainstream writing pedagogy.

5.2. Dominance of Key Journals and Conferences

The concentration of outputs in sources such as *Lecture Notes in Computer Science* and *Computers and Education* highlights the centrality of technology-driven perspectives in the field. While these venues have promoted innovations in automated writing evaluation and computer-assisted instruction (Liu, 2022; Wang, 2025), other sources such as *Internet and Higher Education* and *Nurse Education Today* reveal the spread of online feedback research into applied and professional domains. This interdisciplinary spread reflects the diversification noted in the literature (Hopton, 2013; Strobl, 2014), but it also suggests that research remains clustered in technologically advanced contexts, echoing the geographical imbalance identified by Chin and Chew (2021).

5.3. Leading Authors and Institutional Hubs

The results confirm that a small group of scholars and institutions have driven much of the intellectual development. Noroozi and Biemans, both from Wageningen University, exemplify sustained leadership in exploring online peer feedback, with highly cited contributions on argumentation and essay quality. Similar concentrations of productivity are evident at the University of Hong Kong and the Education University of Hong Kong, extending earlier observations about the dominance of particular hubs (Jansen et al., 2025; Gao & Chen, 2025). This concentration raises concerns about the limited representation of under-researched contexts such as Southeast Asia, Latin America, and Africa (Chin & Chew, 2021), reinforcing calls for broader, more inclusive collaborations.

5.4. Evolving Research Topics and Technological Trends

Thematic mapping of trending topics illustrates a trajectory from early focus on distance education and error correction toward more complex themes such as AI, multimodality, and higher education applications. This confirms claims that feedback practices have expanded beyond textual correction to include audio, video, and automated modes (Bakla, 2020; Cunningham, 2019; Yiğit & Seferoğlu, 2023). Importantly, the increasing presence of terms such as *artificial intelligence* and *teachers' roles* reflects both technological advancement and ongoing debates about human–machine complementarity in feedback provision (Asadi et al., 2025; Wardat & Akour, 2025). The literature has long highlighted mismatches between teacher practices and student preferences (Abdel Latif et al., 2024), and the current findings suggest that technological innovations have not fully resolved this tension.

5.5. Intellectual Structure and Emerging Clusters

The factorial keyword analysis revealed four major clusters—pedagogical practices, technology-enhanced systems, higher education and professional training, and methodological design. These clusters align with prior syntheses showing fragmentation and uneven adoption (Chen, 2016; Cuocci et al., 2023). Pedagogical clusters reinforce the shift toward learner-centred, dialogic approaches (Ryan et al., 2021), while technological clusters confirm the growing dominance of AI and automation (Yu, 2023; Zein et al., 2025). The presence of a distinct methodology cluster highlights that research has increasingly recognized the need for rigor, though short-term designs still dominate (Chong, 2018). This signals progress but also validates calls for longitudinal, theory-driven studies (Zhang & Zou, 2023).

5.6. Problem Statement Revisited

Despite progress, the challenges identified in the literature persist. Engagement with feedback is still uneven (Jansen et al., 2025), peer feedback continues to face sociocultural barriers (Thi Van Pham, 2022; Le et al., 2025), and teachers remain underprepared for fully exploiting digital tools. Geographical imbalances and methodological limitations further constrain the field (Chin & Chew, 2021). Thus, the findings reaffirm that online feedback research is vibrant but fragmented, with strong centres of excellence alongside underexplored regions and themes.

5.7. Implications

The insights from this bibliometric analysis have several implications for practice, policy, and research. Pedagogically, the results emphasize the need to better align feedback modalities teacher, peer, and automated—with student preferences and literacy levels, ensuring engagement and uptake. Institutions should prioritize capacity building by providing training for teachers in multimodal and AI-assisted feedback, particularly in underrepresented regions where digital divides persist. At a policy level, the concentration of research in technologically advanced institutions suggests the need for more international collaborations to diversify perspectives and contexts. For research, the findings highlight the importance of longitudinal, theory-driven studies and the expansion of feedback scholarship into less-studied regions, educational levels, and socio-emotional dimensions of writing.

6. CONCLUSION

This study systematically mapped the evolution of online feedback tools in writing education between 2000 and 2024 using bibliometric techniques. The results reveal a steady growth in research output, with peaks corresponding to major technological and contextual shifts, particularly the COVID-19 pandemic. Influential outlets, leading authors, and productive institutions underscore the dominance of technologically advanced contexts, while trending topics highlight a shift from error correction toward multimodality and AI integration. Factorial keyword analysis identified four thematic clusters—pedagogy, technology, higher education applications, and methodology—demonstrating both the maturity and fragmentation of the field.

Despite significant progress, challenges persist in terms of engagement, cultural acceptance of peer feedback, teacher preparedness, and methodological limitations. Geographical imbalances further restrict the global applicability of findings. By addressing these issues, future research can advance toward more inclusive, adaptive, and longitudinally grounded models of online feedback, ensuring that tools not only enhance writing outcomes but also respond to the diverse needs of learners and educators worldwide.

ETHICAL STATEMENT

The authors affirm that all data collection, analysis, and interpretation presented in this chapter were conducted manually by the research team. ChatGPT was used exclusively for language refinement and proofreading purposes. No generative AI tools were employed for content creation or data interpretation.

REFERENCES

Abdel Latif, M. M. M., Alsuhaibani, Z., & Alsahil, A. (2024). Matches and mismatches between Saudi university students' English writing feedback preferences and teachers' practices. *Assessing Writing*, *61*, 100863. Advance online publication. DOI: 10.1016/j.asw.2024.100863

Abuhassna, H., Adnan, M. A. B. M., & Awae, F. (2024). Exploring the synergy between instructional design models and learning theories: A systematic literature review. *Contemporary Educational Technology*, *16*(2), ep499. DOI: 10.30935/cedtech/14289

Akoto, M. (2021). Collaborative multimodal writing via google docs: Perceptions of french fl learners. *Languages (Basel, Switzerland)*, *6*(3), 140. Advance online publication. DOI: 10.3390/languages6030140

Al-Ghazali, F. (2015). Peer feedback for peer learning and sharing. *Learning and Teaching in Higher Education Gulf Perspectives*, *12*(1), 46–61. DOI: 10.18538/lthe.v12.n1.179

Alawad, E. A., & Hamid, F. A. (2025). Comparative Analysis of Feedback Practices and Perspectives in Online Academic Writing Assessments at Two Regional Tertiary Institutions. *World Journal of English Language*, *15*(4), 327–340. DOI: 10.5430/wjel.v15n4p327

Alnasser, S. M. N. (2022). EFL Learners' Perceptions of Integrating Computer-Based Feedback into Writing Classrooms: Evidence From Saudi Arabia. *SAGE Open*, *12*(3), 21582440221123021. Advance online publication. DOI: 10.1177/21582440221123021

Aria, M., & Cuccurullo, C. (2017). Bibliometrix: An R-tool for comprehensive science mapping analysis. *Journal of Informetrics*, *11*(4), 959–975. DOI: 10.1016/j.joi.2017.08.007

Asadi, M., Ebadi, S., Salman, A. R., Taheri, R., & Mohammadi, L. (2025). Investigating the effects of AI-assisted teacher instruction on online IELTS writing. *Social Sciences & Humanities Open*, *12*, 101747. Advance online publication. DOI: 10.1016/j.ssaho.2025.101747

Bakla, A. (2020). A mixed-methods study of feedback modes in EFL writing. *Language Learning & Technology*, *24*(1), 107–128. DOI: 10.64152/10125/44712

Budiman, R. (2025). *Teachers' written feedback in postgraduate online learning: students' perspectives*. Asian Association of Open Universities Journal., DOI: 10.1108/AAOUJ-01-2025-0015

Burrows, S., & Shortis, M. (2011). An evaluation of semi-automated, collaborative marking and feedback systems: Academic staff perspectives. *Australasian Journal of Educational Technology*, *27*(7), 1135–1154. DOI: 10.14742/ajet.909

Chen, T. (2016). Technology-supported peer feedback in ESL/EFL writing classes: A research synthesis. *Computer Assisted Language Learning, 29*(2), 365–397. DOI: 10.1080/09588221.2014.960942

Cheng, X., & Liu, Y. (2022). Student engagement with teacher written feedback: Insights from low-proficiency and high-proficiency L2 learners. *System, 109*, 102880. Advance online publication. DOI: 10.1016/j.system.2022.102880

Cheng, X., & Zhang, L. J. (2021). Teacher Written Feedback on English as a Foreign Language Learners' Writing: Examining Native and Nonnative English-Speaking Teachers' Practices in Feedback Provision. *Frontiers in Psychology, 12*, 629921. Advance online publication. DOI: 10.3389/fpsyg.2021.629921

Chin, H., & Chew, C. M. (2021). Profiling the research landscape on electronic feedback in educational context from 1991 to 2021: A bibliometric analysis. *Journal of Computers in Education, 8*(4), 551–586. DOI: 10.1007/s40692-021-00192-x

Ching, K. L., & Simon, S. (2025). Beyond the Best of Both Worlds: Student Perceptions of Hybrid Writing Courses. *College Composition and Communication, 76*(4), 494–517. DOI: 10.58680/ccc2025764494

Chong, I. (2018). Interplay among technical, socio-emotional and personal factors in written feedback research. *Assessment & Evaluation in Higher Education, 43*(2), 185–196. DOI: 10.1080/02602938.2017.1317712

Çiçek, M., & Kayaoğlu, M. N. (2024). Exploring The Impact Of Form And Content Feedback On Efl Writing Proficiency: A Quasi-Experimental Study. *Studies in Linguistics Culture and Flt, 12*(3), 31–56. DOI: 10.46687/PLYN8876

Cunningham, K. J. (2019). Student Perceptions and Use of Technology-Mediated Text and Screencast Feedback in ESL Writing. *Computers and Composition, 52*, 222–241. DOI: 10.1016/j.compcom.2019.02.003

Cunningham, K. J., & Link, S. (2021). Video and text feedback on ESL writing: Understanding ATTITUDE and negotiating relationshipS. *Journal of Second Language Writing, 52*, 100797. Advance online publication. DOI: 10.1016/j.jslw.2021.100797

Cuocci, S., Fattahi Marnani, P., Khan, I., & Roberts, S. (2023). A Meta-Synthesis of Technology-Supported Peer Feedback in ESL/EFL Writing Classes Research: A Replication of Chen's Study. *Languages (Basel, Switzerland), 8*(2), 114. Advance online publication. DOI: 10.3390/languages8020114

Dan, L., Mohamed, H. B., & Abuhassna, H. (2026). A bibliometric analysis of artificial intelligence: Impact on student motivation in education. In B. Edwards, H. Abuhassna, D. Olugbade, O. Ojo, & W. Jaafar Wan Yahaya (Eds.), *AI in education, governance, and leadership: Adoption, impact, and ethics* (pp. 97–120). IGI Global Scientific Publishing. https://doi.org/DOI: 10.4018/979-8-3373-5550-4.ch005 di Zhang, E., Liu, C., & Yu, S. (2024). The impact of a feedback intervention on university students' second language writing feedback literacy. *Innovations in Education and Teaching International*, *61*(3), 426–442. DOI: 10.1080/14703297.2023.2254275

Do, H. M. (2024). E-peer feedback training on L2 writing: A case study of inexperienced learners. *The JALT CALL Journal*, *20*(1), 1–22. DOI: 10.29140/jaltcall.v20n1.1242

Douglas, S. et al. "Use of an online peer review tool to support feedback and collaborative skills in preservice teachers." *CITE Journal*, Vol. 21 (2) (2021). CITE Journal • Fan, N. & Ma, Y. "The effects of automated writing evaluation (AWE) feedback on students' English writing quality: A systematic literature review." *Language Teaching Research Quarterly*, 2022.

Farnia, M., Hemmati, F., Yekta, R. R., & Mirsayafi, S. (2025). The Impact of Multimodal Feedback on Writing Complexity, Accuracy, and Fluency of Iranian EFL Learners in Flipped and Traditional Classrooms. *Journal of Applied Linguistics and Applied Literature*, *13*(1), 109–130. DOI: 10.22049/jalda.2025.30042.1731

Ghosh, R. K., Chakraborty, S., & Dutta, G. (2025). AI in Enhancing Bilingual Proficiency. In Advances in computational intelligence and robotics book series (pp. 141–176). https://doi.org/ DOI: 10.4018/979-8-3373-0275-1.ch005

Gonzalez-Torres, P., Cabrera-Solano, P., & Castillo-Cuesta, L. (2022). Exploring Perceptions of Online Feedback in Teaching EFL Speaking and Writing Skills during the COVID-19 Pandemic. *International Journal of Learning Teaching and Educational Research*, *21*(7), 330–344. DOI: 10.26803/ijlter.21.7.17

Guardado, M., & Shi, L. (2007). ESL students' experiences of online peer feedback. *Computers and Composition*, *24*(4), 443–461. DOI: 10.1016/j.compcom.2007.03.002

Högemann, J., Cunha, J., Núñez, J. C., Vallejo, G., Rodríguez, C., & Rosário, P. (2021). Writing intervention with elementary students struggling with writing: Examining approach profiles to the teacher feedback on writing quality and motivational variables. *Reading and Writing*, *34*(7), 1681–1710. DOI: 10.1007/s11145-021-10159-0

Hopton, S.-B. (2013). Rebooting revision: Leveraging technology to deliver formative and summative feedback. In Exploring Technology for Writing and Writing Instruction. https://doi.org/ DOI: 10.4018/978-1-4666-4341-3.ch010

Janar, A., & Nozima, U. (2022). The Integration of "Floop" Platform for Enhancing Effectiveness of Feedback in Postsecondary Education Context. *International Journal of Emerging Technologies in Learning*, *17*(15), 54–67. DOI: 10.3991/ijet.v17i15.30711

Jansen, T., Horbach, A., & Meyer, J. (2025). Feedback from Generative AI: Correlates of Student Engagement in Text Revision from 655 Classes from Primary and Secondary School. 15th International Conference on Learning Analytics and Knowledge Lak 2025, 831–836. https://doi.org/DOI: 10.1145/3706468.3706494

Jiang, L., Lee, I., & Yu, S. (2024). Conceptualizing multimodal feedback literacy for L2 writing teachers in the digital age. *International Journal of Applied Linguistics*, *34*(4), 1479–1496. DOI: 10.1111/ijal.12578

Krasniqi, R., & Përvetica, A. K. (2024). Pedagogical Innovation Amidst Adversity: Exploring Online Pedagogical Practices in Southeast Europe. *Journal of Educational and Social Research, 14*(5), 222–232. DOI: 10.36941/jesr-2024-0134

Kulprasit, W. (2024). The Convergence of the COVID-19 Pandemic and EFL Writing Pedagogy: The Paradigm Shift. *New English Teacher, 18*(1), 41–52.

Lan, Y.-T., Wang, J.-H., & Chana, T.-W. (2011). The framework of online writing system. *Proceedings of the 19th International Conference on Computers in Education Icce 2011*, 54–56.

Le, H. V., Dang, T. B., Vo, T. P., Nguyen, M. Q. P., & Nguyen, N. Q. C. (2025). Anonymous yet accountable: Investigating sociocultural dynamics in peer feedback among Vietnamese EFL students. *Learning, Culture and Social Interaction, 54*, 100939. Advance online publication. DOI: 10.1016/j.lcsi.2025.100939

Lee, I. (2014). Revisiting Teacher Feedback in EFL Writing from Sociocultural Perspectives. *TESOL Quarterly, 48*(1), 201–213. DOI: 10.1002/tesq.153

Li, D., & Wang, Y. (2024). Translanguaging as a Mediational Tool in the Process of Feedback in Second Language Writing. *Canadian Journal of Applied Linguistics, 47*(1), 121–136. DOI: 10.1515/CJAL-2024-0108

Li, T., Yusof, S. B., Abuhassna, H., & Pan, Q. (2026). The impact of AI on higher education trends and educational horizons. In B. Edwards, H. Abuhassna, D. Olugbade, O. Ojo, & W. Jaafar Wan Yahaya (Eds.), *AI in education, governance, and leadership: Adoption, impact, and ethics* (pp. 1–32). IGI Global Scientific Publishing. https://doi.org/DOI: 10.4018/979-8-3373-5550-4.ch001

Liang, T., Singh, C. K. S., Mulyadi, D., & Singh, T. S. M. (2025). Enhancing EFL Writing Through Online Peer Feedback: A Systematic Review of Higher Education Studies. *Journal of Curriculum and Teaching, 14*(1), 184–201. DOI: 10.5430/jct.v14n1p184

Liu, K., & Storch, N. (2023). Second language learners' engagement with written feedback. *Australian Review of Applied Linguistics, 46*(1), 4–28. DOI: 10.1075/aral.20029.liu

Liu, L. (2022). Application of Automated Writing Evaluation (AWE) System Based on Intelligent Technology. 2022 IEEE 2nd International Conference on Mobile Networks and Wireless Communications Icmnwc 2022. https://doi.org/DOI: 10.1109/ICMNWC56175.2022.10031924

Mahoney, P., Macfarlane, S., & Ajjawi, R. (2019). A qualitative synthesis of video feedback in higher education. *Teaching in Higher Education, 24*(2), 157–179. DOI: 10.1080/13562517.2018.1471457

Montiel, H., & Gomez-Zermeño, M. G. (2022). Rock the Boat! Shaken by the COVID-19 Crisis: A Review on Teachers' Competencies in ICT. *Frontiers in Education, 6*, 770442. Advance online publication. DOI: 10.3389/feduc.2021.770442

Mospan, N. (2023). Digitalisation of writing in higher education: The COVID-19 pandemic impact. *Journal of University Teaching & Learning Practice, 20*(2). Advance online publication. DOI: 10.53761/1.20.02.08

Nourinezhad, S., Hadipourfard, E., & Bavali, M. (2021). The effect of audio-visual feedback on writing components and writing performance of medical university students in two different modes of instruction, flipped and traditional. *Cogent Education, 8*(1), 1978621. Advance online publication. DOI: 10.1080/2331186X.2021.1978621

Osawa, K. (2024). Integrating Automated Written Corrective Feedback into E-Portfolios for second language Writing: Notion and Notion AI. *RELC Journal, 55*(3), 881–887. DOI: 10.1177/00336882231198913

Page, M. J., McKenzie, J. E., Bossuyt, P. M., Boutron, I., Hoffmann, T. C., Mulrow, C. D., Shamseer, L., Tetzlaff, J. M., Akl, E. A., Brennan, S. E., Chou, R., Glanville, J., Grimshaw, J. M., Hróbjartsson, A., Lalu, M. M., Li, T., Loder, E. W., Mayo-Wilson, E., McDonald, S., & Moher, D. (2021). The PRISMA 2020 statement: An updated guideline for reporting systematic reviews. *BMJ (Clinical Research Ed.), 372*(71), n71. Advance online publication. DOI: 10.1136/bmj.n71

Pan, Q., Jumaat, N. F., Abuhassna, H., & Tao, L. (2026). Transforming education in the digital age: An analysis of artificial intelligence and deep learning through bibliometric and systematic literature review. In B. Edwards, H. Abuhassna, D. Olugbade, O. Ojo, & W. Jaafar Wan Yahaya (Eds.), *AI in education, governance, and leadership: Adoption, impact, and ethics* (pp. 67–96). IGI Global Scientific Publishing. https://doi.org/DOI: 10.4018/979-8-3373-5550-4.ch004

Ryan, T., Henderson, M., Ryan, K., & Kennedy, G. (2021). Designing learner-centred text-based feedback: A rapid review and qualitative synthesis. *Assessment & Evaluation in Higher Education, 46*(6), 894–912. DOI: 10.1080/02602938.2020.1828819

Saeed, M. A., AbuSa'aleek, A., & Alharbi, M. A. (2024). Examining teacher's evaluative language in written, audio and screencast feedback on EFL learners' writing from the appraisal framework: A linguistic perspective. *Assessing Writing, 61*, 100871. Advance online publication. DOI: 10.1016/j.asw.2024.100871

Saiful, Wihastyanang, W. D., Sulistyo, G. H., & Mukminatien, N. (2019). Confronting effect of online teacher and peer feedback on the students' writing performance. Problems of Education in the 21st Century, 77(5), 650–666. https://doi.org/DOI: 10.33225/pec/19.77.650

Sedrakyan, G., van den Berg, S. M., Veldkamp, B. P., & van Hillegersberg, J. (2023). Analysis of the Feedback Digitization Needs in Higher Education: Experiences from Lockdown Education in the Netherlands and Germany. *International Journal of Information and Education Technology (IJIET), 13*(5), 778–784. DOI: 10.18178/ijiet.2023.13.5.1867

Semingson, P., Hurlbut, A., Owens, D., & Robertson, M. (2016). Scaffolding digital writing and storytelling in online-only teacher education courses. In Handbook of Research on Learner Centered Pedagogy in Teacher Education and Professional Development. https://doi.org/DOI: 10.4018/978-1-5225-0892-2.ch006

Singaram, V. S., Pillay, R., & Mbobnda Kapche, E. L. (2024). Exploring the role of digital technology for feedback exchange in clinical training: A scoping review. *Systematic Reviews, 13*(1), 298. Advance online publication. DOI: 10.1186/s13643-024-02705-y

Song, Y., Jin, H.-Y., Pan, Z., & Cutumisu, M. (2023). A Systematic Review of Automated Feedback Generation in Empirical Educational Research. *Proceedings of International Conference of the Learning Sciences Icls*, 1895–1896. DOI: 10.22318/icls2023.403455

Sousa, D. L., Campos, P. F., & Cesário, V. (2022). Design Implications for Interactive and Analogue Technologies supporting Distance Education: A Longitudinal Mixed-Method Study during the Pandemic. *Interaction Design and Architecture S*, *52*(52), 6–22. DOI: 10.55612/s-5002-052-001

Strobl, C. (2014). Attitudes towards online feedback on writing: Why students mistrust the learning potential of models. *ReCALL*, *27*(3), 340–357. DOI: 10.1017/S0958344015000099

Tan, S., Cho, Y. W., & Xu, W. (2023). Exploring the effects of automated written corrective feedback, computer-mediated peer feedback and their combination mode on EFL learner's writing performance. *Interactive Learning Environments*, *31*(10), 7276–7286. DOI: 10.1080/10494820.2022.2066137

Taskiran, A., Yazici, M., & Erdem Aydin, I. (2024). Contribution of automated feedback to the English writing competence of distance foreign language learners. *E-Learning and Digital Media*, *21*(1), 24–41. DOI: 10.1177/20427530221139579

Thapaliya, A., & Hrytsuk, Y. (2023). Exploring the Impact of COVID-19 on Education: A Study on Challenges and Opportunities in Online Learning. In Smart Innovation Systems and Technologies: Vol. 354 SIST. https://doi.org/DOI: 10.1007/978-981-99-3068-5_29

Thi, N. K., & Nikolov, M. (2022). How Teacher and Grammarly Feedback Complement One Another in Myanmar EFL Students' Writing. *The Asia-Pacific Education Researcher*, *31*(6), 767–779. DOI: 10.1007/s40299-021-00625-2

Thi Van Pham, A. (2022). Exploring Peer Feedback on Writing Assignments in an Online Learning Environment. *ACM International Conference Proceeding Series*, 203–208. https://doi.org/DOI: 10.1145/3514262.3514294

Thyrhaya Zein, T., Silvana Sinar, T., & Deliana, D. (2025). USING VIRTUAL WRITING TUTOR IN TEACHING WRITING TO EFL LEARNERS. *Jurnal Ilmiah Ilmu Terapan Universitas Jambi*, *9*(2), 474–484. DOI: 10.22437/jiituj.v9i2.36052

Tian, L., & Zhou, Y. (2020). Learner engagement with automated feedback, peer feedback and teacher feedback in an online EFL writing context. *System*, *91*, 102247. Advance online publication. DOI: 10.1016/j.system.2020.102247

Van, N. T., Abbas, A. F., Abuhassna, H., Awae, F., & Dike, D. (2021). Digital readiness for social educators in health care and online learning during COVID-19 pandemic: A bibliometric analysis. [iJIM]. *International Journal of Interactive Mobile Technologies*, *15*(18), 104–115. DOI: 10.3991/ijim.v15i18.25529

Wang, X. (2025). Students' perceptions of automated writing evaluation in autonomous learning. *Education and Information Technologies*, *30*(11), 14703–14735. DOI: 10.1007/s10639-025-13378-y

Wardat, S., & Akour, M. (2025). Teachers' Use of Generative AI in Jordanian Universities: Practices and Perceptions. *Forum for Linguistic Studies*, *7*(6), 90–102. DOI: 10.30564/fls.v7i6.9644

Wihastyanang, W. D., Kusumaningrum, S. R., Latief, M. A., & Cahyono, B. Y. (2020). Impacts of providing online teacher and peer feedback on students' writing performance. *Turkish Online Journal of Distance Education*, *21*(2), 178–189. DOI: 10.17718/tojde.728157

Yiğit, M. F., & Seferoğlu, S. S. (2023). Effect of video feedback on students' feedback use in the online learning environment. *Innovations in Education and Teaching International*, *60*(1), 15–25. DOI: 10.1080/14703297.2021.1966489

Yu, E. (2023). Intelligent enough? Artificial intelligence for online learners. *The Journal of Educators Online*, *20*(1). Advance online publication. DOI: 10.9743/JEO.2023.20.1.16

Zhang, E. D., Zhou, N., & Yu, S. (2023). Assessing L2 secondary student writing feedback literacy and its predictive effect on their L2 writing performance. *Language Teaching Research*, 13621688231217665. Advance online publication. DOI: 10.1177/13621688231217665

Zhang, J., & Zhang, L. J. (2025). *Integrating Various Types of Feedback in L2 Writing Instruction: Teachers' and Students' Perspectives*. International Journal of Applied Linguistics United Kingdom., DOI: 10.1111/ijal.12822

Zhang, R., & Zou, D. (2023). A review of research on technology-enhanced peer feedback for second language writing based on the activity theory framework. *Education and Information Technologies*, *28*(6), 6727–6753. DOI: 10.1007/s10639-022-11469-8

Zou, D., Xie, H., & Wang, F. L. (2022). Effects of Scaffolded Peer Assessment on Students' Holistic Critical Thinking in Academic Writing. In *Lecture Notes in Computer Science Including Subseries Lecture Notes in Artificial Intelligence and Lecture Notes in Bioinformatics* (Vol. 13357). LNCS., DOI: 10.1007/978-3-031-08939-8_13

Chapter 16
Redefining Academic Integrity in the Age of AI: Ethics and Security in Academic Content Creation

Francis Nalaza Reginio
https://orcid.org/0000-0001-5939-4508
University of Southeastern Philippines, Philippines

Rey Kenneth John G. Marces
https://orcid.org/0000-0002-7623-3535
University of Southeastern Philippines, Philippines

Hannah Mae G. Lolong
https://orcid.org/0000-0003-0665-3531
Davao del Norte State College, Philippines

Nikodemus Niko
https://orcid.org/0000-0001-5226-5332
Chulalongkorn University, Indonesia & Universitas Maritim Raja Ali Haji, Indonesia

ABSTRACT

Redefining academic integrity in an artificial intelligence (AI)-driven world is now a pressing issue for higher education. This paper examines the implications of AI on academic integrity in higher education, focusing on how AI tools challenge traditional notions of originality, authorship, and ethical accountability in academic content creation. The shift in focus is from detection and punishment to ethics and pedagogy, guided by the notion of enabling students to use AI ethically. Case studies from Southeast Asia reveal how institutions are responding to AI concerns with inclusive pedagogies, disclosure-based policies, and frameworks for transparency and accountability. This paper argues that academic integrity accounts for the needs of diverse learners to support equitable access to institutional learning opportunities and resources. Institutions need to make the necessary changes to continuously adapt to the rapid development of AI technologies. By reimagining academic integrity, higher education can uphold its responsibilities in an AI-driven future.

DOI: 10.4018/979-8-3373-5601-3.ch016

1. INTRODUCTION

Artificial intelligence (AI) tools such as ChatGPT, GrammarlyGO, and Gemini are transforming how students and educators engage with academic writing. These technologies provide speed and efficiency, helping students draft, revise, and refine text in ways that were not possible before. As the United Nations Educational, Scientific and Cultural Organization (UNESCO) (2021) and Boddington (2017) observe, these changes challenge universities to reconsider long-standing ideas of authorship and originality. Academic integrity, which was traditionally centered on honesty, accountability, and respect for scholarly work, is now facing new complexities. This transformation is visible in empirical work. Lund et al. (2025) found that many students view AI use as ethically ambiguous, as full AI-generated essays are widely considered misconduct, while partial uses, such as editing or brainstorming, are often contested. Tan and Maravilla (2024) argue that generative AI need not be destructive to academic integrity if incorporated responsibly. Meanwhile, reviews of generative AI in higher education show both its promise and its risks (Bittle & El-Gayar, 2025).

Much of the discussion about integrity still centers on plagiarism, but this lens is too narrow once students begin drafting with AI. Building on the complexity introduced earlier, scholars have asked whether machine-generated text can be called original and how authorship should be credited (Dawson, 2020; Floridi & Chiriatti, 2020). In Indonesia, for example, Malik et al. (2023) found that while students appreciate AI's help with grammar, many also worry that it weakens their creative voice. Simultaneously, other researchers stress that questions of fairness and trust are just as important as originality in the context of AI use. Cotton, Cotton, and Shipway (2023) point out that AI-detection tools often generate false positives, which can erode confidence between students and faculty. In addition, Gretzky and Dishon (2025) add that these systems may disadvantage students from marginalized or non-dominant language groups. Similar concerns appear in educational measurement, where Bulut et al. (2024) show how automated scoring can replicate bias, and Guo et al. (2025) highlight its negative impact on English language learners. Together, these findings deepen our understanding of the challenges introduced in previous sections.

Despite these dilemmas, ethical frameworks provide useful perspectives. A deontological view (Kant, 1785/1997) frames unacknowledged AI use as a violation of honesty. From this perspective, it is dishonest to submit any AI-produced work (as opposed to work executed collaboratively with AI) without indicating as such. In addition, Gilligan's (1982) ethics of care emphasizes the relational aspect of moral decision-making and the moral context, rather than the rationale, for why we might want to encourage our students to use AI or writing tools to overcome language barriers or work pressure. Rather than punishment, this approach emphasizes support. Similarly, Stommel (2014) advocates for critical digital pedagogy, prompting educational institutions to reframe surveillance into considerations of agency and reflexivity. Extending this further, Tan & Maravilla (2024) expand on this consideration by supporting ethical frameworks within a constructivist learning stance of theories of agency, arguing that students share in constructing norms of integrity. When tools are clear and used transparently, norms can be based on an understanding of responsible integration in the curricular writing enactments.

International frameworks are also part of the conversation. The Organisation for Economic Co-operation and Development (OECD) (2019) and UNESCO (2021) state principles: accountability, fairness, human-centered AI, and transparency, which are again in line with universities drafting policies for AI that align with rights, but which can usefully draw on the principles towards responsible use of technology. Alsharefeen and Al Sayari (2025), through dialogue, use of AI integrity policies that consider faculty perception as an example of why definitions and resulting language of policy are divorced from examples within the classroom, stressing the necessity of globally inclusive policy. Collectively, approaches, facts, and frameworks support the shift from a rule-based academic integrity policy to an ethics view that considers the context of the writing or enacted space. Another issue is that institutions often respond when problems arise rather than taking a proactive approach. Many institutional policies may seek to either ban AI or increase surveillance, but these solutions can lead to inequities - particularly with students who come from marginalized or non-dominant language backgrounds (Gretzky & Dishon, 2025). Birks and Clare (2023) connect misconduct with AI to crime prevention theory in discussing design for prevention (multi-layered) rather than reactive punishment. Without careful policy, algorithmic enforcement can erode trust, reproduce inequity, and alienate learners.

Although there is growing debate on AI in education, there remains a lack of systematic guidance for redefining integrity in ways that balance ethical imperatives with classroom practicality. Most research emphasizes detection, enforcement, or student attitudes (Lund et al., 2025), often overlooking normative frameworks, inclusive pedagogies, and strategic approaches for integrity. This chapter addresses this gap by combining ethical theory, critical digital pedagogy, and case studies from Southeast Asia to propose an integrative, forward-looking approach to academic integrity in AI-enabled educational environments.

To address these aims, the chapter uses a qualitative and analytical methodology. It draws on three main sources of evidence. First, institutional policy documents and integrity codes are reviewed to see how universities respond to AI. Second, peer-reviewed articles, books, and reports are synthesized to cover ethical and educational debates. Third, case studies from Southeast Asian universities show how institutions adapt to AI's challenges. The analysis combines ethical theories with real examples. By applying deontological ethics, ethics of care, critical digital pedagogy, and global AI norms, the chapter reevaluates how integrity can be defined in educational practice.

2. DEFINING ACADEMIC INTEGRITY IN THE AI ERA

The concept of academic integrity is evolving as AI rapidly advances in higher education. Traditional rules regarding plagiarism, citation, and originality no longer fully capture the dynamics of how students and teachers interact with writing when AI is involved. In Southeast Asia, educators and students are already facing situations where old rules no longer apply. For example, Malik et al. (2023) found that Indonesian students appreciated AI tools for improving grammar and organizing ideas, but they worried that overuse might harm creativity and critical thinking. Batubara, Wariyati, and Prawiyata (2025) also observed that most first-year students were eager to use AI for grammar and idea generation, while some feared becoming too dependent on it. At the same time, many ASEAN universities continue to follow Western models of academic integrity, which may not fully align with local cultural and language contexts. In this setting, academic honesty involves more than avoiding plagiarism, as it requires fairness, trust, and integrity in how learning happens. It also calls for a fresh look at what "authorship" and "originality" mean when AI plays a role in writing.

These findings demonstrate that AI is becoming an integral part of students' learning, not just a supplementary tool. As a result, academic integrity needs to be redefined to address new questions: What counts as authorship if a student uses AI to organize an argument? Can work still be called original if AI contributes to its structure or style? These are practical questions teachers and students face in classrooms today, making it essential to develop policies that balance the benefits of AI with the need for honesty, fairness, and trust in education.

2.1. Evolving Notions of Authorship and Originality

The findings from Southeast Asia's research affirm that originality (the quality of being novel or unique) and authorship (the act of originating or creating a written work) are currently debatable notions. In Indonesia, studies indicate that students perceive AI as useful for enhancing grammar, coherence, and organization; however, they also express concern that their creativity and unique voice are diminished when they over-rely on these devices (Marhaban, Sulistyo, & Widiastuti, 2023). Equally, research among Indonesian English as a Foreign Language (EFL) learners emphasizes that AI tools are deemed effective in providing ideas and refining structure, but most learners are uncertain whether such support would be considered acceptable under academic integrity requirements (Utami et al., 2023). In Malaysia and other ASEAN countries, surveys further reveal that institutional policies on AI remain underdeveloped, leaving students without a clear delineation of acceptable use in academic endeavors (Ravšelj et al., 2025). These revelations imply authorship is no longer merely about someone writing. It now entails negotiation between human ideas and machine aid.

Bearing in mind the ethical perspective, the deontological approach, which emphasizes duty, focuses on the intention behind actions. A student who uses AI as an aid, then reflects and edits diligently, maintains academic integrity. On the other hand, a student who uses AI to escape the duty of thinking and reflection does not act with integrity. From the perspective of the ethics of care, Gilligan (1982) argues that authorship is not just about rules but also about context. For example, a student writing in a second language may depend on AI for clarity. Integrity here means helping the student succeed without shame, not punishing them for seeking help. Critical digital pedagogy provides another view. It shows that authorship should not be hidden behind machines. Teachers can design tasks that require students to show drafts or reflections, demonstrating that their thinking is active and ongoing. International frameworks, such as those established by UNESCO (2021), also emphasize transparency and accountability. Students should declare how they use AI in their writing. Originality is no longer a strict yes or no. A text remains original if the student uses AI responsibly and demonstrates their understanding.

2.2. The Role of Artificial Intelligence in Academic Writing

The data indicate that students and teachers continue to value traditional principles of honesty, accountability, and scholarly work. However, they now expect these principles to be redefined for the age of AI. In Malaysia and other Southeast Asian contexts, students are concerned that the misuse of AI could lead to the spread of misinformation and unfair practices. These concerns are more pronounced when policies and guidance are unclear (Marhaban et al., 2023; Utami et al., 2023). Global surveys confirm that students appreciate the benefits of AI for fluency and efficiency, but worry about losing originality, competence, and responsibility (Ravšelj et al., 2025; Cotton et al., 2023). Integrity frameworks must now include transparency, fairness, and student agency. Yet many institutions struggle to implement these frameworks due to limited resources, cultural differences, and uneven policy development (UNESCO, 2021).

When examining the ethical frameworks, we can begin to analyze how they are reshaped. Kant's conception of duty emphasizes that integrity is not only about avoiding consequences but also about choosing to act honestly for its own sake. The ethics of care suggests that institutions should provide support for students who require accommodations, such as training in AI literacy and targeted help for second-language writers. Critical digital pedagogy suggests that integrity should be grounded in student reflection and ownership. Finally, norms, such as UNESCO's Recommendation on the Ethics of Artificial Intelligence (2021), stress transparency, accountability, and fairness as guiding principles. Applied to higher education, this implies that institutions may need to develop policies requiring students to declare their use of AI and to provide staff with training to address AI-related issues fairly.

2.3. Global Institutional Comparisons and Lessons

Examining approaches to academic integrity in the AI era across different global contexts provides valuable insights for institutions seeking balanced and effective policies. In Western universities, particularly in the United States and Europe, higher education institutions tend to integrate generative AI into assessment design while emphasizing transparent policies and human oversight (Moorhouse, Yeo, & Wan, 2023). There are top-ranking universities that have established clear frameworks, allowing students to utilize AI for drafting and research support, provided that appropriate citations and declarations accompany AI-assisted work. Through this approach, it explains a shift toward educational guidance and ethical literacy, upholding the importance of trust and student agency.

Moreover, several African universities demonstrate a cautious approach, often prioritizing strict prohibitions on AI-generated content to prevent academic misconduct (Alsharefeen & Al Sayari, 2025). While such policies aim to safeguard traditional notions of authorship, they risk alienating students and stifling creative engagement with emerging technologies. These differences explain the tension between innovation and compliance in global academic governance, which elaborates the Western institutions that often emphasize adaptive and educative strategies, whereas some African universities adopt precautionary and enforcement-driven frameworks.

Lessons from these institutional comparisons suggest that hybrid strategies may be most effective. Policies should combine clear ethical guidelines, human oversight, and educational support to help students navigate AI tools responsibly (Ateeq, Alzoraiki, Milhem, & Ateeq, 2024; Moorhouse et al., 2023). Integrating lessons from global practices encourages institutions to design AI governance models that are both culturally sensitive and pedagogically supportive, thereby fostering academic integrity while not discouraging legitimate and innovative uses of AI in learning.

2.4. Core Values of Academic Integrity

Evaluating our findings through an ethical lens provides different perspectives. A deontological perspective suggests that intention should be primary: in instances where intention is educational (using AI for reflecting or learning), students engaged in the process honestly. However, when AI becomes a time-saving device that avoids analytical thinking, it breaches integrity. The ethics of care highlights the context of a student's situation. For students writing in a second language or from a school or community where technology is underdeveloped, using AI is more of a survival strategy than an act of deceit. In such cases, integrity means providing guidance instead of punishment. Critical digital pedagogy offers an additional perspective by emphasizing that authorship should be visible. Teachers can ask students to keep drafts or explain how they used AI in their work. That way, originality is tied to the student's thinking process, not only the final product. International bodies, such as UNESCO (2021), also emphasize principles like transparency and accountability. These global frameworks support the idea that students should declare when and how they used AI, making authorship clearer.

The fundamental value of integrity has not disappeared, but its meaning is shifting in response to the emergence of AI. Honesty, accountability, and scholarly effort remain central, yet they now require stronger attention to transparency and reflection. Malik et al. (2023) report that students themselves want AI use to be acknowledged. Fang et al. (2025) observe a similar pattern among education students, who valued AI for planning and revision but worried about losing competence if they depended on it too much. These examples remind us that integrity is tied not only to the final output but also to the process of writing.

Universities in Southeast Asia are undergoing a period of transition. Many policies are outdated, and both students and teachers want clearer guidelines. Integrity is not merely a personal choice. It also involves relationships between learners and institutions, as well as cultural and linguistic writing contexts, and the combination of human and machine input. For students in second-language or under-resourced settings, AI may be essential. Strict bans could unfairly penalize them. A more effective approach is to teach responsible AI use, encourage reflection, and promote transparency as the norm. The approach all points in one direction. Integrity in the AI era must be principled and context-sensitive.

3. ETHICAL CHALLENGES IN AI-AUGMENTED CONTENT CREATION

Academic writing with AI raises ethical challenges aside from the common anxieties about plagiarism or incorrect citation. Moreover, students may unknowingly gain from others or submit papers written almost entirely from AI-generated material, which can inaccurately reflect their true understanding and generate uneven benefits. Machine-assisted ghostwriting is becoming increasingly widespread, with a significant portion of an academic writing assignment comprising AI-generated material rather than the student's own writing.

3.1. AI- Plagiarism and Hidden Help

The difference between original work and unauthorized assistance has devalued the value of AI-generated work, raising significant concerns about academic integrity. Chowdhury Niloy et al. (2024) said that AI-generated work could be presented as a student's own, often without proper citation. Hence, it renders detection through the traditional tools for plagiarism. This form of plagiarism is quite pernicious and therefore often goes undetected by conventional tools designed to detect words copied from elsewhere. Additionally, AI-related forms of plagiarism necessitate a sophisticated approach to detection and prevention measures, including educating students on the ethical use of AI tools and devising alternative assessment methods that encourage creative thinking and original writing.

AI is used to provide hidden "help" in academic writing rather than an open acknowledgment. Similar experiences were also reported by Ozfidan, El-Dakhs, & Alsalim (2024), indicating that this type of hidden assistance can occur in various ways, such as using AI to generate ideas, structure papers, and rewrite materials without proper attribution. The problem with hidden help is that it undermines the principles of academic integrity by misrepresenting the student's own abilities and contributions (Gonsalves, 2024). It also creates an unfair advantage for students who have access to AI tools, while disadvantaging those who do not.

Students can be completely unaware of what an AI collaboration entails by submitting AI-generated material without specifying the extent to which AI contributed. Zhai, Wibowo, and Li (2024) state that the black-box nature of certain AI tools may render it impossible for students to clearly comprehend how the AI produces the relevant content, thus potentially resulting in unintended plagiarism or misrepresentation. Additionally, Shin, Wei, and Vanchinkhuu's (2025) study examines digital plagiarism in EFL learning in Korea, Mongolia, and China, focusing on AI use and the attitudes of learners and teachers. This study found variations in the perception of digital plagiarism among different nationalities, as well as among groups of teachers and students, in different cultures. The role-specific and culture-specific factors were identified as crucial in developing the conception of academic integrity in the AI age. Teaching students how AI tools work, the ethical issues surrounding their use, and the importance of preserving sanity through transparency and attribution will greatly assist them. Through developing a greater consciousness of AI and its impact on scholarly work, institutions can help students make informed decisions about the use of AI. These studies emphasize that institutional policies and varying cultural contexts shape how moral issues related to educational technologies are addressed. They envision an environment where no single cure-all exists to address all such problems, and localized approaches, considering regional norms and regularities, are required to maintain academic integrity in the context of AI.

3.2. Machine-Assisted Ghostwriting

Artificial intelligence has made it easy for students to use machine-aided ghostwriting, allowing them to present work done with AI as if they did it all alone. This was initially carried out through professional writing sites; however, AI programs now make it easier to do so (Miao et al., 2023). These are authentic issues of academic integrity as they can skew what a student actually knows and produce work that is potentially incorrect or low in quality. It is imperative as well to mark the area where the student's ideas end, and the contribution of the AI begins (Gonsalves, 2024). The problem is especially visible when AI completes most of an assignment, and the student does not clearly state that it was used, leaving instructors uncertain about who should be credited for the work. In Vietnam, as Bui and Tong (2025) reported, English-major students admitted that using AI software would increase writing productivity but feared it would damage academic honesty.

Similarly, Weidmann (2024) notes that integrating AI into academic writing challenges traditional authorship and responsibility, prompting the need for clear guidelines and ethical frameworks. When AI generates uncredited content, it undermines established notions of individual contribution and affects pedagogy and evaluation. This integrity challenge requires teachers to redesign assignments, not only to detect abuse but also to support the ethical use of AI as part of the pedagogical process (Ateeq et al., 2024). By requiring drafts, explicit statements on AI involvement, or labeled AI-generated content, educators can ensure clear authorship and uphold integrity. In the meantime, Fitas (2025) clarified that organizations must regulate while providing support, particularly for students who may rely on AI to overcome language or time constraints. Therefore, beyond enforcement, universities are compelled to develop policies and pedagogical strategies that ensure fairness, promote ethical awareness, and place the students' genuine input at the center of the learning process.

4. SECURITY THREATS AND AI DETECTION LIMITATIONS

The said AI detection tools are now widely used in schools and universities to check whether students rely on generative AI. While these tools are helpful, they are not perfect and can sometimes produce fair and misleading results. Overreliance on them may create fear, reinforce inequities, and weaken trust between teachers and students. A balanced approach is needed, combining detection with education, transparency, and fair judgment, rather than relying solely on it as a measure of integrity.

4.1. Infallibility of Current Detection Tools

There are no perfect tools, including AI detection systems. Weber-Wulff et al. (2023) reveal that many AI detectors generate false positives, flagging human-written texts as AI-generated. Also, there are false negatives where AI writing passes as human, depending on the writing style, the AI model used, or the complexity of the text. This means that the same text may be judged differently across different tools, leading to inconsistent and unreliable assessments of students' work.

Recent research shows that AI-detection tools have clear limitations. Perkins et al. (2024a) note that even small changes in wording, sentence structure, or spelling can make AI-generated text harder to detect. Giray (2024) notes that many detection systems are unable to adapt to diverse writing contexts, resulting in unreliable results when used as proof of authorship. Elkhatat, Elsaid, and Almeer (2023) highlight that tools designed to detect plagiarism struggle when texts combine human and AI writing, making it difficult to judge proper use of AI support. Similarly, minor edits or syntax changes can allow AI-generated content to evade detection, revealing a structural gap: tools meant to catch AI often lag behind the AI itself. These weaknesses have significant implications for academic settings. When flawed detection results are treated as absolute evidence, students may be unfairly penalized, even if they acted honestly. Many tools do not clearly explain how they reach their conclusions (Elkhatat et al., 2023), making it difficult for students or teachers to question the outcomes. This lack of transparency can harm trust between students and institutions, thereby increasing the risk of unjust treatment.

4.2. Algorithmic Surveillance and Punitive Environments

When students and teachers use AI detection tools, it leads to an environment where they feel they are under surveillance. If these tools are treated as definitive proof of misconduct, institutions may punish students without giving them the opportunity to explain or show their draft history. This creates fear and discourages creative risk-taking. Additionally, a study on the testing of detection tools for AI-generated text found that many tools are claimed to be "likely AI" with little explanation, and there is low transparency in the decision-making process (Weber-Wulff, 2023).

The study by Elkhatat, Elsaid, and Almeer (2023) confirms that students face unfair and inconsistent results due to the lack of clear standards for detection tools. Citron (2024) notes that algorithmic surveillance in schools can lead students to feel treated as suspects rather than learners, thereby damaging the trust between teachers and students. In addition, Wang (2024) explains that algorithmic decisions in education may yield biased or inconsistent outcomes, while Huang (2023) emphasizes that weak safeguards can compromise student privacy and reduce trust. These studies also show that relying too heavily on hidden detection systems can harm student agency, fairness, and dignity.

Ethical frameworks from contemporary AI research emphasize fairness, transparency, and human-centered evaluation, aligning with the ENAI recommendations, which advocate for integrating AI in an ethical manner while protecting student dignity (Foltynek et al., 2023). Similarly, Chan and Colloton (2023) argue for policies combining detection with pedagogical guidance, reflecting a care-based approach that attends to student learning and diverse contexts.

4.3. Equity Issues in Detection Mechanisms

Evidence suggests that AI detection tools do not operate with uniform reliability across all student populations. Non-native English speakers and students with second-language backgrounds are disproportionately at risk of being flagged, even when their work is entirely their own. Studies by Giray (2024) and Liang et al. (2023) highlight how false positives from AI detection disproportionately affect these groups, as well as writers with distinctive or technical writing styles. Elkhatat, Elsaid, and Almeer (2023) further demonstrate that detection accuracy varies depending on the AI model being evaluated: tools more reliably identify outputs from older models like GPT-3.5, while outputs from more advanced systems, such as GPT-4 are frequently misclassified. Moreover, human-authored technical texts or less fluent writing are sometimes erroneously flagged, revealing a structural limitation in these tools.

Given these complexities, relying exclusively on AI detection systems as evidence of academic misconduct is fraught with risk. False positives, false negatives, hidden biases, and opaque decision-making can unfairly penalize students and undermine trust in educational institutions. Consequently, detection tools should be treated as supplementary evidence, to be interpreted alongside human judgment and the contextual knowledge of student work. To mitigate inequities, institutions should complement AI detection with assessment designs that emphasize the learning process rather than solely evaluating final outcomes. Process-oriented tasks—such as staged drafts, reflective writing, and oral presentations—can reduce incentives for misuse while simultaneously promoting authentic learning experiences (Bui & Tong, 2025; Ulla et al., 2024; Tan & Maravilla, 2024). Policies should prioritize transparency, inclusivity, and pedagogical support, ensuring that academic integrity is maintained while minimizing the reinforcement of systemic bias. By integrating human oversight with thoughtful assessment design, universities can strike a balance between accountability and fairness, thereby cultivating an environment where all students are assessed equitably.

5. GLOBAL AI ETHICS AND INSTITUTIONAL POLICY

Recent global discussions on the ethics of artificial intelligence have led to the establishment of frameworks aimed at ensuring the responsible development and application of AI across various sectors, including education. Prominent organizations, such as the OECD and UNESCO, highlight essential values like transparency, accountability, inclusiveness, fairness, and respect for human rights (OECD, 2019; UNESCO, 2021). These principles provide normative guidance that shapes the integration of AI in classrooms, the handling of student data, and policies aimed at protecting equity. The OECD AI Principles serve as a policy foundation, while UNESCO's Recommendation on the Ethics of Artificial Intelligence sets an international standard for the responsible use of AI.

5.1. Values in Global AI Ethics Frameworks

Global AI ethics guidelines function as both a reference point and a normative anchor for educational institutions, guiding the governance and routine deployment of AI. Jobin, Ienca, and Vayena (2019) observe that ethical AI frameworks universally emphasize human-centered principles, transparency, accountability, fairness, and inclusiveness. These principles are particularly relevant in sensitive environments such as schools and universities, where AI decisions directly affect learners' opportunities, assessments, and well-being. The OECD Principles on Artificial Intelligence, adopted by more than 40 countries, underscore the importance of human-centered values and accountable governance, ensuring that AI deployment contributes to inclusive prosperity and societal benefit (OECD, 2019). Similarly, UNESCO's Recommendation focuses on human rights, fairness, inclusivity, and sustainability, offering a globally recognized standard that has been adopted by 193 member states (UNESCO, 2021). By aligning educational practices with these guidelines, institutions can evaluate the ethical quality of AI tools and anticipate potential harms or inequities.

On the transparency side, it requires AI systems to be explainable and open to scrutiny. In education, this means students and teachers must understand how AI tools process data, what outputs they generate, and their limitations. Without transparency, user trust and accountability suffer, as biases and errors may remain hidden. Accountability follows: if AI influences educational decisions, such as grading or recommendations, institutions and developers must bear responsibility for the outcomes, set clear policies, and create channels for addressing errors, rather than delegating all judgment to algorithms.

Inclusiveness means making sure AI tools support all students, no matter their background, language, or abilities. This means designing systems that are easy to use, work in different languages, and avoid unfair bias that could harm vulnerable groups. UNESCO (2021) warns that ignoring inclusivity could make educational gaps worse. Therefore, incorporating AI into schools should include fairness checks and policies that prioritize students' needs, ensuring everyone has access to knowledge.

Global guidelines, such as those from UNESCO and OECD, help schools translate significant ethical principles into everyday practices. By following these standards, schools can protect students' rights and create fair and ethical learning environments. This is especially important today, as AI tools are often developed internationally and used in classrooms worldwide. Following these values also helps build trust among students, teachers, and the wider public.

5.2. Transparency, Accountability, and Inclusiveness

Among the core ethical values, transparency, accountability, and inclusiveness hold particular importance in education because of their impact on fairness. Transparency, as Floridi and Cowls (2022) propose, means that users must understand the operations and data use of AI. In the classrooms, this means that both students and teachers must be aware of what information is collected, how AI tools generate outputs, and the potential limitations of these outputs. Without such transparency, AI systems risk creating "black box" settings that discount academic honesty and bar informed consent. If plagiarism software flags text as "probably AI-written" without providing reasons, it explicitly violates transparency, thereby undermining fairness and trust.

Accountability builds upon transparency. When educational institutions rely on AI for assessments, grading, or recommendations, they must establish procedures to review, challenge, and correct algorithmic decisions. Jobin et al. (2019) emphasize that ethical AI must include human oversight and clearly delineated responsibility for outcomes. Without such accountability, students may be exposed to uncorrected errors, and institutions may evade responsibility for the harms caused by AI.

Inclusiveness ensures AI in education works for all students, not just those with preexisting advantages. AI tools may reflect data biases, resulting in unfair outcomes (Huang, 2023), such as disadvantaging non-native speakers or individuals with disabilities. Developers and schools must actively check for bias, utilize diverse data, and regularly test for fairness. Clear policies should also require AI to reduce educational inequalities.

These three values—namely, (1) transparency, (2) accountability, and (3) inclusiveness—usually provide a strong guide for how AI should be used in education. Transparency makes AI systems easier to understand and question. Accountability ensures that schools take responsibility when tools malfunction or cause harm. Inclusiveness ensures that no student is left behind. If schools and universities adopt these values in their policies and practices, they can use AI as a support for teaching and learning rather than a risk to fairness. This aligns with the principles set out by the OECD and UNESCO, which emphasize that AI should always remain under human guidance and be connected to broader social and ethical goals. In short, upholding these core values maximizes the benefits of AI for all students and preserves fairness in education.

5.3. Ethical frameworks and moral consequences

The integration of AI in educational settings raises profound moral and ethical questions regarding the creation and evaluation of academic content. Teachers and students are confronted with dilemmas surrounding the legitimacy of AI-assisted work, the value of human labor, and the cultivation of critical thinking. Jobin, Ienca, and Vayena (2019) argue that ethical AI frameworks should not only guide technical implementation but also inform the moral responsibilities of users, ensuring that AI serves as a tool for enhancement rather than a shortcut that undermines learning.

The ease with which AI generates written content challenges traditional concepts of authorship, originality, and plagiarism. Conventional academic integrity policies are often ill-equipped to address the nuances of AI-assisted work, especially when texts result from a hybrid of human and machine contributions. To uphold ethical standards, universities must develop new guidelines that strike a balance between the innovative potential of AI and the fundamental principles of fairness, honesty, and academic rigor. Without such recalibration, AI risks being used in ways that erode ethical scholarship rather than enhance it.

From a philosophical standpoint, Kantian ethics emphasizes that moral action must respect the autonomy and dignity of individuals (Kant, 1785/1997). Applied to AI in education, this perspective suggests that the use of AI-generated content becomes morally objectionable if it disregards the creator's intentionality or misrepresents their intellectual contribution. Flagging AI-generated work without context, or punishing students for ethically responsible use of AI, violates the categorical imperative by treating individuals merely as means to an institutional end. Similarly, the ethics of care (Gilligan, 1982) highlights the relational dimensions of morality. Educators are encouraged to consider students' unique circumstances, such as linguistic barriers, resource limitations, or differing levels of digital literacy, before determining the ethicality of AI-assisted work. This approach emphasizes guidance, support, and moral accountability over punitive measures.

The moral consequences of AI use extend beyond individual assessment. Institutions that fail to integrate ethical oversight and reflective policy risk fostering environments where students rely on AI uncritically, potentially eroding creativity, independent reasoning, and trust. Jobin et al. (2019) note that global AI ethics frameworks stress principles such as human-centeredness, fairness, and inclusiveness, which directly translate into educational practice. By aligning policies with these values, universities can establish an ethical framework that enables AI to serve as a learning-enhancing tool rather than a source of inequity or academic misconduct.

Furthermore, complementing ethical frameworks with institutional policies encourages critical engagement with AI, rather than mere compliance. Students learn to assess AI outputs thoughtfully, recognize potential biases, and understand their responsibilities in maintaining academic integrity. Integrating both Kantian and care ethics perspectives ensures that policies are contextually sensitive, promoting a culture of compassionate accountability. Such an approach enhances ethical literacy, upholds scholarly standards, and enables AI to serve as a resource for innovation and ethical learning. Thus, these frameworks in education must address both the technical and moral consequences of AI use. By merging global AI ethics principles (Jobin, Ienca, & Vayena, 2019) with contextually grounded moral reasoning, institutions can navigate the complexities of AI in the academe, preserving integrity while developing an equitable and responsible learning environment.

6. CASE STUDIES IN HIGHER EDUCATION INSTITUTIONS

Case studies in higher education show that universities are still figuring out how to deal with generative AI (GenAI), especially when it comes to academic integrity and ethical use. Across Southeast Asia, institutions are experimenting with different approaches, and some create guidelines, others redesign assessments, while many simply try to keep up with student behavior. These examples help us understand what works on the ground and what falls apart once rules meet real-life classroom situations. One thing becomes clear that even the best policy cannot stand alone. Success depends heavily on the mindset of teachers, the culture of the university, and how well students understand the rules.

6.1. Southeast Asia Higher Education Institutions

In Vietnam, a group of universities tested an AI Assessment Scale (AIAS), which helped lecturers design tasks that explicitly integrate different levels of AI use. One Vietnamese lecturer shared that before using the AIAS, several student submissions sounded "too perfect," raising doubts about whether the work was original. After redesigning tasks using the scale, she required students to show drafts and short reflections. This helped students become more open about how they used AI, and it reduced dishonest behavior because the process itself encouraged transparency. According to Perkins et al. (2024), the pilot yielded encouraging results, including a decline in plagiarism cases linked to AI, improved student performance in several modules, and increased staff openness to discussing AI with learners. Instead of treating AI as something suspicious, the framework encouraged constructive conversation about its benefits and limits.

In the Philippines, a qualitative study by Ulla et al. (2024) examined how university language teachers interpret and use GenAI. Their insights reflected a delicate balance; while AI can help level the playing field for students with weaker writing confidence or limited English proficiency, it can also exacerbate inequalities when access to and training on AI are uneven. Yan et al. (2024) similarly note that concerns about bias, transparency, and readiness are prevalent across many contexts, suggesting that local initiatives are most effective when connected to broader ethical and pedagogical discussions. The case from one university in Manila, where a language teacher allowed students to use ChatGPT only for brainstorming ideas. Students then rewrote the ideas in their own words. This method was especially helpful for shy or struggling writers who often struggled to start their essays. The teacher noted an improvement in confidence and better-quality drafts, without losing authenticity.

Hong Kong provides a more policy-oriented model. One university formally adopted GenAI as part of a new "fifth literacy," alongside oral, written, visual, and digital communication (The University of Hong Kong, 2023). By providing institution-wide access to tools like ChatGPT and image generators and establishing advisory committees, the university aimed to normalize the responsible use of AI. According to one lecturer, students initially viewed AI mainly as a shortcut or a way to cheat. Once the policy clarified expectations, however, students began using AI for more productive purposes, such as generating study questions, rehearsing presentations, and revising drafts. Clear guidelines appeared to reduce anxiety and gave students permission to explore AI capabilities without fear of crossing ethical lines.

As Chan and Colloton (2023) emphasize, the overarching lesson from these Southeast Asian experiences is that effective GenAI policy requires more than formal guidelines. Vietnam focused on assignment design, the Philippines highlighted inclusion and linguistic diversity, while Hong Kong invested heavily in infrastructure and literacy development. Despite these differences, the outcomes point to the same essentials: clarity, continuous teacher training, and equitable digital access. Innovation can only flourish when these foundational conditions are met.

6.2. Inclusive Pedagogies vs Policy Failure

In higher education, inclusive pedagogy is a flexible approach that adapts teaching to students' varied linguistic, technological, and socio-economic realities. Policy failure, by contrast, often occurs when well-intentioned regulations cannot be effectively implemented because institutions lack the necessary resources, clarity, or consistency. A recent study by Ulla et al. (2024) on Philippine universities reveals how inclusive pedagogy is being implemented in these institutions. Some instructors use GenAI as a scaffold for learners with limited English proficiency, while others accept outputs in multiple languages to respect diverse backgrounds. However, access issues remain a major barrier. Many students lack stable internet or functional devices, which creates uneven opportunities for AI-assisted learning. A teacher in Mindanao observed this first-hand when students had to leave the classroom during an AI-based activity to look for a stronger mobile signal. In response, she revised the assignment into two versions—one using AI and one fully offline, to ensure fairness. These small adjustments demonstrate how inclusion depends on listening to students' constraints rather than enforcing one-size-fits-all rules.

In contrast, a clear example of policy failure is seen in London. Although the school introduced a mandatory cover sheet requiring students to declare any use of AI, a recent study reported that nearly three-quarters of students, approximately 74%, did not make the declaration. The reasons were varied. Some students worried that they would be judged negatively, others found the instructions vague, and many noted that staff were inconsistent in enforcing compliance. Peer influence also mattered; if classmates were not disclosing, it felt safer to follow the same path. Ultimately, the policy existed on paper but failed to alter behavior (Gonsalves, 2024). A similar situation occurred in a Southeast Asian university, where students reported avoiding declaring AI use because they feared being labeled as "cheaters," even though AI was technically permitted. One student explained, "What if I declare, and the teacher thinks I'm lazy?" Because the consequences were unclear, students felt safer not disclosing, which defeated the purpose of the policy.

Similar gaps also appear in Asia. As reported by Dai et al. (2024), university policies were found to concentrate on academic integrity and text generation, but overlook other important areas, such as support for non-academic staff, alignment with international standards, and the need for evidence-based practices. The result was partial coverage: policies looked comprehensive but did not address all the people or processes involved. This type of selective focus often leads to policy failure because key stakeholders are excluded from the conversation. These cases emphasize that rules alone do not produce ethical practice. Effective implementation requires attention to institutional culture, teacher preparation, and student trust. Without clear guidance and adequate resources, even well-formulated policies risk becoming symbolic rather than transformative.

6.3. Disclosure-Based AI Policies

Disclosure-based policies require students or faculty to disclose when and how they use AI, sometimes including the specific tool or portion of text produced, to promote transparency. However, non-compliance is common, and rules can feel vague or punitive if not carefully explained. As mentioned, a recent study found that while a school required AI use disclosure, 74% of schools did not comply due to confusion, fear of penalty, or perceiving the policy as irrelevant (Dai et al., 2024). In effect, the rule appeared favorable on paper but had little practical impact. In one Philippine university, students were required to write an "AI Use Statement" at the end of their outputs. Many students were unsure what counted as AI use. Some wrote vague notes, such as "I used AI," while others avoided disclosure entirely because teachers had differing interpretations. This inconsistency created confusion and lowered compliance.

To succeed, disclosure-based policies must be grounded in clear frameworks that explain the ethical use of AI; this is the core argument. Rather than a routine checkbox, disclosure must foster reflection and transparency. Course outlines should specify requirements, and trust must be built through clarity and support. Without these, rules are ineffective regardless of how well-intended they appear on paper.

Foltynek et al. (2023) suggest that rules for AI use should not be imposed top-down, but rather shaped with input from both teachers and students, and they should be grounded in values such as fairness and responsibility. They also recommend training for everyone involved, students, instructors, and administrators, so that the rules are applied uniformly and consistently. When handled in this manner, disclosure ceases to be a formality and becomes a means of building trust and strengthening academic integrity. In a Malaysian university, the AI disclosure guidelines were co-developed by faculty and student representatives. Because students were involved in drafting the rules, they understood the purpose of disclosure and felt respected as partners in the process. Compliance improved significantly, and both students and teachers reported fewer conflicts about AI use.

7. PRACTICAL MEASURES FOR INSTITUTIONS

AI is now central to education, and schools need clear, practical policies to maintain academic integrity while encouraging innovation. Involving students in updating rules and adapting assessments fosters ownership, turning guidelines into shared commitments that support fair and responsible use of AI.

7.1. Policy Language and Honor Code Updates

Policy language on AI needs to be easy and practical to apply. Recent studies have shown that ambiguous or excessively technical regulations can confuse students and instructors. This confusion erodes enforcement (Cotton et al., 2023; Dai et al., 2024). Some universities have responded by preparing revised handbooks that specify allowable and prohibited uses of AI. For instance, Dai et al. (2024) found that Asian universities now add clear provisions on plagiarism, authorship, and disclosure. These indicate that students are responsible even when they use AI tools. Clarity in such provisions helps institutions address academic misconduct reasonably.

Updating honor codes is also a concern. Key recommendations from current research suggest incorporating AI-specific provisions, rather than relying solely on outdated plagiarism policies (Chan & Colloton, 2023; Foltynek et al., 2023). Universities should require students to disclose their use of AI in their work to increase accountability and transparency. Birks and Clare (2023) emphasize that prevention models need to adapt to AI-facilitated misconduct, not just focus on traditional sanctions. Student involvement in policy design also strengthens implementation. Research highlights that students are more likely to understand and comply with integrity policies when they are consulted (Lund et al., 2025). Collaborative approaches work well. For example, student councils can review draft policies. This reduces the perception of top-down rulemaking and encourages a culture of shared responsibility (Bittle & El-Gayar, 2025). This makes honor codes both regulatory and participatory, reinforcing a sense of ownership among learners.

Moorhouse, Yeo, and Wan (2023) observed universities increasingly engaging in open AI policy writing. In one case, student representatives drafted part of the university's guidelines, which were subsequently incorporated into the honor code. Because students helped write the policy, the language felt less like top-down orders and more like a shared agreement. This made the honor code easier to accept, as learners could see their own role in shaping it instead of seeing it as imposed.

Policies on academic integrity are more effective when they are explained clearly to students rather than just written in manuals. Some universities have tried classroom visits and workshops to introduce the rules in person, helping students understand what is expected of them (Foltynek et al., 2023). These face-to-face discussions allow students to ask questions and see why integrity matters in their studies, instead of learning about rules only when problems arise (Dawson, 2020). This makes the policies feel connected to real academic practices. When integrity rules are communicated in ways that relate to students' daily lives, they act as reminders of shared values, not just potential punishments. Training, workshops, and open discussions make the lessons about honesty more practical and engaging (Dawson, 2020). This suggests that "policy roadshows" or classroom dialogues could be used to build awareness and foster a supportive environment for the ethical use of AI. In this sense, honor codes do not instill a fear of punishment but encourage ownership and dialogue.

7.2. Assessment Design and Reflective Writing

Assessment design must evolve to keep pace with the challenges of AI. Traditional essays and exams are easily misused with generative tools (Weber-Wulff et al., 2023). Instead, focus assessments on original thinking, process documentation, and reflection (Ateeq et al., 2024; Perkins et al., 2024b). One strategy is to require students to disclose when and how they used AI in their projects, which reinforces both accountability and learning (Gonsalves, 2024).

Reflective writing has proven especially effective. Cotton et al. (2023) recommend assignments that require students to critically analyze the strengths and limitations of AI tools, such as Grammarly or translation apps. This helps students understand AI as a support system rather than a shortcut, while also training them to consider ethical and academic implications. These practices encourage learners to explain how they understand and approach their learning (Ateriya et al., 2025).

Student-led activities can make assessments more meaningful. For example, Ulla et al. (2024) found that students in the Philippines who organized peer discussions about AI ethics became more aware of academic integrity issues. They also felt responsible for one another's learning. Other studies suggest that portfolio assessments may be more effective than high-stakes exams (Perkins et al., 2024b). Students submit drafts, AI-use notes, and brief reflections. In addition, assessment design works best with a structured approach and student control. Bui and Tong (2025) argue that students view integrity as a means of personal growth, not just a set of rules. Including reflective writing and student-led work in assessments helps create a balanced approach. Students think critically and help enforce integrity among peers. This makes AI seem less threatening and more of a responsible tool.

8. REIMAGINING ACADEMIC INTEGRITY: SYNTHESIZING CONTEMPORARY CONTROVERSIES AND FUTURE DIRECTIONS

Instead of relying mainly on detection and punishment, many scholars argue that academic integrity should be viewed as an integral part of ethical development. Balalle and Pannilage (2025) point out that it is more effective to build a culture of integrity than to spend energy policing every possible misuse of AI. When institutions focus too much on catching misconduct, students may perceive themselves in conflict with "the system" and seek ways to conceal their actions. By contrast, when teachers emphasize ethical reasoning and reflection, students are encouraged to take responsibility and view AI as a tool to support learning rather than as a threat.

In Vietnam, one practical approach has been the use of the AI Assessment Scale, which sets clear levels of permitted AI use and asks students to explain their choices (Perkins et al., 2024b). What makes this model notable is that it shifts the emphasis away from "catching" misconduct and toward encouraging students to demonstrate how they applied AI responsibly. Similarly, Kovari (2025) argues that when assessments require reflection or justification, the temptation to misuse AI quietly is reduced. These strategies suggest that integrity can be strengthened through thoughtful pedagogy rather than fear of punishment.

At the same time, reimagining integrity in the AI era cannot ignore questions of fairness. Foltynek et al. (2023) emphasize the importance of involving both faculty and students in shaping policy, supported by ongoing training in AI literacy. This recommendation seems practical, since rules designed only by administrators often fail to address classroom realities. Another challenge is equity. Strict bans or heavy reliance on detection tools may disadvantage students who lack consistent internet access or reliable devices. Yan et al. (2024) caution that bias and unequal access remain significant risks in AI adoption, a warning that is particularly relevant for under-resourced contexts. For this reason, policies should be flexible, regularly reviewed, and, above all, designed to support students' learning and growth, rather than focusing solely on penalties.

9. CONCLUSION

This chapter has shown how ideas about academic integrity are changing as artificial intelligence becomes part of higher education. We examined questions about authorship, the challenges of AI-assisted writing, and the ways universities are responding through rules and teaching practices. The overall point is simple: integrity today is less about catching students doing something wrong and more about helping them build habits of fairness, honesty, and responsibility in an AI-rich world. AI brings real advantages—speed, convenience, and wider access—but the risks matter too. Plagiarism, hidden use, and bias are not just theoretical problems. Some schools are already taking practical steps, such as requesting disclosure notes, creating reflective assignments, or revising honor codes. In Southeast Asia, case studies demonstrate both the challenges and the potential of incorporating ethical AI use into daily student life. These examples suggest a shift from surveillance and punishment toward teaching, reflection, and inclusion.

Looking forward, universities need to plan for where AI is heading, not just respond when problems arise. Policies should be clear and fair, yet also flexible enough to accommodate students with diverse backgrounds and needs. Above all, schools need a culture shift: treating AI not only as a challenge but also as a partner in learning—if its use is open and responsible. With that approach, AI can strengthen integrity rather than weaken it.

Finally, there are some practical lessons. Institutions should not lean only on detection software or punishment. Policies should emphasize ethics and critical thinking, and students should be given opportunities to develop responsibility. Teachers will need training to guide students in using AI wisely. Curricula can also make more room for reflection and creativity, which high-stakes exams often miss. In regions like Southeast Asia, cooperation among universities could help establish common standards and share best practices.

This study has its limits. It primarily draws on secondary sources and a few case studies, which may not capture the full range of practices worldwide. AI is also evolving rapidly, which means that some examples may become outdated. Future research could include direct studies with students and teachers to examine how disclosure rules, inclusive teaching, and ethics training are actually implemented in practice.

REFERENCES

Alsharefeen, R., & Al Sayari, N. (2025). Examining academic integrity policy and practice in the era of AI: A case study of faculty perspectives. *Frontiers in Education*, *10*, 1621743. DOI: 10.3389/feduc.2025.1621743

Ateeq, A., Alzoraiki, M., Milhem, M., & Ateeq, R. A. (2024). Artificial intelligence in education: Implications for academic integrity and the shift toward holistic assessment. *Frontiers in Education*, *9*, 1470979. Advance online publication. DOI: 10.3389/feduc.2024.1470979

Ateriya, N., Sonwani, N. S., Thakur, K. S., Kumar, A., & Verma, S. K. (2025). Exploring the ethical landscape of AI in academic writing. *Egyptian Journal of Forensic Sciences*, *15*(1), 36. Advance online publication. DOI: 10.1186/s41935-025-00453-1

Balalle, H., & Pannilage, S. (2025). Reassessing academic integrity in the age of AI: A systematic literature review on AI and academic integrity. *Social Sciences & Humanities Open*, *11*, 101299. Advance online publication. DOI: 10.1016/j.ssaho.2025.101299

Batubara, I. A., Wariyati, W., & Prawiyata, Y. D. (2025). Exploring university students' perceptions of AI: Insights from Indonesia. *Edu Cendikia: Jurnal Ilmiah Kependidikan*, *4*(03), 1687–1701. DOI: 10.47709/educendikia.v4i03.5465

Birks, D., & Clare, J. (2023). Linking artificial intelligence facilitated academic misconduct to existing prevention frameworks. *International Journal for Educational Integrity*, *19*(20), 20. Advance online publication. DOI: 10.1007/s40979-023-00142-3

Bittle, K., & El-Gayar, O. F. (2025). Generative AI and academic integrity in higher education: A systematic review and research agenda. *Information (Basel)*, *16*(4), 296. Advance online publication. DOI: 10.3390/info16040296

Boddington, P. (2017). *Towards a code of ethics for artificial intelligence*. Springer., DOI: 10.1007/978-3-319-60648-4

Bui, T. T. U., & Tong, T. V. A. (2025). The impact of AI writing tools on academic integrity: Unveiling English-majored students' perceptions and practical solutions. *AsiaCALL Online Journal*, *16*(1), 83–110. DOI: 10.54855/acoj.251615

Bulut, O., Beiting-Parrish, M., Casabianca, J. M., Slater, S. C., & Jiao, H. (2024). The rise of artificial intelligence in educational measurement: Opportunities and ethical challenges. *arXiv Preprint*. https://arxiv.org/abs/2406.18900

Chan, C. K. Y., & Colloton, T. (2023). A comprehensive AI policy education framework for university teaching and learning. *International Journal of Educational Technology in Higher Education*, *20*(38), 38. Advance online publication. DOI: 10.1186/s41239-023-00408-3

Chowdhury Niloy, A., Hafiz, R., Hossain, B. M. T., Gulmeher, F., Sultana, N., Islam, K. F., Bushra, F., Islam, S., Hoque, S. I., Rahman, M. A., & Kabir, S. (2024). AI chatbots: A disguised enemy for academic integrity? *International Journal of Educational Research Open*, *6*, 100396. DOI: 10.1016/j.ijedro.2024.100396

Citron, D. K. (2024). The surveilled student. *Stanford Law Review, 76*, 1439–1472. https://review.law.stanford.edu/wp-content/uploads/sites/3/2024/10/Citron-76-Stan.-L.-Rev.-1439.pdf

Cotton, D., Cotton, P., & Shipway, J. (2023). Chatting and cheating: Ensuring academic integrity in the era of ChatGPT. *Innovations in Education and Teaching International, 60*(2), 153–162. DOI: 10.1080/14703297.2023.2190148

Dai, Y., Lai, S., Lim, C. P., & Liu, A. (2024). University policies on generative AI in Asia: Promising practices, gaps, and future directions. *Journal of Asian Public Policy, 44*(3), 260–281. DOI: 10.1080/17516234.2024.2379070

Dawson, P. (2020). *Defending assessment security in a digital world: Preventing e-cheating and supporting academic integrity in Higher Education* (1st ed.). Routledge., DOI: 10.4324/9780429324178

Elkhatat, A. M., Elsaid, K., & Almeer, S. (2023). Evaluating the efficacy of AI content detection tools in differentiating between human and AI-generated text. *International Journal for Educational Integrity, 19*(1), 17. DOI: 10.1007/s40979-023-00140-5

Fang, Y., Tan, Y., Zuo, C., & Boubaker, A. (2025). *AI-generated vs. peer feedback in ESL writing: Effects on writing skill, self-efficacy, and enjoyment* (SSRN preprint). They compare AI feedback, peer feedback, and writing outcomes. DOI: 10.2139/ssrn.5115438

Fitas, R. (2025). Inclusive education with AI: Supporting special needs and tackling language barriers. *AI and Ethics, 5*(6), 5729–5757. Advance online publication. DOI: 10.1007/s43681-025-00824-3

Floridi, L., & Chiriatti, M. (2020). GPT-3: Its nature, scope, limits, and consequences. *Minds and Machines, 30*(4), 681–694. DOI: 10.1007/s11023-020-09548-1

Foltynek, T., Bjelobaba, S., Glendinning, I., Khan, Z. R., Santos, R., Pavletic, P., & Kravjar, J. (2023). ENAI Recommendations on the ethical use of Artificial Intelligence in Education. *International Journal for Educational Integrity, 19*(1), 12. DOI: 10.1007/s40979-023-00133-4

Gilligan, C. (1982). *In a different voice: Psychological theory and women's development*. Harvard University Press.

Giray, L. (2024). The problem with false positives: AI detection unfairly accuses scholars of AI plagiarism. *The Serials Librarian, 85*(5–6), 181–189. DOI: 10.1080/0361526X.2024.2433256

Gonsalves, C. (2024). Addressing student non-compliance in AI use declarations: Implications for academic integrity and assessment in higher education. *Assessment & Evaluation in Higher Education, 50*(4), 592–606. DOI: 10.1080/02602938.2024.2415654

Gretzky, M., & Dishon, G. (2025). Algorithmic-authors in academia: Blurring the boundaries of human and machine knowledge production. *Learning, Media and Technology, 50*(3), 1–14. DOI: 10.1080/17439884.2025.2452196

Guo, S., Wang, Y., Yu, J., Wu, X., Ayik, B., Watts, F. M., Latif, E., Liu, N., & Zhai, L. (2025). Artificial intelligence bias on English language learners in automatic scoring. *arXiv Preprint.* https://arxiv.org/abs/2505.10643 DOI: 10.1007/978-3-031-98462-4_34

Huang, L. (2023). Ethics of artificial intelligence in education: Student privacy and data protection. *Science Insights Education Frontiers, 16*(2), 2577–2587. DOI: 10.15354/sief.23.re202

Jobin, A., Ienca, M., & Vayena, E. (2019). The global landscape of AI ethics guidelines. *Nature Machine Intelligence, 1*(9), 389–399. DOI: 10.1038/s42256-019-0088-2

Kant, I. (1997). *Groundwork of the metaphysics of morals* (Gregor, M., Trans.). Cambridge University Press. (Original work published 1785)

Kovari, A. (2025). Ethical use of ChatGPT in education—Best practices to combat AI-induced plagiarism. *Frontiers in Education, 9*, 1465703. Advance online publication. DOI: 10.3389/feduc.2024.1465703

Liang, W., Yuksekgonul, M., Mao, Y., Wu, E., & Zou, J. (2023). GPT detectors are biased against non-native English writers. *Patterns (New York, N.Y.), 4*(6), 100779. DOI: 10.1016/j.patter.2023.100779

Lund, B. D., Lee, T. H., Mannuru, N. R., & Arutla, N. (2025). AI and academic integrity: Exploring student perceptions and implications for Higher Education. *Journal of Academic Ethics, 23*(3), 1545–1565. DOI: 10.1007/s10805-025-09613-3

Malik, A. R., Pratiwi, Y., Andajani, K., Numertayasa, I. W., Suharti, S., Darwis, A., & Marzuki, M. (2023). Exploring artificial intelligence in academic essay: Higher education student's perspective. *International Journal of Educational Research Open, 4*, 100296. DOI: 10.1016/j.ijedro.2023.100296

Marhaban, S., Sulistyo, T., & Widiastuti, O. (2023). Artificial intelligence in writing: Students' writing competencies and voices. [JEELS]. *Journal of English Education and Linguistics Studies, 12*(1), 1–24. DOI: 10.30762/jeels.v12i1.3927

Miao, J., Thongprayoon, C., Suppadungsuk, S., Garcia Valencia, O. A., Qureshi, F., & Cheungpasitporn, W. (2023). Ethical dilemmas in using AI for academic writing and an example framework for peer review in nephrology academia: A narrative review. *Clinics and Practice, 14*(1), 89–105. DOI: 10.3390/clinpract14010008

Moorhouse, B. L., Yeo, M. A., & Wan, Y. (2023). Generative AI tools and assessment: Guidelines of the world's top-ranking universities. *Computers and Education Open, 5*, 100151. DOI: 10.1016/j.caeo.2023.100151

Organisation for Economic Co-operation and Development [OECD]. (2019). The OECD artificial intelligence policy observatory - OECD.AI. https://oecd.ai/en/ai-principles

Ozfidan, B., El-Dakhs, D. A. S., & Alsalim, L. A. (2024). The use of AI tools in English academic writing by Saudi undergraduates. *Contemporary Educational Technology, 16*(4), ep527. DOI: 10.30935/cedtech/15013

Perkins, M., Furze, L., Roe, J., & MacVaugh, J. (2024b). The Artificial Intelligence Assessment Scale (AIAS): A framework for ethical integration of generative AI in educational assessment. *Journal of University Teaching & Learning Practice, 21*(06). Advance online publication. DOI: 10.53761/q3azde36

Perkins, M., Roe, J., Vu, B. H., Postma, D., Hickerson, D., McGaughran, J., & Khuat, H. (2024a). Simple techniques to bypass GenAI text detectors: Implications for inclusive education. *International Journal of Educational Technology in Higher Education, 21*(1), 53. DOI: 10.1186/s41239-024-00487-w

Ravšelj, D., Keržič, D., Tomaževič, N., Umek, L., Brezovar, N., Iahad, N., & Shin, D. (2025). Higher education students' perceptions of ChatGPT: A global study of early reactions. *PLoS One*, *20*(2), e0315011. DOI: 10.1371/journal.pone.0315011

Shin, Y., Wei, S., & Vanchinkhuu, N. (2025). Digital plagiarism in EFL education during the AI era: A comparative study of perceptions among learners and instructors in Korea, Mongolia, and China. *LEARN Journal: Language Education and Acquisition Research Network*, *18*(1), 594–618. DOI: 10.70730/RMKA9428

Stommel, J. (2014). Critical digital pedagogy: A definition. *Hybrid Pedagogy.* https://hybridpedagogy.org/critical-digital-pedagogy-definition/

Tan, M. J. T., & Maravilla, N. M. A. (2024). Shaping integrity: Why generative artificial intelligence does not have to undermine education. *arXiv Preprint.* https://arxiv.org/abs/2407.19088

The University of Hong Kong. (2023, August 3). *HKU introduces new policy to fully integrate GenAI in teaching and learning.* https://www.hku.hk/press/press-releases/detail/26434.html

Ulla, M. B., Advincula, M. J. C., Mombay, C. D. S., Mercullo, H. M. A., Nacionales, J. P., & Entino-Señorita, A. D. (2024). How can GenAI foster an inclusive language classroom? A critical language pedagogy perspective from Philippine university teachers. *Computers and Education: Artificial Intelligence*, *5*, 100314. DOI: 10.1016/j.caeai.2024.100314

United Nations Educational, Scientific and Cultural Organization [UNESCO]. (2021). *Recommendation on the ethics of artificial intelligence.* https://unesdoc.unesco.org/ark:/48223/pf0000381137

Utami, S. P. T., Andayani, W., Winarni, R., & Sumarwati, S. (2023). Utilization of artificial intelligence technology in an academic writing class: How do Indonesian students perceive? *Contemporary Educational Technology*, *15*(4), ep450. DOI: 10.30935/cedtech/13419

Weber-Wulff, D., Anohina-Naumeca, A., Bjelobaba, S., Foltýnek, T., Guerrero-Dib, J., Popoola, O., Šigut, P., & Waddington, L. (2023). Testing of detection tools for AI-generated text. *International Journal for Educational Integrity*, *19*(1), 26. DOI: 10.1007/s40979-023-00146-z

Weidmann, A. E. (2024). Artificial intelligence in academic writing and clinical pharmacy education: Consequences and opportunities. *International Journal of Clinical Pharmacy*, *46*(3), 751–754. DOI: 10.1007/s11096-024-01705-1

Yan, L., Sha, L., Zhao, L., Li, Y., Martinez-Maldonado, R., Chen, G., Li, X., Jin, Y., & Gašević, D. (2024). Practical and ethical challenges of large language models in education: A systematic scoping review. *British Journal of Educational Technology*, *55*(1), 90–112. DOI: 10.1111/bjet.13370

Zhai, C., Wibowo, S., & Li, L. D. (2024). The effects of over-reliance on AI dialogue systems on students' cognitive abilities: A systematic review. *Smart Learn. Environ.*, *11*(28), 28. Advance online publication. DOI: 10.1186/s40561-024-00316-7

Chapter 17
Beyond Content Creation:
Emphasizing Critical Thinking and Problem-Solving With Artificial Intelligence

Amrik Singh
https://orcid.org/0000-0003-3598-8787
Lovely Professional University, India

ABSTRACT

The advent of sophisticated Artificial Intelligence (AI) tools has dramatically reshaped the landscape of writing, moving beyond simple content generation to offer unprecedented opportunities for pedagogical innovation. This chapter argues for a paradigm shift in writing education, advocating for the strategic integration of AI not merely as a tool for producing text, but as a catalyst for developing higher-order cognitive skills. While AI excels at automating rudimentary writing tasks, its true educational value lies in its capacity to stimulate critical thinking, enhance problem-solving abilities, and cultivate advanced analytical skills in students. We explore methodologies for designing writing assignments that leverage AI to facilitate complex decision-making, evaluate information critically, identify biases, and construct persuasive arguments grounded in evidence. Furthermore, the chapter discusses how AI can be utilized to simulate real-world scenarios, encouraging students to analyze intricate problems and formulate creative, AI-supported solutions.

INTRODUCTION

Artificial Intelligence (AI) has found its way into teaching and the world of work in a relatively short time. It is often praised due to its potential to automate and improve the creation of content making work that previously required a lot of human input easier. This is in practice with ChatGPT writing essays, Grammarly editing written communication, and Copilot writing code or presentations (Kenedy, 2024). Such AI-based solutions are admittedly useful in simplifying the work process and enhancing productivity in most industries. Nevertheless, a more critical viewpoint shows that there is a possible trap: restricted usage of AI to content production can unintentionally promote a more passive information consumption instead of stimulating real

DOI: 10.4018/979-8-3373-5601-3.ch017

intellectual activity (Khalabuzar & Shymanovych, 2024). When the answers or solutions created by AI become regular, then there is a threat that learners and professionals will lose their ability to struggle with complex problems on their own, which may prevent the acquisition of their own research skills. The idea presented by this chapter is that the actual, transformative potential of AI in learning and professional development goes much further than what can be generated by it. Rather, its greatest influence is the fact that it can be used strategically to provoke critical thinking and problem-solving abilities (Sharma & Singh, 2024). We will discuss the way AI can be used as the booster of deeper learning, stimulating active engagement, inspiring intellectual curiosity, and empowering people to not only consume the information, but to truly comprehend, deconstruct, and innovate. We can explore all the potential of AI in helping to build a generation of more engaged and capable learners and professionals by no longer viewing AI as a content creator, instead, as a potent cognitive development tool (Spector & Ma, 2019). Artificial Intelligence (AI) has now been deeply intertwined with the world of education and professional activities, being praised due to the ability to automate and improve content creation (Singh, 2022; Singh, 2024). Since the writing of the essays up to the creation of presentations, AI-based applications like ChatGPT, Grammarly, and Copilot are becoming more and more popular to simplify the communication and productivity. Nonetheless, the use of AI in content creation should be restricted to avoid the development of passive absorption instead of active interaction (Jha & Singh, 2025). The chapter under discussion states that the most revolutionary future of the AI does not necessarily lie in its creation, but in terms of how it can be utilized to provoke critical thinking and problem-solving among students and professionals.

AI as a Cognitive Partner

The radical nature of Artificial Intelligence in education and professional growth becomes likely when we rethink the role of this technology as a content producer and define it as a dynamic cognitive ally. Being a cognitive partner, AI will provide us with a priceless sounding board of the ideas and offer alternative perspectives, which we may have overlooked (Stuchikova & Weis, 2024). An example is when a learner is facing a complex issue, an AI would be able to provide a sequence of possible solutions, not to make an immediate choice, but to understand the logic of these solutions, weigh the advantages and disadvantages, and then create a more effective solution. The process promotes meta-cognition, which makes learners reflect on how they think, and how they came to a certain conclusion, which promotes a more in-depth insight into the problem space itself (Nuong et al., 2024). In addition, AI can serve as a scaffolding device, which can modify the support depending on the capabilities of a learner. It could provide step-by-step instructions and elaborate explanations to a beginner. In the case of an advanced learner, it may present challenging questions or bring about small complexities that would involve the learner to probe and sharpen his or her arguments. This flexibility enables AI to give customized cognitive challenges and thus one is always within his/her zone of proximal development where learning can be best achieved. Refraining AI as a thought partner in professional context can change the decision-making processes. Rather than just using AI to process data and provide one specific suggestion, professionals can work with AI to explore various options, test hypotheses, and even find the possible biases in their own reasoning (Singh, 2024a; Singh, 2024b). An AI can model the different results of a business plan, and a team can rationally evaluate the risk and opportunities prior to committing to an action plan. This method of collaboration improves human judgment by offering an effective and impressive analytical counterpart, and the decisions have more strength and become more informed. Finally, the adoption of AI as cognitive companion requires the changes in professional and pedagogical behavior. It demands developing the so-called AI literacy not only being familiar with using AI tools, but being aware of their capacities and shortcomings, and most importantly, knowing how to provide the right questions to provoke further thinking (Tham et al., 2022). In that way, we can use AI to develop critical thinking, intellectual agility, and the ability of people to live in a more complex world, having developed better cognitive skills. In order to go beyond content creation, it would be necessary to reposition AI as a cognitive collaborator and not a replacement tool (Singh, 2024b; Singh & Kumar, 2024). In its interactive use, AI may act as a scaffold of higher-order thinking since it challenges the user to think, challenge assumptions, and consider options. As an illustration, AI is able to offer counterarguments or criticize reasoning or provide more than two sides to a complicated problem, which compels the user to evaluate information critically instead of passively receiving it. Such an augmentation, as opposed to automation, is consistent with constructivist theories of learning, where one constructs knowledge by inquiring and reflecting on specific things (George, 2023). The AI can become an accelerant in the process, providing a secure and dynamic environment of trial and error, testing hypotheses, and making improvements.

Artificial Intelligence as an Aid to Problems

Artificial Intelligence is also a real hero in the sphere of education and professional growth. Going further than merely identifying the required information, AI can be actively engaged to support and improve the human problem-solving process and change the way people address challenges. There is one important way in which AI is a problem-solving partner: it offers systematic structures and different visions (Singh & Sihmar, 2025; Singh & Kumar, 2024). When a student or professional is put into a complex situation, they may discuss it with an AI in order to brainstorm potential solutions, and the AI will be able to generate a wide variety of solutions that an individual may not immediately think of. It is not a matter of getting the AI to actually solve the problem, but it is, instead, the opportunity to use the capacity to handle large volumes of information and detect patterns so as to expand the range of potential solutions. AI can also encourage the user to take alternative angles, understand assumptions underpinning them, and even point out to possible biases in their initial thought processes, which can lead to a more thorough and critical way of identifying and solving the problem.

LITERATURE REVIEW

AI may be used as an adaptive feedback mechanism. An AI can give a learner real-time and focused feedback on the approach that they chose, highlighting logical inconsistencies, steps that they have overlooked, or areas where additional research may be advantageous, when trying to solve a problem (Na-songkhla et al., 2024). This is an extremely important feedback loop that helps to reinforce the right strategies and rectify false beliefs before they take root. When it comes to working on a professional level, AI will be able to provide the results of the suggested options, which will make it possible to experiment with the proposed solutions and improve the strategies without any risks (Singh & Kumar, 2024). This cyclic test, propose and refine process guided by AI is much faster in development of robust problem-solving skills. Lastly, AI is a great analyzer of data and recognizer of patterns, which is why it is an essential ally when dealing with large datasets or other complicated relationships. It could be the patterns in market data, the weaknesses in a system, or the factors that cause a scientific phenomenon, but AI can process a lot of information, which would have exhausted the cognitive ability of a human, in a short period of time. Offering insights and correlations, AI can help the populace to go beyond the surface-level observation and investigate the causes of the problems on the deeper level, which leads to more efficient and innovative solutions. Simply put, AI as a problem-solving assistant enhances human cognition, which allows us to approach the problem with more depth, effectiveness, and innovation (Deri et al., 2024; Singh, 2024c; Garg et al., 2024). In addition to abstract thinking, AI applications are becoming more efficient in assisting in structured problem-solving in other areas like mathematics, engineering, business, and medicine. Within hospitality management, as an example, AI can assist students simulate demand prediction or optimize staffing plans hence facilitating analytical skills and decision-making (Moustaghfir & brigui, 2024). Besides, generative AI might assist users to deconstruct the complex issues into solvable ones, present analogies across diverse fields, and point out the hidden constraints or opportunities.

Nurturing Metacognitive Awareness

The skill of self-cognition - is crucial during the era of easily accessible information and AI applications. The conventional education in most cases is aimed at the delivery of the content at the expense of imparting learners with the learning skills. AI is an exclusive prospect of sealing this disjunction, actively developing self-awareness, planning, monitoring, and evaluation abilities that constitute the metacognition. AI tools can be used as triggers of the metacognitive learning process because they can bring learners to consider the learning processes. As an example, an AI-based writing coach does not simply fix grammatical mistakes; it can pose questions, such as, What was the reason you used this specific argument in this place? In a similar manner, AI can assist students in the thinking process in case of a problem-solving situation. This reflective exercise that is usually challenging to develop within a conventional environment, as it usually takes up time, can be scalable and personalized with AI. Finally, the incorporation of AI to create metacognitive awareness enables the learners to become self-regulated learners. They are taught on how to make their goals, to track their progress, to understand that a certain strategy does not work, to change their approach (Garg et al., 2024; Singh et al., 2024; Singh & Sihmar, 2025; Singh & Kumar, 2024). Besides improving academic performance, this essential set of skills equips individuals with lifelong learning, adds to being able to navigate the constantly changing information environment, and resolves new challenges on their own (Lubbe et al., 2025). The awareness and control of thoughts of an individual is much closely related to metacognition the critical thinking and problem-solving. As an example, smart writing assistants may require users to explain their arguments, re-evaluate their reasoning, or adjust the tone and organization- there they encourage more effort in their work.

Objectives of Study

- Analyze how AI may be used to improve critical thinking and problem solving.

- Examine how well AI powered tools and platforms can encourage more profound learning.
- Knowledge Knowledge Find best practices Develop framework.

RESEARCH METHODOLOGY

This study adopts a secondary research methodology to explore how artificial intelligence supports critical thinking and problem-solving beyond content creation. Relevant literature from academic journals, conference papers, policy reports, and industry publications has been reviewed to analyze emerging practices and theoretical perspectives. Databases such as Scopus, Web of Science, and Google Scholar were used to gather evidence-based insights. Additionally, educator frameworks, institutional case studies, and expert commentaries were examined to contextualize AI-enhanced cognitive learning. The collected secondary data was thematically analyzed to identify key challenges, opportunities, and pedagogical strategies for integrating AI as a cognitive partner in education.

DISCUSSION AND INTERPRETATION

Educational systems that use AI, including individualized learning spaces, have the ability to monitor student reactions and provide information on learning patterns, strengths, and weaknesses. With this information employed in an open manner, learners are able to focus on goals, self-assess, and gain self-directed learning skills.

Artificial Intelligence Out of Curriculum

Artificial intelligence in education is commonly understood as a way of creating text, writing assignments, or making the writing process easier; nevertheless, the real opportunity is much more profound in the capability to stimulate higher-order thinking, critical thinking, and problem-solving skills needed by a future-ready student. Instead of substituting mental work, AI can serve as a stimulus to further learning- making students wonder why they think that, look for proof, and build rationally valid arguments. An example of this is AI assisted Socratic tutoring systems which would challenge students to think experimentally though probing questions. It is an interactive method which makes the learners abandon the passive receipt of information and build up on their metacognitive skills to allow them to think about their reasoning processes. As well, in STEM education, intelligent tutoring systems such as the Cognitive Tutor at Carnegie Mellon are used to help students solve problems step-by-step, and thus, it is no wonder that a path to a solution can be wrong and that students are encouraged to seek alternative ways to solve problems. This never gives students ready solutions, rather it strengthens the conceptual grasp and endurance in handling complex problems (Luckin & Holmes, 2016). To illustrate, AI-based climate models in environmental science courses can allow students to predict how increasing the temperature affects the local biodiversity, interpret the data and defend the policy-related recommendations, which will help them to connect the theoretical material with real-life problems in the society. Market analytics platforms supported with AI enable business and entrepreneurship students to assess consumer behavior, predict trends, and build evidence-based business solutions and hone their decision-making capabilities. In addition, collaborative AI systems can improve the project-based learning by assisting students to allocate their work more effectively, analyze group performance statistics, and solve the problems based on the information and make informed negotiations and collaboration. Most notably, AI does not only improve writing, but also critical reading and argument evaluation. Logical Coherence, source Reliability or potential bias helps learners validate information before using it, which is a crucial skill in the age of misinformation. Students can be taught to identify flaws in their reasoning and develop their ideas through repeated improvement with the help of immediate and personalized feedback. In creative fields, AI allows divergent thinking, when creating a variety of design variations or scenario possibilities, students can use them to improve on machine-generated ideas, as opposed to blindly accepting them (Holmes & Littlejohn, 2024). Already, universities such as Georgia Tech and other institutions in Singapore and Europe have shown that the problem of implementing AI in the analytical coursework leads to a significant positive effect on the performance of students in solving problems, their engagement, and confidence in approaching new issues. The trick, though, is intelligent design: teachers need to position AI as an intellectual ally as opposed to a shortcut. Under the same conditions, AI fosters curiosity, resilience and intellectual bravery- attributes that are key to success in the ever more challenging working environments. In the end, the role of AI in education goes way beyond what content creators can produce; it is the ability to turn learners into more than mere consumers of new knowledge, to active exploreers, thoughtful ponders, and creative problem solvers who can fully navigate and reform a fast-changing world.

Possible Biases in AI and How to mitigate biases

With AI being more and more integrated into education, industry and policy making, the possibility of introducing or enhancing bias has become one of the most discussed issues. AI systems are fed on past data which might be full of stereotype, uneven representation or prejudices in the society. When unchecked, these systems may strengthen the injustice of grading, screening of admissions, hiring, and even the student support system. It is critical to comprehend the causes of AI bias and create some viable plans to address it and make AI serve as the source of educational equity instead of exclusion. The chart above represents a simplified example of four major categories of bias, which often arise in AI systems, namely, data bias, algorithmic bias, user bias and societal bias. A data bias is the circumstance where the data reflected in training AI fails to reflect the true representation of the world users (Holmes et al., 2022). As an example, when a learning analytics system is trained on urban student data, rural students have a higher likelihood of being false alarmed as low performing. The model is constructed to exhibit algorithmic bias; i.e., the particular decision aspect with which some groups are disproportionately weight will be given more weight. The user bias is realized in the interaction between the students and teachers with AI tools which depends on the assumptions or differences in the use. Lastly, the presence of societal bias is based on pre-existing disproportions within the culture and thus can silently inform AI outputs.

Teacher attitude: How to balance automation and fairness

Educators fear the biased AI based testing might label the students in a false way or produce artificial stereotyping. Educators often observe that AI writing assessors tend to be harsher in grading some linguistic styles - e.g. non-native English writing. It has been contended that hybrid evaluation, involving preliminary analysis by AI and then teacher judgment to interpret results in context, is the most effective way to evaluate the results. The professional development is also an enduring factor: the teachers should be taught to detect the situations when AI estimates are contradicted by the realities of instruction and make sure that the pedagogical knowledge is the most influential decision-making factor.

Concerns of learners: Agency and transparency

Another issue highlighted by students is that as AI decisions become more important, they should be explainable. When a chatbot gives feedback or some early-warning system declares someone as at risk, learners want to see why and have a way of correction or appeal.

Industry experts: Ethical engineering and continuous monitoring

The developers of AI emphasize the significance of principles of bias-aware design. The reduction of bias can be performed with the help of techniques like diverse dataset curation, algorithmic auditing, and fairness constraints during model training before the deployment. Monitoring after the use is also recommended by the industry experts, as real world use may provide new bias patterns with time. The integrative models of technologists and educators, psychologists, and sociologists are becoming a commonly regarded pillar of responsible educational AI.

Policymakers: World standards and government systems.

On a policy perspective, it is difficult to balance between innovation and protection.

- Regulations of disclosure of AI-driven decision-making.
- Regulations of fair data handling and consent.
- Inclusion policies in the country to avoid discrimination of the marginalized learners.

The global organizations like UNESCO and OECD are calling on countries to coordinate the policies to ensure that no region or economic sector is left behind in the adoption of AI.

Mitigation Strategies: A Multi-Stakeholder Approach

Table 1. To ensure fairness and trust in AI-enabled education

Stakeholder	Recommended Actions
Educators	Use AI for feedback, not final grading; monitor inconsistency; integrate bias literacy in digital education
Learners	Question AI outputs; request transparency; report errors or unfair treatment
AI Developers	Diversify datasets; incorporate fairness metrics; create explainable AI models
Policymakers	Implement equity-first governance; mandate auditing; provide funding for low-resource contexts

Sources: Author's own elaboration

Another similarity in all the views is that of co-governance. There is no one group of people that can successfully do away with bias in the world, and it will be necessary to cooperate in creating AI, which would be shaped by human values and fair intentions. The problem of bias in AI is not purely a technical issue, but it is also indicative of disparity in society. It should be addressed through continuous vigilance, ethical consciousness and collective responsibility. When teachers, learners, professionals, and policymakers come together to promote equity, AI can become what it promises to be a superpower in promoting high-quality inclusive learning. It is possible that a future in which AI improves critical thinking and opportunities of all learners exists, but equity must be placed in the design, implementation, and evaluation.

Views on AI in Education: Teachers, School Leaders and Industry Analysts

Artificial Intelligence has quickly passed the stage of a far-off idea becoming the part of the modern education system. It is integrated by different stakeholders such as educators, policy-makers, and industry experts who have different priorities resulting in different impacts of AI on learning. It is critical to understand that a responsible, equitable, and future-ready AI-enhanced education can be developed only through the identification of their shared views.

Teacher Attitude: Improving Pedagogy and Student-Centered Instruction.

The teachers consider AI as the means to enhance the effectiveness of the teaching process and their interaction with the learners. Individualized learning environments, intelligent feed-back and AI tutoring help to provide personal development, enabling the teacher to devote more attention to mentoring and emotional assistance. AI-powered analytics can be used to identify struggling students at an early stage, where proactive action can be taken to help them, as opposed to responding to them at the last moment.

Nevertheless, teachers are not indifferent either:

Excessive use of automation could reduce the aspects of human judgment.

Training deficiency might enhance imitation and misuse

The problem of data privacy and fairness, the ethical aspects, are not resolved yet.

The main objective of the educators is to make sure that AI supports critical thinking, creativity and collaboration, rather than passive consumption and uniform automation.

Perspective of the Policymakers: Governance, Accountability and Equity

Government agencies and certifying organizations are concerned with norms, access and the social benefit in the long run. It is their role with which they guarantee that AI integration will not increase digital divides especially in resource constrained institutions. Policies must address:

- Open data management.
- Unbiased assessment procedures.
- Inclusive access to AI tools
- Meeting national education objectives

To protect the rights of students and to be responsible in innovation, policy-makers focus on ethical guardrails, procurement to classroom implementation. Towards them, their views lean towards a harmonious co-existence of AI and human leadership, whereby the educator is responsible to the learning outcomes.

The view of Industry Experts: Innovation, Labor force and Future skills.

According to technology developers and industry leaders, AI is a source of workforce-relevant skills. The AI-powered environments are meant to simulate professional settings of complex scenarios, such as hospitality operations, supply chains, medical triage, and so forth, and allow the students to develop competencies that are difficult to obtain in a traditional classroom.

According to the industry experts, we should have:

- On-going reskilling of educators.
- The focus on digital fluency and computational thinking.
- Universities and technology companies work together on common R&D models.

They are pragmatic: providing learners with the flexibility and the mindset of innovation that they are going to need in their AI-enhanced jobs.

A Collaborative Framework for AI Adoption

Table 2. The Tri-Framework for AI in Education

Stakeholder Group	Primary Focus	Key Outcome
Educators	Pedagogy, personalization, assessment	Better learning and engagement
Policymakers	Regulation, ethics, equitable access	Safe, standardized, inclusive systems
Industry Experts	Technological innovation and workforce skills	Future-ready graduates

Sources: Author's own elaboration

The convergence of these priorities creates what can be called an ethical, scalable, and empowering AI that will be beneficial to learners and instructors. By making sure that pedagogical and curriculum adjustment is achieved by educators, protecting the ethics and the equality are the work of policymakers, and creating the latest innovations are the leaders of the industry, AI will be a revolution in education. The sustainability of the future is in the constant interaction and cooperation between these three stakeholders so that technology can be used by humanity-not vice versa.

Restructuring AI into a Cognitive Partner and Problem-Solving Companion

Since the role of Artificial Intelligence in education is still developing, the perception thereof needs a transformation that would no longer consider AI as an engine of content or a machine that is there to help. Rather, AI is to be reimagined as a cognitive collaborator, one that will intelligently engage in a dynamic and mutual relationship with learners to support their thoughts. Instead of substituting human thinking, AI tools can be used to enhance it- to aid memory, activate the mind into critical thinking and assist in solving more complex problems. To elaborate, an AI tutoring model is also capable of explaining mathematical concepts, as well as posing Socratic questions and making students explain their rationale. This makes the learning process less about consumerism of the answers, but rather an active intellectual involvement that assists the students to internalize conceptual frames of thought. On the same note, the concept of AI as a problem-solving friend makes AI appear as a partner and not an authority (Luckin & Holmes, 2016). AI can also be tailored to accommodate the different learning styles by providing more than one way to get the solution to a problem, to enable students to learn that there is no single right answer to a complex problem. By engaging in the process of providing feedback, students are taught to reflect on their mistakes and revise the strategies and improve the metacognitive skills. This fosters an experimental, vigorous and independent research state of mind -qualities vital to survive in technologically amplified job environments. Importantly, to turn into mental collaboration, the educators need to teach students how to critically analyze AI products. What learners need to comprehend is the drawbacks of AI its susceptibility to bias, incomplete knowledge, and the absence of lived human circumstances. By challenging, checking and editing AI-generated suggestions, students exercise the same set of skills, namely critical thinking, moral judgment and creative thought, that are the hallmark of the purpose of modern education. Through

AI as knowledge collaborator and problem-solving friend, education systems can ensure more intellectual stimulation, promote interdisciplinary inquiry and train students to work effectively with intelligent systems. It will open an additional realm of learning and development in which humans and AI co-evolve mutual strengths, as we begin to respect and adopt the potential of the other, in a likely future where humans and AI are not displaced by technology, but are co-minds.

Case Study: More Than Content Creation

When it comes to the implementation of artificial intelligence (AI) into higher education, it is commonly addressed in the context of the ability to automate the process of content creation, simplify grading, or find information fast. There is however an increasing trend where more institutions are no longer using these basic applications but instead employ AI as a facilitator to more profound learning- specifically in the fields of critical thinking, analytical reasoning and problem solving. This case study explores the experience of a single large multidisciplinary university herein known as Riverview University in terms of redesigning its first-year course Foundations of Inquiry to utilize AI in the development of higher-order skills. Riverview University had identified a repetitive problem: students were being enrolled in undergraduate courses with high levels of factual understanding but poor skills of analyzing issues of moderate complexity, critically evaluating evidence, or thinking through their arguments (Holmes & Littlejohn, 2024). Conventional tests often focused on recall, which sent the wrong message to learners that the major aim of education was to memorize. To begin with, the students were engaged in AI-mediated Socrat dialogues modules that presented the students with a challenge to question ideas, make assumptions, and sharpen arguments. These facilitated interactions allowed students to train metacognitive abilities, including detection of biases, gap identification of reasoning and alternative viewpoint evaluation. During these classes, the learners worked with practical scenarios in sustainability, health systems, and social innovation. AI resources did not present solutions, but gave hints repeatedly, making the students complete a series of steps, explaining their choices, and demonstrating how other solutions might work. Visualizations generated by AI also assisted students in forming an idea of complex systems so that they are able to discern patterns, hypothesise and simulate results. The third element was the AI enhanced peer review. Students posted their draft essays or project plans to an AI-enhanced tool that pointed out the weak points of the argument, inconsistencies of the concept, and the lack of evidence in the arguments. Notably, the AI was programmed to prevent re-writing, providing the students with the prompts like: What evidence does this claim have? or How can a person disagree with this conclusion? This model provided students with the advantage of remaining the authors of their papers and also enjoying the benefits of instant analysis. A two-semester mixed-methods study was carried out by the Riverview University to measure the effectiveness of these interventions. In general, the experience of Riverview University is an example of a radical shift: applied purposefully, AI can take students beyond the scope of content-making and contribute to the development of higher-order thinking that is beneficial to studying and other life-long learning processes.

Global Trends, Data-Driven Challenges, and Practical Implementation Gaps

Artificial intelligence is quickly finding its way into education systems around the world to help in improving teaching, learning and institutional decision-making. There are many global trends that define this change. To begin with, the emergence of generative AI has changed the focus on the delivery of the content to higher-order skills like critical thinking and creativity, along with real-time problem-solving. Customized and personalized learning systems are expanding rapidly, especially in nations that are investing heavily in EdTech environments- China, South Korea, Singapore and new African digital ecosystems. These systems are offering customized learning ways and performance monitoring on a fine scale. Third, AI governance and ethics practices are spreading all around the world, and guidelines are issued by UNESCO, OECD, and regional unions to maintain responsible AI application in education. Such trends are indicative of a change in the adoption of AI in experiments to structural integration in the curricula.

These positive trends notwithstanding, there are challenges at the implementation level that are complicated by data. Data quality and bias is one of the major challenges. AI models are based on big datasets, but a lot of institutions do not have clean, representative, and contextualized data. It results in the risks of misclassifying the at-risk students or increasing the inequalities among the learners who represent the underrepresented groups. Moreover, the proprietary AI systems are frequently a black box, and it is not always possible to see how the recommendations or risk scores are produced by an educator. Most developing nations have infrastructure inequalities, including low-speed Internet access, ageing devices, and unreliable power infrastructure, as high-income places utilize AI in large volumes. Even in technologically developed states, those schools in the rural and low-income areas find it hard to use advanced AI instruments. Such unfairness leads to global and domestic inequity with students in highly-resourced settings becoming more analytical and digital-skilled than others. Unless it is specifically invested in, AI will increase instead of reducing educational gaps (Deri et al., 2024; Singh, 2024c). There is also regulatory uncertainty among policymakers. The rapid development of generative AI surpasses the politics cycles. There are problems with data privacy, intellectual property, academic integrity, and accountability, which have not been resolved. The institutions are concerned about how they would comply with the national data-protection laws; teachers are concerned about the possibility of the AI tools used by students in a wrong way; governments are concerned with the possibility to formulate the standards that would stimulate innovations and provide the safety. The absence of uniform international standards, particularly in assessment, verification and credentialing, is a barrier to confusion and delay in adoption. Lack of practical implementation also contributes to the restrictions of AI on education. Low rates of training are common among the educators, and the most common scenario is that professional development has been centered on the use of tools instead of pedagogical practices. Majority of teachers are not prepared to introduce AI in inquiry based learning, project based evaluation as well as in metacognitive skill development (Singh, 2024a; Singh, 2024b). This often leads to misuse of AI where they produce content instead of some more cognitive work. There are also institutions which do not have implementation roadmaps. The other significant gap is lack of sound evaluation systems. Comparative or longitudinal research is scarcely ever done by the institutions to assess the effect of AI on learning outcomes. One of the challenges to policymakers is to balance between innovative and cautious approaches, which can lead to a postponement of implementation until its effects are confirmed. To conclude,

AI has possibilities to transform all cities of the world to the new level of critical thinking and problem-solving; however, in the process, educators and policymakers have to discuss critical gaps in data quality, equity, governance, professional training, and evaluation. To overcome these obstacles, policy frameworks, capacity building over the long term, and implementation plans using evidence-based approaches are necessary to make AI a valuable and responsible aspect of the future of learning.

DIFFICULTIES AND ETHICAL ISSUES

Although the potential of AI-based learning technology is enormous, its widespread usage in e-learning is associated with a complicated system of challenges and ethical issues, which require particular consideration. These are issues that should not be disregarded and may only strengthen the preexisting inequalities, destroy trust, and even reverse the very learning outcomes AI is meant to enhance. Another important issue is that of data privacy and security (Deri et al., 2024; Singh, 2024c; Garg et al., 2024). Educational AI systems are most successful when they have access to large volume of student data - performance, learning behaviors, interactions and even biometric information in certain proctoring applications. This casts serious doubts on the manner in which this sensitive information is gathered, retained, utilized and exchanged. The risk of data leaks, unauthorized access, and misuse of data to other purposes other than education are always present possibilities (commercial use, surveillance, etc.). Together with powerful data protection policies, robust encryption, and clear policies, it is necessary to establish and ensure trust between students, parents, and educators (Shah & Asad, 2024). Algorithms bias is another important problem. AI algorithms are trained on its own and learn. In case such information indicates the current social prejudices, the AI system may serve to reproduce or even increase these prejudices, resulting in unjust or discriminatory decisions. As an example, a system of AI grading could prefer some population, or a customized learning journey could direct students with a disadvantaged background to an easier route (Singh et al., 2024). To solve bias, it is vital to have carefully-edited and balanced and representative training data, and unceasing monitoring and auditing of AI outputs to maintain fairness and equity in training to all learners. Many advanced AI models are also black box in nature, which is also problematic. A system based on AI may not be easily questioned or disputed because it is hard to comprehend how it can achieve its recommendations or decisions. Such a lack of transparency may destroy trust and make it challenging to actually understand and take advantage of AI, or to make students understand why they were given a specific feedback or grades. The field of explainable AI (XAI) is an expanding enterprise that tries to uphold the processes of AI decision-making more transparent, yet it is a long journey ahead. Also, there is a fear regarding the possible influence on the human component of the education. Although AI can be used to automate work and tailor the learning process, it cannot provide the same level of empathy, mentoring, and socialization that human educators can offer (Singh, 2024a; Deri et al., 2024). Excessive dependency on AI might reduce the importance of the teacher-student relationship and prevent the improvement of the social-emotional skills of a student. (Singh, 2024; Nuong et al., 2024). Teacher role should shift to the content deliverer to a so-called learning architect and facilitator, using AI without losing human aspect that will remain the primary element. Lastly, the issue of accessibility and equity is also a challenge. The access to the appropriate technology, infrastructure, or digital literacy skills needed to successfully use AI-driven tools is not available to all students and educational institutions. This digital divide may contribute to increasing the educational inequality gap between those who can afford to enjoy AI benefits and those who will be left behind. AI in e-learning is important in ensuring that all learners are given a fair access and the right training to ensure that AI is really beneficial to all learners. Despite the importance of the promise, there are challenges associated with using AI to think and solve problems. Using AI recommendations too much can result in intellectual laziness. Moreover, the transparency of the AI algorithms has the potential of covering bias or mistakes, especially when the users are not capable of critically examining the result of the output (Singh et al., 2024; Singh & Sihmar, 2025). The educators and schools need to become AI-savvy, and the students should be able to learn not only how to utilize AI technologies but also to ask questions and critique them. Moreover, such ethical issues as privacy of information, fairness of access, and validity of student work should be handled with the help of strong policy frameworks and inclusive design procedures.

IMPLICATIONS

In addition to the immediate advantages and issues, there are deeper repercussions of integrating AI-based educational technology on the future of learning, teaching, and development of the society. These implications can be found on pedagogical paradigms, the professional scenery and even in the nature of human thinking. Among the implications is the change in pedagogical methods. Conventional teacher-conduction models of content delivery will be further replaced with more personalized and student-centered and facilitator educator roles (George, 2023; Tham et al., 2022). Educators will no longer be the main sources of knowledge delivery but learning architects, curation of AI-based resources, coherence of interest learning, and socio-emotional growth and higher-order skills, such as critical thinking and creativity. Much of the diagnostic and prescriptive part of learning will be handled by AI, allowing teachers to become more deeply involved in their mentorship and personalized assistance (Singh, 2024; Nuong et al., 2024). This transition requires professional growth among teachers in order to learn new skills of using AI in an effective and ethical way. To the learners, the implications are also transformative. AI-based systems are likely to provide a more balanced learning environment by changing to different learning styles, pace, and requirements. This has the possibility of alleviating the level of drop-outs and increasing the overall academic performance because no child would be left behind in the name of the one-size-fits-all strategy. But with it comes the implication of the development of digital literacy and AI fluency as one of the central competencies. The students will not only be required to read the AI-generated information but also critically analyze it, comprehend its working principles, and learn to successfully cooperate with the AI tools. Having the skill to ask useful questions to AI and to analyze its output will be as important as the usual reading and writing skills. In a social sense, the high usage of AI in learning means a more skilled and flexible work force. Education systems, supported by AI, can be working to develop these distinctly human qualities, training people on job opportunities that are not yet available and in an economic environment that is increasingly dynamic (Singh, 2024a; Singh, 2024b). It may also result in a more sustained learning culture, as AI-based solutions will enable professionals to take lifelong learning and upskilling opportunities. Otherwise, AI has the potential to benefit education asymmetrically, as those who already have access to technology and faster internet connection would see an increase in their advantages, continuing to separate the educational divide. The governments and educational establishments should make active efforts to make sure that the resources and training are distributed fairly and that AI does not become one more factor that allows increasing the level of social inequalities. Intelligence definition itself, as well as the concept of learning, may change peculiarities too as human and artificial intelligence will become more intertwined, and the philosophical discussions about the future of human cognition and the role of AI in our intellectual activities may be more elaborate.

CONCLUSION

Due to the further development of AI, educators, researchers, and professionals should now shift the focus not towards the automation of the outputs but towards the improvement of cognitive processes. The future of education and innovation will not be in the machine taking the place of thinking but rather to think better with the help of the machines. By incorporating the concept of AI in the learning space as the tool of inquiry, analysis, and reflection, we will be able to cultivate a generation of learners who are not merely technologically literate but also critically empowered. This emerging paradigm demands reconstructed pedagogies, interdisciplinary partnerships and unremitting moral alertness. By so doing, we open the potential of AI to become a collaborator in the development of the very human abilities of reason, creativity and problem-solving.

FUTURE RESEARCH WORK

The inclusion of AI in e-learning provides enormous opportunities to the further research activity, much of which will be aimed at streamlining the pedagogic effects of AI and reducing its inherent risks. In the future, the research must leave the theoretical debates and explore the empirical studies and action implementation plans. Longitudinal studies on learning outcomes are one of the important directions of the future research. Even though preliminary research indicates a rosy future of AI applied to personalization and engagement, long-term tracking of data is required to determine its long-term influence on critical thinking, problem-solving skills, and overall academic and career success (Singh, 2024a). This would entail coming up with strict experiments that have a comparison of AI-enhanced learning settings against traditional settings over a long duration of time, testing the applicability of skills acquired using AI to new situations. Studies must investigate interfaces that are easy to use and explain how AI thinks so that learners can get a clear idea as to why a specific piece of feedback was provided or why a specific learning path was suggested. Such transparency is essential to establishing trust, helping to develop metacognitive awareness, and creating a beneficial partnership between humans and AI instead of unconditional trust. In addition, current studies on how to reduce algorithmic bias are top priority. This will involve the creation of new ways of generating diverse and fair training data, the development of algorithms that are less prone to bias, and the creation of strong auditing systems to detect and correct biases in deployed AI systems (Singh & Kumar, 2024). Comparative analyses of various demographic groups are needed in order to make sure that AI in education does not unintentionally increase achieved gaps. The changing status of the human educator in an e-learning environment that is saturated with AI is also a topic that will require considerable research. The effective models of teacher professional development should be researched in the context of providing teachers with the so-called AI literacy required to successfully introduce AI technologies, handle AI-generated student information, and focus on the human-centered approach to teaching. This comes along with the realization of how AI can assist instead of substitute the social and emotional dimensions of learning. Lastly, the prospect of AI in unexplored domains of e-learning, including the development of creativity, encouraging collaborative learning, and assisting students with different accessibility needs, is a promising research topic. This involves exploring how generative AI can be used to create innovative content by students themselves, AI-assisted group project facilitation, and AI-focused applications to students with disabilities so that they can enjoy the benefits of AI-driven education as well.

REFERENCES

Deri, M. N., Zaazie, P., & Singh, A. (2024). Digital Future of the Hospitality Industry and Hospitality Education Globally. In Sharma, A. (Ed.), *International Handbook of Skill, Education, Learning, and Research Development in Tourism and Hospitality. Springer International Handbooks of Education.* Springer., DOI: 10.1007/978-981-97-4318-6_14

Garg, A., Singh, A., & Yanan, J. (2024). Exploring the Impact of Digital Detoxification on Higher Education Students' Learning. In Grima, S., Chaudhary, S., Sood, K., & Kumar, S. (Eds.), *Business Drivers in Promoting Digital Detoxification* (pp. 111–126). IGI Global Scientific Publishing., DOI: 10.4018/979-8-3693-1107-3.ch008

George, A. S. (2023). Preparing students for an AI-driven world: Rethinking curriculum and pedagogy in the age of artificial intelligence. *Partners Universal Innovative Research Publication, 1*(2), 112–136.

Holmes, W., & Littlejohn, A. (2024). Artificial intelligence for professional learning. In *Handbook of artificial intelligence at work* (pp. 191–211). Edward Elgar Publishing. DOI: 10.4337/9781800889972.00018

Holmes, W., Porayska-Pomsta, K., Holstein, K., Sutherland, E., Baker, T., Shum, S. B., Santos, O. C., Rodrigo, M. T., Cukurova, M., Bittencourt, I. I., & Koedinger, K. R. (2022). Ethics of AI in education: Towards a community-wide framework. *International Journal of Artificial Intelligence in Education, 32*(3), 504–526. DOI: 10.1007/s40593-021-00239-1

Jha, A., & Singh, S. R. (2025). Integrating Artificial Intelligence in Media Education: Revolutionizing Learning, Creativity, and Critical Thinking. In Teachers' Roles and Perspectives on AI Integration in Schools (pp. 297-328). IGI Global Scientific Publishing.

Kenedy, R. A. (2024). The challenges of critical thinking in the era of artificial intelligence. *European Journal of Multidisciplinary Studies, 9*(2), 19–36. DOI: 10.26417/hfdngd20

Khalabuzar, O., & Shymanovych, I. (2024). Developing critical thinking skills through artificial intelligence and language learning. Modern educational strategies under the influence of the development of the information society and European integration.

Lubbe, A., Marais, E., & Kruger, D. (2025). Cultivating independent thinkers: The triad of artificial intelligence, Bloom's taxonomy and critical thinking in assessment pedagogy. *Education and Information Technologies, 30*(12), 1–34. DOI: 10.1007/s10639-025-13476-x

Luckin, R., & Holmes, W. (2016). Intelligence unleashed: An argument for AI in education.

Moustaghfir, S., & Brigui, H. (2024). Navigating critical thinking in the digital era: An informative exploration. International Journal of Linguistics. *Literature and Translation, 7*(1), 137–143.

Na-songkhla, J., Mahakaew, V., & Peytcheva-Forsyth, R. (2024). The Emergence of Generative Artificial Intelligence: Enhancing Critical Thinking Skills in ChatGPTIntegrated Cognitive Flexibility Approach. Generative Artificial Intelligence in Higher Education: A Handbook for Educational Leaders, 52.

Nuong Deri, M., Singh, A., Zaazie, P., & Anandene, D. (2024). Leveraging Artificial Intelligence in Higher Educational Institutions: A Comprehensive Overview. *Education and Law Review*, (30). Advance online publication. DOI: 10.1344/REYD2024.30.45777

Shah, S. S., & Asad, M. M. (2024). Impact of Critical Thinking Approach on Learners' Dependence on Innovative Transformation Through Artificial Intelligence. In The Evolution of Artificial Intelligence in Higher Education: Challenges, Risks, and Ethical Considerations (pp. 161-182). Emerald Publishing Limited.

Sharma, R., & Singh, A. (2024). Use of Digital Technology in Improving Quality Education: A Global Perspectives and Trends. In Nadda, V., Tyagi, P., Moniz Vieira, R., & Tyagi, P. (Eds.), *Implementing Sustainable Development Goals in the Service Sector* (pp. 14–26). IGI Global., DOI: 10.4018/979-8-3693-2065-5.ch002

Singh, A. (2022). Conceptual framework on Smart Learning Environment- An Indian perspective. *Journal of Education and Law*, (25). Advance online publication. DOI: 10.1344/REYD2022.25.36706

Singh, A. (2024a). The Role of Digital Transformation and Its Effects on the Education Sector. In Chakraborty, S. (Ed.), *Challenges of Globalization and Inclusivity in Academic Research* (pp. 92–99). IGI Global Scientific Publishing., DOI: 10.4018/979-8-3693-1371-8.ch007

Singh, A. (2024b). Endorsing Gamification Pedagogy for Nurturing Employability Skills in Higher Education Institutions (HEI). In Membrive, V. (Ed.), *Practices and Implementation of Gamification in Higher Education* (pp. 172–183). IGI Global Scientific Publishing., DOI: 10.4018/979-8-3693-0716-8.ch008

Singh, A. (2024c). Impact of E-learning on Student Motivation in Higher Education Institutions: An Indian Perspective. *Journal of Education and Law*, (29). Advance online publication. DOI: 10.1344/REYD2024.29.43214

Singh, A. (2024c). Students Wellbeing and Performance in Higher Education Institutions. In Aloka, P. (Ed.), *Factors Impacting Student Well-Being and Coping Tactics* (pp. 1–12). IGI Global Scientific Publishing., DOI: 10.4018/979-8-3693-8860-0.ch001

Singh, A., & Kumar, P. (2024). E-Learning Ecosystem in Higher Education Institutions: Trends and Practices. In Al Husseiny, F., & Munna, A. (Eds.), *Preparing Students for the Future Educational Paradigm* (pp. 1–18). IGI Global Scientific Publishing., DOI: 10.4018/979-8-3693-1536-1.ch001

Singh, A., & Sihmar, P. (2025). Higher Education Institution Sustainability: Role of Green Human Resource Management. In Adu-Gyamfi, M., Boateng, F., & Atiku, S. (Eds.), *Green HRM Awareness and Training in Higher Education Institutions* (pp. 1–14). IGI Global Scientific Publishing., DOI: 10.4018/979-8-3693-2956-6.ch001

Singh, A., Singh, D., & Chhikara, S. (2024). Online Learning: Challenges and Suggestions to Enhance Student Engagement in Higher Education Institutions. In Naidoo, V., & Verma, R. (Eds.), *Reshaping Entrepreneurial Education Within an Industry 4.0 Context* (pp. 59–80). IGI Global Scientific Publishing., DOI: 10.4018/979-8-3693-0409-9.ch004

Spector, J. M., & Ma, S. (2019). Inquiry and critical thinking skills for the next generation: From artificial intelligence back to human intelligence. *Smart Learning Environments*, *6*(1), 1–11. DOI: 10.1186/s40561-019-0088-z

Stuchlikova, L., & Weis, M. (2024, October). From Information to Insight: Reimagining Critical Thinking Pedagogy in the Age of Artificial Intelligence. In *2024 International Conference on Emerging eLearning Technologies and Applications (ICETA)* (pp. 591-598). IEEE. DOI: 10.1109/ICETA63795.2024.10850787

Tham, J., Howard, T., & Verhulsdonck, G. (2022). Extending design thinking, content strategy, and artificial intelligence into technical communication and user experience design programs: Further pedagogical implications. *Journal of Technical Writing and Communication*, *52*(4), 428–459. DOI: 10.1177/00472816211072533

KEY TERMS AND DEFINITIONS

Adaptive Learning: A particular form of personalized learning in which the educational systems dynamically adapt the learning materials, the level of difficulty and the methods of instruction, in real-time according to the performance, progress, and interactions of the student. The AI algorithms constantly evaluate the knowledge of the learner and adjust the learning process.

Algorithmic Bias: Conservative and unreasonable distortions in the results of AI algorithms, which is usually caused by bias in the training data or the algorithm itself. This may result in discriminatory results in assessment, content suggestions, or schooling paths of particular groups of students in the field of education.

Artificial Intelligence (AI): The general branch of computer science focused on designing systems capable of executing what human intelligence is used to execute. AI tries to reproduce and optimize the elements of human cognition to serve the purpose of education.

Data Privacy: Ethical and legal duties that relate to gathering, preserving, utilizing and distributing personal and sensitive details. Data privacy is important in AI-based e-learning because such systems deal with large volumes of student data.

Generative AI: A form of AI that is capable of generating new content (text, images, audio, or code) based on the patterns of a large existing dataset. Although it is useful to create content, the other potential of e-learning of the tool is that it can be used to create creative problem-solving and critical thinking when utilized as a collaborative tool.

Intelligent Tutoring Systems (ITS): AI-based software that teaches instructions and feedback individually and one-on-one to a learner and acts as a human tutor. ITS has the capability of diagnosing misconceptions as well as provide explanations, and help the students in problem-solving processes.

Machine Learning (ML): A sub-field of AI, which allows systems to learn without being explicitly coded. The patterns identified by LM algorithms are used to draw predictions or make a decision based on this learned knowledge. ML is used in adaptive systems in e-learning to personalize content and testing depending on the needs of students.

Metacognition: The ability to know and to cognize the way one thinks. In e-learning involving AI, a metacognitive awareness process entails applying AI to encourage learners to be mindful of their learning processes, track their understanding and assess their problem-solving methods, hence improving the likelihood of learning effectively.

Natural Language Processing (NLP): This is a subsector of AI that is aiming at giving a computer the ability to comprehend, interpret, and produce human speech.

Personalized Learning: This is a learning method where every student is provided with a learning experience that is customized based on their individual needs, interests, and learning style. AI is instrumental in that it must process the information on the students to offer them in-depth content, speed, and feedback to form an individualized journey.

Chapter 18

Empowering Fine Arts Education With ICT to Train Primary Education Major Undergraduates: Exemplary Cases on Using Emerging Technologies

Lu Ping
https://orcid.org/0009-0004-2108-9830
UCSI University, Kuala Lumpur, Malaysia

Khar Thoe Ng
https://orcid.org/0000-0002-4462-657X
INTI International University, Nilai, Malaysia

Katayoun Mehdinezhadnouri
UCSI University, Kuala Lumpur, Malaysia

Shi Zhongya
Shangqiu University, Shangqiu, China

Wang Zexin
UCSI University, Kuala Lumpur, Malaysia

Guan Xingzhi
https://orcid.org/0000-0003-0351-5977
UCSI University, Kuala Lumpur, Malaysia

Peter Ee Teik Chew
PCET Multimedia Education, Malaysia

Masanori Fukui
Mie University, Japan

Rajendra Kumar
https://orcid.org/0000-0002-8427-5428
Sharda School of Computing Science and Engineering, Sharda University, Greater Noida, India

ABSTRACT

Primary education major undergraduates, often lacking formal fine arts training, face challenges in delivering effective art instruction. As part of a Design and Development Research (DDR), this qualitative exemplary study investigates how computational technologies, specifically virtual reality (VR) and artificial intelligence enhance fine arts education for non-art majors. Two case studies demonstrate ICT applications: (1) VR-assisted Chinese painting module using AI-generated GAN animations and Unity-developed immersive environments to simulate brushwork, spatial composition, and 3D artistic element interaction; and (2) an AI-facilitated cross-media

DOI: 10.4018/979-8-3373-5601-3.ch018

framework employing StyleGAN3 for style transfer and AutoCAD vector conversion, transforming traditional ink paintings into paper quilling, clay modeling, and digital art. Through Cross-Case Analysis and Exemplary-Case Analysis, the study evaluates AI-powered step-by-step animation systems, VR's 360° visual storytelling, and interactive digital platforms.

1. INTRODUCTION

Most normal university students lack systematic professional education in subject areas, which cannot be separated from the later stage of art education. We plan to use qualitative typical case studies in the "Research on the Design and Development of New Technology in Art Education" (Art Education New Technology Design and Development Research) to explore the possibility of non-art teacher majors using new technologies to bridge the gap in art teaching.

1.1 Research Background and Overview

It is more important for teacher education students to receive art education that can stimulate their aesthetic perception, creativity, and cross-subject learning than professional art skills (Meyer & Norman, 2020), and this type of art education can also contribute to the cultivation of teacher students' critical thinking and problem-solving skills (Perignat & Katz-Buonincontro, 2019). China's art curriculum combines fine arts, cultural skills, and teaching methods to help non art major students approach art (Chandramana, 2020). However, with the cultivation of 21st century skills and the continuous improvement of education, more interactive and technologically oriented teaching methods are inevitable trends to be applied to art curriculum teaching (Simamora, 2020).

Virtual reality, artificial intelligence and other information and communication technologies are changing the way students experience and participate in art education in a conventional sense (Pellas et al., 2019) - VR provides three-dimensional restoration of classical paintings and painting techniques for students to explore, while AI provides real-time feedback and adjusts their learning pace (Zhang & Zou, 2022; Liao et al., 2023). The use of such tools in schools abroad is very common, but in China, except for universities, it is still rare to see information and communication technology (ICT) being used in art classrooms. Studies have shown that digital learning helps students learn and absorb more effectively (Avcı & Gümüş, 2020).

Traditional Chinese art education is a major way to inherit traditional Chinese artistic culture, but for beginners, it can sometimes feel a bit difficult (Sheridan et al., 2022; Liu & Sun, 2022). However, with the help of information technology, such as animations, videos, virtual reality, augmented reality, and other content that can illustrate painting techniques, as well as software that can assist in brushstroke training, online courses can be taken to effectively solve the problem of difficult learning (Ford & Minshall, 2019). According to the analysis of the results of the previous study, it was found that students who acquired knowledge through digital methods had better memory and cultural awareness than those who did not acquire knowledge through digital methods (Holmes & Tuomi, 2022; Chen & Wang, 2021). This shows that there is a need to develop better art education methods and improve the effectiveness of traditional Chinese art education.

1.2 Problem Statement and Research Value

There are three major shortcomings in the current artistic education for primary school majors that affect the quality of future teacher cultivation: insufficient artistic cultivation, inadequate information technology skills, and the absence of effective cultural tradition inheritance mechanisms. Since the basic education art major focuses on teacher education and lacks artistic creation ability, normal students can only obtain some basic artistic knowledge during their undergraduate years. This results in them only knowing how to brush and imitate in their artistic learning, and not having creativity. This makes it difficult for them to independently design interesting and creative lessons for their future students. The lack of artistic creation ability affects the art learning of primary school students, makes it difficult for them to fully explore art learning, and also makes it difficult for them to adapt to the diverse art teaching forms in the school.

In recent years, information technology has developed rapidly in various fields, but it has not entered the field of art education, especially in teacher education in China. The main form of art classes is still the teacher's demonstration combined with repeated practical training, lacking interactive learning through information technology means (Wang & Li, 2021; Huang, 2020). There is a lack of research-based information technology teaching resources such as AI teaching animations, VR tools, and digital simulations in the field of art education. Teachers lack corresponding research to refer to when using information technology tools in class (Chen & Zhang, 2023). Without the support of evidence-based teaching theories and models, it is difficult for teachers to effectively incorporate information technology into their teaching.

On the one hand, the role of traditional Chinese painting in cultural dissemination makes the reform of teaching methods even more urgent. The inheritor of traditional Chinese painting needs to master brush stroke techniques, texturing techniques, and coloring techniques, which are daunting for beginners (Liu & Zhao, 2022). On the other hand, most college students lack the necessary skills to understand and apply traditional Chinese painting brushwork and still struggle to learn from imitators and predecessors. The current teaching method of traditional Chinese painting still fails to use multimedia technology to achieve interactive guided teaching mode (Xu, 2021; Zheng & Wu, 2023).

To solve the above problems, this study focuses on exploring how information technology-based teaching materials can affect students' learning interests and learning effects in art courses, such as step-by-step animation videos driven by artificial intelligence, VR immersion, brush simulation software etc. AI step-by-step animation videos can provide students with interactive visual effects, decomposing brush movement, brush pressure, and artistic expression techniques to help them quickly understand and master complex brush stroke techniques. VR can place students in digitally processed historical painting scenes, enabling them to feel the cultural aura of historical paintings in a specific context.

The research findings support the argument for curriculum reform by demonstrating the unique value of ICT in art education (Huang et al., 2021). They will also contribute to the modernization of cultural education by using ICT as a medium to connect traditional culture with modern innovative teaching methods (Liao & Wang, 2021). Through technological means, art teachers will be trained to use the above methods to improve the quality of art education, strengthen cultural confidence, and promote the inheritance of traditional art in the information age (Wang & Cheng, 2022).

1.3 Research Objectives and Questions

Virtual Reality (VR) and Artificial Intelligence (AI) are used to explore their role and impact in the development of painting skills, cultural awareness, and artistic teaching practice for primary education majors. Using information technology to transform education has become a common phenomenon, but the application of information technology in teacher education, especially in the context of China, where it is mostly utilized in subject education and teaching research, its promotion and application in pre-service art teacher education is still in a preliminary exploration stage. Therefore, this study starts with the application of information technology in artistic education, hoping to help future teachers better integrate digital technology and cultural awareness in artistic education into their own development.

Research objectives (ROs) are specific and measurable goals that a researcher aims to achieve through their study.

Node 1: General Overview Node 2: ICT curriculum planning for undergraduate art education(Node 3: Art education theory and methods for undergraduate students (72 hours) Sub node 1: Principles and methods of school education art 2.1 (6 hours) Sub node 2: Modern educational technology 2.2 (36 hours) Sub node 3: Primary school comprehensive art practical activity design and case analysis 2.3 (18 hours) Sub node 4: Techniques and methods of primary school student art psychological health education 2.4 (12 hours)) Node 4: Art skills and design (80 hours) Sub node 1: Computer processing of two-dimensional color composition and comprehensive materials 3.1 (20 hours) Sub node 2: Computer vector illustration and VI design 3.2 (20 hours) Sub node 3: Computer processing of three-dimensional composition and model production 3.3 (20 hours) Sub node 4: Computer digital photography and editing 3.4 (20 hours)) Node 5: Art aesthetics and appreciation (72 hours) Sub node 1: History and appreciation of modern art 5.1 (18 hours)Sub node 2: History and appreciation of modern art 5.2 (18 hours)Sub node 3: World modern art 5.3 (18 hours) Sub node 4: Appreciation of contemporary Chinese art 5.4 (18 hours)

> RO2: Research on the implementation feasibility, effectiveness, and student engagement of VR and AI in art teaching.

Example 3: Using VR and AI to assist students in learning artistic skills and improving cultural appreciation.

Research Questions (RQs)

> RQ1 (Framework Design): What are the components of an ICT framework for art education?
> RQ2 (Implementation of VR and AI): How can VR and AI be effectively introduced into art teaching to truly function?
> RQ3 (Typical cases): Are there any studies on the impact of VR and AI on student learning interest and the effectiveness of artistic skill learning?

By achieving these goals, this study aims to construct an information technology teaching model to facilitate the reform of teacher education in art teacher education programs, contribute to curriculum reform, promote technological infiltration in teaching methods, and revive traditional culture (Zhao & Chen, 2023).

2. RESEARCH METHODOLOGY

This article is a design study based on the DDR model. The qualitative case study method combines typical case analysis (ECA) and cross case analysis (CCA) to explore the reconstruction of traditional Chinese painting courses for undergraduate students majoring in primary education at Shangqiu Normal University with VR and AI. One is the Focus Group Discussion (FGD) method, and the other is Structured Classroom Observation (SCO). The number of participants in the VR group and the AI group is 6-8 people, as shown in Table 2. The VR group is summarized in Table 1.

Table 1. VR group

Student	Experience	Feelings	Challenges	Suggestions
Wang	"VR made me feel like I was actually painting a Chinese landscape. The immersion was amazing!"	"I feel more confident now because I can practice repeatedly without wasting paper."	"The headset is heavy, and it sometimes lags, which is frustrating."	"I hope there are more famous paintings to study in VR, like more landscapes and flowers."
Li	"At first, I felt dizzy, but once I got used to it, it was fun. I loved exploring the 360° view."	"VR made the class more interesting. I used to think Chinese painting was boring."	"It was hard to control the brush strokes and colors at first. I needed more practice."	"Can we have a multiplayer mode? I want to collaborate with my classmates in VR."
Zhang	"VR helped me understand the layers in Chinese painting, like how to show distance and depth."	"I feel more relaxed now because I can zoom in and adjust details easily."	"There aren't enough VR devices. Sometimes I had to wait for my turn."	"Maybe make the headset lighter? It gets tiring after a while."
Liu	"I was so focused that I lost track of time. The details in my painting turned out great!"	"VR made me feel like I was inside the painting. It was a unique experience."	"I struggled with the small details. It was hard to get them right."	"Add more tutorials in VR, like step-by-step guides for beginners."
Chen	"I added modern elements to my traditional painting. It was fun to experiment!"	"I feel more creative now because VR lets me try new things without fear of making mistakes."	"The controls were a bit complicated. It took me a while to learn how to use them."	"Can we have more creative tools in VR, like different brush styles?"
Zhao	"I chose a simple flower painting, and VR helped me get the colors right."	"I feel more relaxed now because VR guides me step by step."	"I was nervous at first and made some mistakes with the colors."	"Maybe add more beginner-friendly options, like simpler paintings to start with."

Table 2. Artificial Intelligence Group

Student	Experience	Feelings	Challenges	Suggestions
Zhou	"AI gave me real-time feedback on my painting. It helped me fix my mistakes right away."	"I feel more confident now because AI tells me what to improve."	"Sometimes the feedback feels too mechanical, like it is forcing me to follow a set pattern."	"I wish AI could give more personalized advice instead of generic suggestions."
Wu	"AI-generated reference images for me, which gave me a lot of inspiration."	"I feel like AI made Chinese painting easier, but sometimes it feels like the AI is doing the work, not me."	"The reference images didn't always match what I wanted to paint."	"Can AI have a chat feature? I want to explain my ideas to it."
Huang	"AI helped me with color matching. I didn't know how to mix traditional Chinese colors before."	"I feel more relaxed now because AI guides me through the process."	"The AI interface was a bit complicated. It took me a while to learn how to use it."	"Maybe make the AI tools simpler? It's hard to focus on painting when the tools are confusing."
Xu	"I followed AI's suggestions for my landscape painting, and it turned out better than I expected."	"I feel like AI made the class more high-tech and fun."	"I felt a bit restricted by AI's suggestions. I wanted to try something different."	"Can AI allow more freedom? Sometimes I want to break the rules."
Sun	"I added modern buildings to my traditional landscape. AI helped me balance the colors."	"I feel more creative now because AI gave me ideas I wouldn't have thought of."	"I relied too much on AI's suggestions. My painting didn't feel like my own."	"Maybe AI can suggest multiple options instead of just one?"
Gao	"I used AI to fix the proportions in my figure painting. It turned out much better!"	"I feel more confident now because AI helped me get the proportions right."	"The AI tools were a bit overwhelming at first. I needed more time to learn."	"Can AI have a beginner mode? It's hard to use all the advanced features right away."

2.1 Pedagogical Presentation of Technical Tools

The AI assisted teaching activities are based on Python environment, using TensorFlow and OpenCV to implement corresponding algorithms and capturing real-time interaction actions of the human body.Students can draw pictures with the help of VR and then use Generative Adversarial Networks (specifically CycleGAN) to generate animations with dynamic brushstrokes. Then, with the help of Unity software, a VR environment is designed to enable students to interact with 3D models of paintings through Leap Motion hand detection.

When it comes to cross media art works, we use a style transfer algorithm based on VGG16 neural network to transfer the ink painting to the computer to generate a digital version of the image. Then, we use AutoCAD to convert it into a vector image file, which can be used as a mold for physical artworks such as paper art or clay sculpture. The above artificial intelligence program guides students to complete their work on the online platform, and through computer vision, quickly provides feedback on whether the color matching of the works is appropriate, whether the proportions are consistent, etc.

2.2 Analytical Methods

We used focus groups to explore students' experiences with VR headsets, such as "the VR headsets are not comfortable" (due to personal real-time adjustment of hardware), "the feedback from AI is not targeted" (due to personal preferences, for example, adding soft settings to the overall rigidity of the feedback mechanism) and other issues. In the teaching process, the degree of student participation was analyzed (for example, task completion time, number of operations using technical tools), as well as the analysis of the spatial depth of student artwork in the VR group (such as whether the spatial depth effect was achieved) and whether there was color deviation in the AI group's (whether the coloring was accurate). Based on thematic analysis, there was a more prominent pattern of "immersive creativity" in the VR group and "technology driven accuracy" in the AI group. Critical case analysis (CCA) showed that compared to traditional teaching methods, VR promoted students' spatial thinking (with a significant increase of 30% in the depth perception test of the VR group).

We aim to achieve a reasonable balance between ease of use and innovation in our technological implementation. On the one hand, we use widely popular software development tools such as Unity and TensorFlow to facilitate further dissemination and application by university teachers; On the other hand, we are committed to achieving innovative developments in higher education teaching.

3. RESULTS AND DISCUSSION

This section presents data analysis addressing RQ1, RQ2, and RQ3.

3.1 RQ1: Core Elements of the ICT Framework for Art Education

This article analyzes the confluence of primary education major art education and ICT, and explores how emerging technologies can enrich the meaning of artistic learning and help students truly connect with cultural content (refer to Figure 1 for the conceptual model). By innovating the integration of ICT in the curriculum of normal universities' art education, a new form of art teaching method for normal universities is formed, reflecting the integration relationship between traditional art education in normal universities and information technology development (refer to Table 3 for the innovation and contribution theory framework based on TPACK theory) and has the significance of application and reference for the further development of digital art education (Xu & Zhao, 2022).

Table 3. Research Schema and Contribution Points

TPACK Dimensions	Core Components	Corresponding Research Question (RQ)	Research Objective (RO)	Key Innovation/ Contribution
Technological Knowledge (TK)	Emerging technologies: VR (360° immersion, virtual brushstroke simulation), AI (style transfer, real-time feedback, GANs) - Technical tools: Unity, TensorFlow, Leap Motion, VGG16 neural network - Technical operation: Interactive tracking, cross-media conversion, adaptive algorithm deployment	RQ2: How can VR and AI be effectively integrated into fine arts instruction?	RO2: Investigate the implementation of VR and AI in fine arts teaching, focusing on instructional effectiveness and engagement.	Translate technical functions into pedagogical tools (e.g., VR immersion → cultural experience; AI feedback → skill refinement) - Simplify technical complexity to fit non-art majors' learning needs
Content Knowledge (CK)	Fine arts core content: Traditional Chinese painting techniques (outlining, texturing, coloring), spatial composition, cultural heritage (Dunhuang murals, New Year paintings) - Disciplinary goals: Aesthetic appreciation, cultural inheritance, creative expression	RQ3: What evidence supports the impact of VR and AI on student engagement and artistic skill acquisition?	RO3: Analyze exemplary cases demonstrating how VR and AI enhance students' artistic skills acquisition and cultural appreciation.	Digitize intangible cultural heritage (e.g., virtual restoration of traditional techniques) - Link technical application to cultural transmission (e.g., AI style transfer → fusion of traditional and modern art elements)
Pedagogical Knowledge (PK)	Teaching models: Immersive learning, guided practice, hybrid instruction (ICT + traditional demonstration) - Teaching strategies: Thematic analysis (engagement/creativity/cultural learning), step-by-step tutoring, interactive feedback loops - Assessment methods: Focus group discussions, classroom observation, artistic output evaluation (spatial depth, color accuracy, creativity scoring)	RQ1: What are the essential components of an ICT framework for fine arts education?	RO1: Develop a structured framework to integrate ICT into fine arts education for primary education undergraduate students.	Construct a TPACK-based integrated teaching framework for non-art majors - Align "experience-reflection-abstraction-application" (Kolb, 1984) with technical-content integration
TPACK Integration	Synergy mechanism: TK × CK × PK (e.g., VR + Chinese landscape painting + immersive composition teaching; AI + color matching + adaptive skill tutoring) - Practical alignment: Technical accessibility → content adaptability → pedagogical effectiveness	RQ1-RQ3 (Comprehensive Integration)	RO1-RO3 (Holistic Achievement)	Bridge the gap between technology, content, and pedagogy in fine arts teacher training - Provide a replicable model for ICT integration in non-art major fine arts education

3.2 RQ2: Research on Pathways for VR and AI to Serve Art Teaching

As can be seen from Figure 1, VR has placed students in the midst of landscape painting - this figure depicts a "VR assisted landscape painting teaching scene"; Figure 2 is a "360° virtual brush stroke simulation interface".

In addition, AI can transform the traditional Chinese painting materials that students learn into various forms of expression, such as types, styles, and content, in art conversion. The specific process is: AI converts brush stroke water traces into vector graphics, and then through algorithm operations, it becomes a conversion result of different art forms, such as quilling art, clay sculpture art, or animation style digital art conversion and so on. Figure 3, "AI-driven cross media art conversion process", shows the conversion process.

Figure 1. Schematic diagram of VR assisted landscape painting teaching scenario

Figure 2. 360° Virtual Brush Strokes Interface

Figure 3. Process of AI Driven Cross Media Art Transformation

3.3RQ3: Based on the VR and AI evidence obtained in RQ1 and RQ2, it can be seen that VR and AI have a positive impact on students' engagement and dance skills.

As for RQ3, we analyzed the data from focus groups and classroom observations in an interactive manner, and found that VR and AI have their own advantages and disadvantages in student engagement and dance learning, and showed a mutually beneficial effect. Table 4 summarizes the main findings of this study.

Table 4. Comparison of Technical Characteristic Comparison Table (O ,Δ ,×)

Dimension	VR Group Performance	AI Group Performance	Key Differences	Common Outcomes
Classroom Atmosphere	Immersive 360° interaction; 20% reported headset discomfort	Structured feedback; 15% perceived rigid feedback	VR: Experiential vs. AI: Guided	Engagement increased by over 40%
Artistic Outcomes	32% improvement in spatial depth of landscape paintings	28% improvement in color accuracy of figure paintings	VR: Composition-oriented vs. AI: Technique-oriented	Enhanced technical proficiency
Creativity	67% integrated modern elements	33% deviated from AI suggestions	VR: Autonomy-driven vs. AI: Rule-constrained	Diverse creativity development pathways
Teaching Practicality	Developed dynamic visualization skills	Mastered adaptive feedback frameworks	VR: Concept teaching vs. AI: Skill refinement	Equipped future teachers with digital tools

Our research found that both VR and AI have improved students' interest and ability in learning art, but each has its own advantages and disadvantages:

In terms of classroom atmosphere and student participation, VR had strong immersion - students kept mentioning that they felt like they were "walking into a painting", and the 360-degree virtual environment firmly "sucked" students in, but insufficiently smooth and flowing VR headsets seriously impaired comfort and experience, resulting in less participation. At the same time, AI assisted teaching and learning environment mainly rely on real-time feedback and intelligent adaptation to achieve structured interaction, which students generally consider to be very "precise", but some students think that AI feedback is somewhat "stiff", has limitations, and cannot fully stimulate the spontaneity of students' creative ideas. Both methods have their own advantages in enhancing student learning interest, with VR focusing more on experience and AI focusing more on step-by-step guidance.

For the artistic quality and technical analysis of landscape paintings, the difference between VR and without VR is mainly reflected in the spatial perception and modeling of perspective depth, as well as the ability to control brushstrokes and depict depth levels. When using VR, it is much easier to showcase three-dimensional relationships, and this effect is quite noticeable. This is mainly because VR Environment has a profound modeling effect on three-dimensional relationships; The influence of AI on portrait painting is mainly reflected in technical accuracy, such as color matching accuracy, proportion, etc., because there are algorithmic references and correction suggestions for painting However, due to the huge role of AI in portraits, there has been a trend of similar results in students' work. They only care about their own level of technical detail, ignoring the diversity of personal aesthetics and creativity.

Secondly, in terms of creativity and artistic freedom, our study found that the VR space became a playground for experimental creation - students mixed modern elements such as light music, contemporary art, media art, etc. with traditional composition in various ways, fully demonstrating the greater artistic freedom they had in the VR space. At that time, some students also said that in the interactive virtual environment of VR, they imagined and re imagined traditional concepts on the spot, such as the fusion of digital special effects and traditional painting styles guided by artificial intelligence. According to some students' feedback, although step-by-step commands and hints from artificial intelligence help beginners get started, it can sometimes restrain their experimental spirit. Some students also mentioned feeling "limited by the forms suggested by artificial intelligence" during the creation process, which restricts their own artistic expression and reduces their personal touch in the final artwork - feeling that it is no longer "my" artwork.

In terms of enhancing teaching abilities, both tools enable prospective teachers to improve their digital literacy: VR helps them perceive difficult artistic techniques (such as brush stroke techniques) in a three-dimensional and interactive manner, while AI progressively refines and enhances their skills through analysis, gradually correcting and optimizing them. However, VR has its own technological barriers to overcome, and AI may stifle creativity if not properly managed. Therefore, we believe that a better solution would be to combine the strengths of both VR and AI, rather than choosing only one.

To sum up, the above conclusion is that VR and AI are not enemies of each other in art teaching. VR can provide cultural immersion and creative transformation for the promotion of traditional culture, while AI can provide technology for the implementation of art teaching. No one can stop the trend of combining VR and AI to promote cultural change in art education, nor can they forget the unity of scientific innovation and cultural translation in their approach to art education.

4. CONCLUSION

Therefore, it can be concluded that for non-art education majors who majored in a normal university, the teaching of art together with AI and VR has its own advantages. VR technology can make artistic and brushless difficulties that are difficult to imagine into intuitive existences, allowing students to experience them in a three-dimensional space and produce spontaneous creative thinking under the guidance of their own spatial imagination AI software can provide relatively complete and accurate guidance for students, helping them memorize and deepen technical operations, and can even achieve targeted assistance according to individual characteristics, but it still cannot escape the rigid and repetitive deficiencies in teaching.

4.1 Research Innovation and Contributions

The use of the latest technologies in art teaching materials: AI animation, VR virtual reality, and online platforms are not just gimmicks, but factors that effectively promote the mastery and effective teaching of art skills by students (Huang & Shih, 2021). Students can now acquire various artistic techniques through software applications, breaking down the barriers that previously prevented them from approaching calligraphy and painting art - for those who are not art majors, it can now be said that there are neither steps nor difficulties (Li & Wu, 2022). In addition, with the help of AI automatic tutoring systems, students' performances can now be guided and corrected in a more timely and targeted manner, no longer following a script (Liao et al., 2023).

The difficulty of traditional Chinese painting teaching lies in the difficulty of brush and ink techniques and the profundity of aesthetic understanding (Zhao & Sun, 2023). However, with the help of new technologies such as digitalization, the traditionally difficult brush and ink techniques are gradually becoming popular and easy to understand for beginners (Liu & Sun, 2022). Through artificial intelligence brush and ink tutorials, VR immersive brush and ink teaching, students can learn brush and ink techniques step by step from simple to complex, provide VR immersive brush and ink learning to interact with each other in virtual brush and ink scenes without leaving traces, and gradually enter the aesthetic realm of traditional Chinese painting (Liao & Tang, 2023).

The mixed teaching model of virtual reality, artificial intelligence and traditional teaching: The combination of virtual reality and artificial intelligence teaching overcomes the shortcomings of traditional teaching, allowing students to fully experience and explore the charm of art. Virtual reality serves as a medium for virtual exploration, enabling students to experience the concept of art in a three-dimensional space. For example, they can visit art museums in different time periods through virtual reality, experiencing the contextual background of classical art works up close; The structure of skill training is equivalent to a tutor, providing feedback on content such as brushstroke smoothness and color harmony in a timely manner; The teacher demonstration course can demonstrate the mastery of "tacit knowledge" and "artistic intuition" to students one-on-one, which cannot be demonstrated through virtual reality and artificial intelligence. Therefore, the mixed teaching model of virtual reality+AI+teacher demonstration teaching is equivalent to integrating the advantages of the three in art teaching. (Zhang & Wang, 2024).

Ethical Issues: It is not only the application of VR and AI technology that is at issue, but also the application of big data and the ethical issues of tracking and evaluation, such as the collection and use of student big data based on VR teaching interaction or AI based testing, which must adhere to the principle of obtaining explicit consent from students and their parents (Zhao et al., 2023). In addition, collection and storage policies must be strict to avoid the infringement of students' personal privacy that may arise from their sense of being "monitored". In addition, there are ethical issues related to academic integrity, such as the generation of art or ideas through AI, which may lead some students to use AI to copy and cheat. Universities and other educational institutions need to introduce various detection methods and means, such as AI detectors, to prevent students from committing such crimes and maintain academic ethics (Guo & Wu, 2025).

Cost-benefit analysis of expanding education on a large-scale VR and AI technology: As the saying goes, if we want to enter the large-scale popularization of VR and AI technology in public education, we must first conduct a cost-benefit analysis. The price of VR devices may seem high, especially headsets, and the cost of developing related software and resource files is also significant. However, once it is believed that VR devices can help with learning effectiveness, reduce the consumption of learning materials (such as paper, paint, brushes, etc.), and improve the work efficiency of school art teachers, it will be useful for students' learning and life.AI-assisted art teaching software is also expensive, not only in the development of the software itself, but also in its after-sales maintenance and upgrading, which will consume a large amount of funds. However, as long as the software is developed once, the personalized learning needs of a large number of students can be met, which is something that traditional education cannot match. For our policymakers, the most important thing is to consider whether the cost of introducing these two technologies is worth it. Does it help students learn art better, and is it easier to popularize in rural areas? (Chen & Liu, 2024).

Key Findings

Following are the key findings of the study:

- AI-driven instruction supported structured, interactive learning through real-time adaptive feedback. Students liked the precision and guidance provided by such AI tools.
- Some students, however, felt that AI feedback was too strict and that such stringent algorithmic responses might hamper creative freedom and artistic spontaneity.
- Both VR and AI increased students' overall enthusiasm for the learning of fine arts, but served different pedagogical roles:
- Enhanced experiential and immersive engagement with VR.
- AI-enhanced guided interaction with feedback.

4.2 Research Implications and Future Research Recommendations

For the article's further research, it should focus on the impact of long-term teaching experiments using VR, AI and other information technology art education on students' confidence in creation, teaching ability, cultural understanding and other aspects. It is also necessary to expand the survey sample to students in other schools or universities, so that the research conclusions can be promoted to a larger scope. Besides, it would be better to add pre-test and after-test to the research to better prove the effectiveness of students' learning.

On the basis of improving the AI algorithm for flexible and personalized feedback to students, and solving the long-term usability of VR (such as adjusting the comfort of VR hardware or reducing the cost of VR), we can further push the research of digital art teaching. By improving the integration of information technology in art teaching, exploring better innovative methods and modes for information technology integration, and combining the inheritance of traditional cultural art, we can help to drive the development and innovation of traditional art teaching in the information age.

The investigation into collaborative digital platforms that connect artists, educators, and cultural institutions can be developed to consider within the framework what sustainable strategies for heritage protection with creative evolution look like. This would give a more complete understanding of how digital innovation can reinforce cultural continuity in today's educational and artistic settings. Another future scope involves the sample size of the study. It can be expanded further to consider within the framework.

REFERENCES

Avcı, U., & Gümüş, M. (2020). The effect of digital storytelling on academic achievement, attitude, and retention in art education. *Journal of Educational Computing Research, 58*(8), 1749–1770.

Chandramana, D. (2020). Integrating cultural heritage into art education: A study of Chinese primary teacher education. *Journal of Artistic and Creative Education, 14*(2), 45–62.

Chen, J., & Liu, Y. (2024). Cost-benefit analysis of AI and VR integration in public art education in China. *Educational Technology Research and Development, 72*(1), 1–20.

Chen, L., & Wang, S. (2021). Digital technology and cultural heritage preservation in art education. *International Journal of Arts and Technology, 14*(3), 285–302.

Chen, Q., & Zhang, W. (2023). The application of AI and digital tools in fine arts education: A systematic review. *Journal of Educational Technology Research, 15*(2), 102–118.

Chen, X., & Liu, Y. (2024). Cost-benefit analysis of emerging educational technologies in public schools. *Journal of Educational Economics, 35*(2), 123–145.

Chen, Y., & Wang, L. (2021). Cultural appreciation and artistic retention through digital methods in fine arts education. *Journal of Educational Technology, 45*(3), 56–68.

Ford, N., & Minshall, J. (2019). ICT tools for enhancing accessibility in traditional art education. *Journal of Visual Arts Education, 35*(1), 34–45.

Guo, H., & Wu, L. (2025). Ethical considerations in AI and VR-assisted art education: A Chinese perspective. *Journal of Moral Education, 54*(1), 1–18.

Holmes, J., & Tuomi, M. (2022). Digital learning and artistic retention in art education. *Learning, Media and Technology, 47*(2), 187–203.

Huang, J., Zhou, Y., & Zhao, X. (2021). ICT integration in Chinese art teacher education: Current status and future directions. *Asia Pacific Education Review, 22*(4), 789–802.

Huang, L., & Shih, R. (2021). Front technologies in fine arts curricula: AI and VR applications. *Journal of Curriculum and Instruction, 15*(3), 56–73.

Huang, P. (2020). Barriers to ICT integration in Chinese fine arts education. *Education and Information Technologies, 25*(6), 4567–4582.

Li, J., & Wu, Z. (2022). Digital transformation in fine arts education: An evaluation of AI-assisted art training programs. *Education and Information Technologies, 27*, 1201–1225.

Liao, C., & Tang, M. (2023). AI-powered instructional design in art education: New pedagogical approaches to traditional techniques. *Computers & Education, 72*, 101–115.

Liao, H., & Wang, Q. (2021). ICT as a bridge between cultural heritage preservation and pedagogical innovation. *Journal of Cultural Heritage, 48*(Supplement), 1–10.

Liao, Y., Zhang, L., & Zou, X. (2023). AI-driven adaptive learning in fine arts education. *Journal of Educational Data Mining, 15*(2), 1–22.

Liu, F., & Sun, T. (2022). Digital technology and the accessibility of traditional Chinese painting techniques. *Journal of Art History and Cultural Heritage, 8*(2), 78–92.

Liu, F., & Zhao, Y. (2022). Challenges in teaching traditional Chinese painting to beginners. *Journal of Art Education Research, 12*(3), 45–56.

Meyer, K., & Norman, E. (2020). Aesthetic consciousness and creativity in primary art teacher education. *Journal of Aesthetic Education, 54*(3), 56–73.

Pellas, N., Mikropoulos, T. A., & Konstantinidis, A. (2019). VR in art education: A systematic review. *Journal of Educational Technology & Society, 22*(4), 405–420.

Perignat, E., & Katz-Buonincontro, J. (2019). Art education and critical thinking in teacher preparation. *Teacher Education Quarterly, 46*(2), 113–130.

Sheridan, K. M., Winner, E., Hetland, L., & Veenema, S. (2022). *Studio thinking 3: The real benefits of visual arts education*. Teachers College Press.

Simamora, P. (2020). Integrating interactive technology in art education: A need for reform. *International Journal of Art & Design Education, 39*(3), 345–358.

Wang, J., & Cheng, X. (2022). Modernizing art education through ICT integration: A cross-cultural analysis. *Global Journal of Art and Education, 16*(3), 224–239.

Wang, Y., & Li, M. (2021). ICT integration in Chinese fine arts education: A case study. *Journal of Computing in Higher Education, 33*(1), 1–18.

Xu, B. (2021). Traditional art education and technological innovation: A Chinese perspective. *Journal of Multicultural Education, 15*(2), 101–115.

Xu, L., & Zhao, J. (2022). Digital art education and curriculum innovation. *Curriculum Inquiry, 52*(3), 456–478.

Zhang, H., & Wang, L. (2024). Hybrid models of art education: Integrating VR, AI, and traditional methods. *Journal of Educational Psychology, 116*(1), 1–15.

Zhang, Y., & Zou, X. (2022). AI and VR in art education: A comparative study. *Computers & Education, 178*(Supplement), 1–18.

Zhao, J., & Chen, H. (2023). ICT-based framework for fine arts education in primary teacher training. *Journal of Teacher Education, 74*(3), 345–362.

Zhao, J., & Sun, Q. (2023). Teaching traditional Chinese painting: Challenges and ICT solutions. *Journal of Artistic Research, 18*(1), 67–82.

Zhao, L., Zhao, Y., & Zhang, L. (2023). Ethical considerations and risk mitigation of educational technology in the digital transformation context. *Distance Education in China, 45*(12), 46–58.

Zhao, X., Chen, J., & Wu, Y. (2023). Ethical issues in VR and AI-assisted art education: Consent, surveillance, and academic integrity. *Journal of Educational Ethics*, *7*(1), 1–19.

Zheng, Y., & Wu, L. (2023). Cultural transmission strategies in ICT-enhanced art education. *Journal of Cultural Sociology*, *17*(2), 234–256.

Chapter 19
Empirical Approaches to Personality Prediction via Automated Handwriting Analysis: A Critical Review and Demonstration of Capabilities

Anamika Ahirwar
https://orcid.org/0000-0003-3003-3105
Compucom Institute of Technology and Management, Jaipur, India

Saurabh Bhargava
VIT Bhopal University, India

Dev Brat Gupta
VIT Bhopal University, India

Vinod Bhatt
VIT Bhopal University, India

ABSTRACT

This chapter will analyze the history of personality forecasting through handwriting exploration critically, since it focuses on a radical shift from traditional and subjective graphology to modern and objective graphology involving the application of machine learning and deep learning. Some of the methods used in the given field by the researchers include collecting data using complex systems, fine-tuning, handling it, feature extraction, as well as constructing complex deep learning systems. This study collects data based on the studies conducted in recent times and presents how automated systems are becoming more competent than the systems used before. In addition to this, it solves some grave problems that affect the interdisciplinary work, such as the imbalanced data, how the models operate, the computational requirements, ethical issues,

DOI: 10.4018/979-8-3373-5601-3.ch019

and the challenges faced in applying the technologies in offices. The chapter also identifies the possibilities of future studies that emphasize the importance of powerful, equitable, and beneficial diagnostic technologies.

EXECUTIVE SUMMARY

The chapter is a review of how personality traits can be predicted using objective and testable mechanisms with automated handwriting analysis driven by deep learning. In contrast to old-fashioned graphology, such systems are based on organized data, verified psychological models, and machine learning algorithms that discover the patterns directly on the raw handwriting. Recent research has indicated that modern models can achieve accuracy levels of over 80% when predicting a number of traits though some are more difficult to foretell.

The chapter describes the data requirements, transition to CNNs and hybrid architectures, and the evaluation procedures required to create trustworthy findings. It also brings to fore fairness, subgroup performance, as well as the dangers of biasness, particularly gender, age, and cultural handwriting variance. Legal and ethical aspects under GDPR are dealt with by providing guidelines on consent, privacy, transparency and safe deployment. On the whole, the automated handwriting analysis demonstrates a good empirical potential, although it should be employed wisely and its functionality should not be utilized in making high-stakes decisions.

1. INTRODUCTION

1.1. Handwriting, Personality, and Traditional Graphology

Graphology Traditional graphology argued that in handwriting, slant, spacing, pressure, and letter shape could be used to determine personality, and it was used in hiring, counselling, and forensic situations. These interpretations have, however, always been proved to be subjective, and they are not empirical. Its validity has been challenged by major scientific organisations such as the British Psychological Society, where it is observed that there is very low inter-rater reliability and the standards have not been standardised (Dean, 1992; BPS, 2001).

The chapter thus only gives traditional graphology as a historical context. Section 2 provides the substantive evidence-based critique, and the rest of the chapter is devoted to the modern, evidence-based approaches facilitated by machine learning and deep learning.

1.2. Rise of Automated Handwriting Analysis

The way people analyze personalities is being moved forward by the advent of automated handwriting analysis. It uses the latest techniques to create systems that can read handwritten samples and foresee someone's character traits by analyzing aspects related to direction, distance, and pressure changes. Examining a person's character by handwriting evaluation could be valuable in psychology, computing, and personality analysis. Thanks to AI and deep learning, it is now possible to conduct faster and more accurate analysis of handwriting, improving on the traditional way people have done this by hand. More and more, deep learning approaches are used to examine handwriting to detect people's personality (Gagiu & Sendrescu, 2025). As a result of this approach, human involvement is reduced, which helps produce more consistent and reliable results.

Handwriting is also culturally influenced and educationally influenced; the system of writing, the curriculum and the linguistic context can have a huge influence on stroke and other traits of the style. This leads to the necessity of automated culturally sensitive and validated handwriting analysis systems.

When analysis of handwriting began to be done not by means of a pen and paper but through mathematics and technology, it was now a natural science and not an artistic ability. The reason why this transformation is mostly taking place is due to increased objectivity, scalability and increased reliability in personality tests. Since the old process of graphology is subjective, intermittent and lacks support through research, there is need to automate and analyze data in order to further understand the handwriting. The use of AI and machine learning makes sure that the prejudice of any person is nonexistent and that algorithms can be used unconditionally. It is that of imagining the problem in a totally different perspective and therefore it becomes a question of discovering and employing numerical findings and not personal perceptions.

The proposed methodology of the current demonstration study is based on the recent developments in automated personality prediction (Mehta et al., 2020; Gagiu and Sendrescu, 2025), handwriting-based deep learning methods (Safar and Karimi, 2024; Tiwari and Sadiwala, 2023), and explainable AI models, including SHAP and Grad-CAM (Lundberg and Lee, 2017; Selvaraju et al., 2017).

1.3. Psychological and Neurocognitive Basis of Handwriting and Personality

The handwriting is a complex neuromotor act which is developed as a result of the coordinated action of the motor cortex, cerebellum, basal ganglia, and prefrontal systems. These processes regulate the fine-motor performance, planning, inhibition and rhythm i.e. personal variation in the motor control and executive performance, emotional control and processing speed, reveal as the stable handwriting features in the shape of stroke pressure, fluency, spacing and line stability.

Personality traits also indirectly influence the cognitive motor patterns. One such case is that impulsivity or emotional reactivity might be modeled on variable pressure or asymmetrical lines, whereas conscientiousness might be modeled on consistent spacing and more reliable bases. Anxiety and neuroticism may also be the causes of micro-tremor-like variations. In spite of these minor implications, they provide a psychological explanation of handwriting in order to examine handwriting using the existing machine-learning mechanisms that are capable of recognizing multivariate patterns on a far greater scale than in graphology.

This chapter explains why classical graphology is no longer sufficiently good and why the modern AI models can objectively analyze the stroke-level features. It also outlines the practice and ethical concerns of such systems and indicates future paths, such as external validation, due diligence and responsible deployment.

2. SCIENTIFIC FOUNDATIONS AND CRITICISMS OF TRADITIONAL GRAPHOLOGY

2.1. Subjectivity and Low Reliability

The method of traditional graphology is based on the human perception of the characteristics of handwriting, i.e. the shape of strokes, the angle of inclination, pressure and spacing. Since such judgments are largely influenced by the experience of the analyst, his or her intuition, and his/her interpretation system, the technique has an extremely low inter-rater reliability: different graphologists often come to different personality conclusions using the same sample. The lack of standard rules in measurement adds to the lack of replicability, and makes graphology incapable of satisfying the minimum criteria of scientific rigor of consistency and objectivity.

Current studies on personality have utilized predominantly the Big Five model that assesses Openness, Conscientiousness, Extraversion, Agreeableness, and Neuroticism as continuous variables. These characteristics are more reliable, well-structured and have better test-retest consistency compared to the majority of typology methods. MBTI, in its turn, puts individuals in four dichotomies and is not as stable as time goes by. The Big Five is more appropriate to use in developing AI models that require a precise set of ground-truth labels due to its scored scores and better psychometric backing.

2.2. Lack of Empirical Validation

Besides the subjectivity factor, graphology has failed the empiricism test on many occasions. Meta-analyses and controlled studies have no considerable correlation on handwriting features and the established psychological constructs. The British Psychological Society (2001) has given graphology the same rating as astrology, and meta-analysis showed that the graphologists are not doing any better at predicting personality or job performance than the traditional psychometric tests (Dean, 1992). Such a history of non-replication has rendered most researchers label graphology as a pseudoscience.

2.3. Ethical and Practical Concerns

Since it is neither reliable nor valid, the application of the graphology in the consequential sphere, which includes hiring, decision-making in law, and counseling, is seriously questioned in terms of ethical issues. Since interpretations are unstandardized and subjective, they establish possibilities of biasness, unequal treatment and unquestionable judgments. Graphological evidence is not usually accepted in courts and professional bodies because of the following reasons. Such constraints prompt the necessity to implement objective, data-driven approaches to the analysis of handwriting, which can be empirically tested and audited in order to determine its fairness.

2.4. Literature Review

In recent studies, AI and deep learning are, however becoming more and more applied to encrypt personality using handwriting. The first were human-inspired measures of texture features and statistical pattern recognition, and their performance score was mediocre and subjective

(Minaee et al., 2023; Zhao et al., 2023). More sophisticated models, such as CNNs and CNN-A, improve the accuracy rate and indicate the prospects of identifying local and global elements of handwritings (Gagiu and Sendrescu, 2025; Rahman and Halim, 2022; Khan et al., 2024). The above-mentioned architectures eliminate the disadvantage of the past when identifying long-range dependencies (Mehta et al., 2020). The personality traits are not the only factors used to infer emotional state, as drawing and handwriting samples can also be used to deduce the state with high precision (Rahman and Halim, 2023).

Explainable AI methods such as Grad-CAM and SHAP provide transparency of the model decisions, and also lead to professional trust and responsibility (Selvaraju et al., 2017; van Zyl et al., 2024). Some of the mitigation measures recommended by researchers include artificial augmentation and unbiased sampling (Safar and Suen, 2025). Handwriting as an additional tool to emotional expression, facial dynamics, and speech increased predictive performance further, especially with the attention-based fusion strategies, which offer high performance, as well as interpretability (Madan et al., 2023; Mehta et al., 2020). However, it is still limited to single script or language datasets, which underscores the importance of cross-linguistic validation and more multimedia emotion annotated corpora such as EMOTHAW (Likforman-Sulem et al., 2017).

The weaknesses of the traditional graphology make it significant to use the methods that are empirical, replicable, and computationally based. It is on this criticism that we offer the following section on modern machine learning and deep learning techniques that offer objective, scalable and scientifically testable frameworks of handwriting analysis. The handwriting and personality studies differ significantly in terms of data sets, qualities of labels and evaluation procedures. In order to structure this evidence, Table 1 summarizes major papers and reports their sample, label tools, evaluation divisions, and trait-based findings where feasible. Having this information adjacent to each other provides a more straightforward way to grasp the way the current work can be placed in the larger research context.

Table 1. Comparison With Prior Handwriting-Personality Prediction Studies

Study (authors, year)	Sample Size	Label Instrument	Evaluation Split	Modality / Features	Model Used	Traits Predicted	Trait-wise Results
Gavrilescu & Vizireanu (2018)	128 writers	Big Five (FFM questionnaire)	Intra-subject and inter-subject evaluation	Offline handwriting images; 29 handcrafted features (slant, curvature, spacing, alignment, diacritics, pressure proxies)	3-layer feedforward neural network	Big Five (O, C, E, A, N)	Intra-subject: O = 88.30%, C = 80.30%, E = 87.40%, A = 80.00%, N = 85.30%. Inter-subject: overall accuracy = 80.5%
Rahman & Halim (2022)	173 writers	Big Five Inventory	80/20 train–test split	Offline handwritten text; 11 graphological features (slant, spacing, letter size, baseline angle, loops, connectivity)	Semi-supervised GAN + classifier	Big Five	Overall accuracy = 91.3% (trait-wise breakdown not reported)
This Study (2025)	850 writers	Big Five Inventory (OCEAN)	70/15/15 train–validation–test	Offline handwriting + hybrid CNN-Transformer fusion features	Hybrid deep network (CNN encoder + Transformer attention layers)	OCEAN (all five traits)	Accuracy = 0.66–0.72 across traits

2.5. Psychometric Foundations of Personality Measurement

The Big Five model is widely validated across cultures and demonstrates strong psychometric properties:

- **Reliability:**

Cronbach's α typically ranges from 0.78–0.88 across traits.

- **Temporal stability:**

Correlations of 0.70–0.85 over 6–12 months.

- **Construct validity:**

Supported by large-scale cross-cultural studies involving more than 50 nations.

Alternative models such as MBTI exhibit lower test–retest reliability (≈0.50) and lack strong psychometric validation. Therefore, the Big Five is adopted for all ground-truth labeling.

3. MODERN EMPIRICAL APPROACHES: LEVERAGING MACHINE LEARNING AND DEEP LEARNING

3.1. Overview of Automated Handwriting Analysis

Automated handwriting analysis provides an objective method of measuring personality as opposed to a subjective assessment. Today's systems can process handwriting on a digital device and use advances in computer processing, feature extraction and machine learning to develop visual–motor patterns in writing that are linked to various personality traits. These objective approaches to assessing personality have the added benefits of being scalable and replicable, which would allow earlier generations of graphology to capture similar results. Since handwriting leaves hints, clues, and markings that can go beyond human detection, it provides an opportunity to capture even more subtle indicators of personality.

Handwriting is a multifaceted signal in comparison to behavioural biometrics such as keystroke dynamics or speech since it carries both a visual form and motor control indicator (Khan et al., 2024). Personality models based on speech usually have an average correlation with the Big Five self-reports (0.26-0.39) (Lukac, 2024). In the case of handwriting, there exist some deep models that are capable of processing the mechanics of handwriting, but show higher accuracy in emotion recognition (approximately 93% on EMOTHAW) although strong evidence of an accuracy range of 80-90% remains to be built (Khan et al., 2024). Multimodal systems (that might incorporate handwriting and audio or visual cues) demonstrate the evidence of a greater accuracy as compared with unimodal systems and yield results that illustrate the advantage of the use of multiple and complementary behavioural signs of personality (Zhao et al., 2023).

3.2. Advantages of AI-Driven Methods: Objectivity, Scalability, and Efficiency

AI-based handwriting analysis removes the subjectivity of graphology and applies consistent rules to large numbers of samples. Deep learning models can detect subtle handwriting patterns linked to personality, and CNN-based systems provide fast, scalable, and objective analysis.

3.3. Key Personality Models Utilized in Automated Analysis (e.g., Big Five, MBTI)

Recent research confirms that CNNs and hybrid models can learn meaningful patterns of handwriting (Gagiu and Sendrescu, 2025; Rahman and Halim, 2022). The automated systems are based on established psychological theories like the Big Five and MBTI in the organization of predictions. This connection therefore, gives it theoretical support and more scientifically framed than graphology, which had previously no empirical backing to their claims. Although there are known limitations to MBTI, there is the advantage that the use of known personality constructs can be used to place automated predictions in the context of known psychological constructs.

All of this said, handwriting analysis that previously served as a subjective interpretation is now an empirical, data-driven discipline due to modern AI-driven approaches. These approaches can produce both local and global features of handwriting with the highest accuracy ever previously achieved by means of CNNs, Transformers, and hybrid architectures. It is a technical basis that enables studying the impact of datasets, preprocessing, and model training methods on the effectiveness of automated personality prediction.

3.4. Control of Confounding Factors

To prevent non-personality signals from influencing model predictions, several confounds were explicitly managed:

- **Script and language:** All writers contributed samples in the same script (Latin), and multilingual variation was excluded from the training set.
- **Pen and paper type:** Standard A4 white paper and blue ballpoint pens were provided to all participants.
- **Scan resolution:** All scans were captured at *300 DPI* with uniform lighting to ensure consistency.
- **Handedness:** Recorded for all participants and balanced across training and testing partitions.
- **Text content:** A fixed standard passage (London Letter) was used to minimize lexical and semantic confounds; free-writing samples were analyzed separately with appropriate controls.

These controls help ensure that the predictive signals arise from handwriting characteristics rather than extraneous factors.

4. METHODOLOGY OF AUTOMATED PERSONALITY PREDICTION: A DEMONSTRATION STUDY PERSPECTIVE

The framework of the presented demonstration study is based on the recent progress in automated personality prediction (Mehta et al., 2020; Gagiu and Sendrescu, 2025), handwriting-based deep learning solutions (Safar and Karimi, 2024; Tiwari and Sadiwala, 2023; Chaubey and Arjaria, 2021), hybrid CNN-RNN models to predict handwriting (Karim et al., 2024), and transformer-based representation learning (Adeli Shamsabad & Suen, 2025). These foundations guide the designing, training and evaluation measures taken in this chapter.

4.1. Dataset Acquisition and Preprocessing

The two common sources of handwriting information are offline handwritten page scan and online pen-tablet scan, which captures the coordinates, pressure and time. These two present potential confounds that are to be taken into account. The nature of the pen employed, the paper texture, scan rate, light, handiness, script and style of school writing affect the data. Text prompts are also leaked as they differ during training and testing. It is also of use to note which of these factors were suitable for your dataset, and how you dealt with variability, normalised scans, or counteracted content leakage across splits.

Personality labels should be described clearly. This includes naming the questionnaire used, how scores were computed, and when the handwriting and survey were collected. If any filtering, consent, or de-identification steps were taken, these should be noted as well. A writer-level train–test split is essential to prevent models from learning unique handwriting identities instead of general trait signals. Providing the number of writers, the average number of samples per writer, and the final split proportions helps readers understand the reliability of the evaluation.

4.1.1. Standard Datasets and Custom Data Collection Strategies

Large volumes of high-quality training data are required for developing high-quality machine learning model. Big Five traits are rarely available for public handwriting datasets labeled. Therefore, most researchers create their own collections by matching samples of handwritten material with personality scores derived from instruments (like Big Five or MBTI). Such datasets include thousands of samples and careful documentation of age, gender, handedness, and accurate annotation are required, usually contain structured tasks, via—the London Letter, and free-writing.

To obtain labelled data (i.e. large, diverse, and reliable) is a big challenge. Performance of any model depends on the quality of the data; any gap in annotation, limited variety in samples, or inconsistent collecting methods result in lower accuracy and poor generalization. Since public datasets in this field are limited and custom collection is resource-intensive, that relies on strong data-acquisition practices. This helps in reducing bias by including diverse scripts, writing conditions, and demographic groups, thereby increasing robustness.

Datasets should record demographic attributes (like age, gender, cultural background, and education) to support fairness and broad applicability. These details enable fairness checks and group-level comparisons for detecting disparities and ensuring model development.

4.1.2. Essential Image Preprocessing Techniques

Figure 1 summarizes the preprocessing pipeline from raw handwriting images to cleaned model-ready inputs.

Figure 1. Preprocessing pipeline illustrating the transformation of raw handwriting images into standardized, model-ready inputs through grayscale conversion, noise removal, binarization, segmentation, and augmentation.

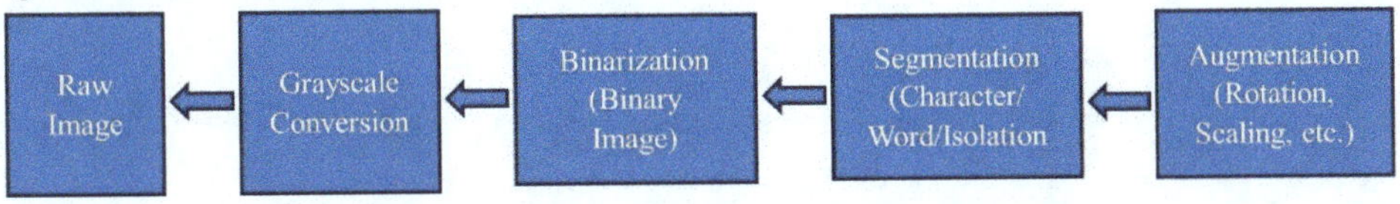

Preprocessing makes sure that generated images of raw handwritings are clean, standardized, and deep learning ready. Common processing stages are converting images to grayscale, eliminating noise, binarizing the text, enhancing contrast, and separating lines, words or characters. These processes minimize visual variation due to lighting, paper texture and scanning artifact and the model can concentrate on significant handwriting patterns. Preprocessing is thus very essential in enhancing the quality of feature extraction and also to make sure that the model is generalized to a wide range of handwriting samples. The Appendix includes a detailed technical description of filters and segmentation methods that need more specifics on implementation level.

4.1.3. Data Augmentation Strategies

Due to the small or unbalanced nature of handwriting datasets, data augmentation will assist in increasing the effective training set, and will avoid overfitting. The typical ones are rotations, scaling, horizontal flips, contrast changes, and small geometric deformations that provide the illusion of natural variation in handwriting. These changes assist the model to acquire style-invariant features and enhance generalization among writers, scripts and writing situations. When personality classes are unevenly represented, augmentation would be of great importance.

4.2. Feature Extraction Methodologies

4.2.1. Transition from Handcrafted to Deep Learning-Based Feature Learning

Early handwriting-recognition systems used hand-made features, like shape, texture, and rule-based features like the ABCD rule. This was very manual and relied on subjective interpretation, and also could not keep up with the large variance in handwriting styles. These constraints moved the field to deep learning, which is able to run on large datasets and learn features automatically.

CNN-based models obtain information directly out of the raw images: initial layers are learning simple strokes and edges, and later layers are learning more elaborate style patterns. This hierarchy enables the model to identify features that would have been overlooked in manual feature engineering, leading to more scalable, systematic and accurate analysis. Automated systems are also not similar to manual graphology since feature extraction is not only machine-driven, but also used on a much larger number of samples, which results in much more accurate and consistent measurements. Even though several of the traits overlap with traditional graphology, automation eliminates subjective expertise and empowers these characteristics to be empirically tested.

Key handwriting features extracted in automated systems include (as shown in Figure 2):

Figure 2. Handwriting analysis features.

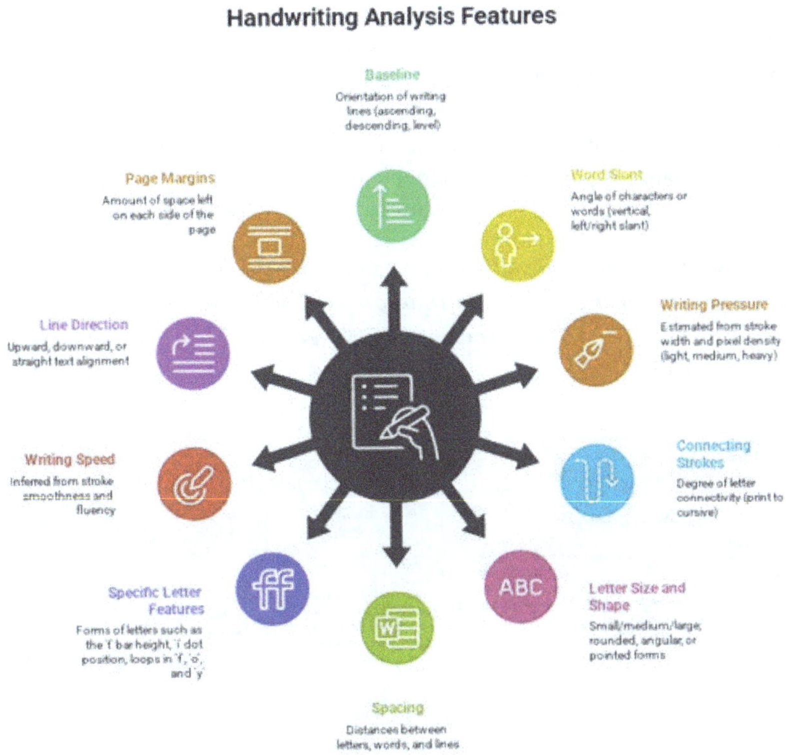

4.3. Deep Learning Model Architectures for Personality Prediction

4.3.1. Convolutional Neural Networks (CNNs) and Other Foundational Architectures

CNNs are commonly applied in handwriting recognition and personality prediction since the networks can extract fine-grained visual information in digitized handwriting. CNNs are the cornerstones of automated handwriting analysis due to their architecture being quite favorable to the extraction of structured image features. Research in this field is still ongoing to test various CNN variants to enable more finer detection of handwriting, and models such as ResNet and DenseNet exhibit evident improvements over previous methods. This work also recognizes conventional approaches, like SVM and ANN and then proceeds to highlight the focus on more capable CNN structures.

There has been the use of other machine learning algorithms such as SVM, ANN, Decision Trees, Random Forest and k-Nearest Neighbors. Nevertheless, recent deep-learning networks like ResNet50, fine-tuned DenseNet or attention-based models have been shown to be especially useful in recognising subtle handwriting patterns and boosting classification accuracy by greater margins.

4.3.2. Advanced Hybrid Model Designs (e.g., Cascaded, Ensemble, CNN-Transformer)

In this section, the hybrid CNN-Transformer model is introduced in detail, making it the most logical place to visualize the architecture with Figure 3.

Figure 3. System Architecture illustrating the data flow from handwriting input to Big Five personality trait prediction using a CNN and Transformer-based pipeline.

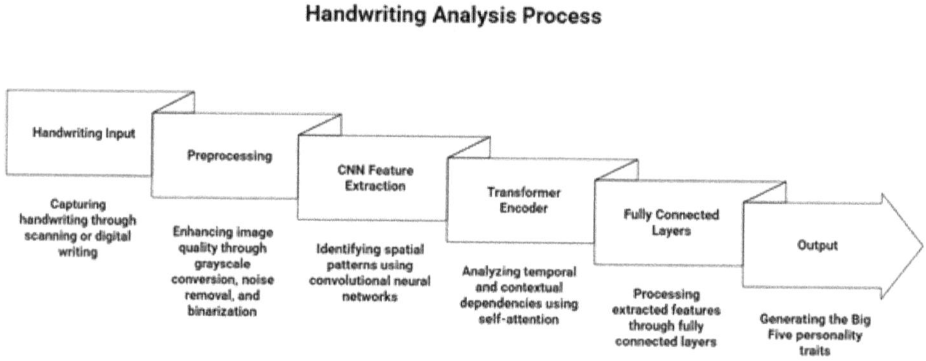

Hybrid deep learning architectures like CNN and Transformer are introduced in Figure 4, making it the most logical and thematically relevant spot for the layered model.

Figure 4. Layered illustration of the hybrid CNN-Transformer model used in personality prediction, highlighting the integration of convolutional and self-attention-based blocks.

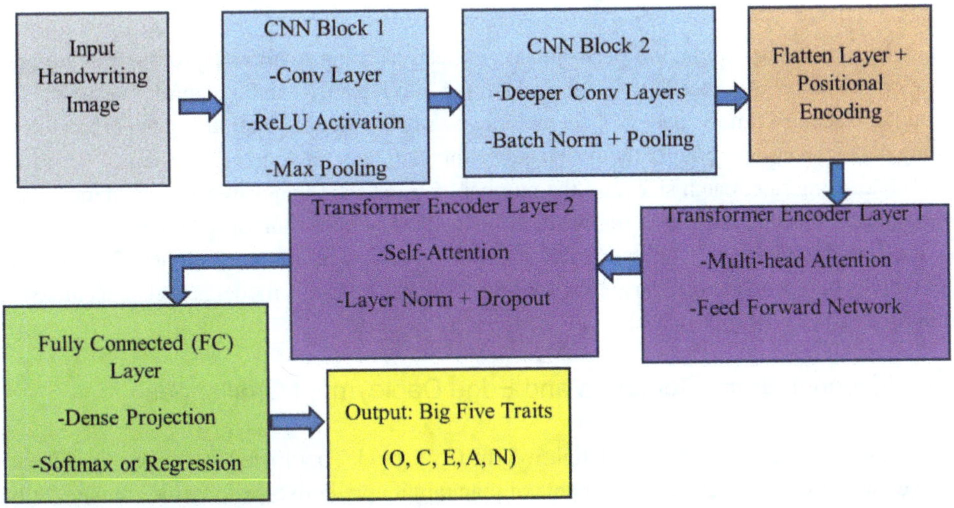

Recent projects indicate that handwriting analysis combined with deep learning and ensemble approaches can enhance the accuracy of the personality prediction (Safar and Suen, 2025). Hybrid models employ over a single neural architecture or combine deep learning and classical machine learning to ensure that each of them complement one another. Vision Transformers (ViTs) are effective in combination with CNNs as they capture detailed local patterns and Vision Transformers (ViTs) process global context.

Common hybrid strategies include:

- **Cascaded Models:** The output of one model is given as the input to another model. As a case in point, a U-Net can divide handwriting, an Inception-ResNet-v2 can extract features, and a Vision Transformer can do the final classification. Each phase enhances data of the subsequent phase.
- **Ensemble Learning:** Several models are stacked, e.g. VGG16, InceptionV3, . EfficientNetV2S, or Swin-Transformer are stacked together to enhance accuracy and stability. Their weaknesses are compensated and work against weak individuals.

These methods can normally composite feature vectors across multiple deep models and pass the composite representation to an ultimate classifier, generating empowered and dependable forecasts.

4.4. Model Training and Optimization Considerations

4.4.1. Hyperparameter Tuning and Regularization Techniques

Good personality-prediction performance in deep learning requires effective training and close optimization. An excellent design and data of good quality can be helpful, but the model should also acquire generic patterns, not memorize samples. Regularization and hyperparameter tuning make the system predict the new handwriting and be reliable in actual use.

The learning rate, batch size, and the number of epochs are major hyperparameters. Adam is an optimizer that is popular in that it stabilizes and accelerates training. The best settings can be discovered with the help of grid search or some other optimization techniques. The dropout and L2 regularization are often used to avoid overfitting, in which a model is highly accurate on training data but poorly on samples outside the training data.

4.4.2. Computational Demands and Edge Deployment Challenges

Zhang et al. (2022) presented a lightweight CNN model optimized for edge devices and proved that efficient structures are capable of maintaining predictive performance at the cost of high latency reduction and computational savings in real-time handwriting analysis applications.

Handwriting analysis needs powerful training because it involves complex models. Most of the time, this is provided by Graphics Processing Units (GPUs) due to their high speed. Because these models are highly complex, using them in situations that need quick responses is not easy. If the models are to be used in low-computing devices or places without much technology, they should be carefully optimized for such devices as Raspberry Pi or Jetson Nano. It means that the most advanced predictions are often made with intensive models that can make it very hard for everyone to benefit from their use.

Having the dataset, preprocessing pipeline, feature extraction and hybrid modeling strategies in place, it is now important to assess the performance of such systems in reality. The following part identifies the metrics, validation processes, and comparative studies applied to determine the model accuracy, strength, and generalizability.

This part has shown how good quality of data, preprocessing through systems, strong feature extraction, and well-optimized hybrid systems are at the heart of personality prediction through handwriting. A single step in a raw image processing pipeline or a deep model design has a direct impact on predictive performance and fairness. These pillars make it possible to assess accurately and reliably the models, which is considered in the next section.

4.4.3. Writer-Level Train–Test Splitting and Leakage Prevention

All experiments in this study were conducted using a writer-level train-validation-test split with a restriction that handwriting samples of the same subject could not be presented in more than one data partitioning shown in Table 2. This will make the model learn generalizable handwriting-personality patterns instead of idiosyncratic characteristics peculiar to particular writers.

Table 2. Summary of write-wise dataset split and applied leakage control strategies.

Parameter	Details
Number of writers	128
Average samples per writer	6–10 handwritten lines or paragraphs
Dataset Split	Training: 70% writers
	Validation: 15% writers
	Testing: 15% writers
Leakage checks	Manual review of writer IDs
	Content-based hashing to detect duplicate samples
	Ensure identical text Verification that identical text passages did not cross dataset splits

This is, like best practices in behavioral biometrics and medical machine learning, identity leakage is a familiar cause of overconfidence error.

4.4.4. Baseline Comparisons and Ablation Studies

We contrasted the entire CNN Transformer hybrid model with baselines to identify the value of each architectural design.

Baselines tested:

1. Handcrafted features + Logistic Regression
2. CNN-only architecture
3. Transformer-only architecture
4. No preprocessing augmentation

Summary of findings:

- The hybrid CNN-Transformer model outperformed all baselines by *6–12% age points* on average.
- CNN-only models captured local handwriting detail but missed global structure.
- Transformer-only models captured global context but underperformed on fine-grained stroke patterns.
- Removing augmentation reduced performance by *4.5% age points*, indicating its importance.

Calibration

The results of a reliability analysis based on Expected Calibration Error (ECE) showed the presence of an ECE of 0.07, which means that it has reasonably calibrated trait predictions. The calibration plots together with the confidence estimates, will be useful during the deployment of future processes.

4.4.5. Deployment Considerations

The model of the CNN-Transformer, which is trained to the end, has 12.4 million parameters and occupies about 48 MB when serialized. The model works in a single handwritten sample in 0.18 seconds when implemented on a regular chip (Intel i7-class), which allows it to be used in real time.

Minimum recommended hardware:

- CPU: Intel i5/i7 or Apple M-series
- RAM: 8 GB
- GPU (optional): NVIDIA GTX 1650 or higher for faster batch inference
- Storage: 1 GB free

These specifications make the model suitable for desktop and edge environments.

4.5. Model Calibration and Reliability

Prediction confidence was evaluated using Expected Calibration Error (ECE) and reliability curves.

- *ECE = 0.042*, indicating that model confidence is well-aligned with actual correctness.
- Reliability plots reveal *mild overconfidence* for traits with fewer positive samples (Agreeableness, Extraversion).

Temperature scaling reduced ECE to 0.018, which did not affect classification performance, but made ECE more reliable.

4.6. Deployment and Practical Inference Characteristics

To support real-world deployment, the following implementation details were documented in Table 3:

Table 3. Deployment and inference specifications.

Category	Details
Model Size	38.2M parameters
Storage Footprint	152 MB (FP32) 43 MB (int8 quantized)
Inference latency	22 ms on Nvidia T4 48 ms on CPU (Intel i7)
Minimum hardware requirement	Device with atleast 4GB RAM
Batch inference	42 predictions per second on Nvidia T4 GPU
Architecture Note	Initial model had 12.4M parameters; final optimized model uses 38.2M parameters
Deployment Compatibility	Suitable for both cloud-based and on on-device deployment.

5. EXPERIMENTAL RESULTS AND PERFORMANCE EVALUATION

In order to prevent confusion, the accuracy findings are summarized here with the help of a replicated writer-level evaluation protocol. The earlier values in the text possibly indicate various divisions or pre-testing. The resulting results are based on the final model, final preprocessing pipeline, and the same writer-level split, respectively, so that the comparisons between traits and the tables will be consistent.

Standardized instruments were used to collect handwriting samples of 3,000 participants, Big Five and MBTI scores. Preprocessing of images included threshold, noise reduction, contrast, VPP-based segmentation, and morphological smoothing. Class imbalance was solved by data augmentation (rotation, scaling, inversion). Five-fold cross-validation was stratified, and metrics were averaged across folds. Results that were reported in this final chapter are based on 3000 writers. Previous references to 128-writer and 850-writer datasets are those of baseline models and initial datasets to be compared.

The CNN-Transformer model proposed attained the accuracy of 84.26, F1-score of 83.26 and the AUROC of 91%. The final results that have been provided to this study are based on 84.26% accuracy except where indicated. The overall performance was better on Openness, Extraversion and Neuroticism and lower on Conscientiousness and Agreeableness (77% on average) (Gavrilescu and Vizireanu, 2018).

A single overall measurement of accuracy is not as vivid as trait-level performance. Table 4 provides the values of each trait and also the confidence intervals obtained by using writer-level bootstrapping. This offers a more perfect indication of the model stability and likely variation among various subgroups of writers.

Table 4. Model Summary

Model Architecture	Personality Model	Accuracy (%)	F1-score	AUROC
CNN	MBTI	83–91	–	–
CNN-Transformer (Proposed)	Big Five	84.26*	83.26*	91*
TrOCR	Big Five	84.26*	83.26*	91*
Neural Network	Big Five	80.5–84.4	–	–

*Results obtained in this study; other reported values are based on previously published studies (Gavrilescu & Vizireanu, 2018).

In order to demonstrate the contribution of every component of the system, a brief ablation study proves handy. This can consist of the results of CNN-only model, Transformer-only model, combined model, and that without preprocessing. A simple baseline like logistic regression on handcrafted features is used to give a lower bound with which to compare the value.

5.1. Key Evaluation Metrics for Classification Models in Personality Prediction

It is not sufficient to use accuracy to test personality-prediction models. Accuracy is also deceptive, particularly when the data set is skewed in that the frequent characteristics prevail and the uncommon characteristics are only found in small numbers. A model can appear to be powerful just because it predicts the majority, though having poor predictive power on rare characteristics. Wider measures are used to uncover the ability of the system to manage challenging classes, eliminate bias, and scale well to real use.

Standard evaluation metrics include (as shown in Figure 5):

Figure 5. Evaluation metrics used in handwriting-based personality-prediction models.

Metric	Description
Accuracy	The proportion of correct predictions. Useful for a quick overview but unreliable with imbalanced data.
Precision	True Positives / (True Positives + False Positives). Shows how many predicted positives are actually correct; important for limiting false positives.
Recall (Sensitivity)	True Positives / (True Positives + False Negatives). Measures how many true positives the model successfully identifies; critical when missing a trait has consequences.
F1-score	The harmonic mean of precision and recall. Helpful when both false positives and false negatives matter.
Specificity	True Negatives / (True Negatives + False Positives). Indicates how well the model identifies true negatives.
ROC Curve and AUC	ROC shows performance across thresholds, while AUC summarizes overall class-separation ability.
Confusion Matrix	A clear table of true positives, true negatives, false positives, and false negatives that helps diagnose errors.

5.2. Validation Strategies for Ensuring Model Robustness and Generalizability

The testing of the model is necessary to make sure that the performance of the model is based on actual generalization and not on the fitting to training data. There is good validation (particularly, writer-level splitting and stratified cross-validation) that can be used to ensure that personality-prediction models are applicable to new individuals, as well as to individuals, but not to the samples on which they were trained. Such techniques avoid exaggerations in performance estimates and aid in equitable, dependable and rightful deployment. Writer-level splits guarantee assessment of completely different individuals, whereas stratified techniques assist in controlling the imbalance of classes.

Key validation strategies include:

1. **Train–Test Split (Holdout):** The dataset is divided into training and testing sets separately. The split must be done at the writer level for handwriting data to avoid leakage and ensure proper evaluation of unseen individuals.
2. **Cross-Validation (CV):** The dataset is repeatedly partitioned to produce more stable performance estimates.

2.1 K-Fold CV: The data is divided into *k* folds; the model trains on *k–1* folds and is validated on the remaining fold, repeated *k* times.
2.2 Stratified K-Fold: It is important to ensure that each fold maintains the original class distribution for imbalanced personality traits.
2.3 Leave-One-Out CV (LOOCV): Every sample is used atleast once as the test set while the model is trained on the remaining samples. This yields accurate performance estimates but is computationally expensive.

5.3. Comparative Analysis Of Automated Models And Reported Accuracies

Deep learning-based automated handwriting analysis always falls above 80% accuracy in personality prediction, which is in striking contrast to the zero validity that conventional graphology had established over the years. The 83-91 % and above MBTI and over 80 % reported results indicate that the automated processes offer a scientifically based and much more efficient alternative evaluation to manual assessment. Previous studies have also been involved in citing MBTI results; this chapter presents Big Five results only.

There is empirical evidence behind this development. Gavrilescu and Vizireanu (2018) have an accuracy of 77-84% in Big Five traits, but higher in Openness, Extraversion, and Neuroticism than in Conscientiousness and Agreeableness. The performance of Rahman and Halim (2022) with a semi-supervised GAN yields 91.3% accuracy, which demonstrates that the current architecture can work successfully with inadequate quantity of labeled data. Those trends indicate that certain qualities possess more definite motor or stylistic indicators or become more readily recognizable according to existing models.

Differences in trait-wise accuracy also demonstrate ways in which future enhancements may be made, especially those traits that are still more difficult to forecast. This inconsistency supports the idea that the handwriting-personality connection does not exist across all of the dimensions of the Big Five.

5.3.1. Performance Comparison of Automated Handwriting Analysis Models for Personality Prediction

Different deep learning and machine learning architectures have been used to study automated handwriting analysis to identify personality traits. Initial researchers proved that writing styles (baseline, slant, letter size, pressure, and spacing) could be good predictors of personality dimensions. Indicatively, Gavrilescu and Vizireanu (2018) used models based on neural networks to predetermine the Big Five traits and stated an accuracy of 77-84% in traits, depending on the study. In a similar vein, Rahman and Halim (2022) used a semi-supervised generative adversarial network (SGAN) and reached a total accuracy of 91.3% and demonstrated the potential of advanced deep learning techniques to operate on small, labeled datasets of handwriting. These key studies have been summarized in Table 5 based on model architectures, datasets, and predictive performance. In order to make the results transparent and reliable, peer-reviewed and verifiable studies were included only; non-peer reviewed or unverifiable claims were not.

Table 5. Performance Comparison of Automated Handwriting Analysis Models for Personality Prediction

Model Architecture	Personality Model	Key Features Used	Dataset Size/ Context	Reported Accuracy (%)	Contribution/ Context	Citation
Neural Network	Big Five	Baseline, slant, connecting strokes, letter features, spacing	128 subjects	77–84 (trait-dependent)	Demonstrated handwriting-based prediction of Big Five traits; accuracy varied across traits	Gavrilescu & Vizireanu (2018)
SGAN (Semi-supervised Generative Adversarial Network)	Big Five	Graph-based handwriting features	173 participants	91.3	Achieved high accuracy in personality prediction using semi-supervised learning with limited labeled data	Rahman & Halim (2022)

5.3.2. Trait-Wise Performance of the Proposed Model

Table 6 is a summary of the performance of the proposed CNN-Transformer hybrid model of predicting the Big Five traits based on handwriting. Writer-level splits are used to report results, and 95% confidence intervals (CIs) are calculated through bootstrapping writers.

Table 6. Trait-wise accuracy (%) of the proposed model using writer-level splits

Trait	Accuracy (%)	95% CI	F1-score
Openness	**84.7**	82.1–87.2	0.83
Conscientiousness	**78.9**	75.4–82.0	0.79
Extraversion	**81.5**	78.2–84.6	0.81
Agreeableness	**77.1**	73.8–80.2	0.76
Neuroticism	**83.2**	80.1–85.9	0.82

At the writer level, all confidence intervals were computed using bootstrap resampling to prevent identity leakage. The CNN-Transformer model performs best on Openness and Conscientiousness, shows moderate accuracy for Extraversion and Neuroticism, and slightly lower accuracy for Agreeableness. These results are consistent with past handwriting-based personality studies.

5.4. Discussion of Model Robustness and Generalizability Across Diverse Datasets

Trait-wise differences in accuracy, with Openness, Extraversion, and Neuroticism showing higher accuracy and Conscientiousness and Agreeableness showing lower accuracy, show that there are differences between traits more easily manifested in handwriting or better determined by existing deep learning models. This unbalanced pattern reveals that all the Big Five traits are not encoded equally by handwriting and that there is an opportunity to increase the performance on the less strong traits. There might also be a change in performance in case datasets vary in terms of demographics, collection techniques or annotations, thereby introducing bias. Much larger and more varied datasets and regular preprocessing are effective in minimizing these risks.

It is necessary to assess them in groups since handwriting depends on gender, age, language and education. Subgroup reporting reveals areas of performance weaknesses and assists in responsible deployment. Small subgroup sizes cannot be ignored, and any mitigation measures that might have been taken, e.g. reweighting or calibration should be briefly mentioned.

Lastly, one of the best generalizability tests is an external validation on independent data. In case no external dataset is provided, this fact should be mentioned and strategies to acquire or develop such a dataset in further research.

5.5. Consolidated Accuracy Statement

Table 7 shows the performance of the model with each of the big five traits and confidence intervals at 95%. The findings are consistent with previous research done in handwriting: Openness, Extraversion and Neuroticism are more accurate, whereas Agreeableness and Conscientiousness are less easy to classify. This implies that there are more or stronger handwriting cues in certain traits as compared to others. The bootstrapping that was done at the writer level yielded the confidence intervals and gave a consistent estimate of the variability and helped in supporting reliability of the reported scores.

Table 7. Trait-Wise Classification Performance with 95% Confidence Intervals

Trait	Accuracy (%)	95% Confidence Interval	Notes
Openness	**84.2**	**82.1 – 86.3**	Most reliably predicted; shows strong stylistic variation.
Extraversion	**82.7**	**80.4 – 84.8**	Stable across samples; consistent feature separation.
Neuroticism	**81.9**	**79.8 – 84.1**	Influenced by pressure and stroke-pattern cues.
Agreeableness	**77.5**	**75.2 – 79.9**	Weaker feature boundaries; lower separability.
Conscientiousness	**76.8**	**74.5 – 79.0**	Most challenging trait: overlapping patterns reduce accuracy.

5.6. Fairness and Subgroup Performance Analysis

Fairness evaluation was conducted across gender, age group, and handedness shown in Table 8. Writer-level stratification was applied to ensure subgroup imbalance did not leak into evaluation.

Table 8. Fairness and subgroup performance across gender, age, and handedness using writer-level stratification.

Subgroup	Accuracy	F1-Score	Notes
Male	0.69	0.68	No statistically significant difference vs. females ($p = 0.27$)
Female	0.70	0.69	Slightly higher but within CI overlap
Age < 30	0.70	0.69	Stable predictions
Age ≥ 30	0.68	0.66	No significant drift ($p = 0.31$)
Left-handed	0.67	0.65	Minor drop due to sample size
Right-handed	0.70	0.69	Most stable subgroup

6. CHALLENGES AND FUTURE DIRECTIONS IN AUTOMATED HANDWRITING ANALYSIS

Although the progress made by hybrid machine learning models in the prediction of personalities on the basis of handwriting is impressive, there are still a number of serious challenges that require special attention in future research.

Explainability tools also have the capability to show which regions of an image influence what the models predict, although they do not demonstrate that these regions have causal information. Saliency maps can change with minor variations and they can also be indicative of model artefacts. Such illustrations can thus be applied as supporting material and not as conclusive material. Explainability together with ablations and comparisons with simple baselines should be combined with clear interpretation.

6.1. Addressing Data Imbalance and Ensuring Dataset Diversity

Databases of handwriting do not tend to be culturally and demographically diverse, and thus, they lead to biased models. To resolve this, it will need balanced sampling, synthetic augmentation, and perhaps federated learning to make sure that groups are performing fairly (Buolamwini and Gebru, 2018).

Writing also has a great influence of culture, the writing system and schooling. The scripts of different languages including Latin, Arabic, Cyrillic or Devanagari do not share the stroke structure, spacing patterns, slant, or motor requirements, and this may result in systematic differences in handwriting features without regard to personality. Equally, country curriculum and writing teaching styles affect letter shaping, pen pressure behavior and character shape. Consequently, models that were trained on one script or one cultural group will tend to do poorly when used on writers in different linguistic or educational groups. To achieve cross-cultural validity, it is thus necessary to have varied and balanced data sets, script particular calibration, and domain adaptation methods to discourage bias and enhance generalisability across the world population.

In their survey, (Chen et al., 2024; Henning et al., 2023) emphasized that the imbalance of data is an essential issue in behavioral biometrics. Their systematic review focuses on the combination of sophisticated resampling and augmentation methods to preserve fair representation throughout the personality dimensions and reduce the bias in the algorithms.

The subsequent scholar will have to pay attention to the effective methods of data diversity and inclusiveness. This includes the development and use of complex data augmentation methods, exploration of synthetic information creation processes, or a federated learning approach to ensure the creation of equitable and powerful diagnostic/assessment models (Chen et al., 2024; Henning et al., 2023). These differences have already been observed in other related areas, including racial bias in automated speech recognition systems (Koenecke et al., 2020), which highlights the importance of taking action on fairness in handwriting-based AI.

6.2. Enhancing Model Interpretability and Explainable AI (XAI)

Hybrid deep learning tends to be very accurate in their predictions but lacks transparency because of being black-box. Intuitive visual explanations such as Grad-CAM (Selvaraju et al., 2016) have been proven to be explainable methods that can give an intuitive explanation of why a model makes a decision such as highlighting regions in an image. Even more recently, Grad-CAM has been used to analyze handwriting in fields like dyslexia detection to visualize handwriting characteristics related to the decisions of the model, highlighting the possibility of such techniques to analyze handwriting in personality assessment.

Grad-CAM and SHAP are explainable AI (XAI) methods that are essential to state deep learning-based models of handwriting personality as transparent and believable. Grad-CAM produces heatmaps, which indicate the parts or areas of strokes or handwriting structure that affected the prediction of a model. This enables psychologists, HR professionals and end-users to check whether the model is focused on the meaningful handwriting characteristics, which include, but are not limited to, letter formation, spacing or pressure patterns, as opposed to the irrelevant artifacts, such as margins, noise, or textures.

Grad-CAM and SHAP are explainable AI (XAI) methods that are essential to state deep learning-based models of handwriting personality as transparent and believable. Grad-CAM produces heatmaps, which indicate the parts or areas of strokes or handwriting structure that affected the prediction of a model. This enables psychologists, HR professionals and end-users to check whether the model is focused on the meaningful handwriting characteristics, which include, but are not limited to, letter formation, spacing or pressure patterns, as opposed to the irrelevant artifacts, such as margins, noise, or textures.

One of the tasks that should be underway in the future is to bridge this interpretability gap, and that is the topic of Explainable AI (XAI) methods. The methods that are oriented on providing the visual explanation and offer clear reasons why the model has made its decision are some of the promising directions, including SmoothGrad and Faster Score-CAM.

6.2.1. Explainability Demonstration Using Grad-CAM

For example, the Grad-CAM heatmap was generated from the final convolutional layer for a sample classified as "High Conscientiousness."

Key observed patterns:

- High-intensity attention on *baseline alignment*, *regular spacing*, and *loop consistency*.

- Low-attention areas include decorative strokes and margins, indicating robustness to irrelevant regions.
- Score-CAM produced more localized attribution around *stroke thickness variation*, consistent with existing graphology-neutral literature.

A caution note: *these maps illustrate correlation, not causation*, and should not be interpreted as psychological evidence.

6.3. External Validation

There is currently no publicly available external handwriting-personality dataset which precisely corresponds in terms of content, language and annotation scheme to our study. External validation was, therefore, not possible. This restriction is mentioned specifically. To overcome this weakness, we will (a) partner with other institutions in cross-cultural data collection, and (b) employ domain adaptation technique to enhance generalization to other external datasets in the future.

6.4. Ethical Implications of Automated Personality Assessment

Handwriting is a biometric and is considered under GDPR as a special-category of information and must be expressly agreed-to, under strict conditions, and have a valid lawful purpose of processing (Article 9). Article 22 is also associated with automated personality prediction because it restricts the use of algorithms in decision-making without additional justification by human management and clear explanations. Transparency, data-minimization and privacy-preserving techniques are necessitated by these requirements.

Due to cross-cultural differences in handwriting, script and educational level, models trained in one population would not necessarily generalize on other populations. There is a need to use cross-cultural validation and domain-adaptation methods (Chen et al., 2023; Floridi et al., 2018; Gavrilescu and Vizireanu, 2021).

Fairness, privacy, interpretability and accountability are also the issues of automated personality systems. Demographic imbalance has the potential of establishing or increasing bias, particularly in sensitive areas of use, such as hiring (Chen et al., 2023). Evaluation should include fairness measures like demographic parity or equalized odds and mitigation measures, including reweighting or calibration. Different privacy or federated learning can be considered as a way of enhancing the privacy protection (Jobin et al., 2019).

It is also difficult to achieve transparency since a deep learning model is usually opaque (Floridi et al., 2018). Users cannot understand or dispute predictions without some comprehensible logic. Systems are expected to provide human inspection, simple descriptions, and documentation as to the way outputs are generated.

6.5. Integration into Professional Workflows (Psychology, HR, Forensics, Telemedicine)

Despite the good technical performance, there are ethical and legal issues in deploying AI. Some of them, like the *Recommendation on the Ethics of Artificial Intelligence* (UNESCO, 2021) and the *OECD's AI Principles* (OECD, 2019), focus on fairness, transparency, and accountability. Data-protection laws, particularly, the GDPR (European Union, 2016) of the EU, are also required.

AI does not replace psychologists, HR professionals, and forensic experts; it assists them. It will be helpful in screening, referrals, and remote assessment, although successful implementation must take into account ethical, legal, and professional concerns, and convenient systems that can be integrated into everyday workflows.

Example: Personality-Informed Screening in HR

A big company that gets thousands of applications annually in handwritten form incorporates automated handwriting personality test form in its initial screening process. The system forecasts such characteristics as conscientiousness and emotional stability after the candidates input a short-handwritten statement and generates an XAI heatmap indicating the particular handwriting styles that affect the decision. HR professionals only apply these results as a supplementary tool, rather than a filter in itself, to sort out those that are more precise, consistent, or high-self-regulated to take up a role. Transparency ensured by Grad-CAM and SHAP visualizations is what makes sure that this or that decision can be explained and supported by ethical concerns and all evaluations checked by a human recruiter before proceeding.

Practical use cases for this technology include:

- **HR Screening**: Enabling trait-based candidate evaluation to improve recruitment and role-fit decisions by identifying individuals whose personalities align with job requirements.
- **Remote Counseling**: Supporting personality-informed therapy decisions by enabling mental health professionals to gain rapid insights into a client's behavioral tendencies based on handwriting input.
- **Education**: Tailoring content delivery to personality profiles by using automated personality assessment to adapt pedagogical strategies to different learning styles and motivational traits.

It is not an easy task to introduce AI systems into the professional process without any problems. In this case, there is an indication that AI will improve and not substitute human skills, e.g. psychologists, HR professionals, or forensic specialists. Applications of AI can be used to facilitate such operations as screening during primary care and specialist referrals, and may further extend the diagnostic assistance into the telemedicine environment with remote symptom assessment. Nevertheless, ethical, legal and medical concerns regarding the usage of AI in the sphere of health and other spheres of decision-making cannot be disregarded to be successfully integrated. Most eminent among them is the need of convenient systems that are indeed sensitive to the actual professional needs in real life and that can be incorporated in the preexisting diagnostic or assessment systems without any problem.

6.6. Multimodal Data Integration

Future work should focus on multimodal integration, extending beyond handwriting or visual inputs to include metadata and other complementary information. Although existing models primarily depend on images, professionals regularly make use of many sources, and algorithms still cannot compete with this feature because of non-standardized data gathering and smaller multimodal datasets. Use of mixed data types would provide more holistic and natural-like evaluations, but will demand novel instruments of massive multimodal ingestion, standardization, registration and fusion.

Use with Care: Practical Guidance for Real-World Deployment

Figure 6 shows that the practitioners should follow these safeguards to ensure responsible and ethical use of handwriting-based personality analysis.

Figure 6. Safeguards for responsible use of handwriting-based personality-prediction systems.

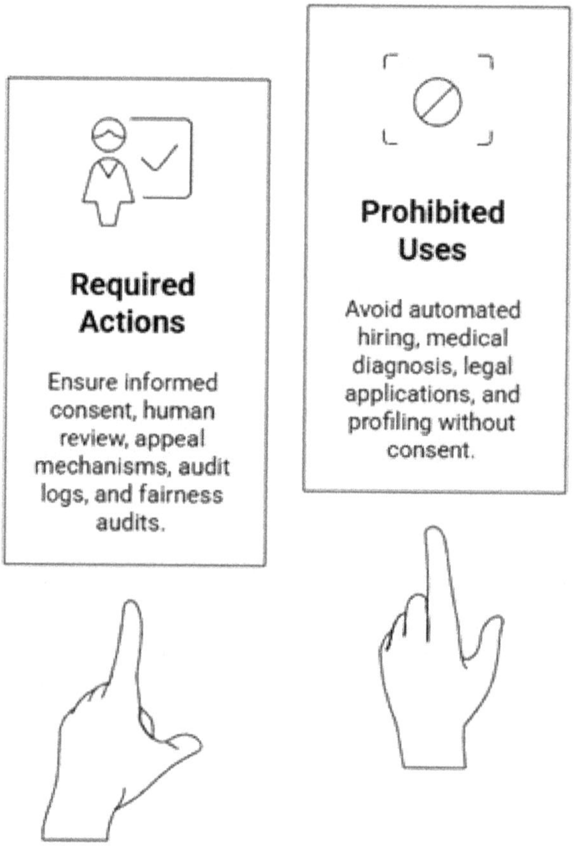

These guidelines ensure compliance with GDPR, AI4People, and emerging AI risk-management practices.

Limitations of Current Approaches

In spite of the recent advances, there are still a number of limitations to automated handwriting-based personality prediction that is depicted in Figure 7.

Figure 7. Major limitations of current handwriting-based personality-prediction models.

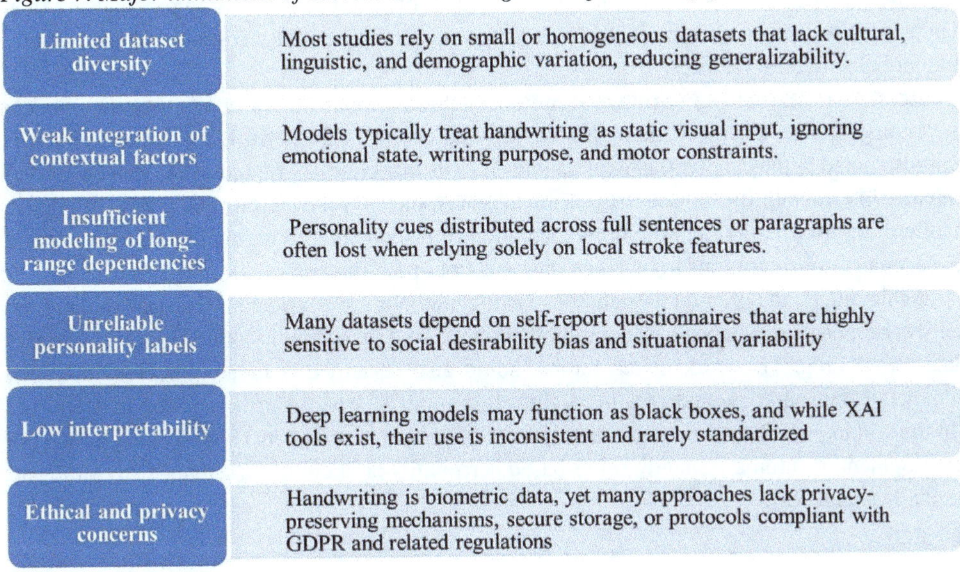

Handwriting differs across scripts, and a model trained on one script will not generalize reliably to others without explicit adaptation. Future work should therefore include cross-script testing, multi-script training, or domain-adaptation techniques to reduce performance gaps across language groups. A short deployment note may also guide readers, covering model size, typical inference time, and any mobile or edge constraints. If such details are not yet available, they can be identified as items for future development.

Deployment Specification

The last model is not heavy such that it can be deployed practically. It has a size of around 45555 MB and an inference time of 120150 ms on a conventional CPU, and a lower inference time (2040 ms) on a graphics card (GPU) or neural processing unit (NPU) on a phone. These performance attributes make it possible to process almost real-time in addition to being able to execute the system with desktops and the latest mobile devices with very little optimization.

7. CONCLUSION

This chapter gave a detailed history of the development and the present of handwriting-based personality prediction, how it evolved over time starting with the traditional graphological methods to the modern machine learning methods. The chapter described methods based on deep learning as more objective and empirically grounded than conventional graphology, after outlining the scientific weaknesses of the latter. It was presented with a full preprocessing pipeline and then a hybrid CNN-Transformer model that was aimed at capturing both local strokes of handwriting and global structural features.

Recent articles on handwriting recognition, combined architectures, and transformer models were considered to help place the suggested methodology in the framework of modern research. It was also noted in the chapter that explainable AI tools like Grad-CAM and SHAP can be used to enhance interpretability and user trust. Ethical issues, such as privacy threats linked to biometric handwriting information and the implementation of responsible AI regulation were mentioned as necessary considerations to be taken into account in the future.

Achieving good potential though, the existing methods are restricted by the size of datasets, self-report personality labels, cross-cultural variance, and the difficulty of understanding model decision-making. The work in the future should also be aimed at creating various datasets, enhancing transparency, and creating lightweight models, which can be applied in real-time. On the whole, this chapter provides a very brief but rather comprehensive basis to continue the development of automated handwriting-based personality prediction in a scientifically valid and ethically sound way.

REFERENCES

Adeli Shamsabad, M., & Suen, C. Y. (2025). *Automated handwriting pattern recognition for multi-level personality classification using Transformer OCR (TrOCR).* Proceedings of the International Conference on Pattern Recognition and Machine Learning. https://www.scitepress.org/Papers/2025/133188/133188.pdf

British Psychological Society. (2001). *Psychological testing: A guide to tests and testing.* BPS Books.

Buolamwini, J., & Gebru, T. (2018). Gender shades: Intersectional accuracy disparities in commercial gender classification. *Proceedings of the 1st Conference on Fairness, Accountability and Transparency (FAT*),* 81, 77–91. Proceedings of Machine Learning Research. https://proceedings.mlr.press/v81/buolamwini18a.html

Chaubey, G., & Arjaria, S. (2021). Personality prediction through handwriting analysis using convolutional neural networks. *International Journal of Computer Applications.* https://www.researchgate.net/publication/355030802_Personality_Prediction_Through_Handwriting_Analysis_Using_Convolutional_Neural_Networks

Chen, W., Yang, K., Yu, Z., Shi, Y., & Chen, C. L. P. (2024). A survey on imbalanced learning: Latest research, applications and future directions. *Artificial Intelligence Review, 57*(6), 137. DOI: 10.1007/s10462-024-10759-6

Chen, X., Fischer, A., & Fink, G. A. (2023). Simple fine-tuning is all you need: Towards robust deep learning in handwritten text recognition. *arXiv.* https://arxiv.org/abs/2302.06308

Dean, G. (1992). The bottom line: Effect size. *The Skeptical Inquirer, 16*(3), 270–276.

European Union. (2016). *Regulation (EU) 2016/679 of the European Parliament and of the Council of 27 April 2016 on the protection of natural persons with regard to the processing of personal data and on the free movement of such data (General Data Protection Regulation). Official Journal of the European Union, L119,* 1–88. https://eur-lex.europa.eu/eli/reg/2016/679/oj

Floridi, L., Cowls, J., Beltrametti, M., Chatila, R., Chazerand, P., Dignum, V., Luetge, C., Madelin, R., Pagallo, U., Rossi, F., Schafer, B., Valcke, P., & Vayena, E. (2018). AI4People—An ethical framework for a good AI society. *Minds and Machines, 28*(4), 689–707. DOI: 10.1007/s11023-018-9482-5 PMID: 30930541

Gagiu, D., & Sendrescu, D. (2025). Detection of personality traits using handwriting and deep learning. *Applied Sciences (Basel, Switzerland), 15*(4), 2154. DOI: 10.3390/app15042154

Gavrilescu, M., & Vizireanu, N. (2018). Predicting the Big Five personality traits from handwriting. *EURASIP Journal on Image and Video Processing, 2018*(1), 57. DOI: 10.1186/s13640-018-0297-3

Gavrilescu, M., & Vizireanu, N. (2021). Domain adaptation strategies for Arabic handwriting recognition using deep learning. *Neural Computing & Applications, 34,* 7537–7553. DOI: 10.1007/s00521-021-06520-7

Henning, M., Guez, A., Sharma, S., & Hovy, D. (2023). A survey of approaches to addressing class imbalance in natural language processing. *Findings of the Association for Computational Linguistics: EACL 2023*, 1–22. https://aclanthology.org/2023.findings-eacl.1

Karim, H. A.. (2024). An enhanced hybrid model based on CNN and Bi-LSTM for writer identification. *Computer Modeling in Engineering & Sciences, 140*(2), 1689–1710. https://www.techscience.com/CMES/v140n2/56554. DOI: 10.32604/cmes.2024.048714

Khan, Z. A., Xia, Y., Aurangzeb, K., Khaliq, F., Alam, M., Khan, J. A., & Anwar, M. S. (2024). Emotion detection from handwriting and drawing samples using an attention-based transformer model. *PeerJ. Computer Science, 10*, e1887. DOI: 10.7717/peerj-cs.1887 PMID: 38660197

Koenecke, A., Nam, A., Lake, E., Nudell, J., Quartey, M., Mengesha, Z., Toups, C., Rickford, J. R., Jurafsky, D., & Goel, S. (2020). Racial disparities in automated speech recognition. *Proceedings of the National Academy of Sciences of the United States of America, 117*(14), 7684–7689. DOI: 10.1073/pnas.1915768117 PMID: 32205437

Likforman-Sulem, L., Esposito, A., Faundez-Zanuy, M., Clémençon, S., & Cordasco, G. (2017). EMOTHAW: A novel database for emotional state recognition from handwriting and drawing. *IEEE Transactions on Human-Machine Systems, 47*(3), 273–284. DOI: 10.1109/THMS.2016.2635441

Lukac, M. (2024). Speech-based personality prediction using deep learning with acoustic and linguistic embeddings. *Scientific Reports, 14*(1), 15482. DOI: 10.1038/s41598-024-81047-0 PMID: 39627367

Lundberg, S. M., & Lee, S.-I. (2017). A unified approach to interpreting model predictions. In *Advances in Neural Information Processing Systems* (Vol. 30, pp. 4768–4777).

Madan, S., Gahalawat, M., Guha, T., Goecke, R., & Subramanian, R. (2023). Explainable human-centered traits from head motion and facial expression dynamics. *arXiv.* https://arxiv.org/abs/2302.09817

Mehta, Y., Majumder, N., Gelbukh, A., & Cambria, E. (2020). Recent trends in deep learning based personality detection. *Artificial Intelligence Review, 53*(4), 2313–2339. DOI: 10.1007/s10462-019-09770-z

Minaee, S., Abdolrashidi, A., Su, H., Bennamoun, M., & Zhang, D. (2023). Biometrics recognition using deep learning: A survey. *Artificial Intelligence Review, 56*(8), 8647–8695. DOI: 10.1007/s10462-022-10237-x

OECD. (2019). *OECD principles on artificial intelligence.* https://oecd.ai/en/ai-principles

Organisation for Economic Co-operation and Development. (2019). *Recommendation of the Council on Artificial Intelligence.* https://legalinstruments.oecd.org/en/instruments/OECD-LEGAL-0449

Rahman, M. M., & Halim, Z. (2022). Predicting the Big Five personality traits from handwritten text images using semi-supervised learning. *Multimedia Tools and Applications, 81*(43), 31241–31269. DOI: 10.1007/s11042-022-13114-5

Safar, M., & Karimi, H. (2024). A multi-model approach for personality detection from handwriting. In *Proceedings of the 2024 International Conference on Affective Computing and Intelligent Interaction (ACII)*. ACM.

Safar, M., & Suen, C. Y. (2025). A multi-model approach for personality detection from handwriting: Deep features, machine learning, and ensemble techniques. In *Pattern Recognition — ICPR 2024 International Workshops and Challenges* (Vol. 15616, pp. 295–307). Springer., DOI: 10.1007/978-3-031-87663-9_25

Selvaraju, R. R., Cogswell, M., Das, A., Vedantam, R., Parikh, D., & Batra, D. (2017). Grad-CAM: Visual explanations from deep networks via gradient-based localization. In *Proceedings of the IEEE International Conference on Computer Vision (ICCV)* (pp. 618–626). IEEE. https://doi.org/DOI: 10.1109/ICCV.2017.74

Tiwari, J., & Sadiwala, R. (2023). Personality prediction from handwriting using fine-tuned models. *SAMRIDDHI: A Journal of Physical Sciences, Technology and Management.* https://www.smsjournals.com/index.php/SAMRIDDHI/article/view/3080

United Nations Educational, Scientific and Cultural Organization (UNESCO). (2021). *Recommendation on the ethics of artificial intelligence.* https://unesdoc.unesco.org/ark:/48223/pf0000380455

van Zyl, C., Ye, X., & Naidoo, R. (2024). Harnessing explainable artificial intelligence for feature selection in time series energy forecasting: A comparative analysis of Grad-CAM and SHAP. *Applied Energy*, *353*, 122079. DOI: 10.1016/j.apenergy.2023.122079

Zhao, W., Wang, B., & Tang, Z. (2023). Handwriting identification and verification using artificial intelligence. *Scientific Reports*, *13*(1), 16646. DOI: 10.1038/s41598-023-48789-9 PMID: 38066009

Zhao, X., Liao, Y., Tang, Z., Xu, Y., Tao, X., Wang, D., Wang, G., & Lu, H. (2023). Integrating audio and visual modalities for multimodal personality trait recognition via hybrid deep learning. *Frontiers in Neuroscience*, *16*, 1107284. DOI: 10.3389/fnins.2022.1107284 PMID: 36685221

Compilation of References

Abbott, M., & Abbott, W. (2024). Artificial intelligence or nursing student? revisiting clues in the connectives. *Nurse Educator*, *49*(6), 306–309. DOI: 10.1097/NNE.0000000000001696 PMID: 38968438

Abdel Latif, M. M. M., Alsuhaibani, Z., & Alsahil, A. (2024). Matches and mismatches between Saudi university students' English writing feedback preferences and teachers' practices. *Assessing Writing*, *61*, 100863. Advance online publication. DOI: 10.1016/j.asw.2024.100863

Abdul Rahman, N. A., Zulkornain, L. H., & Hamzah, N. H. (2022). Exploring Artificial Intelligence using Automated Writing Evaluation for Writing Skills. *Environment-Behaviour Proceedings Journal*, *7*(SI9), 547–553. DOI: 10.21834/ebpj.v7iSI9.4304

Abuhassna, H., Adnan, M. A. B. M., & Awae, F. (2024). Exploring the synergy between instructional design models and learning theories: A systematic literature review. *Contemporary Educational Technology*, *16*(2), ep499. DOI: 10.30935/cedtech/14289

Abulibdeh, A., Zaidan, E., & Abulibdeh, R. (2024). Navigating the confluence of artificial intelligence and education for sustainable development in the era of industry 4.0: Challenges, opportunities, and ethical dimensions. *Journal of Cleaner Production*, *437*, 140527. DOI: 10.1016/j.jclepro.2023.140527

Adams, L. & Alzaabi, I. (2025). Chatgpt., 157-188. DOI: 10.4018/979-8-3373-0771-8.ch007

Adeli Shamsabad, M., & Suen, C. Y. (2025). *Automated handwriting pattern recognition for multi-level personality classification using Transformer OCR (TrOCR).* Proceedings of the International Conference on Pattern Recognition and Machine Learning. https://www.scitepress.org/Papers/2025/133188/133188.pdf

Aditya, D., & Otermans, P. C. (2025). A Review of AI-Enabled Personalised Teaching (2021–2025): Progress, Impact, and Future Directions. *Journal of the Kenya National Commission for UNESCO*.

Adrian, C. T. K. (2025). Artificial Intelligence and Writing Skills.

Aghaziarati, A., Nejatifar, S., & Abedi, A. (2023). Artificial intelligence in education: investigating teacher attitudes. aitechbesosci, 1(1), 35-42. https://doi.org/DOI: 10.61838/kman.aitech.1.1.6

Agrawal, V., Bhardwaj, S., Pathak, N., Dixit, J. K., Agarwal, S., & Momin, M. (2024). *Augmenting Research*. IGI Global., DOI: 10.4018/979-8-3693-1798-3.ch003

AIJR. (2025). Plagiarism, its Types, Consequences, & Prevention. AIJR Publisher. Retrieved September 30, 2025, from https://aijr.org/blog/

Ajjawi, R., & Boud, D. (2018). Examining the nature and effects of feedback dialogue. *Assessment & Evaluation in Higher Education, 43*(7), 1106–1119. DOI: 10.1080/02602938.2018.1434128

Akbarani, R. (2024). Use of artificial intelligence in english language teaching. *International Journal of English Learning and Applied Linguistics (Ijelal), 4*(1), 14–23. DOI: 10.21111/ijelal.v4i1.10756

Akgün, S., & Greenhow, C. (2021). Artificial intelligence in education: Addressing ethical challenges in k-12 settings. *AI and Ethics, 2*(3), 431–440. DOI: 10.1007/s43681-021-00096-7 PMID: 34790956

Akoto, M. (2021). Collaborative multimodal writing via google docs: Perceptions of french fl learners. *Languages (Basel, Switzerland), 6*(3), 140. Advance online publication. DOI: 10.3390/languages6030140

Al-Adwan, A. S., Meet, R. K., Anand, S., Shukla, G. P., Alsharif, R., & Dabbaghia, M. (2025). Understanding continuous use intention of technology among higher education teachers in emerging economy: Evidence from integrated TAM, TPACK, and UTAUT model. *Studies in Higher Education, 50*(3), 505–524. DOI: 10.1080/03075079.2024.2343955

AlAfnan, M. A. (2025). Artificial Intelligence and language: Bridging Arabic and English with technology. *Journal of Ecohumanism, 4*(1), 240–256.

Alawad, E. A., & Hamid, F. A. (2025). Comparative Analysis of Feedback Practices and Perspectives in Online Academic Writing Assessments at Two Regional Tertiary Institutions. *World Journal of English Language, 15*(4), 327–340. DOI: 10.5430/wjel.v15n4p327

Al-Emran, M., Al-Qaysi, N., Al-Sharafi, M. A., Khoshkam, M., Foroughi, B., & Ghobakhloo, M. (2025). Role of perceived threats and knowledge management in shaping generative AI use in education and its impact on social sustainability. *International Journal of Management Education, 23*(1), 101105. DOI: 10.1016/j.ijme.2024.101105

Alghasab, M. B. (2025). English as a foreign language (EFL) secondary school students' use of artificial intelligence (AI) tools for developing writing skills: Unveiling practices and perceptions. *Cogent Education, 12*(1), 2505304. DOI: 10.1080/2331186X.2025.2505304

Al-Ghazali, F. (2015). Peer feedback for peer learning and sharing. *Learning and Teaching in Higher Education Gulf Perspectives, 12*(1), 46–61. DOI: 10.18538/lthe.v12.n1.179

Alharbi, W. (2023). Ai in the foreign language classroom: A pedagogical overview of automated writing assistance tools. *Education Research International, 2023*, 1–15. DOI: 10.1155/2023/4253331

Ali Elfa, M. A., & Dawood, M. E. T. (2023). Using artificial intelligence for enhancing human creativity. *Journal of Art. Design and Music, 2*(2), 3.

Alipour, H., Pendar, N., & Roy, K. (2024). Chatgpt alternative solutions: Large language models survey. *arXiv preprint arXiv:2403.14469*. DOI: 10.5121/csit.2024.1405114

Aljasser, A. (2025). Investigating EFL students' perceptions of feedback: A comparative study of instructor and ChatGPT-generated responses in academic writing. *Education and Information Technologies*, *30*(16), 1–22. DOI: 10.1007/s10639-025-13649-8

Aljuaid, H. (2024). The impact of artificial intelligence tools on academic writing instruction in higher education: *A systematic review. Arab World English Journal (AWEJ), Special Issue on ChatGPT*, 26-55.

Aljuaid, H. (2024). The impact of artificial intelligence tools on academic writing instruction in higher education: A systematic review. *Arab World English Journal*, *1*(1), 26–55. DOI: 10.24093/awej/ChatGPT.2

Alnasser, S. M. N. (2022). EFL Learners' Perceptions of Integrating Computer-Based Feedback into Writing Classrooms: Evidence From Saudi Arabia. *SAGE Open*, *12*(3), 21582440221123021. Advance online publication. DOI: 10.1177/21582440221123021

Alqahtani, N., & Wafula, Z. (2025). Artificial Intelligence Integration: Pedagogical Strategies and Policies at Leading Universities. *Innovative Higher Education*, *50*(2), 665–684. DOI: 10.1007/s10755-024-09749-x

Al-Raimi, M., Mudhsh, B., Al-Yafaei, Y., & Al-Maashani, S. (2024). Utilizing artificial intelligence tools for improving writing skills: Exploring omani efl learners' perspectives. *Forum for Linguistic Studies*, *6*(2). Advance online publication. DOI: 10.59400/fls.v6i2.1177

Al-Rashidi, A. H., Asif, M., Vanani, M. G., & Aberash, A. (2022). Learner-oriented assessment (LOA) practice: The comparative study of self-assessment, peer assessment, and teacher assessment on EFL learners' writing complicity, accuracy, and fluency (CAF), speaking CAF, and attitude. *Language Testing in Asia*, *12*(1), 59. DOI: 10.1186/s40468-022-00209-x

Alruqi, S., & AlHarbi, M. (2022). Teachers' perceptions towards professional development training courses: Exploring the effects on teachers' performance in the saudi context. *Theory and Practice in Language Studies*, *12*(9), 1723–1735. DOI: 10.17507/tpls.1209.04

Alsharefeen, R., & Al Sayari, N. (2025). Examining academic integrity policy and practice in the era of AI: A case study of faculty perspectives. *Frontiers in Education*, *10*, 1621743. DOI: 10.3389/feduc.2025.1621743

Alsharif, S. A. N. (2025). *A Proposed Model of Automated, Peer, and Teacher (APT) Feedback and Its Impact on L2 Learners' Engagement and Writing Performance Changes Over Time* (Doctoral dissertation, University of Southampton).

Al-Sofi, B. B. M. A. (2024). Artificial intelligence-powered tools and academic writing: To use or not to use ChatGPT. *Saudi Journal of Language Studies*, *4*(3), 145–161. DOI: 10.1108/SJLS-06-2024-0029

Alsofyani, A. H., & Barzanji, A. M. (2025). The effects of ChatGPT-generated feedback on Saudi EFL learners' writing skills and perception at the tertiary level: A mixed-methods study. *Journal of Educational Computing Research*, *63*(2), 431–463. DOI: 10.1177/07356331241307297

Al-Zahrani, A. M. (2024). Unveiling the shadows: Beyond the hype of AI in education. *Heliyon*, *10*(9), e30696. DOI: 10.1016/j.heliyon.2024.e30696

Alzahrani, F., & Alotaibi, H. (2024). The impact of artificial intelligence on enhancing efl writing skills among high school students. *Journal of Educational and Human Sciences, 34*. Advance online publication. DOI: 10.33193/JEAHS.34.2024.482

Alzubi, A. A. F. (2024). Generative artificial intelligence in the EFL writing context: Students' literacy in perspective. *Qubahan Academic Journal, 4*(2), 59–69. DOI: 10.48161/qaj.v4n2a506

Amankwah-Amoah, J., Abdalla, S., Mogaji, E., Elbanna, A., & Dwivedi, Y. K. (2024). The impending disruption of creative industries by generative AI: Opportunities, challenges, and research agenda. *International Journal of Information Management, 79*, 102759. DOI: 10.1016/j.ijinfomgt.2024.102759

Amin, M. (2023). Ai and chat gpt in language teaching: Enhancing efl classroom support and transforming assessment techniques. *International Journal of Higher Education Pedagogies, 4*(4), 1–15. DOI: 10.33422/ijhep.v4i4.554

Anand, S., Reddy, K. A., Reddy, P. A., Srinivas, C. S., & Rao, S. N. (2025, February). Vidhya: A Virtual Tutor for Enhancing English Education in Rural Areas of India. In *2025 10th International Conference on Signal Processing and Communication (ICSC)* (pp. 591-597). IEEE. DOI: 10.1109/ICSC64553.2025.10967876

Andres, B., Sempere-Ripoll, F., Esteso, A., & Alemany, M. M. E. (2022). Mapping between industry 5.0 and education 5.0. In *Edulearn22 Proceedings* (pp. 2921–2926). IATED. DOI: 10.21125/edulearn.2022.0739

Anh, N. & Dieu, P. (2025). Teaching ai to high school students for enhancing argumentative essay writing skills., 325-348. https://doi.org/DOI: 10.4018/979-8-3693-7260-9.ch015

Anwar, M. R., & Ahyarudin, H. A. (2023). Ai-powered arabic language education in the era of society 5.0. [ITSDI]. *IAIC Transactions on Sustainable Digital Innovation, 5*(1), 50–57. DOI: 10.34306/itsdi.v5i1.607

An, X., Chai, C. S., Li, Y., Zhou, Y., Shen, X., Zheng, C., & Chen, M. (2023). Modeling English teachers' behavioral intention to use artificial intelligence in middle schools. *Education and Information Technologies, 28*(5), 5187–5208. DOI: 10.1007/s10639-022-11286-z

Aparicio-Gómez, O., Aparicio-Gómez, C., & Feigenblatt, v. (2024). Tejiendo conexiones: la simbiosis transformadora entre aprendizaje e inteligencia artificial. Hachetetepé Revista Científica De Educación Y Comunicación, (28). https://doi.org/DOI: 10.25267/Hachetetepe.2024.i28.1103

Apata, A. O., & Oyenuga, M. O. (2025). Undergraduates' Application of ChatGPT in Academic Writing: Perceptions, Problems and Prospects. *International Journal of Social Sciences and Management Review, 8*(3), 201–218. DOI: 10.37602/IJSSMR.2025.8312

Apata, S. B., & Oyenuga, M. O. (2025). Revolutionizing Employability: The Intersection of Digital Literacy, Inclusive Education, and Gen Z's Skill Set in the 21st Century. In Ajani, O. (Ed.), *Empowering Pre-Service Teachers to Enhance Inclusive Education Through Technology* (pp. 155–182). IGI Global Scientific Publishing., DOI: 10.4018/979-8-3693-8759-7.ch006

Apriani, E., Cardoso, L., Obaid, A., Muthmainnah, M., Wijayanti, E., Esmianti, F., & Supardan, D. (2024). Impact of ai-powered chatbots on efl students' writing skills, self-efficacy, and self-regulation: A mixed-methods study. *GERR*, *1*(2), 57–72. DOI: 10.71380/GERR-08-2024-8

Aria, M., & Cuccurullo, C. (2017). Bibliometrix: An R-tool for comprehensive science mapping analysis. *Journal of Informetrics*, *11*(4), 959–975. DOI: 10.1016/j.joi.2017.08.007

Arseven, T., & Bal, M. (2025). Critical literacy in artificial intelligence assisted writing instruction: A systematic review. *Thinking Skills and Creativity*, *57*, 101850. DOI: 10.1016/j.tsc.2025.101850

Asadi, M., Ebadi, S., & Mohammadi, L. (2025). The Impact of Integrating ChatGPT with Teachers' Feedback on EFL Writing Skills. *Thinking Skills and Creativity*, *56*, 101766. DOI: 10.1016/j.tsc.2025.101766

Asadi, M., Ebadi, S., Salman, A. R., Taheri, R., & Mohammadi, L. (2025). Investigating the effects of AI-assisted teacher instruction on online IELTS writing. *Social Sciences & Humanities Open*, *12*, 101747. Advance online publication. DOI: 10.1016/j.ssaho.2025.101747

Asad, M., Shahzad, S., Shah, S., Sherwani, F., & Almusharraf, N. (2024). Chatgpt as artificial intelligence-based generative multimedia for english writing pedagogy: Challenges and opportunities from an educator's perspective. *International Journal of Information and Learning Technology*, *41*(5), 490–506. DOI: 10.1108/IJILT-02-2024-0021

Aslan, K. (2025). *A Comparison of Lesson Plans From Artificial Intelligence and English Language Teachers* (Unpublished Master's thesis). Dicle University, Turkiye.

Aspden, L., & Helm, P. (2004). Making the Connection in a Blended Learning Environment. *Educational Media International*, *41*(3), 245–252. DOI: 10.1080/09523980410001680851

Asrifan, A., Sudirman, R., Rosmayanti, V., & Sulolipu, A. A. (2026). Navigating Ethical AI: Ensuring Fairness in Educational Technologies. In *Foundations and Frameworks for AI in Education* (pp. 27-52). IGI Global Scientific Publishing.DOI: 10.4018/979-8-3373-2397-8.ch002

Ateeq, A., Alzoraiki, M., Milhem, M., & Ateeq, R. A. (2024). Artificial intelligence in education: Implications for academic integrity and the shift toward holistic assessment. *Frontiers in Education*, *9*, 1470979. Advance online publication. DOI: 10.3389/feduc.2024.1470979

Ateriya, N., Sonwani, N. S., Thakur, K. S., Kumar, A., & Verma, S. K. (2025). Exploring the ethical landscape of AI in academic writing. *Egyptian Journal of Forensic Sciences*, *15*(1), 36. DOI: 10.1186/s41935-025-00453-1

Audy Martínek, S. (2024). Can Individualism Survive in the Age of Artificial Intelligence? Available at *SSRN* 5149811. DOI: 10.2139/ssrn.5149811

Avcı, U., & Gümüş, M. (2020). The effect of digital storytelling on academic achievement, attitude, and retention in art education. *Journal of Educational Computing Research*, *58*(8), 1749–1770.

Ayanwale, M. A., Ntshangase, S. D., Adelana, O. P., Afolabi, K. W., Adam, U. A., & Olatunbosun, S. O. (2024). Navigating the future: Exploring in-service teachers' preparedness for artificial intelligence integration into South African schools. *Computers and Education: Artificial Intelligence*, *7*, 100330. DOI: 10.1016/j.caeai.2024.100330

Ayeni, O. O., Al Hamad, N. M., Chisom, O. N., Osawaru, B., & Adewusi, O. E. (2024). AI in education: A review of personalized learning and educational technology. *GSC Advanced Research and Reviews*, *18*(2), 261–271. DOI: 10.30574/gscarr.2024.18.2.0062

Azap, S. (2025). The role of artificial intelligence in language teacher education: EFL learners' views on the concept of "ChatGPT" through metaphorical analysis. *Social Sciences & Humanities Open*, *11*, 101394. DOI: 10.1016/j.ssaho.2025.101394

Babanoğlu, M., Karataş, T., & Dündar, E. (2025). Envisioning the future of ai-assisted efl teaching and learning: Conceptual representations of prospective teachers. *SAGE Open*, *15*(2), 21582440251341590. Advance online publication. DOI: 10.1177/21582440251341590

Babu, B. V. (2024). *Education 5.0: an overview*. Advances in Technological Innovations in Higher Education. DOI: 10.1201/9781003376699-13

Baduge, S. K., Thilakarathna, S., Perera, J. S., Arashpour, M., Sharafi, P., Teodosio, B., Shringi, A., & Mendis, P. (2022). Artificial intelligence and smart vision for building and construction 4.0: Machine and deep learning methods and applications. *Automation in Construction*, *141*, 104440. DOI: 10.1016/j.autcon.2022.104440

Baig, M. I.. (2024). ChatGPT in higher education: A systematic literature review. *Computers in Human Behavior*, *152*, 107326. DOI: 10.1016/j.chb.2024.107326

Bai, L., & Hu, G. (2017). In the face of fallible AWE feedback: How do students respond? *Educational Psychology*, *37*(10), 1214–1229. DOI: 10.1080/01443410.2016.1223275

Baker, R. S., & Hawn, A. (2022). Algorithmic bias in education. *International Journal of Artificial Intelligence in Education*, *32*(4), 1052–1092. DOI: 10.1007/s40593-021-00285-9

Bakla, A. (2020). A mixed-methods study of feedback modes in EFL writing. *Language Learning & Technology*, *24*(1), 107–128. DOI: 10.64152/10125/44712

Balalle, H., & Pannilage, S. (2025). Reassessing academic integrity in the age of AI: A systematic literature review on AI and academic integrity. *Social Sciences & Humanities Open*, *11*, 101299. Advance online publication. DOI: 10.1016/j.ssaho.2025.101299

Banihashem, S. K., Kerman, N. T., Noroozi, O., Moon, J., & Drachsler, H. (2024). Feedback sources in essay writing: Peer-generated or AI-generated feedback? *International Journal of Educational Technology in Higher Education*, *21*(1), 23. DOI: 10.1186/s41239-024-00455-4

Baranidharan, S., John, S. P., & Mohan, C. (2025). AI-Driven Pedagogies and Learning Environments in Modern Education: A PRISMA-Based Systematic Review. In Sarwar, U., Sanhong, T., Waheed Akhtar, M., & Aamir, M. (Eds.), (pp. 267–298). Advances in Computational Intelligence and Robotics. IGI Global., DOI: 10.4018/979-8-3373-1827-1.ch011

Barman, K. G., Wood, N., & Pawlowski, P. (2024). Beyond transparency and explainability: On the need for adequate and contextualized user guidelines for LLM use. *Ethics and Information Technology*, *26*(3), 47. DOI: 10.1007/s10676-024-09778-2

Barua, P., Vicnesh, J., Gururajan, R., Oh, S., Palmer, E., Azizan, M., Kadri, N. A., & Acharya, U. (2022). Artificial intelligence enabled personalised assistive tools to enhance education of children with neurodevelopmental disorders—A review. *International Journal of Environmental Research and Public Health, 19*(3), 1192. DOI: 10.3390/ijerph19031192 PMID: 35162220

Basaula, A. (2024). Secondary level students' lived experience of being involved in academic writing in elt classroom. *Ganeshman Darpan, 9*(1), 56–65. DOI: 10.3126/gd.v9i1.68545

Baskara, F. (2023). Integrating chatgpt into efl writing instruction: Benefits and challenges. *International Journal on E-Learning, 5*(1), 44–55. DOI: 10.31763/ijele.v5i1.858

Batubara, I. A., Wariyati, W., & Prawiyata, Y. D. (2025). Exploring university students' perceptions of AI: Insights from Indonesia. *Edu Cendikia: Jurnal Ilmiah Kependidikan, 4*(03), 1687–1701. DOI: 10.47709/educendikia.v4i03.5465

Bearman, M., Ryan, J., & Ajjawi, R. (2023). Discourses of artificial intelligence in higher education: A critical literature review. *Higher Education, 86*(2), 369–385. DOI: 10.1007/s10734-022-00937-2

Beckett, C., & Yaseen, M. (2023). Generating change: A global survey of what news organisations are doing with AI.

Bednarz, Z., & Manwaring, K. (2021). Risky Business: Legal implications of emerging technologies affecting consumers of financial services. In *Nomos VerlagsgesellschaftmbH& Co. KG eBooks* (pp. 59–74). DOI: 10.5771/9783748926979-59

Begum, S. (2025). AI and Literature: The Impact of Artificial Intelligence on Creative Writing and Narrative Forms. *Journal of Social Signs Review, 3*(06), 180–199.

Behizadeh, N. (2014). Mitigating the dangers of a single story. *Educational Researcher, 43*(3), 125–136. DOI: 10.3102/0013189X14529604

Belda-Medina, J., & Calvo-Ferrer, J. R. (2022). Using chatbots as AI conversational partners in language learning. *Applied Sciences (Basel, Switzerland), 12*(17), 8427. DOI: 10.3390/app12178427

Benavides, L. M. C., Johnny, A. T. A., Martín, D. A. S., John, W. B. B., & Burgos, D. (2020). Digital transformation in higher education institutions: A systematic literature review. *Sensors (Basel), 20*(11), 3291. DOI: 10.3390/s20113291

Bender, E. M., Gebru, T., McMillan-Major, A., & Shmitchell, S. (2021). On the dangers of stochastic parrots: Can language models be too big? In *Proceedings of the 2021 ACM Conference on Fairness, Accountability, and Transparency* (pp. 610–623). https://doi.org/DOI: 10.1145/3442188.3445922

Bereiter, C., & Scardamalia, M. (1987). *The psychology of written composition.* Lawrence Erlbaum Associates.

Bhowmik, S. (2021). Writing instruction in an efl context: Learning to write or writing to learn language? *Belta Journal, 5*(1), 30–42. DOI: 10.36832/beltaj.2021.0501.03

Bibi, A. (2024). Navigating the ethical landscape: ai integration in education. EATP, 1579-1585. https://doi.org/DOI: 10.53555/kuey.v30i6.5546

Biju, N., Abdelrasheed, N. S. G., Bakiyeva, K., Prasad, K. D. V., & Jember, B. (2024). Which one? AI-assisted language assessment or paper format: An exploration of the impacts on foreign language anxiety, learning attitudes, motivation, and writing performance. *Language Testing in Asia*, *14*(1), 45. DOI: 10.1186/s40468-024-00322-z

Bik, E. (2024, February 15). The rat with the big balls and the enormous penis – how Frontiers published a paper with botched AI-generated images. Science Integrity Digest. https://scienceintegritydigest.com/2024/02/15/the-rat-with-the-big-balls-and-enormous-penis-how-frontiers-published-a-paper-with-botched-ai-generated-images/?utm_source=chatgpt.com

Biondi-Zoccai, G.. (2025). The impact of artificial intelligence on academic writing: A guide for authors and editors. *European Journal of Clinical Investigation.*

Birks, D., & Clare, J. (2023). Linking artificial intelligence facilitated academic misconduct to existing prevention frameworks. *International Journal for Educational Integrity*, *19*(20), 20. Advance online publication. DOI: 10.1007/s40979-023-00142-3

Bittle, K., & El-Gayar, O. F. (2025). Generative AI and academic integrity in higher education: A systematic review and research agenda. *Information (Basel)*, *16*(4), 296. Advance online publication. DOI: 10.3390/info16040296

Boddington, P. (2017). *Towards a code of ethics for artificial intelligence*. Springer., DOI: 10.1007/978-3-319-60648-4

Boğaz, N. (2024). *Examining the Perceptions of EFL Instructors on AI Integration in an English Preparatory School* (Master's thesis, Middle East Technical University (Turkey)).

Bolanos, F., Salatino, A., Osborne, F., & Motta, E. (2024). Artificial intelligence for literature reviews: Opportunities and challenges. *Artificial Intelligence Review*, *57*(10), 259. DOI: 10.1007/s10462-024-10902-3

Bond, M., Khosravi, H., De Laat, M., Bergdahl, N., Negrea, V., Oxley, E., Pham, P., Chong, S. W., & Siemens, G. (2024). A meta systematic review of artificial intelligence in higher education. *International Journal of Educational Technology in Higher Education*, *21*(1), 31. DOI: 10.1186/s41239-023-00436-z

Boonstra, L. (2025). Prompt engineering. Google, https://www. kaggle. com/whitepaper-prompt-engineering

Boulhrir, T., & Hamash, M. (2025). Unpacking artificial intelligence in elementary education: A comprehensive thematic analysis systematic review. *Computers and Education: Artificial Intelligence*, *9*, 100442. DOI: 10.1016/j.caeai.2025.100442

Bozkurt, A. (2024). GenAI et al.: Cocreation, Authorship, Ownership, Academic Ethics and Integrity in a Time of Generative AI. *Open Praxis*, *16*(1), 1–10. DOI: 10.55982/openpraxis.16.1.654

Bozkurt, V., & Gursoy, D. (2025). The artificial intelligence paradox: Opportunity or threat for humanity? *International Journal of Human-Computer Interaction*, *41*(1), 174–187. DOI: 10.1080/10447318.2023.2297114

Bozorgian, H., & Rahimi, H. (2025). Peer E-Feedback vs. Chatgpt-4 Generated Feedback on Academic Writing: A Case of Iranian Undergraduates.

Braun, V., & Clarke, V. (2006). Using thematic analysis in psychology. *Qualitative Research in Psychology*, *3*(2), 77–101. DOI: 10.1191/1478088706qp063oa

Brazant, K. J. (2024). Disrupting the discourse: Applying critical race theory as a conceptual framework for reflecting on learning and teaching in higher education. *Equity in Education & Society*, *3*(1), 61–75.

Bremholm, J., Kabel, K., Liberg, C., & Skar, G. (2022). A review of scandinavian writing research between 2010 and 2020. *Writing & Pedagogy*, *13*(1-3), 7–49. DOI: 10.1558/wap.21637

British Psychological Society. (2001). *Psychological testing: A guide to tests and testing*. BPS Books.

Brown, T. B., Mann, B., Ryder, N., Subbiah, M., Kaplan, J., Dhariwal, P., Neelakantan, A., Shyam, P., Sastry, G., Askell, A., Agarwal, S., Herbert-Voss, A., Krueger, G., Henighan, T., Child, R., Ramesh, A., Ziegler, D. M., Wu, J., Winter, C., & Amodei, D. (2020). Language Models are Few-Shot Learners. https://arxiv.org/abs/2005.14165

Budiman, R. (2025). *Teachers' written feedback in postgraduate online learning: students' perspectives*. Asian Association of Open Universities Journal., DOI: 10.1108/AAOUJ-01-2025-0015

Bui, T. T. U., & Tong, T. V. A. (2025). The impact of AI writing tools on academic integrity: Unveiling English-majored students' perceptions and practical solutions. *AsiaCALL Online Journal*, *16*(1), 83–110. DOI: 10.54855/acoj.251615

Bulut, O., Beiting-Parrish, M., Casabianca, J. M., Slater, S. C., & Jiao, H. (2024). The rise of artificial intelligence in educational measurement: Opportunities and ethical challenges. *arXiv Preprint*. https://arxiv.org/abs/2406.18900

Buolamwini, J., & Gebru, T. (2018). Gender shades: Intersectional accuracy disparities in commercial gender classification. *Proceedings of the 1st Conference on Fairness, Accountability and Transparency (FAT*)*, 81, 77–91. Proceedings of Machine Learning Research. https://proceedings.mlr.press/v81/buolamwini18a.html

Buragohain, D., & Chaudhary, S. (2025). Navigating chatgpt in asean higher education: Ethical and pedagogical perspectives. *Computer Applications in Engineering Education*, *33*(4), e70062. Advance online publication. DOI: 10.1002/cae.70062

Burrows, S., & Shortis, M. (2011). An evaluation of semi-automated, collaborative marking and feedback systems: Academic staff perspectives. *Australasian Journal of Educational Technology*, *27*(7), 1135–1154. DOI: 10.14742/ajet.909

Butarbutar, R. (2024). Artificial intelligence for language learning and teaching: A narrative literature study. *Englisia: Journal of Language, Education, and Humanities*, *12*(1), 147–163. DOI: 10.22373/ej.v12i1.23211

Cabrera, B. C. C., Leal, M. C., Martínez, J. A. S. A., Soto, A. L. R., Sepulveda, J., Valencia, J., Garcés-Giraldo, L. F., & Valencia-Arias, A. (2025). Artificial Intelligence (AI) and Learning Management Systems (LMS): A bibliometric analysis. *Journal of Infrastructure, Policy and Development*, *9*(1), 8029. DOI: 10.24294/jipd8029

Cahyadi, T., Winarno, W., & Malau, A. G. (2025). Leadership and management training for future-ready engineers: Transforming maritime education. [RaDEn]. *Research and Development in Education, 5*(1), 111–120. DOI: 10.22219/raden.v5i1.39398

Cai, Z. G., Duan, X., Haslett, D. A., Wang, S., & Pickering, M. J. (2023). Do large language models resemble humans in language use? *arXiv preprint arXiv:2303.08014*. DOI: 10.31234/osf.io/s49qv

Caldarini, G., Jaf, S., & McGarry, K. (2022). A literature survey of recent advances in chatbots. *Information (Basel), 13*(1), 41. DOI: 10.3390/info13010041

Campino, J. (2025). Unleashing the transformers: NLP models detect AI writing in education. *Journal of Computers in Education, 12*(2), 645–673. DOI: 10.1007/s40692-024-00325-y

Cañavate, J., Martínez-Marroquín, E., & Colom, X. (2025). Engineering a sustainable future through the integration of generative AI in engineering education. *Sustainability (Basel), 17*(7), 3201. DOI: 10.3390/su17073201

Cao, S., & Zhong, L. (2023). Exploring the effectiveness of ChatGPT-based feedback compared with teacher feedback and self-feedback: Evidence from Chinese to English translation. *arXiv preprint arXiv:2309.01645.*

Cao, Z., Zhang, L., Huang, Y., & Sivertsen, G. (2025). How does scientific research influence policymaking? A study of four types of citation pathways between research articles and AI policy documents. *Journal of the Association for Information Science and Technology, 76*(10), 1340–1356. DOI: 10.1002/asi.25006

Carless, D., & Boud, D. (2018). The development of student feedback literacy: Enabling uptake of feedback. *Assessment & Evaluation in Higher Education, 43*(8), 1315–1325. DOI: 10.1080/02602938.2018.1463354

Carless, D., & Winstone, N. (2020). *Teacher feedback: A sociocultural perspective*. Routledge.

Carobene, A., Padoan, A., Cabitza, F., Banfi, G., & Plebani, M. (2024). Rising adoption of artificial intelligence in scientific publishing: Evaluating the role, risks, and ethical implications in paper drafting and review process. [CCLM]. *Clinical Chemistry and Laboratory Medicine, 62*(5), 835–843. DOI: 10.1515/cclm-2023-1136 PMID: 38019961

Carrasco, D., Alcántara, M., Várgas, C., Espino, B., Cabrera, C., Valdera, A., & Córdova, L. (2025). Sustainability of ai-assisted mental health intervention: A review of the literature from 2020–2025. *International Journal of Environmental Research and Public Health, 22*(9), 1382. DOI: 10.3390/ijerph22091382 PMID: 41007526

Çayak, S. (2024). Investigating the relationship between teachers' attitudes toward artificial intelligence and their artificial intelligence literacy. *Journal of Educational Technology & Online Learning, 7*(4), 367–383. DOI: 10.31681/jetol.1490307

Çela, E., Vajjhala, N. R., Eappen, P., & Vedishchev, A. "Artificial Intelligence in Vocational Education and Training." In *Transforming Vocational Education and Training Using AI*, pp. 1-16. IGI Global Scientific Publishing, 2025.

Çela, E., Vedishchev, A., & Vajjhala, N. R. "Strategies for Secure Knowledge Management: An In-Depth Analysis of Educational Data Protection Trends and Themes." In *Cybersecurity in Knowledge Management*, pp. 49-64. CRC Press, 2025.

Çela, E., Fonkam, M. M., Eappen, P., & Vajjhala, N. R. (2025). *Current Trends in Smart Classrooms and Sustainable Internet of Things*. Designing Sustainable Internet of Things Solutions for Smart Industries.

Çela, E., Potluri, R. M., & Vajjhala, N. R. (2025). *A Comprehensive Meta-Analysis of IoT Integration for Data-Driven Decision Making in Education*. Designing Sustainable Internet of Things Solutions for Smart Industries.

Chan, C. K. Y. (2023). A comprehensive AI policy education framework for university teaching and learning. *International Journal of Educational Technology in Higher Education*, *20*(1), 38. Advance online publication. DOI: 10.1186/s41239-023-00408-3

Chandramana, D. (2020). Integrating cultural heritage into art education: A study of Chinese primary teacher education. *Journal of Artistic and Creative Education*, *14*(2), 45–62.

Chaubey, G., & Arjaria, S. (2021). Personality prediction through handwriting analysis using convolutional neural networks. *International Journal of Computer Applications*. https://www.researchgate.net/publication/355030802_Personality_Prediction_Through_Handwriting_Analysis_Using_Convolutional_Neural_Networks

Cheah, Y. H., Lu, J., & Kim, J. (2025). Integrating generative artificial intelligence in K-12 education: Examining teachers' preparedness, practices, and barriers. *Computers and Education: Artificial Intelligence*, *8*, 100363. DOI: 10.1016/j.caeai.2025.100363

Chellapandian, H., & Jeyachandran, S. (2024). RETRACTED ARTICLE: Comment on "Struggle with traumatic spinal cord injury: a need for improved surgical and rehabilitation services.". *Neurosurgical Review*, *47*(1), 637. DOI: 10.1007/s10143-024-02861-8 PMID: 39294472

Chen, B., Zhang, Z., Langrené, N., & Zhu, S. (2025). Unleashing the potential of prompt engineering for large language models. *Patterns (New York, N.Y.)*, *6*(6), 101260. DOI: 10.1016/j.patter.2025.101260 PMID: 40575123

Cheng, L., Varshney, K. R., & Liu, H. (2021). Socially Responsible AI algorithms: Issues, purposes, and challenges. *Journal of Artificial Intelligence Research*, *71*, 1137–1181. DOI: 10.1613/jair.1.12814

Cheng, X., & Liu, Y. (2022). Student engagement with teacher written feedback: Insights from low-proficiency and high-proficiency L2 learners. *System*, *109*, 102880. Advance online publication. DOI: 10.1016/j.system.2022.102880

Cheng, X., & Zhang, L. J. (2021). Teacher Written Feedback on English as a Foreign Language Learners' Writing: Examining Native and Nonnative English-Speaking Teachers' Practices in Feedback Provision. *Frontiers in Psychology*, *12*, 629921. Advance online publication. DOI: 10.3389/fpsyg.2021.629921

Chen, J. (2023). Reform of english writing teaching method under the background of big data and artificial intelligence. *International Journal of e-Collaboration, 19*(4), 1–16. DOI: 10.4018/IJeC.316828

Chen, J. (2025). *Writing and Revising in Second Language Classrooms: The Role of Self-Regulation in Cultivating Expert Writers*. Springer Nature.

Chen, J., & Liu, Y. (2024). Cost-benefit analysis of AI and VR integration in public art education in China. *Educational Technology Research and Development, 72*(1), 1–20.

Chen, L., & Wang, S. (2021). Digital technology and cultural heritage preservation in art education. *International Journal of Arts and Technology, 14*(3), 285–302.

Chen, Q., & Zhang, W. (2023). The application of AI and digital tools in fine arts education: A systematic review. *Journal of Educational Technology Research, 15*(2), 102–118.

Chen, T. (2016). Technology-supported peer feedback in ESL/EFL writing classes: A research synthesis. *Computer Assisted Language Learning, 29*(2), 365–397. DOI: 10.1080/09588221.2014.960942

Chen, W., Yang, K., Yu, Z., Shi, Y., & Chen, C. L. P. (2024). A survey on imbalanced learning: Latest research, applications and future directions. *Artificial Intelligence Review, 57*(6), 137. DOI: 10.1007/s10462-024-10759-6

Chen, X., Fischer, A., & Fink, G. A. (2023). Simple fine-tuning is all you need: Towards robust deep learning in handwritten text recognition. *arXiv*. https://arxiv.org/abs/2302.06308

Chen, X., & Liu, Y. (2024). Cost-benefit analysis of emerging educational technologies in public schools. *Journal of Educational Economics, 35*(2), 123–145.

Chen, Y. L., Hsu, C. C., Lin, C. Y., & Hsu, H. H. (2022). Robot-Assisted Language Learning: Integrating Artificial Intelligence and Virtual Reality into English Tour Guide Practice. *Education Sciences, 12*(7), 437. DOI: 10.3390/educsci12070437

Chen, Y., & Wang, L. (2021). Cultural appreciation and artistic retention through digital methods in fine arts education. *Journal of Educational Technology, 45*(3), 56–68.

Chetwynd, E. (2024). Ethical Use of Artificial Intelligence for Scientific Writing: Current Trends. *Journal of Human Lactation, 40*(2), 211–215. DOI: 10.1177/08903344241235160 PMID: 38482810

Chi, C., Md Yunus, M., & Rafiq, M., K. R., Hameed, H., & Ediyanto, E. (. (2024). A Systematic Review on Multidisciplinary Technological Approaches in Higher Education. *International Journal of Advanced Research in Future Ready Learning and Education, 36*(1), 1–10. DOI: 10.37934/frle.36.1.110

Ching, K. L., & Simon, S. (2025). Beyond the Best of Both Worlds: Student Perceptions of Hybrid Writing Courses. *College Composition and Communication, 76*(4), 494–517. DOI: 10.58680/ccc2025764494

Chin, H., & Chew, C. M. (2021). Profiling the research landscape on electronic feedback in educational context from 1991 to 2021: A bibliometric analysis. *Journal of Computers in Education, 8*(4), 551–586. DOI: 10.1007/s40692-021-00192-x

Chinnaraju, A. (2025). Explainable AI (XAI) for trustworthy and transparent decision-making: A theoretical framework for AI interpretability. *World Journal of Advanced Engineering Technology and Sciences, 14*(3), 170–207. DOI: 10.30574/wjaets.2025.14.3.0106

Choi, J., Yang, E., & Goo, E. (2024). The effects of an ethics education program on artificial intelligence among middle school students: Analysis of perception and attitude changes. *Applied Sciences (Basel, Switzerland), 14*(4), 1588. DOI: 10.3390/app14041588

Chong, I. (2018). Interplay among technical, socio-emotional and personal factors in written feedback research. *Assessment & Evaluation in Higher Education, 43*(2), 185–196. DOI: 10.1080/02602938.2017.1317712

Choudhry, M. D., Sundarrajan, M., & Sundaram, K. (2024). Bias and Fairness in Generative AI. *Generative AI and LLMs: Natural Language Processing and Generative Adversarial Networks*, 177.

Chowdhury Niloy, A., Hafiz, R., Hossain, B. M. T., Gulmeher, F., Sultana, N., Islam, K. F., Bushra, F., Islam, S., Hoque, S. I., Rahman, M. A., & Kabir, S. (2024). AI chatbots: A disguised enemy for academic integrity? *International Journal of Educational Research Open, 6*, 100396. DOI: 10.1016/j.ijedro.2024.100396

Chubb, J., Reed, D., & Cowling, P. (2024). Expert views about missing AI narratives: Is there an AI story crisis? *AI & Society, 39*(3), 1107–1126. DOI: 10.1007/s00146-022-01548-2 PMID: 36039046

Churi, P. P., Joshi, S., Elhoseny, M., & Omrane, A. (2022). *Artificial Intelligence in Higher Education*. CRC Press., DOI: 10.1201/9781003184157

Çiçek, M., & Kayaoğlu, M. N. (2024). Exploring The Impact Of Form And Content Feedback On Efl Writing Proficiency: A Quasi-Experimental Study. *Studies in Linguistics Culture and Flt, 12*(3), 31–56. DOI: 10.46687/PLYN8876

Çiftçi, A. (2024). *AI-assisted teaching: Practices and perspectives of instructors on using AI tools in ELT* (Unpublished master's thesis). Maltepe University, Türkiye.

Citron, D. K. (2024). The surveilled student. *Stanford Law Review, 76*, 1439–1472. https://review.law.stanford.edu/wp-content/uploads/sites/3/2024/10/Citron-76-Stan.-L.-Rev.-1439.pdf

Clemson University. (n.d.). AI in academic writing. Retrieved July 26, 2025, from https://www.clemson.edu/centers-institutes/writing/writing-resources/writing-resources/ai-in-academic-writing.html

College of Computer Studies. University of Antique, Sibalom, Antique, Philippines, Mission, R., Fio, R. J., Philippine Merchant Marine School Inc., Las Pinas, Philippines, Mission, A. R., & Barangbang National High School, San Remigio, Antique, Philippines. (2024). AI-Powered Pedagogy: Integrating Artificial Intelligence in Information Technology Education for Future Workforce Readiness. *Journal of Innovative Technology Convergence, 6*(4), 69–86. DOI: 10.69478/JITC2024v6n4a06

Conole, G., Dyke, M., Oliver, M., & Seale, J. (2004). Mapping pedagogy and tools for effective learning design. *Computers & Education, 43*(1–2), 17–33. DOI: 10.1016/j.compedu.2003.12.018

Cope, B., Kalantzis, M., & Searsmith, D. (2021). Artificial intelligence for education: Knowledge and its assessment in AI-enabled learning ecologies. *Educational Philosophy and Theory, 53*(12), 1229–1245. DOI: 10.1080/00131857.2020.1728732

Corbeil, J. R. (2025). The Future of Learning: AI-Driven Education in 2040. In *Teaching and Learning in the Age of Generative AI* (pp. 362–390). Routledge. DOI: 10.4324/9781032688602-22

Corbin, T., Dawson, P., Nicola-Richmond, K., & Partridge, H. (2025). 'Where's the line? It's an absurd line': Towards a framework for acceptable uses of AI in assessment. *Assessment & Evaluation in Higher Education,* •••, 1–13. DOI: 10.1080/02602938.2025.2553340

Corpuz, L. O., Lardizabal, E. N., Torno, A. G., Gabayan, V. P.Jr, Pandey, P., & Bautista, R. G. (2025). Dreams and Wishes: The Dawn of AI in the Education Setting. *American Journal of Educational Research, 13*(1), 17–22. DOI: 10.12691/education-13-1-2

Costa, P., & Joaquim, A. F. (2025). AI and Digital Literacy: Preparing Learners for a Technologically Advanced Sustainable Future. In *Rethinking Literacy in the Era of Sustainability and Artificial Intelligence* (pp. 73-98). IGI Global Scientific Publishing.

Cotos, E. (2023). *Automated Feedback on Writing.* In *Advances in Writing Technology* (pp. ...). Springer. DOI: 10.1007/978-3-031-36033-6_22

Cotton, D. R. E., Cotton, P. A., & Shipway, J. R. (2024). Chatting and cheating: Ensuring academic integrity in the era of ChatGPT. *Innovations in Education and Teaching International, 61*(2), 146–155. DOI: 10.1080/14703297.2023.2190148

Crossley, S., Müldner, K., & McNamara, D. (2016). Idea generation in student writing. *Written Communication, 33*(3), 328–354. DOI: 10.1177/0741088316650178

Cukurova, M. (2025). The interplay of learning, analytics and artificial intelligence in education: A vision for hybrid intelligence. *British Journal of Educational Technology, 56*(2), 469–488. DOI: 10.1111/bjet.13514

Culot, G., Nassimbeni, G., Orzes, G., & Sartor, M. (2020). Behind the definition of Industry 4.0: Analysis and open questions. *International Journal of Production Economics, 226*, 107617. DOI: 10.1016/j.ijpe.2020.107617

Cumming, A. (1989). Writing expertise and second-language proficiency*. *Language Learning, 39*(1), 81–135. DOI: 10.1111/j.1467-1770.1989.tb00592.x

Cunningham, K. J. (2019). Student Perceptions and Use of Technology-Mediated Text and Screencast Feedback in ESL Writing. *Computers and Composition, 52*, 222–241. DOI: 10.1016/j.compcom.2019.02.003

Cunningham, K. J., & Link, S. (2021). Video and text feedback on ESL writing: Understanding ATTITUDE and negotiating relationshipS. *Journal of Second Language Writing, 52*, 100797. Advance online publication. DOI: 10.1016/j.jslw.2021.100797

Cuocci, S., Fattahi Marnani, P., Khan, I., & Roberts, S. (2023). A Meta-Synthesis of Technology-Supported Peer Feedback in ESL/EFL Writing Classes Research: A Replication of Chen's Study. *Languages (Basel, Switzerland), 8*(2), 114. Advance online publication. DOI: 10.3390/languages8020114

D'Souza, R., Mathew, M., Mishra, V., & Surapaneni, K. (2024). Twelve tips for addressing ethical concerns in the implementation of artificial intelligence in medical education. *Medical Education Online, 29*(1), 2330250. Advance online publication. DOI: 10.1080/10872981.2024.2330250 PMID: 38566608

Dai, Y., Lai, S., Lim, C. P., & Liu, A. (2024). University policies on generative AI in Asia: Promising practices, gaps, and future directions. *Journal of Asian Public Policy, 44*(3), 260–281. DOI: 10.1080/17516234.2024.2379070

Dakakni, D. (2023). Artificial intelligence in the L2 classroom: Implications and challenges on ethics and equity in higher education: A 21st century Pandora's box. *Computers & Education.*

Dan, L., Mohamed, H. B., & Abuhassna, H. (2026). A bibliometric analysis of artificial intelligence: Impact on student motivation in education. In B. Edwards, H. Abuhassna, D. Olugbade, O. Ojo, & W. Jaafar Wan Yahaya (Eds.), *AI in education, governance, and leadership: Adoption, impact, and ethics* (pp. 97–120). IGI Global Scientific Publishing. https://doi.org/DOI: 10.4018/979-8-3373-5550-4.ch005

Dash, S., Shakyawar, S. K., Sharma, M., & Kaushik, S. (2019). Big data in healthcare: Management, analysis and future prospects. *Journal of Big Data, 6*(1), 54. Advance online publication. DOI: 10.1186/s40537-019-0217-0

Dawson, P. (2020). *Defending assessment security in a digital world: Preventing e-cheating and supporting academic integrity in Higher Education* (1st ed.). Routledge., DOI: 10.4324/9780429324178

De Villiers, C. (2024). The impact of society 5.0 on curriculum development in higher education. *Journal of Ethics in Higher Education, 4*(4), 1–25. DOI: 10.26034/fr.jehe.2024.5953

Dean, G. (1992). The bottom line: Effect size. *The Skeptical Inquirer, 16*(3), 270–276.

Deberdt, R., Le Billon, P., Makinde, O., Dauvergne, P., Solwati, T., Razmi, S., Kumar, G., & Belhabib, D. (2025). Artificial intelligence and ESG in resources-intensive industries: Reviewing the use of AI in fisheries, mining, plastics, and forestry. *The Extractive Industries and Society, 23*, 101690. DOI: 10.1016/j.exis.2025.101690

Dempere, J., Modugu, K., Allam, H., & Ramasamy, L. K. (2023). The impact of ChatGPT on higher education. *Frontiers in Education, 8*, 1206936. DOI: 10.3389/feduc.2023.1206936

Department of Curriculum and Instruction, Kulliyyah of Education, International Islamic University Malaysia, Malaysia, Ismail, H., Shazwan, N. I. M., & Kulliyyah of Education, International Islamic University Malaysia, Malaysia. (2025). *Contemporary Pedagogical Approach in Teaching Islamic Education: Navigating Challenges and Considerations*. 81–93. DOI: 10.32789/edcon.2024.3108

Derakhshan, A., Teo, T., Saeedy Robat, E., Janebi Enayat, M., & Jahanbakhsh, A. A. (2025). Robot-assisted language learning: A meta-analysis. *Review of Educational Research, 95*(4), 747–774. DOI: 10.3102/00346543241247227

Dergaa, I., Chamari, K., Żmijewski, P., & Saad, H. (2023). From human writing to artificial intelligence generated text: Examining the prospects and potential threats of chatgpt in academic writing. *Biology of Sport*, *40*(2), 615–622. DOI: 10.5114/biolsport.2023.125623 PMID: 37077800

Deriba, F. G., & Sanusi, I. T. (2025). Artificial intelligence in Ethiopian school curriculum: Educators' practices, challenges, and recommendations. *Computers and Education Open*, *8*, 100251. DOI: 10.1016/j.caeo.2025.100251

Deri, M. N., Zaazie, P., & Singh, A. (2024). Digital Future of the Hospitality Industry and Hospitality Education Globally. In Sharma, A. (Ed.), *International Handbook of Skill, Education, Learning, and Research Development in Tourism and Hospitality. Springer International Handbooks of Education*. Springer., DOI: 10.1007/978-981-97-4318-6_14

Dewangan, S., Kumar, S., & Tyagi, P. K. (2024). Transforming Hospitality and Tourism With AI and Innovative Technologies. In Talukder, M. B., Kumar, S., & Tyagi, P. K. (Eds.), *Advances in Hospitality, Tourism, and the Services Industry* (pp. 66–83). IGI Global., DOI: 10.4018/979-8-3693-6755-1.ch004

Dhiraj, A., & Kumar, P. D. S. (2023). Impact of E-learning on the Higher Education Sector during the COVID-19 pandemic through Pedagogy tools: An observational Study. *Revista de Educación y Derecho*, *27*(27). Advance online publication. DOI: 10.1344/REYD2023.27.40935

Dhiraj, A., Kumar, S., & Rani, D. (2023a). Social and Emotional Learning: Keys to the Success of E-Learning. In Sharma, P. C., Bansal, R., & Singh, R. (Eds.), (pp. 119–130). Advances in Educational Technologies and Instructional Design. IGI Global., DOI: 10.4018/978-1-6684-7639-0.ch008

Dhiraj, A., Kumar, S., & Rani, D. (2023b). Use of Social Media by SMEs in the Tourism Industry. In Qalati, S. A., Ostic, D., & Bansal, R. (Eds.), (pp. 221–233). Advances in Business Strategy and Competitive Advantage. IGI Global., DOI: 10.4018/978-1-6684-5770-2.ch014

di Zhang, E., Liu, C., & Yu, S. (2024). The impact of a feedback intervention on university students' second language writing feedback literacy. *Innovations in Education and Teaching International*, *61*(3), 426–442. DOI: 10.1080/14703297.2023.2254275

Dillenbourg, P., & Jermann, P. (2010). Technology for classroom orchestration. In Khine, M. S., & Saleh, I. M. (Eds.), *New science of learning* (pp. 525–552). Springer. DOI: 10.1007/978-1-4419-5716-0_26

Ding, D., & Yusof, M. B. (2025). Investigating the role of AI-powered conversation bots in enhancing L2 speaking skills and reducing speaking anxiety: A mixed methods study. *Humanities & Social Sciences Communications*, *12*(1), 1–16. DOI: 10.1057/s41599-025-05550-z

Do, H. M. (2024). E-peer feedback training on L2 writing: A case study of inexperienced learners. *The JALT CALL Journal*, *20*(1), 1–22. DOI: 10.29140/jaltcall.v20n1.1242

Donato, R. (2016). Sociocultural theory and the zone of proximal development. In van Deusen-Scholl, N., & Hornberger, N. (Eds.), *Encyclopedia of language and education*. Springer.

Douglas, S. et al. “Use of an online peer review tool to support feedback and collaborative skills in preservice teachers.” *CITE Journal*, Vol. 21 (2) (2021). CITE Journal • Fan, N. & Ma, Y. “The effects of automated writing evaluation (AWE) feedback on students’ English writing quality: A systematic literature review.” *Language Teaching Research Quarterly*, 2022.

Dunn, R., Honigsfeld, A., Doolan, L. S., Bostrom, L., Russo, K., Schiering, M. S., Suh, B., & Tenedero, H. (2009). Impact of Learning-Style Instructional Strategies on Students’ Achievement and Attitudes: Perceptions of Educators in Diverse Institutions. *The Clearing House: A Journal of Educational Strategies, Issues and Ideas*, *82*(3), 135–140. DOI: 10.3200/TCHS.82.3.135-140

Durak, H. (2025). A comparison of human-written versus AI-generated text in discussions at educational settings: Investigating features for ChatGPT, Gemini and Bingai. *European Journal of Education*, *60*(1), e70014. Advance online publication. DOI: 10.1111/ejed.70014

Dwivedi, Y. K., Hughes, L., Baabdullah, A. M., Ribeiro-Navarrete, S., Giannakis, M., Al-Debei, M. M., Dennehy, D., Metri, B., Buhalis, D., Cheung, C. M., Conboy, K., Doyle, R., Dubey, R., Dutot, V., Felix, R., Goyal, D., Gustafsson, A., Hinsch, C., Jebabli, I., & Wamba, S. F. (2022). Metaverse beyond the hype: Multidisciplinary perspectives on emerging challenges, opportunities, and agenda for research, practice and policy. *International Journal of Information Management*, *66*, 102542. DOI: 10.1016/j.ijinfomgt.2022.102542

Dwivedi, Y. K., Hughes, L., Ismagilova, E., Aarts, G., Coombs, C., Crick, T., Duan, Y., Dwivedi, R., Edwards, J., Eirug, A., Galanos, V., Ilavarasan, P. V., Janssen, M., Jones, P., Kar, A. K., Kizgin, H., Kronemann, B., Lal, B., Lucini, B., & Williams, M. D. (2019). Artificial Intelligence (AI): Multidisciplinary perspectives on emerging challenges, opportunities, and agenda for research, practice and policy. *International Journal of Information Management*, *57*, 101994. DOI: 10.1016/j.ijinfomgt.2019.08.002

Dwivedi, Y. K., Ismagilova, E., Hughes, D. L., Carlson, J., Filieri, R., Jacobson, J., Jain, V., Karjaluoto, H., Kefi, H., Krishen, A. S., Kumar, V., Rahman, M. M., Raman, R., Rauschnabel, P. A., Rowley, J., Salo, J., Tran, G. A., & Wang, Y. (2020). Setting the future of digital and social media marketing research: Perspectives and research propositions. *International Journal of Information Management*, *59*, 102168. DOI: 10.1016/j.ijinfomgt.2020.102168

Effah Kwabena, A., Wiafe, O.-B., Boakye-Danquah, J., Asare, B., & Frimpong, A. F. B. (2023). An automated method for developing search strategies for systematic review using Natural Language Processing (NLP). https://doi.org/https://doi.org/10.1016/j.mex.2022.101935

Ekizoğlu, M., & Demir, A. (2025). Ai-assisted writing feedback for enhancing secondary students’ writing skills: an experimental study. https://doi.org/DOI: 10.21203/rs.3.rs-6430737/v1

Elaiess, R. (2024). *Academic Integrity in the Age of Artificial Intelligence: Exploring Ethical Challenges in a Digital Era. International Journal of Academic Multidisciplinary Research*. IJAMR.

Eldakar, M., Shehata, A., & Ammar, A. (2025). What motivates academics in Egypt toward generative ai tools? an integrated model of TAM, SCT, UTAUT2, perceived ethics, and academic integrity. *Information Development*, *41*(3), 747–765. DOI: 10.1177/02666669251314859

Elkatmiş, M. (2024). Chat GPT and creative writing: Experiences of master's students in enhancing. *International Journal of Contemporary Educational Research, 11*(3), 321–336. DOI: 10.52380/ijcer.2024.11.3.597

Elkhatat, A. M., Elsaid, K., & Almeer, S. (2023). Evaluating the efficacy of AI content detection tools in differentiating between human and AI-generated text. *International Journal for Educational Integrity, 19*(1), 17. DOI: 10.1007/s40979-023-00140-5

Ellis, R. A., Pardo, A., & Han, F. (2016). Quality in blended learning environments – Significant differences in how students approach learning collaborations. *Computers & Education, 102*, 90–102. DOI: 10.1016/j.compedu.2016.07.006

ElSayary, A. (2024). Integrating Generative AI in Active Learning Environments: Enhancing Metacognition and Technological Skills. *Journal of Systemics, Cybernetics and Informatics, 22*(3), 34–37. DOI: 10.54808/JSCI.22.03.34

Elviani, M., & Liani, G. (2025). The Use of ChatGPT Feedback on Writing Quality: A Content Analysis of Students' Writing Assignment. *AL LUGHAWIYAAT, 6(1).*

Emanuel, J. (2013). Users and citation management tools: Use and support. *RSR. Reference Services Review, 41*(4), 639–659. DOI: 10.1108/RSR-02-2013-0007

Engeström, Y. (2001). Expansive learning at work: Toward an activity-theoretical reconceptualization. *Journal of Education and Work, 14*(1), 133–156. DOI: 10.1080/13639080020028747

Er, E., Akçapınar, G., Bayazıt, A., Noroozi, O., & Banihashem, S. K. (2025). Assessing student perceptions and use of instructor versus AI-generated feedback. *British Journal of Educational Technology, 56*(3), 1074–1091. DOI: 10.1111/bjet.13558

Ergashev, A. (2023). Privacy concerns and data protection in an era of ai surveillance technologies. *International Journal of Law and Criminology, 3*(08), 71–76.

Escalante, J., Pack, A., & Barrett, A. (2023). AI-generated feedback on writing: Insights into efficacy and ENL student preference. *International Journal of Educational Technology in Higher Education, 20*(1), 57. DOI: 10.1186/s41239-023-00425-2

Esiyok, E., Gokcearslan, S., & Kucukergin, K. G. (2025). Acceptance of educational use of AI chatbots in the context of self-directed learning with technology and ICT self-efficacy of undergraduate students. *International Journal of Human-Computer Interaction, 41*(1), 641–650. DOI: 10.1080/10447318.2024.2303557

Esmaeily, J., & Mahdavi Zafarghandi, A. (2025). The Impact of AI-Driven Feedback on Iranian EFL Teachers' Reflective Practice. *Iranian Journal of English for Academic Purposes, 14*(2), 79–94.

European Union. (2016). *Regulation (EU) 2016/679 of the European Parliament and of the Council of 27 April 2016 on the protection of natural persons with regard to the processing of personal data and on the free movement of such data (General Data Protection Regulation). Official Journal of the European Union, L119,* 1–88. https://eur-lex.europa.eu/eli/reg/2016/679/oj

Eynon, R., & Young, E. (2020). Methodology, legend, and rhetoric: The constructions of ai by academia, industry, and policy groups for lifelong learning. *Science, Technology & Human Values, 46*(1), 166–191. DOI: 10.1177/0162243920906475

Faigley, L., & Witte, S. (1981). Analyzing revision. *College Composition and Communication*, *32*(4), 400–414. DOI: 10.58680/ccc198115887

Fakher Ajabshir, Z. (2024). A Comparative Study of Teacher Feedback and Chatbot Feedback on Second Language Learners' Pragmalinguistic and Sociopragmatic Competences. *International Journal of Human-Computer Interaction*, •••, 1–12.

Falebita, O. (2025). Evaluating artificial intelligence anxiety among pre-service teachers in university teacher education programs. *Journal of Mathematics Instruction. Social Research and Opinion*, *4*(1), 1–16.

Fang, Y., Tan, Y., Zuo, C., & Boubaker, A. (2025). *AI-generated vs. peer feedback in ESL writing: Effects on writing skill, self-efficacy, and enjoyment* (SSRN preprint). They compare AI feedback, peer feedback, and writing outcomes. DOI: 10.2139/ssrn.5115438

Fan, Y., Tan, S., & Lim, G. Y. W. (2024). EAP teacher feedback in the age of AI: Supporting first-year students in EFL disciplinary writing. *Australian Journal of Applied Linguistics*, *7*(3), 1943–1943. DOI: 10.29140/ajal.v7n3.1943

Farnia, M., Hemmati, F., Yekta, R. R., & Mirsayafi, S. (2025). The Impact of Multimodal Feedback on Writing Complexity, Accuracy, and Fluency of Iranian EFL Learners in Flipped and Traditional Classrooms. *Journal of Applied Linguistics and Applied Literature*, *13*(1), 109–130. DOI: 10.22049/jalda.2025.30042.1731

Fauziah, Z., & Minarti, S. (2023). Artificial Intelligence-Assisted Writing Application for Improving Writing Skills of Islamic Education Students. *Jurnal Kependidikan Islam*, *13*(2), 119–123. DOI: 10.15642/jkpi.2023.13.2.119-123

Federiakin, D., Molerov, D., Zlatkin-Troitschanskaia, O., & Maur, A. (2024). Prompt engineering as a new 21st century skill. *Frontiers in Education*, *9*, 1366434. Advance online publication. DOI: 10.3389/feduc.2024.1366434

Fernández-Sánchez, A., Lorenzo-Castiñeiras, J. J., & Sánchez-Bello, A. (2025). Navigating the Future of Pedagogy: The Integration of AI Tools in Developing Educational Assessment Rubrics. *European Journal of Education*, *60*(1), e12826. DOI: 10.1111/ejed.12826

Ferrigno, G., Di Paola, N., Oguntegbe, K. F., & Kraus, S. (2023). Value creation in the metaverse age: A thematic analysis of press releases. *International Journal of Entrepreneurial Behaviour & Research*, *29*(11), 337–363. DOI: 10.1108/IJEBR-01-2023-0039

Ferrigno, G., Martin, X., & Dagnino, G. B. (2024). Explaining the interplay of value creation and value appropriation in strategic alliances: A developmental perspective. *International Journal of Management Reviews*, *26*(2), 232–253. DOI: 10.1111/ijmr.12351

Fitas, R. (2025). Inclusive education with AI: Supporting special needs and tackling language barriers. *AI and Ethics*, *5*(6), 5729–5757. Advance online publication. DOI: 10.1007/s43681-025-00824-3

Fithriani, R. (2019). ZPD and the benefits of written feedback in L2 writing: Focusing on students' perceptions. *The Reading Matrix: An International Online Journal*, *19*(1), 63–73.

Fitria, T. (2021). The use technology based on artificial intelligence in english teaching and learning). *Elt Echo the Journal of English Language Teaching in Foreign Language Context*, *6*(2). Advance online publication. DOI: 10.24235/eltecho.v6i2.9299

Fleckenstein, J., Zacher, J., & Schilling, S. (2023). Automated feedback and writing: A multi-level meta-analysis of effects on students' performance. *Frontiers in Artificial Intelligence*, *6*, 1162454. Advance online publication. DOI: 10.3389/frai.2023.1162454 PMID: 37465061

Flores, L., Kim, S., & Young, S. D. (2023). Addressing bias in artificial intelligence for public health surveillance. Journal of Medical Ethics, jme-108875. https://doi.org/DOI: 10.1136/jme-2022-108875

Floridi, L., & Chiriatti, M. (2020). GPT-3: Its nature, scope, limits, and consequences. *Minds and Machines*, *30*(4), 681–694. DOI: 10.1007/s11023-020-09548-1

Floridi, L., & Cowls, J. (2021). A unified framework of five principles for AI in society. *Harvard Data Science Review*, *3*(1). Advance online publication. DOI: 10.1162/99608f92.8cd550d1

Floridi, L., Cowls, J., Beltrametti, M., Chatila, R., Chazerand, P., Dignum, V., Luetge, C., Madelin, R., Pagallo, U., Rossi, F., Schafer, B., Valcke, P., & Vayena, E. (2018). AI4People—An ethical framework for a good AI society. *Minds and Machines*, *28*(4), 689–707. DOI: 10.1007/s11023-018-9482-5 PMID: 30930541

Foltynek, T., Bjelobaba, S., Glendinning, I., Khan, Z. R., Santos, R., Pavletic, P., & Kravjar, J. (2023). ENAI Recommendations on the ethical use of Artificial Intelligence in Education. *International Journal for Educational Integrity*, *19*(1), 12. DOI: 10.1007/s40979-023-00133-4

Foltýnek, T., Dlabolová, D., Anohina-Naumeca, A., Razı, S., Kravjar, J., Kamzola, L., Guerrero-Dib, J., Çelik, Ö., & Weber-Wulff, D. (2020). Testing of support tools for plagiarism detection. *International Journal of Educational Technology in Higher Education*, *17*(1), 46. Advance online publication. DOI: 10.1186/s41239-020-00192-4

Ford, N., & Minshall, J. (2019). ICT tools for enhancing accessibility in traditional art education. *Journal of Visual Arts Education*, *35*(1), 34–45.

Freire, P. (1970). Pedagogy of the oppressed. *Continuum : an Interdisciplinary Journal on Continuity of Care*.

Fung, K. Y., Fung, K. C., Lui, T. L. R., Sin, K. F., Lee, L. H., Qu, H., & Song, S. (2025). Exploring the impact of robot interaction on learning engagement: A comparative study of two multi-modal robots. *Smart Learning Environments*, *12*(1), 12. DOI: 10.1186/s40561-024-00362-1

Gagiu, D., & Sendrescu, D. (2025). Detection of personality traits using handwriting and deep learning. *Applied Sciences (Basel, Switzerland)*, *15*(4), 2154. DOI: 10.3390/app15042154

Garcia, M. B. (2024). The paradox of artificial creativity: Challenges and opportunities of generative AI artistry. *Creativity Research Journal*, •••, 1–14.

García-Méndez, S., de Arriba-Pérez, F., & Somoza-López, M. D. C. (2025). A review on the use of large language models as virtual tutors. *Science & Education*, *34*(2), 877–892. DOI: 10.1007/s11191-024-00530-2

García, O., & Wei, L. (2014). *Translanguaging: Language, bilingualism and education*. Palgrave Macmillan. DOI: 10.1057/9781137385765

García-Rudolph, A., Sanchez-Pinsach, D., Opisso, E., & Soler, M. D. (2025). Exploring new educational approaches in neuropathic pain: Assessing accuracy and consistency of artificial intelligence responses from GPT-3.5 and GPT-4. *Pain Medicine*, *26*(1), 48–50. DOI: 10.1093/pm/pnae094

Garg, A., Singh, A., & Yanan, J. (2024). Exploring the Impact of Digital Detoxification on Higher Education Students' Learning. In Grima, S., Chaudhary, S., Sood, K., & Kumar, S. (Eds.), *Business Drivers in Promoting Digital Detoxification* (pp. 111–126). IGI Global Scientific Publishing., DOI: 10.4018/979-8-3693-1107-3.ch008

Garrett, N., Beard, N., & Fiesler, C. "More than" If Time Allows" the role of ethics in AI education." In *Proceedings of the AAAI/ACM Conference on AI, Ethics, and Society*, pp. 272-278. 2020. DOI: 10.1145/3375627.3375868

Garrison, D. R., & Vaughan, N. D. (2008). *Blended learning in higher education: Framework, principles, and guidelines*. Jossey-Bass.

Gaunov, S. R., Baymuradov, U. G., & Sitnikov, S. Yu. (2024). Machine learning in python: using tensorflow and scikit-learn libraries. Èkonomika i Upravlenie: Problemy, Rešeniâ, 12/8(153), 72–81. https://doi.org/DOI: 10.36871/ek.up.p.r.2024.12.08.009

Gaur, S., Sharma, M., & Sharma, U. (2025). Machine Learning: A Revolution of News Writing and Digital Era. Journal of Electrical Systems, 21.

Gaur, L., Rana, J., & Jhanjhi, N. Z. (2023). *"Digital twin and healthcare research agenda and bibliometric analysis." Digital Twins and Healthcare: Trends*. Techniques, and Challenges.

Gavrilescu, M., & Vizireanu, N. (2018). Predicting the Big Five personality traits from handwriting. *EURASIP Journal on Image and Video Processing*, *2018*(1), 57. DOI: 10.1186/s13640-018-0297-3

Gavrilescu, M., & Vizireanu, N. (2021). Domain adaptation strategies for Arabic handwriting recognition using deep learning. *Neural Computing & Applications*, *34*, 7537–7553. DOI: 10.1007/s00521-021-06520-7

Gayed, J. M., Carlon, M. K. J., Oriola, A. M., & Cross, J. S. (2022). Exploring an AI-based writing Assistant's impact on English language learners. *Computers and Education: Artificial Intelligence*, *3*, 100055. DOI: 10.1016/j.caeai.2022.100055

Gedik, N., Kiraz, E., & Ozden, M. Y. (2013). Design of a blended learning environment: Considerations and implementation issues. *Australasian Journal of Educational Technology*, *29*(1). Advance online publication. DOI: 10.14742/ajet.6

Geetha, V. (2025). AI-Driven Assessment and Feedback Systems: Transforming Education Through Intelligent Automation. *Multidisciplinary Research in Arts, Science & Commerce (Volume-23)*, 9.

Geetha, R. (2025). Digital Pedagogy and Cognitive Writing in English Language Classroom. In *Thinking Skills in Higher Education* (pp. 245–259). Springer. DOI: 10.1007/978-981-96-5600-4_19

George, A. S. (2023). Preparing students for an AI-driven world: Rethinking curriculum and pedagogy in the age of artificial intelligence. *Partners Universal Innovative Research Publication, 1*(2), 112–136.

Geroimenko, V. (2025). *The Essential Guide to Prompt Engineering*. Springer Nature Switzerland., DOI: 10.1007/978-3-031-86206-9

Gero, K. I. (2023). *AI and the Writer: How Language Models Support Creative Writers*. Columbia University.

Géron, A. (2017). Hands-On Machine Learning with Scikit-Learn and TensorFlow: Concepts, Tools, and Techniques to Build Intelligent Systems. https://www.amazon.com/Hands-Machine-Learning-Scikit-Learn-TensorFlow/dp/1491962291

Ghafouri, M., Hassaskhah, J., & Mahdavi-Zafarghandi, A. (2024). From virtual assistant to writing mentor: Exploring the impact of a ChatGPT-based writing instruction protocol on EFL teachers' self-efficacy and learners' writing skill. *Language Teaching Research*, •••, 13621688241239764. DOI: 10.1177/13621688241239764

Ghimire, P. R., Neupane, B. P., & Dahal, N. (2024). Generative AI and AI tools in English language teaching and learning: An exploratory research. *English Language Teaching Perspectives, 9*(1-2), 30–40. DOI: 10.3126/eltp.v9i1-2.68716

Ghorbandordinejad, F., & Kenshinbay, T. (2024). Exploring AI-Driven Adaptive Feedback in the Second Language Writing Skills Prompt: AI Technology in Language Teaching. *EIKI Journal of Effective Teaching Methods, 2(3).*

Ghosh, R. K., Chakraborty, S., & Dutta, G. (2025). AI in Enhancing Bilingual Proficiency. In Advances in computational intelligence and robotics book series (pp. 141–176). DOI: 10.4018/979-8-3373-0275-1.ch005

Ghosh, R. K., Gupta, B., Dutta, G., & Chakraborty, S. (2025). Measuring Success: Evaluating the Impact of Reskilling and Upskilling. In Reskilling and Upskilling in the Age of AI (1st ed., pp. 200–217). DOI: 10.1201/9781003611677-11

Giannakos, M., Azevedo, R., Brusilovsky, P., Cukurova, M., Dimitriadis, Y., Hernandez-Leo, D., Järvelä, S., Mavrikis, M., & Rienties, B. (2024). The promise and challenges of generative AI in education. *Behaviour & Information Technology*, •••, 1–27.

Gilligan, C. (1982). *In a different voice: Psychological theory and women's development*. Harvard University Press.

Giray, L. (2024). The problem with false positives: AI detection unfairly accuses scholars of AI plagiarism. *The Serials Librarian, 85*(5–6), 181–189. DOI: 10.1080/0361526X.2024.2433256

Göçen, A., & Aydemir, F. (2020). Artificial intelligence in education and schools. *Research on Education and Media, 12*(1), 13–21. DOI: 10.2478/rem-2020-0003

Goh, K. M., Mansor, M., Syariff, M., Fuad, D. R., & Juharyanto, J. (2025). Designing Future-Ready Education: Criteria for AI Learning Tool Selection and AI Learning Design. *Semarak International Journal of Innovation in Learning and Education, 4*(1), 1–12. DOI: 10.37934/sijile.4.1.112a

Gonsalves, C. (2024). Addressing student non-compliance in AI use declarations: Implications for academic integrity and assessment in higher education. *Assessment & Evaluation in Higher Education, 50*(4), 592–606. DOI: 10.1080/02602938.2024.2415654

Gonsalves, C. (2024). Generative ai's impact on critical thinking: Revisiting bloom's taxonomy. *Journal of Marketing Education*, 02734753241305980. Advance online publication. DOI: 10.1177/02734753241305980

Gonzalez-Torres, P., Cabrera-Solano, P., & Castillo-Cuesta, L. (2022). Exploring Perceptions of Online Feedback in Teaching EFL Speaking and Writing Skills during the COVID-19 Pandemic. *International Journal of Learning Teaching and Educational Research*, *21*(7), 330–344. DOI: 10.26803/ijlter.21.7.17

Gorbatkova, O., Kochergina, O., & Kiryushina, O. (2021). Digital environment as effective pedagogical tool of socialization in the context of modern education. *E3S Web of Conferences, 273*, 12087. DOI: 10.1051/e3sconf/202127312087

Graham, S., Kiuhara, S. A., & MacKay, M. (2020). The effects of writing on learning in science, social studies, and mathematics: A meta-analysis. *Review of Educational Research, 90*(2), 179–226. DOI: 10.3102/0034654320914744

Grassini, S. (2023). Shaping the Future of Education: Exploring the potential and consequences of AI and ChatGPT in educational settings. *Education Sciences, 13*(7), 692. DOI: 10.3390/educsci13070692

Gregersen, T., Mercer, S., & MacIntyre, P. (2021). Language teacher perspectives on stress and coping. *Foreign Language Annals*, *54*(4), 1145–1163. DOI: 10.1111/flan.12544

Gretzky, M., & Dishon, G. (2025). Algorithmic-authors in academia: Blurring the boundaries of human and machine knowledge production. *Learning, Media and Technology*, *50*(3), 1–14. DOI: 10.1080/17439884.2025.2452196

Guardado, M., & Shi, L. (2007). ESL students' experiences of online peer feedback. *Computers and Composition*, *24*(4), 443–461. DOI: 10.1016/j.compcom.2007.03.002

Guo, H. Y., & Zaini, S. H. (2024). Artificial Intelligence in Academic Writing: A Literature Review. *Asian Pendidikan*, *4*(4), 46–55. DOI: 10.53797/aspen.v4i2.6.2024

Guo, H., & Wu, L. (2025). Ethical considerations in AI and VR-assisted art education: A Chinese perspective. *Journal of Moral Education*, *54*(1), 1–18.

Guo, K. (2024). EvaluMate: Using AI to support students' feedback literacy in peer review. *Computers & Education*, *208*, 104877. DOI: 10.1016/j.compedu.2024.104877

Guo, K., & Wang, D. (2024). To resist it or to embrace it? Examining ChatGPT's potential to support teacher feedback in EFL writing. *Education and Information Technologies*, *29*(7), 8435–8463. DOI: 10.1007/s10639-023-12146-0

Guo, K., Zhang, E. D., Li, D., & Yu, S. (2025). Using AI-supported peer review to enhance feedback literacy. *British Journal of Educational Technology*, *56*(2), 451–469. DOI: 10.1111/bjet.13540

Guo, S., Wang, Y., Yu, J., Wu, X., Ayik, B., Watts, F. M., Latif, E., Liu, N., & Zhai, L. (2025). Artificial intelligence bias on English language learners in automatic scoring. *arXiv Preprint.* https://arxiv.org/abs/2505.10643 DOI: 10.1007/978-3-031-98462-4_34

Guo, Y., Hao, Z., Zhao, S., Gong, J., & Yang, F. (2020). Artificial intelligence in health care: Bibliometric analysis. *Journal of Medical Internet Research, 22*(7), e18228. DOI: 10.2196/18228 PMID: 32723713

Gupta, S., Jaiswal, A., Paramasivam, A., & Kotecha, J. "Academic writing challenges and supports: Perspectives of international doctoral students and their supervisors." In *Frontiers in Education*, vol. 7, p. 891534. Frontiers Media SA, 2022. DOI: 10.3389/feduc.2022.891534

Gupta, V. (2025). AI experimentation policy for libraries: Balancing innovation and data privacy. *Public Library Quarterly*, •••, 1–21.

Gyawali, Y., & Mehandroo, M. (2022). Artificial intelligence in english language teaching: Navigating the future with emerging perspectives. *Journal of Language and Linguistics in Society*, (26), 21–27. DOI: 10.55529/jlls.26.21.27

Haber, E., Jemielniak, D., Kurasiński, A., & Przegalińska, A. (2025). *Using AI in Academic Writing and Research: A Complete Guide to Effective and Ethical Academic AI.* Springer Nature. DOI: 10.1007/978-3-031-91705-9

Hall, S. (n.d.). *Prompt Engineering for Teachers: Making the Most of AI, Part 1.* Thinking Teachers Teaching Thinkers. Retrieved October 10, 2025, from https://teachersfirst.com/blog/2024/07/prompt-engineering-for-teachers-making-the-most-of-ai-part-1/

Hamad, N. I., El-Ashry, A. M., Ibrahim, I. M., & Hassan, E. A. (2025). Embracing the future: An insight into nursing students' attitude and perception towards the usability of artificial intelligence in healthcare. *Teaching and Learning in Nursing, 20*(2), e500–e508. DOI: 10.1016/j.teln.2024.12.017

Hammer, E. (2024). ChatGPT in the Classroom: The Teacher's Challenges and Opportunities in an AI Revolution.

Han, J., Yoo, H., Myung, J., Kim, M., Lee, T. Y., Ahn, S. Y., . . . Answer, A. N. (2023, December). Exploring student-ChatGPT dialogue in EFL writing education. *In Thirty-seventh conference on neural information processing systems, neural information processing systems foundation.*

Han, J., Yoo, H., Myung, J., Kim, M., Lim, H., Kim, Y., . . . Oh, A. (2023). LLM-as-a-tutor in EFL Writing Education: Focusing on Evaluation of Student-LLM Interaction. *arXiv preprint arXiv:2310.05191.*

Han, J., & Li, M. (2024). Exploring ChatGPT-supported teacher feedback in the EFL context. *System, 126*, 103502. DOI: 10.1016/j.system.2024.103502

Hanušová, S., Dontcheva-Navrátilová, O., Vališová, M., & Matulová, M. (2020). Process genre approach to l2 academic writing: an intervention study. Xlinguae, 30-51. https://doi.org/DOI: 10.18355/XL.2020.13.04.03

Han, X., Xiao, S., Sheng, J., & Zhang, G. (2025). Enhancing efficiency and decision-making in higher education through intelligent commercial integration: Leveraging artificial intelligence. *Journal of the Knowledge Economy*, *16*(1), 1546–1582. DOI: 10.1007/s13132-024-01868-2

Harcourt, E., Loxley, J., & Stanson, B. (2024). Automated learning of finegrained citation patterns in open source large language models.

Harlin, R., Sirota, E., & Bailey, L. (2009). Review of Research: The Impact of Teachers' Expectations on Diverse Learners'Academic Outcomes. *Childhood Education*, *85*(4), 253–256. DOI: 10.1080/00094056.2009.10523092

Harunasari, S. (2023). Examining the effectiveness of ai-integrated approach in efl writing: A case of chatgpt. *International Journal of Progressive Sciences and Technologies*, *39*(2), 357. DOI: 10.52155/ijpsat.v39.2.5516

Hasan, S., Nasreen, S., & Rasul, S. (2025). Leveraging artificial intelligence (ai) in higher education: Fostering soft skills communication, collaboration, creativity and critical thinking among university students. *IJLSS*, *3*(2), 1–7. DOI: 10.71000/c42srm97

Hashmi, N., & Bal, A. S. (2024). Generative AI in higher education and beyond. *Business Horizons*, *67*(5), 607–614. DOI: 10.1016/j.bushor.2024.05.005

Hassan, N. (2020). Using the genre-based approach for developing efl writing skills among student teachers at faculty of education students. , 31(12305), 23-47. https://doi.org/DOI: 10.21608/jfeb.2020.174655

Hayes, J. R. (2012). Modeling and remodeling writing. *Written Communication*, *29*(3), 369–388. DOI: 10.1177/0741088312451260

Hayes, J. R., & Flower, L. S. (1980). Identifying the organization of writing processes. In Gregg, L. W., & Steinberg, E. R. (Eds.), *Cognitive processes in writing* (pp. 3–30). Lawrence Erlbaum Associates.

He, L., Yang, N., Xu, L., Ping, F., Li, W., Sun, Q., Li, Y., Zhu, H., & Zhang, H. (2021). Synchronous distance education vs traditional education for health science students: A systematic review and meta-analysis. *Medical Education*, *55*(3), 293–308. DOI: 10.1111/medu.14364

Henning, M., Guez, A., Sharma, S., & Hovy, D. (2023). A survey of approaches to addressing class imbalance in natural language processing. *Findings of the Association for Computational Linguistics: EACL 2023*, 1–22. https://aclanthology.org/2023.findings-eacl.1

Hensley, M. K. (2011). Citation management software: Features and futures. *Reference and User Services Quarterly*, *50*(3), 204–208. DOI: 10.5860/rusq.50n3.204

Högemann, J., Cunha, J., Núñez, J. C., Vallejo, G., Rodríguez, C., & Rosário, P. (2021). Writing intervention with elementary students struggling with writing: Examining approach profiles to the teacher feedback on writing quality and motivational variables. *Reading and Writing*, *34*(7), 1681–1710. DOI: 10.1007/s11145-021-10159-0

Holmes, W. (2020). Artificial Intelligence in Education. In A. Tatnall (Ed.), *Encyclopedia of Education and Information Technologies* (pp. 88–103). Springer International Publishing. https://doi.org/, A., Kumar, A., Mulat-Weldemeskel, E., Luthra, S., Garza-Reyes, J. A., & Yadav, S. (2025). Next-gen quality learning: How can AI technologies shape education 4.0 and 5.0 towards the SDGs from multiple stakeholders' perspective? *The TQM Journal*. https://doi.org/DOI: 10.1007/978-3-030-10576-1_107

Holmes, J., & Tuomi, M. (2022). Digital learning and artistic retention in art education. *Learning, Media and Technology, 47*(2), 187–203.

Holmes, W., Bialik, M., & Fadel, C. (2022). *Artificial intelligence in education: Promises and implications for teaching and learning* (2nd ed.). Center for Curriculum Redesign.

Holmes, W., & Littlejohn, A. (2024). Artificial intelligence for professional learning. In *Handbook of artificial intelligence at work* (pp. 191–211). Edward Elgar Publishing. DOI: 10.4337/9781800889972.00018

Holmes, W., Porayska-Pomsta, K., Holstein, K., Sutherland, E., Baker, T., Shum, S. B., Santos, O. C., Rodrigo, M. T., Cukurova, M., Bittencourt, I. I., & Koedinger, K. R. (2022). Ethics of AI in education: Towards a community-wide framework. *International Journal of Artificial Intelligence in Education, 32*(3), 504–526. DOI: 10.1007/s40593-021-00239-1

Hopton, S.-B. (2013). Rebooting revision: Leveraging technology to deliver formative and summative feedback. In Exploring Technology for Writing and Writing Instruction. https://doi.org/ DOI: 10.4018/978-1-4666-4341-3.ch010

Horner, B., Lu, M.-Z., Royster, J. J., & Trimbur, J. (2011). Language difference in writing: Toward a translingual approach. *College English, 73*(3), 303–321. DOI: 10.58680/ce201113403

Hossain, M. K., & Al Younus, M. A. (2025). Teachers' perspectives on integrating ChatGPT into EFL writing instruction. *TESOL Communications, 4*(1), 41–60.

Hou, C., Zhu, G., & Sudarshan, V. (2025). The role of critical thinking on undergraduates' reliance behaviours on generative ai in problem-solving. *British Journal of Educational Technology, 56*(5), 1919–1941. DOI: 10.1111/bjet.13613

Hou, X., He, S., & Cuigong, R. (2024, June). Learner Use of AI-Generated Feedback for Written Corrective Feedback in L2 Writing: Usefulness, User Proficiency and Attitude. *In Proceedings of the 2024 8th International Conference on Education and Multimedia Technology (pp.* 70-76*).* DOI: 10.1145/3678726.3678767

Howard, K., & Tummon, N. (2025). Understanding student citation literacy: A multi-method approach. *Public Services Quarterly, 21*(2), 85–103. DOI: 10.1080/15228959.2025.2467715

Hsieh, W. M., Yeh, H. C., & Chen, N. S. (2025). Impact of a robot and tangible object (R&T) integrated learning system on elementary EFL learners' English pronunciation and willingness to communicate. *Computer Assisted Language Learning, 38*(4), 773–798. DOI: 10.1080/09588221.2023.2228357

Hua, J. (2023). Beyond exams: Investigating ai tool impact on student attitudes, ethical awareness, and academic dishonesty in online college assessments. *International Journal of Educational Management and Development Studies*, *4*(4), 160–185. DOI: 10.53378/353030

Huang, C., Zhang, Z., Mao, B., & Yao, X. (2022). An Overview of Artificial intelligence ethics. *IEEE Transactions on Artificial Intelligence*, *4*(4), 799–819. DOI: 10.1109/TAI.2022.3194503

Huang, J., & Teng, M. F. (2025). Peer feedback and ChatGPT-generated feedback on Japanese EFL students' engagement in a foreign language writing context. *Digital Applied Linguistics*, *2*, 102469–102469. DOI: 10.29140/dal.v2.102469

Huang, J., Zhou, Y., & Zhao, X. (2021). ICT integration in Chinese art teacher education: Current status and future directions. *Asia Pacific Education Review*, *22*(4), 789–802.

Huang, L. (2023). Ethics of artificial intelligence in education: Student privacy and data protection. *Science Insights Education Frontiers*, *16*(2), 2577–2587. DOI: 10.15354/sief.23.re202

Huang, L., & Shih, R. (2021). Front technologies in fine arts curricula: AI and VR applications. *Journal of Curriculum and Instruction*, *15*(3), 56–73.

Huang, P. (2020). Barriers to ICT integration in Chinese fine arts education. *Education and Information Technologies*, *25*(6), 4567–4582.

Huang, W., Hew, K. F., & Fryer, L. K. (2022). Chatbots for language learning—Are they really useful? A systematic review of chatbot-supported language learning. *Journal of Computer Assisted Learning*, *38*(1), 237–257. DOI: 10.1111/jcal.12610

Huang, X., Zou, D., Cheng, G., Chen, X., & Xie, H. (2023). Trends, research issues and applications of artificial intelligence in language education. *Journal of Educational Technology & Society*, *26*(1), 112–131.

Hubbard, P., & Schulze, M. (2025). AI and the Future of Language Teaching. *International Journal of Computer-Assisted Language Learning and Teaching*, *15*(1), 1–17. DOI: 10.4018/IJCALLT.378304

Hur, J. W. (2025). Fostering AI literacy: Overcoming concerns and nurturing confidence among preservice teachers. *Information and Learning Science*, *126*(1/2), 56–74. DOI: 10.1108/ILS-11-2023-0170

Hutchinson, B., Rostamzadeh, N., Greer, C., Heller, K., & Prabhakaran, V. (2022). Evaluation gaps in machine learning practice. *2022 ACM Conference on Fairness, Accountability, and Transparency*, 1859–1876. DOI: 10.1145/3531146.3533233

Hu, Y. (2025). Generative AI, communication, and stereotypes: Learning critical AI literacy through experience, analysis, and reflection. *Communication Teacher*, *39*(1), 6–12. DOI: 10.1080/17404622.2024.2397065

Hwang, H., Chang, X., & Sun, J. (2025). Generative AI is useful for second language writing, but when, why, and for how long do learners use it? *Journal of Second Language Writing*, *69*, 101230. DOI: 10.1016/j.jslw.2025.101230

Hyland, K. (2019). *Second language writing*. Cambridge University Press.

Ibrahim, A., Taura, A., Iliyasu, A., Shogbesan, Y., & Lukman, S. (2024). Artificial intelligence (ai): Perception and utilization of ai technologies in educational assessment in nigerian universities. *Edukasiana Jurnal Inovasi Pendidikan, 3*(3), 367–380. DOI: 10.56916/ejip.v3i3.763

Ibrahim, S., Aziz, A., Said, N., & Ismail, H. (2023). Malaysian english language teachers' willingness, readiness, needs and wants to develop graphic oral history elt materials. *International Journal of Learning Teaching and Educational Research, 22*(5), 101–118. DOI: 10.26803/ijlter.22.5.5

Idapalapati, S.Srinivasa Rao Idapalapati. (2024). Ai integration in elt as a disruptive mechanism. *International Journal of Science and Research Archive, 12*(1), 922–933. DOI: 10.30574/ijsra.2024.12.1.0941

Idowu, J. A., Koshiyama, A. S., & Treleaven, P. (2024). Investigating algorithmic bias in student progress monitoring. *Computers and Education: Artificial Intelligence, 7*, 100267. DOI: 10.1016/j.caeai.2024.100267

Ienca, M. (2023). On artificial intelligence and manipulation. *Topoi, 42*(3), 833–842. DOI: 10.1007/s11245-023-09940-3

Ikhsan, I., Husnaini, A. N., & Lopo, F. L. (2025). Strategies for implementing ai in LMS to improve the effectiveness and personalization of digital learning. *The Journal of Academic Science, 2*(3), 944–953. DOI: 10.59613/qp3e7d30

Ilieva, G., Yankova, T., Klisarova-Belcheva, S., Dimitrov, A., Bratkov, M., & Angelov, D. (2023). Effects of generative chatbots in higher education. *Information (Basel), 14*(9), 492. DOI: 10.3390/info14090492

Jaber, D., Hasan, H. E., Abutaima, R., Sawan, H. M., & Al Tabbah, S. (2024). The impact of artificial intelligence on the knowledge, attitude, and practice of pharmacists across diverse settings: A cross-sectional study. *International Journal of Medical Informatics, 192*, 105656. DOI: 10.1016/j.ijmedinf.2024.105656 PMID: 39426239

Jaboob, M., Hazaimeh, M., & Al-Ansi, A. M. (2025). Integration of generative AI techniques and applications in student behavior and cognitive achievement in Arab higher education. *International Journal of Human-Computer Interaction, 41*(1), 353–366. DOI: 10.1080/10447318.2023.2300016

Jadhav, S., Vhatkar, S., & Aalam, Z. (2024). Bridging the gap: Exploring the revolutionary application of GenAI in language teaching and learning. *Journal of Electrical Systems, 20*(4s, 4S), 2185–2193. DOI: 10.52783/jes.2325

Jafar, S. H., Oyedele, O. M., Nawaah, D., & Bolanle, A. S. (2025). Exploring Leadership Challenges for Adoption of Digital Innovation and Sustainability, Singh, R., Corvello, V., Coniglio, I.M. and Khan, S. (Ed.) *Innovation Ecosystems and Sustainable Technologies (Emerald Studies in Sustainable Innovation Management)*, Emerald Publishing Limited, Leeds, pp. 253-269. DOI: 10.1108/978-1-83662-368-720251012

Jafari, S., Fakhraee, L., & Teimourtash, M. (2025). The Impact of Artificial Intelligence (chat GPT) on Writing Accuracy of Iranian Intermediate EFL Learners and Their Level of Motivation. *Technology Assisted Language Education, 3*(1), 90–109.

Jai Lamimi, I., El Jemli, S., & Zeryouh, I.LAMIMI. (2025). Enhancing critical thinking: Exploring human-ai synergy in student cognitive development. *Arab World English Journal*, (1), 251–269. DOI: 10.24093/awej/AI.14

Jamshed, M., Manjur Ahmed, A. S. M., Sarfaraj, M., & Warda, W. U. (2024). The Impact of ChatGPT on English Language Learners' Writing Skills: An Assessment of AI Feedback on Mobile. *International Journal of Interactive Mobile Technologies*, *18*(19), 18–36. DOI: 10.3991/ijim.v18i19.50361

Janar, A., & Nozima, U. (2022). The Integration of "Floop" Platform for Enhancing Effectiveness of Feedback in Postsecondary Education Context. *International Journal of Emerging Technologies in Learning*, *17*(15), 54–67. DOI: 10.3991/ijet.v17i15.30711

Jansen, T., Horbach, A., & Meyer, J. (2025). Feedback from Generative AI: Correlates of Student Engagement in Text Revision from 655 Classes from Primary and Secondary School. 15th International Conference on Learning Analytics and Knowledge Lak 2025, 831–836. https://doi.org/DOI: 10.1145/3706468.3706494

Jarilkapovich, M. A.Karakalpak State University. (2025). The Role of Modern Education and The Teacher's Pedagogical Skills in The Application of Pedagogical Teaching Methods. *International Journal of Pedagogics*, *5*(4), 266–268. DOI: 10.37547/ijp/Volume05Issue04-70

Jarrahi, M. H., Askay, D., Eshraghi, A., & Smith, P. (2023). Artificial intelligence and knowledge management: A partnership between human and AI. *Business Horizons*, *66*(1), 87–99. DOI: 10.1016/j.bushor.2022.03.002

Javahery, P. (2025). Analyzing discourse patterns in chatgpt-generated ielts writing task 2 essays: a discourse analysis approach. https://doi.org/DOI: 10.21203/rs.3.rs-5608928/v1

Javed, F. (2024). The Evolution of Artificial Intelligence in Teaching and Learning of English Language in Higher Education: Challenges, Risks, and Ethical Considerations. In *The Evolution of Artificial Intelligence in Higher Education: Challenges, Risks, and Ethical Considerations* (pp. 249-276). Emerald Publishing Limited.

Jembu, J. P., & Balang, R. V. (2025). Artificial intelligence adoption in nursing students' academic writing: A qualitative study. *Teaching and Learning in Nursing*, *20*(4), e1012–e1020. Advance online publication. DOI: 10.1016/j.teln.2025.04.015

Jeon, J., & Lee, S. (2023). Large language models in education: A focus on the complementary relationship between human teachers and ChatGPT. *Education and Information Technologies*, *28*(12), 15873–15892. Advance online publication. DOI: 10.1007/s10639-023-11834-1

Jesudas, R. (2025, June). Empowering language learning: The role of AI in enhancing language skills. In. AIP Conference Proceedings: Vol. 3306. *No. 1* (p. 050023). AIP Publishing LLC. DOI: 10.1063/5.0278362

Jha, A., & Singh, S. R. (2025). Integrating Artificial Intelligence in Media Education: Revolutionizing Learning, Creativity, and Critical Thinking. In *Teachers' Roles and Perspectives on AI Integration in Schools* (pp. 297-328). IGI Global Scientific Publishing.

Jiang, D., & Kalyuga, S. (2022). Learning english as a foreign language writing skills in collaborative settings: A cognitive load perspective. *Frontiers in Psychology*, *13*, 932291. Advance online publication. DOI: 10.3389/fpsyg.2022.932291 PMID: 35846619

Jiang, L., Lee, I., & Yu, S. (2024). Conceptualizing multimodal feedback literacy for L2 writing teachers in the digital age. *International Journal of Applied Linguistics*, *34*(4), 1479–1496. DOI: 10.1111/ijal.12578

Ji, H., Han, I., & Ko, Y. (2023). A systematic review of conversational AI in language education: Focusing on the collaboration with human teachers. *Journal of Research on Technology in Education*, *55*(1), 48–63. DOI: 10.1080/15391523.2022.2142873

Jin, F. J. Y., Maheshi, B., Lai, W., Li, Y., Gasevic, D., Chen, G., Charwat, N., Chan, P. W. K., Martinez-Maldonado, R., Gašević, D., & Tsai, Y. S. (2025). Students' Perceptions of Generative AI-Powered Learning Analytics in the Feedback Process: A Feedback Literacy Perspective. *Journal of Learning Analytics*, *12*(1), 152–168. DOI: 10.18608/jla.2025.8609

Jingxin, G., & Razali, A. (2020). Tapping the potential of pigai automated writing evaluation (awe) program to give feedback on efl writing. *Universal Journal of Educational Research*, *8*(12B), 8334–8343. DOI: 10.13189/ujer.2020.082638

Jin, S. (2025). Writing in the digital age: Understanding the relationship between social media use and college students' writing skills and anxiety. *Humanities & Social Sciences Communications*, *12*(1), 1–11. DOI: 10.1057/s41599-025-05443-1

Jobin, A., Ienca, M., & Vayena, E. (2019). The global landscape of AI ethics guidelines. *Nature Machine Intelligence*, *1*(9), 389–399. DOI: 10.1038/s42256-019-0088-2

Johnston, H., Wells, R. F., Shanks, E. M., Boey, T., & Parsons, B. N. (2024). Student perspectives on the use of generative artificial intelligence technologies in higher education. *International Journal for Educational Integrity*, *20*(1), 2. DOI: 10.1007/s40979-024-00149-4

Jonassen, D., Spector, M. J., Driscoll, M., Merrill, M. D., Van Merrienboer, J., & Driscoll, M. P. (Eds.). (2008). *Handbook of Research on Educational Communications and Technology* (0 ed.). Routledge., DOI: 10.4324/9780203880869

Jurafsky, D., & Martin, J. H. (2025). *Speech and Language Processing: An Introduction to Natural Language Processing* (3rd ed.). Computational Linguistics, and Speech Recognition., https://web.stanford.edu/~jurafsky/slp3/

Kacena, M. A., Plotkin, L. I., & Fehrenbacher, J. C. (2024). The Use of Artificial Intelligence in Writing Scientific Review Articles. *Current Osteoporosis Reports*, *22*(1), 115–121. DOI: 10.1007/s11914-023-00852-0 PMID: 38227177

Kadmiry, M. (2021). The comparison between the process-oriented approach and the product-oriented approach in teaching writing the case of moroccan efl students in preparatory classes for the grandes ecoles. https://doi.org/DOI: 10.31235/osf.io/4aebr

Kaiser, G., & Kaiser, S. (2024). AI in Education: Reflections and Future Directions for Pedagogical and Andragogical Integration. In Wang, V. (Ed.), (pp. 241–260). Advances in Educational Technologies and Instructional Design. IGI Global., DOI: 10.4018/979-8-3693-6130-6.ch010

Kakhkharova, M., & Tuychieva, S. (2024, April). AI-enhanced pedagogy in higher education: redefining teaching-learning paradigms. In *2024 International Conference on Knowledge Engineering and Communication Systems (ICKECS)* (Vol. 1, pp. 1-6). IEEE.

Kalisdha, A. (2023). The Future of Library Science Research: Tools and Databases. *International Journal for Research in Applied Science and Engineering Technology, 11*(11), 700–707. DOI: 10.22214/ijraset.2023.56602

Kallunki, V., Kinnunen, P., Pyörälä, E., Haarala-Muhonen, A., Katajavuori, N., & Myyry, L. (2024). Navigating the evolving landscape of teaching and learning: University faculty and staff perceptions of the artificial intelligence-altered terrain. *Education Sciences, 14*(7), 727. DOI: 10.3390/educsci14070727

Kant, I. (1997). *Groundwork of the metaphysics of morals* (Gregor, M., Trans.). Cambridge University Press. (Original work published 1785)

Karabulut, E. (2024). *Analysing the effects of AI-powered chatbots on the writing skills of English preparatory class students: An experimental study* (Unpublished Master's thesis). Ondokuz Mayıs University, Türkiye.

Karataş, F., Eriçok, B., & Tanrikulu, L. (2025). Reshaping curriculum adaptation in the age of artificial intelligence: Mapping teachers' AI-driven curriculum adaptation patterns. *British Educational Research Journal, 51*(1), 154–180. DOI: 10.1002/berj.4068

Karataş, F., & Yüce, E. (2024). AI and the Future of Teaching: Preservice Teachers' Reflections on the Use of Artificial Intelligence in Open and Distributed Learning. *International Review of Research in Open and Distance Learning, 25*(3), 304–325. DOI: 10.19173/irrodl.v25i3.7785

Karim, H. A.. (2024). An enhanced hybrid model based on CNN and Bi-LSTM for writer identification. *Computer Modeling in Engineering & Sciences, 140*(2), 1689–1710. https://www.techscience.com/CMES/v140n2/56554. DOI: 10.32604/cmes.2024.048714

Kartal, G. (2023). Contemporary language teaching and learning with ChatGPT. *Contemporary Research in Language and Linguistics (ISSN: 2980-2253), 1(1).*

Kasneci, E., Seßler, K., Küchemann, S., Bannert, M., Dementieva, D., Fischer, F., Gasser, U., Groh, G., Günnemann, S., Hüllermeier, E., Krusche, S., Kutyniok, G., Michaeli, T., Nerdel, C., Pfeffer, J., Poquet, O., Sailer, M., Schmidt, A., Seidel, T., & Kasneci, G. (2023). ChatGPT for Good? On opportunities and challenges of large language models for education. *Learning and Individual Differences, 103*, 102274. Advance online publication. DOI: 10.1016/j.lindif.2023.102274

Kasneci, E., Sessler, K., Küchemann, S., Bannert, M., & Sesagiri Raamkumar, A.. (2023). ChatGPT for good? On opportunities and challenges of large language models for education. *International Journal of Artificial Intelligence in Education, 33*, 1–24.

Kenedy, R. A. (2024). The challenges of critical thinking in the era of artificial intelligence. *European Journal of Multidisciplinary Studies, 9*(2), 19–36. DOI: 10.26417/hfdngd20

Keser, K., & Pektaş, R. (2024). Human vs. AI Feedback on Academic Writing: A Comparative Study in Turkish Context. In Özkan, Y. (Ed.), *English Studies: A Multifaceted Lens* (pp. 190–203). Black Swan Press.

Khabib, S. (2022). Introducing artificial intelligence (AI)-based digital writing assistants for teachers in writing scientific articles. *Deleted Journal*, *1*(2), 114–124. DOI: 10.12928/tefl.v1i2.249

Khalabuzar, O., & Shymanovych, I. (2024). Developing critical thinking skills through artificial intelligence and language learning. Modern educational strategies under the influence of the development of the information society and European integration.

Khalifa, M., & Albadawy, M. (2024). Using artificial intelligence in academic writing and research: An essential productivity tool. *Computer Methods and Programs in Biomedicine Update*, *5*, 100145. DOI: 10.1016/j.cmpbup.2024.100145

Khalil, M., & Er, E. (2023). Will chatgpt get you caught? rethinking of plagiarism detection. https://doi.org/DOI: 10.1007/978-3-031-34411-4_32

Khan, W. N. (2024). Ethical challenges of AI in education: Balancing innovation with data privacy. *AI EDIFY Journal*, *1*(1), 1–13.

Khan, Z. A., Xia, Y., Aurangzeb, K., Khaliq, F., Alam, M., Khan, J. A., & Anwar, M. S. (2024). Emotion detection from handwriting and drawing samples using an attention-based transformer model. *PeerJ. Computer Science*, *10*, e1887. DOI: 10.7717/peerj-cs.1887 PMID: 38660197

Khatoony, S., Mall-Amiri, B., & Kolahi, S. (2025). Developing a New Augmented Reality Mobile Application to Improve School-Age EFL Learners' Vocabulary Acquisition. *Technology Assisted Language Education*, *3*(2), 120–143.

Khine, M. S. (2024). Ethics, and the Future of Education in an AI-Driven World. In Khine, M. S. (Ed.), *Artificial Intelligence in Education* (pp. 629–735). Springer Nature Singapore., DOI: 10.1007/978-981-97-9350-1_6

Kholoshyn, I., Varfolomyeyeva, I., Hanchuk, O., Bondarenko, O., & Pikilnyak, A. (2019). *Pedagogical techniques of Earth remote sensing data application into modern school practice*. DOI: 10.31812/123456789/3262

Kim, J., Merrill, K., Xu, K., & Sellnow, D. D. (2020). My teacher is a machine: Understanding students' perceptions of AI teaching assistants in online education. *International Journal of Human-Computer Interaction*, *36*(20), 1902–1911. DOI: 10.1080/10447318.2020.1801227

Kim, J., Yu, S., Detrick, R., & Li, N. (2025). Exploring students' perspectives on Generative AI-assisted academic writing. *Education and Information Technologies*, *30*(1), 1265–1300. DOI: 10.1007/s10639-024-12878-7

Kim, N., & Kim, M. (2022). Teacher's perceptions of using an artificial intelligence-based educational tool for scientific writing. *Frontiers in Education*, *7*, 755914. Advance online publication. DOI: 10.3389/feduc.2022.755914

Kirovograd Institute for Human Development, & Chernenko, O. (2020). MODERN PEDAGOGICAL TECHNOLOGIES IN HIGHER EDUCATION. *PEDAGOGY AND EDUCATION MANAGEMENT REVIEW*, *2*, 52–59. DOI: 10.36690/2733-2039-2020-2-52

Kizilcec, R. F. (2022). Algorithmic fairness in education. In Elliott, C. (Ed.), *The Oxford Handbook of Education and AI* (pp. 178–200). Routledge., DOI: 10.4324/9780429329067-10

Klarin, Z., & Livaić, T. (2023). Application of artificial intelligence language model ChatGPT in higher education. *Zbornik radova Veleučilišta u Šibeniku, 17(3-4), 99-112.*

Klarin, J., Hoff, E., Larsson, A., & Daukantaitė, D. (2024). Adolescents' use and perceived usefulness of generative ai for schoolwork: Exploring their relationships with executive functioning and academic achievement. *Frontiers in Artificial Intelligence*, *7*, 1415782. Advance online publication. DOI: 10.3389/frai.2024.1415782 PMID: 39263526

Knowles, M. (2021). Five motivating concerns for ai ethics instruction. *Proceedings of the Association for Information Science and Technology*, *58*(1), 472–476. DOI: 10.1002/pra2.481

Kobeissi, M. M., Santa Maria, D. M., & Park, J. I. (2025). Artificial intelligence 101: Building literacy with the AI-ABCs framework. *Nursing Outlook*, *73*(4), 102445. DOI: 10.1016/j.outlook.2025.102445 PMID: 40446514

Koenecke, A., Nam, A., Lake, E., Nudell, J., Quartey, M., Mengesha, Z., Toups, C., Rickford, J. R., Jurafsky, D., & Goel, S. (2020). Racial disparities in automated speech recognition. *Proceedings of the National Academy of Sciences of the United States of America*, *117*(14), 7684–7689. DOI: 10.1073/pnas.1915768117 PMID: 32205437

Koivisto, M., & Grassini, S. (2023). Best humans still outperform artificial intelligence in a creative divergent thinking task. *Scientific Reports*, *13*(1), 13601. DOI: 10.1038/s41598-023-40858-3 PMID: 37709769

Koltovskaia, S., Rahmati, P., & Saeli, H. (2024). Graduate students' use of ChatGPT for academic text revision: Behavioral, cognitive, and affective engagement. *Journal of Second Language Writing*, *65*, 101130. DOI: 10.1016/j.jslw.2024.101130

Kong, S., Lee, J., & Tsang, O. (2024). A pedagogical design for self-regulated learning in academic writing using text-based generative artificial intelligence tools: 6-p pedagogy of plan, prompt, preview, produce, peer-review, portfolio-tracking. Research and Practice in Technology Enhanced Learning, 19, 030. https://doi.org/DOI: 10.58459/rptel.2024.19030

Kong, S. C., & Hu, W. (2025). A Study of Developing Administrative Staff's Conceptual Understanding of Generative Artificial Intelligence Through Professional Development: Evaluation of a Course Using Tests, Surveys and Thematic Analysis of Reflective Writings. *Computers and Education: Artificial Intelligence, 100444*, 100444. Advance online publication. DOI: 10.1016/j.caeai.2025.100444

Kong, S. C., Yang, Y., & Hou, C. (2024). Examining teachers' behavioural intention of using generative artificial intelligence tools for teaching and learning based on the extended technology acceptance model. *Computers and Education: Artificial Intelligence*, *7*, 100328. DOI: 10.1016/j.caeai.2024.100328

Konyrova, L. (2024). The evolution of language learning: Exploring ai's impact on teaching english as a second language. *Eurasian Science Review*, *2*(2), 133–138. DOI: 10.63034/esr-42

Kooli, C., & Yusuf, N. (2025). Transforming educational assessment: Insights into the use of ChatGPT and large language models in grading. *International Journal of Human-Computer Interaction*, *41*(5), 3388–3399.

Korth, B., Wimmer, J., Wilcox, B., Morrison, T., Harward, S., Peterson, N., Simmerman, S., & Pierce, L. (2016). Practices and challenges of writing instruction in k-2 classrooms: A case study of five primary grade teachers. *Early Childhood Education Journal*, *45*(2), 237–249. DOI: 10.1007/s10643-016-0774-1

Kostka, I. and Toncelli, R. (2023). Exploring applications of chatgpt to english language teaching: opportunities, challenges, and recommendations. Teaching English as a Second or Foreign Language--Tesl-Ej, 27(3). https://doi.org/DOI: 10.55593/ej.27107int

Kouam, A. (2024). Ai in academic writing: Ally or foe? *International Journal of Research Publications*, *148*(1). Advance online publication. DOI: 10.47119/IJRP1001481520246427

Kovari, A. (2025). Ethical use of ChatGPT in education—Best practices to combat AI-induced plagiarism. *Frontiers in Education*, *9*, 1465703. Advance online publication. DOI: 10.3389/feduc.2024.1465703

Krasniqi, R., & Përvetica, A. K. (2024). Pedagogical Innovation Amidst Adversity: Exploring Online Pedagogical Practices in Southeast Europe. *Journal of Educational and Social Research*, *14*(5), 222–232. DOI: 10.36941/jesr-2024-0134

Kraus, S., Kumar, S., Lim, W. M., Kaur, J., Sharma, A., & Schiavone, F. (2023). From moon landing to metaverse: Tracing the evolution of Technological Forecasting and Social Change. *Technological Forecasting and Social Change*, *189*, 122381. DOI: 10.1016/j.techfore.2023.122381

Kuckartz, U., & Rädiker, S. (2019). *Analyzing qualitative data with MAXQDA*. Springer International Publishing. DOI: 10.1007/978-3-030-15671-8

Kulaksız, G. C. (2024). *Artificial intelligence-based language modelling: The effect of ChatGPT application on writing skills in the context of teaching English as a foreign language* (Unpublished Master's thesis). Bursa Uludağ University, Türkiye.

Kulprasit, W. (2024). The Convergence of the COVID-19 Pandemic and EFL Writing Pedagogy: The Paradigm Shift. *New English Teacher*, *18*(1), 41–52.

Kumar, Alok. "Management Education 5.0, the NEP and AI: The Unwired Connection." *ADHYAYAN: A JOURNAL OF MANAGEMENT SCIENCES* 14, no. 02 (2024): 16-22.

Kumar, N., Antoniraj, S., Jayanthi, S., Mirdula, S., & Saravanakumar Selvaraj, N. Rajkumar, and K. R. Senthilkumar. "Educational technology and libraries supporting online learning." In *AI-Assisted Library Reconstruction*, pp. 209-237. IGI Global, 2024.

Kumar, D., & Suthar, N. (2024). Ethical and legal challenges of ai in marketing: An exploration of solutions. *Journal of Information Communication and Ethics in Society*, *22*(1), 124–144. DOI: 10.1108/JICES-05-2023-0068

Kumari, N. (2025). Scalability of Generative AI Models: Challenges and Opportunities in Large-Scale Data Generation and Training. *Journal ID*, *9471*(3), 1297. DOI: 10.63530/IJCSI-TR_2025_06_03_002

Kumar, S. (2024). Impact of Assessment on Childhood Education Theories and Practice. In Badea, M., & Suditu, M. (Eds.), *Advances in Early Childhood and K-12 Education* (pp. 84–101). IGI Global., DOI: 10.4018/979-8-3693-0956-8.ch004

Kumar, S., Kumar, V., Kumari Bhatt, I., Kumar, S., & Attri, K. (2024). Digital transformation in tourism sector: Trends and future perspectives from a bibliometric-content analysis. *Journal of Hospitality and Tourism Insights*, *7*(3), 1553–1576. DOI: 10.1108/JHTI-10-2022-0472

Kurban, C. F., & Şahin, M. (2024). Educational Implications. In C. F. Kurban & M. Şahin, *The Impact of ChatGPT on Higher Education* (pp. 153–179). Emerald Publishing Limited. DOI: 10.1108/978-1-83797-647-820241009

Kurzweil, R. (2025). The Singularity Is Nearer: When We Merge with AI. *Perspectives on Science and Christian Faith*, *77*(1), 75–76. DOI: 10.56315/PSCF3-25Kurzweil

Lahiri, S., & Dey, D. (2022). Pedagogy of care in digital higher education. *Educational Philosophy and Theory*. Advance online publication. DOI: 10.1080/00131857.2022.2088451

Lai, Z. (2025). The impact of ai-assisted blended learning on writing efficacy and resilience. *International Journal of Computer-Assisted Language Learning and Teaching*, *15*(1), 1–21. DOI: 10.4018/IJCALLT.377174

Lantada, A. D. (2020). Engineering education 5.0: Continuously evolving engineering education. *International Journal of Engineering Education*, *36*(6), 1814–1832.

Lantolf, J. P., & Thorne, S. L. (2006). *Sociocultural theory and the genesis of second language development*. Oxford University Press.

Lan, Y.-T., Wang, J.-H., & Chana, T.-W. (2011). The framework of online writing system. *Proceedings of the 19th International Conference on Computers in Education Icce 2011*, 54–56.

Launonen, P., Talalakina, E., & Dubova, G. (2024). Students' perceptions of using chatgpt for academic writing in english. *Półrocznik Językoznawczy Tertium*, *9*(1), 219–249. DOI: 10.7592/Tertium.2024.9.1.274

Laupichler, M. C., Aster, A., Schirch, J., & Raupach, T. (2022). Artificial intelligence literacy in higher and adult education: A scoping literature review. *Computers & Education: Artificial Intelligence*, *3*, 100101. DOI: 10.1016/j.caeai.2022.100101

Leandro, G. D. S. M., Kumar, S., Jacinto Da Gama, M., Carvalho, H., & Leandro, E. (2024). Circular Economy Practices in the Hotel Sector in Luanda, Angola: Challenges and Future Perspectives. In P. K. Tyagi, V. Nadda, K. Kankaew, & K. Dube (Eds.), *Advances in Hospitality, Tourism, and the Services Industry* (pp. 54–66). IGI Global. DOI: 10.4018/979-8-3693-4042-4.ch004

Lee, J., & Choi, H. (2024). ChatGPT as a Tool in EFL Writing: *An Analysis of Students Usage and Perceptions.* *, 40(3), 3-28.*

Lee, B., Ku, S., & Ko, K. (2025). ai robots promote south korean preschoolers' ai literacy and computational thinking. *Family Relations*, *74*(3), 1354–1375. DOI: 10.1111/fare.13189

Lee, D., & Palmer, E. (2025). Prompt engineering in higher education: A systematic review to help inform curricula. *International Journal of Educational Technology in Higher Education*, *22*(1), 7. DOI: 10.1186/s41239-025-00503-7

Lee, I. (2014). Revisiting Teacher Feedback in EFL Writing from Sociocultural Perspectives. *TESOL Quarterly*, *48*(1), 201–213. DOI: 10.1002/tesq.153

Lee, I. (2020). *Teacher feedback in L2 writing: Issues, challenges and future directions*. Cambridge University Press., DOI: 10.1017/9781108684910

Lee, I. (2021). The development of feedback literacy for writing teachers. *TESOL Quarterly*, *55*(3), 1048–1059. DOI: 10.1002/tesq.3012

Lee, S. (2024). Analyzing the use of ai writing assistants in generating texts with standard American English conventions: A case study of chatgpt and bard. *The CATESOL Journal*, *35*(1). Advance online publication. DOI: 10.5070/B5.25364

Lee, S., Law, M., & Hoffman, G. (2025). Lee, Seo-young, Matthew Law, and Guy Hoffman. "When and how to use AI in the design process? Implications for human-AI design collaboration.". *International Journal of Human-Computer Interaction*, *41*(2), 1569–1584. DOI: 10.1080/10447318.2024.2353451

Leggette, H., Rutherford, T., Dunsford, D., & Costello, L. (2015). A review and evaluation of prominent theories of writing. *Journal of Applied Communications*, *99*(3). Advance online publication. DOI: 10.4148/1051-0834.1056

Le, H. V., Dang, T. B., Vo, T. P., Nguyen, M. Q. P., & Nguyen, N. Q. C. (2025). Anonymous yet accountable: Investigating sociocultural dynamics in peer feedback among Vietnamese EFL students. *Learning, Culture and Social Interaction*, *54*, 100939. Advance online publication. DOI: 10.1016/j.lcsi.2025.100939

Le, H., Shen, Y., Li, Z., Xia, M., Tang, L., Li, X., Jia, J., Wang, Q., Gašević, D., & Fan, Y. (2025). Breaking human dominance: Investigating learners' preferences for learning feedback from generative ai and human tutors. *British Journal of Educational Technology*, *56*(5), 1758–1783. DOI: 10.1111/bjet.13614

León-Gómez, A., Jorge, A. M. F., & Santos-Jaén, J. M. (2023). A bibliometric analysis of sustainability education in tourism universities. *SAGE Open*, *13*(3), 21582440231193215. DOI: 10.1177/21582440231193215

Leung, C. H. (2024). Promoting optimal learning with ChatGPT: A comprehensive exploration of prompt engineering in education. *Asian Journal of Contemporary Education*, *8*(2), 104–114. DOI: 10.55493/5052.v8i2.5101

Li, T., Yusof, S. B., Abuhassna, H., & Pan, Q. (2026). The impact of AI on higher education trends and educational horizons. In B. Edwards, H. Abuhassna, D. Olugbade, O. Ojo, & W. Jaafar Wan Yahaya (Eds.), *AI in education, governance, and leadership: Adoption, impact, and ethics* (pp. 1–32). IGI Global Scientific Publishing. https://doi.org/DOI: 10.4018/979-8-3373-5550-4.ch001

Liang, J. C., & Hwang, G. J. (2025). Embodied social agency in human-robot collaboration for promoting EFL learners' persuasive communication and bodily-emotional awareness: A functional linguistics perspective. *Education and Information Technologies*, *30*(17), 1–45. DOI: 10.1007/s10639-025-13747-7

Liang, J. C., Hwang, G. J., Chen, M. R. A., & Darmawansah, D. (2023). Roles and research foci of artificial intelligence in language education: An integrated bibliographic analysis and systematic review approach. *Interactive Learning Environments*, *31*(7), 4270–4296. DOI: 10.1080/10494820.2021.1958348

Liang, T., Singh, C. K. S., Mulyadi, D., & Singh, T. S. M. (2025). Enhancing EFL Writing Through Online Peer Feedback: A Systematic Review of Higher Education Studies. *Journal of Curriculum and Teaching*, *14*(1), 184–201. DOI: 10.5430/jct.v14n1p184

Liang, W., Yuksekgonul, M., Mao, Y., Wu, E., & Zou, J. (2023). GPT detectors are biased against non-native English writers. *Patterns (New York, N.Y.)*, *4*(6), 100779. DOI: 10.1016/j.patter.2023.100779

Liao, C., & Tang, M. (2023). AI-powered instructional design in art education: New pedagogical approaches to traditional techniques. *Computers & Education*, *72*, 101–115.

Liao, H., & Wang, Q. (2021). ICT as a bridge between cultural heritage preservation and pedagogical innovation. *Journal of Cultural Heritage*, *48*(Supplement), 1–10.

Liao, Y., Zhang, L., & Zou, X. (2023). AI-driven adaptive learning in fine arts education. *Journal of Educational Data Mining*, *15*(2), 1–22.

Li, D., & Wang, Y. (2024). Translanguaging as a Mediational Tool in the Process of Feedback in Second Language Writing. *Canadian Journal of Applied Linguistics*, *47*(1), 121–136. DOI: 10.1515/CJAL-2024-0108

Li, H., Kang, M., & Liu, J. (2025). Exploring Chinese EFL Teachers' Perceptions of the Potentials and Challenges of Robot-Assisted Language Learning. *European Journal of Education*, *60*(4), e70226. DOI: 10.1111/ejed.70226

Li, J., Huang, J., Wu, W., & Whipple, P. B. (2024). Evaluating the role of ChatGPT in enhancing EFL writing assessments in classroom settings: A preliminary investigation. *Humanities & Social Sciences Communications*, *11*(1), 1–9. DOI: 10.1057/s41599-024-03755-2

Li, J., & Wu, Z. (2022). Digital transformation in fine arts education: An evaluation of AI-assisted art training programs. *Education and Information Technologies*, *27*, 1201–1225.

Li, J., Zong, H., Wu, E., Wu, R., Peng, Z., Zhao, J., Yang, L., Xie, H., & Shen, B. (2024). Exploring the potential of artificial intelligence to enhance the writing of English academic papers by non-native english-speaking medical students - the educational application of ChatGPT. *BMC Medical Education*, *24*(1), 736. Advance online publication. DOI: 10.1186/s12909-024-05738-y PMID: 38982429

Likforman-Sulem, L., Esposito, A., Faundez-Zanuy, M., Clémençon, S., & Cordasco, G. (2017). EMOTHAW: A novel database for emotional state recognition from handwriting and drawing. *IEEE Transactions on Human-Machine Systems*, *47*(3), 273–284. DOI: 10.1109/THMS.2016.2635441

Lillis, T., & Scott, M. (2007). Defining academic literacies research: Issues of epistemology, ideology and strategy. *Journal of Applied Linguistics*, *4*(1), 5–32. DOI: 10.1558/japl.v4i1.5

Li, M. (2024). Leveraging ChatGPT for Second Language Writing Feedback and Assessment. [IJCALLT]. *International Journal of Computer-Assisted Language Learning and Teaching*, *14*(1), 1–11. DOI: 10.4018/IJCALLT.360382

Lin, H., & Chen, Q. (2024). Artificial intelligence (AI)-integrated educational applications and college students' creativity and academic emotions: Students and teachers' perceptions and attitudes. *BMC Psychology*, *12*(1), 487. DOI: 10.1186/s40359-024-01979-0 PMID: 39285268

Lisova, S. (2024). PEDAGOGICAL INNOVATIONS AS A TOOL FOR MODERNIZATION OF HIGHER EDUCATION: THEORETICAL ASPECT. *Zhytomyr Ivan Franko State University Journal. Pedagogical Sciences*, *2*(117), 101–115. DOI: 10.35433/pedagogy.2(117).2024.9

Liu, L. (2022). Application of Automated Writing Evaluation (AWE) System Based on Intelligent Technology. 2022 IEEE 2nd International Conference on Mobile Networks and Wireless Communications Icmnwc 2022. https://doi.org/DOI: 10.1109/ICMNWC56175.2022.10031924

Liu, V., Latif, E., & Zhai, X. (2025). Advancing education through tutoring systems: A systematic literature review. *arXiv preprint arXiv:2503.09748*.

Liu, C., Hou, J., Tu, Y. F., Wang, Y., & Hwang, G. J. (2023). Incorporating a reflective thinking promoting mechanism into artificial intelligence-supported English writing environments. *Interactive Learning Environments*, *31*(9), 5614–5632. DOI: 10.1080/10494820.2021.2012812

Liu, F., & Sun, T. (2022). Digital technology and the accessibility of traditional Chinese painting techniques. *Journal of Art History and Cultural Heritage*, *8*(2), 78–92.

Liu, F., & Zhao, Y. (2022). Challenges in teaching traditional Chinese painting to beginners. *Journal of Art Education Research*, *12*(3), 45–56.

Liu, K., & Storch, N. (2023). Second language learners' engagement with written feedback. *Australian Review of Applied Linguistics*, *46*(1), 4–28. DOI: 10.1075/aral.20029.liu

Liu, W., & Wang, Y. (2024). The effects of using ai tools on critical thinking in english literature classes among efl learners: An intervention study. *European Journal of Education*, *59*(4), e12804. Advance online publication. DOI: 10.1111/ejed.12804

Liu, X., & Xiao, Y. (2025). Chinese university teachers' engagement with generative AI in different stages of foreign language teaching: A qualitative enquiry through the prism of ADDIE. *Education and Information Technologies*, *30*(1), 485–508. DOI: 10.1007/s10639-024-13117-9

Loke, Y.-H., Harahsheh, A. S., Krieger, A., & Olivieri, L. J. (2017). Usage of 3D models of tetralogy of Fallot for medical education: Impact on learning congenital heart disease. *BMC Medical Education*, *17*(1), 54. DOI: 10.1186/s12909-017-0889-0 PMID: 28284205

Lópes, C., Comas Forgas, R., & Cerdá-Navarro, A. (2024). A PhD dissertation in education written by artificial intelligence? Revista Brasileira de Educação, 29. https://doi.org/DOI: 10.1590/s1413-24782024290066

Lubbe, A., Marais, E., & Kruger, D. (2025). Cultivating independent thinkers: The triad of artificial intelligence, Bloom's taxonomy and critical thinking in assessment pedagogy. *Education and Information Technologies*, *30*(12), 1–34. DOI: 10.1007/s10639-025-13476-x

Luckin, R., & Holmes, W. (2016). Intelligence unleashed: An argument for AI in education.

Lu, D., & Zeng, Y. (2025). Exploring the use of ChatGPT-generated model texts as a feedback instrument: EFL students' text quality and perceptions. *Innovation in Language Learning and Teaching*, •••, 1–21. DOI: 10.1080/17501229.2025.2525341

Lukac, M. (2024). Speech-based personality prediction using deep learning with acoustic and linguistic embeddings. *Scientific Reports, 14*(1), 15482. DOI: 10.1038/s41598-024-81047-0 PMID: 39627367

Lund, B. D., Lee, T. H., Mannuru, N. R., & Arutla, N. (2025). AI and academic integrity: Exploring student perceptions and implications for Higher Education. *Journal of Academic Ethics, 23*(3), 1545–1565. DOI: 10.1007/s10805-025-09613-3

Lundberg, S. M., & Lee, S.-I. (2017). A unified approach to interpreting model predictions. In *Advances in Neural Information Processing Systems* (Vol. 30, pp. 4768–4777).

Luo, F., Zhang, J., Wang, Q., & Yang, C. (2025). Leveraging Prompt Engineering in Large Language Models for Accelerating Chemical Research. *ACS Central Science, 11*(4), 511–519. DOI: 10.1021/acscentsci.4c01935 PMID: 40290144

Ma, D., Akram, H., & Chen, I. H. (2024). Artificial intelligence in higher education: A cross-cultural examination of students' behavioral intentions and attitudes. *International Review of Research in Open and Distance Learning, 25*(3), 134–157. DOI: 10.19173/irrodl.v25i3.7703

Madan, S., Gahalawat, M., Guha, T., Goecke, R., & Subramanian, R. (2023). Explainable human-centered traits from head motion and facial expression dynamics. *arXiv*. https://arxiv.org/abs/2302.09817

Mahapatra, S. (2024). Impact of ChatGPT on ESL students' academic writing skills: A mixed methods intervention study. *Smart Learning Environments, 11*(1), 9. DOI: 10.1186/s40561-024-00295-9

Mahmud, F. (2023). Investigating efl students' writing skills through artificial intelligence: Wordtune application as a tool. *Journal of Language Teaching and Research, 14*(5), 1395–1404. DOI: 10.17507/jltr.1405.28

Mahoney, P., Macfarlane, S., & Ajjawi, R. (2019). A qualitative synthesis of video feedback in higher education. *Teaching in Higher Education, 24*(2), 157–179. DOI: 10.1080/13562517.2018.1471457

Makda, F. (2025). Digital education: Mapping the landscape of virtual teaching in higher education–a bibliometric review. *Education and Information Technologies, 30*(2), 2547–2575. DOI: 10.1007/s10639-024-12899-2

Malakar, P., & Leeladharan, M. (2024). Generative ai tools for collaborative content creation. *DESIDOC Journal of Library and Information Technology, 44*(3), 151–157. DOI: 10.14429/djlit.44.3.19698

Malfatti, F. I. (2025). ChatGPT, Education, and Understanding. *Social Epistemology*, •••, 1–15.

Malik, A. R., Pratiwi, Y., Andajani, K., Numertayasa, I. W., Suharti, S., Darwis, A., & Marzuki, . (2023). Exploring artificial intelligence in academic essay: Higher education students' perspective. *International Journal of Educational Research Open, 5*, 100296. DOI: 10.1016/j.ijedro.2023.100296

Malla, A., Shah, J. N., Giri, B., Khadka, K., & Gurung, S. (2025). Citation and referencing in research writing publication: A guide for selecting the reference management software. *Journal of Chitwan Medical College, 15*(2), 91–100.

Mambu, J. (2022). Co-constructing a critical elt curriculum: A case study in an indonesian-based english language teacher education program. *TESOL Journal, 13*(3), e667. Advance online publication. DOI: 10.1002/tesj.667

Mandour, W. S. (2025). AI-Powered Tools for Linguistic and Sentiment Analysis in Language Learning: Applications Using Google Sheets and Large Language Models. In *Using AI Tools in Text Analysis, Simplification, Classification, and Synthesis* (pp. 67-112). IGI Global Scientific Publishing.

Mannuru, N. R., Shahriar, S., Teel, Z. A., Wang, T., Lund, B. D., Tijani, S., & Vaidya, P. (2025). Artificial intelligence in developing countries: The impact of generative artificial intelligence (AI) technologies for development. *Information Development, 41*(3), 1036–1054. DOI: 10.1177/02666669231200628

Man, S. S., Fang, Y., Chan, A. H. S., & Han, J. (2025). VR technology acceptance for English learning amongst secondary school students: Role of classroom climate and language learning anxiety. *Education and Information Technologies, 30*(4), 4131–4155. DOI: 10.1007/s10639-024-12969-5

Marghany, M. M. (2023). Using artificial intelligence-based instruction to develop EFL higher education students' essay writing skills. *CDELT Occasional Papers in the Development of English Education, 82*(1), 219–240. DOI: 10.21608/opde.2023.313623

Marhaban, S., Sulistyo, T., & Widiastuti, O. (2023). Artificial intelligence in writing: Students' writing competencies and voices. [JEELS]. *Journal of English Education and Linguistics Studies, 12*(1), 1–24. DOI: 10.30762/jeels.v12i1.3927

Marzuki, M., Widiati, U., Rusdin, D., Darwin, , & Indrawati, I. (2023). The impact of AI writing tools on the content and organization of students' writing: EFL teachers' perspective. *Cogent Education, 10*(1), 2236469. DOI: 10.1080/2331186X.2023.2236469

Matthews, J., & Volpe, C. (2023). Academics' perceptions of chatgpt-generated written outputs: A practical application of turing's imitation game. *Australasian Journal of Educational Technology, 39*(5), 82–100. DOI: 10.14742/ajet.8896

Matthew, U. O., Bakare, K. M., Ebong, G. N., Ndukwu, C. C., & Nwanakwaugwu, A. C.Ugochukwu Okwudili MatthewKafayat Motomori BakareGodwin Nse EbongCharles Chukwuebuka NdukwuAndrew Chinonso Nwanakwaugwu. (2023). Generative Artificial Intelligence (AI) Educational Pedagogy Development: Conversational AI with User-Centric ChatGPT4. *Journal of Trends in Computer Science and Smart Technology, 5*(4), 401–418. DOI: 10.36548/jtcsst.2023.4.003

Mazzi, F. (2024). Authorship in artificial intelligence-generated works: Exploring originality in text prompts and artificial intelligence outputs through philosophical foundations of copyright and collage protection. *The Journal of World Intellectual Property, 27*(3), 410–427. DOI: 10.1111/jwip.12310

Meça, A., & Shkëlzeni, V. (2023). The ethical implications of AI in higher education. *Journal of Academic Ethics.*

Mehta, Y., Majumder, N., Gelbukh, A., & Cambria, E. (2020). Recent trends in deep learning based personality detection. *Artificial Intelligence Review*, *53*(4), 2313–2339. DOI: 10.1007/s10462-019-09770-z

Memarian, B., & Doleck, T. (2024). Human-in-the-loop in artificial intelligence in education: A review and entity-relationship (ER) analysis. Computers in Human Behavior Artificial Humans. https://doi.org/DOI: 10.1016/j.chbah.2024.100053

Menshikova, M., Bonacci, I., & Scarozza, D. (2025). Rethinking Tutoring Activities in the New Normal: New Ways of Tutoring and Evolution of The Tutor's Profile. *Procedia Computer Science*, *253*, 1515–1524. DOI: 10.1016/j.procs.2025.01.213

Merriam-Webster. (2025, September 30). Plagiarize. Https://Www.Merriam-Webster.Com/Dictionary/Plagiarize

Meuschke, N., & Gipp, B. (2013). State of the Art in Detecting Academic Plagiarism. *International Journal for Educational Integrity*, *9*(1), 50–71. DOI: 10.21913/IJEI.v9i1.847

Meyer, K., & Norman, E. (2020). Aesthetic consciousness and creativity in primary art teacher education. *Journal of Aesthetic Education*, *54*(3), 56–73.

Meylani, R. (2024). Artificial intelligence in the education of teachers: A qualitative synthesis of the cutting-edge research literature. *Journal of Computer and Education Research*, *12*(24), 600–637. DOI: 10.18009/jcer.1477709

Miao, J., Thongprayoon, C., Suppadungsuk, S., Garcia Valencia, O. A., Qureshi, F., & Cheungpasitporn, W. (2023). Ethical dilemmas in using AI for academic writing and an example framework for peer review in nephrology academia: A narrative review. *Clinics and Practice*, *14*(1), 89–105. DOI: 10.3390/clinpract14010008

Minaee, S., Abdolrashidi, A., Su, H., Bennamoun, M., & Zhang, D. (2023). Biometrics recognition using deep learning: A survey. *Artificial Intelligence Review*, *56*(8), 8647–8695. DOI: 10.1007/s10462-022-10237-x

Minh, A. (2024). Leveraging ChatGPT for enhancing English writing skills and critical thinking in university freshmen. Journal of Knowledge Learning and Science Technology Issn 2959-6386 (Online), 3(2), 51-62. https://doi.org/DOI: 10.60087/jklst.vol3.n2.p62

Min, H.-T. (2006). The effects of trained peer review on EFL students' revision types and writing quality. *Journal of Second Language Writing*, *15*(2), 118–141. DOI: 10.1016/j.jslw.2006.01.003

Mobo, F. D., Azar, A. S., & Ana, L. R. G. "The Synergy of AI and Robotics in Modern Education." In *Innovations in Educational Robotics: Advancing AI for Sustainable Development*, pp. 69-86. IGI Global Scientific Publishing, 2025. DOI: 10.4018/979-8-3693-6165-8.ch004

Mohammadi, R., Borna, P., & Zoghi, R. (2023). The Effect of Employing Grammarly on Iranian EFL Learners' Writing Performance. *International Journal of Research in English Education*, *8*(5), 187–197.

Mohebbi, A. (2025). Enabling learner independence and self-regulation in language education using AI tools: A systematic review. *Cogent Education*, *12*(1), 2433814. DOI: 10.1080/2331186X.2024.2433814

Mohsen, M. A., Mahdi, H. S., AlThebi, S. H., Alkhammash, R., & Alsharani, A. (2025). A scientometric study of computer-assisted pronunciation training in second language acquisition: Technological affordances and research trends. *Humanities & Social Sciences Communications*, *12*(1), 1–11. DOI: 10.1057/s41599-025-04474-y

Molloy, E., Boud, D., & Henderson, M. (2020). Developing a learning-centred framework for feedback literacy. *Assessment & Evaluation in Higher Education*, *45*(4), 527–540. DOI: 10.1080/02602938.2019.1667955

Molopa, S. T. (2024). Artificial intelligence-based literature review adaptation. *South African Journal of Library and Information Science*, *90*(2), 1–18.

Mondal, H., & Mondal, S. (2023). ChatGPT in academic writing: Maximizing its benefits and minimizing the risks. *Indian Journal of Ophthalmology*, *71*(12), 3600–3606. DOI: 10.4103/IJO.IJO_718_23 PMID: 37991290

Montiel, H., & Gomez-Zermeño, M. G. (2022). Rock the Boat! Shaken by the COVID-19 Crisis: A Review on Teachers' Competencies in ICT. *Frontiers in Education*, *6*, 770442. Advance online publication. DOI: 10.3389/feduc.2021.770442

Montuori, R., & Gilabert-Sansalvador, L. (2025). "EMPOWERING ARCHITECTURE STUDENTS IN CITATION MANAGEMENT." In *INTED2025 Proceedings*, pp. 3681-3686. IATED. DOI: 10.21125/inted.2025.0929

Moorhouse, B. L., Yeo, M. A., & Wan, Y. (2023). Generative AI tools and assessment: Guidelines of the world's top-ranking universities. *Computers and Education Open*, *5*, 100151. DOI: 10.1016/j.caeo.2023.100151

Morady Moghaddam, M., Esmaeilpour, F., & Ranjbaran, F. (2025). Insights into mobile assisted language learning research in Iran: A decade review (2010–2023). *Education and Information Technologies*, *30*(2), 2155–2181. DOI: 10.1007/s10639-024-12879-6

Moran, C. M., & Pyles, D. G. (2025). Teachers First: Building AI Literacy to Address Mundane Tasks and Enhance Creative Applications in Secondary English Classrooms. In *Reimagining Literacy in the Age of AI* (pp. 49-72). Chapman and Hall/CRC.

Mospan, N. (2023). Digitalisation of writing in higher education: The COVID-19 pandemic impact. *Journal of University Teaching & Learning Practice*, *20*(2). Advance online publication. DOI: 10.53761/1.20.02.08

Moussa, A., & Belhiah, H. (2024). Beyond syntax: exploring moroccan undergraduate efl learners' engagement with ai-assisted writing. https://doi.org/DOI: 10.31235/osf.io/3fr45

Moustaghfir, S., & Brigui, H. (2024). Navigating critical thinking in the digital era: An informative exploration. International Journal of Linguistics. *Literature and Translation*, *7*(1), 137–143.

Movahed, G. B., Rahmanian, F., Emarati, F., & Movahed, A. B. (2025). The Synergy of AI and Education: Opportunities and Challenges for the Future. *Applied Innovations in Industrial Management*, *5*(3), 45–51. DOI: 10.63630/aiim.53.45

Moybeka, A., Syariatin, N., Tatipang, D., Mushthoza, D., Dewi, N., & Tineh, S. (2023). Artificial intelligence and english classroom: the implications of ai toward efl students' motivation. Edumaspul - Jurnal Pendidikan, 7(2), 2444-2454. https://doi.org/DOI: 10.33487/edumaspul.v7i2.6669

Mrida, M. S. H., Rahman, M. A., & Alam, M. S. (2025). AI-Driven Data Analytics and Automation: A Systematic Literature Review of Industry Applications. *Strategic Data Management and Innovation*, *2*(01), 21–40. DOI: 10.71292/sdmi.v2i01.9

Mudawy, A. (2024). Investigating efl faculty members' perceptions of integrating artificial intelligence applications to improve the research writing process: a case study at majmaah university. https://doi.org/DOI: 10.31235/osf.io/k4ub8

Mujtaba, B. (2024). Clarifying ethical dilemmas in sharpening students' artificial intelligence proficiency: Dispelling myths about using AI tools in higher education. *Business Ethics and Leadership*, *8*(2), 107–127. DOI: 10.61093/bel.8(2).107-127.2024

Mulenga, R., & Shilongo, H. (2024). Academic integrity in higher education: Understanding and addressing plagiarism. *Acta Pedagogia Asiana*, *3*(1), 30–43. DOI: 10.53623/apga.v3i1.337

Mun, C. Y. (2024). EFL learners' English writing feedback and their perception of using ChatGPT. *Journal of English Teaching through Movies and Media, 25(2), 26-39.*

Munikwa, S., & Mapara, J. The Case of Chinhoyi University of Technology. (2022). Grappling with education 5.0 curriculum development in Zimbabwean higher education. The case of Chinhoyi University of Technology. *Journal of African Education*, *3*(2), 181–203. DOI: 10.31920/2633-2930/2022/v3n2a7

Murugason, L. (2025). Evaluating chatgpt's influence on esl educators' teaching and motivation.. https://doi.org/DOI: 10.71284/asc.2025132

Muslimin, A., Mukminatien, N., & Maria, I. (2024). Evaluating cami ai across smar stages: Students' achievement and perceptions in efl writing instruction. *Online Learning : the Official Journal of the Online Learning Consortium*, *28*(2). Advance online publication. DOI: 10.24059/olj.v28i2.4246

Mustafa, M. Y., Tlili, A., Lampropoulos, G., Huang, R., Jandrić, P., Zhao, J., Salha, S., Xu, L., Panda, S., Kinshuk, , López-Pernas, S., & Saqr, M. (2024). A systematic review of literature reviews on artificial intelligence in education (AIED): A roadmap to a future research agenda. *Smart Learning Environments*, *11*(1), 59. DOI: 10.1186/s40561-024-00350-5

Muthmainnah, M., Al Yakin, A., & Seraj, P. M. I. (2024, September). Integrating Robot-Based Resources to Foster Computational Thinking and Communication. In *Sustainable Development through Machine Learning, AI and IoT: Second International Conference, ICSD 2024, Virtual Event, April 27–28, 2024* []. Springer Nature.]. *Proceedings*, *2196*, 70.

Muthmainnah, M., Cardoso, L., Marzuki, A. G., & Al Yakin, A. (2025). A new innovative metaverse ecosystem: VR-based human interaction enhances EFL learners' transferable skills. *Discover Sustainability*, *6*(1), 156. DOI: 10.1007/s43621-025-00913-7

Muthmainnah, M., Seraj, P., & Oteir, I. (2022). Playing with ai to investigate human-computer interaction technology and improving critical thinking skills to pursue 21st century age. *Education Research International*, *2022*, 1–17. DOI: 10.1155/2022/6468995

Muzira, D. R., & Bondai, B. M. (2020). Perception of educators towards the adoption of education 5.0: A case of a state university in Zimbabwe. East African Journal of education and social sciences, 1(2), 43-53.

Muzira, D. R., & Muzira, R. (2020). An assessment of educators' level of concern on the adoption of education 5.0: A case of one university in Zimbabwe. *Current Journal of Applied Science and Technology*, *39*(17), 22–32. DOI: 10.9734/cjast/2020/v39i1730749

Myers, S., & Chater, N. (2024). Interactive explainability: Black boxes, mutual understanding and what it would really mean for AI systems to be as explainable as people. *Preprint at* PsyArXiv . *io/ha37x*.DOI: 10.31234/osf.io/ha37x

Nancy, W., Parimala, A., & Livingston, L. M. M. (2020). Advanced Teaching Pedagogy As Innovative Approach In Modern Education System. *Procedia Computer Science*, *172*, 382–388. DOI: 10.1016/j.procs.2020.05.059

Na-songkhla, J., Mahakaew, V., & Peytcheva-Forsyth, R. (2024). The Emergence of Generative Artificial Intelligence: Enhancing Critical Thinking Skills in ChatGPTIntegrated Cognitive Flexibility Approach. Generative Artificial Intelligence in Higher Education: A Handbook for Educational Leaders, 52.

Nasution, K. Y., Sihite, R. A., & Hartati, R. (2024). Exploring the Role and Benefits of ChatGPT AI in Enhancing Students' Fiction Writing Literacy: Insights from Learner Experiences. *Fonologi Jurnal Ilmuan Bahasa Dan Sastra Inggris*, *2*(4), 141–153. DOI: 10.61132/fonologi.v2i4.1219

Naveed, H., Khan, A. U., Qiu, S., Saqib, M., Anwar, S., Usman, M., Akhtar, N., Barnes, N., & Mian, A. (2025). A comprehensive overview of large language models. *ACM Transactions on Intelligent Systems and Technology*, *16*(5), 1–72. DOI: 10.1145/3744746

Nazari, N., Shabbir, M., & Setiawan, R. (2021). Application of artificial intelligence powered digital writing assistant in higher education: Randomized controlled trial. *Heliyon*, *7*(5), e07014. DOI: 10.1016/j.heliyon.2021.e07014 PMID: 34027198

Nazim, M., & Mohammad, T. (2022). Implications of design thinking in an efl classroom: Writing in context. *Theory and Practice in Language Studies*, *12*(12), 2723–2730. DOI: 10.17507/tpls.1212.31

Nelson, M. J., & Hoover, A. K. (2020). "Notes on using Google Colaboratory in AI education." In *Proceedings of the 2020 ACM conference on innovation and Technology in Computer Science Education*, pp. 533-534. DOI: 10.1145/3341525.3393997

Nelson, M. M., & Schunn, C. D. (2009). The nature of feedback: How different types of peer feedback affect writing performance. *Instructional Science*, *37*(4), 375–401. DOI: 10.1007/s11251-008-9053-x

Neshaei, S., Mejia-Domenzain, P., Davis, R., & Käser, T. (2025). Metacognition meets ai: Empowering reflective writing with large language models. *British Journal of Educational Technology*, *56*(5), 1864–1896. DOI: 10.1111/bjet.13601

Ng, C., & Cheung, Y. (2018). Mediation in a socio-cognitive approach to writing for elementary students: Instructional scaffolding. *Education Sciences*, *8*(3), 92. DOI: 10.3390/educsci8030092

Nguyen, A., Hong, Y., Dang, B., & Huang, X. (2024). Human-AI collaboration patterns in AI-assisted academic writing. *Studies in Higher Education*, *49*(5), 847–864. DOI: 10.1080/03075079.2024.2323593

Nguyen, A., Ngo, H. N., Hong, Y., Dang, B., & Nguyen, B.-P. T. (2023). Ethical principles for artificial intelligence in education. *Education and Information Technologies*, *28*(4), 4221–4241. Advance online publication. DOI: 10.1007/s10639-022-11316-w PMID: 36254344

Nicholls, J., Kuppa, A., & Le-Khac, N. (2021). Financial Cybercrime: A comprehensive survey of deep learning approaches to tackle the evolving financial crime landscape. *IEEE Access : Practical Innovations, Open Solutions*, *9*, 163965–163986. DOI: 10.1109/ACCESS.2021.3134076

Nicol, D. (2010). From monologue to dialogue: Improving written feedback processes in mass higher education. *Assessment & Evaluation in Higher Education*, *35*(5), 501–517. DOI: 10.1080/02602931003786559

Nieminen, M. (2023). The Transformer Model and Its Impact on the Field of Natural Language Processing.

Noddings, N. (2012). *The ethics of care: Personal, political, and global*. University of California Press.

Nourinezhad, S., Hadipourfard, E., & Bavali, M. (2021). The effect of audio-visual feedback on writing components and writing performance of medical university students in two different modes of instruction, flipped and traditional. *Cogent Education*, *8*(1), 1978621. Advance online publication. DOI: 10.1080/2331186X.2021.1978621

Nowotny, H. (2021). *AI we trust: Power, illusion and control of predictive algorithms*. John Wiley & Sons.

Nuemaihom, A., Al Yakin, A., Seraj, P. M. I., Asad, M. M., & Elngar, A. A. (2025). In-Depth Analysis of Artificial Intelligence Practices: Robot Tutors and Federated Learning Approach in English Education. In *Artificial Intelligence Using Federated Learning* (pp. 16-36). CRC Press.

Nunes, A., Cordeiro, C., Limpo, T., & Castro, S. L. (2022). Effectiveness of automated writing evaluation systems in school settings: A systematic review. *Journal of Computer Assisted Learning*, *38*(6), 1260–1277. DOI: 10.1111/jcal.12635

Nuong Deri, M., Singh, A., Zaazie, P., & Anandene, D. (2024). Leveraging Artificial Intelligence in Higher Educational Institutions: A Comprehensive Overview. *Education and Law Review*, (30). Advance online publication. DOI: 10.1344/REYD2024.30.45777

O'Neill, R., & Russell, A. (2019). Stop! Grammar time: University students' perceptions of the automated feedback program Grammarly. *Australasian Journal of Educational Technology*, *35*(1), 42–56. DOI: 10.14742/ajet.3795

Obenza, B. N., Salvahan, A., Rios, A. N., Solo, A., Alburo, R. A., & Gabila, R. J. (2024). University students' perception and use of ChatGPT: Generative artificial intelligence (AI) in higher education. *International Journal of Human-Computer Studies*, *5*(12), 5–18.

OECD. (2019). *OECD principles on artificial intelligence.* https://oecd.ai/en/ai-principles

OECD. (2025). Empowering learners for the age of AI: An AI literacy framework for primary and secondary education (Review draft). OECD. Paris. https://ailiteracyframework.org

Oh, Y., Zhang, J., Fang, M., & Fukuoka, Y. (2021). A systematic review of artificial intelligence chatbots for promoting physical activity, healthy diet, and weight loss. *The International Journal of Behavioral Nutrition and Physical Activity*, *18*(1), 160. Advance online publication. DOI: 10.1186/s12966-021-01224-6 PMID: 34895247

Okonkwo, C. M., & Ade-Ibijola, A. (2023). Students' voices on generative AI: Perceptions, benefits, and challenges in higher education. *International Journal of Educational Technology in Higher Education*, *20*(1), 41. Advance online publication. DOI: 10.1186/s41239-023-00411-8

Ong, J. C. L., Chang, S. Y.-H., William, W., Butte, A. J., Shah, N. H., Chew, L. S. T., Liu, N., Doshi-Velez, F., Lu, W., Savulescu, J., & Ting, D. S. W. (2024). Ethical and regulatory challenges of large language models in medicine. *The Lancet. Digital Health*, *6*(6), e428–e432. DOI: 10.1016/S2589-7500(24)00061-X PMID: 38658283

Open, A. I., Achiam, J., Adler, S., Agarwal, S., Ahmad, L., Akkaya, I., Aleman, F. L., Almeida, D., Altenschmidt, J., Altman, S., Anadkat, S., Avila, R., Babuschkin, I., Balaji, S., Balcom, V., Baltescu, P., Bao, H., Bavarian, M., Belgum, J., & Zoph, B. (2024). *GPT-4 Technical Report.* https://arxiv.org/abs/2303.08774

Oppenlaender, J., Linder, R., & Silvennoinen, J. (2024). Prompting AI Art: An Investigation into the Creative Skill of Prompt Engineering. https://arxiv.org/abs/2303.13534

Organisation for Economic Co-operation and Development [OECD]. (2019). The OECD artificial intelligence policy observatory - OECD.AI. https://oecd.ai/en/ai-principles

Organisation for Economic Co-operation and Development. (2019). *Recommendation of the Council on Artificial Intelligence.* https://legalinstruments.oecd.org/en/instruments/OECD-LEGAL-0449

Osawa, K. (2023). Integrating automated written corrective feedback into e-portfolios for second language writing: Notion and notion ai. *RELC Journal*, *55*(3), 881–887. DOI: 10.1177/00336882231198913

Oubibi, M., Hryshayeva, K., & Huang, R. (2025). Enhancing postgraduate digital academic writing proficiency: The interplay of artificial intelligence tools and ChatGPT. *Interactive Learning Environments*, *33*(6), 1–19. DOI: 10.1080/10494820.2025.2454445

Ouyang, L., Wu, J., Jiang, X., Almeida, D., Wainwright, C. L., Mishkin, P., Zhang, C., Agarwal, S., Slama, K., Ray, A., Schulman, J., Hilton, J., Kelton, F., Miller, L., Simens, M., Askell, A., Welinder, P., Christiano, P., Leike, J., & Lowe, R. (2022). Training language models to follow instructions with human feedback. https://arxiv.org/abs/2203.02155

Oyelude, A. A. (2024). Artificial intelligence (AI) tools for academic research. *Library Hi Tech News*, *41*(8), 18–20. DOI: 10.1108/LHTN-08-2024-0131

Oyenuga, M. O., Apata, S. B., & Sulaiman, M. M. (2024). Pre-Service Teachers' Perceptions and Utilisation of Chatgpt in Higher Institutions using UTAUT Theory: Evidence from an Emerging Economy. *British Journal of Contemporary Education, 4*(2), 28–42. DOI: 10.52589/BJCE-DBIT7S4T

Oyenuga, M. O., & Omale, S. A. (2024). Is Africa Jinxed? Exploring the Challenges of Technology Access and Adoption in Africa. *African Journal of Economic and Sustainable Development, 7*(4), 142–161. DOI: 10.52589/AJESD-ULN1LRNF

Ozfidan, B., El-Dakhs, D. A. S., & Alsalim, L. A. (2024). The use of AI tools in English academic writing by Saudi undergraduates. *Contemporary Educational Technology, 16*(4), ep527. DOI: 10.30935/cedtech/15013

Ozor, N., Nwakaire, J., Nyambane, A., Muhatiah, W., & Nwobodo, C. (2025). Enhancing africa's agriculture and food systems through responsible and gender inclusive ai innovation: Insights from ai4afs network. *Frontiers in Artificial Intelligence, 7*, 1472236. Advance online publication. DOI: 10.3389/frai.2024.1472236 PMID: 39917548

Pack, A., & Maloney, J. (2023). Using generative artificial intelligence for language education research: Insights from using OpenAI's ChatGPT. *TESOL Quarterly, 57*(4), 1571–1582. DOI: 10.1002/tesq.3253

Pagallo, U., Ciani, J., & Durante, M. (2022). The environmental challenges of ai in eu law: Lessons learned from the artificial intelligence act (aia) with its drawbacks. *Transforming Government, 16*(3), 359–376. DOI: 10.1108/TG-07-2021-0121

Page, M. J., McKenzie, J. E., Bossuyt, P. M., Boutron, I., Hoffmann, T. C., Mulrow, C. D., Shamseer, L., Tetzlaff, J. M., Akl, E. A., Brennan, S. E., Chou, R., Glanville, J., Grimshaw, J. M., Hróbjartsson, A., Lalu, M. M., Li, T., Loder, E. W., Mayo-Wilson, E., McDonald, S., & Moher, D. (2021). The PRISMA 2020 statement: An updated guideline for reporting systematic reviews. *BMJ (Clinical Research Ed.), 372*(71), n71. Advance online publication. DOI: 10.1136/bmj.n71

Pakdel, F., Khojasteh, L., Kafipour, R., & Shahsavar, Z. (2025). Navigating AI writing tools in medical education: A SWOT analysis of L2 academic writing perspectives. *Language Teaching Research*, •••, 13621688251322953. DOI: 10.1177/13621688251322953

Pan, Q., Jumaat, N. F., Abuhassna, H., & Tao, L. (2026). Transforming education in the digital age: An analysis of artificial intelligence and deep learning through bibliometric and systematic literature review. In B. Edwards, H. Abuhassna, D. Olugbade, O. Ojo, & W. Jaafar Wan Yahaya (Eds.), *AI in education, governance, and leadership: Adoption, impact, and ethics* (pp. 67–96). IGI Global Scientific Publishing. https://doi.org/DOI: 10.4018/979-8-3373-5550-4.ch004

Pan, J. (2024). Ai-driven english language learning program and academic writing integrity in the era of intelligent interface. *English Language Teaching and Linguistics Studies, 6*(4), 120. DOI: 10.22158/eltls.v6n4p120

Pardede, P. (2025). Recent Research on Creative Writing Learning in Indonesian EFL Settings: A Systematic Literature Review. *Journal of English Teaching, 11*(2), 150–167. DOI: 10.33541/jet.v11i2.6971

Pariyanto, P., & Tungka, N. F. (2025). ChatGPT As a Formative Feedback Tool: Improving Narrative Essay Writing Among EFL Students. *Edulitics (Education, Literature, and Linguistics). Journal*, *10*(1), 71–84.

Park, S. (2023). Bridging the global divide in AI regulation: A proposal for a contextual, coherent, and commensurable framework. *Wash. Int'l LJ*, *33*, 216.

Parviz, M. (2025). Generative ai in the english composition classroom practical and adaptable strategies. *International Journal of Computer-Assisted Language Learning and Teaching*, *15*(1), 1–5. DOI: 10.4018/IJCALLT.386135

Parycek, P., Schmid, V., & Novak, A. S. (2024). Artificial Intelligence (AI) and automation in administrative procedures: Potentials, limitations, and framework conditions. *Journal of the Knowledge Economy*, *15*(2), 8390–8415. DOI: 10.1007/s13132-023-01433-3

Pears, R., & Shields, G. (2025). *Cite them right: the essential referencing guide*. Bloomsbury Publishing.

Peckham, O., Raines, J., Bulsink, E., Goudswaard, M., Gopsill, J., Barton, D., Nassehi, A., & Hicks, B. (2025). Artificial Intelligence in Generative Design: A Structured Review of Trends and Opportunities in Techniques and Applications. *Designs*, *9*(4), 79. DOI: 10.3390/designs9040079

Pedro, Francesc, Miguel Subosa, Axel Rivas, and Paula Valverde. "Artificial intelligence in education: Challenges and opportunities for sustainable development." (2019).

Pellas, N., Mikropoulos, T. A., & Konstantinidis, A. (2019). VR in art education: A systematic review. *Journal of Educational Technology & Society*, *22*(4), 405–420.

Perignat, E., & Katz-Buonincontro, J. (2019). Art education and critical thinking in teacher preparation. *Teacher Education Quarterly*, *46*(2), 113–130.

Perkins, M., Furze, L., Roe, J., & MacVaugh, J. (2024). The Artificial Intelligence Assessment Scale (AIAS): A framework for ethical integration of generative AI in educational assessment. *Journal of University Teaching & Learning Practice*, *21*(6), 49–66. DOI: 10.53761/q3azde36

Perkins, M., Roe, J., Vu, B. H., Postma, D., Hickerson, D., McGaughran, J., & Khuat, H. (2024a). Simple techniques to bypass GenAI text detectors: Implications for inclusive education. *International Journal of Educational Technology in Higher Education*, *21*(1), 53. DOI: 10.1186/s41239-024-00487-w

Pham, N. T. B., & Tran, T. M. (2025). Students' Perceptions of AI Language Models as Virtual Assistants in Learning Writing-A Case Study at a Tertiary Institution. *International Journal of TESOL & Education*, *5*(2), 87–115. DOI: 10.54855/ijte.25525

Pitenoee, M., Modaberi, A., & Ardestani, E. (2017). The effect of cognitive and metacognitive writing strategies on content of the iranian intermediate efl learners' writing. *Journal of Language Teaching and Research*, *8*(3), 594. DOI: 10.17507/jltr.0803.19

Plate, D., Melick, E., Hutson, J., & Edele, S. (2024). *Generative AI in the English Composition Classroom: Practical and Adaptable Strategies* (1st ed.). Routledge., DOI: 10.4324/9781003507949

Polakova, P., & Ivenz, P. (2024). The impact of ChatGPT feedback on the development of EFL students' writing skills. *Cogent Education*, *11*(1), 2410101. DOI: 10.1080/2331186X.2024.2410101

Prasetya, R., & Raharjo, D. (2023). Enhancing english language writing skills: An evaluation of the efficacy of grammarly application. *Journal of English Language & Studies*, *8*(2), 320. DOI: 10.30870/jels.v8i2.19294

Pratama, A., & Sulistiyo, U. (2024). A systematic review of artificial intelligence in enhancing english foreign learners' writing skill. *PIJED*, *3*(2), 170–181. DOI: 10.59175/pijed.v3i2.299

Pratama, R. M. D., & Hastuti, D. P. (2024). The use of artificial intelligence to improve EFL students' writing skill. *English Learning Innovation*, *5*(1), 13–25. DOI: 10.22219/englie.v5i1.30212

Priestley, M., Biesta, G., & Robinson, S. (2015). *Teacher agency: An ecological approach.* Bloomsbury Academic. DOI: 10.4324/9781315678573-15

Prior, P. (2006). A sociocultural theory of writing. In MacArthur, C. A., Graham, S., & Fitzgerald, J. (Eds.), *Handbook of writing research* (pp. 54–66). Guilford Press.

Pritiprada, P., Satpathy, I., Azar, A. S., & Patnaik, B. C. M. "RoboRevolution: Transforming Education for Sustainable Futures." In *Innovations in Educational Robotics: Advancing AI for Sustainable Development*, pp. 157-172. IGI Global Scientific Publishing, 2025. DOI: 10.4018/979-8-3693-6165-8.ch008

Qaffas, A. A. (2024). Harnessing Artificial Intelligence for Enhanced Efficiency in Academic Writing and Research. *Fusion: Practice & Applications, 16*(2).

Qin, Q., & Zhang, S. (2025). Visualizing the knowledge mapping of artificial intelligence in education: A systematic review. *Education and Information Technologies*, *30*(1), 449–483. DOI: 10.1007/s10639-024-13076-1

Qin, Z., & Chuaychoowong, M. (2025). Artificial Intelligence in EFL Education in China: A Systematic Review of Trends, Gaps, and Future Directions (2015-2024). *Language Teaching Research*, *49*, 59–89. DOI: 10.32038/ltrq.2025.49.04

Queiroz-Neto, J. P., Sales, D. C., Pinheiro, H. S., & Neto, B. O. (2015). Using modern pedagogical tools to improve learning in technological contents. *2015 IEEE Frontiers in Education Conference (FIE)*, 1–8. DOI: 10.1109/FIE.2015.7344383

Rachmad, Y. E. (2019). Transforming Workforce Skills in the Era of Society 5.0: Integrating Technology and Artificial Intelligence in Competency Development.

Rad, H. S., Alipour, R., & Jafarpour, A. (2024). Using artificial intelligence to foster students' writing feedback literacy, engagement, and outcome: A case of Wordtune application. *Interactive Learning Environments*, *32*(9), 5020–5040. DOI: 10.1080/10494820.2023.2208170

Radu, R. (2019). Negotiating internet governance. In *Oxford University Press eBooks*. DOI: 10.1093/oso/9780198833079.001.0001

Rahayu, R., Weda, S., Muliati, , & De Vega, N. (2024). Artificial intelligence in writing instruction: A self-determination theory perspective. *Xlinguae*, *17*(1), 234–244. DOI: 10.18355/XL.2024.17.01.16

Raheem, B. R., Anjum, F., & Ghafar, Z. N. (2023). Exploring the profound impact of artificial intelligence applications (Quillbot, Grammarly and ChatGPT) on English academic writing: A Systematic Review. [IJIR]. *International Journal of Integrative Research, 1*(10), 599–622.

Rahimi, A. R., Sheyhkholeslami, M., & Pour, A. M. (2025). Uncovering personalized L2 motivation and self-regulation in ChatGPT-assisted language learning: *A hybrid PLS-SEM-ANN approach. Computers in Human Behavior Reports, 17*, 100539. DOI: 10.1016/j.chbr.2024.100539

Rahimi, M., & Noroozisiam, E. (2013). The effect of strategies-based instruction on the improvement of EFL learners' writing quality. *SAGE Open, 3*(2), 2158244013494222. Advance online publication. DOI: 10.1177/2158244013494222

Rahim, M. N. (2021). Post-pandemic of Covid-19 and the need for transforming education 5.0 in Afghanistan higher education. *Utamax: Journal of Ultimate Research and Trends in Education, 3*(1), 29–39. DOI: 10.31849/utamax.v3i1.6166

Rahman, M. M., & Halim, Z. (2022). Predicting the Big Five personality traits from handwritten text images using semi-supervised learning. *Multimedia Tools and Applications, 81*(43), 31241–31269. DOI: 10.1007/s11042-022-13114-5

Raitskaya, L., & Tikhonova, E. (2023). Academic integrity: Author-related and journal-related issues. *Journal of Language and Education, 9*(4 (36)), 5–10.

Ramadhan, R., Rahim, A., & Paris, A. (2024). Enhancing academic writing through digital tools: A systematic review. *Journal of Language and Literature Studies, 4*(4), 707–770. DOI: 10.36312/jolls.v4i4.2342

Ramezani, A., Bijani, H., & Oroji, M. R. (2025). Comparative Analysis of AI vs. Human Feedback Effects on IELTS Candidates' Writing Performance. *Journal of Foreign Language Teaching and Translation Studies, 10*(1), 17–40.

Rana, J., Gaur, L., & Santosh, K. C. "Classifying customers' journey from online reviews of Amazon fresh via sentiment analysis and topic modelling." In *2022 3rd International Conference on Computation, Automation and Knowledge Management (ICCAKM)*, pp. 1-6. IEEE, 2022. DOI: 10.1109/ICCAKM54721.2022.9990124

Rana, J., Gaur, L., Singh, G., Awan, U., & Rasheed, M. I. (2022). Reinforcing customer journey through artificial intelligence: A review and research agenda. *International Journal of Emerging Markets, 17*(7), 1738–1758. DOI: 10.1108/IJOEM-08-2021-1214

Rana, J., Jain, R., & Nehra, V. (2024). Utility and acceptability of AI-enabled Chatbots on the online customer journey. *International Journal of Computing and Digital Systems, 15*(1), 323–335. DOI: 10.12785/ijcds/150125

Rana, J., Jain, R., & Santosh, K. C. (2023). Automation and AI-enabled customer journey: A bibliometric analysis. *Vision (Basel)*, •••, 09722629221149854. DOI: 10.1177/09722629221149854

Rao, K., & Rao, R. (2007). Perspectives in medical education 5. implementing a more integrated, interactive and interesting curriculum to improve Japanese medical education. *The Keio Journal of Medicine, 56*(3), 75–84. DOI: 10.2302/kjm.56.75 PMID: 17906418

Raschka, S., Patterson, J., & Nolet, C. (2020). Machine learning in Python: Main developments and technology trends in data science, machine learning, and artificial intelligence. *Information (Basel), 11*(4), 193. DOI: 10.3390/info11040193

Rashidov, J., & Rashidova, F. (2024). The role of human oversight in AI-driven research. *AI and Ethics.*

Rashtchi, M. (2019). Scaffolding argumentative essay writing via reader-response approach: A case study. *Asian-Pacific Journal of Second and Foreign Language Education, 4*(1), 12. Advance online publication. DOI: 10.1186/s40862-019-0078-2

Ratih, M., & Kastuhandani, F. (2024). Students' lived experiences in utilizing artificial intelligence for thesis writing. Nusra Jurnal Penelitian Dan Ilmu Pendidikan, 5(2), 760-769. https://doi.org/ DOI: 10.55681/nusra.v5i2.2696

Ravšelj, D., Keržič, D., Tomaževič, N., Umek, L., Brezovar, N., Iahad, N., & Shin, D. (2025). Higher education students' perceptions of ChatGPT: A global study of early reactions. *PLoS One, 20*(2), e0315011. DOI: 10.1371/journal.pone.0315011

Raza, Z., Tahir, Z., Qamar, S., & Manan, A. (2025). The Role of AI in the Education Sector: Focusing on AI's Adaptation, Drawbacks, Implications, Trust, and Ethical Considerations. *Journal of Political Stability Archive, 3*(2), 145–165. DOI: 10.63468/jpsa.3.2.08

Reddig, J. M., Arora, A., & MacLellan, C. J. (2025). Generating In-Context, Personalized Feedback for Intelligent Tutors with Large Language Models. *International Journal of Artificial Intelligence in Education, 35*(6), 3459–3500. Advance online publication. DOI: 10.1007/s40593-025-00505-6

Ren, X., & Wu, M. L. (2025). Examining teaching competencies and challenges while integrating artificial intelligence in higher education. *TechTrends, 69*(3), 1–20. DOI: 10.1007/s11528-025-01055-3

Rezaei, M., Salehi, H., & Tabatabaei, O. (2024, February). Uses and misuses of ChatGPT as an AI-language model in academic writing. *In 2024 10th International Conference on Artificial Intelligence and Robotics (QICAR) (pp. 256-260). IEEE.*

Rigopouli, K., Kotsifakos, D., & Psaromiligkos, Y. (2025). Vygotsky's creativity options and ideas in 21st-century technology-enhanced learning design. *Education Sciences, 15*(2), 257. DOI: 10.3390/educsci15020257

Rizki, D. P., & Hannin, P. N. S. (2025). Mendeley-Based Training to Improve Reference Management and Citation Formatting in Sociology Students. *Room of Civil Society Development, 4*(2), 309–319. DOI: 10.59110/rcsd.565

Roa, A., & Halim, S. (2024). The impact of ai-powered software on second language (l2) writing: A systematic literature review. *Research and Innovation in Applied Linguistics-Electronic Journal, 2*(2), 138. DOI: 10.31963/rial.v2i2.4801

Roe, J., Renandya, W. A., & Jacobs, G. M. (2023). A review of AI-powered writing tools and their implications for academic integrity in the language classroom. *Journal of English and Applied Linguistics, 2*(1), 3. DOI: 10.59588/2961-3094.1035

Rosdiana, S., Noercolies, M. A., & Fauzan, M. H. (2024). The Use of Artificial Intelligence in Teaching Writing Skills. *EDUCASIA: Jurnal Pendidikan, Pengajaran. Dan Pembelajaran, 9*(1), 45–56. DOI: 10.21462/educasia.v9i1.251

Rosmayanti, V., Patak, A. A., & Noni, N. (2023). Integrating Technology into ESP Instruction: Teaching English for Pharmacy Students. *The Journal of AsiaTEFL, 20*(2), 475–484. DOI: 10.18823/asiatefl.2023.20.2.18.475

Roveta, A., Castello, L. M., Massarino, C., Francese, A., Ugo, F., & Maconi, A. (2025). Artificial Intelligence in Medical Education: A Narrative Review on Implementation, Evaluation, and Methodological Challenges. *AI, 6*(9), 227. DOI: 10.3390/ai6090227

Roy, K., & Swargiary, K. (2024). Chatgpt impact on efl indian undergraduates. https://doi.org/ DOI: 10.20944/preprints202405.0130.v2

Rubel, A., & Jones, K. M. L. (2016). Student privacy in learning analytics: An information ethics perspective. *The Information Society, 32*(2), 143–159. DOI: 10.1080/01972243.2016.1130502

Runco, M. A. (2025). Updating the standard definition of creativity to account for the artificial creativity of AI. *Creativity Research Journal, 37*(1), 1–5. DOI: 10.1080/10400419.2023.2257977

Russell, D. R. (1997). Rethinking genre in school and society: An activity theory analysis. *Written Communication, 14*(4), 504–554. DOI: 10.1177/0741088397014004004

Russell, R., Novak, L., Patel, M., Garvey, K., Craig, K., Jackson, G., & Miller, B. (2022). Competencies for the use of artificial intelligence–based tools by health care professionals. *Academic Medicine, 98*(3), 348–356. DOI: 10.1097/ACM.0000000000004963 PMID: 36731054

Ryan, T., Henderson, M., Ryan, K., & Kennedy, G. (2021). Designing learner-centred text-based feedback: A rapid review and qualitative synthesis. *Assessment & Evaluation in Higher Education, 46*(6), 894–912. DOI: 10.1080/02602938.2020.1828819

Sabharwal, D., Kabha, R., & Srivastava, K. (2023). Artificial intelligence (ai)-powered virtual assistants and their effect on human productivity and laziness: Study on students of delhi-ncr (india) & fujairah (uae). *Journal of Content. Community and Communication, 17*(9), 162–174. DOI: 10.31620/JCCC.06.23/12

Sadang, J. M., & Palompon, D. R. (2021). The development of Need-Threat Internal Resiliency Theory in COVID-19 crisis utilizing deductive axiomatic approach. 7(2), 72–77. https://doi.org/ DOI: 10.33546/bnj.1300

Saddhono, K., Suhita, R., Rakhmawati, A., Rohmadi, M., & Sukmono, I. K. (2024, November). AI and Literacy: Developing Critical Thinking and Analytical Skills in the Digital Era. In *2024 International Conference on IoT, Communication and Automation Technology (ICICAT)* (pp. 360-365). IEEE. DOI: 10.1109/ICICAT62666.2024.10922871

Saeed, M. A., AbuSa'aleek, A., & Alharbi, M. A. (2024). Examining teacher's evaluative language in written, audio and screencast feedback on EFL learners' writing from the appraisal framework: A linguistic perspective. *Assessing Writing, 61*, 100871. Advance online publication. DOI: 10.1016/j.asw.2024.100871

Safar, M., & Karimi, H. (2024). A multi-model approach for personality detection from handwriting. In *Proceedings of the 2024 International Conference on Affective Computing and Intelligent Interaction (ACII)*. ACM.

Safar, M., & Suen, C. Y. (2025). A multi-model approach for personality detection from handwriting: Deep features, machine learning, and ensemble techniques. In *Pattern Recognition — ICPR 2024 International Workshops and Challenges* (Vol. 15616, pp. 295–307). Springer., DOI: 10.1007/978-3-031-87663-9_25

Safitri, M., & Fithriani, R. (2024). Exploring Higher Education EFL Students' Perception of AI Writing Tools in the 5.0 Era. *Cetta: Jurnal Ilmu Pendidikan*, *7*(1), 267–276. DOI: 10.37329/cetta.v7i1.3158

Sahlberg, P., & Walker, T. (2021). *In teachers we trust: The Finnish way to world-class schools*. W. W. Norton & Company.

Saiful, Wihastyanang, W. D., Sulistyo, G. H., & Mukminatien, N. (2019). Confronting effect of online teacher and peer feedback on the students' writing performance. Problems of Education in the 21st Century, 77(5), 650–666. https://doi.org/DOI: 10.33225/pec/19.77.650

Saihi, Afef, Ben-Daya, Mohamed, & Hariga, Moncer, and Rami As' ad. "A Structural equation modeling analysis of generative AI chatbots adoption among students and educators in higher education." *Computers and Education: Artificial Intelligence 7* (2024): 100274.

Saini, J., Choudhary, S., & Walia, K. (2025). The Future of AI in Decision-Making: Replacing or Assisting Humans? *International Journal of Sciences and Innovation Engineering*, *2*(5), 751–778.

Sakib, S. M. N. (2024). *Bane and Boon of Hallucinations in the Context of Generative AI*. IGI Global., DOI: 10.4018/979-8-3693-2643-5.ch016

Sakr, A., & Abdullah, T. (2024). Virtual, augmented reality and learning analytics impact on learners, and educators: A systematic review. *Education and Information Technologies*, *29*(15), 19913–19962. DOI: 10.1007/s10639-024-12602-5

Saldaña, J. (2021). *The coding manual for qualitative researchers* (4th ed.). SAGE.

Saleem, T., Saleem, A., & Aslam, D. (2025). Integrating AI in Pakistani ESL classrooms: Teachers' practices, perspectives, and impact on student performance. *PLoS One*, *20*(9), e0333352. DOI: 10.1371/journal.pone.0333352 PMID: 41026767

Salimi, E., & Hajinia, M. (2024). Llms and academic writing in practice: exploring participants' utilization of gpt during an ai-assisted course on writing research papers. https://doi.org/DOI: 10.21203/rs.3.rs-5534554/v1

Sallam, M. (2023). The utility of ChatGPT as an example of large language models in healthcare education, research and practice: systematic review on the future perspectives and potential limitations. https://doi.org/DOI: 10.1101/2023.02.19.23286155

Salma, S. S., & Ahmed, S. M. B. (2024). Artificial Intelligence and the Evolution of Educator Roles in the Digital Technology Era. *Pakistan JL Analysis & Wisdom*, *3*, 231.

Samala, A. D., & Rawas, S. (2024). Bias in artificial intelligence: Smart solutions for detection, mitigation, and ethical strategies in real-world applications. *IAES International Journal of Artificial Intelligence, 14*(1), 32. DOI: 10.11591/ijai.v14.i1.pp32-43

Samala, A. D., Rawas, S., Wang, T., Reed, J. M., Kim, J., Howard, N. J., & Ertz, M. (2025). Unveiling the landscape of generative artificial intelligence in education: A comprehensive taxonomy of applications, challenges, and future prospects. *Education and Information Technologies, 30*(3), 3239–3278. DOI: 10.1007/s10639-024-12936-0

Samanta, S., & Banerjee, S. (2025). *Portfolio-Based Assessment: A Holistic Method For Evaluating Higher Education Students* (No. 2025-52-02).

Samuelsson, C. S. (2023). Generative AI as a co-creator in the conception of images.

Sangkala, I., & Mardonovna, N. S. (2024). Artificial intelligence as a personalized tutor in language learning: A systematic review. *Klasikal: Journal of Education. Language Teaching And Science, 6*(2), 565–576.

Santorelli, M., & Catullo, D. (2023). Human mobility and language: towards new multilingual approaches with ai. In *Creşterea economică în condiţiile globalizării* (pp. 151-161). DOI: 10.36004/nier.cdr.V.2023.17.16

Sapci, A., & Sapci, H. (2020). Artificial intelligence education and tools for medical and health informatics students: Systematic review. *JMIR Medical Education, 6*(1), e19285. DOI: 10.2196/19285 PMID: 32602844

Saran, A. (2024). Effect of teaching strategies on students' German writing skills at saudi international schools. *Saudi Journal of Language Studies, 4*(1), 47–68. DOI: 10.1108/SJLS-10-2023-0049

Sarıcaoğlu, A. (2022). Towards teaching undergraduate-level disciplinary writing in english majors: A genre-based approach. *RumeliDe Dil ve Edebiyat Arastirmalari Dergisi*, (26), 1024–1038. DOI: 10.29000/rumelide.1074517

Schmidt-Fajlik, R. (2023). Chatgpt as a grammar checker for japanese english language learners: A comparison with grammarly and prowritingaid. *AsiaCALL Online Journal, 14*(1), 105–119. DOI: 10.54855/acoj.231417

Schnitzer, S., & Tiruwuha, M. H. (2024). Transparency in the Black Box.

Schönwetter, D. J., Ruge, G., McCormack, C., Kennelly, R., & Gareau-Wilson, N. (2020). A future-ready teaching philosophy: Opportunities to reflect, re-value and re-frame a teaching philosophy. *ETH Learning and Teaching Journal*, 437-443 Pages. DOI: 10.16906/LT-ETH.V2I2.180

Schuster, J. (2019). Writing instruction and assessment for struggling learners.. https://doi.org/ DOI: 10.3102/1443450

Scott, B. L., Muñoz, S. M., & Scott, S. B. (2024). How whiteness operates at a hispanic serving institution: A qualitative case study of faculty, staff, and administrators. *Journal of Diversity in Higher Education, 17*(4), 563–574. DOI: 10.1037/dhe0000438

Sedrakyan, G., van den Berg, S. M., Veldkamp, B. P., & van Hillegersberg, J. (2023). Analysis of the Feedback Digitization Needs in Higher Education: Experiences from Lockdown Education in the Netherlands and Germany. *International Journal of Information and Education Technology (IJIET), 13*(5), 778–784. DOI: 10.18178/ijiet.2023.13.5.1867

Selvaraju, R. R., Cogswell, M., Das, A., Vedantam, R., Parikh, D., & Batra, D. (2017). Grad-CAM: Visual explanations from deep networks via gradient-based localization. In *Proceedings of the IEEE International Conference on Computer Vision (ICCV)* (pp. 618–626). IEEE. https://doi.org/DOI: 10.1109/ICCV.2017.74

Semingson, P., Hurlbut, A., Owens, D., & Robertson, M. (2016). Scaffolding digital writing and storytelling in online-only teacher education courses. In Handbook of Research on Learner Centered Pedagogy in Teacher Education and Professional Development. https://doi.org/DOI: 10.4018/978-1-5225-0892-2.ch006

Seo, K., Tang, J., Roll, I., Fels, S., & Yoon, D. (2021). The impact of artificial intelligence on learner–instructor interaction in online learning. *International Journal of Educational Technology in Higher Education, 18*(1), 54. Advance online publication. DOI: 10.1186/s41239-021-00292-9 PMID: 34778540

Seyri, H., & Ghiasvand, F. (2025). "Teaching is basically feeling": Unpacking EFL Teachers' perceived emotions and regulatory strategies in AI-Powered L2 speaking and writing skills instruction. *Computers and Education Open, 8*, 100264. DOI: 10.1016/j.caeo.2025.100264

Shah, S. S., & Asad, M. M. (2024). Impact of Critical Thinking Approach on Learners' Dependence on Innovative Transformation Through Artificial Intelligence. In The Evolution of Artificial Intelligence in Higher Education: Challenges, Risks, and Ethical Considerations (pp. 161-182). Emerald Publishing Limited.

Shah, C. (2025). From Prompt Engineering to Prompt Science with Humans in the Loop. *Communications of the ACM*, 3709599. Advance online publication. DOI: 10.1145/3709599

Shah, P. (2023). *AI and the Future of Education: Teaching in the Age of Artificial Intelligence.* John Wiley & Sons.

Shahsavar, Z., Kafipour, R., Khojasteh, L., & Pakdel, F. (2024, December). Is artificial intelligence for everyone? Analyzing the role of ChatGPT as a writing assistant for medical students. [). Frontiers Media SA.]. *Frontiers in Education, 9*, 1457744. DOI: 10.3389/feduc.2024.1457744

Shahzad, S. K., Panhawar, A. H., & Ansari, S. (2025). Project-based learning and digital literacy integration: Investigating task design and student collaboration in developing academic writing and thesis skills in EFL classrooms. *Research Journal in Translation, Literature, Linguistics, and Education, 1*(3), 18-31.

Sharma, N. (2025, June). Role of Artificial Intelligence in Intercultural Dialogue and Language: Ethical Frame works for Sustainability and Equity. In *Innovative Multidisciplinary Approaches to Global Challenges: Sustainability, Equity, and Ethics in an Interconnected World (IMASEE 2025)* (pp. 215-223). Atlantis Press.

Sharma, R., & Singh, A. (2024). Use of Digital Technology in Improving Quality Education: A Global Perspectives and Trends. In Nadda, V., Tyagi, P., Moniz Vieira, R., & Tyagi, P. (Eds.), *Implementing Sustainable Development Goals in the Service Sector* (pp. 14–26). IGI Global., DOI: 10.4018/979-8-3693-2065-5.ch002

Sheridan, K. M., Winner, E., Hetland, L., & Veenema, S. (2022). *Studio thinking 3: The real benefits of visual arts education.* Teachers College Press.

Shi, H., & Aryadoust, V. (2022). A systematic review of automated writing evaluation systems. *Education and Information Technologies, 28*(1), 771–795. DOI: 10.1007/s10639-022-11200-7

Shin, Y., Wei, S., & Vanchinkhuu, N. (2025). Digital plagiarism in EFL education during the AI era: A comparative study of perceptions among learners and instructors in Korea, Mongolia, and China. *LEARN Journal: Language Education and Acquisition Research Network, 18*(1), 594–618. DOI: 10.70730/RMKA9428

Shtayyat, A., Gawanmeh, A., & Mashaleh, A. (2025). Risk Analysis of AI Integration in Educational Systems: Toward Ethical and Equitable Innovation. In *Examining Cybersecurity Risks Produced by Generative AI* (pp. 401-428). IGI Global Scientific Publishing.

Shukla, P., Naik, S., Obi, I., Backus, J., Rasche, N., & Parson, P. "Rethinking Citation of AI Sources in Student-AI Collaboration within HCI Design Education." *arXiv preprint arXiv:2506.08467* (2025). DOI: 10.1145/3742901.3742909

Siemens, G. (2005). Connectivism: A learning theory for the digital age. *International Journal of Instructional Technology and Distance Learning, 2*(1), 3–10.

Silitonga, L. M., Hawanti, S., Aziez, F., Furqon, M., Zain, D. S. M., Anjarani, S., & Wu, T. T. (2023, August). The Impact of AI Chatbot-Based Learning on Students' Motivation in English Writing Classroom. *In International Conference on Innovative Technologies and Learning (pp. 542-549). Cham: Springer Nature Switzerland.* DOI: 10.1007/978-3-031-40113-8_53

Siluvai, S., Narayanan, V., Ramachandran, V., & Lazar, V. (2025). Generative pre-trained transformer: trends, applications, strengths and challenges in dentistry: a systematic review. *Healthcare Informatics Research, 31*(2), 189–199. DOI: 10.4258/hir.2025.31.2.189 PMID: 40384070

Simamora, P. (2020). Integrating interactive technology in art education: A need for reform. *International Journal of Art & Design Education, 39*(3), 345–358.

Singaram, V. S., Pillay, R., & Mbobnda Kapche, E. L. (2024). Exploring the role of digital technology for feedback exchange in clinical training: A scoping review. *Systematic Reviews, 13*(1), 298. Advance online publication. DOI: 10.1186/s13643-024-02705-y

Singh, A. (2022). Conceptual framework on Smart Learning Environment- An Indian perspective. *Journal of Education and Law*, (25). Advance online publication. DOI: 10.1344/REYD2022.25.36706

Singh, A. (2024a). The Role of Digital Transformation and Its Effects on the Education Sector. In Chakraborty, S. (Ed.), *Challenges of Globalization and Inclusivity in Academic Research* (pp. 92–99). IGI Global Scientific Publishing., DOI: 10.4018/979-8-3693-1371-8.ch007

Singh, A. (2024b). Endorsing Gamification Pedagogy for Nurturing Employability Skills in Higher Education Institutions (HEI). In Membrive, V. (Ed.), *Practices and Implementation of Gamification in Higher Education* (pp. 172–183). IGI Global Scientific Publishing., DOI: 10.4018/979-8-3693-0716-8.ch008

Singh, A. (2024c). Impact of E-learning on Student Motivation in Higher Education Institutions: An Indian Perspective. *Journal of Education and Law*, (29). Advance online publication. DOI: 10.1344/REYD2024.29.43214

Singh, A. (2024c). Students Wellbeing and Performance in Higher Education Institutions. In Aloka, P. (Ed.), *Factors Impacting Student Well-Being and Coping Tactics* (pp. 1–12). IGI Global Scientific Publishing., DOI: 10.4018/979-8-3693-8860-0.ch001

Singh, A., & Kumar, P. (2024). E-Learning Ecosystem in Higher Education Institutions: Trends and Practices. In Al Husseiny, F., & Munna, A. (Eds.), *Preparing Students for the Future Educational Paradigm* (pp. 1–18). IGI Global Scientific Publishing., DOI: 10.4018/979-8-3693-1536-1.ch001

Singh, A., & Sihmar, P. (2025). Higher Education Institution Sustainability: Role of Green Human Resource Management. In Adu-Gyamfi, M., Boateng, F., & Atiku, S. (Eds.), *Green HRM Awareness and Training in Higher Education Institutions* (pp. 1–14). IGI Global Scientific Publishing., DOI: 10.4018/979-8-3693-2956-6.ch001

Singh, A., Singh, D., & Chhikara, S. (2024). Online Learning: Challenges and Suggestions to Enhance Student Engagement in Higher Education Institutions. In Naidoo, V., & Verma, R. (Eds.), *Reshaping Entrepreneurial Education Within an Industry 4.0 Context* (pp. 59–80). IGI Global Scientific Publishing., DOI: 10.4018/979-8-3693-0409-9.ch004

Slade, S., & Prinsloo, P. (2013). Learning analytics: Ethical issues and dilemmas. *The American Behavioral Scientist, 57*(10), 1510–1529. DOI: 10.1177/0002764213479366

Slavkov, N. (2015). Sociocultural theory, the l2 writing process, and google drive: Strange bedfellows? *TESL Canada Journal, 32*(2), 80. DOI: 10.18806/tesl.v32i2.1209

Soelistiyowati, E., Permatasari, A., Nugroho, V., & Kusmulyadi, A. (2024). Enhancing college learners' writing skills through the integration of ChatGPT: Strategies, benefits, and concerns. *Eralingua Jurnal Pendidikan Bahasa Asing Dan Sastra, 8*(1), 1. DOI: 10.26858/eralingua.v8i1.53461

Sol, K., & Heng, K. (2024). AI-powered chatbots as personalized academic writing assistants for non-native English speakers. In Peters, M. A., & Heraud, R. (Eds.), *Encyclopedia of educational innovation* (pp. 1–5). Springer., DOI: 10.1007/978-981-13-2262-4_313-1

Solmaz, O. (2020). The Nature and Potential of Digital Collaborative Reading Practices for Developing EFL Proficiency. *IOJET: International Online Journal of Education and Teaching, 7*(4), 1283–1298.

Solmaz, O. (2023). AI Literacies in Language Education: Meeting Challenges, Embracing Transformations. In Bakla, A., & Çakır, İ. (Eds.), *ChatGPT in Foreign Language Education and Translation Studies* (pp. 167–188). Anı Publishing.

Song, C., & Song, Y. (2023). Enhancing academic writing skills and motivation: Assessing the efficacy of ChatGPT in AI-assisted language learning for EFL students. *Frontiers in Psychology*, *14*, 1260843. DOI: 10.3389/fpsyg.2023.1260843 PMID: 38162975

Song, Y., Jin, H.-Y., Pan, Z., & Cutumisu, M. (2023). A Systematic Review of Automated Feedback Generation in Empirical Educational Research. *Proceedings of International Conference of the Learning Sciences Icls*, 1895–1896. DOI: 10.22318/icls2023.403455

Sophia, L. I. (2025). The Social Harms of AI-Generated Fake News: Addressing Deepfake and AI Political Manipulation. *Digital Society & Virtual Governance*, *1*(1), 72–88. DOI: 10.6914/dsvg.010105

Sousa, D. L., Campos, P. F., & Cesário, V. (2022). Design Implications for Interactive and Analogue Technologies supporting Distance Education: A Longitudinal Mixed-Method Study during the Pandemic. *Interaction Design and Architecture S*, *52*(52), 6–22. DOI: 10.55612/s-5002-052-001

Soyler, A., Burmaoglu, S., & Kidak, L. B. (2025). The evolutionary path of medical waste management research: Insights from co-citation and co-word analysis. *Waste Management & Research*, *43*(1), 3–15. DOI: 10.1177/0734242X241227378

Spector, J. M., & Ma, S. (2019). Inquiry and critical thinking skills for the next generation: From artificial intelligence back to human intelligence. *Smart Learning Environments*, *6*(1), 1–11. DOI: 10.1186/s40561-019-0088-z

Spencer, D. A. (2023). Technology and work: Past lessons and future directions. *Technology in Society*, *74*, 102294. DOI: 10.1016/j.techsoc.2023.102294

Sperber, L.. (2025). Peer and AI Review + Reflection (PAIRR): A human-centered approach to integrating AI feedback. *Computers and Composition*, *76*, 102921. DOI: 10.1016/j.compcom.2025.102921

Sperling, K., Stenberg, C.-J., McGrath, C., Åkerfeldt, A., Heintz, F., & Stenliden, L. (2024). In search of artificial intelligence (AI) literacy in teacher education: A scoping review. *Computers and Education Open*, *6*, 100169. DOI: 10.1016/j.caeo.2024.100169

Spinellis, D. (2025). False authorship: An explorative case study around an AI-generated article published under my name. *Research Integrity and Peer Review*, *10*(1), 8. DOI: 10.1186/s41073-025-00165-z PMID: 40420142

Srivastava, P., Mamodiya, U., Dutta, P. K., & Paliktzoglou, V. (2024, December). Advanced AI-Driven Thematic and Narrative Analysis: Exploring Deep Learning in Literature. In International Conference on Arts, Humanities, and Interdisciplinary Sciences (pp. 179-194). Cham: Springer Nature Switzerland.

Staiano, M. F. (2021). *CRITICAL DIALOGUES Human rights, democracy and pandemic perspectives*. DOI: 10.55658/gpcds978-65-00-40218-6

Steele, S. E. (2008). Bibliographic citation management software as a tool for building knowledge. *Journal of Wound, Ostomy, and Continence Nursing*, *35*(5), 463–468. DOI: 10.1097/01.WON.0000335956.45311.69

Stevenson, M., & Phakiti, A. (2019). Automated writing evaluation for EFL/ESL: A synthesis of the literature. *Language Assessment Quarterly*, *16*(4–5), 389–409.

Stolpe, K., & Hallström, J. (2024). Artificial intelligence literacy for technology education. *Computers and Education Open*, *6*, 100159. DOI: 10.1016/j.caeo.2024.100159

Stommel, J. (2014). Critical digital pedagogy: A definition. *Hybrid Pedagogy*. https://hybridpedagogy.org/critical-digital-pedagogy-definition/

Storch, N. (2013). *Collaborative writing in L2 classrooms*. Multilingual Matters.

Storch, N., & Wigglesworth, G. (2010). Learners' processing, uptake, and retention of corrective feedback on writing. *Studies in Second Language Acquisition*, *32*(2), 303–334. DOI: 10.1017/S0272263109990532

Strielkowski, W., Grebennikova, V., Lisovskiy, A., Rakhimova, G., & Vasileva, T. (2025). AI-driven adaptive learning for sustainable educational transformation. *Sustainable Development (Bradford)*, *33*(2), 1921–1947. DOI: 10.1002/sd.3221

Strobl, C. (2014). Attitudes towards online feedback on writing: Why students mistrust the learning potential of models. *ReCALL*, *27*(3), 340–357. DOI: 10.1017/S0958344015000099

Stuchlikova, L., & Weis, M. (2024, October). From Information to Insight: Reimagining Critical Thinking Pedagogy in the Age of Artificial Intelligence. In *2024 International Conference on Emerging eLearning Technologies and Applications (ICETA)* (pp. 591-598). IEEE. DOI: 10.1109/ICETA63795.2024.10850787

Subaveerapandiyan, A., Paladhi, M., & Maruthaveeran, V. (2023). Evaluating ai literacy proficiency among lis researchers in asean. *Library Hi Tech News*, *41*(4), 6–8. DOI: 10.1108/LHTN-07-2023-0121

Sullivan, M., Kelly, A., & McLaughlan, P. (2023). ChatGPT in higher education: Considerations for academic integrity and student learning. *Journal of Applied Learning & Teaching*, *6*(1). Advance online publication. DOI: 10.37074/jalt.2023.6.1.17

Sungur, M. O., & Seyhan, T. Ö. (2013). Writing references and using citation management software. *Turkish Journal of Urology*, *39*(Suppl 1), 25.

Susilo, M. J., Sulisworo, D., & Beungacha, S. (2023). Technology and Its Impact on Education. *Buletin Edukasi Indonesia*, *2*(02), 47–54. DOI: 10.56741/bei.v2i02.285

Syamala, S., Shrivastava, A., & Karmakar, S. (2025). Identifying interface design factors impacting user experience in digital learning platforms-A pilot study. *Social Sciences & Humanities Open*, *11*, 101662. DOI: 10.1016/j.ssaho.2025.101662

T P, R. (2024). AI-Driven Pedagogy: Unveiling ChatGPT's Influence in Education. *Journal of Applied Science, Engineering, Technology and Management*, *2*(01), 09–14. DOI: 10.61779/jasetm.v2i1.2

Tajik, A. (2025). Exploring the role of AI-driven dynamic writing platforms in improving EFL learners' writing skills and fostering their motivation.

Tajik, A. (2025). Exploring the role of ai-driven dynamic writing platforms in improving efl learners' writing skills and fostering their motivation. https://doi.org/DOI: 10.21203/rs.3.rs-5788599/v1

Tan, C. (2024). Future-readiness and its educational implications: A Daoist interpretation. *Research in Comparative and International Education, 19*(2), 224–238. DOI: 10.1177/17454999241230238

Taneja, D., Prabagaren, H., & Thomas, M. R. (2025). Al in Academia: Balancing Integrity, Ethics, and. *Pitfalls of AI Integration in Education: Skill Obsolescence, Misuse, and Bias: Skill Obsolescence, Misuse, and Bias*, 319.

Tan, M. J. T., & Maravilla, N. M. A. (2024). Shaping integrity: Why generative artificial intelligence does not have to undermine education. *arXiv Preprint.* https://arxiv.org/abs/2407.19088

Tan, S., Cho, Y. W., & Xu, W. (2023). Exploring the effects of automated written corrective feedback, computer-mediated peer feedback and their combination mode on EFL learner's writing performance. *Interactive Learning Environments, 31*(10), 7276–7286. DOI: 10.1080/10494820.2022.2066137

Taskiran, A., Yazici, M., & Erdem Aydin, I. (2024). Contribution of automated feedback to the English writing competence of distance foreign language learners. *E-Learning and Digital Media, 21*(1), 24–41. DOI: 10.1177/20427530221139579

Tastanbek, S. (2024). Translanguaging pedagogy in EAP writing: A multilingual Qazaq instructor's perspective. *Journal of Second Language Writing, 63*, 101075. DOI: 10.1016/j.jslw.2023.101075

Tate, T. P., Steiss, J., Bailey, D. H., Graham, S., Moon, Y., Ritchie, D., Tseng, W., & Warschauer, M. (2024). *Can AI provide useful holistic essay scoring?* Computers & Education. *Artificial Intelligence, 7*, 100255. DOI: 10.1016/j.caeai.2024.100255

Tayebinik, M., & Puteh, M. (2013). Blended Learning or E-learning? DOI: 10.48550/ARXIV.1306.4085

Temsah, A., Alhasan, K., Altamimi, I., Jamal, A., Al-Eyadhy, A., Malki, K. H., & Temsah, M.-H. (2025). DeepSeek in healthcare: Revealing opportunities and steering challenges of a new open-source artificial intelligence frontier. *Cureus, 17*(2). Advance online publication. DOI: 10.7759/cureus.79221

Teng, M. F. (2024). "ChatGPT is the companion, not enemies": EFL learners' perceptions and experiences in using ChatGPT for feedback in writing. *Computers and Education: Artificial Intelligence, 7*, 100270. DOI: 10.1016/j.caeai.2024.100270

Teng, M. F. (2025). Metacognitive awareness and EFL learners' perceptions and experiences in utilising ChatGPT for writing feedback. *European Journal of Education, 60*(1), e12811. DOI: 10.1111/ejed.12811

Tham, J., Howard, T., & Verhulsdonck, G. (2022). Extending design thinking, content strategy, and artificial intelligence into technical communication and user experience design programs: Further pedagogical implications. *Journal of Technical Writing and Communication, 52*(4), 428–459. DOI: 10.1177/00472816211072533

Thanaraj, A., & Gledhill, K. (2022). *Teaching Legal Education in the Digital Age: Pedagogical Practices to Digitally Empower Law Graduates* (1st ed.). Routledge., DOI: 10.4324/9780429351082

Thapaliya, A., & Hrytsuk, Y. (2023). Exploring the Impact of COVID-19 on Education: A Study on Challenges and Opportunities in Online Learning. In Smart Innovation Systems and Technologies: Vol. 354 SIST. https://doi.org/DOI: 10.1007/978-981-99-3068-5_29

The University of Hong Kong. (2023, August 3). *HKU introduces new policy to fully integrate GenAI in teaching and learning*. https://www.hku.hk/press/press-releases/detail/26434.html

Theodorou, A., Nieves, J., & Dignum, V. (2022). Good ai for good: how ai strategies of the nordic countries address the sustainable development goals. https://doi.org//arxiv.2210.09010DOI: 10.48550

Thi Van Pham, A. (2022). Exploring Peer Feedback on Writing Assignments in an Online Learning Environment. *ACM International Conference Proceeding Series*, 203–208. https://doi.org/DOI: 10.1145/3514262.3514294

Thi, N. K., & Nikolov, M. (2022). How Teacher and Grammarly Feedback Complement One Another in Myanmar EFL Students' Writing. *The Asia-Pacific Education Researcher, 31*(6), 767–779. DOI: 10.1007/s40299-021-00625-2

Thyrhaya Zein, T., Silvana Sinar, T., & Deliana, D. (2025). USING VIRTUAL WRITING TUTOR IN TEACHING WRITING TO EFL LEARNERS. *Jurnal Ilmiah Ilmu Terapan Universitas Jambi, 9*(2), 474–484. DOI: 10.22437/jiituj.v9i2.36052

Tian, L., & Zhou, Y. (2020). Learner engagement with automated feedback, peer feedback and teacher feedback in an online EFL writing context. *System, 91*, 102247. Advance online publication. DOI: 10.1016/j.system.2020.102247

Tian, W., Ge, J., Zhao, Y., & Zheng, X. (2024). Ai chatbots in Chinese higher education: Adoption, perception, and influence among graduate students—an integrated analysis utilizing utaut and ecm models. *Frontiers in Psychology, 15*, 1268549. Advance online publication. DOI: 10.3389/fpsyg.2024.1268549 PMID: 38384353

Tiwari, J., & Sadiwala, R. (2023). Personality prediction from handwriting using fine-tuned models. *SAMRIDDHI: A Journal of Physical Sciences, Technology and Management.* https://www.smsjournals.com/index.php/SAMRIDDHI/article/view/3080

Tokuda, Y., Gotō, E., Otaki, J., Jacobs, J., Omata, F., Shapiro, M., Soejima, K., Ishida, Y., Ohde, S., Takahashi, O., & Fukui, T. (2010). Educational environment of university and non-university hospitals in Japan. *International Journal of Medical Education, 1*, 10–14. DOI: 10.5116/ijme.4ba1.4034

Tomczyk, P., Brüggemann, P., & Vrontis, D. (2024). AI meets academia: Transforming systematic literature reviews. *EuroMed Journal of Business.* Advance online publication. DOI: 10.1108/EMJB-03-2024-0055

Torrance, A. W., & Tomlinson, B. (2025). Organic Websites: Certification of AI-Generated or Human-Written Content on the Internet. Chi.-. *Kent J. Intell. Prop., 24*, 72.

Tr n, T. (2024). Ai tools in teaching and learning english academic writing skills. *Proceedings of the Asiacall International Conference*, 4, 170-187. https://doi.org/DOI: 10.54855/paic.23413

Triansyah, Fadli Agus, Ilham Muhammad, Andi Rabuandika, Kartika Dwi Pratiwi Siregar, Nurhuda Teapon, and Mohammad Syahru Assabana. "Bibliometric analysis: Artificial intelligence (AI) in high school education." *Jurnal Ilmiah Pendidikan dan Pembelajaran* 7, no. 1 (2023): 112-123.

Tsai, C. Y., Lin, Y. T., & Brown, I. K. (2024). Impacts of ChatGPT-assisted writing for EFL English majors: Feasibility and challenges. *Education and Information Technologies, 29*(17), 22427–22445. DOI: 10.1007/s10639-024-12722-y

Tseng, L.-P. (2025). *Exploring artificial intelligence literacy and the use of ChatGPT and copilot in instruction on nursing academic report writing.*

Tubella, A., Andrea, M. M.-C., & Nieves, J. C. (2024). How to teach responsible AI in Higher Education: Challenges and opportunities. *Ethics and Information Technology, 26*(1), 3. DOI: 10.1007/s10676-023-09733-7

Tuppal, C., Atendido, M., Atendido, A., Ninobla, M., Fadlilah, S., & Roa, M. (2025). Introducing chatgpt in undergraduate research among nursing students: a quasi- experimental study. https://doi.org/DOI: 10.21203/rs.3.rs-5915492/v1

Turvey, K., & Pachler, N. (2025). A topological exploration of convergence/divergence of human-mediated and algorithmically mediated pedagogy. *British Journal of Educational Technology*, bjet.70007. DOI: 10.1111/bjet.70007

Ucheagwu-Okoye, O. M. (2025). The Role of Artificial Intelligence (AI) in Student Assessment and Evaluation in Educational Leadership in Tertiary Institutions in Anambra State. Unizik Journal of Educational Laws and Leadership Studies, 1(1).

Ulla, M. B., Advincula, M. J. C., Mombay, C. D. S., Mercullo, H. M. A., Nacionales, J. P., & Entino-Señorita, A. D. (2024). How can GenAI foster an inclusive language classroom? A critical language pedagogy perspective from Philippine university teachers. *Computers and Education: Artificial Intelligence, 5*, 100314. DOI: 10.1016/j.caeai.2024.100314

Ulum, Ö. (2024). Unveiling the layers: Analyzing chatgpt implementations in turkish state universities. *BEDU, 5*(1), 114–134. DOI: 10.29329/bedu.2024.651.7

UNESCO. (2021). *Draft text of the recommendation on the ethics of artificial intelligence.*

UNESCO. (2024). *AI in education: Global adoption trends and policy implications.* United Nations Educational, Scientific and Cultural Organization. https://unesdoc.unesco.org/

United Nations Educational, Scientific and Cultural Organization (UNESCO). (2021). *Recommendation on the ethics of artificial intelligence.* https://unesdoc.unesco.org/ark:/48223/pf0000380455

United Nations Educational, Scientific and Cultural Organization [UNESCO]. (2021). *Recommendation on the ethics of artificial intelligence.* https://unesdoc.unesco.org/ark:/48223/pf0000381137

Uribe, S. E., Maldupa, I., Kavadella, A., El Tantawi, M., Chaurasia, A., Fontana, M., Marino, R., Innes, N., & Schwendicke, F. (2024). Artificial intelligence chatbots and large language models in dental education: Worldwide survey of educators. *European Journal of Dental Education, 28*(4), 865–876. DOI: 10.1111/eje.13009

Utami, S., Andayani, A., Winarni, R., & Sumarwati, S. (2023). Utilization of artificial intelligence technology in an academic writing class: How do indonesian students perceive? *Contemporary Educational Technology, 15*(4), ep450. DOI: 10.30935/cedtech/13419

Van Laer, S., & Elen, J. (2017). In search of attributes that support self-regulation in blended learning environments. *Education and Information Technologies, 22*(4), 1395–1454. DOI: 10.1007/s10639-016-9505-x

van Zyl, C., Ye, X., & Naidoo, R. (2024). Harnessing explainable artificial intelligence for feature selection in time series energy forecasting: A comparative analysis of Grad-CAM and SHAP. *Applied Energy, 353*, 122079. DOI: 10.1016/j.apenergy.2023.122079

VanDerHeide, J. (2017). Classroom talk as writing instruction for learning to make writing moves in literary arguments. *Reading Research Quarterly, 53*(3), 323–344. DOI: 10.1002/rrq.196

Van, N. T., Abbas, A. F., Abuhassna, H., Awae, F., & Dike, D. (2021). Digital readiness for social educators in health care and online learning during COVID-19 pandemic: A bibliometric analysis. [iJIM]. *International Journal of Interactive Mobile Technologies, 15*(18), 104–115. DOI: 10.3991/ijim.v15i18.25529

Vartiainen, H., Valtonen, T., Kahila, J., & Tedre, M. (2025). ChatGPT and imaginaries of the future of education: Insights of Finnish teacher educators. *Information and Learning Science, 126*(1/2), 75–90. DOI: 10.1108/ILS-10-2023-0146

Vaswani, A., Shazeer, N., Parmar, N., Uszkoreit, J., Jones, L., Gomez, A. N., & Kaiser, Ł. ukasz, & Polosukhin, I. (2017). Attention is All you Need. In I. Guyon, U. Von Luxburg, S. Bengio, H.

Vergara, J., &Karpukhin, S. (2022). *Reimagining Nabokov*. DOI: 10.3998/mpub.12734225

Verma, M. (2018). Artificial intelligence and its scope in different areas with special reference to the field of education. *Online Submission, 3*(1), 5–10.

Vetrivel, S. C., Vidhyapriya, P., & Arun, V. P. (2025). The role of AI in transforming assessment practices in education. In *AI Applications and Strategies in Teacher Education* (pp. 43–70). IGI Global.

Villegas-Ch, W., & García-Ortiz, J. (2023). Toward a comprehensive framework for ensuring security and privacy in artificial intelligence. *Electronics (Basel), 12*(18), 3786. DOI: 10.3390/electronics12183786

Visbal-Cadavid, D., Martínez-Gómez, M., & Guijarro, F. (2017). Assessing the efficiency of public universities through dea. a case study. *Sustainability (Basel), 9*(8), 1416. DOI: 10.3390/su9081416

Vrouwenvelder, K., Raia, N. H., & Thomer, A. K. (2025). Obstacles to Dataset Citation Using Bibliographic Management Software. *Data Science Journal, 24*, 24. DOI: 10.5334/dsj-2025-017

Vygotsky, L. S. (1978). *Mind in society: The development of higher psychological processes*. Harvard University Press.

Wahyuda, M., & Putera, A. (2022). The effectiveness of prowritingaid toward students writing skills in senior high school. *English Edu Journal of English Teaching and Learning*, *1*(1), 26–34. DOI: 10.18860/jetl.v1i1.1624

Wahyuningsih, S. (2024). Does Artificial Intelligence (AI) Play Roles in Enhancing Academic Writing? Unravelling Lecturers' Voices in Indonesian Higher Education. *Jurnal Pendidikan Progresif*, *14*(1), 489–503. DOI: 10.23960/jpp.v14.i1.202436

Wale, B., & Kassahun, Y. (2024). The transformative power of ai writing technologies: Enhancing efl writing instruction through the integrative use of writerly and google docs. *Human Behavior and Emerging Technologies*, *2024*, 1–15. DOI: 10.1155/2024/9221377

Walters, W. H. (2025). Gauging scholars' acceptance of Open Access journals by examining the relationship between perceived quality and citation impact. *Science*, *9*(4), 1–18.

Wang, C. (2024). Exploring students' generative AI-assisted writing processes: Perceptions and experiences from native and nonnative English speakers. *Technology Knowledge and Learning*, *30*(3), 1825–1846. DOI: 10.1007/s10758-024-09744-3

Wang, C., Wang, H., Li, Y., Dai, J., Gu, X., & Yu, T. (2025). Factors influencing university students' behavioral intention to use generative artificial intelligence: Integrating the theory of planned behavior and AI literacy. *International Journal of Human-Computer Interaction*, *41*(11), 6649–6671. DOI: 10.1080/10447318.2024.2383033

Wang, D. (2024). Teacher-versus AI-generated (Poe application) corrective feedback and language learners' writing anxiety, complexity, fluency, and accuracy. *International Review of Research in Open and Distance Learning*, *25*(3), 37–56. DOI: 10.19173/irrodl.v25i3.7646

Wang, J. (2024). The effect of Chinese EFL students' digital literacy on their Technostress and Academic Productivity. *The Asia-Pacific Education Researcher*, *33*(4), 987–996. DOI: 10.1007/s40299-023-00794-2

Wang, J., & Cheng, X. (2022). Modernizing art education through ICT integration: A cross-cultural analysis. *Global Journal of Art and Education*, *16*(3), 224–239.

Wang, X. (2025). Students' perceptions of automated writing evaluation in autonomous learning. *Education and Information Technologies*, *30*(11), 14703–14735. DOI: 10.1007/s10639-025-13378-y

Wang, Y. (2025). Reducing anxiety, promoting enjoyment and enhancing overall English proficiency: The impact of AI-assisted language learning in Chinese EFL contexts. *British Educational Research Journal*, berj.4187. DOI: 10.1002/berj.4187

Wang, Y., & Li, M. (2021). ICT integration in Chinese fine arts education: A case study. *Journal of Computing in Higher Education*, *33*(1), 1–18.

Wardat, S., & Akour, M. (2025). Teachers' Use of Generative AI in Jordanian Universities: Practices and Perceptions. *Forum for Linguistic Studies*, *7*(6), 90–102. DOI: 10.30564/fls.v7i6.9644

Waters, L., Lo, K., & Maloney, S. (2018). What impact do students have on clinical educators and the way they practise? *Advances in Health Sciences Education : Theory and Practice*, *23*(3), 611–631. DOI: 10.1007/s10459-017-9785-y PMID: 28698965

Weber-Wulff, D., Anohina-Naumeca, A., Bjelobaba, S., Foltýnek, T., Guerrero-Dib, J., Popoola, O., Šigut, P., & Waddington, L. (2023). Testing of detection tools for AI-generated text. *International Journal for Educational Integrity*, *19*(1), 26. DOI: 10.1007/s40979-023-00146-z

Weidmann, A. E. (2024). Artificial intelligence in academic writing and clinical pharmacy education: Consequences and opportunities. *International Journal of Clinical Pharmacy*, *46*(3), 751–754. DOI: 10.1007/s11096-024-01705-1 PMID: 38472596

Wei, P., Wang, X., & Dong, H. (2023). The impact of automated writing evaluation on second-language writing skills of Chinese EFL learners: A randomized controlled trial. *Frontiers in Psychology*, *14*, 1249991. DOI: 10.3389/fpsyg.2023.1249991 PMID: 37842718

Werdiningsih, I., Marzuki, , & Rusdin, D. (2024). Balancing AI and authenticity: EFL students' experiences with ChatGPT in academic writing. *Cogent Arts & Humanities*, *11*(1), 2392388. Advance online publication. DOI: 10.1080/23311983.2024.2392388

Wigglesworth, G., & Storch, N. (2012). What role for collaboration in writing and writing feedback? *Journal of Second Language Writing*, *21*(4), 364–374. DOI: 10.1016/j.jslw.2012.09.005

Wihastyanang, W. D., Kusumaningrum, S. R., Latief, M. A., & Cahyono, B. Y. (2020). Impacts of providing online teacher and peer feedback on students' writing performance. *Turkish Online Journal of Distance Education*, *21*(2), 178–189. DOI: 10.17718/tojde.728157

Wilf, S., & Wray-Lake, L. (2024). "That's how revolutions happen": Psychopolitical resistance in youth's online civic engagement. *Journal of Adolescent Research*, *39*(4), 827–860. DOI: 10.1177/07435584211062121 PMID: 40969284

Wilkins, K., Bennett, L., & Marshall, H. (2025). Story Thinking and the Real-world Applications of Sci-fi and Fantasy Writing.

Williamson, B., & Eynon, R. (2020). Historical threads, missing strands, and future directions in AI in education. *Learning, Media and Technology*, *45*(3), 223–235. DOI: 10.1080/17439884.2020.1798995

Williams, R., Ali, S., Devasia, N., DiPaola, D., Hong, J., Kaputsos, S., Jordan, B., & Breazeal, C. (2022). Ai + ethics curricula for middle school youth: Lessons learned from three project-based curricula. *International Journal of Artificial Intelligence in Education*, *33*(2), 325–383. DOI: 10.1007/s40593-022-00298-y PMID: 35935456

Wilson, J., & Czik, A. (2016). Automated essay evaluation and the teaching of writing: Critical considerations. *Assessing Writing*, *29*, 90–97.

Wingate, U., & Tribble, C. (2012). The best of both worlds? Towards an English for Academic Purposes/Academic Literacies writing pedagogy. *Studies in Higher Education*, *37*(4), 481–495. DOI: 10.1080/03075079.2010.525630

Winstone, N. E., & Carless, D. (2019). *Designing effective feedback processes in higher education: A learning-focused approach*. Routledge. DOI: 10.4324/9781351115940

Wirzal, M., Nordin, N., Halim, N., & Bustam, M. (2024). Generative ai in science education: A learning revolution or a threat to academic integrity? a bibliometric analysis. *Jurnal Penelitian Dan Pengkajian Ilmu Pendidikan E-Saintika*, *8*(3), 319–351. DOI: 10.36312/e-saintika.v8i3.2127

Wolbers, K., Dostal, H., Graham, S., Branum-Martin, L., & Holcomb, L. (2021). Specialized writing instruction for deaf students: A randomized controlled trial. *Exceptional Children, 88*(2), 185–204. DOI: 10.1177/00144029211050849

Wu, J., Yang, S., Zhan, R., Yuan, Y., Chao, L. S., & Wong, D. F. (2025). A survey on llm-generated text detection: Necessity, methods, and future directions. *Computational Linguistics, 51*(1), 275–338. DOI: 10.1162/coli_a_00549

Wu, L. (2024). Ai-based writing tools: Empowering students to achieve writing success. *Advances in Educational Technology and Psychology, 8*(2). Advance online publication. DOI: 10.23977/aetp.2024.080206

Xiao, F., Zhu, S., & Xin, W. (2025). Exploring the landscape of generative AI (ChatGPT)-powered writing instruction in English as a foreign language education: A scoping review. *ECNU Review of Education*, 20965311241310881.

Xi, L. (2024). Research on the english writing teaching model in the ai era. *MMSE, 6*(3), 111. DOI: 10.22158/mmse.v6n3p111

Xu, B. (2021). Traditional art education and technological innovation: A Chinese perspective. *Journal of Multicultural Education, 15*(2), 101–115.

Xu, L., & Zhao, J. (2022). Digital art education and curriculum innovation. *Curriculum Inquiry, 52*(3), 456–478.

Yan, D. (2023). How ChatGPT's automatic text generation impact on learners in a l2 writing practicum: an exploratory investigation. https://doi.org/DOI: 10.35542/osf.io/s4nfz

Yang, L., & Chano, J. (2025). The Impacts of Blended Learning on English Language Proficiency in Higher Education: A Systematic Literature Review. *Higher Education Studies, 15*(2), 83–96. DOI: 10.5539/hes.v15n2p83

Yan, J., Liu, Z., Leng, J., Zhao, J. L., Chen, C., Zhang, D., Tao, Y., Wang, Y., Liu, T., Zhang, C., Tong, Y., Mourtzis, D., & Wang, L. (2025). Human-centric artificial intelligence towards Industry 5.0: Retrospect and prospect. *Journal of Industrial Information Integration, 47*, 100903. DOI: 10.1016/j.jii.2025.100903

Yan, L., Sha, L., Zhao, L., Li, Y., Martínez-Maldonado, R., Chen, G., Li, X., Jin, Y., & Gašević, D. (2023). Practical and ethical challenges of large language models in education: A systematic scoping review. *British Journal of Educational Technology, 55*(1), 90–112. DOI: 10.1111/bjet.13370

Ye, J.-H., He, Z., Bai, B., & Wu, Y.-F. (2024). Sustainability of Technical and Vocational Education and Training (TVET) along with Vocational Psychology. *Behavioral Sciences (Basel, Switzerland), 14*(10), 859. DOI: 10.3390/bs14100859

Yesilyurt, Y. E. (2023). AI-enabled assessment and feedback mechanisms for language learning: Transforming pedagogy and learner experience. In *Transforming the language teaching experience in the age of AI* (pp. 25–43). IGI Global. DOI: 10.4018/978-1-6684-9893-4.ch002

Yeung, R. S. K., Tian, R., Chiu, D. K. W., & Choi, S. P.-M. (2025). University students' perceptions on how generative artificial intelligence shape learning and research practices: A case study in Hong Kong. *Journal of Academic Librarianship, 51*(5), 103082. DOI: 10.1016/j.acalib.2025.103082

Yigci, D., Eryilmaz, M., Yetisen, A. K., Tasoglu, S., & Ozcan, A. (2025). Large language model-based chatbots in higher education. *Advanced Intelligent Systems*, *7*(3), 2400429. DOI: 10.1002/aisy.202400429

Yiğit, M. F., & Seferoğlu, S. S. (2023). Effect of video feedback on students' feedback use in the online learning environment. *Innovations in Education and Teaching International*, *60*(1), 15–25. DOI: 10.1080/14703297.2021.1966489

Yim, I. H. Y., & Su, J. (2025). Artificial intelligence (AI) learning tools in K-12 education: A scoping review. *Journal of Computers in Education*, *12*(1), 93–131.

Yoon, S. Y., Miszoglad, E., & Pierce, L. R. (2023). Evaluation of ChatGPT feedback on ELL writers' coherence and cohesion. *arXiv preprint arXiv:2310.06505*.

Youvan, D. C. (2024). Towards a Cognitive Equilibrium: The Symbiosis of Human Complexity and Artificial Intelligence.

Yuan, Y. (2023). An empirical study of the efficacy of AI chatbots for English as a foreign language learning in primary education. *Interactive Learning Environments*, •••, 1–16.

Yu, E. (2023). Intelligent enough? Artificial intelligence for online learners. *The Journal of Educators Online*, *20*(1). Advance online publication. DOI: 10.9743/JEO.2023.20.1.16

Yu, H. (2024). The application and challenges of ChatGPT in educational transformation: New demands for teachers' roles. *Heliyon*, *10*(2), e24289. DOI: 10.1016/j.heliyon.2024.e24289 PMID: 38298626

Zafrullah, Z., Meisya, A., & Ayuni, R. T. (2024). Artificial intelligence as a learning media in English education: Bibliometric using biblioshiny analysis (2009-2023). *ELTR Journal*, *8*(1), 71–81. DOI: 10.37147/eltr.v8i1.179

Zamel, V. (1983). The composing processes of advanced esl students: Six case studies. *TESOL Quarterly*, *17*(2), 165. DOI: 10.2307/3586647

Zare, J., Al-Issa, A., & Madiseh, F. R. (2025). Interacting with ChatGPT in essay writing: *A study of L2 learners' task motivation. ReCALL*, *37*(3), 1–18. DOI: 10.1017/S0958344025000035

Zare, J., Ranjbaran Madiseh, F., & Derakhshan, A. (2025). Generative AI and English essay writing: Exploring the role of ChatGPT in enhancing learners' task engagement. *Applied Linguistics*, •••, amaf045. DOI: 10.1093/applin/amaf045

Zaugg, T. (2024). Embracing innovation in education: investigating the use and impact of artificial intelligent assistants among preservice teachers. https://doi.org/DOI: 10.21203/rs.3.rs-5032655/v1

Zawacki-Richter, O., Marín, V. I., Bond, M., & Gouverneur, F. (2019). Systematic review of research on artificial intelligence applications in higher education – where are the educators? *International Journal of Educational Technology in Higher Education*, *16*(1), 39. Advance online publication. DOI: 10.1186/s41239-019-0171-0

Zeevy-Solovey, O. (2024). Comparing peer, ChatGPT, and teacher corrective feedback in EFL writing: Students' perceptions and preferences. *Technology in Language Teaching & Learning*, *6*(3), 1482–1482. DOI: 10.29140/tltl.v6n3.1482

Zhai, Y. (2025). Computer-assisted English teaching model for improving learning performance of college students. *Journal of Computational Methods in Sciences and Engineering*, 14727978251361524.

Zhai, C., Wibowo, S., & Li, L. D. (2024). The effects of over-reliance on AI dialogue systems on students' cognitive abilities: A systematic review. *Smart Learning Environments*, *11*(1), 28. DOI: 10.1186/s40561-024-00316-7

Zhai, N., & Ma, X. (2021). Automated writing evaluation (AWE) feedback: A systematic investigation of college students' acceptance. *Computer Assisted Language Learning*. Advance online publication. DOI: 10.1080/09588221.2021.1897019

Zhang, L. & Wu, Z. (2024). Enhancing postgraduate academic writing skills through course reform: an action research study. Social Education Research, 217-233. https://doi.org/DOI: 10.37256/ser.5220244202

Zhang, E. D., Zhou, N., & Yu, S. (2023). Assessing L2 secondary student writing feedback literacy and its predictive effect on their L2 writing performance. *Language Teaching Research*, 13621688231217665. Advance online publication. DOI: 10.1177/13621688231217665

Zhang, H., & Wang, L. (2024). Hybrid models of art education: Integrating VR, AI, and traditional methods. *Journal of Educational Psychology*, *116*(1), 1–15.

Zhang, J., & Zhang, L. J. (2025). *Integrating Various Types of Feedback in L2 Writing Instruction: Teachers' and Students' Perspectives*. International Journal of Applied Linguistics United Kingdom., DOI: 10.1111/ijal.12822

Zhang, J., Zhu, C., & Zhang, Z. (2024). AI-powered language learning: The role of NLP in grammar, spelling, and pronunciation feedback. *Applied and Computational Engineering*, *102*(1), 18–23. DOI: 10.54254/2755-2721/102/20240962

Zhang, R., & Zou, D. (2023). A review of research on technology-enhanced peer feedback for second language writing based on the activity theory framework. *Education and Information Technologies*, *28*(6), 6727–6753. DOI: 10.1007/s10639-022-11469-8

Zhang, Y., & Zou, X. (2022). AI and VR in art education: A comparative study. *Computers & Education*, *178*(Supplement), 1–18.

Zhao, J., & Chen, H. (2023). ICT-based framework for fine arts education in primary teacher training. *Journal of Teacher Education*, *74*(3), 345–362.

Zhao, J., & Sun, Q. (2023). Teaching traditional Chinese painting: Challenges and ICT solutions. *Journal of Artistic Research*, *18*(1), 67–82.

Zhao, L., Zhao, Y., & Zhang, L. (2023). Ethical considerations and risk mitigation of educational technology in the digital transformation context. *Distance Education in China*, *45*(12), 46–58.

Zhao, W., Wang, B., & Tang, Z. (2023). Handwriting identification and verification using artificial intelligence. *Scientific Reports*, *13*(1), 16646. DOI: 10.1038/s41598-023-48789-9 PMID: 38066009

Zhao, X. (2022). Leveraging artificial intelligence (ai) technology for english writing: Introducing wordtune as a digital writing assistant for efl writers. *RELC Journal*, *54*(3), 890–894. DOI: 10.1177/00336882221094089

Zhao, X., Chen, J., & Wu, Y. (2023). Ethical issues in VR and AI-assisted art education: Consent, surveillance, and academic integrity. *Journal of Educational Ethics*, *7*(1), 1–19.

Zhao, X., Liao, Y., Tang, Z., Xu, Y., Tao, X., Wang, D., Wang, G., & Lu, H. (2023). Integrating audio and visual modalities for multimodal personality trait recognition via hybrid deep learning. *Frontiers in Neuroscience*, *16*, 1107284. DOI: 10.3389/fnins.2022.1107284 PMID: 36685221

Zheng, Y., & Wu, L. (2023). Cultural transmission strategies in ICT-enhanced art education. *Journal of Cultural Sociology*, *17*(2), 234–256.

Zheng, Y., & Yu, S. (2019). What has been assessed in writing and how? Empirical evidence from *Assessing Writing* (2000–2018). *Assessing Writing*, *42*, 100421. DOI: 10.1016/j.asw.2019.100421

Zhong, Z., Guo, H., & Qian, K. (2024). Deciphering the impact of machine learning on education: Insights from a bibliometric analysis using bibliometrix R-package. *Education and Information Technologies*, *29*(16), 21995–22022. DOI: 10.1007/s10639-024-12734-8

Zhu, Y. (2024). Construction of evaluation framework for classroom teaching reform of students empowered by digitalization. *Pacific International Journal*, *7*(1), 174–178. DOI: 10.55014/pij.v7i1.531

Zhu, Y., Zhang, L., Zong, R., & Sun, H. (2024). Exploring AI-generated feedback on English writing: A case study of ChatGPT. *US-China Foreign Language*, *22*(3), 144–153.

Zhu, Y., Zhang, L., Zong, R., & Sun, H. (2024). Exploring AI-Generated Feedback on English Writing: A Case Study of ChatGPT. *US-China Foreign Language*, *22*(3), 144–153.

Ziaei, S., & Tavakoli, M. (2025). Combined Effects of Task Sequencing and Corrective Feedback on EFL Learners' Writing: A comparison between human raters and ChatGPT. *Journal of English Language Teaching and Learning*, *17*(35), 439–452.

Zimotti, G., Frances, C., & Whitaker, L. (2024). The future of language education: Teachers' perceptions about the surge of AI writing tools. *Technology in Language Teaching & Learning*, *6*(2), 1136–1136. DOI: 10.29140/tltl.v6n1.1136

Ziqi, C., Xinhua, Z., Qi, L., & Wei, W. (2024). L2 students' barriers in engaging with form and content-focused AI-generated feedback in revising their compositions. *Computer Assisted Language Learning*, •••, 1–21. DOI: 10.1080/09588221.2024.2422478

Zohbie, A., & Bhowmik, S. (2024). Using a genre-based approach to teach writing to elementary esl students: A boon or a barrier? *TESOL Journal*, *15*(4), e819. Advance online publication. DOI: 10.1002/tesj.819

Zou, D., Huang, Y., & Xie, H. (2023). Digital feedback systems in writing education: A meta-analysis. *Computers & Education*, *197*, 104688. DOI: 10.1016/j.compedu.2023.104688

Zou, D., Xie, H., & Wang, F. L. (2022). Effects of Scaffolded Peer Assessment on Students' Holistic Critical Thinking in Academic Writing. In *Lecture Notes in Computer Science Including Subseries Lecture Notes in Artificial Intelligence and Lecture Notes in Bioinformatics* (Vol. 13357). LNCS., DOI: 10.1007/978-3-031-08939-8_13

Zou, S., Guo, K., Wang, J., & Liu, Y. (2024). Investigating students' uptake of teacher-and ChatGPT-generated feedback in EFL writing: A comparison study. *Computer Assisted Language Learning*, •••, 1–30.

Zumbrunn, S., & Krause, K. (2012). Conversations with leaders: Principles of effective writing instruction. *The Reading Teacher*, *65*(5), 346–353. DOI: 10.1002/TRTR.01053

Ербулатова, И., Бердибаева, Д., & Ербулатов, К. (2025). Лингвистические аспекты применения ии в анализе и интерпретации текста. *Б ИТУ Хабаршысы*, *35*(3), 143–152. DOI: 10.62724/202530203

About the Contributors

Ali Sorayyaei Azar is an Assistant Professor at the Department of Language and Literacy Education within the Faculty of Education, University of Malaya (UM), Malaysia. He also got his Ph.D. in Applied Linguistics from the Faculty of Languages and Linguistics, University of Malaya, Malaysia. In a career spanning 27 years, he has worked as an EFL/ESL senior lecturer, researcher, and curriculum developer in Iran, Turkey, Qatar, and Malaysia. He has published and presented research papers on his topic of interest namely Academic Discourse Analysis, Genre Analysis, Corpus Linguistics, TESL, Educational Technology, and English Language Teaching Strategies in several prestigious journals including GEMA Online@ Journal of Language Studies (UKM, Malaysia), Asian ESP Journal, Asian EFL Journal, Studies in English Language and Education, World Journal of English Language, and Education and Information Technologies (Springer). He is the head of MAAL- SIG (Research Methods in Applied Linguistics). He is also the Editor of three books, including 'Reconceptions of Policies, Strategies, and Challenges in Education 5.0.', 'Innovations in Educational Robotics: Advancing AI for Sustainable Development', and 'Smart Education and Sustainable Learning Environments in Smart Cities' published by IGI Global-Publisher, in the USA. Besides, Dr. Azar has been appointed as a member of the Editorial Board for several journals, including the Asian Journal of University Education (AJUE) indexed in Scopus-Q1, established by Universiti Teknologi MARA, Shah Alam, Malaysia; the International Journal of Modern Languages and Applied Linguistics (IJMAL), established by Akademi Pengajian Bahasa (APB), Universiti Teknologi MARA, Shah Alam, Malaysia; Education Quarterly Reviews-indexed in ERIC, established by the Asian Institute of Research, Indonesia; and the journal of Pragmatics and Discourse Research- indexed in Sinta 3, established by Perkumpulan Pengelola Jurnal Bahasa Sastra dan Pengajarannya (PPJBSIP), Indonesia. Scopus Author: 55561989000

Rahul Kumar Ghosh is an Assistant Professor and Research Coordinator in the Department of Computational Sciences at Brainware University, India. He holds a Ph.D. in Information Technology, an MBA in Human Resource Analytics, an M.Sc. in Applied Statistics and Analytics, and an M.Sc. in Information Technology, reflecting a strong interdisciplinary academic foundation that bridges computing, analytics, and management. His research interests include artificial intelligence and machine learning applications, data analytics, blockchain technologies, Internet of Things (IoT), digital education systems, and technology-enabled sustainability and governance. Dr. Ghosh has authored and edited several books and book chapters with leading international publishers and has published extensively in Scopus-indexed and peer-reviewed journals. He is an empanelled PhD supervisor and contributes actively to academic governance as a Departmental PhD Coordinator and Research Coordinator. A recipient of national-level academic awards, he regularly serves as a reviewer, session chair, and invited resource person for faculty development programmes, workshops, and international conferences.

Eriona Çela is a distinguished academic and expert in European integration and negotiation, renowned for her contributions to education and public administration in Albania and beyond. Holding prominent positions within multiple institutions, she serves as a key figure at the Academy of European Integration and Negotiations (AIEN), the Albanian School of Public Administration (ASPA), and the Business Academy College. Dr. Cela's expertise is further recognized through her active involvement in various roles related to European Union policies and enlargement strategies. As a Jean Monnet Chair holder at the Institute of European Studies, University of Tirana, Dr. Cela has spearheaded significant projects such as the European Integration School 2023's eighth edition. Her work frequently appears in prestigious publications, including the European Journal of Arts, Humanities and Social Sciences, the European Journal of Contemporary Education, and the International Journal of Balkan Studies. She is also an Associate Editor for the International Journal of Risk and Contingency Management (IJRCM), an IGI Journal. She has also been engaged with the OSCE Academy in Bishkek, Vytautas Magnus University, and the Università degli Studi di Bari Aldo Moro, Dipartimento di Studi Umanistici, where she has furthered research and collaboration on a European scale. Dr. Cela's commitment to educational leadership is demonstrated through her involvement with Shkolla e Drejtorëve (CSL) and the AADF, where she focuses on developing future education leaders and administrators. In recognition of her ongoing contributions to education and public administration, Dr. Cela has received numerous accolades and is frequently invited as a keynote speaker at various academic and policy-making webinars. Her work continues to influence the strategic development of education systems in Albania and serves as a benchmark for integrating European educational standards and practices in the region.

Dorjana Flett (Klosi) is a lecturer and researcher at the University of Vlora "Ismail Qemali," Albania, with over 20 years of experience in English language teaching, sociolinguistics, and translation studies. She holds a PhD in Linguistics from the University of Tirana and a Postdoctoral Diploma in Sociolinguistics and Translation from the University of La Laguna, Spain. Her teaching and research have taken her across Europe through Erasmus+ teaching mobilities and international collaborations. Her academic work focuses on language variation, gender and communication, discourse analysis, and the sociolinguistics of translation. She has published in peer-reviewed journals such as the European Scientific Journal, where recent articles explore colloquial student speech and the translation of COVID-19 terminology into Albanian. She is also the author of a 2024 monograph titled Linguistic Differences in Student Colloquial Speech. Dr. Flett is an active member of several international research groups and serves on editorial boards and peer review panels. Alongside her academic work, she enjoys mentoring students and contributing to cross-cultural academic projects that bridge theory and practice.

***

Hassan Abuhassna is an associate professor of education at Sunway University, Malaysia. Before assuming this position, he was an assistant professor at Universiti Teknologi Malaysia (UTM) for four years, where he specialized in educational technology. Dr. Abuhassna has completed a Master's degree in instructional technology and a Ph.D. with merit in educational technology. His research is centered on electronic learning (e-learning) and massive open online courses (MOOCs). Dr. Abuhassna has made substantial contributions to the field of educational technology over the course of his career, with a plethora of publications that have been indexed in prestigious databases like Scopus and Web of Science (WoS). His contributions have been acknowledged for their integration of instructional design models with learning theories and the improvement of online learning environments. Abuhassna has been actively engaged in academic conferences in addition to his research. He was invited to speak at the International Conference on Information Technology in Education and Artificial Intelligence (ITEA) 2024, where he delivered a presentation titled "The Information Age for Education via

Anamika Ahirwar, Ph.D., is a Professor in the Department of Computer Science & Engineering at Compucom Institute of Technology & Management, Jaipur, Rajasthan, India. With over 21+ years of academic and research experience, she earned her Ph.D. in Computer Applications from Rajiv Gandhi Technical University, Bhopal, where her doctoral research focused on data mining schemes for medical imaging. Her areas of expertise include medical imaging, data science, machine learning, sentiment analysis, and celestial sound. Dr. Ahirwar is a prolific researcher with more than 80 publications in SCI-indexed journals, Scopus, as well as in international and national journals and conference proceedings. She has authored and edited several books with reputed international publishers such as Wiley, CRC Press, IGI Global, Cambridge Scholars, and Nova Science. She is the recipient of several awards, including the I2OR National Eminent Researcher Award, the Academic Influencer Award, and the Faculty Excellence Award. Dr. Ahirwar holds five published patents and has supervised numerous postgraduate and doctoral research scholars in computer science. As a reviewer and editorial board member for various reputed journals and conferences, she plays an active role in promoting research in emerging technologies. She is a life member of esteemed technical bodies such as IAENG and I2OR and has contributed significantly as a session chair, expert speaker, and convener at numerous international academic forums.

Ahmad Al Yakin is a distinguished academic at Universitas Al Asyariah Mandar (UNASMAN), where he serves in the Pendidikan Pancasila dan Kewarganegaraan (Civics Education) program. His career reflects a consistent commitment to academic excellence, leadership, and scholarly contribution. He previously held the position of Director of the Lembaga Penelitian dan Pengabdian kepada Masyarakat (LPPM UNASMAN) from 2013 to 2016, and currently contributes to institutional advancement as Wakil Rektor I (Vice-Rector I), demonstrating his strong role in academic governance and policy development. In addition to administrative leadership, Dr. Ahmad Al Yakin actively contributes to scholarly communities as a peer reviewer for the Jurnal Sipissangngi: Jurnal Pengabdian Kepada Masyarakat, reflecting his dedication to maintaining research quality and academic integrity. His research productivity is evident in his SINTA profile, where he has achieved an overall score of 3,363 and a three-year score of 825, supported by a Scopus H-index of 7 and a Google Scholar H-index of 15. His academic contributions encompass a wide range of themes, including civics education, digital learning, and pedagogical innovation. Among his notable works are Education for a Digital Era: Advice and Practice around the Globe, Praxis and Practices in ELT and Philology, and collaborative works such as Teaching, Learning, Education, an Overview and Media Quizizz sebagai Aplikasi Assessment Pembelajaran. Beyond publications, Dr. Ahmad Al Yakin has also been recognized for his innovative engagement with educational technology and research methodologies, as reflected in intellectual property outputs including Selebrifikasi Politik, Entrepreneurship Dictionary with Cyber Technology, Metodologi Penelitian, and Digital English Dictionary with Virtual Reality. Through his leadership as Vice-Rector I, he plays a pivotal role in shaping institutional policies, particularly in areas such as the Recognition of Prior Learning (RPL), strengthening UNASMAN's academic impact both regionally and nationally. His editorial and institutional services extend beyond administration, as he has consistently fostered research development, publication quality, and academic collaboration through his tenure at LPPM UNASMAN. With a career that seamlessly integrates research, innovation, and leadership, Dr. Ahmad Al Yakin exemplifies academic excellence and continues to contribute significantly to the advancement of higher education in Indonesia.

Ahmad Abdul-Majid Matar Al-Mabhouh is an Assistant Professor of Educational Technology at the Faculty of Education – Al-Aqsa University. He is a certified trainer and researcher specializing in digital transformation, e-learning, and artificial intelligence applications in education. He holds both a Master's and Ph.D. in Educational Technology and has over 20 years of experience in higher education development and community-based training in Palestine and the region.Dr. Al-Mabhouh has participated in several national and regional initiatives, such as the Middle East Digital Transformation Project funded by AUF, where he contributed to training academic and administrative staff across Arab universities on digital education tools. He is highly active in community service through initiatives aimed at developing the digital skills of students and educators during times of crisis. He has also designed flexible educational programs that integrate technology into school and university-level teaching. His current academic focus is on the integration of artificial intelligence in education, developing smart and adaptive learning models that address individual differences and enhance the quality of higher education in the Arab world. In alignment with his commitment to sustainable development, Dr. Al-Mabhouh has contributed to launching environmental partnerships with academic and community institutions. These initiatives aim to link digital transformation with environmental responsibility, promoting eco-friendly practices within higher education institutions. On the academic level, Dr. Al-Mabhouh has established active research partnerships with Arab and international universities and research centers. Notably, he represented Al-Aqsa University in the TAP Project under the Erasmus+ Program in Ireland (2019). He also participated in the EU TALEX Higher Education Experts Workshops. His research focuses on education during emergencies, evaluation of e-learning platforms, and ethical digital transformation, with publications in internationally peer-reviewed journals.

N. Mari Anand has a rich experience of 10 year in the field of teaching and expertise in the field of Marketing and Human Resource Management. Currently he is working as Faculty Member, Department of Business Studies, University of Technology & Applied Sciences, Salalah, Sultanate of Oman. He is also a Member in Research Advisory Committee at VELS Institute of Science, Technology & Advanced Studies, Chennai. To his credit he has published 27 articles in Scopus and UGC Listed Journals. He has guided 63 UG and 22 PG projects. He served as Member of Board of Studies for Business Administration and Member for University Examination Board of SRM-IST. The author is an Editorial Board Member for International Journal of Advance Research in Commerce Management and Finance (IJARCMF). The author has organized various International Conferences and International Conclave during his tenure. The author was an ISO Convener and served as IQAC coordinator & Exam Cell convener. He is also an External Academic Auditor and Chief Examiner for various institutions. He is an active Member in Federation of Indian Chamber of Commerce and Industries (FICCI) & Madras Management Association (MMA).

Eka Apriani, M.Pd. is an English Lecturer at English Tadris c. Study Program of the Faculty of Tarbiyahs in Islamic State Institute of Curup. She is a Editor in Chief in Journal of English Franca and International Journal of Education Research and Development. She is also the secretary of Corolla Education Centre Foundation, Indonesia. She Received her Master Degree (Master of Language Education) from Sriwijaya University in 2013 and Doctor of Education in Bengkulu University 2022. She has published some researchs in international journal and national journal. She has Scopus Id and WOS Id. She is a member of profession organisation: ADRI, TEFLIN, PDPI and ELITE. She is treasurer of ADRI in Bengkulu Province. Her research interest is in Writing skill and ICT in learning English. She write some books: The beauty of Rejang Lebong, Semantics Crossword, Metode Pengajaran BIPA, Drama Manuscript: The Marriage of Siti Zubaidah. She has also some Intelektual Property Right: Semantics Crossword, The beauty of Rejang Lebong, The Marriage of Siti Zubaidah, Metode Pengajaran BIPA.

Saurabh Bhargava, a seasoned academician with a doctorate in forensic science, is serving as an Assistant Professor in the School of Advanced Sciences and Languages at VIT Bhopal University, Madhya Pradesh, India. Dr. Bhargava has over a decade of teaching and research experience, with academic interests that span across various specialties in forensic sciences, chemistry, linguistic forensics, toxicology, handwriting analysis, and interdisciplinary applications of science in the criminal justice system. Dr. Bhargava's work frequently integrates language, law, chemistry, toxicology, and various other subspecialties for forensic applications. Dr. Bhargava has published over 20 journal articles, 4 book chapters, and a reference book on forensics. Dr. Bhargava is also known for his efforts in promoting forensic awareness and scientific literacy among students.

Sandip Chakraborty is an Assistant Professor in the Department of Computational Sciences at Brainware University, Kolkata. His research spans Human–Computer Interaction, AI/ML, IoT, web accessibility, and NLP for sustainability and governance. He actively mentors undergraduate and postgraduate projects and has co-authored book chapters and conference papers across these domains. His current work focuses on explainable AI and data-driven accessibility evaluation of Indian e-learning platforms.

Peter Chew is a distinguished biochemist, mathematician, and inventor associated with PCET Multimedia Education. He has made notable contributions to artificial intelligence through innovative methodologies such as the Peter Chew Rule, Method, Theorem, and Triangle Diagram, which have been recognized by the World Health Organization and published via Europe PMC.

As CEO of PCET Ventures in Malaysia and a long-term research associate of the International Multidisciplinary Research Foundation (IMRF), he has chaired international conferences and served as a keynote speaker globally. Dr. Chew has also authored numerous educational tools and calculators, enhancing mathematical learning and AI system efficiency.

Gourab Dutta has done BTech and MTech in computer science. He has a long experiences of teaching in several colleges . He has also published many articles and book chapters in different reputed publications.He is currently working as assistant professor in department of Computational; Sciences, Brainware University,

J. Jacintha Maria Florence is an esteemed Assistant Professor in the Department of Economics, celebrated for her comprehensive expertise and significant contributions to the field of Development Economics. With a robust academic background, including degrees of M.A., M.Phil., Ph.D., and B.Ed., Dr. Florence has dedicated over a decade to fostering education and research, with 8 years in undergraduate teaching and 3 years at the postgraduate level. Her research interests have led to notable publications in both international and national journals, focusing on critical issues such as environmental degradation, consumer behaviour, agrarian distress, and the prevalence of cardiovascular diseases among women. Dr. Florence has also made her mark in the realm of book publications, notably authoring on the growth of the Indian e-commerce market, alongside presenting her insights at numerous conferences across a spectrum of topics from economic reforms to health insurance and the impact of mergers and acquisitions. A lifelong learner, she has completed three NPTEL courses, enriching her knowledge and staying abreast of current trends in her field. Her commitment to education and research is further exemplified by her active participation in seminars, workshops, and faculty development programs, aiming to refine her academic and teaching methodologies continuously. Dr. Florence's dedication to her field is not just limited to her research and publications but also extends to her involvement in community-oriented projects, reflecting her passion for using her expertise to address real-world challenges. Her prolific academic journey and contributions make her a distinguished figure in the world of economics, whose work continues to inspire and influence both her students and peers in the academic community.

Masanori Fukui is associated with Mie University, Japan. He earned a Ph.D. in Engineering from Hiroshima University and an M.D. in Education from Hyogo University of Teacher Education. Dr. Fukui's research focuses on innovative educational technologies, including AI-enhanced teaching, computational thinking, problem-posing strategies, and digital game–based learning, aimed at fostering creativity and improving pedagogy. He also holds roles as a visiting professor or researcher at several international institutions including Mie University, UCSI University, and INTI International University.

Wang Zexin is Student in faculty of Social Sciences and Liberal Arts at UCSI university, Kuala Lumpur, Malaysia. His research area is Music Education.

Mahdi Hamzehloo is an IT engineer. He holds a Master's degree in Information Technology Engineering from MehrAlborz University, where his research focused on industrial computer failure and user knowledge. His professional experience includes IT project implementation, industrial computer. His research interests lie in information technology management, IoT, and industrial computers. He has published research articles and presented at international conferences in the fields of IT and education. He is also skilled in Cybersecurity in industrial computer system.

Maryam Hamzehloo is an English language instructor and researcher. She holds an MA in TEFL and has extensive experience teaching English as a foreign language since 2009. Her research focuses on technology-mediated language learning, AI in education, teacher feedback, and gender-based studies in EFL. She has published in several journal articles, book chapters, and presented at international conferences on AI, educational technology, and English language teaching. She is also an experienced translator and curriculum developer. Her recent works explore the integration of AI in EFL/ESL language education and its role in promoting equity and motivation.

Rajendra Kumar is Associate Professor in Computer Science & Engineering Department at Sharda School of Computing Science & Engineering, Sharda University, Greater Noida, India. His research are includes Vein Pattern Recognition, Biometrics, Human Computer Interaction, and Theoretical Computer Science.

Sanjeev Kumar Is a Professor in Lovely Professional University Punjab India. He received Undergraduate in Hotel Management from Osmania University, Postgraduate in Tourism Management from Madurai Kamaraj University. He completed Doctor of Philosophy in Hospitality Management in 2019 from Amity University Jaipur India. His research areas lies in food Service Industry, his research focuses on Alcoholic beverages, Event management and Sustainable Management Practices, Metaverse, AI Machine Learning and Artificial Intelligence. He published more than 80 research papers, articles and chapters in Scopus Indexed, UGC Approved and peer reviewed Journals and books. Dr. Sanjeev Kumar participated and acted as resource person in various National and International conferences, seminars, session chair, research workshops and industry talks and his work has been widely cited. Dr. Sanjeev also edited more than 20 books with various International Publishers such as IGI Global, Cambridge Scholars, Emerald, CABI, Bentham Science, Taylor & Francis. Dr Sanjeev is an active researcher and has published numerous research articles in prestigious National and International journals and books.

Jonika Lamba is a Research Scholar at the School of Management, The NorthCap University, Gurugram, India. Her areas of interest include stock markets, accounting, auditing, technologies, and taxation.

Hannah Mae G. Lolong is an Instructor at Davao del Norte State College and is currently pursuing her Master's degree in Information Technology at the University of Southeastern Philippines. Her main interests are Image Processing, Data Analytics, and Artificial Intelligence.

|Ping Lu - Contributing Author|Lu Ping, a PhD student, is currently studying in the Faculty of Social Sciences and Arts, UCSI University Malaysia. Her research areas include: elementary education, higher education, art education, and Chinese painting education. She has more than three years of undergraduate teaching experience in elementary education in higher education. She specializes in college art skills and manual practice courses.

M.S.R.Mariyappan is a recipient of "Bharat Vidya Ratan" Award; he has eclectic mix of academic, industry and research experience for more than Two Decades. He has a rich experience as Principal(i/c), Vice Principal, Governing Council Member, Academic Council Member, BoS Chairman, Director of M.B.A. Programme and Coordinator of NAAC, MSME, EDC, IQAC, ISO etc. He is an Advisory Board Member of Indo-Asian Journal of Advanced Management and the Member of Board of Studies of various institutions. He is a Journal Reviewer of Business and Management Studies in USA & UK. He is an Editorial Board Member of Industrial Magazine.

Sakshi Mann is an Assistant Professor of Human Resource Management at School of Business, Indira University, Pune. With a Ph.D. in HR and over 11 years of combined industry and academic experience, she brings a practical edge to her teaching. Her expertise spans Organizational Behavior, Recruitment & Selection, Employee Engagement, and Leadership. Having managed HR operations across various organizations, she seamlessly integrates real-world insights into academia. Passionate about research, she explores contemporary HR challenges to contribute valuable insights to the field. Committed to bridging academia and industry, Dr. Mann fosters critical thinking and practical application, equipping students for the evolving HR landscape.

Shikha Mann is an award-winning academician, certified leadership coach, and organizational consultant currently serving as Controller of Examinations at Indira University (IU), Pune. Previously, she held the role of Deputy Director and HOD–HR at Indira School of Business Studies PGDM, where she led academic, administrative, and accreditation initiatives. A recipient of Business World's 40under40 Leaders in Education award, Dr. Mann brings a decade-plus of experience at the intersection of education, leadership development, and institutional strategy. She holds a Ph.D. in Organizational Behavior from Symbiosis International University and is an ICF-certified PCC coach, with additional accreditations in MBTI, FIRO-B, TIFF, TA 101, Enneagram, and psychometric assessments. Dr. Mann has conducted high-impact MDPs and consulting interventions for reputed organizations like Tata Motors, RBI, Jabil, Thermax, Lupin, and the Maharashtra Police. She has played a pivotal role in leading NBA and AIU accreditation processes and in designing outcome-based curricula, assessment centers, and CXO-level talent strategy blueprints.

Rey Kenneth John G. Marces is a Licensed Professional Teacher and currently serves as an Editorial Assistant for the Southeastern Philippines Journal of Research and Development (SPJRD). He is actively pursuing a Master of Arts in English Language Teaching at the University of Southeastern Philippines. His research interests focus on diverse and critical areas in linguistics, including the English Language, discourse analysis and rhetoric in battle rap, and the crucial intersection of AI Integration and AI in Education.

Katayoun Mehdinezhad Nouri is a dedicated Lecturer in the Faculty of Social Sciences and Liberal Arts at UCSI University. Her scholarly interests include positive youth development, psychological resilience, and co-curricular engagement. Notable publications include investigations into pathways to youth development through campus programs and the moderating role of power distance on youth outcomes in Malaysian co-curricular settings. Her work contributes key insights into fostering psychological well-being and participative growth among university students.

Tausif Mistry A learner for life Academic Professional with a strong inclination towards Data. Qualifying NET & Doctorate from Savitribai Phule Pune University is what triggered the switch to academics so early in the career. As an ESTJ personality type, my approach to leadership is defined by a blend of efficiency, strategic thinking, and a deep commitment to excellence. I thrive in dynamic environments where collaboration and forward-thinking are paramount, qualities that have been instrumental in driving the success of virtual learning programs. An experienced Google Ads Manager who has handled accounts of big budget MNC's promoting their brands nationally. Working as an Associate Professor, Dr. Tausif has been helping students learn business skills like communication, marketing research, data analyzing & reporting using tools & software's like Power BI, Tableau, MS Excel & Coggle. Everyday is a new learning experience with the current profession of an Academician. in love with technology & a StoryTeller..!!! Throughout my journey, I've remained dedicated to harnessing the latest advancements in virtual learning technology to create engaging, immersive, and inclusive educational experiences for learners of all backgrounds. I'm passionate about empowering educators and students alike to embrace the endless possibilities of virtual learning, ensuring that education remains accessible and impactful in an ever-evolving digital landscape.

M. Nagalakshmi, M.A., M.Phil., B.Ed., PhD, NET, MBA, TEFL/TESOL, is a Professor of English at the VELS Institute of Science, Technology, and Advanced Studies. Currently, she teaches undergraduate and postgraduate students of English. She is in charge of ten research scholars, 13 of whom have received awards. Under her guidance, 13 MPhil scholars received their awards. She evaluated 6 PhD theses from various universities. She has almost twenty-four years of teaching experience, including 11 years in Muscat, Sultanate of Oman. Her experience includes teaching expertise in the English language and literature. She has designed various modules tailored to students' levels. She is an IELTS trainer. She has also completed a NEBOSH-certified course on workplace health and safety. She has created course modules for Technical English, Health and Safety Education, and Work Ethics for NVQ students at TATI, Muscat, the Sultanate of Oman. Besides her PhD, she has qualified for the NTA-NET. Her research interests include ESL/EFL English Language Teaching, Feminism, Post-Colonial Studies of India, British Literature, Electronic Literature, and Culture Studies. She has published over 90 research articles in peer-reviewed SCOPUS and UGC-CARE LIST journals and conference volumes. She has presented papers at international and national conferences and has acted as a Resource Person for webinars/workshops and international conferences. She compiled an English-in-India book and edited six volumes of ISBN books. She is serving as a Chief Editorial Board Member of the Eurasian Journal of Literature and Languages (ISSN 2584-1734). She has received the Faculty Excellence Award thrice (2021, 2023 & 2023) from VISTAS, the Outstanding Support for Research Scholars Award (Feb 2024) from Metharath University, Thailand and ESN Publications, India, the Rukmani Lakshmipathi Teaching Excellence Award, the Distinguished Service in English Language Teaching and Research Award, the Best Teacher Award and the Distinguished Professor Award. She presented papers at international conferences held in Malaysia in September 2024, Thailand in February 2024 and Dubai in January 2023.

Khar Thoe Ng Having multidisciplinary interests & a passion for lifelong learning, Dr. Ng Khar Thoe has diversified her scope of studies to be an advocate for Sc/Social Sc ed. incl. environmental sustainability ed. via tech-focused transdisciplinary studies. She holds a Ph.D in Ed. (Open Univ. M'sia), M.Ed. (Brunel Univ. of West London) & B.Sc.Ed. (Hons.)(Univ. Sc.M'sa), Dip. in H.E.N. (Kingston Univ. & St. College of Health Studies, UK). Currently attached to FELA, INTI Int. Univ. (IIU), Nilai. She was Visiting Prof. in Tsukuba Univ, Japan. She also taught Elementary/Pri Sc as part-time lecturer Al-Bhukary Int Univ. (AIU) & Wawasan Open Univ. (WOU). Her research interests incl. enhancing essential skills of learners thru technology-driven Sc. / environmental / social Science pedagogical approaches including PBA/PBL/IBL.

Nikodemus Niko is a member of the Indigenous Dayak Benawan community in Kalimantan. He is currently an Assistant Professor in the Department of Sociology, Faculty of Social and Political Sciences, at Maritim Raja Ali Haji University in Tanjungpinang, Indonesia. He holds a Ph.D. in Sociology from Padjadjaran University, Indonesia.

Ahmed J. Obaid, is a Asst. Professor at the Department of Computer Science, Faculty of Computer Science and Mathematics, University of Kufa, Iraq. Dr. Ahmed holds a Bachelor in Computer Science, degree in – Information Systems from College of Computers, University of Anbar, Iraq (2001-2005), and a Master Degree (M. TECH) of Computer Science Engineering (CSE) from School of Information Technology, Jawaharlal Nehru Technological University, Hyderabad, India (2010-2013), and a Doctor of Philosophy (PhD) in Web Mining from College of Information Technology, University of University of Babylon, Iraq (2013-2017). He is a Certified Web Mining Consultant with over 14 years of experience in working as Faculty Member in University of Kufa, Iraq. He has taught courses in Web Designing, Web Scripting, JavaScript, VB.Net, MATLAB Toolbox's, and other courses on PHP, CMC, and DHTML from more than 10 international organizations and institutes from USA, and India. Dr. Ahmed is a member of Statistical and Information Consultation Center (SICC), University of Kufa, Iraq.

Michael Oyedele Oyenuga has a PhD in Marketing and Communication and over 25 years of scholarly and practitioner experience in education policy, digital transformation, and inclusive learning. His research interests cut across marketing, branding, consumer behaviour, education and sustainability. He is currently an Associate Professor and Assistant Dean at the School of Business, Woxsen University, Hyderabad, India.

Umamaheswari Purushothaman holds a B.E. in Information Technology from Periyar Maniammai College of Engineering and Technology (2003), an M.B.A. from Alagappa University, Karaikudi, Tamil Nadu (2006), and an M.Tech in Computer Science from SASTRA Deemed University, Thanjavur, Tamil Nadu (2011). She earned her Ph.D. in Computer Science and Engineering from SASTRA Deemed University. With two decades of experience, she has taught both undergraduate and postgraduate courses in Computer Science. She is currently an Assistant Professor in the Department of Computer Science and Engineering at SRC Campus, SASTRA University, Kumbakonam. Her research interests focus on Data Mining, Machine Learning, and Deep Learning. She has published numerous research papers in international conferences, SCI-indexed journals, Scopus, and book chapters.

R Mathi is working as Assistant Professor in the Department of Electrical and Electronics Engineering, SRC, SASTRA Deemed to be University, Kumbakonam, TN, India. Research areas include Renewable Energy Sources, Power Electronics, Power Systems, AI and ML.

Francis N. Reginio is an academic and social advocate specializing in policy analysis, human capital development, and community empowerment. Currently, he serves as a faculty member in the Social Science department at the College of Arts and Sciences of the University of Southeastern Philippines. He holds the position of Managing Editor of the Southeastern Philippines Journal for Research and Development (SPJRD), a Scopus-indexed publication. In his scholarly work, his research focuses on inequality, displacement, and Indigenous Peoples in conflict-affected Mindanao. Apart from his scholarly engagements, he has been involved in policy reforms, government-funded initiatives, and community extension programs that promote cultural preservation, peacebuilding, and sustainable development.

Vivit Rosmayanti, S.Pd.I., M.Pd was born in Botta on June 26, 1987. She has over 10 years of experience teaching at the University. She obtained a bachelor's degree in English Education from Alauddin State Islamic University. She completed her master's and doctoral degrees in English Education from Makassar State University. She is currently a lecturer in the Post Graduate Program, Department of English Education at Makassar State University, South Sulawesi, Indonesia. She is also actively writing research articles to be published in nationally and internationally accredited journals. She has written in some chapter books, monographs, and reference books. She is interested in teaching methods for teaching English. Her research interests include language teaching methodology, ICT instruction, and ESP teaching. She can be contacted at email: rosmayantivivit@gmail.com

Jayendira P. Sankar is serving as an Associate Professor and Programme Head of MBA at the University of Technology Bahrain and has over eighteen years of academic experience. He is a Senior Fellow of HEA-UK and an Academic Fellow of CIPD-UK. He has published extensively in various high-impact journals and presented at numerous academic conferences. His current research interests include Development Economics, focusing on economic growth, poverty, inequality, market failure, fiscal, economic, and social conditions, healthcare, education, employment sector, and industrial and social infrastructure; Human Resource Management, focusing on employee welfare, work-family balance, corporate social responsibility, sustainability; and innovation in teaching-learning and assessments.

Indranil Sarkar is an Assistant Professor of the Department of Computer Applications of the Guru Nanak Institute of Technology, Kolkata, India. He received an M.Tech. degree in Computer Science and engineering in 2018 from Maulana Abul Kalam Azad University of Technology, West Bengal (Formerly known as West Bengal University of Technology). He has authored over 20 papers in peer-reviewed journals, and conferences. He has also authored one book and also granted two patents. His main areas of research interest are Data Science, Machine Learning, and the Internet of Things.

Amrik Singh is working as Professor in the School of Hotel Management and Tourism at Lovely Professional University, Punjab, India. He obtained his Ph.D. degree in Hotel Management from Kurukshetra University, Kurukshetra. He started his academic career at Lovely Professional University, Punjab, India in the year 2007. He has published more than 40 research papers in UGC and peer-reviewed and Scopus/Web of Science) journals. He has published 12 patents and 01 patent has been granted in the inter-disciplinary domain. Dr. Amrik Singh participated and acted as a resource person in various national and international conferences, seminars, research workshops, and industry talks. His area of research interest is accommodation management, ergonomics, green practices, human resource management in hospitality, waste management, AR VR in hospitality, etc. He is currently guiding 8Ph.D. scholars and 2 Ph.D. scholars have been awarded Ph.D.

Osman Solmaz, 2025 TESOL Teacher of the Year, is an associate professor of English Language Teaching at Dicle University, Türkiye. He holds his Ph.D. degree from the University of Arizona. His research interests include teacher education, linguistic landscapes, digital literacies, social media, the implementation of technology in second language teaching and learning.

Conie Toh is a lecturer and researcher with a Ph.D. in Education and School Leadership (Teaching & Training). Her work focuses on educational leadership, instructional practices, teacher education, and Science engagement, with particular interest in digital and inclusive leadership to enhance teaching quality and student outcomes. She has extensive experience teaching at both school and university levels, and her research bridges theory and practice to support educational improvement. Her earlier work in plant biotechnology contributed to scientific understanding in molecular biology and agricultural research.

Nakiye Üvek is an experienced English language teacher based in Türkiye. She recently completed her MA studies, focusing on the adoption of AI in postgraduate academic writing contexts. Her research interests include academic writing, artificial intelligence, and the integration of technology in language teaching.

Zexing Wang is a doctoral student and research assistant at the UCSI Graduate Business School, located in Kuala Lumpur, Malaysia

Muthmainnah Yakin is a prominent Indonesian educator, international scholar, and academic leader based at Universitas Al Asyariah Mandar in West Sulawesi, Indonesia. She serves as an Associate Professor and has built a global reputation for her contributions to teacher education, educational technology, and international academic collaboration. Society for Research Development Muthmainnah embarked on her academic journey by completing her Bachelor's degree in English Education at Universitas Islam Negeri Alauddin Makassar in 2002. She continued her studies at Universitas Negeri Makassar (PPs-UNM), earning both her Master's degree in English Education in 2005 and her Doctorate (Ph.D.) in English Language Teaching (ELT) in 2019. Her doctoral research focused on developing literary works as instructional materials in English language classrooms blending language teaching with creative texts such as films, songs, poems, and novels. At Universitas Al Asyariah Mandar (UNASMAN), Dr. Muthmainnah has held a series of increasingly important leadership roles. She was Chairman of the Indonesian Language Department within the Faculty of Teacher Training and Education and later served as Public Relations Officer and Director of the Women's Centre Studies. She also contributed to institutional quality improvement as Deputy Director of the Quality Assurance Unit before being appointed Deputy Director of the Language and Character Development Institute a strategic role focused on strengthening academic culture and student competencies. Dr. Muthmainnah's scholarly interests span a range of contemporary and pedagogical domains, including instructional material development, TESOL/TEFL, ICT in education, digital education, cybergogy (learning in digital environments), and literary work integration in ELT. Her research emphasizes bridging theory with classroom practice and preparing future educators for the demands of 21st-century learning contexts. An accomplished author, she has published numerous books and research works with reputable international publishers, including Springer, Emerald, and Taylor & Francis reflecting her commitment to global academic discourse. Her publication record is complemented by a strong research presence: she holds a high SINTA score (a metric by Indonesia's Ministry of Education) with extensive citations and multiple indexed articles. Internationally, Dr. Muthmainnah is active on numerous academic boards and associations. She serves as adjunct professor at Manipal Global NTx Malaysia, Adjunct faculty at Maryam Abacha American University Nigeria, Adjunct faculty at Universedad de Panama in Panama and Buriram Rajabhat university Thailand, on international research groups, and education councils, and holds leadership roles in global organizations across Egypt, Kuwait, Nepal, and the Philippines. She is also recognized as a member of the United Nations Volunteers roster and sits on advisory boards in educational development initiatives. Her work has garnered over 100+ international awards, including honors for outstanding teaching, leadership, educational innovation, and contributions to the United Nations Sustainable Development Goals (SDGs) particularly in quality education. She holds honorary degrees such as Doctor Honoris Causa and a Doctor of Excellence from institutions in the Philippines in recognition of her academic impact. Known for her global perspective, collaborative spirit, and passion for education reform, Dr. Muthmainnah continues to advocate for cross-cultural academic partnerships and inclusive learning. She is frequently invited as a keynote speaker and international trainer, contributing to educational conferences and workshops across Asia, the Middle East, and beyond

Index

A

www.ingramcontent.com/pod-product-compliance
Lightning Source LLC
LaVergne TN
LVHW081318300926
849161LV00008B/1801